W9-AFS-217

CAPTAIN JAMES COOK

1. Captain James Cook, by Nathaniel Dance, 1776

Stanford University Press
Stanford, California
© 1974 by Timothy H. Beaglehole
Originating publisher: A. & C. Black Ltd, London, 1974
Printed in Great Britain
ISBN 0 8047 0848 7
LC 73 87124

The Life of
CAPTAIN JAMES COOK

by

J. C. BEAGLEHOLE

STANFORD UNIVERSITY PRESS

STANFORD, CALIFORNIA

CONTENTS

ILLUSTRATIONS

SKETCH MAPS

ACKNOWLEDGEMENTS

The reproductions have been made by the courtesy of the Trustees of the National Art Gallery and Dominion Museum, Wellington, New Zealand, 44; His Excellency the Governor-General of New Zealand, Government House, Wellington, 27; the Trustees of the British Museum, 3, 6–13, 15a, 15b, 22–5, 29, 35, 37; the Trustees of the National Maritime Museum, Greenwich, frontispiece, 5, 16, 19b, 20, 28, 30a, 33, 34, 36, 40, 41; the Committee of the National Library of Australia, Canberra, 14, 30b, 31; the Peabody Museum, Salem, Massachusetts, 39; the Controller of H.M. Stationery Office, 26, 38, 42; the Hydrographer of the Navy, 4; the Trustees of the Mitchell Library in the Public Library of New South Wales, Sydney, 17, 18, 21, 43; the Right Hon. the Earl of Birkenhead, 19a; the Whitby Literary and Philosophical Society, 2.

PREFACE

NEARLY forty years ago J. C. Beaglehole said he was going to write the life of Cook: the preliminary step—and how lightly that was once viewed—would be a new and scholarly edition of the Journals. Preliminary, perhaps; in the event this called for twenty years' work. In July 1967, a few months after his retirement from the Chair of British Commonwealth History at Victoria University of Wellington, he began the first chapter of the life. In the next two years there were long interruptions while he gave lectures for Cook bicentenary celebrations in Britain, New Zealand and Australia. The last page was written on 26 March 1971. At the time of his death, on 10 October 1971, he was revising the typescript and had reached the middle of chapter XIX.

This biography, the summation of a lifetime's study of Pacific exploration, is the writing towards which my father's whole work as an historian was directed. His devotion to the eighteenth century, his antipodean wit, his recreating imagination, his fascination with the Pacific—over so much of which he was to travel in Cook's tracks from Nootka Sound in the north to Dusky Bay in the south—come together in a book which, in some ways perhaps, only a New Zealander could have written.

In completing the revision and seeing the book through the press I have had help from many quarters for which I am deeply grateful: in New Zealand from Mrs Janet Paul and Dr David Mackay, and Mrs Ilse Jacoby who carefully typed the whole text; in England from Mrs Alison Quinn (who compiled the index), Miss Phyllis Mander-Jones (for the bibliography), both of whom scrutinised the proofs with a critical and scholarly eye, from Mrs Yolande Jones, Dr Averil Lysaght, Mr J. D. Newth, Dr Helen Wallis and Dr Glyndwr Williams.

Over many years my father became indebted to men and women in almost every part of the world for scholarly assistance. Many are listed in the prefaces to his editions of the Cook and Banks Journals. It is impossible for me to list them all here, and all will, I am sure, accept that this book itself is the real acknowledgement of their advice and help and will, on their part, share our gratitude that a lifetime's work has been so magnificently completed.

T. H. BEAGLEHOLE
Victoria University of Wellington

CAPTAIN JAMES COOK

I

The North Sea

THE VILLAGE of Marton-in-Cleveland, in the north-east corner of the North Riding of Yorkshire, where Cook was born, had not in the early part of the eighteenth century been touched by fame. No traveller, that we know of, committed to his journal any particular notice of the scatter of farm houses and cottages, on its gentle rise a quarter of a mile south of the road between Stockton and Guisborough; so far from prominence was it that it may indeed have shrunk since its earlier days, within its parish of five miles by two. It lay in an agricultural district, though moors and hills were not far away—a district well farmed, according to the standards of the time; the virtues of whose inhabitants were—so we learn from the worthy John Tuke,[1] who published his observations in 1794—uncontaminated by the neighbourhood or vices of manufacture. Farmers were sober, industrious, orderly, thrifty; so, by force of example, were the lower and labouring classes, decent in their demeanour, deserving of every indulgence from their superiors that might render their situation comfortable and easy. We may perhaps see in Cleveland, then, sixty or seventy years earlier, if not outstanding genius or intellectual or social passions, at least a certain general respectability—the sort of English soil from which, now and again, the most astonishing and unpredictable phenomenon will shoot up to dominate the imagination, a soil otherwise for long years undisturbed. This district was not entirely secluded. A man of curiosity would find the sea not far distant. A few miles to the north the river Tees met larger waters, though the Marton horizon was not yet made sinister by the fires and smokes of Middlesbrough at its mouth; across country some fifteen miles, a little north of east, the small harbour of Staithes fronted the fury of the North Sea; and rather more than twenty miles away, a little south of east, stood the comparatively large town of Whitby, sheltered by high land where the Esk exchanged its wooded valley for tidal flats and flowed north through its gateway of cliffs

[1] John Tuke, *A General View of the Agriculture of the North Riding of Yorkshire* (London, 1794).

I

into the coastal waters. You passed from the Esk to the world. This reflection, one may guess, was not often entertained by the lower and labouring classes of Cleveland, that district so predominantly agricultural, nor within it by the parish of Marton, five miles by two.

Beyond the North Riding lay the county of Durham, and then Northumberland; Northumberland marched with the Border and on the other side of the Border was Roxburghshire. In the north-east corner of Roxburghshire was Ednam, the village where the poet Thomson was born; here also was born another person of more immediate interest to us.[1] The parish register of Ednam records that on 24 December 1692 John Cook of that parish, at some time kirk elder, and Jean Duncan of the parish of Smaillhome, 'gave up their names for proclamation', and that before marriage Jean produced a certificate of her good behaviour. This couple were married on the following 19 January 1693 by Mr Thomas Thomson, minister, later to be father of the poet. On 4 March 1694 Mr Thomson baptised their son called James. According to the tradition of one family claiming descent from this John, the father of James, he had connections with building, milling, and sheep-rearing, all on a modest scale, and certainly made no fortune at Ednam, where James was the only son born to him, so far as the parish records can tell us.[2] He had other sons, born elsewhere (though where is unknown), and he himself and his wife Jean disappear from sight. Not so James. Whether obscurely impelled to travel, even if not far, or driven across the border by the hard times which followed the Jacobite rebellion of 1715, and seeking employment like other Scots in some rising alum works, he came south to Yorkshire—a man obviously without training in any trade, willing to do the humblest farm labour, sober, respectable, industrious, fitting without friction into the respectable and respectful lower classes at Cleveland; and, it seems, intelligent. 'God give you grace', his mother is alleged to have said to him when he departed from his home; and Grace is what he was given, in the person of a young woman of Stainton-in-Cleveland whose surname was Pace. They were married in the parish church of Stainton on 10 October 1725, when he was thirty-one and she twenty-three, and settled first in the village of Morton, in the parish of Ormesby, near Guisborough. It is in this parish register that the baptism of their first child, a son John, is noted, 10 January 1726/7. This son lived into his early twenties, but other-

---

[1] John Walker Ord, *History and Antiquities of Cleveland* (London, 1846), 547.
[2] I am indebted for some relevant information to a letter from Mr Clifford Cook, of Ashby-de-la-Zouch, Leicestershire.

wise attracted no attention. James and Grace moved shortly to Marton, the village already briefly described, a mile to the westward; and here, in a two-roomed, clay-built thatched cottage, their second child and second son was born, on 27 October 1728, being baptised in the village church of St Cuthbert on 3 November as 'James, yᵉ son of a day labourer'. It is evident that the Cook family was strongly conservative in their choice of names for elder sons. There were six other children born to the couple, of whom four died young: Mary, born 1732, who died in her fifth year; Jane, born 1738, who also died in her fifth year; another Mary, born 1740, who died at ten months; and a son William, born 1745, who died at the age of three. There were two survivors besides James beyond the year 1750, his sisters Margaret and Christiana. James Cook, born and baptised in that cold time of the year 1728, an infant strong, tough, and if the child is physically as well as mentally the father of the man, large-boned, with a clutch on survival, was the child whose career we have now to pursue. What combination of factors, in the mingled blood of a Lowland Scots labourer and a Yorkshire village woman, went to produce that remarkable career, we may ask without useful answer. Sobriety, orderliness, industry, all virtues to be respected, we might quite well be prepared for and deduce. Genius, of whatever sort, takes us unawares: is not, even in retrospect, deducible. We can ponder, if we choose, over the unlikely origins, in place and circumstance, of a maritime distinction so extraordinary.

A fitful light, as usual with the annals of the poor, plays on the boy's earliest years. A few months after his birth his parents went to another cottage—presumably, as they now had two sons, a larger one—and at some time thereafter his birthplace became the village ale-house, at the sign of the Bear. His father worked most regularly for a Mr Mewburn. When the baby became a small boy he went to learn his letters with Mrs Walker, whose husband farmed Marton Grange; the Walker family story was that this education of a promising youth was in return for his services round the place, running errands and watering stock.[1] No doubt he engaged in the other

[1] The Walker family story tended to move over into legend. Ord, who tells Cook's story in a very large footnote, 545 ff., writes in his elevated style, 'Dame Walker was the daughter of the wealthiest farmer in the neighbourhood; and her husband, a respectable yeoman of the first class, resided at Marton Grange. Young Cook, then a mere lad, tended the stock, took the horses to water, and ran errands for the family; and in return for such services, the good old lady, finding him an intelligent, active youth, was pleased to teach him his alphabet and reading. Dame Walker was great-great-great grandmother to the author on the maternal side.'—The 'intelligent, active youth' would then be six or seven years old, and 'the good old lady', if she died in 1789, aged 89, as Ord says, would be in her mid-thirties.

pursuits of small boys in a small village. About 1736 there was a further family removal to Ayton or Great Ayton ('Yatton' of the natives), a move which argues steadiness, sobriety and intelligence on the part of James Cook senior; for he had been made 'hind', or foreman, to Mr Thomas Skottowe, of Airyholme farm; virtually, it appears, he was the farm-manager. Ayton was four miles from Marton, a much larger village—even, we are told, with some good buildings; its situation was pleasant, on the edge of the sombre Cleveland hills, among which stood out the kingly shape of Rosebury or Roseberry Topping; it had its own small river, a branch of the Leven. It was not far from a market-town, Stokesley; and with its watermills and rural manufactories, weaving, tanyards, brewery, brick-kiln, and so forth,[1] could entertain a growing boy with some variety, when he was let off from farm-work or school. Skottowe belonged to the gentry rather than to the class of yeomen-farmers— Cook was to come across one of his sons in official position at a later date—a benevolent as well as substantial man; and noticing that the boy had some brains, he paid the small fees asked for him at the Postgate School at Ayton, where Mr Pullen the master taught him writing, arithmetic and his catechism, and perhaps more read-ing than Mrs Walker could. The school, the charitable foundation in 1704 of Michael Postgate, a local yeoman-farmer, was rebuilt in 1785, part of an oblong block of schoolhouse and poorhouse com-bined, so that the present-day pilgrim will find nothing on which to exercise emotion but original stones. James was said to have been good at his sums: he certainly left no lasting impression of academic brilliance, or displayed visible ambition for a nobler scholarship. We may guess that he helped his father well enough with the horses and about the farmyard; a country-bred boy, in his after career he had a good eye for the land as well as the sea. There may be hind-sight and a little of fancy in one of the small bits of reminiscence that have survived from the 1740's; but as this does not set him out as a paragon of leadership it may not improbably be true, high flown as is the historian of Cleveland.

During young Cook's continuance at this village seminary it appears that he was never much regarded by the other boys of the school, and was generally left behind in their juvenile excursions; a circumstance, which can only be attributed to his steady adherence to his own plans and schemes, never giving way to the *contre-projets* of his associates. This, instead of conciliating their regard, naturally rendered them averse from

[1] John Graves, *The History of Cleveland* (Carlisle, 1808), 197. I take it that Great Ayton had not changed essentially between 1736 and the beginning of the next century.

his company. It has been asserted by those who knew him at this early period of his life, that he had such an obstinate and sturdy way of his own, as made him sometimes appear in an unpleasant light; notwithstanding which, *there was a something* in his manners and deportment, which attracted the reverence and respect of his companions.

The seeds of that undaunted resolution and perseverance which afterwards accelerated his progress to immortality, were conspicuous, even in his boyish days. Frequently, on an evening, when assembled together in the village, to set out in search of birds' nests, Cook might be seen in the midst of his comrades, strenuously contending that they should proceed to some particular spot: This he would sometimes do, with such inflexible earnestness, as to be deserted by the greater part of his companions.[1]

How long Cook remained a village seminarist, with the leisure occupations of birds' nesting and argument, before he emerged on the world as a master of reading, writing, and arithmetic and (a little less so) of spelling; whether he spent the succeeding period exclusively in the employ of his father or Mr Skottowe and how wide was his farm practice, how far he rambled from Ayton, who made the next suggestion for the career of a likely lad—of all these things we are ignorant. But it seems as if something—proficiency in arithmetic?—marked him out as perhaps equal to the demands of commerce; for we next find him, in 1745, at the age of seventeen, a shop-boy with Mr William Sanderson, grocer and haberdasher, of Staithes. This was not regular apprenticeship, there were no indentures, it was trial on both sides; Sanderson was a wise and amiable man. The building which contained his house and shop was close to the sea, and as early as 1812 was pulled down lest it should be washed away, to be rebuilt in its present position in Church Street by his successors in business;[2] the counter on which the youth measured out raisins and ribbon was removed in 1835 to Middlesbrough, 'Captain Cook's Shop' is but dubiously his. Over the original site the waves flow deep. The importance of this shop-keeping interlude is not commercial. What Cook learnt from it, obviously, was that he did not want to be a shop-keeper. We need give only the most fleeting attention to the famous story of his exchange of a shilling of his own for a bright new shilling in the till, one of those issued by the South Sea Company, which excited his curiosity, and Sanderson's displeasure at fancied dishonesty—a trivial affair blown up to dramatic proportions by more than one romancer. Sanderson and his family had and kept James in high regard. The important thing was Staithes itself. Cook might have become a sailor

[1] Graves, 456, n.
[2] Arthur Kitson, *Captain James Cook* (London, 1907), 7.

without Staithes, but there it was, the little fishing port—the most considerable fishing port, indeed, on that part of the coast—at the foot of a gash in the cliffs, alive, active. Strong Yorkshire figures took out their boats or brought them in, heaved up their baskets of fish, bent working over their pointed flat-bottomed cobles; strong Yorkshire voices sounded over the wash of the waves; ropes were coiled, nets dried in the wind; the smell of the beach, of seaweed and tar was different from that of the farmyard, it blew into the shop; the children playing on the beach, in and out of the boats, the youths of seventeen, seemed a different race from those land-bound beings a few miles westward; how could another youth of seventeen, glimpsing all this at door or window, or gazing out towards the procession of sails north and south on the horizon, half the traffic of the North Sea, and then turning back to the groceries and ribbons, not be stirred to restlessness? Nothing can be more reasonably certain than that Cook had his first taste, as well as sight, of the sea at Staithes, and that the experience was convincing. Nevertheless, he did not run away, he finished his shop-life by no act of romantic daring; he stood it for eighteen months in all sobriety, we are led to believe, and then the good Sanderson himself, having made requisite enquiries, went over to Whitby with him and arranged his formal apprenticeship, as 'a three-years servant', to Mr John Walker.

The word respectable recurs. John Walker was greatly to be respected, a Quaker ship-master, ship-owner, and coal-shipper, who made a firm with his brother Henry, though it was to John exclusively that the young Cook was bound apprentice. The Quaker connection was powerful in the town—its first meeting house was built in 1676—and a Quaker dignity and restraint marked many of the stone and brick dwellings of the old town, among them John Walker's own house in Haggersgate, on the west side of the river, where Cook lodged with his master, and that of John Walker's mother, the late seventeenth-century building in Grape Lane on the east side, to which Walker removed in 1752.[1] The youth, coming to his first metropolis (Whitby's inhabitants numbered upwards of ten thousand) as well as his first port, may have noticed solidity as well as bustle; and Whitby's long and honourable history, even where it was built on sand-banks, ran back far beyond the reigns of the Georges, far beyond the ruined abbey on its east cliff through the centuries of the building and re-building of its parish church of St

[1] Mrs Walker's house and its attic in Grape Lane are popularly regarded as the premises where Cook lived and slept, but the dates make this impossible. John Walker's house in Haggersgate no longer exists. There seems to have been no connection between these Walkers and the farming family of Marton.

Mary near by, the very image of a seafaring people's church. Its streets were none of them far from the river, and though these might smell less of fish than did the narrow beach of Staithes, Whitby had its fishermen, and there were other smells connected with the sea— of mud-flats at ebb of tide, of shipyards, of sail-makers' lofts, of rope-walks. The whale-fishery had not yet begun; but Whitby men at the middle of the century owned over two hundred ships, trading on the English coast, to the Baltic, the Mediterranean, America; even, when chartered by the Honourable Company, to India and China. Ship-building and boat-building had gone on from time immemorial; towards the end of the seventeenth century really big ships, on the reckoning of the time, began to come from the yards. A revolution in transport was to destroy the old industry; in the next century railway companies bought and filled in the docks, turned shipyards into station-yards, obliterated all that sober glory. Whitby in its ship-building prime had five principal yards, as well as the innumerable builders of small craft and cobles. When Cook entered the service of Walker, in 1746, the firms so closely identified with his voyages, Thomas Fishburn and the Langborns, had not yet established themselves, but the west bank of the river was busy, and John Walker the ship-owner had not far to go from his house in Haggersgate to the yard where his ships were built. The picture is one of industry, enterprise, propriety, and the few later letters we have of Walker to Cook reflect in him, at least, a sober and benevolent soul. A seaport, on the other hand, is not all sobriety and benevolence; Whitby had its numerous taverns; its quarrels and riots, over press-gang or smuggling; its crimes and punishments and unhealthinesses and uproars of the eighteenth century in general. As an introduction to life, whether urban or maritime, it was for a country boy adequate. Has his life so far seemed obscure and dull? It will not in the future seem dull to him.

The coal trade, too, in which the Walkers were concerned, was one of the great trades of Britain, and opened vistas of the real metropolis. Coal was the 'grand commodity of the northern counties';[1] a thousand ships or more carried coal, four hundred of them to London, in the annual trade from the Tyne—at this time a million tons of it, and the quantity increased every year. In the year a ship might make as many as ten voyages, granted the most favourable conditions, though they were generally fewer. It was no wonder that this trade was regarded as—to use the ancient, the hallowed phrase

[1] Quoted in E. Lipson, *Economic History of England* (5th ed., 1948), II, 113.

—'a nursery of seamen': not a writer who mentions it but mentions it thus. Nurseries of seamen, however, carried with them a paradox: so far from being the abodes of a gentle tenderness, they were the hardest nurseries that ever existed. The east coast of England was a treacherous coast, unlighted, unbuoyed, its charts rudimentary, its harbours bar-harbours, its tides to be watched; the North Sea was a treacherous sea. The dangers were not merely the offshore dangers of sunken rocks and rocky shelves, breakers and sand-spits and sand-banks, tidal streams, storms and thick weather, but the banks far out from land, the storms and thick weather from England to the Baltic. Gales might be propitious, weather clear, all well, two or three hundred ships might sail out of Newcastle harbour on one tide, after long-continued easterly winds, and reach London in safety; losses might not be considered, from one year's end to the other, outrageous; yet men in Cook's day remembered, and long after his day remembered, the things that they had known—innumerable groundings, single wrecks that they had survived, the ship that sank with all hands before their eyes; the sixteen ships that crossed the bar of Shields together, the six that were left after the northerly tempest that all at once fell on them, the twenty-three lost on the Norfolk coast in one dreadful night of storm.[1] But apart from such shattering misfortune, the good master, in a well found vessel, who knew his coast and kept an offing, came through; prided himself on his reputation as a seaman, resented any slight cast upon it; might even legitimately hope, as an able and prudent man, to retire owner or part-owner of his ship and live in decent comfort. The competent seaman could hope to be a master. There was in that trade a great deal of competence. It was concerned not merely with the management of ships in general, but with the management of a particular sort of ship under particular conditions.

Apprentices worked hard, a man who had been one not many years after Cook tells us.[2] They learnt the ropes and learnt their ship. Seamen as well as mates and masters were responsible, competent, and strict instructors, and the senior apprentice exercised a sort of delegated authority. The boy normally got one half-day's shore leave in a week. He was given care of some particular part of the

[1] Henry Taylor, *Memoirs of The Principal Events in the Life of Henry Taylor* (North Shields, 1811). Taylor, nine years younger than Cook, went to sea in the coal trade when about 13, as a six-years' apprentice, and became master of a ship when 21. His experience, coal trade and North Sea, was much like Cook's, and his picture of the life is the best we have. He left the sea at 35, to become a ship and insurance broker at North Shields, and to carry on a valuable propaganda for coastal lights (with which, indeed, his book is largely concerned).
[2] i.e. Taylor.

ship's stores, which he had to have ready immediately it was called for. The lazy unhandy boy was set to tasks a smart apprentice considered degrading, like sweeping the decks or cleaning out the boats; the smart boy, as he felt at home, had paths to distinction, the race to be first up the rigging or at the windlass pawls. 'To haul out the weather earing when the topsails were to reef, to ship the first handspike, and to cat the anchor, were objects contended for by men and boys, as point of honor.'[1] To be one of a score who managed a ship of three or four hundred tons, aloft and below, only a quarter of whom, in addition to master and mate, were out of indentures, was no small thing. To handle her, not merely in a gale at sea, but in the narrow entrance of a small river harbour, or over the shifting sandbanks of the Thames, with other shipping about, to keep her off the bottom or know when she could safely rest upon it, to bring her to anchor or get her under weigh in a crowd, these might be feats of learning or technique indeed. And the ship, the instrument of this art, was a specialised thing—in appearance the clumsiest thing, it might be thought, that could be created. The broad-bottomed blunt-bowed Whitby collier was no sprite of the sea: she was a 'cat-built' vessel, or simply a 'cat'. The cat was defined by the *Dictionary of the Marine*[2] as 'a ship employed in the coal trade, formed from the Norwegian model. It is distinguished by a narrow stern, projecting quarters, a deep waist, and by having no ornamental figure on the prow . . . generally built remarkably strong', and carrying from four to six hundred tons; a vessel, that is, of severe lack of beauty, which a figure-head could hardly have conferred; a vessel also that could be converted from carrying coals to carrying any large amount of cargo for its size; a vessel for its purpose, under the right conduct, thoroughly handy. Go even now to Whitby, from which the colliers and the ship-yards have vanished, with its bar harbour, its outside kelp-covered rocks, the drying mud and shingle of the flats at low tide, when the Esk gives up the struggle to cover that not so wide estuary: one look makes plain a whole period of ship design and building. The collier was built to 'take the ground' as well as to float upon the waters.

Into this life plunged the young Cook, fugitive from retail trade —young, but at eighteen or nearly eighteen rather old for a beginning apprentice—and joined the men and boys so thickly recruited from the Yorkshire coastal villages. While seamen are in the nursery they do not have individual prominence; and, as might be expected,

[1] Taylor, 158.
[2] William Falconer, *A Universal Dictionary of the Marine*. I have used the 1789 edition.

we get few personal details of the youth during these years. The muster-rolls of a number of Walker's ships still exist, however, through which, with other indications, we can follow his life in general terms. Between voyages he lived in the stable environment of his master's house, where, it is said, Walker encouraged him to study the theory of navigation—whatever that means: one supposes he learnt something about the compass and its variation, and latitude, and studied sail-plans, and what charts he could get hold of, and plans of ships, and improved on the arithmetic he had brought away from the Postgate School. He had another friend in Walker's house besides Walker, the housekeeper Mary Prowd, who coddled his studies in a quiet corner with a private table and candle. The industrious apprentice got full sympathy. But his real learning had to be, in the first place, seamanship; in the second place, as a coastal seaman, actual memorisation of his coast and the dangers that lay off it, the peculiarities of harbours and the winds that blew in them —the sort of knowledge and its application, including a good deal of rule of thumb, that would become second nature to him. So the men from whom the 'servant' Cook chiefly learnt, apart from those by whose side he bent sails or heaved at the windlass, were probably John Jefferson, master of the *Freelove* and the *Three Brothers*, and his mate Robert Watson; for we have record of Walker himself sailing as master only for two passages of the *Freelove* from London in 1747, and for a month on the maiden passage of the *Three Brothers* to London, with Jefferson, a man of 32, as his co-master then. Watson was five years younger. Good men could rise young in that service. Walker's function from then, it is clear, was that of owner.

Cook's first voyage was in the *Freelove*, a ship—that is a three-masted vessel, square-rigged—of 341 tons, 106 feet in length with a beam of 27 feet—somewhat the equivalent, indeed, of the vessel in which, twenty-two years later, he was first to go exploring, and built as a collier at Great Yarmouth, Norfolk, in 1746. Walker must have acquired her immediately, or almost immediately, she was built. She carried a complement of nineteen—master, mate, carpenter, cook, five seamen, and ten 'servants' or apprentices. The birthplace and domicile of all these last is given in the muster-roll as Whitby, and they ranged in age from nineteen down to fifteen.[1] Cook was one of the oldest, but he was not nineteen in 1747 until 27 October; the date when he entered is given as 26 February and the date of his discharge as 22 April, his period aboard for this voyage being one month and 25 days, like four other of the apprentices. Unfortunately

[1] The surviving muster-rolls are now preserved in the Whitby Museum.

the places of entry and discharge are not given, so we are at a loss to know where he went. The master and some of the seamen were entered on 20 February and discharged on 7 June; one apprentice served for only twenty-three days; the reckonings do not always match when they should. The next record is of an autumn and winter passage from London, where the same apprentices (some with different ages, Cook now with birthplace Marton and domicile Great Ayton) were entered on 29 September 1747. Two seamen were discharged at Shields, which indicates a cargo of Tyne coal to Whitby, where the generality of the company left the ship on 17 December, Cook's stay on board being this time two months and nineteen days; and other indications are that for the last month the ship was manned almost entirely by the 'servants'. It is evident that these youths were beginning to know the east coast from the Thames at least as far north as Tynemouth, and that much was expected of them. Whether, when their coal was unloaded at a Thames-side wharf, they got leave from their ship long enough to go up to the city and fill their eyes with its sights, whether James was smitten with the metropolis, whether Walker recommended him to the London Quaker connection, we have no means of useful conjecture.

Walker had a new ship under construction, and it is said that Cook took part in her rigging and fitting out, invaluable experience again. She was the *Three Brothers*, apparently a quite large vessel.[1] Jefferson became her master, and took into her with him a number of the *Freelove* men, including six of the apprentices. Cook was one of these, and was in the ship continuously from 14 June 1748 to 8 December 1749. For the early part of this time she was in the coal trade; then, with stalls for forty horses, was chartered by government for some months as a transport, carrying troops that had been engaged in Flanders from Middleburg to Dublin and Liverpool.[2] After the completion of this service Cook signed on for the first time as a seaman, 20 April 1750, his apprenticeship over and perhaps with a little pride

[1] Kitson, 11, says she was 'of some 600 tons', and she 'was still in existence near the close of the last [i.e. 19th] century.' It seems doubtful whether a 600-ton ship could have been managed by a crew of nineteen, the number given in her muster-roll. An entry in the catalogue of a Cook exhibition at the National Maritime Museum, Greenwich, in 1956–7, refers to her as 'over 400 tons', but gives no authority. Richard Weatherill, *The Ancient Port of Whitby and its Shipping* (Whitby, 1908), has no particulars.

[2] I follow Kitson, 12, in this; but Navy Board letters shown at the exhibition referred to in the previous note, on the chartering of a *Three Brothers*, William Drake master, convinced the officials concerned that the ship, 'in which Cook was then serving', sailed from Gravesend for Flanders in March 1747 and for Williamstadt in February 1748. Cook however was in the *Freelove* in 1747, and appears in the *Three Brothers* (master John Jefferson) only in June 1748—and she was then a new ship. The name *Three Brothers* may have been a popular one: the National Maritime Museum mentions another, 97 tons, taken up for transport duties at Whitehaven in December 1746.

at his heart. His ship for the rest of the year was in the trade to Norway. His acquaintance with the sea, with coasts and with ports, was extending. He may have fancied this North Sea trade; for we next find him, all his old shipmates left behind, in the *Mary* of Whitby, owned by John Wilkinson and commanded by William Gaskin— some relative of Walker—for eight months to and from the Baltic, February to 5 October 1750, when he was discharged at London. He was next in a Sunderland ship, unspecified, till he returned to the *Three Brothers* for 1751 and 1752, her master being Robert Watson, the mate of his first voyage. In December of this latter year Watson moved as master to the *Friendship*, another new Walker ship, and with him went James Cook, mate. The mate remained in the *Friendship* for two and a half years, with successive masters, after Watson, in John Swainston and Richard Ellerton: with the last-named of these men he seems to have formed a positive friendship. There is no doubt that he had learnt a great deal. The practice of seamanship, as well as its theory, has been adverted to, the rule of thumb, the line of coast alive in the mind. He had not been confined to one shore: he knew the North Sea and its further side, at least in ports from the Netherlands to Norway; he had been through the Channel and into the Irish Sea; but it was the east coast of England that had given him his most intimate experience, the experience of the inshore sailor. We shall see the deposit of that experience active in his mind on coasts far distant, as dangerous, still unknown.

We must beware of too much eloquence. James Cook, at this point of his career, in his twenty-seventh year, knew his business pretty well. It was the business, however, of a good seaman, rather than of a highly educated one. He certainly disposed of no refined technique of navigation, and it would be hard to think of anyone who at that time did, though there were a number of treatises and text-books on the current practice of the art, as well as a variety of suggestions for its improvement. We may conjecture that at home with Walker, or later, in the course of self-education, he studied something of the earlier sort. He could hardly have read the famous *Elements of Navigation* of John Robertson, mathematical teacher and librarian to the Royal Society, over which eighteenth-century sailors pored, unless he were a very up-to-date student indeed, because its first edition appeared only in 1754. We may conjecture a little further, and guess, if he read a book, it was another extremely well known in its day, the *Practical Navigation* of John Seller, which, though first published in 1669, went through edition after edition for seventy years. Seller, a compass-maker and chart publisher of Wapping, gave rules, described instruments—the ring-dial, the cross-staff, the backstaff, the azimuth compass, the nocturnal dipping-needle—provided tables: 'the whole being delivered in a manner so well adapted to the general humour of mariners', as one critic observed, that it could not help having a long run.[1] But if Walker fancied a different work, there were half a dozen or more he could choose from—some *Art* or *Elements* or *Treatise* or *Complete Tutor*—to place before his servant. One way or another, the young man would have learnt a little elementary astronomy and geometry, and how to use the more popular instruments; how to find a latitude and work out his position with the traverse board, how to allow for leeway and the other incidents of a ship's behaviour at sea. It is very possible that he had his own backstaff, or Davis's quadrant as it was now called, that old friend of mariners; probably he knew all about Hadley's quadrant, since Hadley invented it in 1731, though it may be doubtful whether he could afford to own one. He would probably on his experience not have seen much reason to differ from Halley—'the celebrated Doctor Halley'—that the system of navigation in his time depended on the three L's of Lead, Latitude and Look-out,[2] or to think that times had changed much. Look-out and Lead did not need to be taught theoretically. Henry Taylor, whose memoirs are so instructive about the conditions of the coal trade in which both he and Cook served, nevertheless found it worth while to point out that 'Another necessary duty, especially on this coast, is that of frequently casting the lead. . . . Even in crossing the North Sea it is necessary to have recourse to the lead';[3] and he adds a cautionary tale about a master who scorned it. In thick or hazy weather one practically navigates

[1] The words quoted are those of Dr James Wilson, in the preliminary 'Dissertation on the Rise and Progress of the Modern Art of Navigation' which he contributed to the second and third editions (1764 and 1772) of Robertson's book; he goes on, 'the last [edition] I have seen, was in 1739; but some late writers seem to have abated the run of this book.' Its full title was *Praxis Nautica: Practical Navigation: or, an Introduction to the whole Art.* The *Dictionary of the Marine* lists a number of the 'late writers'—e.g. Edward Hauxley, *Navigation Unveil'd* (1743), a perfectly conventional treatment in spite of its dramatic title; John Barrow, *Navigatio Britannica* (1750); and so on. Cook must have encountered Robertson's book later on. It is interesting to note that William Wales, the astronomer of the second voyage, brought out new editions of it in 1780, 1786 and 1796; so that it too had a long life.

[2] Quoted, by William Hutchinson, 'Mariner, And Dock Master at Liverpool', on p. 110 of his valuable volume beginning *A Treatise* and boiling down to *Practical Seamanship.* Hutchinson, in his second edition of 1787, adds (p. 106), 'The latitude when it can be got by a good observation, with a good instrument, must be allowed to be the only guide we have in navigation; because it not only gives to a certainty, the ship's place, North and South, but it likewise helps us to form a judgment how far a dependance may be put on our reckoning, East or West; in proportion as the latitude by the account kept of the ship's way, agrees or disagrees with the latitude observed in the passage in general; so more or less dependance accordingly may be put upon the longtitude the ship is reckoned to be in.' This is rather unsophisticated for 1787.

[3] Taylor, 32.

by the lead, knowing where to expect such and such a depth of water and what sort of bottom. This means a highly admirable skill, certainly; it does not mean scientific navigation.

Cook's experience, to recur to that, was still a narrow experience: although not confined to the Narrow Seas, its widest sea was the North Sea. If the argument should be advanced by some battered captain that the North Sea should be experience enough for anyone, the answer would be No, for the complete sailor its coastwise and short voyage sailing was not enough. The coal trade, the Baltic trade were not the only nurseries of seamen. The Newfoundland trade was another highly-esteemed nursery, though not one into which Yorkshire boys normally entered. There were various Atlantic trades, and there were the long passages, out to India and China and back, which bred men 'the most perfect in the open seas'.[1] Cook had never yet been on a long voyage. To the immediate view, there were hundreds of mates like him, with the same training and the same experience—some of them with much more of it. Any Whitby owner of average judgment could easily pick up a good mate. It might not be quite so easy to pick up a first-rate master, particularly among men in their twenties; but there were hundreds of experienced and competent masters. However that may be, the young Cook had certainly gained the complete confidence of that sober person John Walker; for Walker now offered him the command of the *Friendship*, as next in the succession of her captains. To become master of a ship eleven years after becoming an apprentice could hardly be other than satisfactory to any man; and Cook must have been tempted. Instead, he volunteered into the royal navy as an able seaman.

[1] Hutchinson, 129; 'From all that I have seen, the seamen in the *East India* trade are the most perfect in the open seas, and those in the coal trade to *London* the most perfect in difficult narrow channels, and tide ways. . . .'

II

The Navy

HE VOLUNTEERED at Wapping on 17 June 1755; and the only recorded reason is that he determined to 'take his future fortune' that way;[1] or, much the same thing as recollected by Walker, 'he had always an ambition to go into the Navy'.[2] Among merchant seamen this was unusual. As between the two services there might seem to be no possible claim that the navy had on the rational man. If such a man, for his own purposes, wanted a different sort of ship from colliers, or a longer voyage than those of the coal or Baltic trades, he could join an Atlantic vessel, or enter the service of the East India Company. The disadvantage of that choice was that any seaman in the merchant service was in time of war subject to the depredations of the press gang, on shore or afloat, in his home port or as he finished a hard passage at Bombay or Calcutta. But there were years of peace as well as years of war; and in any case Cook, as the master of a merchant ship, could not have been pressed. We do not take at face value Dr Johnson's reflections on the sailor's life in general, that no man would be a sailor, who had contrivance enough to get himself into a jail; 'for, being in a ship is being in a jail, with the chance of being drowned'. Men enough went to sea to give the lie to that remark; the merchant service at least was adequately manned. The navy was a different matter. Its physical conditions were worse; its pay was worse; its food was worse, its discipline was harsh, its record of sickness was appalling. To the chance of being drowned could be added the chance of being flogged, hanged or being shot, though it was true that deaths in battle were infinitely fewer than deaths from disease. The enemy might kill in tens, scurvy and typhus killed in tens of hundreds. 'Manned by violence and maintained by cruelty', as were the fleets of Britain to the mind of that great man Admiral Vernon (and his head on so many inn

---

[1] Phrase from Kippis, 4.
[2] '. . . as Mr John Walker observes in a memorandum now lying before me', says E. H. Locker in his *Gallery of Greenwich Hospital*, part I (1831), 2.

signs was an index to his dearness to the mind of the people), it is staggering to the mind of the historian that these fleets could attain a reasonable efficiency of movement and survival, quite apart from winning battles and wars. Officers entered the navy voluntarily, from higher social classes, to make a career; but it was commonly thought in the profession that they should enter not later than their early adolescence, to be inured to its rigours soon enough for other modes of life to be deprived of attraction. A midshipman might do the duty of a seaman, and get a seaman's pay, but he was a young gentleman, and aspired to become a lieutenant as soon as he had served the requisite term of years, and come of age, and passed his examination. He was in embryo a professional man. The ordinary seaman might be the scum of the dockyards, or an unfortunate landsman picked up by the press-gang, or something in between sent on board drunk by a crimp and unable to desert; the able sea-man, however he got on board, and even if he had settled down to make the best of it, could hardly regard himself as a dedicated naval person, or his instincts as professional instincts. Men could be trained as seamen; they could, even under the conditions of the time, give loyalty and devotion to a good officer; a really good officer might even make a ship seem almost a humane place. The appearance of many men when they were first dragged on board a ship, however, might almost break an officer's heart; and in spite of all the diffi-culties of bringing the navy from a peace footing to a war footing— raising its general complement, that is, from 16,000 to 80,000—there were numbers of miserable beings passed from ship to ship, unfor-tunates whom nobody wanted and the system yet could not bear to lose. In 1755 the navy was going on to a war footing. England and France were on the edge of world conflict, though each still pre-ferred to maintain the fiction of peace, and in England there was a 'hot press'. It brought in little of value, only 'very indifferent lands-men'. The arrival of Cook at the Wapping rendezvous must therefore have been an agreeable incident in the day of the lieutenant in charge: a man young though mature enough, strong-faced, tall, well set-up, healthy, a seaman—and a volunteer, a prize indeed; with nothing against his intelligence, perhaps, except that he was a volunteer. The lieutenant must have looked at him with curiosity as well as gratification. Presumably, if Walker offered him the com-mand of a ship, there must have been some correspondence between them, and to the respectable Quaker the step his protégé was taking can hardly have appeared proper or wise. No correspondence has survived. The £2 bounty can hardly have been an attraction to

Cook, or the able seaman's wage of £1 4s a month. There were precedents, though few, that he might have heard of, of men rising from the lower to the quarter deck; but if that sort of ambition stirred in him, there is no evidence that he ever confided it in anyone. If he was finding the coasting trade dull, and thought that naval service, whatever its drawbacks, offered a lively mind more variety and more excitement, this was as good a time as any to make the change. We can henceforth follow his career a little more clearly. It is still, over a period, largely an anonymous career: not quite anony- mous, because he was a man enrolled, we know where he was, and one or two things he did in the course of duty; but for the most part his personal history is subsumed in the history of a ship. We view his experience, we do not know what effect his experience had on him.

The volunteer was sent to the *Eagle*, Captain Joseph Hamar,[1] a 60-gun ship then moored at Spithead. She had come out of dock in Portsmouth harbour on 8 May, with only her lower masts and bow- sprit standing, no rigging, and a vast deal to do to fit her for sea. There was still plenty to do when Cook made his first appearance in her, on 25 June. His appearance, we are to gather, was highly satisfactory to Captain Hamar, because a month later he was rated master's mate.[2] We have the log he dutifully began to keep, the first of many: 'Log Book on Board his Maj⁵ Ship Eagle, Kept by Jam⁵ Cook Masters Mate Commencing the 27ᵗʰ June 1755, And Ending the 31ˢᵗ of December 1756'; and the first of innumerable entries registering wind and weather. The master was the very capable Thomas Bisset. Work on the ship went forward; at the beginning of July the fleet at Portsmouth was ceremonially visited by the First Lord of the Admiralty, Lord Anson, and the Duke of Cumberland; ships and admirals came and went; the master's mate recorded such happenings as '[20 July] Rec⁴ on Board 12 Chalder of Coals & 3 Cask's of Char Coal, wᵗʰ other Stoars for Pursser, Emp⁴ in Makeing Points & Pointing Ropes Ends'—or the arrival of 'his Maj⁵ Ship Giberalter'; on 27 July all the volunteers on board got two months' pay in advance; and at last, on 4 August, the *Eagle* sailed: 'weigh'd & Came to Sail, Saw a water Spout to yᵉ S.W.'[3] On that day too the mate, in an incursion into the learned unusual

[1] Kitson and others spell his name Hamer, but he signs himself in his log/journal, Adm 51/292, 'Jos. Hamar'.
[2] 'Immediately', not 'a month later', if we are to take literally the title-page of his *Eagle* log, now in the ATL. But Kitson correctly gives the date of his promotion as 24 July, going on the muster book, Adm 36/5533. It is possible that he began to keep a log even as A.B., inscribing the title-page later.
[3] The quotations and dates given in this chapter are from Cook's log, ATL, unless otherwise attributed.

among seamen, begins to use the astronomical symbols for the days of the week: he is already a slightly unusual young man.

The primary aim of the navy was the interruption of French communication with the possessions of France in North America, an aim in which it had so far not been markedly successful. The earlier intention for the *Eagle* was that she should cross the Atlantic to the Leeward Islands. In July, however, this plan was changed, and Hamar was ordered on a cruise outside St George's Channel, between the Scilly Islands and Cape Clear on the Irish coast. He was to put himself under the command of Admiral Hawke. It was a cruise of no great glory. One day out a sail to the south was taken to be a French ship of war, and chased, but proved a Dutch merchantman. From day to day small vessels were chased, stopped and examined; and Hamar, short-handed as he was, did not miss the chance to press men when he could from the London-bound—three one day, four another.[1] Half-way through August the weather turned squally. At the beginning of September there were hard gales; early in the morning of the 1st, off the Old Head of Kinsale 'a Monstrous great Sea Carry'd away the Driver Boom in a deep Roll' (it is Hamar writing), and a few hours later the captain was convinced his main mast was sprung between decks. He decided to go into Plymouth for repairs, and there he was anchored on 5 September. After two surveys in a week the mast-makers could find nothing wrong; and then Hamar, ordered to sea again immediately by an indignant Admiralty, and ready for sailing, decided instead to put his ship in dock to clean and tallow her bottom. This was too much for the Admiralty, who did not like its commands ignored, and before the end of the month Hamar was superseded. On 1 October came on board in his stead Captain Hugh Palliser.[2] His arrival meant much more to Cook than either dreamed.

Palliser was another Yorkshireman, from the West Riding, well-rooted in the gentry; the son of an army captain. Five years older than Cook, he had had twenty years' more naval experience: he had gone to sea at the age of twelve, in an uncle's care, passed his examination and become a lieutenant when eighteen (which was three years too early for a commission according to the regulations), been in the action off Toulon in February 1744, and got his first command in 1746, the year in which Cook began as Walker's apprentice. He had served in the West Indies and on the Coromandel coast of India

[1] Bisset's log, Adm 52/578, 8 and 9 August 1755.
[2] Hamar, Adm 51/292, 29 September, 'This day Captⁿ Palliser Superceeded me in the Comand of the Eagle'.—Cook, 1 October, 'Came on Board, Capt Palliser & tooke Possesion of ye Ship'.

as well as on the English coast, and in September 1755 had just returned from convoying transports out to Virginia. He was a capable man, although certainly never hindered in professional advancement, to his new command he brought a good deal of energy. He sailed from Plymouth in the *Eagle* for the first time on 8 October. The cruise this time was down Channel and about its western approaches, under the general orders of West and Byng, rear-admiral and vice-admiral; but for the greater part of five weeks the *Eagle* was on her own. They were weeks of gales and squalls, hard on the sails, and no doubt hard on the sailors, as the ship chased anything in sight—vessels which usually turned out to be English, Spanish, Swedes, Hamburgers or Dutch, though she took two or three French ones, fishermen homeward bound from Newfoundland. In one chase forty leagues west of Ushant, 18 October, in a hard gale, her main topmast went by the board and the Frenchman escaped under cover of night; but next day, with a jury topmast, the *Eagle* fell in with the *Monmouth*, and the Frenchman being sighted again, the *Monmouth* took her. The prizes were sent in to Plymouth. The *Eagle*, with more than two hundred prisoners, continued cruising, ran into gales again in early November, carried away her main top-gallant mast in a squall, and on the 13th was with West and Byng in the Bay of Biscay.

She was present at the end of the *Espérance*, a French seventy-four short of fifty guns, which had eluded Boscawen's fleet on the other side of the Atlantic only to be maimed in the storms and brought up by West's squadron almost within reach of home: in a fight that for hopeless heroism was like that of the *Revenge* she was finally battered into surrender. She was to enter no British harbour as a prize, and Cook's log registers her last hours, on the afternoon of the 15th: 'Rec^d on B^d from ye Esperance 26 Prisoners att 4 ye Esperance on fire there being no Posabillity of Keeping her above water'. And so she went down. A few days after this funeral rite Byng, having returned to the Channel, ordered West and half-a-dozen ships, including the *Eagle*, into Plymouth Sound for cleaning and refitting; and here she remained from 21 November to 13 March 1756. On 27 November Palliser wrote to the Admiralty Secretary with the perennial captain's plaint. He had a great many men on board, he said, who were supernumeraries belonging to other ships, and had been received at different times from them or from hospital, to make up a sufficient crew to go to sea. What ships they properly belonged to he could not tell, and nobody wanted them: forty-four were alleged to belong to the *Ramillies*, she needed only six, and her boatswain thought only three worth taking. 'When their Lordships shall think proper to Compleat this Ships Complement I hope they'll be pleased to Order her a few good Men, for I assure you I have been much distressed this last Cruize having so very few Seamen on board.'[1] One of his best seamen, James Cook, in February spent a few days in hospital with an unspecified minor illness;[2] some of the others were flogged round the fleet for desertion; otherwise (and even thus) it was the routine of winter weeks in harbour.

The winter, so it seems, was marked for Cook by further promotion. 'AM had a Survey on Boatswain's Stores, when Succeeded ye Former Boatswain'. This was on 22 January. It may have been only temporary. As boatswain he would have been responsible for ropes, sails, cables and anchors, flags, and (not unnaturally) boats; his pay would have risen from £3 16s to £4 a month. It was very satisfactory, though Palliser still refers to him as a mate, he continues to appear in other records as master's mate, and as such he may continue to be referred to here.

The cruise last completed laid down the pattern for the next fifteen months, in and out of Plymouth Sound and hanging round the French coast, a period broken by one savage duel with the enemy and two interludes of semi-independence for the master's mate. Palliser reports on his proceedings for March–April.[3] He had sailed on 13 March for his station off Cape Barfleur, the eastern point of the Cherbourg peninsula, where he had not arrived because of strong winds till the 19th; on the 21st he had been joined by the *Windsor*, and cruised in company with her until they both joined the *Antelope*, Captain Gayton, Palliser's senior officer, who ordered him further west off the Isle of Batz on the Breton coast. He and Captain Faulkner of the *Windsor* agreed to keep company as far as that island in case a French convoy then in Cherbourg should sail that night and elude Gayton. They encountered no convoy, only two little sloops, smugglers from Guernsey with tea and brandy for the English coast: the weather was too bad and they were too short of men to detain these sloops, so they took out their cargoes and let them go. On 4 April they joined company with a British squadron of three ships and two cutters; Palliser sent one of the cutters into Guernsey to fetch out pilots, and sent Cook into the other. Cook's log entries for two weeks now relate to this experience, beginning with the morning of 5 April: 'Brot too on ye Star: Tack when I

[1] Palliser to Clevland, 27 November 1755, Adm 1/2292.
[2] Kitson, 20.
[3] Palliser to Clevland, 13 April 1756, Adm 1/2293; and his log, Adm 51/292, Part III.

went on Board yᵉ Cruzer Cutter, to take yᵉ Command of her with Men, Arms, and Ammanishon. Modᵗ & Clowdy. In Company wᵗʰ yᵉ Eagle, Falmouth, Greyhound, & Firret Sloop.' Next day he makes a little drawing of the coast about Morlaix, with its buildings and rocks—already trying his hand, as if by instinct, on a 'coastal profile'. On the 8th, off the Tragoz rocks, two large French sails, taken for frigates, were chased but made their escape into Morlaix, where the British could not follow; then on the 12th an order was received from Captain Keppel to repair to Plymouth Sound, whence next day Palliser wrote to the Admiralty. He was out again on the 16th. Meanwhile Cook was off on his own, in and out of sight of the squadron, having some hard squalls and rain, no doubt enjoying the exercise of authority as he fired a few shots to bring vessels to— until he went on board the *Falmouth*, the commodore's ship, on the 21st, to return to Plymouth. Here on the 27th he and his men transferred to the *St Albans*, another 60-gun ship, which sailed on the 30th and joined the fleet of 'Admˡ Buscowon', Vice-Admiral of the Blue, off Ushant—a formidable array, and the master's mate copies out the line of battle. On 3 May he was once more on board the *Eagle*, now part of Boscawen's fleet. Boscawen met no French fleet—the British purpose was blockade—but as explicit war came nearer (it was declared on 18 May) the *Eagle*'s men began to die, and her log is a melancholy record. There was a little relief on 20 May, when in the Bay of Biscay she and the *St Albans* took two prizes, one 'a ship from Santimingo' with sugar and coffee (as Cook notes), and put boarding parties in both to carry them to port.[1] It was Cook who took command of 'yᵉ Triton prize' and got her into Plymouth at the end of the month, only to be sent round to London with her. By the end of June he had her moored securely in the Thames, had taken an inventory of her rigging and stores, sent his men back to Plymouth, and followed them himself. Rejoining his ship on 1 July, he was plunged into a very busy month of refitting.

Palliser had been sent into Plymouth by Boscawen to land his sick men and his prisoners. He arrived on 3 June, on which day his surgeon and four men died, to add to the twenty-two who had been buried in the previous month; he put 130 men in hospital, 'most of which are extreamly Ill', including the two surgeon's mates; and as he had thirty-five men away in prizes, and was thirty-four short of his complement, he reported himself in a very weak condition.[2] He landed 143 prisoners. There was a standing order at Plymouth to

[1] *Eagle* log, 22 May 1756 to 1 July.
[2] Palliser to Clevland, 3 June, 4 June 1756, Adm 1/2293.

dock, clean and refit any ship that came in from Boscawen, and while this was being done to the *Eagle* Palliser took further thought. The sickness and mortality that had raged in his ship, he reported, was in great measure owing to the want of clothes: his men were nearly all landsmen, who had never been at sea till they were sent on board the *Eagle*, 'Naked when they came on board being for the most part Vagabones not one in Twenty of them that had more than Shirt and one ragged Coat'. The established allowance of slops was not enough; when they became sickly he had to give them more, and he now wished to be indemnified for this over-expenditure of clothing.[1] The Lords were not unsympathetic: he was ordered 'To let the men be supplied with what they absolutely want and no more, and to take care they do not sell any part thereof'. He reported readiness for sea again on 6 July—which, if we are to take Cook's log seriously, can hardly have been so, though no doubt the ship was out of dock[2] and was ordered to rejoin Boscawen. In the interval, 'very much indisposed in a Fever', he had requested leave of absence for himself, with the temporary appointment of another captain.[3] Charles Proby, so designated, being detained by adverse winds in the Downs, Palliser was recovered and on board again by the time, 2 August, rumour spread of a French squadron in the Channel,[4] so that on the 4th he could sail again under the orders of Rear-Admiral Harrison. The French squadron seems to have been merely the figment of a Swedish mariner's imagination.[5] The *Eagle* first helped to convoy a large number of merchantmen down Channel; then, one of a dozen ships, took part in the blockade directed by Boscawen, cruising some sixty miles west of Ushant, chasing whatever appeared, seizing an occasional prize: it was a long cruise, that hardly rose above routine, and by the time she was back once more at Plymouth, on 11 November, her men had again begun to die. That was the other routine. When an advance payment of prize money

[1] Palliser to Clevland, 17 June 1756 and endorsement, Adm 1/2293.
[2] Palliser to Clevland, 6 July, Adm 1/2293: but Cook's log notes continuous work on the ship, rigging, loading, etc., till they sailed on 4 August.
[3] Palliser to Clevland, 18 July, Adm 1/2293.
[4] Palliser to Clevland, 2 August, Adm 1/2293.
[5] Kitson, 22, gives the story more at large: 'The report originated with the master of a Swedish trader, who, under examination, swore that he had seen nine ships off the Isle of Wight, flying a white flag, all large, and he estimated two to be 90-gun ships. He stated that he was boarded by a boat from one that he believed to be the flagship, and that after the boarding officer had returned to his ship, a gun was fired, and the whole squadron made sail. Very careful enquiry was made, and the portion of the Channel mentioned by the Swede was thoroughly searched, but no signs or tidings could be found of any French men-of-war having been in the neighbourhood, and the Swede paid the penalty of what seemed to be only an exercise of his imagination, by suffering a detention of some months in Portsmouth.'

was made in mid-December[1] it would have seemed to able seamen and warrant officers little enough to compensate for those dull and stormy months.

She left again, her crew increased to 420, on 29 December—the blockade was winter work as well as summer—only to meet a very hard gale of wind off the Isle of Wight on 4 January 1757, 'which blowed away most of our sails',[2] and forced her to put first into Spithead and then back to the Sound until 30 January, when she sailed with the fleet of Vice-Admiral West. This was a Biscayan cruise rather than an off-Channel one, and lasted till 15 April. Palliser was given fourteen days' leave for 'some business of consequence in town' while the usual cleaning and refitting went on.[3] On 25 May, in company with the *Medway*, another 60-gun ship, Captain Proby, she departed to rejoin Boscawen. Five days later she had her moment of glory. It was an Atlantic action, its place given by Palliser as about latitude 48° and 2° W of the Lizard—that is about 180 miles southwest of Ushant. At 1 o'clock in the morning, through driving rain, a sail was seen to the north-west of the two English ships. They immediately gave chase: 'let out the Reefs, & set Studding Sails & Clear'd Ship for Action', wrote Palliser in his log. The *Medway*, in the lead, omitted to clear for action, and was forced to bring to when nearly up with the chase to do so; by this time she had hoisted French colours. Proby, the senior captain, at first urged Palliser on, then wished him to shorten sail so that he himself might get into the action; Palliser, however, did not understand—possibly did not want to understand—the signals, and Proby managed only a few raking shots.

'At ¼ before 4', writes Palliser, 'Came along side the [chase] & Engaged at about Two Ships lengths from her the Fire was very brisk on both Sides for near an hour, she then Struck to us, She proved to be the Duc D'Acquitaine last from Lisbon, mounting 50 Guns all 18 Pounders, 493 Men, We had 7 men Killed in the Action & 32 Wounded, Our Sails & Rigging cutt almost all to Peices, soon after She Struck her Main & Mizen Masts went by the Board Employed the Boats fetching the Prisoners & carrying Men on board the Prize, Employed Knotting & Splicing the Rigging. Our Cutter was lost alongside the Prize by the going away of her Main Mast.'[4]

At the end of the day the prize's foremast also went by the board, and three of the *Eagle*'s men died of their wounds; another died two

[1] Palliser log, 17 December 1756, Adm 51/292/III.
[2] Palliser to Clevland, 6 January, 13 January 1757, Adm 1/2294; Palliser log, 30 January.
[3] Palliser to Clevland, 17 April 1757, Adm 1/2294.
[4] Palliser log, 30 May, Adm 51/292/III.

days later. Eighty (notwithstanding Palliser's first count) were wounded. The French losses were fifty killed and thirty wounded. The *Eagle* herself had suffered badly, her masts and rigging and sails 'very much shattered', sails indeed 'rent almost to rags', almost all the running rigging shot away, her sides full of shot-holes, and stuck, like her masts and yards, with bars of iron.[1] She was in no case to do much about her conquest, which the *Medway* took in tow. The latter had had only ten men injured from an accidental explosion of powder. The *Duc d'Aquitaine* was an East Indiaman of 1500 tons, commanded by 'the Sieur D'Esquelen'; she had landed a rich cargo at Lisbon, whence she had sailed on her way round to Lorient, equipped for war and hoping to intercept a British convoy about to sail from Lisbon in charge of the 20-gun *Mermaid*, but before this desperate action had taken only an English brig from Cadiz.[2] This the Sieur obligingly ransomed for £200, and let go.

The three ships put back into Plymouth together. Palliser found that his report made the Lords exceedingly happy, and he in his turn was made happy by their compliments. The prize was surveyed, found worth taking into the navy in spite of the 97 shot-holes through both her sides, and fitted out as a 64-gun ship under the same name. The *Eagle*, put into order again within a month, on 12 July sailed for Halifax across the Atlantic, to join Rear-Admiral Holburne, second-in-command to Boscawen, who was now blockading the formidable stronghold of Louisburg. His fleet, formidable too, was thwarted by foul weather as well as French daring; and by the end of September the *Eagle*, victim of a violent storm, had begun to stagger home across the Atlantic, leaking, with jury-masts and improvised sails, and men going down sick in tens and scores. She reached safety; but Palliser's days in her were almost at an end. He handed over the command in February 1758. He had been without two of his most valuable warrant officers for many months. Bisset, the master, had been appointed to the *Pembroke*, a ship still building, on 28 April 1757, and had a good deal to do with her even before she was launched. He thus missed the *Duc d'Aquitaine* affair. In this affair his mate, James Cook, stood an enemy's fire for the first time, and escaped cannon-balls and bars of iron. As he, too, was given preferment, between it and the following cruise, he also escaped the wretched experience of that October Atlantic crossing. It might have seemed a question, briefly, not whether the master's mate might have preferment, but what preferment he should have: for about this time, as we may guess, Palliser received a letter from Mr William Osbaldestone,

---

[1] Palliser to Clevland, 5 June, list of 'Visible Defects', Adm 1/2294.   [2] ibid.

member of Parliament for Scarborough, written on the stimulus
of John Walker of Whitby, suggesting that Cook might be commissioned. That is, the great principle of 'interest', spring of so much
naval advancement, was being tried on his behalf, and broke down—
the principle that what really counted in the profession was the influence which important persons, on the fringe of authority, could
bring to bear on important persons in authority. Really important
persons—a Lord of the Admiralty, perhaps—applied to by a noble
earl, or the son of a noble earl, or an influential contractor to the
navy, might quite light-heartedly lay aside a hallowed regulation to
oblige some favoured child of grace. But Mr Osbaldestone was not
one of the great members of parliament; Hugh Palliser, though he
had done very well, was still only a naval captain, not at all the son of
an earl, and he could not dispense with regulations or exert influence
on those who could; Mr Osbaldestone and Mr Walker perhaps
showed a little naïveté in applying to him. True, the war meant a
great demand not merely for able seamen but (though a lesser one)
for officers, particularly lieutenants, the rank at which commissions
started. There were still, however, plenty of unemployed though
qualified men to be employed; and the regulations had it that no
midshipman or mate without at least six years' naval service could
take his lieutenant's examination. An order had recently been issued
for the strict enforcement of this regulation. Here was a mate with
two years' service. Palliser was bound to reply as he did, that Cook
had been too short a time in the service for a commission, but that a
master's warrant might be given him, 'by which he would be raised
to a station that he was well qualified to discharge with ability and
credit'.[1] This was just; there can be no doubt that Palliser spoke up
for his mate. On 29 June 1757 James Cook attended at the Trinity
House, Deptford, passed his own examination, and came away with
a certificate stating that he was qualified 'to take charge as Master of
any of His Majesty's Ships from the Downs thro' the Channel to the
Westward and to Lisbon'; and, one presumes, in any other direction.[2]
On 30 June he was discharged from the *Eagle* and entered as master
in the *Solebay*, a 24-gun frigate, Captain Robert Craig.

[1] Kippis, 4–5, 'From the information of Sir Hugh Palliser'.
[2] Minute Books of the Trinity House, Deptford, 29 June 1757.

III

The Master

THE POSITION of master in a ship of the navy was an honourable and responsible one, without parallel at the present day; rooted in history, to the time when for purposes of war the royal servants hired a ship with her 'master' and crew all together, and installed in her the necessary military persons to 'fight' her, men skilled in arms but innocent of navigation. The transformation of these men into officers acquainted with the ways of the sea and of ships came in due course, but the master remained, of inferior social position, appointed not by commission from the Admiralty but by warrant from the Navy Board; perhaps with a minimum of formal education (and a good many of his superiors might have not much more) but trained by hard experience and his own ability; the chief professional on board though not the highest ranking one, the man who never ceased to retain control, as a professional thing, of the ship's navigation. He was subject of course to the orders from the captain, who got his orders from an admiral or the Admiralty; but it would be an unwise captain who ignored, or overrode, his subordinate's particular expertness. Apart from navigation the master was responsible, over the boatswain, for masts, yards, sails and rigging, for stores, for general management. In between navigation and management he had a special responsibility for pilotage and harbour-work, and for what may be called the investigative side of his trade, for taking soundings and bearings and correcting or adding to charts—often enough for making new ones. He was responsible for the ship's log. His responsibilities were endless, his signature always in demand. This did not mean that captain, lieutenants, mates, midshipmen were merely ornamental. They had duties, laid down in the black and white of the naval *Regulations and Instructions*; some of their duties were, on paper, very like a master's; but the master's were cumulative. He wore no uniform. His competence was certified when he passed his examination. In the end his capacity to find his position at sea was outdistanced by officers with scientific accomplishment enough to master the relevant astronomy and mathematics; but there was more to a master than dead reckoning. In the hierarchy of pay he might, depending on the rating of his ship, get more than a lieutenant. The value of a good master was beyond computation in gold or rubies. For this very reason there was a tendency for masters to remain masters: who would wish to waste such a man by giving him a commission? It was into this select brotherhood, more than into a particular ship, that Cook now entered.

The *Solebay*'s duty was the patrol of the eastern coast of Scotland and of the Orkney and Shetland islands, against smuggling and 'treasonable intercourse' with France or Holland. Her base was at Leith on the Firth of Forth; there she had just returned and was at anchor in Leith Road when Cook joined her on 30 July 1757. He must have had leave in the month since his discharge from the *Eagle*, but how he spent it one can but speculate. He had pay in his pocket, and one guesses that he made his way from Plymouth to London, where, at the Black Swan in Holborn, he took the coach for Yorkshire, to visit his parents, and John Walker and his other friends at Whitby, on his way to Scotland. One guesses also, from the flourishes encircling his signature in the new log that he began to keep on entering his ship, that he derived a little, and proper, pride in now being 'James Cook; Master' of one of His Majesty's ships. It is a routine log,[1] and the cruise it chronicles was one without particular incident, notable perhaps for no more than giving Cook his only view of the Scottish coast—which was a view, however, that he remembered. Sailing on 2 August, and calling at one or two points on the mainland—Stoneham in Kincardineshire, Buchan Ness, the easternmost point of the Aberdeenshire coast—and then at the islet of Copinsay in the eastern Orkneys and at Fair Isle, by the 9th of the month she was in Lerwick harbour in the Shetlands, and the master was registering the other ships riding there, their comings and goings; on the 19th she was at Stromness, and after some days round and about these waters was back in her anchorage at Leith at the end of the month. Cook remained with her till 7 September—or at least his log ends at that date;[2] and we have again a gap in his chronology, because it was not till 18 October that a warrant was made out giving him his next appointment, not till 27 October that

[1] Cook's 'Solebays Logg' is a small quarto, Adm 52/1033, 30 July—7 September 1757, according to its title-page, but the date of the first entry is corrected from 30 to 31 July. At the end of the book, after a large interposition of blank pages, is a small section heralded 'Solebays Journal / James Cook / Master', and the dates—which, however, adds nothing of value to the log. Craig's log is Adm 51/908.

[2] Kitson, 29, says, 'on 17th September James Cook was superseded by John Nichols as Master'; but there could quite easily have been a nine days' vacancy in the position.

he entered upon it.[1] In this appointment he followed Bisset, whose mate he had been in the *Eagle,* and it was a very satisfactory one indeed. For the warrant made him master of the *Pembroke,* the almost new 64-gun ship, 1250 tons, Captain John Simcoe, a ship of the line and a captain that might well be the cause of some pride in warrant officers. This was better than a collier and the North Sea.

Simcoe had taken command of his ship while she was still on the stocks at Plymouth, and had watched over her launching on 2 June and her fitting out.[2] When Cook joined her she was in Portsmouth harbour, just returned from Lisbon, busily fitting and provisioning for another cruise. The business of the port! Did a ship of the line, more than a collier, stir the mind? Portsmouth or Plymouth more than Whitby was an animating place, with the activity of naval war, the noise of dockyards, the coming and going of sails, the noble ships —single ships, squadrons, fleets—the bringing in of prizes, the crowd of small craft, the sound of guns: guns were always going off in salutes, salutes to admirals, salutes for anniversaries, the king's birthday, the king's accession, the king's coronation; the waters and the air were never still. It could not be said, in October 1757, that the atmosphere was that of present victory; but there were considerable workings. A man, not a pressed landsman, might tread the deck with a certain elation. So the master could not have felt depressed when the *Pembroke* on 8 December weighed and came to sail from St Helen's, where she had been anchored for a fortnight, and with other ships made down Channel. This was a cruise of a sort he was familiar with from his days in the *Eagle,* across the Bay of Biscay, somewhat further south than before, so that Finisterre and not Ushant became the point of reference, in the old routine of chase—one day he remarks on 'the whole Fleet in Chase';[3] a number of seamen died, that routine repeated; and on 9 February 1758 a home-port again, moored at Plymouth.

This sort of activity was necessary though humdrum. The *Pembroke,* however, with Cook in her, was on the edge of greater things —was, in fact, about to play her part in one of the great reversals of history; and a reversal in an American theatre. The war that had been waged between Britain and France since 1754—undeclared

[1] Kitson, 29: 'entered upon his duties on 27th October, the twenty-ninth anniversary of his birth'. This does not allow for the change in the calendar instituted in 1752. The 27 October of his birth was Old Style: a strict reckoning of his birthday after 1752 would have been eleven days later, i.e. 7 November New Style. Bisset[t]'s log, Adm 52/978, finishes on 26 October, on which date he was appointed to the *Stirling Castle.*

[2] Simcoe to John Clevland, secretary to the Admiralty, 19 April, 14 May, 2 June 1757.—Adm 1/2471.

[3] Adm 52/978, 3 January 1758.

till May 1756, declared thereafter—was a transatlantic, American war, to British colonists the 'French and Indian war'—the continuation, in spite of all efforts at peaceful settlement, of the war that had its illusory end in 1748; and it became, inevitably, an Atlantic and then a European war. The American, the frontier, the backwoods, war could not be sustained indefinitely on either side without recourse to naval power; the critical lines of communication and supply, in final analysis, were Atlantic lines, the continental struggle merged into oceanic struggle. There was, on both sides, the usual preying on commerce; both sides lost enormously in merchant ships. Cook had seen a little of this, in his cruises in the *Eagle*, as she chased the fishing-vessels from Newfoundland or the snows from the West Indies. There were the single ship actions—and he had seen the end of the *Espérance*, had helped to batter the *Duc d'Aquitaine* into surrender. In both the *Eagle* and the *Pembroke* he had had his introduction to that perennial and tedious strategy, the blockading of the coasts of France, the endless watchfulness through fair weather and foul. But none of this had tended towards victory: indeed, looking back from the end of 1757 the British could see little but defeat, or when not defeat, frustration—and it was in the hysteria consequent on such frustration that they had shot their Admiral Byng. Regular army officers had failed in America, General Braddock had been killed, colonial forces had failed, forts had been lost, the colonial line of defence pushed hither and thither, Indians had massacred, French strategy had been brilliant. There were, however, two factors which gave the French civil and military command in Canada some unease, even at the peak of prestige. They could see signs, first of all, that they had strained their manpower: their regular regiments were good, but the French *habitant* had had his fill of wilderness fighting. Secondly, to do this fighting and the miscellaneous army service that went with it, he had been taken away from his proper work of cultivation; and Canada faced a serious food shortage. Hence the importance to the French of their lines of communication, free movement from France of troops and provisions; hence the eyes at Quebec through the next eighteen months straining for signs of the transports that would bring troops, but even more important— additional troops being additional mouths—flour. And hence the strategy of French naval power—even the risks it was prepared to take in stripping away guns for the sake of supplies: a strategy of convoy and protection, of conservation of line-of-battle ships, not of seeking out some grand general encounter of fleets which might bring glory, but even with glory disaster. Against this the British built up their own vast strategy, by land and sea. Inside it we are able to see, fitfully, the emerging Cook, a figure of slight importance, yet not altogether unimportant; through him, fitfully, we see the strategy.

The safety of the French possessions in North America, and their enlargement, was pinned not merely on successful wilderness fighting but on the two great fortresses which guaranteed the Gulf of St Lawrence and the immense river—Louisburg and Quebec. Who had those had Canada: if they could be captured there would be an immediate revolution in the war, which would negate all French successes on the frontiers of the British colonies, and remove at once the pressure that constricted these to their narrow coastal ribbon. This was plain to Lord Loudon, British commander-in-chief in North America from mid-1756, and he had determined to go straight for Quebec as in his 1757 campaign, assembling troops and making his dispositions carefully for that purpose. If he could get Quebec, he was persuaded—and he was a careful planner—Louisburg could be attended to later. While he was planning, the extraordinary Pitt had at last come to power in England, backed by popular support and with ideas of his own. These dislocated Loudon's, without ensuring all the preliminaries to success. Pitt was convinced that Louisburg and Quebec must both be taken, but in that order; and he could argue powerfully that he was right, on the military principle that in proceeding to one objective, you should not leave a dangerous threat to your communications behind you. Undoubtedly Louisburg would have been that, if a powerful French fleet were based upon it. For Louisburg was a harbour as well as a fortress, just below Cape Breton, the northern tip of the south-eastern coast of Cape Breton island: as a harbour, it could accommodate a large fleet; as a fortress it commanded the approach between Newfoundland and Cape Breton island to the Gulf of St Lawrence; as a considerable town and a port, it was a thriving centre of trade and of the French fishery, and had been in the previous war the thriving headquarters of privateering enterprise against British colonial commerce. It was this last characteristic that led the redoubtable Colonel Pepperrell of Massachusetts, together with Admiral Warren, to attack and take the place in 1745. It had been handed back at the peace in exchange for Madras, regardless of colonial rage; since when the French, determined that it should not be taken again, had poured money and work into its improvement. It had a strong garrison. It had also, through a good part of the year, the protection of the dense fogs that hung over that part of the Atlantic ocean, a beckoning to shipwreck of which potentially intruding fleets were much aware. There was one other material factor in the naval disposition of the area. This was the British base of Halifax, on the Nova Scotian coast, a day or two's sail south-west of Louisburg, as a counterpoise to which it had been deliberately founded in 1749, immediately after the peace, with four thousand colonists sent out from Britain. It was not a heavily fortified place, nor had it grown rapidly into a metropolis; but it had an admirable double harbour and safe anchorage, and British fleets, and their masters, would get to know it extremely well, though perhaps never positively to love it.

Pitt, then, in 1757 wanted Louisburg, and set Loudon to take it. He was generous with reinforcements, despatching them with the squadron commanded by Holburne. But even a Pitt could not command the weather. Contrary winds and gales kept Holburne from Halifax till July, by which time the French, well up in British plans, had been able to install a strong fleet and their own reinforcements in Louisburg; and from late June to late autumn the protective fog was thick. The fortress could be still more strongly fortified. Loudon after a council of war very wisely decided to abandon the project for that season; the French fleet, needed at home, declined to waste time and resources fighting Holburne; and towards the end of September a great southerly hurricane caught the British ships eight or ten leagues off Louisburg, forced them towards the shore for two days, and in another day, if it had continued, would have destroyed them all. It was this tempest that had so badly battered the *Eagle*. Loudon paid for his wisdom, as he had grimly anticipated, by his recall. Pitt demanded brilliance, not Fabian strategy. He planned again for 1758; in that year he wanted both Louisburg and Quebec. His new general was Jeffrey Amherst, and one of Amherst's three brigadiers, for the Louisburg enterprise, was James Wolfe. Sir Charles Hardy's squadron was patrolling the desperate coast, in fogs and storms, from early April—unable even then, when driven away from the land by pressing danger, to prevent five French ships of the line and three frigates from slipping into harbour. The British fleet command was given to Boscawen, a great fighting admiral, who sailed from Plymouth on 22 February[1] with eight line-of-battle ships and some smaller vessels. One of the ships of the line was the *Pembroke*. They picked up transports, crossed the Atlantic by way of Tenerife and Bermuda, and were at Halifax by 9 May, the *Pembroke* having had

[1] The date is from Simcoe's *Pembroke* log, Adm 51/686; but the dates given in various sources by no means coincide.

twenty-six men die on the passage, and putting a large number into hospital as soon as she reached port. Five men also immediately deserted with her yawl. She had to be left behind when Boscawen, on 28 May, stood slowly away for Louisburg with 157 vessels of war and transports. By the time she had received her men back from hospital and could leave with a convoy it was 7 June; it was the 12th when she was anchored off Louisburg, in the formidable company of Vice-Admiral Boscawen, Rear-Admiral Hardy, Commodore Durell, and the great assemblage of fleet and transports. She found that a landing had been forced by Wolfe, aided by good luck, on the morning of 8 June, at Kennington Cove, the west part of Gabarus Bay, just to the south and west of Louisburg; that the French had retreated to the fortress which the British, in doubtful weather, had already invested; and that all was going forward to set up batteries for a bombardment.

This time luck was indeed on the side of the British, ill-hap on the side of the French. The French fleet returning home from the Louisburg operation of the previous year brought ship-fever with it: two thousand men died on the passage, and at Brest ten thousand more. A Mediterranean action of March 1758 revenged the defeat of Byng. A great fleet that it was hoped to send across the Atlantic was kept at home to meet a rumoured British movement against the coasts of France. Hawke in the Bay of Biscay prevented any actual large despatch of ships. Of those that did succeed in slipping into Louisburg harbour four out of five ships of the line had come *en flûte* —that is, with stores in the room of guns. The fortress was effectively cut off from relief. The military and naval commanders at Louisburg could not agree, though that is unlikely to have affected the outcome. On the other hand Boscawen and Amherst co-operated to perfection; seamen not merely put the troops, the heavy naval guns and supplies on shore—losing a hundred boats in the process—but helped to serve the guns and siege works; and the weather, though unkind, was not unkind enough to render the fleet other than a secure base. Strong gales in the middle of June made the *Pembroke* and other ships cut their cables and put to sea, but they were back in two days. The French blocked the harbour-mouth by sinking four ships in it, but blocking the harbour was of little avail when the attack was from the land. On 26 June the siege guns opened up, and the batteries were steadily pressed closer to the walls. On 15 July a fast frigate, the *Aréthuse*, escaped with the ominous tidings for France. On 21 July a shell from a heavy battery exploded the magazine of the *Célèbre*, 64, and set fire to two other ships of the line as well: all three burnt to the water. Another was sunk at the harbour entrance. Bastions and barracks were going up in flames. On the night of 25 July Boscawen sent in two boats from each of his ships, with six hundred men, in thick fog, 'in order to cut away the 2 men-of-warr' that remained, 'the Ben Fison of 64 guns, the Prudon 74 guns' (it is the master of the *Pembroke* writing);[1] the *Bienfaisant* was towed off, but the *Prudent*, aground at low tide, could not be moved and was set on fire. On 26 July the Governor surrendered.

The day after the surrender, the master of the *Pembroke* was ashore at Kennington Cove, where Wolfe had made his landing seven weeks before. His curiosity was much aroused by the behaviour of a man carrying a small square table, supported by a tripod; the man would set his table down so that he could squint along the top in various directions, after which he would make notes in a pocket-book. This man in his turn noticed Cook, and they struck up a conversation. He was a military engineer and surveyor in a regiment under Wolfe; he was making a plan of the place and its encampments, and the instrument he was using was known as a plane table; with it he was observing angles. His name was Samuel Holland. His biography may be lightly touched on. He was Dutch, born in the same year as Cook. At the age of seventeen, he had joined the army of his own country; after some years as an artillery officer had crossed to England, where in 1755 he was commissioned lieutenant in the 60th Regiment, then being raised; he was a valuable person, not merely ambitious, but well trained professionally, an excellent draughtsman, a good linguist. He went to America in Loudon's train in 1756, and he had been present at some famous actions before Louisburg. Neither he nor Cook knew that their encounter that day was not less important than the great event they had just witnessed, for Cook expressed an ardent desire to be instructed in the use of the instrument, and, says Holland, 'I appointed the next day in order to make him acquainted with the whole process; he accordingly attended, with a particular message from Capt. Simcoe expressive of a wish to have been present at our proceedings; and his inability, owing to indisposition, of leaving his ship; at the same time requesting me to dine with him on board; and begging me to bring the Plane Table pieces along. I, with much pleasure, accepted that invitation, which gave rise to my acquaintance with a truly scientific gentleman, for the which I ever hold myself much indebted to Capt. Cook. I remained that night on board, in the morning landed to continue my survey at

[1] Adm 52/978.

White Point [the other end of Gabarus Bay], attended by Capt. Cook and two young gentlemen' whom Simcoe wished also to be instructed in the business.[1] Probably the two young gentlemen were midshipmen of a mathematical cast of mind. The course of demonstration may possibly have lasted longer than that day, because through most of August, the 3rd to the 28th, the *Pembroke* was moored in Louisburg harbour, and one cannot imagine that Cook and Holland parted immediately.

According to Holland, it was agreed by Wolfe and Simcoe that the British force could go straight on and take Quebec that autumn, as Pitt had planned,[2] but the admirals thought the season was too late; the only further action therefore taken by Amherst was to send Wolfe with three battalions, escorted by Sir Charles Hardy and a squadron which included the *Pembroke*, to raid and destroy French settlements at the Bay of Gaspé and other places on the Gulf of St Lawrence and at the entrance to the river—the northern part of what is now New Brunswick. It was inglorious service, though it did deprive Quebec of further provision, in the way of fish, as well as render the fishing population miserable and take a few of them prisoner. A few small prizes were taken also, what provision they had was transferred to the squadron—the *Pembroke* got some bread, butter and wine—and the seven line-of-battle ships, having burnt a sloop and a schooner, returned to Louisburg, where they lay at anchor from 2 October to 14 November. Rather more interesting and useful than these minor acts of war was a small piece of work done by Mr Cook; and we can perhaps see in this directly the influence of his captain and of his new acquaintance Samuel Holland. It was a survey of Gaspé bay and harbour, 'taken in 1758', which resulted in his first engraved and printed chart, dedicated to the Master and Wardens of the Trinity House of Deptford 'by James Cook Master of his Majesty's Ship the Pembroke', and published by the well-known firm Mount and Page of Tower Hill in 1759.[3] How it came to them we do not know: we may presume through Simcoe. Cook had his own little command for a week, taking a schooner round to 'Marquin Bay' to get coals.[4] On 14 November the fleet, under Durell, sailed for Halifax, where on the morning of the 19th the *Pembroke* was moored for the long winter. Boscawen returned to England in

[1] Holland to Lieut-Governor John Graves Simcoe, 11 January 1792. His letter is printed in Ontario Historical Society, *Papers and Records*, XXI (1924), 18–19.
[2] ibid., 19.
[3] R. A. Skelton, *James Cook Surveyor of Newfoundland* (San Francisco, 1965), 22; R A. Skelton and R. V. Tooley, *The Marine Surveys of James Cook in North America 1758–1768* (London, 1967), 13. No MS of this chart is known.
[4] Adm 51/686, 10 October, 12 October 1758.

his flagship, taking Wolfe with him to recuperate his health; Amherst remained in America, as commander-in-chief.

For Halifax, cold and windy as it was, this praise at least can be given, that its harbour did not freeze over, not even in the particularly long and hard winter of 1758-9, however much floating ice from the north knocked at the shores outside. Nor was that winter for seamen in general a time of vast excitement: there was little for anyone to record in his log beyond the wind and the weather—in January a very hard frost, then snow—and the routine of cleaning the ship, its repair, overhauling the hold, the rigging and sails, the receipt of stores, the movement of boats, the coming and going of ships, court martials for offences mostly minor (the fruit, no doubt, often enough of deadly boredom) and floggings round the fleet. Simcoe's men do not seem to have been penalised by this sort of savagery. Day after day a single line serves the *Pembroke*'s master as a record of things remarkable; sometimes he runs to three lines, now and again to more. In December early one morning the house on shore where the sailmakers lodged is burnt down with the sailmakers' assistant and 24 yards of duck;[1] in January Mr Crozier, surgeon's second mate of the *Captain*, is court-martialled on board the *Pembroke* for disobeying the surgeon's orders, and suspended for two months;[2] a few days later one man stabs another 'under ye short rib in a very dangerous manner';[3] in February another surgeon's mate is in trouble 'for Drunkeness Neglect of Duty &c—Broke';[4] in February again we have the consequences of a more complicated affair: 'at 8 AM Punished Felix Flarity for Mutinous Beheavour at Cornwallis's Island Alexdr Lumsden Pursers Steward for Setling in the Ship & Selling Ten Gallns of Wine for a Watch, Jno Tally for Selling the Watch for the Said Wine, & Ben: Hawkings for takeing Wine and Provisions out of the Steward Room, without the Pursers Knowledge, had a Survey on all the Pursers Stores Provisions &c.'[5] Men, of course (for this is the navy, in winter quarters), depart this life. What was of most importance in the master's life, most remarkably remote from routine, from misdemeanours to deaths of bored unhappy men—these public events—was the private excitement, the thing that nobody could conceivably commit to the official pages of a ship's log. For what we know of this thing we are once again indebted to the memories of Samuel Holland; and Holland is transmitting his memories—which, though invaluable, may not be

---

[1] Adm 51/686, 11 December. [2] Adm 51/686, 52/978 (Cook), 6 January 1759.
[3] Adm 51/686, 11 January. [4] Adm 52/978, 19 February.
[5] Adm 52/978, 13 February.

entirely accurate—to the son of Cook's commander. He continues his story from his survey at White Point, on Cape Breton island.

From that period, I had the honor of a most intimate and friendly acquaintance with your worthy father, and during our stay at Halifax, whenever I could get a moment of time from my duty, I was on board the *Pembroke* where the great cabin, dedicated to scientific purposes and mostly taken up with a drawing table, furnished no room for idlers. Under Capt. Simcoe's eye, Mr. Cook and myself compiled materials for a Chart of the Gulf and River St. Lawrence, which plan at his decease was dedicated to Sir Charles Saunders; with no other alterations than what Mr. Cook and I made coming up the River. Another chart of the River, including Chaleur and Gaspe Bays, mostly taken from plans in Admiral Durell's possession, was compiled and drawn under your father's inspection, and sent by him for immediate publication to Mr. Thos. Jeffrey, predecessor to Mr. Faden.[1] These charts were of much use, as some copies came out prior to our sailing from Halifax for Quebec in 1759. By the drawing of these plans under so able an instructor, Mr. Cook could not fail to improve and thoroughly brought in his hand as well in drawing as in protracting, etc., and by your father's finding the latitudes and longitudes along the Coast of America, principally Newfoundland and Gulf of St. Lawrence, so erroneously heretofore laid down, he was convinced of the propriety of making accurate surveys of those parts. In consequence, he told Capt. Cook that as he had mentioned to several of his friends in power, the necessity of having surveys of these parts and astronomical observations made as soon as peace was restored, he would recommend him to make himself competent to the business by learning Spherical Trigonometry, with the practical part of Astronomy, at the same time giving him Leadbitter's works, a great authority on astronomy, etc., at that period, of which Mr. Cook assisted by his explanations of difficult passages, made infinite use, and fulfilled the expectations entertained of him by your father, in his survey of Newfoundland. . . .[2]

Little, unfortunately, is known of John Simcoe,[3] who thus appears as one of the important formative influences on Cook's life; and this lack of knowledge may be the reason why his son, the first lieutenant-governor of Upper Canada, was in 1792 anxious to profit by the memories of Samuel Holland, then the surveyor-general of Quebec. Lieutenant-governor John Graves Simcoe was only seven when his

[1] 'Mr Thos Jeffrey' was Thomas Jefferys, 'Engraver, Geographer to His Royal Highness the Prince of Wales' (to quote his bill heading), map, chart and print seller, of Charing Cross, c. 1750/71. After his death in 1771 he was succeeded in the business by his partner William Faden. See also pp. 51–2 below and p. 52, n. 1 below to this chapter.

[2] Ontario Historical Society, *Papers and Records*, XXI (1924), 19.

[3] See Charnock, *Biographia Navalis*, V, 259. He had the misfortune to be a member of Byng's court martial ('his ship then lying at Portsmouth'). Duncan C. Scott, *John Graves Simcoe* (Toronto, 1905), has a page or two, including the information that he had a predilection also for the army and left a treatise on military tactics which was considered of value in its day—though apparently unpublished.

father died. His second Christian name does note for us one fact about that father—that his friendship with another distinguished naval man of scientific leanings, Captain Samuel Graves, was so warm that he made him a godfather. Simcoe became a captain in the last days of 1743, at the age of twenty-nine, which argues ability; and his ability must have been intellectual as well as practical— mathematical and 'truly scientific' (to use Holland's phrase), if he brought astronomy into the settlement of longitudes as early as 1758. It is scarcely likely that he did that, or did more than exercise unusual care and skill in ordinary observations; and in the deductions and calculation based on them; but there could have been few captains in the service of like capacity, or capable of explaining the difficult passages in the works of Charles Leadbetter to a ship's master en- thusiastic after this sort of education. So the *Young Mathematician's Companion*, that 'compleat Tutor to the Mathematicks', became Cook's companion—or was that too elementary?[1] Did he rather immerse himself in the two volumes of the *Compleat system of Astronomy*, and learn from them the description and use of the sector and the laws of spheric geometry? Did he persevere in the same work to the *New Tables of the Motions of the Planets, fix'd Stars, and the first Satellite of Jupiter, of right and oblique Ascensions and of logistical Logarithms?*, so evocative of the reachings of the astronomical mind in those decades, so fundamental to the technique of a newer navigation, so unattractive to the ordinary dead-reckoning sailor. We may note that the first edition of his *Astronomy* was 'Designed as a Help towards discovering the Longitude at Sea', though the help it could give in its day was no more than the help of inapplicable theory. We do not know the extent of Simcoe's ship-board library. It did not need to be very large to act its evangelistic role in the mind of Mr Cook, 'under Capt. Simcoe's eye', through that uncommonly cold Nova Scotian winter of 1758–9.

The St Lawrence charts compiled at that time (if Holland's memory was correct) could indeed have been nothing more than compilations from the 'plans in Admiral Durell's possession'—but

---

[1] This has been suggested, but the title-page, though endearing, is a trifle deceptive: 'The *Young Mathematician's* Companion, being a compleat Tutor to the Mathematicks; Whereby the *Young Beginner* may be early Instructed; those who have lost the Opportunity of learning in their Youth may with very little Pains, and in a short Time become Pro- ficients in this delightful and instructive Science, and such whose *Business* it is to teach, may receive much *Useful Assistance*. . . . The whole Interspersed with delightful and Useful Questions, and adorned with proper Schemes in order to excite Curiosity, and form the Minds of Youth. By Charles Leadbetter, *Teacher of the Mathematicks*.' London, 1739; 2nd ed. 1748. There are sections on arithmetic, geometry, plain and spherical trigonometry, astronomy, 'Dyalling', and a final one on surveying. The second edition is a full and meaty volume of 354 pp., and probably just what Cook needed.

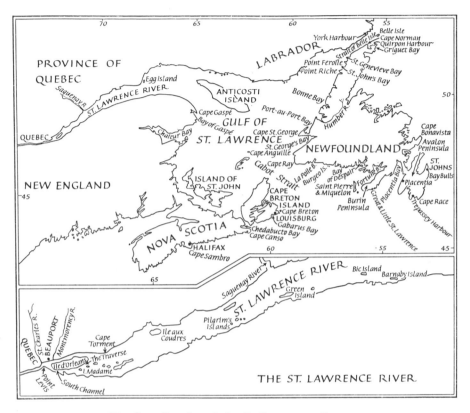

Newfoundland and the St Lawrence Estuary

what were they? There must surely have been some French chart, imperfect as the French charts were; something must surely have been picked up at Louisburg. There was one English chart which could have been used as a basis—the very inexact 'Exact Chart of the River St Laurence' published by Jefferys in 1757; though this may have been corrected in part by Simcoe from his observations when the *Pembroke* was with Wolfe's expedition at the mouth of the river in September 1758 (Chaleur Bay and Gaspé are really in the gulf), for alterations made by Cook and Holland 'coming up the River' could have been made only when the Quebec expedition was already in train, and could not possibly have been incorporated in any published charts which 'came out prior to our sailing from Halifax for Quebec in 1759'. Any well-compiled chart of the Gulf, however, would have been useful, even before the fleet got into the river; and it is possible that Cook's contribution towards the taking of Quebec began in this way.

It is possible, too, or probable, that to this period belongs the first example of 'sailing directions' by Cook himself now extant—one of those 'Descriptions for sailing in and out of Ports, with soundings, Marks for particular Rocks, Shoals, &c. with the Latt^d Long^d, Tides, and Variation of the Compass', which ships' masters were encouraged in general terms to produce and produced not very frequently. These directions are for the 'Harbour of Louisbourg in Cape Breton'.[1] They bear the marks of Cook's own style, a precise and economical composition. He gives the latitude, 46°1^1 N (a few minutes out); the 'Longitude by Computation' is a blank. Although the final figure of the date is gone, it must have been 1758, to match the heading of the column, 'Place and Time when there'; while the wreck of the *Prudent*, used as a mark, further confines the date. After 1760 these sailing directions would lose some of their value; for Cook also used as a mark for mariners the 'Grand Battery'. In the spring of that year Pitt, who seems to have nourished a particular enmity for Louisburg, sent Commodore Byron there with a band of sappers and engineers; and after six months of tunnelling those superb fortifications, Grand Battery included, were blown to pieces level with the ground. In the meanwhile, Cook wrote his careful folio page; perhaps here too we can see some sign of the encouragement of that scientific captain and benevolent educator John Simcoe.

The cold and studious winter drew to its end. All masters and captains were now faced with the completion of the business that

[1] The MS is now in the Houghton Library, Harvard.

had begun the summer before in the reduction of Louisburg, a step towards which had been Cook's and Holland's work on the chart of the St Lawrence. Wolfe, an untried strategist, and as was later to be abundantly made clear, a woefully poor one, had been anxious to move straight on from Louisburg to Quebec, at the end of July—with a reduced army, without preparation, and with campaigning time running out; and surprisingly enough (if Holland is to be believed) he had had the support of Simcoe. Weak as the French at Quebec in reality were, this was still a hare-brained idea, and Boscawen was a much better judge of the possibilities. The attack on the city, nevertheless, all responsible persons agreed, should be pressed as soon as possible; and the reason for sending Durell to winter at Halifax with so strong a squadron was precisely to enable the campaign to begin in the earliest spring by depriving Canada of all hope of relief. The general strategy conceived by Pitt was one of attack from two directions. The first of these was down the upper St Lawrence, to be reached by way of the capture of the French wilderness forts, leading to an advance on Montreal: this operation was to be conducted by Amherst. The second was up the lower St Lawrence to Quebec, with the army and navy acting jointly. Wolfe was selected for the command of the troops, a planned twelve thousand, and he was given three good brigadiers. For the naval command Anson picked Saunders, a taciturn and first-rate though untried admiral—'That brave statue', as Horace Walpole later described him; 'No man said less, or deserved more'—a man of infinite co-operative capacity, and of all the patience necessary for continued co-operation with the temperamental Wolfe. There was little doubt that the two forces would indeed co-operate as well as in the Louisburg operation. There was little doubt that the troops, as highly-trained and efficient as any British army, would do well if they could be brought effectively into contact with the French. There was the difficulty, to make effective contact. Two difficulties presented themselves, rather: one the British began by over-estimating, the other by underestimating. The one was naval; the other was military—or, to be more precise again, a difficulty of combined operations in which the strategic object had perforce to be military. The one was bringing the army to Quebec. The other was bringing to battle the army that defended Quebec.

The one was the navigation, by a great fleet of line-of-battle ships and transports, of the noble four-hundred-mile estuary of the St Lawrence river, at the inner end of which, on the high abrupt cliff, the city and the fortress stood. That navigation the British were sure they could master, but they were aware of dangers, and they were prepared for losses. They were aware of dangers, because the French talked a great deal about them, and though French charts and sailing directions had indeed been captured by Boscawen there was no French chart, there was no chart at all that either a British or a French sailor would rely on. The chart produced by Holland and Cook could be regarded only as provisional. Saunders, in his orders to the masters of transports on 15 May directed them to 'a plan or chart showing the route which His Excellency intends to make from Louisburg Harbour to the Island of Bic'.[1] But this did not touch the main problem. It would help them through Cabot Strait and the Gulf of St Lawrence; and then after Cape Gaspé were two hundred miles, approximately, of deep water and relatively safe sailing, to the small islands of Bic and Barnaby and somewhat beyond—safe so long as a ship avoided the shore on either hand. The islands themselves were shoaled. Then the dangers multiplied. From the rocky shoal-entangled points on the north shore where the tributary Saguenay river abandoned its wild mountains, intricacy grew, among islands and islets, shoals and drying banks and reefs, strong tides, whirling eddies, bewildering currents. Two thirds of the distance from Bic, the channel ran inside the Ile aux Coudres, close to the northern shore of the main, though the great breadth of the river was on the other side; then, clinging near to that shore as far as the high, darkly-wooded Cape Tourmente, it crossed diagonally to the north-eastern end of the Ile d'Orleans, within a whole congeries of dangerous islets; and finally, passing between the eastern shore of that island and the little Ile Madame, with its south-western shoal and reef, followed as the South Channel round the bare flat rock of Orleans into the Basin of Quebec. This diagonal crossing into the South Channel was known as the Traverse; it was virtually uncharted, and here the French had never brought a big ship. Its course was buoyed and marked, inadequately, and the French pilots knew their business. Their navigation marks were now all removed.

There had been previous expeditions for the conquest of Quebec. The first was a New England enterprise commanded by Sir William Phips, the governor of that colony, in 1690. Having made its way successfully to the northern shore of the river before the city, it collapsed in inefficiency and indiscipline. The second, on a larger scale, in 1711, was wrecked on the rocky Egg island, close to the northern shore of the inner gulf, three hundred miles from its objective, on one of the numerous occasions in that age when the

[1] Quoted by Kitson, 38.

British navy did not know where it was. In 1759 it had a much better idea. Not all the French realised this; they tended to rely on the river to defend them. Some did not. Among them was the Marquis de Montcalm, commander-in-chief in Canada, who had a very clear appreciation of the real difficulties of the country, and a sufficiently pessimistic view of the prospect if adequate supply and fortification could not be secured before a hostile fleet and army appeared. At this moment Canada desperately needed food supplies from France. Montcalm wanted powerful batteries at Gaspé, to deny the British a base there; others at the Ile aux Coudres and on the northern shore facing it, to deny them passage through that part of the channel; on Cape Tourmente, to command the Traverse; and, in case a fleet still got through, on the western point of Ile d'Orleans and on Point Lévis or Levis, the elevated point on the other side of the Narrows from the city itself, where the river came down in a swift current to the Basin. He wished to block the Traverse by sinking ten large ships in it. None of these defensive measures was carried out. Few could be carried out, because of the lack of means. Something, it appears, could have been done on the Ile d'Orleans; Point Levis could certainly have had a battery. It was not given; none thought hostile ships could work their way through the Narrows into the upper river under the guns of Quebec, few thought of the possibility of hostile guns planted on the point and bombarding Quebec itself. When the crisis came, there were not enough ships to sink in the Traverse, and all that could be done with it was to take away the marks. Apart from this, the defenders considered, a fleet once in confined waters could be attacked by fire-ships, sweeping down with the current. What Montcalm could do effectively, where he thought danger most threatened—in the direction from which Phips had made his bungling attack of 1690—he did on the north shore of the river, east of Quebec, by a line of entrenchments and fortifications between the St Charles and Montmorency rivers with the village of Beauport between them. If ships could not get past the Narrows, and therefore past the high and steep cliffs which guarded Quebec on the west, then the only way round outside the city to embark on a siege by land, or to tempt its defenders to battle, would be from that eastern quarter. In the meantime, in November 1758, after the British fleet had departed from Louisburg, and at the last possible moment before the ice closed in on the river and made navigation completely impossible, he despatched his aide-de-camp Bougainville to France to plead for the supplies and munitions that were so desperately needed.

Saunders and Wolfe sailed from Spithead on 14 February 1759. They found it impossible to get into Louisburg, the concentration point where they were to embark troops, because of the ice. This was on 21 April. They sailed on to Halifax. Here Durell was still lying, at the end of the month, detained at single anchor by ice and adverse winds, though they had expected him by then to be in the St Lawrence.[1] Not till 5 May could he depart, with thirteen ships of the line, only to fall among great quantities of loose ice. This must have been the first time Cook had encountered that phenomenon at sea, and he registers it in his log for 7 May: 'at 7 [AM] tack^d Close along Side the Ice wch Stretch' away to the ESE as far as Coul'd be distinguished from the Mast Head.'[2] The air was foggy, and the fleet kept together by the noise of guns and small arms. Eight days later Simcoe, who had had to keep to his cabin at Louisburg, died; and we have Cook again, on the evening of 16 May, off the island of Anticosti, bidding farewell to that friend: 'at 6 Buried the Corp's of Capt Jno Simcoe & fired 20 Guns half a Miniute between Each Gun.'[3] The new captain was John Wheelock, from the 20-gun *Squirrel* good promotion, but he was to miss some exciting moments in the *Squirrel* later on.[4] On the 19th the fleet was advancing up the St Lawrence, with a steady north-east wind that brought a shudder to the heart of Montcalm; on the 20th it was anchored off Barnaby Island near Bic. Durell's instructions were to wait there. He improved on them. Leaving a few ships at Bic, he took the greater number, including the *Pembroke*, up to the Ile aux Coudres. He captured three provisioners, and learnt that Bougainville, on his return from France, had been able to slip into the river ahead of him with a small convoy, now safe at Quebec; he captured also a number of French river-pilots, by the simple expedient of tempting them on board by a show of French colours. Though his purpose may have been general reconnaissance—he landed some troops on the island and found it empty of inhabitants, as was Ile d'Orleans, all having departed for the city—he developed reconnaissance into a very useful piece of special work. He ordered one of his senior captains to take four naval vessels—two of which were the *Pembroke* and the *Squirrel*—and his three transports over to the Ile d'Orleans

---

[1] Wolfe thought very meanly of Durell, and others have thought he might have got into the St Lawrence earlier than he did; but after the business was over Saunders 'paid him the highest compliments', and he was included in the House of Commons' vote of thanks. He had been promoted rear-admiral of the blue while at Louisburg, and rear-admiral of the red in February 1759.—Charnock, V, 167–70.

[2] Adm 52/978.   [3] Adm 52/978, 17 May (p.m.)

[4] Wheelock is a rather shadowy figure. He had later West Indies and American service, commanded the *Sultan*, 74, in 1778, and died in early 1779. Charnock, VI, 286.

to destroy 'fire stages', or rafts, which had been reported, and to collect further information. On 8 June these ships were at the beginning of the Traverse. For two days all boats 'manned and armed' were out sounding that formidable passage. They discovered, indeed, a 'New' as well as an 'Old' Traverse. Frequently enough too much credit has been given to Cook for an operation in which all masters took part as a matter of course, and all had a hand in this. At the finish, records this particular master, 'Ret^d satisfied with being aquanted with ye Channel';[1] and this particular division thereupon sailed through it and anchored at the other end. Each ship then sent a boat manned and armed on board the *Squirrel*, 'she being the Western Ship in order to prevent any assault from the Enemy'.[2] The first assault, however, was from the British, who despatched their boats to take a 'sloop' in the northern channel, and in their turn were assailed by Indians from the island and French artillery men who had crossed over to it, so that the *Squirrel* lost her yawl. The French had hastily erected a battery to bombard the ships; it did a little harm, forcing them to change their positions, but could not be maintained for long and was withdrawn.

While these preliminaries, of sounding, marking and direction-finding, were going on, Saunders with his great fleet of ships of war, transports, and supplementary vessels, was slowly and irreversibly moving up the river, and, because of the care taken, in perfect safety: nine ships of the line and thirteen frigates to add to Durell's, and 119 transports. It may be noted that there were few ships of the greatest size: Saunders' flagship, the *Neptune*, carried ninety guns; Durell's, the *Princess Amelia*, eighty; the *Royal William* was an 84-gun ship, the *Northumberland* a seventy; but among the others the *Pembroke* with her sixty guns ranked as one of the largest. Saunders left Halifax on 13 May and Louisburg on the 15th, entered the gulf on 4 June, and on 18 June was anchored off Bic and Barnaby. A week later the whole fleet passed the Traverse, without losing a single vessel of any kind. We have Cook's log for 25 June: 'at 11 AM a Sig^l for all Boats man'd & arm'd, in order to go & Lay in the Traverse, as Buoys for the Ships to come up';[3] the unfortunate French pilots were all employed, threatened with their necks if they failed; and there was the long experience in river-navigation of more than one master of a transport, like Cook familiar with the banks and shoals of home. There is the famous account by the military Captain Knox of 'old Killick' of the transport *Goodwill*, who put his mate at the helm, and went to the stem himself with a speaking trumpet. 'I went forward

[1] Adm 52/978, 10 June 1759.　　[2] Adm 51/686, 15 June 1759.　　[3] Adm 52/978.

with this experienced mariner, who pointed out the channel to me as we passed, shewing me, by the ripple and colour of the water, where there was any danger; and distinguishing the places where there were ledges of rocks (to me invisible) from banks of sand, mud, or gravel. He gave his orders with great unconcern, joked with the sounding-boats who lay off on each side, with different-coloured flags for our guidance; and, when any of them called to him, and pointed to the deepest water, he answered, "aye, aye, my dear, chalk it down, a d–d dangerous navigation—eh, if you don't make a sputter about it, you'll get no credit for it in England, &c." After we had cleared this remarkable place, where the channel forms a complete zig-zag, the Master called to his Mate to give the helm to somebody else, saying, "D— me, if there are not a thousand places in the Thames fifty times more hazardous than this; I am ashamed that Englishmen should make such a rout about it." [1] It may be that old Killick was the merchantman showing off to the navy as well as to a French pilot, and he did after all have the boats and the coloured flags there; nevertheless his performance was a remarkable one, and by such means, added to the preceding careful hydrographic work, was the great enterprise completed. On the morning of 27 June the whole fleet was anchored in the basin of Quebec, stretched between Point Levis and the end of Ile d'Orleans—except the very large *Neptune*, waiting on a special pilot at the Ile aux Coudres. It was a grim sight for Montcalm, and with grim acerbity, thinking of his own people, he remarked to a correspondent that there was now hope of having a good chart of the river 'next year'. [2] Next day it seemed that the weather was turning in favour of the French: a tremendous storm fell on the ships, drove a number of transports ashore, and destroyed many of the boats. Skilful handling saved the fleet, whereupon it was thrown into equal, though a different sort of jeopardy; for Montcalm thought that the night succeeding, with its favourable gale, provided the moment to release his fire ships. He did so, though they were prematurely ignited. It was a terrifying moment for those subject to terror. The nearest vessels had to run for it; two of these raging furies went on shore; the others were grappled by the English boats and towed clear. The navy now had time to breathe. Wolfe had time to look about. The navy had brought him and his troops to Quebec. It seemed within his grasp. The difficulty was to know how to grasp it.

[1] John Knox, *An Historical Journal of the Campaigns in North America* (London, 1769), I, 290–1.
[2] C. P. Stacey, *Quebec, 1759* (Toronto, 1959), 42.

While he wavered and worried, and time slipped by, there was a great deal for masters, and other seamen, to do. Every moment meant boat work. Wolfe's first action had been to land men and stores on the south end of Ile d'Orleans, and set up a hospital there. The position was fortified. At the end of June he began to occupy the Point Levis position, stimulated by Saunders through Wheelock. Opposition was weak, and before long a battery was set up, the *Pembroke*'s long boat helping the artillery: Saunders thus need not fear French guns driving his ships from their anchorage, and the British could bombard the city. Early in July, having discarded the idea of landing above it, Wolfe took some of his troops across to the north shore, east of the Montmorency falls—that is, east of Montcalm's entrenchments and other land defences, with the hope of somehow forcing a battle from that direction. Montcalm was playing for time. If he could hold out through the summer and early autumn, even at the cost of near-starvation, and avoid sacrificing his army to the better-trained British, then the river-ice, or its threat, would do his work for him. The time his enemies had was, after all, limited. Their small boats by no means had it all their own way. The French gun-boats or 'floating batteries' were active on the water; the French guns on shore discouraged too much rashness close in. Prisoners were taken by both sides. On the night of 18–19 July seven ships, including the frigates *Diana* and *Squirrel*, proved the feasibility of getting through the Narrows, under inefficient bombardment from Quebec, returned by the Point Levis guns. The *Diana*, fouled by a sloop, ran aground, the *Richmond* went to her aid, and the *Pembroke* —which otherwise seems to have been anchored off Point Levis from 7 July to 19 September—was involved: 'at 2 pm', says Cook, 'Cut and Slipt pr order of the adml and run up the river in order to cover the Richmond and Dianna wch was Attackd by a Number of the Enemys Row boats, wch Row'd off as Soon as we got up . . . Sent the Long boate and 30 Men on Bd the Dianna to assist in geting her guns out, at 4 fired a 24 pd Shot at the Enemys Row boats going down the River.'[1] That passage through the Narrows and up the river in the end proved the secret of victory.

Meanwhile, and always, it seems, sounding continued. Wherever troops landed they had to be taken there in transports, ships' boats, flat boats; the nature of the shore and currents had to be known. A second, most formidable, attempt to destroy the fleet by fire, by sending down on the tide a hundred fathom-long chain of rafts loaded with combustibles and explosives and shot—this time not

[1] Adm 52/978, 30 July.

ignited too soon—was frustrated by the sailors who once more towed
it off; and then Wolfe decided to abandon skirmishing and try a real
attack. It was to be on part of the French position on the north shore,
at Beauport, beginning with an assault from the water on one of the
enemy redoubts. Two armed transports were to be run aground at
high water as close to this redoubt as possible, bluff-bowed, broad-
bottomed cats like those Cook had known so well in the North Sea.
How close? 'The Master of the Pembroke', wrote Wolfe to his
brigadier Robert Monckton on 28 July, 'assures the Admiral that a
Cat, can go within less than 100 yards of the Redoubt—if so, it will be
a short affair.'[1] After the affair was over he repeated to Saunders,
in explaining away some injustice the admiral thought he had done
to the sailors in his draft despatch home, 'Mr. Cook said he believed
the cats could be carried within 40 or 50 yards of the redoubts. I told
him at the time, that I would readily compound for 150 or 200
yards, which would have been near enough' under certain conditions
which did not at the critical moment present themselves.[2] It was poor
counsel, and the affair was not short. The transports grounded much
further out. The master of the Pembroke was unduly optimistic if he
felt that the shore-line had been adequately investigated, though he
can hardly be held responsible for Wolfe's subsequent change of plan
to a landing from boats at low water, a junction with troops already
on that side of the river, and a direct attempt on the French entrenchments. A close examination, if he had had a chance to carry it
out, might have shown him the barrier of boulders on which the
boats then grounded. He can hardly be held responsible for the defeat
that followed, while the Pembroke and the Centurion, Anson's old ship,
cannonaded the shore. The two cats, damaged past salvage by the
French artillery, were set on fire before being abandoned. We can
otherwise hardly trace Cook, except by implication. His own log is
a most impersonal document, as masters' logs tend to be; indeed for
lengthy periods he may have been so busy as not to have time to
make entries, to judge from the handwriting of the document he
signed. We cannot tell: he may have had time enough to make a
deliberate attempt to improve his handwriting into sophisticated
flourishes, which fortunately failed.

The boat activity continued. At some indeterminate time Cook
may have had the adventure recounted by Kippis, without authority
given. There is nothing inherently impossible about the story,

[1] Stacey, 74.
[2] Wolfe to Saunders, 30 August 1759, in Beckles Willson, *Life and Letters of James Wolfe*
(London, 1909), 461. Saunders was present in a boat himself.

whatever its truth. He was, it is said, out sounding or laying buoys when a party of French and Indians in canoes tried to cut off his boat, which dashed for the Ile d'Orleans shore, Cook leaping out at the bow as the savages leapt into the stern, though they were then driven off by the hospital guard. It has also been said that Bisset, his master of the *Eagle*, now in the *Stirling Castle*, was cut off by the enemy while sounding between the island and the Montmorency falls, and lost his ship's barge and its furniture, as well as one man killed; and it is not improbable that such a story should have been transferred to Cook, as a man who took soundings, and was later more known to fame.[1] The bombardment of the town continued. It was twice set on fire, and the greater part of the lower town consumed. The country on the southern side of the river was ravaged: August was a month of devastation and cruelty. Wolfe fell sick. At the beginning of September he abandoned his Montmorency position and took the greater part of his men to Point Levis, under a hot fire from the town, and then up the river, thinking now in terms of a landing on the north side to cut Montcalm's lines of communication, though with no clear idea where to land. It was an exasperating time for the French, with Bougainville's men marching up and down the other side of the river keeping watch on Rear-Admiral Holmes, who sailed his ships up with the flood, and let them drop down on the ebb-tide. Five of the smaller ships were thus engaged. The largest number, the *Pembroke* and fourteen others, were stationed off Point Levis; there were eleven at Ile Madame, among them the *Princess Amelia*, Durell's flagship; and small vessels were cruising about and watching the shores singly. This was the scene on the British side at that moment.[2]

Wolfe was persuaded that if he could not succeed by the end of September he, and his expedition, would have to go home, leaving Montcalm reprieved for yet another year. The crisis was close. He determined where he should land, at the foot of the cliff not far above the city—not at all the best place to land, and one that gave Admiral Holmes, said that seaman afterwards, 'the most hazardous and difficult Task I was ever engaged in'.[3] Wolfe was fortunate in his naval confrères, to the very end, as he stepped ashore at the Anse du Foulon, on the early morning of 13 September, for the battle that killed him and Montcalm both. Saunders gave himself to

---

[1] The *Stirling Castle's* barge was certainly so taken, on 7 July; but Cook is not likely to have been in it. Bisset may have been, though there is nothing to indicate that he was. Kitson, 45, tells the story about Bisset; Carrington, 28, casts doubt on it.
[2] Adm 1/482, 5 September 1759.
[3] Stacey, 132.

persuading the French that the upriver operation was only a feint, and the real landing was to be at Beauport. We have Wheelock's log for 11 and 12 September: 'at 10 [p.m.] our Master went and laid Sev¹ Buoys on the Shoals of Beauport ... at noon the Enemy attempted to cut away the Buoys our Master laid, but was [driven] off by the fire of the Richmond.'[1] And for the very crisis we have Cook.

Mod^t & Cloudy weath^r at 6 pm unmoord and hov'd in to half a Cable on the Best Bower, at midnight all the Row Boats in the fleet made a faint to Land at Beauport in order to Draw the Enemys Attention that way to favor the Landing of the Troops above the Town on the north Shoar, wch was done with little oposition our Batteries at Point [Levis] Kcept a Continuell fire against the Town all night, at 8 am, the Adm¹ made the Sig¹ for all Boats man'd and Arm'd to go to point Levi Weigh'd and Drop'd higher up, at 10 the English Army Command^d by Gen¹ Wolf, attacked the french under the Com^d of Gen¹ Montcalm in the field of Aberham behind Quebec, and Tottally Defeated them, Continued the Pursute to the very Gates of the City, afterwards the[y] Begun to form the nescesary Desposions for Carring on the Seize, adm¹ Holmes hig^[h]ste'd his flag on Board the Loestoff [*Lowestoft*] above the Town.[2]

It is curious that neither of these sailors mentions the fate of the generals. On 18 September Quebec capitulated, and British troops marched in: 'at 6', says our master's log, 'every Ship in the fleet Sent a Boat mand and Arm'd, und^r the Com^d of Capt Palleser, who whent and took Poss[ess]ion of the Lower Town.'[3]

That log, certainly now in the hand of a different master, Mr John Cleader, chronicles Cook's next movement: 'I, came on board & supersceeded Mr Coock the Master, who was apointed for ye Northumberland'. This movement took place on 23 September, 'per order of Admiral Saunders', says Captain Wheelock.[4]

The 70-gun *Northumberland* carried a complement of five hundred: technically, like the *Pembroke*, she was a 3rd-rate. Her captain was Alexander, Lord Colville, who had been in that post since 1753. A little mystery attaches to the fact that the ship was now, simultaneously with Cook's appointment, given a second captain, William Adams, of the *Hunter* sloop, who had only the previous year been appointed commander: it may have been a personal favour to which Saunders consented, merely to give him rank as post-captain;[5] or

[1] Adm 51/686, 12 September.   [2] Adm 52/978, 13 September.
[3] Adm 52/978, 19 September.
[4] Adm 52/978, Part V. The entry is for 30 September, though Cleader begins to write the log on Monday 24th. Wheelock's log, Adm 51/686, 23 September.
[5] Charnock, VI, 345–6. He died in 1763.

it may have been anticipation on Saunders's part of the early appointment of Colville as commodore, with a captain serving under him.
Adams can have made little impression on the master; for among
the men under whom Cook served, he was one of the few who did not
later have his name conferred upon some cape or bay or island. The
fleet was taking up fresh dispositions prior to moving, and it was
found that the river had still not been mastered; the current and
poor weather made it easy for ships, whether naval vessels or transports, to run ashore on the Ile aux Coudres—fortunately without any
losses. The loss of anchors in the previous months had been considerable. On 18 October Saunders sailed for England, leaving the
city to face the winter and possible French movements with a
garrison under James Murray, one of Wolfe's brigadiers, and two
sloops of war; and a detachment of five ships of the line, three
frigates, and a number of sloops under the command of Colville,
to winter at Halifax. The end of October saw them all moored in
Halifax harbour, the men facing five months of routine, boredom,
punishment for petty offences, and cold, though nothing like the
privations and sickness their army colleagues were experiencing in
Quebec. As for the master of the *Northumberland*, that steady serious
man, we must suppose him plunged once more in calculations
abstruse to his fellows, perhaps exercising his unaided hand at bits
of surveying; because it was probably this season, and the next one
at Halifax, that he was referring to, when the young Lieutenant
King, his eager admirer, in days to come listened to his conversation.
'It was here, as I have often heard him say, that, during a hard
winter, he first read Euclid, and applied himself to the study of
mathematics and astronomy, without any other assistance, than
what a few books, and his own industry, afforded him.'[1] But we can
hardly imagine him denying Holland and Simcoe their due: it
cannot have been in these winters that he 'first' read Euclid, if
Euclid is a synonym adopted by King for Leadbetter; and perhaps
we need take no more from the words than that in winter quarters
Cook studied hard. It seems certain that he also spent time practising
himself in the drawing of charts and in collecting them, in making
notes on navigation and compiling sailing directions, as far afield as
on the East and West Indies. Certainly it must be to this period that
his three extant manuscript charts of Halifax harbour belong.[2]

Meanwhile in England Saunders was going through his papers,

[1] *A Voyage to the Pacific Ocean . . . for making Discoveries in the Northern Hemisphere* (London,
1784), III, 47. King did not get his facts always quite right.
[2] Skelton lists them, *James Cook Surveyor of Newfoundland*, 9, as Public Archives of Canada
T.50/4; British Museum, Add. MS 31360.9; Admiralty Library, MS 20.

and on 22 April 1760, the day that Colville's refitted squadron sailed again from Halifax for Quebec, he was writing to the Admiralty secretary, 'Having got materials ready for publishing a Draught of the River St Laurence, with the Harbours, bays and Islands in that river, I must beg you to acquaint their Lordships of it, that I may receive their directions thereon.'[1] The secretarial annotation is that the Lords approved of his publishing it; and it was published in the same year by Thomas Jefferys of Charing Cross, the leading carto-graphical engraver of his day—a large production, measuring some seven feet by three, in twelve sheets, accompanied by a quarto pamphlet of sailing directions, 'Founded on accurate Observations and Experiments, made by the Officers of his Majesty's Fleet.' It was entitled 'A New Chart of the River St Laurence, from the Island of Anticosti to the Falls of Richelieu: with all the Islands, Rocks, Shoals and Soundings . . . Taken by Order of Charles Saunders, Esqr Vice-Admiral of the Blue, and Commander in Chief of His Majesty's Ships in the Expedition against *Quebec* in 1759.' It bore a note by Saunders, dated 'Pall Mall, May 1st 1760', on its compilation: 'This Chart was drawn from particular Surveys of the following Places; and Published for the Use of the British Navigators, by Command of the Right Honourable the Lords Commissioners of the Ad-miralty.' The 'following Places' were ten in number (including the famous Traverse, both old and new) all appearing as insets on a larger scale, together with seventeen 'profiles' of the coast about the river; and there is the additional note, 'The Distances between the Island of Coudre, the Island of Orleans, the Pillar Rocks, and Shoals in the South Channel were accurately determined by Tri-angles. The other parts of this Chart, were taken from the best French Draughts of this River.' It seems to be the chart which Samuel Holland remembered as being assembled from various pieces by himself and Cook 'under Capt. Simcoe's eye' in the Halifax winter of 1758–9, with their 'alterations . . . made coming up the River': sent by Simcoe 'for immediate publication to Mr. Thos. Jeffrey'. There is no other chart discoverable that answers more closely to Holland's description of 1792, and it is reasonable to assume a certain jumbling of his memories of the time to which he looked back. There are other large charts in manuscript, signed by or attributable to Cook, very much like the main part of this one, which make it seem probable that he had in this one at least a large part; and the reference to distances determined by triangulation in the area in which he was working seems to point directly to him and

[1] Saunders to Clevland, 22 April 1760, Adm 1/482.

the instruction he had had from Holland. Yet, so far as either of them is concerned, we are compelled to infer, clear though some of the inference may be. They were men under orders. Cook had carried out one of the tasks laid down for masters in the navy, that was all. Yet his performance was rather unusual for a master of so few years seniority. He still felt both cautious and modest, if we are to go by his 'remarks' on one of the manuscript charts referred to. 'That part of this plan between the Pilgrims and Green Island is not so correct as I could wish,' he writes, 'as I had not time to make sufficient observations there myself have been obliged to collect those of others.—With respect to the middle bank, which is the only danger in this passage, I find no one person I have yet conversed with to have any true Idea either of its form or extent. . . . I thought proper to make the above remarks in order to point out what may be doubt-full in this chart.'[1] Nevertheless the printed chart became the standard guide not merely for the navy, but for all seamen using the great waterway—for generations of seamen who thumbed their *North American Pilot*, the collection which first appeared in 1775, and incorporated so much of Cook's work.

Colville's departure from Halifax on 22 April was a fortnight earlier than Durell had been able to sail the previous year, though it was a month later than his planned time of departure. Ice floes in the gulf and heavy winds had kept him in harbour; even two days after he had sailed the *Northumberland* with other ships was stuck fast in ice, and remained thus for twenty-four hours, still far short of Cabot Strait, while they had to run through a field of ice as late as 12 May.[2] They were anchored before Quebec, where the garrison

---

[1] This is the large MS chart (22½ in. × 119½ in.) of the St Lawrence in Cook's hand in the National Maritime Museum (from the Hydrographic Department of the Admiralty), inscribed 'To The Right Honble the *Lord Colvill* Rear Admiral of the White Squadron of His Majesty's *Fleet* This *Chart* of the *River St. Laurence* from *Green Island* to *Cape Carrouge* is most Humbly Dedicated by His Lordships most Humble Servant Jam^s Cook.' The reference to Colville as Rear-Admiral indicates that this must have been dedicated, if not drawn, after October 1762 (when the engraved chart had existed for two years), as his promotion came in November of that month; he hoisted his flag in Neptune 7 November. Cf. Skelton, op, cit., 21, 'presumably drawn after September 1759'. There is a copy, not in Cook's hand, in the Hydrographic Department. There is another copy in the Public Archives of Canada: this is pretty obviously by Cook himself, except for two sets of 'Remarks' in a clerkly hand of great neatness. These must all have some close relation with the Saunders/Jefferys chart, which Skelton and Tooley (*Marine Surveys*, 13) un-hesitatingly identify with the chart of Holland's reminiscence (though for the dates, 1759-60, and 'spring of 1760' given by them one should read 1758-9 and 'spring of 1759'). The suggestion seems inescapable that Holland confused his years. In the British Museum, Add. MS 31360 (which is mainly a collection of Pacific charts) is, f. 14, a separate coloured drawing in Cook's hand; 'A Plan of the Traverse or Passage from Cape Torment into the South-Channel of Orleans by Jam^s Cook'.

[2] Adm 51/3925 (Adams), 24-5 April, 12 May 1760; Colville to Clevland, from Halifax, 10 April 1761, Adm 1/482. Colville (summarised) says the ice from the Gulf of St Lawrence and the Gulf of Canso never reached as far west as Halifax; it collected in compact bodies

had been anxiously awaiting them, six days later, and here they remained until 9 October. Murray and his men were anxious, because it was doubtful how much longer they could have sustained the French siege: he had foolishly fought a battle, and fought it foolishly, outside the walls, and lost a great many men; by the end of the winter disease had killed twice as many as had all the previous battles; French as well as British messages had gone out by ship to hasten aid. This time it was the British and not the French that arrived first: three ships from England had in fact preceded Colville. It was Colville's arrival, however, that caused the Chevalier de Lévis to raise his siege and begin the final French retreat. Through the summer Amherst was advancing from New York up the Mohawk river, across Lake Ontario, and down the St Lawrence, and on 7 September 1760 Montreal, and Canada, were surrendered.

The last scenes had been military, not naval ones. There was little for sailors to do at Quebec but see to the embarkation of troops, look after their ships, witness punishments—and, no doubt, make soundings, take angles, chart, sketch the shores, work up notes into sailing directions. The *Northumberland*'s master may have witnessed the hanging at the *Vanguard*'s yardarm of one miserable fellow who with two companions left the hospital at Point Levis without leave; picked up out of a canoe a few days later they were all condemned to death for desertion, but on account of their families 'whose subsistence must depend on their labour' the court martial recommended lenity and the execution of only one; so 'the Commodore having pardon'd two of them, they Cast Lotts who should dye, he whose Lott it was, was Executed Accordingly'.[1] This is not the only execution his journal records. The *Vanguard* parted a cable and fouled the *Northumberland*. The longboat of the *Northumberland*, her anchor caught in a transport's cable, was carried to the bottom, and there was four days' labour in getting her up, and probably some strong words from the master. On 22 September Captain William Adams went to the *Diana*, 32-gun frigate, and Nathaniel Bateman of the 20-gun *Eurus* came to the *Northumberland* in his place, and seems to have made more of an impression on Cook.[2] On 10 October the ship weighed and fell down with the tide, and on 25 October was at Halifax again for another winter: not only for another winter, indeed, but until

---

on the south coast of Cape Breton Island; we ran among it in dark night last year, it closed, and we were stuck for two days till the swell rose and made a small opening; luckily the weather was moderate.

[1] Adm 51/3925 (Adams), 12 July 1760.

[2] Cook made use of his name later on the coast of Australia. His career, with its unhappy end, is noticed in Charnock, VI, 386–7.

early August 1762. In that period her only move seems to have been from her moorings to the careening wharf in September 1761, when she was hove down and given a thorough overhaul.

It is obvious that though the North American squadron continued to exist, there was little for it to do. The naval war was being conducted in the West Indies and the Mediterranean, in the blockade of the French Atlantic ports, in Indian seas. So the chief activity of those months in Halifax harbour once again seems to one who reads the logs to have been the activity of the bosun's mate, as he applied the standard dozen lashes for 'neglect of duty', with more exceptional numbers, even hundreds, for more exceptional offences. Some men seem to have been particularly cursed by fate. Edward Lovely is punished on 6 November 'for thieft'; on 1 April he gets thirteen lashes alongside each ship for 'Severall Crimes and Misdimeniours', and next day twelve lashes similarly, being the remainder of his punishment; on 6 August 1761 Edward Lovely is sentenced to receive '600 Lashes & Vincent Dunnavan belonging to the Norwich to receive 500 lashes the former for absenting himself from the ship and the Latter for Desertion',[1] and they are duly flogged round the fleet, a hundred or eighty lashes alongside each ship. 'Publick Demonstrations of Joy' are the other things that punctuate the time; the memory of the 'Happy Deliverance from the popish Conspiracy' gets its twenty-one guns, as does George II's birthday, with bonfires and illuminations on shore, and then George III's accession, and Queen Charlotte's birthday, and George III's birthday, and the Popish Conspiracy again; and King Charles's restoration—but only fifteen guns for that. It is with a spurt of interest therefore that one comes on the second part of the entry in the Commodore's journal for 19 January 1761. 'Directed Captain Legge to hold a Court-Martial on two Marines of the Falkland, for robbing the Purser of Slop Cloaths', writes Lord Colville. Then, 'Directed the Storekeeper to Pay the Master of the Northumberland Fifty pounds in consideration of his indefatigable Industry in making himself Master of the Pilotage of the River Saint Lawrence, &c.'[2] This can be regarded as a handsome bonus on the master's regular pay of six guineas a month. The entry is certainly a most unusual and most unexpected one in any officer's journal. We conclude that Cook is indeed

---

[1] Adm 51/3925 (Bateman), 6 August 1761. It is hard now to distinguish the different degrees of turpitude. William Buckland got 12 lashes for staying on shore without leave, ibid., 12 August; Robert Boswell got 24 and James Barrett 12 'for absenting themselves from the ship without leave', ibid., 20 August. Presumably the unlucky and savagely treated Lovely, charged in much the same way as these last two, had made a determined effort to desert.

[2] Adm 50/22.

beginning to emerge from that valuable body of persons, the masters of His Majesty's ships, as an unusually valuable person; and that the senior officers with whom he has come in contact are aware of the fact. In the context of naval journals, under their standard headings, he can virtually be classed, along with courts martial and Publick Demonstrations of Joy, as a Remarkable Occurrence.

Possibly the diversion was welcomed when the *Charming Nancy*, a snow from London, struck a rock at the entrance of the harbour and sank, and had to be raised; or when Colville at last thought time had come to exercise his men at gunnery and 'fire'd at Marks'; or when there was a fire in the town and a party rushed on shore to help put it out. There was an outbreak of sickness in January 1762, but that could hardly be called a diversion: a suspicion apparently arose of some contagious element, because the dead were interred with their bedding and clothes, and the crew were set to scrub hammocks and ship.[1] At the end of the previous winter Colville had been addressing the Admiralty on the climate and nature of the place. 'I have now been three Winters at Halifax [he was there with Durell]; and have found by Experience, that in general, this Season is not so boisterous, as 'tis commonly thought. We have much less blowing weather than in England, and much more Sunshine. 'Tis the Frost that makes the coasting Navigation so difficult, and almost impracticable to ships.' That he enlarges on. Then the health of his men: 'we have always been very well supplied with frozen Beef from Boston; which keeps our Seamen healthy while they continue in Port; but the Scurvy never fails to pull us down in great Numbers, upon our going to Sea in the Spring.'[2] Frozen beef was much closer to fresh food than the doubtful brine-sodden substances provided by the English contractors. But this was not enough: sickness, it was obvious, could strike in port. We have plenty of evidence of the nature of the stores normally received on board—beef, beer, butter, bread, pork, pease, oatmeal, vinegar. One day there was even some fruit—and that is abnormal and quite astonishing. There are little evidences of efforts to render conditions between decks less completely intolerable: 'Kept the Ventulaters going night and day',[3] notes Cook at one midsummer moment—and we are surprised to see one of the standing Admiralty instructions put into practice. More was needed than ventilators on hot days and nights, to keep men healthy who had to sling their hammocks in those overcrowded

[1] Adm 52/959 (Cook), 13 February, 2 March, 30 June 1762; Adm 51/3925 (Bateman), 28 December 1761 – 19 February 1762, 18 May 1762.
[2] Colville to Clevland, 10 April 1761, Adm 1/482.
[3] Adm 52/959, 25 July 1761.

'tween-deck dungeons. A great many more men would have run away from the British navy, one fancies, winter or summer, if they had known where to run to—too many to bring back and hang or flog round the fleet and face with that comfortless food. We have certainly no means of knowing, but it is possible that the highly intelligent young master was already thinking about such things as well as about mathematics and astronomy and the best way to put a shoreline down on paper.

On this scene, not of idleness perhaps, but of comparative leisure, on 10 July 1762 a brig arrived with the news that St John's in New-foundland had surrendered to the French. It was a last flurry of French activity in North America, and it caused a good deal of British excitement. Under the provisions of the Treaty of Utrecht in 1713 fishing rights on the coasts of Newfoundland had been divided between the French and the British—the French on the north and west, the British elsewhere. The hostilities of the present war had put an end to the French cod-fishery and placed an enor-mously profitable monopoly in the hands of the British. Now, thought the French, to seize the main town (true, an exceedingly small one) on the island, and to retain it until peace was negotiated, while destroying all possible British fishing establishments, would at once cast great confusion on the fishery and provide an excellent bargain-ing counter. St John's had never been well defended by land, what defences it had were in decay; the British fleet, which must be its only real defence (and the island's) was well scattered. To seize the place would be a gamble, but a gamble worth taking. A squadron of four ships and a bomb-ketch, with eight hundred picked troops, accordingly slipped out of Brest and through the blockade in a fog, received the surrender of St John's on 27 June, devastated the bays to the northward, and then concentrated their forces at the town, which they proceeded to fortify with some efficiency for the first time in its existence. But the gamble was not to succeed. Captain Thomas Graves, a new governor for Newfoundland, not yet arrived, was found at sea in the frigate *Antelope*, and urgently sent marines to reinforce the Isle of Boys, as a defensible position; then he made for Placentia, on the western side of the isthmus of Avalon, roughly opposite St John's, to raise defences there. Amherst, now at New York, apprised in haste, as immediately sent off a body of troops under his brother Lieutenant-Colonel William Amherst to be con-voyed by an armed Massachusetts vessel, the *King George*. This vessel, however, joined Colville, who early in August had moved to Chedabucto Bay, at the north-eastern end of Nova Scotia; and on

10 August the *Northumberland* and *Gosport*, Captain John Jervis—a name bound for renown—sailed for Placentia without the transports. Here they strengthened the garrison with a party of marines, and having met Graves, sailed again with the *Antelope* and *Syren* added to the squadron, to cruise off the east coast of Avalon lest French reinforcements should be on the way. Off the Bay Bulls, south of St John's, Colville impressed fourteen men from a British sloop, and Jervis took a French one; then they moored in the Bay Bulls for a day or two to attend the rigging and take in water, and resumed the cruise. Off Cape Spear on 12 September the transports came up with them; the troops were landed next day at Tor Bay, three leagues to the north of St John's, and at once began their advance. They had artillery; on the 16th they were near enough to clear out a small adjoining harbour called Kitty Vitty or Quidi Vidi, which the French had blocked with shallops. The force was overwhelming, in spite of improved defences; there was nothing the French ships could usefully do, they could not even take off their troops; in a thick fog they slipped out of St John's, as they had slipped out of Brest four months before; and, a gale having blown the British squadron off the immediate coast, got clean away. Colville was highly indignant at this 'shameful flight'; for no doubt he had expected a portion of glory. On 18 September the abandoned French commander gave in; and in the evening, writes the master, 'came on b^d Lieut. Cook of the Gosport, with an acc^t of the Surrender....'[1] Thus fleetingly enters the life of James Cook another James Cook; there is no record of their meeting before or afterwards. The *Northumberland* went into St John's. A day later, the 20th, arrived a man whom Cook had met before. This was Captain Palliser, despatched from England with a small but strong squadron as soon as the news was known. Thus there were concentrated at St John's, together with a number of ships such as the fishing harbour had not earlier seen, three men of signal importance for Cook's career, Colville, Graves and Palliser; and Cook again at this moment gave proof of his technical skill.

In Amherst's force was Captain J. F. W. DesBarres, like Holland a military engineer and surveyor who was to attain great eminence in the near future in North America; and in Conception Bay, to the west of the peninsula on which St John's stood, were the settlements of Carbonear and Harbour Grace, both of importance to the fisheries. Colville, on arriving in England, some weeks later, wrote to the Admiralty.

[1] Adm 52/959, 19 September (p.m.) 1761.

I have mentioned in another Letter that the Fortifications on the Island of Carbonera, were entirely destroyed by the Enemy. Colonel Amherst sent thither Mr. Desbarres an Engineer, who surveyed the Island and drew a Plan for fortifying it with new Works: when these are finished, the Enterprize's six guns will be ready to mount on them. . . . Mr. Cook, master of the Northumberland, accompanied Mr. Desbarres. He has made a Draught of Harbour Grace, and the Bay of Carbonera; both which are in a great measure commanded by the Island, which lies off a Point of Land between them. Hitherto we have had a very imperfect Knowledge of these Places; but Mr. Cook who was particularly carefull in sounding them, has discovered that Ships of any size may ly in safety both in Harbour Grace and the Bay of Carbonera.[1]

This sort of letter could do no master harm at the Admiralty. Nor did Cook confine his attention to Harbour Grace and Carbonear Bay. His ship was moored in Placentia road for a week, in the Bay Bulls for two days, and in St John's harbour for two and a half weeks: of all these places, and of a piece of the coast neighbouring St John's, he drew charts. He also wrote descriptions, appending the dates when he made his notes, incorporating them all in one large 'Description of the Sea Coast of Nova Scotia, Cape Breton Island and Newfoundland', with sailing directions added. He incorporates the similar work he had done in 1758; for the stretch of Nova Scotian coast from Cape Sambro to Cape Canso he mentions that of 1758, 1759, 1760 and 1762. He had never, it is clear, missed a chance for scrutiny; yet of this latter stretch he remarks, 'A good Survey of this coast with the harbours thereon seems to be much wanting, it certainly would be found usefull to this Colony and to Navigation in general.'[2] Most of the latitudes he gives are by observation; most of the longitudes by computation; he includes the variation of the compass from observation. There are other sailing directions, for the St Lawrence, written by him, and attributable to this period since 1759. Certainly it was not in his nature to waste time.

Meanwhile the war was over. In North America the French were confined to New Orleans and the Mississippi valley. The *Enterprize*,

---

[1] Colville to Clevland, 25 October 1762, Adm 1/482.

[2] This particular document has been printed in the *Report of the Board of Trustees of the Public Archives of Nova Scotia For the Year 1958* (Halifax, N.S., 1959), from the holograph in the National Library of Australia, Canberra. With this copy are charts of Harbour Grace and Carbonear, and the river St John (New Brunswick). The Admiralty Library, MS 20, also has the sailing directions, signed by Bateman and Cook, the charts mentioned in the text, and a page of views. All the charts are signed by Cook, except one of Halifax. There are holograph sailing directions for the St Lawrence in both the National Library of Australia and the Public Archives of Canada. Presumably all these manuscripts belong to the material handed to the Admiralty by Cook, as referred to by Colville in his letter quoted on p. 59 below. I have had the advantage of some independent typescript notes made on these *Northumberland* MSS by Mr Skelton.

whose guns were to go to the Carbonear fortification, had come from the West Indies with news of the fall of Havana, the fruit of late and disastrous Spanish entry into the struggle. The *Northumberland* regained her marines from Placentia, and on 7 October sailed from St John's for home in company with Palliser's three ships. With favouring winds, and a few chases, though no prize, they reached Spithead in nineteen days. On 30 October Colville struck his commodore's flag. He was promoted Rear-Admiral of the White. The master too departed. The last entry in his journal is for 11 November: 'Strong gales and Sq^ly with Showers of rain, Clear'd out the Spirit room for takeing in the wine and Brandy, Ship-wrights Still on Board. Ja^s Cook.'[1] With that he stopped work forever in large ships. He drew pay of £291 19s 3d.[2] The shipwrights were still on board because the ship was again getting ready for sea. On 3 December, however, the declaration of cessation of hostilities was read, and on the 8th the whole ship's company was paid off, for good or ill. The master's departure did not mean that he was departing from the navy. As the year came to an end Lord Colville once more addressed the Admiralty on the subject of Mr Cook. 'Sir', he wrote to Mr John Clevland, the Secretary, from London, 30 December 1762:

Mr Cook late Master of the Northumberland acquaints me that he has laid before their Lordships all his Draughts and Observations, relating to the River St Lawrence, Part of the Coast of Nova Scotia, and of Newfoundland.

On this Occasion, I beg leave to inform their Lordships, that from my Experience of Mr Cook's Genius and Capacity, I think him well qualified for the Work he has performed, and for greater Undertakings of the same kind.—These Draughts being made under my own Eye I can venture to say, they may be the means of directing many in the right way, but cannot mislead any.[3]

The sole comment Mr Clevland wrote upon this communication was 'Recd'. It cannot nevertheless have been without its effect.

[1] Adm 52/959, 11 November 1762.
[2] Kitson, 59.
[3] Colville to Clevland, 30 December 1762, Adm 1/482.

IV

Newfoundland

CHARTS, LARGE and small, harbour plans, 'views', descriptions, sailing directions—all these things represent experience, professional education, a mastery of a particular sort. We recur inevitably to Holland's account of the good advice that Simcoe had given in the Halifax winter: 'he told Capt. Cook that as he had mentioned to several of his friends in power, the necessity of having surveys of these parts and astronomical observations made as soon as peace was restored, he would recommend him to make himself competent to the business. . . .' Cook had made himself competent to the business, as if driven by a sober but compulsive ambition. What now? He must sometimes, as a thoughtful man, have considered the past seven and a half years, since he offered himself to the navy at Wapping: he could hardly have been dissatisfied with his advancement since then. He was now thirty-four; he had been fortunate in some of his friends—Walker, Simcoe, Holland—but they were not men who could send him rocketing to eminence, and eminence was a thing he could scarcely have dreamed of. He had worked hard, as it was natural for him to work hard. If he wished to meditate on experience, he could meditate not merely on his introduction to the plane-table and trigonometry and astronomy, but on the North Sea and the Atlantic; on enough battle to satisfy the ordinary man without particular taste for fire-eating; on the behaviour of men crowded by hundreds into ships and the mentality of sailors in general; on naval discipline and its accepted cruelty of hanging and flogging; on the appalling state of naval health. We know, from his subsequent words and actions, that there were things in his experience that revolted him. We would not know it from anything recorded as said or done by him up to this time, or for some time after. He assimilated his experience. He added to it, by getting married.

He took this step within six weeks of departing from the *Northumberland*, on 21 December 1762. Of its preliminaries, any more than of the preliminaries to certain other important steps in Cook's life, we know nothing. His chosen bride was Elizabeth Batts, of the parish of Barking, in Essex. She was aged twenty-one, and if the countenance of old age is any index to the lines of early life, she was a highly personable young woman. It was a respectable rather than socially distinguished union. Elizabeth's mother, originally Mary Smith, was the daughter of a Bermondsey currier, Charles Smith, and Elizabeth was the only child of Mary's first union, to John Batts of Wapping; after Batts's death she married John Blackburn of Shadwell. She had a brother, a second Charles Smith, a shipping agent of the Custom House; whose son, a third Charles, was to be—adding respectability—a wholesale watch-maker of Bunhill Row. Bermondsey, Wapping, Shadwell—they were all riverside districts, of thick dark settlement, the closer to the tide the more disreputable; but they had their better-off streets, where the miserable gave way to the shabby, and the shabby to the agreeable; Shadwell was a natural enough place for a young sailor, who could not have known much of London above the Pool, to go for a lodging when he came off his ship. There is little left of it all now, after the bombings of war; the wharves and warehouses, the cranes and steel barges of the river, the oil tanks and tall chimneys across the river, show us nothing that Cook would have seen; the parish church was rebuilt after Waterloo; his Thameside is with difficulty made vivid in the mind. Possibly—all is conjecture—Elizabeth lived with friends or relatives at Barking, the village with its mill surrounded by open country, beyond the miles of marshland running down to the river; possibly Cook met her when she was visiting her mother in Shadwell, possibly—again—through Mr Charles Smith, shipping-agent, of the Custom House, who would not impossibly be a seaman's acquaintance. Whatever the lines of chance, James Cook of the parish of St Paul, Shadwell, bachelor, and Elizabeth Batts of the parish of Barking, spinster, on 21 December 1762 walked together over the meadows—Elizabeth remembered it—to her parish church, St Margaret's, with its grey stone and old square battlemented tower, and were there married by George Downing, vicar of Little Wakering, Essex, a village about twenty miles away.[1] It was 'Elizabeth Cook late Batts' who added her name beneath her husband's in the register. William Everrest, who witnessed the ceremony, we know was the parish clerk; who the other witnesses were, John Richardson

[1] Why George Downing of Little Wakering? It is an odd little puzzle. The vicar of St Margaret's, Barking, was Christopher Musgrave, though it appears from the Parish Register, 1754–67, that his curate, R. Carter, carried out most of the marriages.

and Sarah Brown, we do not know. This marriage was by Arch-bishop of Canterbury's licence, which indicates that Cook, once he had made up his mind, was not prepared to wait on such impediments to a joint navigation as the calling of banns. We cannot think that Elizabeth, at that moment, looked too forebodingly on the future, though she knew she was taking a sailor for a husband; but she was wise to seize every hour of married life that was open to her. They crossed the river to lodgings in Cook's parish; and there they were to be together till the end of the following April, when Cook went again to sea.

He was to go again to North American waters, and again to where he had last been, to Newfoundland: this time not as the master of a line-of-battle ship, but as a surveyor. Simcoe's advice was bearing fruit. Cook was by no means the only surveyor sent out at this time. Under the treaty of Paris, signed on 10 February 1763, Britain was faced with an enormous acquisition of territory. Settlers were already heading into the interior—was not that the history of America ever since the first landings?—and the mapping of the country called for an effort as vast as its extent. Nor was the imperial territory as it had existed before the war adequately surveyed. The effort made was serious, and in the 60's and 70's an extraordinary amount of valuable work was done, the results of which put to shame contemporary recording of the counties and coasts of England. The two great names on the continent are those of men Cook knew, Holland and DesBarres, the former from 1764 'His Majesty's Surveyor General for the Northern District of North America', and taking within his sphere of competence the province of Massachusetts Bay as well as Canada and the islands of the Gulf of St Lawrence. He worked for the Lords Commissioners of Trade and Plantations, and it is interesting to see the note on one or two of the coastal plans produced by his deputies that shoals and soundings had to be omitted 'for want of Naval Assistance'.[1] The production of charts, however, was not his primary business. DesBarres was working in the first place on the coast of Nova Scotia in a most comprehensive and detailed survey, with naval assistance, and working for the Admiralty. The surveys by Cook, then, were not isolated, they were to fit into a general scheme; but they had a special purpose. This purpose was bound up with the particular geographical position of Newfoundland, which gave it a particular position in the British economy. Newfoundland was no ordinary colony. It was not

[1] Admiralty, Hydrographic Dept., 9/73; A7353/77.

inviting for ordinary settlement; the British government deplored settlement. In relation to the Atlantic cod-fishery it was a sort of great wharf moored in the ocean, as essential as the fishing banks themselves to the welfare of fishermen. Its bays and harbours were fishing bays and harbours; its jetties and stages and buildings were for the purpose of drying and curing fish, and for the accommodation of men thus employed; the men lived on fish, the foot slipped on fish, the air smelt of fish; administration depended on an odd system of fishing 'admirals', with a naval officer in his own ship for governor, and a small number of naval vessels engaged on patrol. The British had never had sole rights to fish the banks or use the shores: to French as well as British the arduous seasonal trade, centred on the other side of the Atlantic two thousand miles off, was a 'nursery of seamen'—a nursery as important to Britain as the North Sea trade; and even Britain victorious in the recent war could not enforce a monopoly. The Treaty of Paris confirmed British sovereignty over Newfoundland, but not entirely so: off the southern coast the islands of St Pierre and Miquelon, traditionally French, were to be returned, and the French were to retain the right to dry their catch on the north-western and northern shores, from Point Riche to Cape Bonavista. Whatever treaty provisions might be, it was clear that for the continued safety of the trade, and for that of traffic in and out of the St Lawrence, whether through Cabot Strait to the south or the Strait of Belle Isle to the north, the Newfoundland coast needed to be charted as well as was humanly possible. The existing charts fell woefully short of this ideal. The French had done something on the east coasts, of which the most recent English survey was one of 1677, not published until 1689; the west coast and the Labrador side of the Strait of Belle Isle were hardly touched by anyone; the south coast, in terms of survey, was not much better. Graves took the matter up.

It seems highly probable that he had in his mind not merely a necessity, but the person to meet it. He had been impressed by Cook's activity after the restoration of the island; had conversed with this unusually active master, and been impressed by the conversation; had been impressed, too, by what was said of him by Colville and Palliser[1]—and Colville can hardly have said less than he said to the Admiralty in his letter of 30 December. There must have been discussion in the new year, after Colville's letter, and a

[1] We can certainly rely on this information given by Kippis, 8, 'From a paper of Admiral Graves's, communicated by the Rev. Dr. Douglas, now Bishop of Carlisle'. The paper is unfortunately lost. Graves's brother refers to it in a letter among the Douglas papers, B.M., Egerton MS 2180.

letter addressed by Graves to the Admiralty secretary, from the *Antelope* in the river Tagus, 2 January 1763, on his return from his first season of government: 'the Newfound Land station which I have been upon two years though only the last year as Governour, has been attended with many untoward and most perplexing accidents, which as they were totally unforeseen cou'd not but embarras the more.'[1] There was another thing, about which Graves went to the Lords, or Board of Trade, and the Lords of Trade to the Crown, in a representation of 29 March. Graves's government in 1763 was enlarged to include Labrador from Hudson Strait round to the St John river, opposite the western end of Anticosti, Anticosti itself and other islands of the Gulf, and he might well have felt over-burdened.

On economic matters his duty was to correspond with the Board of Trade. 'Mr Graves having represented to us', wrote that body, 'that the imperfect Returns hitherto made by the Governors of Newfoundland have been chiefly owing to their want of a Secretary, Surveyor, or other Person, capable of collecting Information, keeping regular accounts and making Draughts of Coasts and Harbours, for which services there has never been any allowances, and that such assistance is now become still more necessary to the Governor of Newfoundland, by the enlargement of his Government, and his instructions to report as accurately as he can the conditions, fisherys, and other material particulars of a country at present little known. We beg leave to humbly submit to your Majesty, whether it may not be expedient that such an allowance should be made.'[2] It does not seem that this plea to make it financially possible for Graves to cope with the paper work consequent on his Royal Instructions had great success, but at least the pressing need for 'Draughts of Coasts and Harbours' was recognised. It is clear that Cook's candidature was pressed on the Admiralty, and that agreement was reached.

There were office delays, of course. Graves's letters to Philip Stephens, who had succeeded Clevland as Admiralty secretary, are not without signs of exasperation. He first writes, if the records are complete, as if all were settled, on 5 April:

I have this moment seen Mr Cook and acquainted him he was to get himself ready to depart the moment the board was pleased to order him, and that he was to have 10 shil^s a day while employed on this service—He has been to enquire for a draughtsman at the Tower, but as this is a Holiday

---

[1] Graves to Clevland, 2 January 1763, Adm 1/1836.
[2] 'Representation' of 29 March 1763, quoted by Kitson, 63–4, from the Shelburne MSS.

he found hardly any one there—There are some who draw there at 1ˢ 6ᵈ a day, and others who have two shillings a day—one of which last establishment he wants to have and is assured that the Board will continue any such Person who chuses to go on their establishment upon an application from your Office made for them. It is from this class/set they allways send draughtsmen with Engineers or Comanding Officers who go abroad—The additional Pay they require from your office Mʳ Cook will acquaint you of tomorrow as soon as he can see them & propose their going. If he does not find their conditions to come wᵗʰ in their own office establishment, I have desired him to advertise for a draughtsman—acquaint you by letter with the terms he can bring them to, and wait your commands, as to the hireing any such, and as to the time of his setting out for the Ship.

There shou'd be a Theodilite and drawings instrumtˢ which will cost about 12 or 15 £ and is a thing the ordnance always allow their People— The officers of the Yard shou'd be orderd to supply me with two or three spare Azimith compasses & a number of Pendants of any colour to put as signals on different Points for takeing the Angles as the Survey goes on—[1]

Cook had been to the Tower because that was the headquarters of the Ordnance Office with its staff of technically-trained draughtsmen, one of which he as much as an 'engineer' would need for assistance. A week went by, and the sign of exasperation appears, in a note headed with some ambiguity 'Tuesday noon 1763'.

Captain Graves Compliments wait upon Mʳ Stephens and beg to know what final answer he shall give to Mʳ Cook late master of the Northumberland who is very willing to go out to Survey the Harbour & Coasts of Labrador and the draughtsman he was to get from the Tower—as they both wait to know their Lordships resolution and the footing they are to be upon. . . .[2]

Graves was evidently casting round for a second-best, in case any part of the great scheme should break down; for he adds to this enquiry another—whether a schoolmaster was allowed to a fourth-rate (which his *Antelope* was) as he had heard of a good draughtsman, in the *Bellona*, who was willing to go out in the *Antelope* on that footing. This was Michael Lane, of later note, and Graves did get him transferred. Nevertheless the governor was still kept in suspense: on 15 April he was writing to Stephens again: 'You will excuse my

[1] Graves to Stephens, 5 April 1763, Adm 1/1836.
[2] Adm 1/1836. I date this note conjecturally as 12 April. The Tuesdays in that month fall on the 5th, 12th, 19th, 26th. It can hardly belong to the 5th, the date of Graves's earlier letter, on which it seems logically to follow, with its reference to getting a draughtsman from the Tower. On the other hand, Graves's letter of 18 April implies that all dubieties were now settled. The dates of Stephens's letter to Cook about instruments, 18 April, and Graves's to Stephens of 15 April, seem to show that Graves was not informed punctually of all the developments.

takeing the liberty to ask if any change of resolution is taken about Mr Cook, the master and an assistant for him, and whither they are to go out with us.'[1] There had been no change of resolution: indeed two days earlier the secretary had written to 'Mr Ja^s Cook, Town' that Cook's letter 'of this date', the 13th, about mathematical instruments, had been communicated to the Lords, and that he was directed to supply himself with the said instruments and to send the bill to the secretary[2]—a missive which suggests, though Cook's own letter is not to be found, that he had already begun to develop the technique of going to the Admiralty himself, explaining what he wanted and the reason for it, and writing the necessary letter on the spot for an immediate answer.

Graves's mind must somehow have been relieved of its immediate worry—which may indeed have fallen on him partly because of his enforced absence from London to deal with some unrest in the *Antelope* at Spithead. On 18 April he reminded Stephens that it had been decided to give him orders to purchase two small vessels of about sixty tons in Newfoundland—'The one to send with Mr Cook upon the Survey of the Coasts and Harbours', the other for anti-smuggling or police duty—as well as to build a new hospital at St John's. The orders had not come. 'A change at the Board takeing place and my being order'd down to my ship on account of a mutiny amongst the Crew—the affair rested where it was and I am afraid is forgotten. . . . I beg you will please to remind their Lordships of these things, that I may go out with proper orders relating to it. The sending out Draughtsmen to Survey the Harbours, seems to Point out the necessity of their having a Small Vessell fit to use on that business.'[3] He enclosed a list of articles given him by Cook 'as necessary in the business of Surveying', which Cook 'apprehends may be supplied from the King's yard by order': to wit,

'Small Flags which may be made from new	
Buntin or out of Old colours	Twelve
Knight's Azimuth Compas	One
Knight's Steering Compas	One
Deep Sea Leads	Two
D° Lines	One
Tallow	lbs Twenty five
Axes	Two
Pick Axes	Two
Common deal Tables to Draw upon	Two

[1] Adm 1/1836.   [2] Stephens to Cook, 13 April 1763, Adm 2/722.
[3] Graves to Stephens, 18 April 1763, Adm 1/1836.

'If the Navy Board have not orders to supply these extra stores, no reason I can offer will have any weight.' Obviously Captain Graves was becoming a trifle weary of 'forms of office'. The Navy Board was ordered to supply the articles from the yard at Plymouth.[1] And the day after Graves wrote his letter from Spithead the Lords at last despatched their formal order.

Whereas we have thought fit to appoint Mr James Cook, a Person well skilled in making Surveys, and Mr William Test belonging to the Drawing Room in the Office of Ordnance, to go to Newfoundland in His Majesty's Ship under your Command in order to be employed in making surveys of the Coast & Harbours of that Island, and in making Drafts and Charts thereof; for which the former will be allowed Ten shillings a day and the latter six shillings in addition to what he receives from the Board of Ordnance: You are hereby required and directed to receive the said two Persons on board, and bear them on a Supernumary [sic] List for Victuals only until your return to England; and to employ them during your stay at Newfoundland as you shall see fit on the Service abovementioned.[2]

On the same day Mr James Cook, Town, and Mr William Test, Tower, were ordered to repair immediately on board the *Antelope* and follow the orders of Captain Graves.[3] Ten shillings a day, one may call to mind, was the wage of a captain of a fourth rate—the wage of Palliser in the *Eagle*.

Then it became obvious that the delays of office were not the only possible delays: Cook, ordered on 19 April to join the ship immediately in Plymouth Sound, did not make his appearance until 4 May, his name in the muster book being followed by a list of fifty-five men who had 'run'—that is, deserted.[4] Mr William Test did not appear at all. Meanwhile, the Admiralty had ordered the Navy Board to reimburse Cook the £68 11s 8d he had spent on surveying instruments;[5] Graves had had time to worry again about the tools Cook wanted—'I hope the Navy Board will have directions . . . or I apprehend they will not (however necessary) furnish any thing out of Course';[6] the Admiralty had told Graves to buy in Newfoundland the small vessels he wanted, and man and victual them from his own ships.[7] Graves groaned again, and acknowledged his orders,

[1] Endorsement on the letter last cited; and Admiralty to Navy Board, 22 April 1763, National Maritime Museum, ADM/A/2546.
[2] Admiralty to Graves, 19 April 1763, Adm 2/90. Graves wrote from Spithead on the 21st. 'By last nights Post I receiv'd' the order (Adm 1/1836); which testifies to fairly rapid communication.
[3] Stephens to Cook/Test, 19 April 1763, Adm 2/90.
[4] Adm 36/4887.
[5] Admiralty to Navy Board, 26 April 1763, NMM, ADM/A/2546.
[6] Graves to Stephens, 29 April 1763, Adm 1/1836.
[7] Admiralty to Graves, 3 May 1763, Adm 1/90.

in a letter of 8 May, which contradicts his muster book: 'Mr Cook arrived here yesterday but without an Assistant, which defect I will endeavour to replace here if possible, under an expectation of the same encouragement their Lordships were to give Mr Test. The first employment I shall give Mr Cook will be to Survey St Pieres & Miquelon, before my getting there to surrender those Islands, to this end it would have been very convenient that one of the Sloops had been ready to sail with me who might have been detached to performe this Service, whilest I made some stay upon the Coast, to afford them the proper time before the surrender of those Islands to the French.'[1] This letter was minuted with information for the captain about the missing draughtsman. The Admiralty had been informed by the Board of Ordnance a fortnight earlier that it would give him the necessary leave of absence but not on pay, as it would have to pay a substitute; since when their Lordships had neither heard nor seen anything of Mr Test. They approved of Graves trying to get someone else. Graves could get no one else before he sailed rather late in the season, Cook with him, on 15 May. Somehow the Admiralty found another man, a Mr Edward Smart, of Lambeth, also an Ordnance draughtsman, and sent him out at the end of the month in the sloop *Spy*, Captain Phillips.[2]

Newfoundland, a great triangle of ancient rock, thrusting out large peninsulas into the ocean as part of its general shape, has an infinite mass of indentations, bays, harbours, arms of the sea, which give it six thousand miles of coastline. This coastline is steep, bare, uninviting, fringed with the dangers of many rocks and shoals, and odd sets of the current; in the long cold winter cut off from access by the masses of Arctic ice swept down by the Labrador current— it is separated from Labrador by only a narrow strait—except for the always ice-free southern shore. Icebergs from the Greenland glaciers appear at any time, the greatest number in the months of spring, and they are dangerous. Fog is the other menace, fortunately not continuous, throughout the year. But the harbours are safe summer ones; although the land is rainy and the summers cool there are warm spells; the offshore banks were alive with cod, and as head-quarters for the seasonal industry of fishing Newfoundland was as

---

[1] Graves to Stephens, from Plymouth Sound, 8 May 1763, Adm 1/1836.
[2] Admiralty to Graves, 27 May 1763, Adm 2/90; Admiralty to 'Mr Smart, at Lambeth', 27 May, Adm 2/722. Test made his career at home. Almost forty years later he became Chief Draughtsman at the Tower, in 1801, and retired in 1815 after 56 years in the Ordnance service.—R. A. Skelton, *James Cook Surveyor of Newfoundland* (San Francisco, 1965), 11, n. Further references to this work are simply to 'Skelton'.

admirable as any place could be in that position and climate. Not far from the south coast, to the west of the Burin peninsula and off the entrance to Fortune Bay, lie St Pierre and Miquelon, already mentioned, small rocky outcrops from the sea, with a harbour in St Pierre hardly touched by ice, and thus valuable in the extreme to the French, whose sovereignty was by the treaty of 1763 so minutely confined. The survey to which Cook was sent was important. Like the fishery, and like the ship-based government of the country, it had to be seasonal. He must be on the coast by early June, and away from it by the end of October. The nature of the coastline made it extraordinarily complex. With all the complexity, it had perhaps one advantage, that a surveyor need never be at a loss for a prominent point to pin his observations to. We have noted the requisition for 'small flags'.

Cook was to carry out many accomplished pieces of surveying, in one part of the world or another, but nothing he ever did later exceeded in accomplishment his surveys of the southern and western sides of Newfoundland from 1763 to 1767. The North-eastern side of the triangle he was hardly to touch. He was so successful because he could deploy all the technique he had acquired from the military 'engineers'; because he could work at times on land as well as from the sea; because, therefore, he could use, sometimes, instruments that required solid earth as their base. The theodolite of which Graves spoke to the Admiralty would have been perfectly useless on the deck of a ship. One must not overstate the matter. It is nevertheless highly significant not only that that is the first 'mathematical instrument' that Cook mentions as necessary, but that when he was looking for a draughtsman he went straight to the Drawing Room at the Tower—to what one might call, in fact, the head office of military survey in England. He went there, one may feel, as the pupil of Holland and the associate of DesBarres, to find a man who was capable of both the desk-work of compiling and drawing, and the instrumental field-work that he had mastered himself. He did not want a plain master's mate for his assistant, any more than he wanted to make only a running survey from the sea. This was the traditional method of surveying a shore: the ship's course, as she sailed along it, would be carefully noted and plotted; the outstanding coastal features equally carefully plotted from cross-bearings taken from the ship; the outline would be filled in by careful sketching.[1] If there

---

[1] 'The errors and omissions inherent in a survey of this sort arose from the difficulty of logging the ship's track and fixing her position with sufficient accuracy, from inability to determine the exact position of soundings and submarine features, and from the masking of some land features by others from the eyes of an observer close inshore.'—Skelton, 11.

was time, the boats would be used for sounding and the accumulation of additional coastal detail. It was a method capable of brilliant exploitation, as Cook exploited it later on for New Zealand or the New Hebrides, or in varying degrees for New South Wales or the north-west coast of North America; but the exploitation, however brilliant, could hardly ever be more than brilliant reconnaissance. As Cook was to say in a note to his journal on the New Hebrides coast, eleven years later than this, 'The word Survey, is not to be understood here, in its literal sence. Sur.'eying a place, according to my Idea, is takeing a Geometrical Plan of it, in which every place is to have its true situation, which cannot be done in a work of this kind.'[1] For Newfoundland, he hoped, he was going to provide a survey in the 'literal', or anyhow the technical, sense. He would use the theodolite and his brass telescopic quadrant, made by Bird. He would measure accurately his base-lines and his angles, fix the positions of his prominent features, plot them on his paper, plot a net of triangles anchored to fixed positions. We can see these on at least one of his surviving charts.[2] He could calculate latitudes accurately with the help of his quadrant. He could not yet bring in longitudes. When he had his land features in correct relation, he would go on to his hydrographic work, would sound, take bearings, draw detail. From his journals as well as his charts we can form some judgment how far he was successful in all this. He no doubt quickened and refined his hand as season succeeded season. The last great Newfoundland chart he produced he felt justified in describing as 'An exact trigonometrical survey'; but that was not yet.

Graves reached Newfoundland in the second week in June, and anchored in Trepassey harbour, just west of Cape Race, the south-eastern point of the country. Besides the 50-gun *Antelope*, he had under his command for the purposes of his government five smaller vessels, and his instructions provided for the deployment of them all in surveying as well as in police duties: 'We have Ordered them to make Charts of all the said Coasts, with Drafts of the Harbours, noting the Depths of Water and Conveniences for fishing, and whatever Observations may Occur worthy of our Knowledge. . . .'[3] This was an affirmation of what was supposed to be routine. Of these vessels, the frigate *Pearl*, 32 guns, was to cruise on the coast of Labra-

---

[1] *Journals of Captain James Cook*, II, 509, n. 4.
[2] 'A Chart of the Sea coast, Bays, and Harbours, in Newfoundland between Green Island and Point Ferrolle. Surveyed . . . by James Cook. Coppy'd from the original survey taken in ye year 1764.'—H.D. 342. R. A. Skelton, in 'Captain James Cook as a Hydrographer', *Mariner's Mirror*, Vol. 40 (1954), 92–119, reproduces a detail of this, pl. 1(*a*).
[3] NMM, Graves MSS, GRV/106, Sect. 9.

dor, between Belle Isle and St John river and round the island of
Anticosti; the 26-gun *Terpsichore*, between Cape Race and Carpoon,
or Quirpon—that is, off the northern coast to its north-east extremity; the 32-gun *Lark* in the strait of Belle Isle, and thence along the
west coast to Cape Ray, the south-western point; the 25-gun *Tweed*
along the south coast, between Cape Race and Cape Ray. The *Tamar*
was to spend her time with the fishing vessels on the Grand Bank.
It was therefore the *Tweed*, Captain Charles Douglas, with which
Cook was to be immediately most closely acquainted. She had been
on her station since the beginning of June. On the 13th she met the
Antelope at Trepassey, and embarked Cook, James Biddon and Peter
Flower, 'Supernumerary born for Victuals only being an Engineer
& his Retinue'.[1] All official documents were now inculcating speed:
the Admiralty's instructions to Graves, Graves's instructions to
Douglas, which Cook was to deliver to him—'you are to proceed
without a moment's loss of time . . . to the Island of St Peter's, where
you are to afford him (who you are to take with you) all the assistance in your power by boats or otherways in taking an accurate
survey of the Island[s] of St Peter and Miquelon with all the
Expedition possible, that no Delay be thereby given to the Delivering
these Islands up to the French.'[2] This was all very well; but the
islands were to have been handed over to the French not later than
10 June,[3] and when Douglas arrived in the harbour of St Pierre not
merely did he find a French frigate, the *Licorne*, already there, but
at the same hour arrived the French governor-designate, M. d'Anjac,
in the *Garonne*, with fifty soldiers and a hundred and fifty men—
merchants and fishermen, women and children. British settlers were
to be removed, these were to be installed: Graves and Douglas were
determined that not an inch of rock nor an ounce of authority should
be ceded until the survey was completed and every secret (if there
were any) laid bare. Douglas was even cautioned against handing
over at all what Graves wrote as 'Langly'—Langley or Langlade,
the present Petite Miquelon, the southern part of that island, now
joined to the northern part by a narrow thread of land: 'that island
has been separated from Miquelon upwards of four years by a passage a mile broad and two fathom deep. It affords little else than wood
but lays between Miquelon and St. Peter's.'[4] In retrospect one can
see some moments of tension, and fancy some moments of comedy.

[1] *Tweed's* muster book, Adm 36/6901, 13 June 1763. They remained on the strength till
the July–August muster.
[2] Adm 1/1704, n.d.   [3] Instructions to Graves, 2 May 1763, Adm 2/90.
[4] Graves to Stephens, 20 October 1763, NMM, GRV/106. The isthmus reasserted
itself in 1781, but not on the charts, and there were many shipwrecks in consequence.

Cook got to work at once, 'with all possible application', on St
Pierre, while Douglas held off the governor, 'who was (you may
believe with some difficulty) persuaded to remain on board with his
troops, untill the fourth day of July when (the survey of St Peter's
being compleated) that Island was deliver'd to him in form: and our
Surveyor began with the other; the weather still continuing foggy
and unfavorable.'[1] In the meantime M. d'Anjac had despatched a
very indignant letter to Graves at Placentia, but was somehow
calmed down. We can see a little of the comings and goings in
Douglas's log: 3 July, 'PM sent our Cutter under ye Command of
a Midshipman to attend Mr Cook whilst he survey'd the Islands of
Miquelon & Langley'; 12 July, 'AM sent ye Longboat with 4 Days
provisions for ye Men wth Mr Cook on ye Island of Langley'; 13
July, 'PM ye Longb^t return'd from Langley not finding Mr Cook
there, he being gone to Miquelon';[2] 25 July, 'Arriv'd here ye Shallop
Tender & Cutter wth Mr Cook he having Finish'd ye Survey of that
part of this Island Called Dunn.'[3] A few days more and Cook had
finished the whole island, which was handed over to the impatient
French on 31 July. He had worked on a large scale. 'A Plan of the
Islands of St Peter's, Langly, and Miquelong, survey'd by order of
H.E. Thos. Graves, Esq., Governor of Newfoundland, by James
Cook', is laid down at three and a half inches to the mile, and
measures seven feet eight inches by two feet five inches.[4] It could be
reduced at need. Douglas, on his part, had done his very best for
Cook. 'I procured him all the time I could,' he wrote later to the
Admiralty secretary, 'by staying at St Peter's under various pretences, untill towards the 17th, and then went to the Road of
Miquelon—where we made shift to keep the Commandant in some
sort of temper, untill the beginning of August; when, thro' the
unwearied assiduity of Mr Cooke, the survey of that Island too,
was compleated.' The dutiful captain had had to expend something
more than tactful words, on which he enlarges modestly.

I flatter myself Sir, that my Lords Comissioners will easily believe, that so
delicate an affair, as keeping the French Governor so long on board; out
of the exercise of his authority, the surveying of his Islands untill the

---

[1] Douglas to Stephens, 3 May 1764, Adm 1/1704.
[2] These dates must again be interpreted according to ship time—i.e. 3 July PM is the
afternoon of 2 July civil time; 12 July AM is the morning of 12 July civil time.
[3] Captain's Logs, *Tweed*, Adm 51/1016. 'Dunn' appears to be what Cook called on his
chart Dunne Harbour, represented now by Grand Barachois—'a basin with a narrow
entrance on its south-eastern side, only practicable for boats' (*Newfoundland Pilot*, I
(8th ed., 1951), 185)—which almost entirely occupies the northern part of the tongue of
land between the two Miquelons, the Chaussee de Miquelon or Isthme de Langlade.
[4] B.M. Add. MS 17963.

beginning of August, due to France since the 10th of June; and to have thereby occasion'd no disturbance, must have caused an expensive intercourse on my side [and he thinks the Lords might be induced to] grant me some consideration for the extraordinary expences I was put to; without having incurred which the Islands in question wou'd have remained unsurvey'd.[1]

The Lords were not unsympathetic, and did not think the suggested £50 was too much to grant.

This survey completed, Douglas took Cook on board again and carried him according to orders to Ferryland, a small harbour on the east coast of the Avalon peninsula about half-way between Cape Race and St John's, whence he joined Graves at St John's. The *Spy* had not yet arrived, and did not arrive until 1 September, so that Cook was still without the help of the skilled assistant Mr Edward Smart. He was, however, to get a vessel of his own. During July Graves had used the authority given him before he left home to buy for the survey, at the price of £372 15s, a 68-ton schooner built in a Massachusetts yard in 1754, 'together with her Boat, Tackle, Furniture and Apparell'.[2] She was called the *Sally*, and became the *Grenville*—in honour, we must suppose, of the man who was then Prime Minister and seems to have been a friend of Graves; and, as Graves reported, she was within three or four days of being ready for service when Cook joined him. As soon as she was ready Cook sailed her up to the northern end of the island to survey Quirpon and Noddy harbours, inside Quirpon island—where, on the western side of Quirpon harbour, he named Graves (now Jacques Cartier) island; 'and from thence to York Harbour to take a compleat survey of that or any other good harbour he shou'd fall in w^t on ye Labradore coast, and to employ himself in like manner on his return when ye Season shoud make it necessary to leave that Coast, this he has done with indefatigable industry haveing survey'd four harbours.'[3] So Graves; and in the absence of a *Grenville* log for that period, or any other more detailed description, we have no idea how long Cook was at each place, or what precisely he did after his return to St John's. He seems to have returned towards the end of September.[4] We have the precise

[1] Douglas to Stephens, London, 3 May 1764, and minute thereon, Adm 1/1704.

[2] The Navy Board made difficulties over paying for it. On 2 December 1763 it asked the Admiralty whether it should pay the bill.—NMM, ADM/B/173. Then it said that under its rules it could not pay; for six months later the Admiralty ordered it to do so—NMM, ADM/A/2561.

[3] Graves to Stephens (draft) *Antelope*, St John's, 20 October 1763; NMM, GRV/106.

[4] The dating is not quite easy. Graves to Stephens, 20 October, says that the *Pearl* had sailed for England, 'there being no occasion to detain her here and carrys some invalids sent hither from Louisbourg for a passage home.'—NMM, GRV/106. On 30 October 'by the Tweed' he says, 'By the Pearl C. Saxton who sailed from hence the

and beautiful detail of his charts, and from what we know of the country we can see that his work would have its discomforts. York or Chateaux (now Chateau) harbour was frozen six months of the year, from Christmas to the end of June; in the summer, if he landed, Cook could walk on moss and eat cranberries, but flies and mosquitoes would fall on him in clouds. His plan is a good one accompanied with sailing directions and 'views'.[1] Presumably when he did reach St John's again he was at last joined by Smart, and could get some relief in copying and computation; and perhaps he had time to consider some of the charts handed in by the other ships on the station.

The governor reported to the Admiralty secretary on 30 October, beginning with the movements of ships. He proceeds:

The Tweed sails with these dispatches and I hope to leave the country about the same time. As Mr Cook whose Pains and attention are beyond my description, can go no farther in surveying this year I send him home in the Tweed in preferance to keeping him on board [the *Antelope*], that he may have the more time to finish the diff^t surveys allready taken of it to be layn before their Lordships—and to copy the different sketches of ye Coasts and Harbours, taken by ye ships on the several stations by which their Lordships will perceive how extreamly erroneous ye present draughts are, & how dangerous to ships that sail by them—and how generally beneficial to Navigation the work now in hand will be when finished indeed I have no doubt in a Year or two more of seeing a perfect good chart of Newfoundland and an exact survey of most of ye good harbours in which there is not perhaps a part of the World that more abounds.

The inclosed Papers are the remarks made by the Captains of the Lark, Tweed and Pearl. Mr Cook will lay before their Lordsh: ye original Survey of St Peters Miquelon & Langley as allso Quirpon & Noddy harbours, Chateaux or York harbour & Croque, these though not so highly finished as a *Copy* may be, yet I am purswaded thier Lordships will think ye properest to be deposited in thier Office.[2]

26th [October?] I acquainted their Lordships with my proceeding[s] till that time. The Schooner Grenvile has since return'd from the Northward w^t our seeing the Terpsichore.' He had sent her with an answer to Captain Ruthven's many queries 'some days since'.— GRV/106.

[1] Hydrographic Dept., B. 188.

[2] NMM, GRV/106. The instructions to captains to carry on the survey were apparently meant to be taken seriously. Douglas to Stephens from the *Tweed*, Spithead, 8 December 1763, illustrates this: 'Be pleased to lay before my Lords Commissioners, the herewith-inclosed Sketch of the Magdalen Islands in the Gulph of St Laurence; where the Sea-Cow fishery is carried on. And be moreover pleased to acquaint their Lordships, that agreeable to the commands of the Right Honourable Board of last April, between the beginning of September and the middle of October I took an incompleat one, of the whole Coast of Newfoundland, within the limits of the station prescribed me by their Lordships; viz: between the Capes Race and Ray. Which Sketch is (pursuant to the desire of the Captain Graves of the Antelope) now in the hands of Mr James Cooke;

The *Tweed* anchored at Spithead on 29 November 1763. Cook, there is little doubt, lost no time in hastening to Mrs Cook and the son that had been born to him seven weeks earlier, another James.[1] Nor could it have been long before he decided he must buy a house. The one he selected was in the hamlet of Mile End Old Town, on the northern side of the parish of Stepney; it was the last in a small terrace, No. 7 Assembly Row, facing on the Mile End Road, over which the coaches lumbered from Cornhill on their way to Essex. The row took its name from the Assembly Rooms near by, the scene of various though fortunately not constant tumultuous gatherings; the house was joined by an archway to a gin distillery, or what Cook was later to refer to as 'Mr Curtis's Wine Vaults'. It was therefore not in a haunt of rural seclusion, as some of the names of neighbouring passage-ways might suggest—Ducking Pond Row, Red Cow Lane, Dog Row, Mutton Lane—but a rush of building had not obliterated all that was green. It was some distance from the dwelling-place of fashion, a house not large, much better nevertheless than lodging in Shadwell for a wife and family, and a man between voyages, entirely respectable, suitable for a master in the navy. Mrs Cook would not be crowded, there was a garden behind to breathe in, market gardens she could visit, meadow and pasture and marsh land not far away. Cook could afford it, on his savings, and his surveyor's ten shillings a day, and his prospect of permanent employment.[2] With such testimonials as his from Graves and Douglas, the Admiralty would not let him go, even if the Navy Board was slow in paying.[3] He and Smart, and Smart's brother, were busy drawing and making copies, and it was intended to send them out again. Smart was not to go out again: he died on 8 March 1764, when Cook was busy in all sorts of ways.[4] He was not too busy to write to Graves, on

---

who was last Summer employ'd to survey the Islands of S[t] Peter and Miquelon: which Survey we were not able to compleat before the beginning of August. One of the reasons of the incompleatness of the Draught last mention'd.'—Adm 1/1704. And see Palliser's letter, p. 84 below.

[1] To be precise, on 13 October 1763, at Shadwell. This is one of the bits of information Kippis (517) got from Mrs Cook.

[2] I owe most of the details in the foregoing passage to Mr A. W. Smith, 'Captain James Cook, Londoner', in *East London Papers*, vol. 11, No. 2 (1968), 94–7. The house stood until 1959. The Assembly Row address remained until 1863, when the name was abolished and the house became 88 Mile End Road. In 1880 the ground floor was converted to a shop, projecting on to the small front garden (most of the other houses in the row were served likewise). No. 88 was in this century successively an emporium for women's apparel and a kosher butchery. An L.C.C. commemorative plaque was affixed to it in 1907, which did not prevent its later demolition. The rest of the row was spared, in shabby disrepair.

[3] Admiralty to Navy Board, 4 January 1764, NMM, ADM/A/2555.

[4] A letter from the Admiralty to the Navy Board, 23 April 1764, refers to his death, and to Smart's (and his brother's) employment, in providing for Smart's pay. A certificate from Cook on the matter was enclosed.—NMM, ADM/A/2558.

15 March, in a way that indicates regard for Graves on his part as great as Graves's regard for him.

Sir,

I learnt this day at the Admiralty of your arrival of which I give you joy, and have to acquaint you, that soon after my arrival, I gave my surveys into the board which was approved of, and was then order'd to draw a fair copie of St Peters and Miquelong to be laid before the King. these and the different Captains Sketches is finished and given in to the board. Those that you intend for the Board of Trade are ready. I had not the honour to see Mr Grenvill when I gave in the Plan, but am convinced it was well received, as he made me an offer soon after (by Mr Whatley Secretary to the Treasury) to go as one of the Surveyors to the Natral Islands, which I was obliged to decline. your favourable recommendation of me to this Gentleman, likewise, to the Admiralty, together with many other signal favours I have received during the short time I have had the honour to be under your command shall ever be had in the most gratfull remembrance and tho' Captain Pallisser, who is appointed to the command in New-foundland is a Gentleman I have been long acquainted with yet I cannot help being sorry that you do not enjoy that officer longer.

It is more than probable the Survey of the Island will go on untill compleatly finished, this usefull and necessary thing the World must be obliged to you for.

I shall do my self the honour to wait upon you as soon as you arrive in town and acquaint you with what has pass'd between Lord Egmont and me in regard to the North part of the Island. I am with great respect

Sir
your most Ob^t and Very Hble Ser^t
Ja^s Cook.[1]

The 'Grenvill' here referred to must certainly have been George Grenville, the First Lord of the Treasury; Egmont was First Lord of the Admiralty, and presumably, he was interested in French infringements of the fishery agreement, on which Graves had already had something to say. Masters in the navy did not ordinarily converse with First Lords of any sort.

Cook was already engaged in discussion with Palliser, so it would seem, on the borderland between geography and diplomacy, perhaps as a sequel to his meeting with Egmont; and a little historical

---

[1] Cook to Graves, 15 March 1764, NMM, GRV/106. The 'fair copie . . . laid before the King' is now in the British Museum map collection, K. Top, cxix. 111. The 'Natral Islands' were presumably the Neutral Islands in the West Indies—St Vincent, Dominica, Tobago and St Lucia (the last an island of superb harbours). They were declared neutral by France and England—i.e. not to be colonised by either power—in 1730 and 1748; but the first three were ceded to England at the Peace of Paris in 1763. The French then clung to St Lucia, which, however, became British in the settlement of 1815.

research was in progress, though not on the 'North part of the Island'. It is to be remembered that fishery disputes were of very long standing. Cook writes a memorandum to Palliser on his investigations, 'Wednesday Evening 5 o Clock 7 March 1764'.

At the Book and Map seller at the large Gateway in Cheap-side Jnᵒ Senex's Map Pub. in 1710 names Cape Ray and calls Pᵗ Rich Cape Pointu—this Map was drawen from the observations communicated to the Royˡ Society at London and the Academy at Paris—

Mitchel's Map—Pub 1755—Cape or Point Rich, which is left out of the late French Maps as if there was no such place seemingly because it is the boundries of their prevelige of fishing which extend from hence Northward round to C. Bonavista.

The *Universal Traveller* or Compleat account of Voyages by Pat. Barclay—1734–54, speaking of Newfoundland, I do not find he once mentions C. Ray or Pᵗ Rich, but says their Journals was so confounded with names common to both sides of the Island that it was a difficult matter to tell which side there where [i.e. they were] upon, in the Gulf or on the NE side—

At Mʳ Vanbushels Gardener at Lambeth

In Ogilbys America Pub in 1671 is a Map without Date, that mentions Cape Ray only—this Historian doth not speak of Cape Ray but in one place, and there he must mean Cape Race—

I have seen no maps to day, but such as we see yesterday, except the above; neither have I met with any Historys or Voyages (and I have looked into several) that makes any mention of what we want—

J. Cook[1]

Palliser was triumphant in rebutting the claim of the French ambassador that Cape Ray and not Point Riche was the really intended southern limit on the west coast of French operations. The enquiries which Cook made of old Newfoundland hands about settlement on the east coast seem less relevant.[2]

There were obviously discussions about the survey as well, between

[1] 'To Hugh Palliser Esqʳ', Adm 1/2300. Palliser must have sent the communication on to the Admiralty. I can trace no Senex map as early as 1710, or any before *The Coast of Newfoundland from Placentia to Cape Bonavista*, No. 50 in his *Atlas maritimus & commercialis*, 1728. The map of Captain John Mitchell, F.R.S. was his *Map of the British and French Dominions in North America*, 1755, used for the peace treaty of 1783. Patrick Barclay, *The Universal Traveller: or, a Complete account of the most remarkable voyages and travels . . . to the present time*, a folio of 795 pp., has the B.M. date 1735. John Ogilby, *America, being the Latest and Most Accurate Description of the New World* . . . London, 1671, another folio. I presume that Mr Vanbushel may have been an acquaintance of Cook's, whom he knew to possess a copy of Ogilby.

[2] *Hist. Rec. N.S.W.*, I, Part 1, 300–1, prints a letter from George Davis to Cook, Poole, 14 March 1764, on the subject. A note on one of Cook's maps ('A Sketch of the Island of Newfoundland. Done from the last Observations. By James Cook 1763'; Admiralty Library, America, Vol. I, No. 21) seems to bear on this same investigation. It concerns the years of settlement at various places 'All of which places the English have continued to fish at, since first settled'.

Palliser and Graves, and Cook must have been brought into them. As a result Palliser made an important suggestion to the Admiralty. The *Grenville* was laid up for the winter at St John's, and in need of stores. Before she could sail on survey she would have to be refitted and re-equipped, and manned from the commodore's, or governor's ship; she would have to return to St John's in time to hand over the men and be laid up again; thus a great deal of time that should be expended on the survey would be used up, with consequent inconvenience and confusion in accounting and command. Would it not be better to appoint 'Mr Cook the Surveyor who is a Master in the Navy . . . master of her, to be charged with all stores and materials belong[ing] to her, with the apointment of a master of a 6th Rate'? The assistant-surveyor should be a seaman with some knowledge of surveying and drawing, and be mate of the vessel, paid as a master's mate of a 6th rate with an additional allowance of 3s or 2s 6d a day: 'I flatter myself their Lordships will think that such a person, who has been brought up in the Navy, is better intitled to encouragemt than any young man who has been brought up in the Tower, that is meerly a draftsman, no seaman & without knowledge of either land or sea Surveying.' (One is forced to conclude either that Mr Edward Smart had been a disappointment, or that there is here a little naval prejudice against the Ordnance service. It had not been Cook's feeling the previous year.) The vessel should bear eighteen or twenty seamen, ten to be borrowed from the several ships on the station, ten to be permanently borne as enough to sail and navigate her at the end of the season, across the Atlantic to Portsmouth, where she would be properly refitted and would arrive for the next season's surveying much earlier and in better condition than if she had been left at St John's. Thus, at no greater additional expense than 2s a day, 'the service will be more compleatly perform'd, & with greater facillity and dispatch.'[1] Palliser enclosed with this letter two very comprehensive lists of 'Extra Stores wanting for the Surveying Service'. The Admiralty was prepared to agree, and to approve a complement for the schooner of master, master's mate, master's servant, and seven seamen; it instructed the Navy Board accordingly, instructed Cook on recruitment, and directed Captain Thompson of the *Lark*, one of Palliser's squadron, to convey them to Newfoundland. The master and master's mate were to be allowed pay as if for a Sixth Rate—that is £4 and £2 2s a month respectively—'and the former to be charged with the Provisions and Stores which shall from time to time to be supplied to the Schooner; and to pass regular

---

[1] Palliser to Stephens, 4 April 1764, Adm 1/2300.

Accounts for the same.'[1] So here he was introduced to the burdens of administration. The Navy Board, 'having received a Certificate of the Corporation of the Trinity House of your Abilities to serve as Master of any of His Majesty's ships of the Fourth Rate', gave him a warrant to take charge of the *Grenville*, and allowed him a servant in addition to his sixth rate pay.[2] Trinity House was being cautious: after all, the *Northumberland*, of which he had been master for three years, was a third rate. Palliser told him to start on the survey as soon as he arrived in Newfoundland, and to keep a particularly attentive eye on the French fisheries.[3]

The *Lark* sailed from Portsmouth on 7 May 1764 for St John's, where, 14 June, began the log of the *Grenville*:[4] 'The first and middle parts moderate and Hazy weather the Later foggy, at 1 PM His Majesty's ship the Lark anchor'd here from England, on board of which came the Master and Company of this Schooner, went on board and took possession of her—Read over to the Crew the Master's Warrant, Articles of War, and Abstract of the Late act of Parliament.' The Articles of War and Abstract were documents Cook was to read over to his crews a good deal, as prescribed by his naval masters. Until 3 July the schooner remained in harbour while she was overhauled and repaired. Palliser arrived in the 50-gun *Guernsey*, whence was taken the man who was to be Cook's mate for the next two and a half years, and in future years an admiral, William

[1] Admiralty to Navy Board, 13 April 1764, NMM, ADM/A/2558. Stephens to Palliser, 13 April, in answer to his of 4 April; agreeing with all his suggestions, and saying, 'Their Lordships have commended Mr Cook to the Navy Board to be appointed Master of the said Vessel & when you acquaint me with the name of the Mate their Lordships will order the Navy Board to pay him an additional Allowance of three Shillings a day Assistant Surveyor.'—Adm 2/724. Cook to Stephens, 21 April (on conduct money, carriage of seamen's chests, and bedding), ATL, *Holograph Letters*; Admiralty to Navy Board, 23 April (conduct money, etc.), 24 April (manning of the *Grenville* two men from *Pearl*, *Tweed*, *Lark*, *Zephyr*, *Spy*); 27 April (Navy Board to repay Cook for repair of surveying instruments and provisions of others).—ADM/A/2558. Stephens to Cook, 23 April (on conduct money, etc.), Adm 2/724, ATL *Hol. Lett.*; to captains *Spy*, *Pearl*, *Tweed*, *Zephyr*, 24 April (on loan of men), Adm 2/90; to Captain Thompson, *Lark*, 24 April (to take out Cook and his men and lend him two men), Adm 2/91; to Palliser, 30 April (on loan of men), Adm 2/724; to Palliser, 2 May (on directions to Cook), printed in H. Carrington, *Life of Captain Cook*, 38. There are a few other formal letters on this season's work in ATL, *Holograph Letters*, item 3 in which seems to be *Grenville* letter book, not in Cook's hand.

[2] Navy Board warrant, 18 April 1764, ATL, *Hol. Lett.*

[3] Palliser to Cook, 29 April 1764, ATL, *Hol. Lett.*

[4] Cook's *Grenville* log and journal, 14 June 1764—15 November 1767, in seven parts, make up Adm 52/1263, parts 1, 2, and 6 the log, parts 3, 5, and 7 the journal: there is not very much difference between them, and neither log nor journal is in Cook's hand, though each part is signed by him. The title-pages of parts 3 and 5 are rather fancy productions, and in part 5 'Schooner' becomes 'Brigg'. Some of the journal, though not by any means all of it, seems to be kept in civil time; the log is now and again a little fuller. Most of the quotations in the present account are from the journal, with occasional recourse to the log, but it does not seem necessary to give constant references beyond the dates in the text.

Parker; and on 4 July the *Grenville* ran out of the harbour and stood north. Palliser had decided that the season's survey should be a continuation of that on the north coast in 1763, from Bauld Cape westward and then down the western coast a certain distance.[1] Two days were spent on the way at anchor in Carouge harbour, a small place some forty miles south of the cape, fitting the boats' oars and making small flags for the survey; then for a week the schooner was moored in Noddy harbour while Sacred Bay, a little to the west, with its numerous islets, rocks and shoals, was sounded and surveyed. We see the system: 14 July, 'went into the Bay Sacre, Measured a Base Line and fix'd Flaggs on the Different Islands, &c.' Flags were fixed on 'Cape de Ognon'—Onion Cape, one of the entrance points. Another week was spent in Pistolet Bay, farther west again, the boats out sounding, Cook busy with his instruments; then they plied up to Cape Norman, the most northern point of the island, with a boat between ship and shore, anchoring for two days south-east of the cape, in a small harbour mainly formed by islands, called Cook's Harbour. On 2 August, 'At Noon took the Suns Meridian altitude on shore and found Cape Norman to be in Latitude 51°39' North'; on 3 August, 'at 6 AM the Master with the Cutter went ashore to Continue the Survey, Stood to the westward about a League off shore, brought too and sounded every mile': the pattern is clear, as the schooner moves from harbour to harbour, the boats sounding, Cook with his theodolite on shore as much as possible, fixing his flags, measuring, sighting, Parker no doubt drawing carefully from offshore. On 6 August the log registers misfortune.

2pm Came on board the Cutter with the Master who unfortunately had a Large Powder Horn blown up & Burst in his hand which shatter'd it in a Terrible manner and one of the people that stood hard by suffered greatly by the same accident and having no Surgeon on board Bore away for Noddy Harbour where a French fishing ship Lay, at 8 sent the Boat in for the French surgeon at 10 the Boat returned with the Surgeon, at 11 Anchord in Noddy Harbour in 6 fathom water.

This untoward affair seems to have disabled Cook as an active surveyor for the rest of the month, though not as a commander. It was his right hand; it healed, but it bore a gash between the thumb and forefinger, and a large scar as far as the wrist, that had an identifying function fifteen years later. The schooner lay in Noddy Harbour till 25 August. Parker was sent off to survey Griguet Bay and the coast as far as White Cape to the south; the men, employed

[1] Palliser to Cook, 19 June 1764, ATL, *Hol. Lett.*

2. Whitby Harbour in the mid-eighteenth century
Water-colour drawing by unknown artist

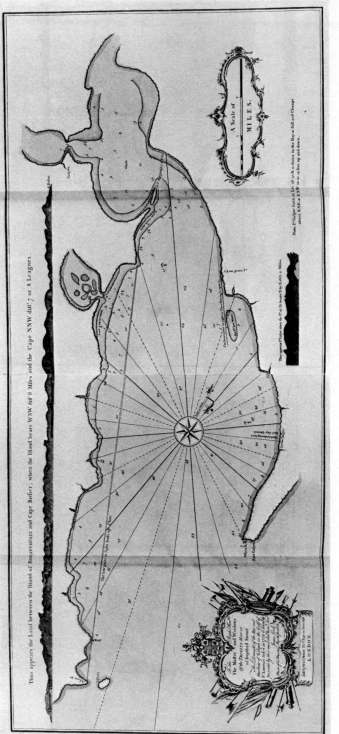

3. 'Draught of the Bay and Harbour of Gaspee', 1758
Cook's first published map

4. 'Plan of the Harbour of Great and Little St Laurence'
By Cook. Inset in a chart of the south coast of Newfoundland, 1765

5. Sir Hugh Palliser, by George Dance

at ship tasks and 'brewing of Spruce Essence'—brewing 'spruce beer', that is—grew a little restive, and even the excellent Peter Flower, Cook's senior hand, was with two others 'Confin'd to the Deck for Drunkness and Mutiny', the ringleader in this crime being further punished 'by running the Gantlope'; but on 26 August the vessel was doubling back to resume her work, and from the end of the month Cook was on shore day by day pretty continually. He marked the 'Indian Path' behind the 'Strait Coast' between Open Bay and Sandy Bay; was anchored for ten days in St Genevieve Bay, during which we have such log entries as that for 14 September, 'PM the Master with the Cutter went on shore with five Days provisions, in order to go on with the Survey', and then day after day, with slight changes of wording, 'the Master with the Cutter Employ'd on the Survey', as he moved on to Old Ferolle—until, on 28 September, 'the Cutter with the Assistant went to Survey the Bay of St Margaret'. This, with Point Ferolle, jutting out between it and the large St John Bay, was the southern limit of the survey on the western coast for 1764, and perhaps the accident of 1 October aided the decision: 'AM sent the Boats to sound off and about point Ferrol, the small Boat got ashore on one of the Ledges which Bilg'd and fill'd, with the Assistance of the Cutter the people were Saved.' Cook spent three days wooding, watering, and brewing, before sailing back round the north and east coasts to St John's, where he was moored on 14 October. On 1 November he sailed for England, had a good deal of stormy weather, put into Cutwater on 4 December, and was at Woolwich on the 12th. Thence he wrote to the Admiralty a letter which anticipated a busy winter. He had fair copies to draw of the surveys he had made this last summer, he said, which would occasion him sometimes to be absent from the schooner he commanded, and he proposed that she should be ordered to Deptford, where she would lie safer than at Woolwich. The Lords acquiesced.[1]

The master had now his own house to go to, for the practice of a few months' domesticity; and here, on 14 December, simultaneously with his own arrival, he and Mrs Cook and the young James were joined by a second son, Nathaniel. We may infer pleasure on Cook's part, perhaps even a temporary inattention to the demands of his profession. If that were so, it could not have lasted long: there were his charts, and there was his ship. While the *Grenville* was at Deptford

---

[1] Cook to Stephens, 13 December 1764, ATL, leaf from *Grenville letter-book* stuck in Hick's *Endeavour* log. Stephens to Cook, 18 December 1764, Adm 2/725; Dixson Library, MS, Q140, 2.

this winter not merely did she have necessary repairs—her bottom was 'Very much eat with worms', he reported—but her rig was altered from a schooner's fore and aft to the square rig of a brig. The suggestion came from Cook himself, in a letter to the Navy Board tactful as well as persuasive:

Gentlemen.

The masts sails and rigging of His Majesty's Schooner the Grenville being all or the most part of them Condemned by Survey, Permit me to set forth the utility of having her rigg'd into a Brigg, as I presume it may now be Done without much additional expence to the Crown, for Schooners are the worst of vessels to go upon any Discovery, for in meeting with any unexpected Danger their staying cannot be Depended upon, and for want of sail to Lay aBack they run themselves ashore before they wear; this I experienced in the Grenville schooner Last summer in the Straights of Belle Islse, when I see the Condition her Bottom is in it supprizeth me that she ever came off. A Brigg hath all these advantages over a schooner besides many more I could name, was I not applying to Gentlemen better acquainted with those things than my self. I only mean to give some reasons for my request, and pray you will be pleas'd to take these into your Consideration, and if they appear reasonable to order her to be rigg'd into a Brigg, as I Cannot help thinking but that it will enable me to Carry on the Survey with greater Dispatch, and Less Danger of Loosing the Vessel than she is at present.[1]

In this proposal the Gentlemen of the Navy Board—'Your Affectionate Friends', as they habitually subscribed themselves—in their turn acquiesced.

Palliser had his own plea, that the permanent complement of the vessel should be raised to twenty, which would avoid the inconveniences of borrowing men from the other ships of his squadron and returning them on time, and the inclination of such men to desert from a ship not their own; and as she was now thus independent she was given also her own armament of six swivel guns and twelve muskets.[2] This refit and the taking in of stores occupied three months from the middle of January 1765. On 28 April Cook sailed from the Downs for the summer's work. He had it planned: passing Cape Race in hard gales and squalls he went straight to an anchor in Great St Lawrence harbour, on the south-western side of Placentia

---

[1] Cook to Navy Board [22 January 1765], Dixson Library, MS, Q 140, 6. The letter, undated, appears among a number in the Dixson Library apparently extracted from the *Grenville's* letter-book; the date is ascertainable from the Navy Board's reply, 6 February 1765 (from the same source), which begins, 'In return to your Letter of 22nd past,'. The remark on worms is in another undated letter, ATL, in the stray letter-book leaf referred to in the previous note.

[2] Palliser to Stephens, 6 March 1765, Adm 1/2300; Stephens to Cook, 5 April, Adm 2/725.

Bay, on 2 June. Here showed the advantage of a self-complete ship and crew: he could at once begin surveying the twin harbours of St Lawrence. To appreciate fully his work over the next five months it is necessary to study the *Grenville's* journal line by line and follow inch by inch the extraordinarily complicated coast that emerged on the chart, the mass of bays and harbours and inlets, capes and headlands, off-lying islands and rocks and shoals—the whole middle section of the southern Newfoundland coast—as Cook moved round the corner, as it were, from his St Lawrence base into Fortune Bay, up one side of it and down the other, and round to what was called (and he called) the Bay of Despair: a name now, by contrary, the Bay d'Espoir, though pronounced by local tenacity Bay Despair. He knew where he was going, there were plenty of names there already—fishermen had been using that coast for two hundred and fifty years; but this was precision. He spent a great deal of time on shore or in the cutter: as early as 12 June we have the entry, 'AM the Cutter with the Master & Pilot Left the Vessel to Continue the Survey along the Coast'. The *Grenville* followed along, or remained at her moorings, as Cook pursued his instrumental work on shore, or took cross-bearings from the ship, and the boats were out sounding —here a day, there two days, a fortnight at Great St Lawrence to begin with, a week in Lawn Bay, a little to the west, a week within the Lamaline islands, a week in Harbour Breton in August, a fortnight in Ship Cove at the northern end of 'Bay Dispair' towards the end of the survey. The nature of the country was indicated by an episode of 14 July, when at Great Garnish, on the southern shore of Fortune Bay, 'at 8 PM took two men on board that had been lost in the woods for near a month, they came from Burin intending to go to St Lawrence and were almost perishing for want of Subsistance'; and Burin was only a few miles north of St Lawrence, on the same side of the Burin peninsula. The nature of the coast is indicated by the accident a week later, when in the morning the ship—the surveying vessel herself, the brig, not the schooner—turning into Long Harbour, at the end of Fortune Bay, ran ashore upon a rock, had to be sheared up with her own yards, lightened of her water and ballast, and was not got off until midnight on a flowing tide. After completing the survey from Ship Cove on 25 September Cook overhauled and cleaned her down thoroughly; it took the carpenter some days properly to repair her forefoot. There was time to brew spruce beer again. He sailed from Ship Cove on 10 October to St John's, was for almost a fortnight in that fishy landlocked harbour, and sailed again, with Palliser and the rest of the squadron, on

5 November. The winter gales were coming up across the Atlantic, but on 17 December the *Grenville* was moored once more in ease at Deptford.

We have two letters of this winter from Palliser to the Admiralty secretary, bearing on the survey. The first reminds us that, while Cook was the full-time surveyor on the Newfoundland station, the captains also employed there were not exempt from the duties of observing and reporting and drawing what charts they could, and that even the commodore and governor found it wise to explain what might look remiss.

Mr Cook the Surveyor having been Employ'd under my Directions upon the Coasts where I have been Employ'd in His Majesty's Ship Guernsey, I beg leave to refer the Board to his Drafts and Remarks, & as the several Services I have had under my care have not allow'd me time to make such Surveys and Remarks myself, I desire you will be Pleas'd to move their Lordships to Signifie to the Navy Board that they have no Objection to their Paying my Wages.[1]

The second comes closer to the interests of the Surveyor himself.

Sir/ Mr Cook Aṗointed by the Right Honble my Lords Commissioners of the Admiralty to Survey the Sea Coast of Newfoundland, under my Direction, having finish'd his Chart of that part of the South Coast of Newfoundland Adjacent to the Islands of St Pierre and Miquelon Including the said Islands; upon a large Scale of one Inch to a Mile, you will herewith receive the said Chart, which be pleas'd to lay before the Right Honble my Lords Commissioners of the Admiralty.

He having also the last Year deliver'd in to the Board his Survey of the North part of Newfoundland upon the same Scale, and having now prepar'd a Chart of that part with the Oṗosite part of the Coast of Labradore, including the Island and Straights of Bell Isle, likewise another of the abovemention'd Survey of part of the South Coast of Newfoundland, both upon a proper Scale to be usefull to the Trade and Navigation of His Majesty's Subjects. as a Publication thereof, I am of Opinion will be a great Encouragement to new Advanturers on the Fishery's upon these Coasts; be pleas'd to move their Lordships to permit Mr Cook to Publish the same.[2]

This letter Mr Stephens minuted on 17 February. 'Their Lordps are pleased to comply with his req^t by permitting Mr Cook to publish them.'

---

[1] Palliser to Stephens, 14 December 1765, Adm 1/2300.
[2] Palliser to Stephens, 3 February 1766, Adm 1/470. Kitson, 79–80, first printed this letter, rather inaccurately, and made the date 1768.

It may seem odd that the Admiralty, having appointed Cook specifically, in the national interest, to improve the general knowledge of the coasts of Newfoundland, and bearing the expenses of an annual survey, should be content to stop there, to accept the careful charts he brought back and put them in a cupboard and do no more. They could be copied, by hand, no doubt, for any particular naval need; but, a large number of seafaring men might have said, how absurd! And if that was to be the fate of the work which every naval captain and master was directed in set and stringent words to carry out, could captains and masters be blamed for sometimes taking instructions lightly? The admiralty had no hydrographic department—did not have one until 1795—and no hydrographer. Britain, for a competitive sea power, lagged ridiculously behind France, where the *Depôt des Cartes et Plans de la Marine* dated from 1720, and where a coruscation of geographers and cartographers were at work. The Admiralty engraved nothing and published nothing; the map and chart trade was a matter for private commerical enterprise, and however conscientious some of those engaged in it might be, the general tendency was not towards scientific exactitude, the old chart appeared and re-appeared for generations, and stationers saw no need to blush. Cook had words of his own, later, with which to record his opinion of this British habit. At least the Admiralty put no obstacle in the way of a public servant like himself who wished to try a better article on the market; he was welcome to take the risk of having his own chart, made at the public expense, engraved and published at his own expense. Fortunately he was able to bear the cost: his surveyor's allowance added to his pay as master gave him a margin above the ordinary needs of subsistence. Very soon, therefore, after receiving Admiralty consent Cook must have gone to J. Larken, a highly accomplished engraver, with his manuscript charts—perhaps at the suggestion of Mount and Page, who had published his chart of Gaspé. He may have had time to oversee the engraving himself if Larken worked hard, but that would have meant the production of two elaborate plates in two months, which is most unlikely. Both were published in 1766. The first was 'A Chart of the Straights of Bellisle with part of the coast of Newfoundland and Labradore from actual surveys Taken by Order of Commodore Pallisser Governor of Newfoundland, Labradore, &ᶜᵃ by James Cook Surveyor 1766.' That is, it was the result of the latter part of Cook's work in 1763 and the *Grenville* survey of 1764. The second, produced in two sheets, was 'A Chart, of Part of the South Coast, of Newfoundland, including the Islands Sᵗ Peters and Miquelon, from an actual survey Taken by order of Commodore Pallisser ... by James Cook, Surveyor ... 1766.'[1] This was a combination of the first part of his work in 1763 and what he had just finished in 1765. Both these charts were on a scale of one inch to one league. Both were accompanied by quarto pamphlets of sailing directions, also by Cook and published at his expense. The first chart was sold by Mount and Page; the second by them, and also by Thomas Jefferys of the St Lawrence chart and Andrew Dury. The two together must be regarded as very distinguished achievement. Yet they did not drive from the market the Newfoundland delineation of 1677, first published in 1689 in *The English Pilot The Fourth Book*, the property of Messrs Mount and Page, which remained steadfastly uninfluenced by Cook, to mislead sailors who patronised that firm rather than Jefferys' until its last edition of 1794.

Apart from this important matter, there is little we know of Cook's activities in the winter of 1765–6. His correspondence is always interesting and enlightening. A letter to him from the Admiralty secretary, of 17 March, in answer to one of his two days earlier, shows both that he was beginning to get quick attention and that he was developing his surveying technique by preparing to spend an even longer time on shore. He now wanted a tent for shelter by night and in bad weather, as he frequently had to be absent from his schooner (he still calls her that) for a week or ten days, and Stephens signifies official approval.[2] The schooner herself, in dock at Deptford, was undergoing a little alteration: 'The Carpenters employ'd sinking the Deck Foreward', says the journal for 3 February. She was out of dock by 22 February and at the 'Catherine Yatch's moorings' till 19 April. Next day she set sail down the river, and on 29 May 1766 found herself rather too close to Cape Race, with 'many Islds of Ice along the Coast'. Cook made straight for the point where he had abandoned the survey at the end of the previous season. The coast was its continuation in nature as well as in line, and his tent got a great deal of use. While Cook was away with the cutter and its crew, Parker, one presumes, supervised the sounding from the boats and wrote up the log and journal. With Cook went— one also presumes—the local men he employed 'to point out to him the hidden dangers', as a means of pushing on the work.[3] The history

---

[1] They are fully described in Skelton, 24–5, and Skelton and Tooley, *Marine Surveys*, 14–16.

[2] Stephens to Cook, 17 March 1766, Adm 2/726.

[3] Admiralty to Navy Board, 12 February 1767, directing that the sum of £16 16s, which Cook had expended on this service, be repaid to him.—ADM/A/2592.

becomes almost a table of dates and anchorages. From 1 to 6 June the *Grenville* was moored in a cove on the west side of Bonne Bay, a small bay between the 'Bay of Despair' and 'Bay Fochee'—Facheux Bay. Next day she sounded the coast along to the latter bay, was moored there with a hawser on shore till the 17th, the following morning sounded about a sunken rock three leagues off Cape La Hune, then surveyed the Penguin islands in the same vicinity, then for ten days was moored in Cape Cove, enclosed by the irregular peninsula of triple-peaked Cape La Hune. Here she was hauled ashore for scrubbing, and beer was brewed. In early July she was in 'Fox Island Harbour', a good deal of summer fog and rain interfering with the survey; then in a cove, probably Ship Cove, in the off-shore Ramea Islands; then, 17–22 July, in a harbour to the westward of White Bear Bay—to judge from the marks on the chart, Wolf Bay or Bay de Loup, where there is good anchorage between the steep-to shores. On 23 July she sailed off shore again to the Burgeo Islands, in thick fog, where she was moored in 'Grandy's Cove' till 5 August. Almost all through this period there was fog—which did not, however, stop the survey—until the last day, when it most fortunately cleared. Cook was able to observe an eclipse of the sun; knowing his habits in conferring names, we may conclude that this was on the minute Eclipse island. Why should he wish to observe an eclipse of the sun? He does not say, though when he observes an eclipse later in his life we are well enough aware of the reason. We may suspect Charles Leadbetter, to whose *Compleat System of Astronomy* he had given such close attention. Leadbetter had a passion for eclipses, he discoursed on them, made tables of them for years ahead, preached their utility to the mariner; for that person 'being well skill'ed in Astronomy, he may, by the Knowledge of Eclipses . . . determine the true Difference of Meridians between *London,* and the Meridian where the Ship then is; which reduc'd into Degrees and Minutes of the Equator, is the true Longitude found at Sea.'[1] There were certain complicating factors with which the mariner could not at that time deal, nor indeed could Leadbetter. Cook preferred to make his observations on land, and having made them, he did not know what to do next. But he fancied they would be of utility: there were other men better able to calculate, and he could hand his figures over. This was true. The exercise might give him a valuable point of reference in constructing an accurate chart. That was important. It

[1] The quotation is from the second and third pages of the Preface to the fairly formidable Leadbetter of 1728. He recommends knowledge also of the 'Immersions and Emersions of *Jupiter's* Satellites, and the Times of the Transits of the Moon by the Fixed Stars and Planets'—quite useless to preach to mariners.

was to have more than immediate importance; for it brought him into the *Philosophical Transactions* of the Royal Society.

Back from the islands to the main, to 'Connure' or Connoire Bay (the engraved chart straightens out the odd phonetic spellings of the log), and then 'Tweed's Harbour', 16–28 August: a name we must probably carry back to Captain Douglas's survey in the *Tweed* in 1763, and see as applying to Cinq Cerf Bay. Then a maze of small harbours and islets off shore which brought the vessel to Port aux Basques, not far short of Cape Ray, for the fortnight 10–23 September, during which her sails and rigging were overhauled, and she was scrubbed and 'boot-topped'.[1] Here the survey was extraordinarily detailed. Around Cape Ray a week was spent in Codroy Road, just south of Cape Anguille. Not merely was the coast between the two capes delineated, but the rivers, for some distance inland. Then Cook turned back on his tracks, to La Poile Bay, on the south coast; he moved about the bay in rain, gales and hard squalls, with much snow and frost, wooding and watering as well as surveying, until 20 October, when he sailed for St John's. He reached it on the 27th. Palliser was there, in the *Guernsey*, with three other vessels of his squadron, including the 32-gun frigate *Niger*, Captain Sir Thomas Adams. On board the *Niger*, lately returned from her patrol of the Strait of Belle Isle, was Joseph Banks, a botanical young gentleman who had been taking a voyage of scientific curiosity. Cook was to see a good deal of him before the decade was out, but it is unlikely that he met him this day, and on the next the *Niger* sailed for Lisbon and England. Had Cook arrived two days earlier they might well have met at the ball with which the governor on 25 October celebrated the anniversary of the Coronation of George III; although (Banks tells us) it was ladies, not gentlemen, that Palliser was short of.[2] Cook himself sailed on 4 November, and with almost continual westerlies was across the Atlantic and up Channel off Beachy Head nineteen days later: on 30 November he was at Deptford, having brought his ship there from Woolwich, by allowance of the Lords, 'for greater safety.'[3]

This winter at home was for Cook much like the last. At Mile End he enjoyed the company of his Elizabeth and his two infant sons. He arranged for the publication of a third chart. This incorporated part of his second one, some of it re-engraved, with the work of the 1766

[1] Boot-topping a ship meant cleaning the upper part of her bottom, and 'paying' or covering it with a mixture of tallow, sulphur, and perhaps other ingredients to discourage marine growth.
[2] *The* Endeavour *Journal of Joseph Banks* (Sydney, 1962), I, 14.
[3] Stephens to Cook, 27 November 1766, Adm 2/726.

season. The engraver was again Larken, and again the title included the compelling phrase 'actual surveys': 'A Chart of Part of the South Coast of Newfoundland including the Islands St Peters and Miquelon with the Southern Entrance into the Gulph of St Laurence from actual Surveys Taken by order of Commodore Pallisser Governor of Newfoundland, Labradore, &c. by James Cook Surveyor, Larken sculp. 1767.'[1] The name of a fourth retailer was added to the imprint, Carington Bowles, so that the way between Cook the publisher and his public was now reasonably open. While his name was thus kept before seafarers, it was brought to the more scientific by Dr John Bevis, a physician, devoted astronomer and person of standing in the Royal Society, who communicated to the Society a brief paper on Cook's eclipse observations. Why Cook should have communicated them to Bevis we cannot say, unless he looked for a man whose interest in eclipses was well known. Bevis himself had to call for help on a fellow astronomer and more expert mathematician, George Witchell, who had worked out a method for clearing an observation for refraction and parallax. The paper was not read until 30 April 1767, after Cook had sailed for the new season's work, and as it has not been correctly printed since it appeared in the *Transactions*[2] may be given in full here as Bevis wrote it.

An Observation of An Eclipse of the Sun at the Island of New-found-land. Aug. 5– 1766

by Mr James Cook, with the Longitudes of the Place of Observation deduced from it, communicated by J. Bevis M.D. F.R.S.

Mr Cook, a good mathematician, and very expert in his Business, having been appointed by the Lords Commissioners of the Admiralty to Survey the Sea coasts of *New-found-land*, *Labradore* &c., took with him a very good apparatus of Instruments, and among them a brass Telescopic Quadrant made by Mr John Bird.

Being Aug. 5th 1766 at one of the Burgeo Islands near Cape *Ray*, Latd. 47°36'19", the South-west extremity of *New-found-land*, and having carefully rectified his Quadrant, he waited for the Eclipse of the Sun; just a minute after the beginning of which he observed the Zenith Distance of the Suns upper Limb 31°57'00", and allowing for Refraction and his Semidiameter, the true Zenith Distance of the Sun's Centre 32°13'30", from whence he concluded the Eclipse to have begun at 0^{h}4'48" Apparent Time, and by a like process to have ended at 3^{h}45'26" App.T.

Note, there were three several observers, with good Telescopes, who all agreed as to the moments of beginning and ending.

Mr Cook having communicated his observation to me, I shewed it to

[1] Described by Skelton, 25; Skelton and Tooley, 16–17.
[2] It was printed in the *Philosophical Transactions* for that year, LVII, 215–6.

Mr George Witchell, who told me he had a very exact observation of the same Eclipse taken at Oxford by the Rev: Mr Hornsby, and he woud compute from the comparison the Difference of Longitude of the places of observation, makeing due allowance for the effect of parallax, and the earths prolate spheroidal figure; and he has since given me the following result.

$5^h23'59''$	Beginn. at Oxford		$7^h\ 7'\ 5''$	End at Oxford
0.46.48	Beginn. at Borgeo Isles		3.39.14	End at Borgeo Isles.
4.37.11			3.27.51	
$-\ \ 51.49$	Effect of Parallax &c		$+\ \ 17.35$	Effect of Parallax &c
3.45.22	Diff. of Meridians		3.45.26	Diff. of Meridians

J. Bevis.

This result, in terms of longitude measured not from Oxford but from London, as Cook put it on his chart, was equivalent to 3h.50m.4sec. or 57°31′ W. The modern determination is 57°37′ W of Greenwich, or 57°27′ from London—which argues remarkably good observation on Cook's part with his telescopic quadrant. From his figure he deduced for his sailing directions the longitudes of a number of other places on the south coast, adding latitudes from observations made on shore. Obviously he had now acquired the taste for astronomical determination of the longitude. On 11 March he wrote to the Admiralty suggesting that he should be given nothing so humdrum as a tent, but a reflecting telescope for the purpose, representing (to use the secretary's words, which would be much of a transcription of his own) 'the great Utility it would be to Navigation to take the Longitude of the Head Lands on the Island of Newfoundland, and on the Continent of America', and the frequent opportunities he had of doing it; and the Lords instructed the Navy Board to furnish him with the article accordingly.[1]

Meanwhile the *Grenville* was having her annual refit. A certain light is cast on naval administration by the note in her master's journal for 10 March, that on that day the ship's company received twelve months wages. The master himself had received a new mate. William Parker at the end of the 1766 voyage was promoted lieutenant, as master's mates frequently were when masters were not. He went to the *Niger*, and was succeeded by Michael Lane. Lane, a product of the mathematical school of Christ's Hospital and a young man of great ability, had been appointed, as we have seen, to the *Antelope* when Graves thought of him as a substitute for the defaulting Mr Test; Palliser in turn had had him transferred to the *Guernsey* in

[1] Stephens to Cook, 24 March 1767, Adm 2/727.

1764;[1] and now it seems Cook approved of him. 'On a second conversation with Mr Cook,' wrote Palliser to Stephens, 'I wish you to alow me to recomend for his assistant (in lieu of the young man I before mention'd) Mr Mich^l Lane Schoolmaster of the Guernsy who draws well, is master of Surveying, was brought up in the blue coat School, served afterwards as Apprentice to Capt Denis, who is his friend & Patron at whose recomendation I took him into the Guernsy.—Mr Cook waits on you with this.—The other young man has a desire to go another way.'[2] Mr Stephens agreed at once, and Mr Lane entered upon his highly distinguished career as a surveyor of the Newfoundland and Labrador coasts.

The *Grenville* was ready to sail by 1 April 1767, when a pilot came on board to carry her to Woolwich, but even a pilot for that short passage in unpleasant weather could not prevent an accident: on the 5th 'at 8 AM a Collier Named the Three Sisters Thomas Bloyd Master of Sunderland in Coming Down the River fell athwart our hause & carried away our Bowsprit Cap & Jibb Boom.' They hauled alongside the *David* sloop, got replacements from on shore, had them rigged in a day or two, picked up their ordnance stores at Woolwich and Gravesend, and were off on the 10th. There was a good deal of bad language over this misadventure, it is alleged, and James Cook, the navy master, was prepared to give Thomas Bloyd the merchant master a piece of his mind, when he found that they had been schoolboys together in the Ayton days, and recrimination was dissolved into reminiscence. It is not impossible; but it is absurd that the incident, though typical enough of Thames navigation with its currents and cross-winds, should have been transferred to Cook's next ship in the next year. Cape Race was picked up on 9 May, when we have another characteristic little note in the journal, 'NB Longitude Made from Scilly to Cape Race 44° 10′ W^t. 'This must have been a dead reckoning longitude.

Repeating his strategy of the previous year Cook went direct to his 1766 breaking-off point, the anchorage in Codroy Road, where he brought to on 15 May—his object being to complete the survey of the west coast, from Cape Anguille to Point Ferolle, his southern limit in 1763. This included a fairly straight stretch of shoreline, but

---

[1] Palliser to Stephens, 7 April 1764, Adm 1/2300; Stephens to Palliser, 7 April, Adm 2/724.

[2] Palliser to Stephens, 2 December 1766, and minute by Stephens thereon, Adm 1/2300. The 'blue coat School' refers to the Mathematical School or side at Christ's Hospital, founded in 1673 specifically for the training of boys for navigation: Captain Denis or Dennis commanded the *Bellona*, in which Lane was schoolmaster; 'apprentice' I do not understand, unless Lane was to further his knowledge of practical navigation under Dennis's care; who 'the other young man' was I do not know.

also three large bays and some smaller ones. As in the previous year, he hired the services of some men who knew the neighbourhood well,[1] and the season's work was quick as well as exceedingly thorough. From Codroy he went into St George's Bay, unsheltered except for the harbour and river at its northern end, encountering on shore 'a Tribe of the Mickmack Indians'; and then round the cliff-sided Cape St George, Red island and a long narrow peninsula into double-bayed Port au Port. It was now the beginning of June, a month when the winds embarrassed though they hardly interrupted the work: 5 June, 'Landed on the Isthmus [at the head of East Bay] & took the true Bearing of C. Anguille'; 6 June, employed all day in sounding the bay; 8 June, sounding, brewing, wooding and watering; 12 June, the foretopsail yard gave way in the slings, and another one had to be cut; 15 June, 'Sounding about a Shoal which lies between [Fox] Island & the Main'; 19 June, 'Sounding in the Vessel only it blowing too hard for the Boat'; 23 June, James Surridge, a seaman, died; 29 June, 'having finished Port aux Port and the Adjacent Coast It blowing very hard Obliged us to put into the Bay of Three Islands.' The three islands were no doubt those at the entrance that Cook called Pearl, Tweed and Guernsey after the ships of Palliser's squadron, but there were others including an Eagle and a Governors, and on the chart we have simply the Bay of Islands. Here he was employed for a week, after which he went for ten days into what the journal refers to as Good Bay—most probably Bonne Bay, in spite of the Small Good Bay where he anchored farther up the coast; a week more almost without anchoring brought him to 'Ingrenachoise'— Ingornachoix—Bay, of which Point Riche is the northern limit, with its three separate inner harbours to be surveyed, Hawke's, Saunders, and Keppel. 'Found riding here a New England Sloop'—he met few other vessels—and then came in H.M. sloop *Favourite*, on the station. On the other side of the Point Riche peninsula is Old Port au Choix, at the southern end of the large open bay of St John, which runs round in the north to Point Ferolle. In this little port he hauled his ship ashore to clean her bottom, and left her while he went in the boat to survey the bay; then for some days he sounded as well from the ship, as far as six leagues out to sea. On 25 August he found 'Our Ladies Bubies NEBN'; they become on the engraved chart (and we have a slight sense of Victorianism, a century too soon) Twin Islands. On 31 August he was back in the Bay of Islands, in York harbour, close to the entrance, at the beginning of twenty-three days of most

---

[1] Minutes of Admiralty Board, 5 April 1768, Adm 3/76. This year they cost him £12 16s.

arduous work; for there was not merely the bay proper and its dozen islands to survey accurately (the week in July was not nearly enough), but also fifteen miles of the Humber arm (the 'River Humber') and the river openings into it, about eighteen miles of the divided Middle ('South') Arm, and nine of the North Arm; and there were still, as there had been from the start of the season, gales and squalls. The end came: on 24 September the *Grenville* worked out of the harbour, carried away her foretopmast three days later, and on 14 October met Palliser and his squadron in St John's harbour. Topmast replaced, she sailed on 23 October, and after a remarkably quick Atlantic passage was in the Channel in sight of the Isle of Wight on 8 November: next day she picked up a Deal pilot.

This return to the Thames brushed disaster more closely than the minor collision at the moment of departure. The afternoon of 10 November turned to vile weather—'a hard Storm of Wind & Excesive heavy Squalls and showers of Rain'—and Cook took in his fore topsail. One may best quote his journal:

at 4 Anchored above the Nore light it bearing ESE in 7 fath^m water with the small Bower and Veerd away to a whole Cable, that bringing her up let go Best Bower and Veerd away upon Both to a Cable & at $\frac{1}{2}$ upon one & $\frac{1}{2}$ Cable upon the other, was then in 6 fath Water, Struck yards & Topmasts. At 6 the Best Bower parted & we taild into shoal water & at 7 She Struck very hard; got a Spring upon the small Bower Cable, & cut the Cable in order to Cast her Head to the S^{o}ward & get her under Sail but the Spring Gave way & She cast to the Northward & directly aShore upon a Shoal called the Knock; got the Topsail Yards & Cross Jack Yards down upon Deck & She lay pretty Easy until the f[l]ood made when the Gale still continuing she struck very hard & lay down upon her Larboard bilge; hoisted out the Boats & hove every thing overboard from off the Decks & Secured all the Hatchways. at 12 at Night there being no prospect of the gale ceasing took all the People away in the Boats, the Cutter made the Best of her way to Sheerness for Assistance. At 10 AM [on the 11th] the Wea^r being mod^t came on Board with proper Assistance from Sheerness Yard in order to get the Vessel off & found she had received Little Damage, began to lighten her by heaving out Shingle Ballast & Pigs of Iron Ballast &c and to lay out Anchors to heave her off.

In the afternoon the weather moderated. 'At high water' continues the journal, 'the Vessel floted, hove her of & made Sail for Sheerness, at 5 anchored between Sheerness & the Nore light, Emp[loyed] Clearing the Decks & putting the Hold to rights.' Next day the necessary spars and stores were brought off from the yard, the Deal pilot (whose part in all this, if any, is unnoticed) was discharged and a river pilot taken on board, a morning was spent rigging the yards and bending sails, and the vessel sailed again. On 15 November, 'At 9 [AM] lashed along side the William & Mary Yatch off Deptford Yard'. That little flurry was over.

When Cook was on shore with the cutter at Sheerness he wrote a hasty note to Stephens, reporting the misadventure, and identifying the scene in rather different words, as 'a shoal called the South End, the Upper End of Shoebury Ness'; and he wrote again immediately they had got the schooner off.[1] Nothing seems to have gone that was not expendable, except perhaps an Indian canoe belonging to Mr Joseph Banks, the *Niger*'s passenger of the 1766 season. Mr Banks had not lost his interest in Newfoundland and Labrador: Palliser had secured some costumes for him at Chateau Bay, and Captain Andrew Wilkinson of the *Niger* this canoe, which he sent home in the *Grenville*. It was either washed overboard or Cook hove it overboard with everything else on deck—'tho I have not been able to see Mr Cook to ask him about it,' wrote Wilkinson, '. . . but if you'll please to send to him he will let you know whether there are any hopes of getting it by Advertising. . . .'[2] We do not know whether Banks took up this suggestion. Cook, arriving home, found that he had now a daughter, a second Elizabeth in the family. He was soon busy over his drawing-table and the composition of his sailing-directions, keeping an eye as usual on the *Grenville* at Deptford. He sent a fourth chart to Larken to be engraved, 'A Chart of the West Coast of Newfoundland . . . by James Cook, Surveyor', the fruit of his summer's work—from the sale of which Carington Bowles was excluded; and there were sailing-directions printed to go with this. He did a small private job of technical drawing for Palliser, to define the Palliser landed property.[3] He resolved the next season's work. Stimulated no doubt by the death among his crew at Port au Port, perhaps also by his own accident in 1764, he decided to ask for the addition of a surgeon's mate to his complement next time the schooner went out. When he asked, early in April, pleading that from the nature of the service the crew were liable to many accidents, as well as to the disorders common to seamen, the Admiralty acquiesced[4]—though the log and journal of

---

[1] Stephens to Cook, 12 November 1767 and 13 November (in answer to Cook's letters), Adm 2/727.

[2] Wilkinson to Banks, 18 December 1767, Kew Banks Correspondence, I, 15; quoted in *The* Endeavour *Journal*, I, 21–2 n. Captain Andrew Wilkinson commanded the *Niger* from 1767 to 1771.

[3] Palliser to Stephens, 30 November 1767, Adm 1/2300: the letter is mainly about manning the *Guernsey*, with the final paragraph, 'Mr Pownel has promis'd to fix a day when Mr Cook may go to the office to take a Sketch of our Estates, from the large plan, and I will apply for a Coppy of the conditions &c^a.'

[4] Stephens to Cook, 11 April 1768, Adm 2/727; Minutes of Adm. Board, 12 April. It may be thought a little strange, administratively, that Stephens's letter conveying the decision should antedate the decision by one day.

the *Grenville* are in fact remarkably free from the notation of sickness or accident, as free as they are from that of crime and punishment. There may be some connection. Cook was a careful man. If there was one thing he respected, it was the lives of seamen. Some of his men served with him continuously, hard as the nature of the service was. They could, one imagines, see a purpose in it. In a service of that kind, apart from unforeseeable accident, men were likely to retain both their health and their discipline; and the work to go on.

The work: having considered Cook's methods, one may also consider, briefly, the finished products of his skill in his mid- and late thirties; and one must consider not so much the engraved versions of his charts produced by Larken, although these are accurate and beautiful enough, as the manuscript originals. It is not always easy, or even quite possible, to separate from the products of his own hand some of the copies made by his assistants in a style faithfully modelled on his, or drawn immediately from his surveys by, for instance Parker. Of the fifty or so 'Cook' charts preserved in various collections, however, we have God's plenty directly attributable to him, whether large coastal charts or 'plans' of ports and harbours. The large charts are indeed tremendous productions: the 'exact trigonometrical survey' of the west coast is about ten feet long, on an inch to the mile scale, and includes much inland topographical drawing showing the courses of rivers and the forms of lakes which as one might expect, were not taken over into the engraved versions; or the south coast chart, like the former in the Hydrographic Department of the Admiralty, three inches to the mile, stated to be 'coppy'd from the original survey taken in the year 1764', and about six feet by three; or the other south coast chart in the same department, an inch to the mile, showing 'the Sea-coast, Bays, Harbours and Islands' between the 'Bay of Despair' and the two St Lawrence harbours, with inset plans of the harbours of Great and Little St Lawrence, Great Jervis, Harbour Breton, Boxey, Blue Pinion, St Jacques, and 'Bande de La'Rier' (Bande de l'Arier or Belloram)—about eight feet by five, and a thing almost overpowering in its detail and colour as well as size. This was raising British hydrographic surveying to a new power.

One may analyse some of his construction and design, noting first that in his technique he follows tradition. With his training, it could hardly have been otherwise; his particular characteristic is the precision, the comprehensive and consistent exactitude, with which he applies the tradition. He draws his charts on a plane projection, generally oriented to magnetic north; rays drawn from the points of the compass roses cover the sea areas; the variation of the compass is often stated. Points where latitude had been determined by observation are sometimes marked by a special symbol, and these latitudes are given in the 'remarks' written on the chart. Longitudes are given but rarely. (It was only in 1767 that Cook got his reflecting telescope, we remember, and opportunities for observation in that season of storms, and phenomena in the skies that could usefully be observed, cannot have been many. Perhaps, indeed, he was a little naive in his hopes.) There is no graduation for latitude or longitude, except in a few fair copies in which the meridian is graduated in degrees and minutes. Soundings are given from low water mark, in great plenty; in the plans of harbours inset on a chart, or in any other place where Cook thought they were particularly called for (if one may discriminate) they are set thick. In harbour plans leading lines are generally drawn—that is, the alignments of landmarks as a guide to the channel: a matter touched on, of course, in the sailing directions prepared to go with the chart. High water hours at new and full moon are shown by roman numerals; there are notes on the tides. There are separate symbols for rocks above and below water. Many charts include at their edges remarks on navigation and on the fishery. Occasionally the manuscripts have pecked lines representing the angles observed by Cook by lines of sight to landmarks; in some fair copies there are pencilled squares, drawn to true north, as a guide for reduction by draughtsman or engraver. All these things may appear on other charts, though rarely all together, or so richly: the distinctive characteristic of Cook's manuscripts, it has been said, is the care and fullness with which topographical detail on land is drawn, a good deal of brown and green brushwork marking relief and land-cover, in the manner of military mapping. Cliffs appear in semi-profile, an old convention. The influence of Samuel Holland, we see, persists, long after that meeting on the shore of Kennington Cove. We can see some trace of it in the work of Cook's assistants, Parker and Lane.[1]

The manuscripts, then, in addition to their technical competence, have some visual interest unmatched by the engravings, accomplished as these are. They have also the interest of displaying Cook's first contributions to topographical nomenclature. There is no difficulty in picking out his most characteristic names: not merely those of the ships on the station, but others like Grenville Rock, Sole bay; those of the English rivers he knew, transferred to wilder streams, Humber,

---

[1] Most of the preceding paragraph is simply a paraphrase of Skelton, 20. I could not hope to approach Mr Skelton's knowledge of the charts, or his critical skill, and he encouraged me to treat him in this way, rather than make a lengthy quotation.

Thames, Medway; names—the association is obvious—like Grave's Island, Parker's River, Hawke Bay, Port Saunders, Keppel Harbour, They are not as picturesque as some of the older names, but they are another contribution to precision. They are engraved and published. The four engraved charts, consolidated into three, were taken into the *Collection of Charts of the Coasts of Newfoundland and Labradore, &c.* which Thomas Jefferys published in 1769–70, with charts by Michael Lane, Joseph Gilbert, master of the *Guernsey*, and other naval officers; and later into that famous volume *The North American Pilot.* Cook's sailing directions, consolidated into *The Newfoundland Pilot*, were also published by Jefferys in 1769. Seventy years later, a hundred and more years later, when the professional hydrographers were again at work in that region of North America, the Gulf and its approaches they considered their predecessors. Most of them, they said roundly, were a danger to the seamen: throw away DesBarres and the rest. Two only could be trusted—Cook, and Lane.[1]

Mr Cook, aware that he was a competent surveyor, but unaware that future ages would regard him as a classic, had plenty to do as the London spring of 1768 came on. Mile End, Deptford, Larken the engraver's, Mr Jefferys' shop, the Admiralty office, Palliser, who had another year to run in his Newfoundland government—one presumes non-professional friends as well as a circle mainly marine: people to see as well as the planning of the season's work, all would have made the weeks busy. He applied to the Admiralty for reimbursement of £28 for the repair of mathematical instruments and the expense of stationery for the ensuing summer, and the Admiralty made the grant on 5 April;[2] he wrote on 9 April asking for a surgeon's mate in his vessel's complement, as we have seen, and that was granted him also. It was already a little late for final planning; the previous year the schooner had sailed on 10 April, even after the misadventure with the collier. At that moment there were forces at work in the world, quite alien to any interest the master had heretofore had, which ordained that he should not sail in the *Grenville* at all. The same minutes of the Admiralty Board that noted the resolve to repay him his instrument and stationery expenses, noted also a resolve to fit out a vessel to convey 'to the Southward' persons intended for a quite different purpose; and the same minutes that dealt

[1] The quotations given by Skelton, 19, from Admiral Bayfield and Captain Boulton are highly illuminating. Admiral Wharton, also a very distinguished hydrographer, added his praise, quoted by Kitson, 80. But perfection is granted to no man, and there were minor dangers hidden from Cook.
[2] Minutes of Adm. Board, Adm 3/76.

with the matter of the surgeon's mate, 12 April, provided, in answer
to Commodore Palliser's desire, that Mr Lane should be appointed
master of the *Grenville* during Mr Cook's absence, at 5s allowance a
day as surveyor over and above the normal schooner's pay, a new
mate to be appointed with an allowance of 2s 6d a day.[1] The navy,
it seems, was to economise. Mr Cook was to be employed elsewhere.

[1] ibid. It was not till 1773 that Lane's allowance was raised to the 10s a day given to
Cook.—Admiralty to Navy Board 15 January 1773; NMM/ADM/A/2663.

V

Scientific Background

THE PERSONS to be conveyed to the Southward were persons 'intended to be sent thither to observe the Transit of Venus'; and by 'the Southward' is to be understood the Southern Hemisphere; and Mr Lane was to take Mr Cook's place in the *Grenville* because it was intended that Mr Cook should command the vessel fitted out for that purpose. We find ourselves, and Mr Cook, plunged suddenly into the middle of eighteenth-century science, or the post-Newtonian physical branch of it. Cook, we know, as he did not know, was about to begin on a series of immense voyages, which would add enormously to knowledge of the surface of the world. The primary purpose of the voyage now envisaged, however, was at once more limited and larger. It concerned the world not in itself, with all its detail of land and water, but the world in the universe. The method was to be astronomical, to determine not the latitude of a cape on an island in the north-west Atlantic, but the dimensions of the universe. Astronomy had its post-Newtonian triumphs in this century already, in between superficial geography, as it were, and the universe. Newton's theory of the shape of the earth had been confirmed by the observations to measure the arc of a meridian by the French expeditions led by La Condamine to Peru in 1735–43 and Maupertius to Lapland in 1736. French science took the lead in organising the observations with which it was hoped to mark the decade of the sixties: observations which, reaching outwards from the earth, would provide the data necessary for the calculation of the distance between the earth and the sun—which distance, in its turn, would serve as a unit for the measurement of the universe itself, as suggested by Kepler. The method for calculating the distance between the earth and the sun was the method of parallax: that is the method with which Cook, as a surveyor, was familiar, of observing angles with his theodolite at each end of his base line, and working out trigonometrically therefrom the distance to his marker. But now, though the base line might be something like the radius of the earth in length, the marker

99

—the sun—was so far away that the parallax counted for hardly anything, and an intermediate help—a sort of observational stepping-stone—was needed. This intermediate help or point was provided by the planet Venus.

It was provided—or we may speak in the present tense and say it is provided in human lives but rarely: at those times only when Venus is in a direct line between the earth and sun, and its black shadow as this passes across the face of the sun can be observed and timed. The time taken by such a 'Transit of Venus' depends on the rate at which the line joining the observer's eye to Venus sweeps across the face of the sun. If the earth were not rotating, this line would move at the same speed for all observers, but because it does rotate, the observer's end of the line moves at a speed determined by his position on the earth and by the apparent size of the earth as seen from Venus. The different times taken for the transit, as measured by different observers, can with much calculation yield the parallax, and hence the total distance from earth to Venus and earth to sun. The mathematician had also to remember that Venus appears to follow slightly different paths across the sun seen from different places. The thing of absolute importance was the so-rarely to be observed 'Transit of Venus' across the face of the sun. Not only were there factors in observation and calculation that had to be allowed for, but the incalculable weather could determine whether the transit would be seen at all.[1] The young, brilliant, short-lived Jeremiah Horrocks had first observed it, in 1639, and the astronomers had realised its potential value for their science; it would occur again on 6 June 1761 and 3 June 1769, and thereafter not till the years 1874 and 1882, and then 2004 and 2012. Edmond Halley, that great man of science, was speaking of the eighteenth-century events when he addressed the Royal Society in 1716, knowing that he, who was born in 1656, could do nothing but prophesy and exhort: 'I could wish that many observations of this famous phenomenon might be taken by different persons at separate places, both that we might arrive at a greater degree of certainty by their agreement, and lest any single observer should be deprived, by the intervention of clouds, of a sight which I know not whether any man living in this or the next age will ever see again, and on which depends the certain and adequate solution of a problem the most noble, and at other times not to be attained to. I recommend it therefore again and

[1] [In the typescript J.C.B. had noted that he was going to rewrite his explanation of the purpose of the observations of the transit. In rewriting the passage I have drawn on the knowledge of my colleague, Dr J. F. Harper. T.H.B.]

again to those curious astronomers who, when I am dead, will have an opportunity of observing these things, that they would remember this, my admonition ... and I earnestly wish them all imaginable success.'[1]

Joseph Nicolas Delisle, one of the elders of a large family of astronomers, mathematicians, geographers and cartographers, was the man who deployed a vast correspondence and organising power, after Halley's death, to ensure that the astronomers of the western world should perform their scientific duty in 1761.[2] From the Jesuits of Peking, westwards through Siberia, India, Turkey and Sweden, south to Rodriguez island in the Indian Ocean, the Cape of Good Hope and St Helena, across the Atlantic to Newfoundland, from a number of points in Europe and some in Britain, a hundred and twenty observers gazed—French, German, Swedish, English, Italian, Portuguese, Russian, Danish, Spanish. There were eminent men among them, the French Pingré at Rodriguez and Chappe d'Auteroche at Tobolsk, the English Bliss at Greenwich and Maskelyne at St Helena. The French took the lead in numbers, even in that desperate time of war, with their empire crashing about them, with thirty-two observers; the English, rapidly becoming masters of the world, came only fourth in the list, with eighteen. The chances of war, travel and cloudy skies baffled some chief observers, who solaced themselves with scientific work of other kinds: in the end, when results were collated, it was undeniable that the observations of 1761, so far as the grand end was concerned, had not been a success. All the more was a supreme effort called for in 1769; and in England the Council of the Royal Society determined that it would not be remiss, that it would make the admonition of Halley sound in the ears of Government. It must have many observers; it must have the

---

[1] It seems worth quoting here the original more resounding Latin of his 1716 paper, *Methodus singularis quâ Solis Parallaxis sive distantia à Terra, ope Veneris intra Solem conspiciendae, tuto determinari poterit:* 'Ac sane vellem diversis in locis ejusdem Phaenomeni observationes à pluribus institui, tum ad majorem adstruendam ex consensu fidem, tum ne Nubium interventu frustraretur singularis Spectator, eo spectaculo quod nescio an denua visuri sunt hujus & subsequentis seculi Mortales; & a quo pendet Problematis nobilissimi & aliunde inaccessi solutio certa & adaequata. Curiosis igitur syderum scrutatoribus, quibus, nobis vita functis, haec observanda reservantur, iterum iterumque commendamus ut, moniti hujus nostri memores, observationi peragendae strenue totisque viribus incumbant; iisque fausta omnia exoptamus & vovemus, praeprimis ne nubili coeli importuna obscuritate exoptatissimo spectaculo priventur; utque tandem Orbium coelestium magnitudines intra arctiores limites coercitae in eorum gloriam famamque sempiternam cedant.'—*Philosophical Transactions*, XXIX (1716), 460.
[2] The little-known importance of Delisle is rightly emphasised in Harry Woolf, *The Transits of Venus* (Princeton, 1959) a volume which, however, devotes less attention to the event of 1769 than to that of 1761.

seats of observation widely spread; it must go to the southern as well as to the northern hemisphere; it must go not merely beyond the Arctic Circle but into the Pacific Ocean.

Into the Pacific Ocean: but where, in that large expanse, with which geography was so inadequately acquainted?—To some point where, for the six hours' duration of the Transit, the phenomenon would be clearly visible, well above the horizon, and the danger of interference from clouds would be minimal. This was obvious to Dr Thomas Hornsby, the professor of astronomy in the University of Oxford, when in 1765 he reminded the Royal Society of its duty; and he reviewed the discoveries recorded as having been made by Spaniards in earlier centuries. He also cast his thought beyond astronomy, and the Royal Society; he was aware that science needed more support than the Royal Society could give it; he remarked that it would be a worthy 'object of attention to a commercial nation to make a settlement in the great Pacific Ocean.'[1] His was not the only voice, in those early days after the Treaty of Paris, to utter this sentiment. Indeed it was by then a commonplace; and we may note that already in the previous year the first of a series of British vessels, a frigate commanded by Commodore Byron, late of the North American station, had sailed for the Pacific—not certainly to make a settlement but to investigate more than one matter deemed worthy of the attention of a commercial nation. In June 1766 the Council of the Society resolved to send observers to various parts of the world, though the only person mentioned by name was the Jesuit father Boscovich, professor of mathematics at Pavia, who might go to California. Then the president of the Society, the Earl of Morton, sounded the Admiralty, suggesting that naval officers who might find themselves in the southern hemisphere at the right time should be directed to take observations and make remarks; to which the Admiralty agreed.[2]

There the thing rested, so far as formal discussion was concerned, until November 1767, when the Council of the Society, perhaps beginning to feel some urgency, set up a Transit Committee. This committee decided that observers should be sent to Fort Churchill in Hudson Bay, to the North Cape, and to the South Seas. It suggested names. The last of these names was that of Mr Dalrymple: 'a proper person to send to the South Seas, having a particular Turn for Discoveries, and being an able Navigator, and well skilled in Observation.'[3] Government should be applied to for a ship. When the

[1] C. Hutton, J. Shaw & R. Pearson, *Phil. Trans.* abgd. XII (1809), 265–74.
[2] Admiralty Secretary to Morton, 15 August 1766, Adm 2/540.
[3] 19 November 1767, Transit Committee, in Council Minutes, Vol. V, 189.

Council met on 3 December, the Astronomer Royal, the Rev. Nevil Maskelyne, confirmed his definition of the best possible station for observing: it would lie in an area between the latitudes of 5° and 35° S, and longitudes 172° E to 124° W in the north, and 139° W to 172° W in the south, a sort of trapezium. Within those limits, according to the history of voyages, were to be found the islands called the Marquesas, in the north-east, and those called Amsterdam and Rotterdam in the west. The former group would be preferable, as it was known to have a good harbour. Other persons made other suggestions, some of them extremely vague—such as that of Dr Bevis, who favoured the first island fit for the purpose in 'the tropick' west of 120° or 130° of longitude west of London. There was also the proposal that Captain Campbell, 'if he pleases to go . . . or some such lover of Astronomy (a Captain of a man of war) would be a proper Person to command the Ship.' Captain John Campbell, a member of the Transit Committee, a first-rate sailor with origins like Cook's in the coal-trade, an able scientist who had developed the sextant from the quadrant, would have been a proper person; but it appears he did not choose to go. Maskelyne was interviewing the possible observers. On 18 December some of them appeared before the Council to state their terms, and obviously the Council thought some of the terms extravagant. Mr Dymond would go to the northward for £250 per annum and expenses; Mr Dunn would go north at a guinea a day, and south at £400 per annum and expenses; Mr Green would go to the south at £300 per annum and expenses; Mr Wales specified a warm climate, £300 per annum and expenses (he went to Hudson Bay).[1] Mr Dalrymple had a different proposition. He had written to the Society's secretary, Dr Morton, already to signify his pleasure at 'the favourable Intentions of the Council of the Royal Society.' He said more: 'Wherever I am in June 1769 I shall most certainly not let slip an opportunity of making an Observation so Important to Science as that of the Transit of Venus—I believe the Royal Society's Intentions make it unnecessary for me to say that there is but one part of the World, where I can engage to make the Observations.' He added, perhaps in view of the mention of Captain Campbell or some other naval man to command the ship, 'However it may be necessary to observe that I can have no thought of undertaking the Voyage as a Passenger going out to make the Observations, or on any other footing than that of having the management of the Ship intended for the Service.'[2] The Council of the Royal

[1] Royal Society Council Minutes, 18 December 1767.
[2] Dalrymple to Dr Morton, 7 December 1767, R. S. Misc. MSS III, f. 14.

Society was quite prepared to accept this condition—no discussion or dissenting voice is recorded—and for the next three and a half months assumed, as Dalrymple himself assumed, that he would command the expedition to the South Seas. It is therefore necessary to scrutinise this remarkable person a little more closely.

No contemporary would deny that Alexander Dalrymple was a passionate man. Few would deny his ability, his knowledge, his enthusiasm, assiduity, vanity. One can see, it is true, a certain lack of balance about many of the arguments of which so much of his life consisted; not the least of his talents was a talent for jumping to conclusions. He talked some sound sense, he did a number of valuable things. Yet he could also cast speculation or unwise belief into terms of the most vehement and wide-ranging dogma, and was pursued by a profound fatality that took his utterances even when they were most vehement and wide-ranging and proved them nonsense. Succeeding generations therefore have tended to accentuate his weaknesses rather than his virtues, his failures rather than his strength. The most practical of sailors owed a debt to Dalrymple the hydrographer and cartographer; scholars of discovery leant hard on his historical work. But, it must be admitted, he could be very foolish. He was born in 1737, a younger son in a large Scots family.[1] His eldest brother was to attain a more conventional, though undoubted, eminence as the jurist Lord Hailes. Alexander, with a minimum of education, was sent out in 1752 to Madras, to the employ of the East India Company, in which he showed his quality first by surviving, and then by the study of all the documents and books he could lay hands on. The documents were the old records of Madras; the books were mainly those of the library of Robert Orme, later the historian of Hindustan, who had come out to join the Council of Fort St George. From the documents he learnt a good deal about the old English spice trade in the East Indies; from the books he derived a vast interest in the history of Spanish exploration in the Pacific, to his learning on which subject he was able to add when he acquired some of the effects of William Roberts, a super-cargo on voyages to Manila, killed in the defence of Fort St George against the French. He decided that he himself wanted to explore: not immediately in the Pacific, but in the East Indies. His ambition was to revive there the British trade which had been ended by the Dutch; and, going further, to use that as an element in a greatly expanded trade with China which would outflank the monopoly of

[1] For Dalrymple's life, see Howard T. Fry, *Alexander Dalrymple (1737–1808) and the Expansion of British Trade* (London, 1970).

Canton. He pictured a base in the Borneo archipelago, part of the Sultanate of Sulu. His industry made him deputy-secretary of Madras by 1758; in 1759 he declined the secretaryship in favour of a preliminary voyage; in 1760 he sailed in the schooner *Cuddalore* for Sulu, to secure a treaty of commerce with the sultan, and to go on to his exploration of the eastern seas; on his next voyage he got the cession to the Company of Balambangan, an island off the north-east coast of Borneo. He took possession of it in January 1763. He was backwards and forwards among the islands until the end of 1764, at one time elected deputy-governor of Manila, acquired by the British in 1762—always concerned with the effective settlement of Balambangan. He had carried his masters at Madras a certain distance with him, but he needed the backing of the Company in England. There he returned in 1765, with his strong plea for East Indian trade; and also with more information, collected at Manila, about the Spanish in the Pacific. He persuaded the Company, though the process lasted three years; eighteen months more went by before the Company could be certain of government encouragement. In the interval Dalrymple had ample time to devote himself to his other great passion. He would never forget the *Cuddalore* and the scented islands among which he had adventured, he would never forget the vision, he would always ignore the difficulties, of the commerce his mind had conjured up; he would drag the pearl-fisheries of Sulu into the most unlikely contexts; but while he was composing pamphlets and memoranda and arguments he was also conjuring up a vision of the south Pacific. Whatever his vision, part of it was always the figure of Alexander Dalrymple.

It is not certain what practical accomplishment Dalrymple had as a sailor. He thought he had a great deal, though he had served no apprenticeship and had never, in the technical sense, commanded a ship. He certainly, as we have seen, persuaded the Royal Society that he was 'an able navigator'. When he returned to England, an intelligent man still short of his thirtieth year, he could not fail to be caught up in intelligent discussion; and two of the objects of discussion were the South Seas and the Transit of Venus. Dalrymple began to cultivate Government and the Royal Society. Commodore Byron was back from his circumnavigation in May 1766; Captain Wallis set out on another in the following July; at the end of that month Lord Shelburne became Secretary of State for the Southern Department, and Lord Shelburne was certainly a person of high intelligence as well as high station. Dalrymple wrote to him, 24 November, a letter that might itself be called exploratory: 'Having had five years' experience in voyages of this kind, thro' seas unknown, and amongst people with whom we have no intercourse, I presume to think myself qualified to be usefully employed in such an undertaking. At the same time, I am not insensible, notwithstanding the instances of Dampier, Halley, etc., how foreign to rules of office it is, to form the most distant expectations, that a person may be employed in the publick Service by Sea, who has no rank in the Navy.'[1] How Shelburne replied to this we do not know: perhaps he did not reply because early in 1767 we have the ambitious man trying again, through an intermediary. He had been made known by his brother Lord Hailes to Adam Smith, and Adam Smith was induced to speak for him; the subject was not now only Dalrymple, but a southern continent.

. . . Whether the continent exists or not may perhaps be uncertain; [wrote Smith with more caution than Dalrymple himself exhibited] but supposing it does exist, I am very certain you will never find a man fitter for discovering it, or more determined to hazard everything in order to discover it.
The terms he would ask are, first, the absolute command of the ship with the naming of all the officers, in order that he may have people who both have confidence in him and in whom he has confidence; and secondly, that in case he should lose his ship by the common course of accident before he gets into the South Sea, that the Government will undertake to give him another. These are all the terms he would insist upon.
The ship properest for such an expedition, he says, would be an old fifty-gun ship without her guns. He does not, however, insist upon this as a *sine qua non*, but will go in any ship with a hundred to a thousand tons. He wishes to have but one ship with a good many boats. Most expeditions of this kind have miscarried from one ship's being obliged to wait for the other, or losing time in looking out for the other.[2]

Once again we do not know how Shelburne replied. Nor was Shelburne the First Lord of the Admiralty. It is clear, however, that Dalrymple was not particularly interested in observing the Transit of Venus, or the far reaches of astronomy; attending Royal Society dinners, contributing to its proceedings a paper on the formation of islands, he had in view what he regarded as a larger purpose. He was convinced that in the prosecution of that purpose, whatever lesser conditions might be imposed, he must be sole director, unimpeded, answerable to no rival command. It is time to consider the matter—

---

[1] P.R.O., Chatham Papers 30/8, Vol. 31, f. 11. According to Kippis, 15–16, it was Dalrymple's idea to be given a brevet commission in the navy, as Bougainville, an army officer, had been.
[2] Adam Smith to Shelburne, 12 February 1767, ATL, Carrington MS Papers 79: 7.

the Cause, as it were, to which he had mortgaged his soul—the Continent.

Terra australis incognita, the unknown southern land—or, more hopefully, *nondum cognita*, not yet known but in due course to be revealed: the brief words trail a long history, are aromatic with an old romance, as of great folios in ancient libraries, compassing all philosophical and geographical knowledge, with pages and double-pages of maps whose very amplitude and pattern ravish the mind; and they present us also with one of the great illusions. It was an illusion raised by abstract thought, buttressed by fragments of dis-covery that seemed to fit into a likely pattern, demolished by ex-perienced fact. There is a southern land, of course, and even now it is not fully known; but it was not this of which so many generations dreamed. The Antarctic is the fact which has survived; and Antarc-tica is not the *provincia aurea*, the golden and spicy province, the land of dye-woods and parrots and castles, the jumble of fable and misinterpretation that was piled on Greek reasoning and Marco Polo.

We do not need, for our present purpose, to probe deeply into the history of classical thought on this subject. We may note the funda-mental speculations of Pomponius Mela, about A.D. 50, and Claudius Ptolemy, the brilliant Alexandrian astronomer of the second century. Both accepted the theory of the spherical earth, though they differed on its nature: Pomponius Mela pictured a sphere consisting of land, or rather a number of continents, sur-rounded by water; Ptolemy one of water, or rather a number of seas, surrounded by land. Ptolemy's *Cosmographia*, first printed in 1477, with maps, was largely the basis of Renaissance geographical thought; but Pomponius Mela, with a southern hemisphere largely ocean, washing the shore of a continent, in this one respect, seems to have been more influential on the future. To both, nevertheless, a continent was essential; the physical argument had to be accepted that to maintain the equilibrium of a spherical earth flowing motion-less in space a landmass in the southern half was necessary to balance the familiar land-mass of Europe, Asia and Africa in the northern half. Two hundred years before Ptolemy was printed, Marco Polo went to China. His account of his travels was widely circulated in manuscript, and was first printed, in German, in 1477, the year of Ptolemy's first printing; and Marco Polo seemed, in a way to vali-date the continental hypothesis. For the text of Marco Polo, as written and printed, became confused. He described his homeward passage from Cathay, first by sea to the rich country of Chamba or Annam, and then for 1200 miles between south and south-west to another country called Locac, 'a good country and a rich', which was the Malay Peninsula. In this country there was gold in incredible quantity, and elephants and much game, and all the porcelain shells which were used for small change in those regions; its people were idolators; it was a wild region, visited by few people; 'nor does the King desire that any strangers should frequent the country, and so find out about his treasure and other resources'.[1] The confusion of the text, however, set Locac 1200 miles between south and west of the island of Java, which Marco Polo had not visited, though he described it from hearsay; and this would carry a traveller well into the southern hemisphere. It was the result of this confusion that riveted itself on the European mind, with corruption even of the name Locac into Lucach or Beach, both of which names appear on sixteenth-century maps: '*Lucach regnum*' has Mercator in his world-chart of 1569; and 'Beach *provincia aurifera quam pauci ex alienis regionibus adeunt propter gentis · inhumanitatem*', 'Beach the golden province where come few foreigners because of its people's in-humanity'. The great 'Typus Orbis Terrarum' of Abraham Ortelius of 1587 displays a tremendous expanse of land—for geographers no less than nature seem to have abhorred a vacuum—stretching right round the world, with appropriate gulfs and projections, one corner of which bears the inscription '*Hanc continentem Australem, nonnulli Magellanicam regionem ab eius inventore nuncupant*': 'This southern continent some call the region of Magellan after its discoverer'. To Ptolemy and Marco Polo, had by that time been added the real discoveries to *Terra australis nondum cognita*, of actual voyagers, not of Magellan alone: there were the East Indies, Tierra del Fuego, Magellan's strait, the Mar del Zur or South Sea, El Mar Pacific, Nova Guinea, the Islas de Salomon: a host of Spanish names mingled with the Latin. The age of exploration was born, the cartographers were endlessly busy; after Columbus came Balboa, first of western men to set eyes upon the Pacific; after him Magellan, first to drive a line across the ocean and reveal its staggering immensity; after him three centuries of agitation, elucidation, and verification. Agitation certainly there was, because no process of discovery ever went on in a serene air of regular and passionless scientific development: elucidation, because the process produced problems, sometimes, more easily than it solved them; verification, because in a day before men could navigate scientifically, no geographical statement could

[1] *The Book of Ser Marco Polo*, ed. H. Yule (3rd ed., London, 1903), II, 276.

be accepted at its face value. It was the fortune of Cook, in good time, not to have to agitate; it was part of his developed character to be as ready to elucidate and verify as to discover.

The great difficulty of Pacific exploration was not merely the immense size of the ocean—'a sea so vast that the human mind can scarcely grasp it', as one of Magellan's chroniclers wrote[1]—a third of the whole earth's surface, in which all the land of earth, if sliced off below sea-level, could be sunk; nor merely that, in spite of its thousands of islands, it contained so much water and so little land. It was not even that, in the exploration of an ocean, apart altogether from the dangers of wreck, disease and starvation, whole wind and current systems had to be learnt. It was that useful exploration depended on the explorer's knowing where he was, at sea, day by day; knowing where he was, in some harbour of a new found country, well enough to report on it reliably when he reached home—if he reached home—so that he or a successor could find the place again. Exploration by land could be arduous enough, but the explorer had landmarks—mountains, rivers, cities—and guides. At sea he had only himself and his skill in navigation. If he were a good seaman he could, taking a sight of the sun or of some known star with cross-staff or quadrant, work out his latitude reasonably well; though another man, equally careful, might reach a different result. That was half a position: then how to find the other half, how to calculate the longitude? For centuries it was impossible; techniques and instruments simply did not go so far. The good sailor might be a master of dead reckoning; he could guess closely the speed of his ship, use his compass, allow something for its variation, observe the current and the swell, estimate leeway, arrive at course made good; but the practical seaman—the sensible seaman, as he deemed himself—when it came to real longitude, threw up his hands. So, in truth, did the seaman who prided himself on his learning, who might write a treatise on navigation for the instruction of others, like Pedro Fernandez de Quiros, highly remarkable among Pacific discoverers.[2] There were striking examples of inaccuracy, like that of the pilot in Magellan's fleet who, trying to calculate the longitude of the Philippine islands, was almost fifty-three degrees out. There were no striking examples of accuracy. Before the latter part of the

[1] This was Maximilian Transylvanus, in a letter to the Cardinal-Archbishop of Salzburg in 1522.

[2] Quiros lays it down that navigation is 'an art that does not admit of ignorance or carelessness', and then has to go on to admit the inevitability of ignorance in matters of longitude. It is not quite true that seamen threw up their hands: they did their best with estimation or 'dead reckoning'. For Quiros see Celsus Kelly, *La Austrialia del Espiritu Santo* (Cambridge, 1966), I, 50-2.

eighteenth century, then, the history of Pacific exploration is a history of faith, hope, accidental discovery, missed objectives, disillusionment, disaster. Nothing once found, it seemed, could ever be found again, unless on the western perimeter of the ocean it were as large as the Philippines or New Guinea or Australia, or as frequented for commerce as the islands of the East Indies. We have the new discoveries firmly placed on the world map of Ortelius. We have, equally firmly placed, a vast amount of fancy—or, as some of the geographers would have preferred to call it, rational deduction. In somebody's mind was always the continent.

After Magellan and a few attempts, costly in men and ships, to follow his route, official Spanish enterprise in the Pacific settled down into regular trading voyages between Acapulco in Mexico and Manila on the other side of the ocean. A feasible return passage was found in the westerly winds of forty degrees north. The Spaniards, on their earlier voyages, encountered a number of the Marshall and Caroline islands, north of the equator, as well as New Guinea, but never the principal group of the northern ocean, Hawaii: they were always well south or well north of it. There were, however, three connected Spanish voyages of great endurance and some success, independent of this regular trade: all in the forty years from 1567, all based on the Peruvian port of Callao, all marked by a quite violent mingling of personal qualities and ambitions, jealousies and rebellions—a history wherein the secular passions for conquest, settlement and gold vied with the Franciscan yearning for *conquista espiritual*, new and noble empire founded on a peaceful Christian subjection of heathen people. These were the voyages of Alvaro de Mendaña and the pilot Pedro Fernandez de Quiros, already mentioned. The first of them was stimulated by a third man, able, energetic and ambitious—Pedro Sarmiento de Gamboa, who in his Peruvian studies had come on the legend of the Inca Tupic Yupanqui. This ruler, so it was said, on a voyage to the west had discovered rich islands: six hundred leagues distant they must be, thought Sarmiento, outliers of the great, and rich, continent. Somehow, for other people, they were mixed up with another legend, the one of King Solomon's Ophir, that abode of gold, now put down as an island or island-group near the East Indian Moluccas. The Viceroy of Peru was persuaded to support a voyage of discovery. He provided two ships, giving the command, however, not to the masterful Gamboa but to his own young nephew Mendaña, a man without seamanship or experience of command, but at once sweet-tempered and tenacious. He was to find the continent and settle there. The ships, built for the fine-weather Peruvian coastal passages and provisioned for a short voyage, manned by argumentative officers and mutinous crews, sailed in November 1567; they were to know starvation, the worst of hurricanes, be given up for lost; they survived and after nearly two years turned up again at Callao with two-thirds of their company safe. They had sailed outwards for eighty days, from one side of the ocean to the other, before they came to the impressive group called after their return the Solomon Islands. There they stayed six months, exploring and observing; found or made the people too hostile to permit settlement; found no gold and no continent; made no spiritual conquest; reached home in the last extremity of privation. Mendaña, at least, was eager to go again.

Not until 1595 could he do so. Official hostility and tardiness had been underlined by the Pacific incursion of Francis Drake, fruit of a theory that, once into the ocean in Magellan's track, you could outwit the Spaniards by quitting it through what we would now call a north-west passage, a strait through the northern parts of America between Pacific and Atlantic. While you were in the Pacific you might discover the continent. Drake had no talent for discovery, nor in any case could he discover what was not there; but the effect of his foray and of others, was to discourage Spanish exploration which might simply present a new attraction to pirates. Nevertheless, Mendaña did, at last, make his second voyage. He could not find his Solomon Islands again, nor could anybody else for two hundred years: so vague indeed were his ideas of longitude that he at first thought he had arrived when he sighted the Marquesas, a sort of half-way point. Coming after many weary weeks to Santa Cruz, not far short of his goal, he decided to settle there. Quarrels, native enmity, and dreadful malaria quashed the attempt; Mendaña himself died; a starving remnant was brought over unknown seas to Manila only through the superb navigation of the chief pilot, the Portuguese seaman Quiros. It was Quiros who, undeterred, took up the mission, a mission to him evangelical as well as geographical. A man of extraordinary qualities, with something Franciscan in his spirit, he combined professional skill with a continental faith that swept him far beyond the touch of reality, that made his path both a triumphant and a dolorous one; so that in the end, foredoomed to failure as he was from the nature of things, it perhaps mattered little that he was a poor leader of men. After much travail, he sailed from Callao in December 1605—further south than Mendaña had done, then north-west through the Tuamotu archipelago, and west when he was in the latitude of Santa Cruz. If he had kept on he would have reached it: three or four degrees beyond it lay the islands of Solomon. He was diverted from an island a little short of it, the latest of a series discovered by him, to turn south, so that he fetched up at something quite different, though close, the land he called Austrialia del Espiritu Santo, the northernmost large island of the New Hebrides group; and here, he was sure, where he proclaimed the city of New Jerusalem, was the much-desired continent. Sickness, at the critical moment infirmity of purpose, unreliable subordinates, finally the cruel luck with the wind, drove him away before a settlement was made, in a vast sweep north that took him to Mexico in October 1606. The wind had parted him from the real hero of the voyage, his principal lieutenant, Luis Vaez de Torres, who made his way from Espiritu Santo to the southern coast of New Guinea, along it through the strait named after him, and so to Manila, thus solving one of the great problems of geography: New Guinea, it was clear, was the northern projection of no continent, it was insular. The solution was not bruited abroad. Quiros returned to Spain, ceaselessly and fruitlessly to importune crown and councils, with memorials and charts, for still another expedition. The Spanish effort was over. His memorials, glowing with their confident transmutation of hopes into matter of fact, spread through Europe. Quiros, who had discovered a dozen islands, became the publicist of the continent. Had he failed in his great purpose? He could hold up a light to the future.

The immediate future, however, needed no light from Spain. The next century of Pacific exploration was almost entirely in the hands of the Dutch: not quite entirely, because one must remember Dampier and the buccaneers on the fringe. The Dutch were the best cartographers of the seventeenth century; they made important advances in naval architecture; they organised a great overseas trade, and a great eastern empire. The empire was a commercial empire; their exploration was an aspect of trade. As the empire was that of the Dutch East Indies Company, so the exploration was that approved of by the Company, the value of discoveries was judged by the Company; though again one must say not entirely so. The Company, or its captains in their passages from the Cape of Good Hope to the East Indies, placed fairly solidly on the map the western coast of Australia—their New Holland—and a good part of the southern coast. Exploring the north coast, they registered its essential outline, though they were never able to decide whether that north coast was altogether continuous, nor whether New

Guinea and New Holland were different countries. An easy passage into the Pacific south of New Guinea might have been of great commercial importance: indeed the first Dutch visit to Australia, that of the *Duyfken*, two months before Torres sailed through the strait, resulted from exploration of its possibility. There is no real reason to think that Australia had been discovered by any European before, or that the 'Dieppe' group of maps, to which an occasional geographer still pins his faith, had anything to do with Australia at all.[1] It may be surprising that there was little tendency to identify this mass of land, set down so hugely between the Pacific and the Indian oceans, with the *Terra australis incognita*; but its shore-line was unpromising, its cliffs and sand-dunes called up no vision of Locac, the Dutch deemed its people poor and abject; and within less than forty years after its first sighting a Dutch seaman had circumnavigated it, without laying eyes on it—except for the island, Van Diemen's Land or Tasmania, that sits off its south-eastern coast. This was the voyage of Abel Janszoon Tasman, a voyage aimed principally at the discovery of the continent, or—there were other objectives—a clear route to Chile and a highly-fancied trade, or the rediscovery of the Solomon Islands. Tasman, in his great round voyage, Batavia to Mauritius, south to 49° and eastward, discovered not merely Van Diemen's Land but the west coast of high surf-struck New Zealand—perhaps this was the continent?—before he turned north to Tonga, escaped the desperately dangerous fringe of Fiji, and passed along the northern coast of New Guinea into the East Indies home.—'God be praised and thanked.' His masters were not highly pleased with this voyage. He had not beaten up any trade.

Not the great Company only, however, had its men in the Pacific, nor did all explorers come from the west. While the Dutch were still experimenting in their approach to eastern trade, through Magellan's strait, one tempest-driven captain, Dirck Gerritsz or Gerrards, in 1599, reported seeing the snow-covered mountains of the great south land, stretching off from latitude 64° in the direction of the Solomon Islands. In 1624 the *Orange*, from a fleet that set out to attack the Spaniards in Peru, reported two sightings, the first in latitude 50°, the second in 41°. This was doing better than the first Dutch expedition which had the continent for its objective, that of Willem Schouten and Jacob Le Maire, in 1615 and 1616, which made no

[1] The 'Dieppe' maps, so called from a group of cartographers at Dieppe in the sixteenth century, and particularly one referred to as the 'Dauphin' map, have been held to be renderings of the Australian coast-line, and to point to Portuguese exploration. Andrew Sharp's discussion (*The Discovery of Australia*, Oxford, 1963, 2-14) is pretty conclusive.

illusory landfalls, but did discover the Strait of Le Maire and Cape Horn, some of the Tuamotus, the northernmost island of the Tongan group, and the Hoorn islands not far from Fiji, passing thereafter north-west round the Solomons and New Guinea to Batavia. Nor, after another century, in 1721–2, did Jacob Roggeveen have more luck. Sponsored by the Dutch West India Company, he also made a Horn passage into the ocean, going far south, almost to latitude 61°. His most striking discovery was Easter Island; he lost a ship in the Tuamotus; found, but would not tarry for, the Samoan group; followed the old route north of New Guinea to Batavia. The number of islands was accumulating; but where was the continent?

We are in the eighteenth century. It was a busy century, in science and speculation and writing, in economic expansion and war, in building and art; a revolutionary century, far beyond the confines of politics and social relations. Mathematical physics and chemistry made immense steps; botany, zoology, physiology, astronomy, geography, were all in movement. The great names are thick. Science had not become part of a polite education, but it was written about, lectured upon, demonstrated, applied, made elegant. Newton was the elder prophet; innumerable followers preached. Leadbetter represents one class of them; Robertson, with his instruction of rising navigators, another. Navigation could not fail to be affected. There was an important discovery in the ascertaining of latitude—the method of 'double altitudes', before and after noon, which could be utilised for days when a noon sighting of the sun was impossible: we shall find double altitudes thick in the records of Cook's voyages. This was due to Cornelis Douwes of Amsterdam, who about 1749 worked out logarithmic tables for the method. Accurate results in calculation depended not merely on tables but upon accurate observation, accurate measurement, and the century was a great age of scientific and mathematical instrument makers. Hadley's octant, farther developed by Captain John Campbell into the sextant, may almost stand as its symbol, though we are not to forget the reflecting telescope, the achromatic telescope, the micrometers. We cannot forget the problem of longitudes. As the century grew, interest grew; we may almost say that excitement grew. The principle involved is plain. Longitude—to put the matter crudely—is wrapped up with time. As the earth makes its daily revolution, time alters regularly from place to place; a difference of one hour is equivalent to fifteen degrees of longitude. One can observe certain astronomical phenomena all round the world, but at different points they occur at different times. If one knows precisely at what time one of them will occur at a fixed point on the earth's surface—Greenwich, for example, or Paris—and observes the time of the same occurrence at any different point—for example again, a spot in the Burgeo Islands—then the difference in hours of time, multiplied by the number 15, will give one the longitude in degrees. As early as 1474 the German astronomer Regiomontanus, stating the principle, had put forward as a basis for calculation 'lunar distances'—that is, the angular distance between the moon and the sun or one of a number of fixed stars. The principle remained undoubted: almost three hundred years were to elapse before the development of instruments and techniques enabled it to be put in practice. An eclipse of the sun would serve, but not for the navigator; for the sun was not eclipsed every day, and the navigator did not know the time of the eclipse at any point of departure. The best Cook could do, after observing in 1766, was to hand in his results to the mathematicians when he arrived home. Much better, some men had said, to send able mathematicians to sea, than to send the observations of seamen to able mathematicians on land; but what good would that do, when all the mathematics in the world could not tell men at sea the time at Greenwich or at Paris?

Astronomers and mathematicians did not lose their interest. There were those who thought that the prospect of a large reward would stimulate sufficient ingenuity; disasters at sea directly attributable to errors in reckoning were all too frequent; the British government, alarmed at some of these, in 1714 offered £20,000 to anyone who could produce a 'generally practicable and useful method' of fixing longitudes at sea within thirty miles at the end of a six weeks' voyage, and lesser rewards to persons who, without solving the problem, made some appreciable contribution towards its solution. The act of Parliament which regulated the matter also set up the Board of Longitude, 'for the discovery of longitude at sea and for examining, trying and judging of all proposals, experiments and improvements relating to the same.'[1] The act was of course an encouragement to the eccentric, almost an inducement to insanity: longitude became all the rage: one need not be surprised to find, among the scenes of active horror in the mad-house print of Hogarth's *Rake's Progress*, of 1736, a comparatively peaceful lunatic working away at a solution. There were, in fact, two ways of solving the problem: the astronomical-mathematical, and the mechanical. About the first enough has been said. The second depended on the production of a clock, a 'watch-machine' so highly sophisticated that it would go at

<hr/>

[1] 12 Anne, cap. 15; and see *Journals* II, xxxix, n. 1.

a uniform rate, permanently and precisely, under any conditions of cold or heat or storm or wave, on land or at sea—so that once set at a point of departure, it would continue to show the time at that point. The difference between that time and the time at any other point, as we have seen, would provide the longitude, and more quickly than by the method of astronomical observation. Both methods came to success almost simultaneously, in the 1760's. The first was made possible by the lunar tables which Tobias Mayer, an astronomer of Göttingen, calculated on Newtonian principles; it was developed by Maskelyne, Cook's junior by four years, who was to become Astronomer Royal in 1765, moving force of the Board of Longitude and of the Royal Society on its astronomical side, and intimately concerned with the great voyages. In 1761 Maskelyne went on a voyage to St Helena to observe that year's transit of Venus. Clouds were spread upon the sky; on the outward and homeward passages, however, he made regular observations with his Hadley's quadrant of lunar distances. Mayer and Maskelyne together gave the longitude. In 1763, the year after Mayer's death, Maskelyne published *The British Mariner's Guide*, which conveyed instruction in his system. In 1766, as Astronomer Royal, he published the first number of the *Nautical Almanac*, which contained tables based on Mayer's, calculated for every day in the following year at three-hour intervals. He had reduced the process, after the initial observation, to arithmetic and not very advanced trigonometry. It was not quite simple: there had to be corrections for refraction and parallax, as George Witchell had applied corrections to Cook's figures for the solar eclipse; the local time of observation also had to be corrected by astronomical means. The calculations, to begin with, took about four hours, but improvement in the system reduced this time to a quarter of an hour—anyhow for a mathematician. The ordinary conservative sea captain tended to look at this estimate rather morosely, and to cling to his dead reckoning. We shall see a more lively interest in Cook, without being able to say exactly when he learnt the technique. As for the 'watch-machine' or chronometer, that life-work of the practical genius John Harrison, it passed with triumph the stringent test of a voyage to Barbados in 1764, when one of its guardians and examiners was Maskelyne himself. Harrison's 'machine' had a cardinal defect, its expense: if that would be sufficiently lowered, the future lay with it. One might be more correct in saying that the future lay with the chronometer, because there were other makers than Harrison; but he had made the vast step. The watch-machine did not instantaneously render the lunar method superfluous, as we shall see. Both are essential parts of the life of Cook.

Meanwhile we may return to discovery, and to thought upon discovery. On the borders of two centuries, the seventeenth and eighteenth, and not in the Pacific at all, we have a voyage that strikes the new note of science. It is the South Atlantic voyage from which Halley, investigating the variation of the compass, brought back his material for the first isogonic map, together with a method of finding longitude through the occultations of the fixed stars— another method useless to sailors without tables or instruments or mathematics. He brought back as well reports of land that were, like so many others, illusory. On the borders of two oceans, the Indian and the Pacific, Dampier failed in a voyage on which he had hoped to reveal the east coast of Australia: at least he cut in two the old conception of New Guinea and could indulge his passion for natural history. Neither Halley nor Dampier showed great capacity for dealing with insubordinate men. The year of Cook's birth was the year in which Vitus Bering, a Dane in the service of Russia, passed the strait named after him; the year 1741, in which Anson, amid gales and fog, entered the South Pacific on the circumnavigation which was to make the ocean sound in all English ears, was that in which Bering, again, amid gales and fog, crossed the North Pacific to the north-west coast of America. Cook was at school at Ayton when the French Bouvet, at the beginning of 1739, sighted in the southern Atlantic the point of snow-covered land he called Cape Circumcision, thinking that he at last had found the continent; had just come out of his apprenticeship when Buffon published his *Theorie de la Terre*, the first volume of the great *Historie Naturelle*, in 1749; in 1752, when the brilliant Maupertius published the *Lettre sur le Progres des Sciences* addressed to Frederick the Great, he was serving his second year in the *Three Brothers*, looking forward perhaps to becoming a mate; in 1756, when the President de Brosses, stimulated by Buffon and Maupertius, published his magistral *Histoire des Navigations aux Terres Australes*, he was in the *Eagle*, master's mate, under Palliser; in 1757, when Philippe Buache, one of the celebrated French geographers, published his memoir on the southern continent and the lands of the Antarctic, their rivers and icy sea,[1] he had advanced no farther in rank or philosophy. The names were French, and if historical scholarship and scientific speculation could have produced a

[1] For the memoir or memoirs of Buache, see Armand Rainaud, *Le Continent Austral* (Paris, 1893), 412–13.

continent the French would have produced it. If it had existed where it was supposed to exist their seamen, within a few years, would have produced it too, whatever the British activity; for the rivalry of the Seven Years' War was continued in the decades after the war in exploration and the free traffic of scientific results, and whatever the suspicions of statesmen and the reports of secret agents it is pleasant to consider the friendship between Dalrymple and French scholars and cartographers—just as it is pleasant to consider the respect in which a more experienced Cook held Bouvet and other French sailors.

There are parallels between French and English thought on the uses of a continent, and we may note that French writings, plans and actions no less than English caused disquiet in a temporarily revived Spanish empire. For a brief while Spain was prepared to name the Pacific as a Spanish preserve as much as it was in the sixteenth century; the return of Anson in 1744 with a galleon's treasure was regarded in England much as the return of Drake in the *Golden Hind* had been. The Falkland Islands were regarded as a key to the Pacific, Spain accordingly would tolerate French settlement there no more than British. Yet how to keep French or British out of that ample ocean, if they were determined to get in, under the excuse either of science or of peaceful trade? There is an obvious connection between the publication in war years, 1744–8, of Dr John Campbell's second edition of 'Harris's Voyages', the *Navigantium atque Itinerantium Bibliotheca* of 1705, and Anson's famous voyage; and Campbell's two thousand folio pages are a continent in themselves, his eloquence, addressed to 'the Merchants of *Great Britain*', rolls with an appropriate thunder. 'Let us maintain Trade, and there is no doubt that Trade will maintain us. Let our past Mistakes teach us to be wise, let our present Wants and Difficulties revive our ancient Industry.' Let us plant a new colony for the benefit of trade. He wastes no time on cosmic principles, will not indulge in hypothesis, knows how far he may safely be dogmatic. 'It is most evident, from Captain *Tasman's* Voyage, that *New Guinea, Carpentaria, New Holland, Antony van Diemen's Land,* and the countries discovered by *de Quiros,* make all one Continent, from which *New Zeland* seems to be separated by a Streight; and, perhaps, is part of another Continent, answering to *Africa,* as this, of which we are now speaking, plainly does to *America.* This Continent reaches from the Equinoctical to 44° of South Latitude, and extends from 122° to 188° of Longitude, making indeed a very large country, but nothing like what *de Quiros* imagined; which shows how dangerous a thing it is to trust too much to Conjecture in such Points as these.'[1] A settlement could be made in this large country; there was reason to believe all that Quiros said about 'Gold, Silver, Pearl, Nutmegs, Mace, Ginger and Sugar-Canes, of an extraordinary Size' that existed there; its trade would be invaluable; from it could be discovered *Terra australis incognita*; such a settlement would greatly increase our shipping and seamen, 'which are the true and natural Strength of this Country, extend our naval Power, and raise the Reputation of this Nation; the most distant Prospect of which is sufficient to warm the Soul of any Man, who has the least regard for his Country, with Courage sufficient to despise the Imputations which may be thrown upon him as a visionary Projector, for taking so much Pains upon an Affair, that can tend so little to his private Advantage.'[2] However the merchants of Great Britain thought of this appeal and their private advantage, their purchases of the work made a reprint necessary in 1764, the year after peace was made, the year of the first post-war Pacific voyage; they bought innumerable volumes of collections of voyages and travels easier to handle than these tremendous folios; they bought with eagerness edition after edition of the single volume of Anson's *Voyage*.

In the commentary of de Brosses on the voyages, collected in his *Histoire*, we have a different spirit; for de Brosses was an intellectual of the eighteenth-century French kind, a *philosophe*, a lover of mankind as well as of the civilisation of his own country. Commerce and naval power, certainly, were not to be despised while Britain so visibly affected the universal monarchy of the sea; but the fame that discoverers should pursue was the fame of scientific knowledge. The President traversed the voyages in the southern hemisphere, in the regions he called Magellanica—the Atlantic; Polynesia—the Pacific; Australasia—the Indian Ocean. Somewhere in those regions must be civilisations that only waited to exchange the lessons of culture with France. Could that whole unknown part of the globe be occupied by nought but the waters of the sea? Capes, fragments of coast, were certain signs of a continent. Must there not be, southwards of Asia, solid land extensive enough to counterweight the northern mass, to maintain in equilibrium the whole rotating globe? It is the classical argument, we see again the Ptolemaic sphere: perhaps it was classical also in the way that the European mind was classical, composing an art and an architecture of elegant and rational balance —so that Buache must have not merely a southern continent, but ice debouching from its rivers through gulfs such as those he designated in the northern hemisphere. De Brosses shows a curious

[1] *Navigantium atque Itinerantium Bibliotheca*, I, xvi.   [2] ibid., 335.

parallelism with the so different Campbell: he too wishes to see the founding of a colony on land already known, as a centre for commerce and a base for exploration, close to the New Jerusalem of Quiros; but a colony unlike Campbell's, one to which beggars, orphans and criminals might be transported, where in its pure air they might slough off vice and rise to heights of mature and noble virtue. Almost we see, rising above some busy port, a statue—not perhaps of Liberty, but at least of Perfectibility. The strain of eighteenth-century benevolence is clear. Would such settlement mean expense? The expense of conquering one little ravaged province of Europe would be a hundred times greater.

On this the war, with all its ravaged provinces, was the harsh commentary. After it was over, a Scotsman, John Callander, in his *Terra Australis Cognita*[1] even snatched the volumes of de Brosses, and gave his argument a fiercely British twist. Callander was a little cautious about the *Terra australis incognita*: some wise and knowing people, he conceded, took it to be merely a chimera. Yet one should not be too hasty, too peremptory: it might exist, and for the sake of science and of navigation be extremely worth the finding. Such, it appears, must have been a popular view. The volumes of voyages had done their work. Twenty years later the first biographer of Cook looked back and fully remembered 'how much his imagination was captivated, in the more early part of his life, with the hypothesis of a southern continent. He has often dwelt upon it with rapture, and been highly delighted with the authors who contended for its existence, and displayed the mighty consequences which would result from its being discovered.'[2] Of these authors, the principal one in England, who seems to have felt a rapture himself, was Alexander Dalrymple, and to Dalrymple we must now return.

Dalrymple regarded himself as a scientific specialist. Trade, which he was so much interested in stimulating in the East Indies, in the South Seas had little interest for him; he gave his attention to a particular sort of voyage, with one single object. His researches had yielded the harvest that he brought out in two volumes in 1770 and 1771 as *A Historical Collection of Voyages . . . in the South Pacific Ocean*, the first devoted to Spanish voyages, the second to Dutch. This was a valuable work. Its argumentative part he had already printed in 1767 in *An Account of the Discoveries made in the South Pacifick Ocean, Previous to 1764*—previous to 1764, presumably, because that was

---

[1] Callander's production appeared in three volumes in Edinburgh, 1766–8. He plundered other books besides de Brosses; see *Journals* I, lxxxi–lxxxiii.

[2] Kippis, 184.

the year in which the first of a new series of voyages, British ones, began. Trade, certainly, was not to be despised, but why should Britain be concerned so much over the trade of her American colonies, with a population of some two million, compared to the probably more than 50 millions of the Southern Continent?—a continent that in the latitude of 40° stretched over 4596 geographic, or 5323 statute miles, 'a greater extent than the whole civilised part of Asia, from Turkey, to the eastern extremity of China. There is at present no trade from Europe thither, though the scraps from this table would be sufficient to maintain the power, dominion, and sovereignty of Britain, by employing all its manufactures and ships.'[1] Magnificent vision! Dalrymple's proofs are both 'philosophical' and historical, 'as well from the analogy of nature, as from the deduction of past discoveries.' The 'analogy of nature' is the argument from counterpoise: the quantity of land in the northern hemisphere implied the 'probable conjecture', the seeming necessity, of a like quantity in the southern, a conformity of hemispheres. Then 'it rests to shew, from the nature of the winds in the South Pacific Ocean, that there *must* be a *Continent* on the *south*'. He shows this. He introduces an ingenious argument from the existence of '*fair-haired* people' in the islands, a fact 'entirely contrary to the common circumstance within the tropic'.[2] He registers all the past 'sightings' of land, from latitude 64° to 40°: '. . . . It cannot be doubted from so many concurrent testimonies, that the Southern Continent has been already *discovered* on the east side; and it appears more than probable, that Tasman's discovery, which he named Staat's Land, but which is in the maps called New Zealand, is the *western* coast of this *Continent*. . . . The north of this *vast Continent* appears to be hitherto undiscovered. . . . Although the *signs of land* seen by Roggevein, previous to the discovery of Easter Island, denote the vicinity of the *continent*, it is from his description of *that* island we are enabled to form some idea of the adjacent *Continent*; no voyage hitherto performed, points out so strongly the *original* of the Peruvian manners and religion.'[3] He proceeds to examine the conduct and courses of the explorers: of Quiros he cannot speak too highly; of Roggeveen, who ignored obvious signs of the continent, he frankly disapproves. He makes it plain that what is needed is a Hero, a Columbus or Magellan, a man of the nobler virtues that flourished in that elder time, one in whom stands forth 'a *sublimity* of *conception*, followed by

---

[1] *Historical Collection*, I, xxviii–xxix.
[2] ibid., 12 ff. after 124. This odd argument is perhaps founded on something that Cook himself was later to observe, the penchant of a number of islanders for bleaching their hair with a plaster of clay.   [3] ibid., xx.

dauntless and *perseverant* resolution. . . .' Much was still within the power of men, 'rather *emulous* of the glorious spirit of *that age*, than *devoted* to the mercenary, or indolent disposition of *the present*';[1] and so on. With a large effort of imagination, one may be able to step back to the year 1767 and read all these words anew. Is one communing with a new Hakluyt or merely participating in a vast and shining day-dream? Day-dream—one can hardly avoid the ultimate conviction—it is, wherein the Hero, the companion in history of heroes, is Alexander Dalrymple. We can now understand the terms of employment that he laid down to Adam Smith, and Adam Smith transmitted to Lord Shelburne; and understand his willingness to serve the Royal Society, without much interest in the Society's grand design.

Meanwhile, even before Dalrymple returned from the East, the British Government had shown itself not quite immune to ideas of Pacific discovery. As long ago as 1749, just after an earlier war, Anson had persuaded his colleagues on the Admiralty to prepare an expedition, and only protests from the agitated Spaniards had prevented it from sailing; and a strain in Anson's strategic thought, the acquisition of the Falkland Islands as the key to the Pacific, had been transmitted to Lord Egmont, First Lord of the Admiralty from 1763 to 1776. Egmont was interested in the continent, wherever it might lie; he was also interested in a grand conception of oceanic control, not merely through control of the Magellanic entrance, the southern, but also through that of a northern passage—the North-West Passage, in fact, in which, despite all failures to find it, there were still devout believers. To control both those entrances would give, obviously a strategic command superior to anything else that could exist. Hence the despatch in June 1764 of the first post-war expedition, that of Commodore the Hon. John Byron, the two ships *Dolphin* and *Tamar*, instructed to examine not the south Pacific but the south Atlantic—any continental mass that might exist 'within Latitudes convenient for navigation and in the Climates adapted to the Produce of Commodities usefull in Commerce', the Falkland Islands, and a 'Pepys Island' alleged to lie in the Atlantic somewhere east of the Falklands; having done which, they were to pass into the Pacific and up to Drake's New Albion, about latitude 38° on the North American coast, examining that coast closely as far northward as possible for a passage through the land, returning through it to England if it existed; if passage there was none, they were to make

[1] *Historical Collection*, I, xvii–xviii.

for China or the Dutch East Indies, returning by way of the Cape of Good Hope.[1] Byron found nothing in the Atlantic beyond the Falklands which he formally annexed for his monarch, charting the northern coast before he sailed into the Strait of Magellan. Here he decided that his ship would not withstand the voyage to New Albion, decided instead to run straight across the Pacific in the hope of finding the Solomons; picked up a few small islands, quite missed the Solomons, and reached England in May 1766 with one resounding story, that of the huge men and women of Patagonia, who had made the British sailors interviewing them seem such pygmies. When the Spanish ambassador enquired of the Duke of Richmond, the secretary of state, what Byron had been looking for, the agreeable nobleman could thus reply, with perfect truth though an economy of it, 'giants'. Lord Egmont, having made sure, as he thought, of the Falklands, could now turn his attention to the continent in the Pacific. He just had time, before he relinquished office, to send out the *Dolphin* again, in August 1766, under the command of Captain Samuel Wallis, to look for this—to quote Wallis's instructions, 'Land or Islands of Great extent, hitherto unvisited by any European Power . . . between Cape Horn and New Zeeland', which he should find by stretching to the westward from the Horn for about 100 or 120 degrees of longitude, 'losing as little Southing as possible'.[2]

There were in France, at the same time, ambitions nourished not dissimilar to those so freely fed in England, though the merchants of France seem to have been less concerned than were individual patriots, administrators, or adventurers. De Brosses had his influence. The Falklands stretched a beckoning strategic hand. There was Bouvet's cape. There were Frenchmen anxious for a continent that would provide a secure port of call for their ships on the long passage to India, there was a French obsession with spiceries, wherein a Pacific settlement might snatch a world-trade from the Dutch, there was a natural French rivalry with the British—why should unimpeded Albion monopolise all the profits of that to-be-discovered hemisphere? The French contemporary of Byron and Wallis is Bougainville, aristocratic, brilliant, a fellow of the Royal Society, the military comrade-in-arms of Montcalm, the disciple of de Brosses, anxious to spend himself and his estate on compensating France abroad for her lost American empire.[3] When Byron surveyed the

[1] Byron's instructions are entered in P.R.O., Adm 2/1332; their policy is examined in *Journals* I, lxxxiv–lxxxvi.

[2] Wallis's instructions also are in P.R.O., Adm 2/1332; and see *Journals* I, xc ff.

[3] Bougainville can be quite fully studied in J. E. Martin-Allanic, *Bougainville navigateur et les découvertes de son temps* (2 vols., Paris, 1964).

north coast of the Falklands there was already a French settlement on the south coast founded by Bougainville. When Spain insisted that neither British nor French would be allowed there she indemnified him both by a money payment and by permission to make a Pacific voyage, which would put de Brosses to the test. When Wallis was entering the ocean Bougainville was at the Falklands handing over his colony. He was nine months behind Wallis on his Pacific traverse, but he made a famous voyage, he installed the French presence, and the astronomer with him, Pierre Antoine Veron, by his use of lunar observations, established the longitude of the Philippine Islands,—and thus, for the first time, the width of the ocean.

All this was quite distinct from the astronomical ambitions of the Royal Society or the Academy of Sciences in Paris. Yet Dr Hornsby in 1765 had seen the possible connection between discovery, or even a settlement made by a commercial nation in the Pacific ocean, and the needs of science. The connection now became very clear. The Royal Society had been actively prosecuting its idea of a South Sea observation of the Transit of Venus. This entailed getting observers to the South Sea, which entailed the expenditure of money. The Royal Society had no money. In February 1768, therefore, the Council as its next step prepared a memorial to its patron, a document nicely calculated to appeal to a patriot king. It pointed out the importance of accurate observation for the improvement of Astronomy, 'on which Navigation so much depends'. It pointed out that 'several of the Great Powers in Europe, particularly the French, Spaniards, Danes and Swedes are making the proper dispositions for the Observation thereof: and the Empress of Russia has given directions for having the same observed in many different places of her extensive Dominions. . . . That the British Nation have been justly celebrated in the learned world, for their knowledge of Astronomy, in which they are inferior to no Nation upon Earth, Ancient or Modern; and it would cast dishonour upon them should they neglect to have correct observations made of this important phenomenon.' The places proper for observing were detailed. The expense would amount to about £4000, 'exclusive of the expense of the ships which must convey and return the Observers that are to be sent to the Southward of the Equinoctial Line and to the North Cape'. The Society's annual income was scarcely sufficient to carry on its necessary business. 'The Memorialists, attentive to the true end for which they were founded by Your Majesty's Royal Predecessor, The Improvement of Natural Knowledge, conceived it to be their duty to lay their sentiments before Your Majesty with all humility, and submit the same to Your Majesty's Royal Consideration.'[1]

His Majesty, well disposed, granted the Society £4000, 'clear of fees'. As this was additional to the ship and its company, to be provided by the Admiralty, one must allow that the British Crown was doing its duty by science. It appears that the Council was still naïve enough to assume that Dalrymple would be appointed commander of the ship. The matter was clarified at a Council meeting of 3 April. A letter from the Admiralty, first, announced the purchase of a ship, 'a Cat of 370 tons', for the expedition, and enquired who was to go and what instructions the Society wanted given to her commander.[2] Secondly, the president reported that he had recommended Mr Dalrymple to the Lords as commander, and had been told that such an appointment would be 'totally repugnant to the rules of the Navy'. Indeed the First Lord, Sir Edward Hawke, either at this interview or at some other time, said roundly that he would suffer his right hand to be cut off rather than sign such another commission as had gone to Halley in the *Paramour* pink in 1698—a civilian in command of a naval vessel on a scientific voyage, whose difficulties with his officers had been painful;[3] or, he might have added, as had gone at the same time to Dampier, who was at least a professional sailor. Dalrymple himself had foreseen the difficulty. He thought it could be solved by his appointing all the ship's officers himself. This was a staggering naïvety, if the navy were to be concerned at all; and who was Dalrymple, with his two or three years in the schooner *Cuddalore*, sailed by Captain Baker, and his longest ocean passage of nineteen days, to suggest—let alone insist— that he should have the command of a voyage to the Pacific Ocean? The answer of course is that Dalrymple was a man with a mission, and that he did not conceive his mission to be limited to observing the transit of Venus. On this same 3 April he attended on the Council; he was told of the Admiralty sentiment; and, quite consistently and finally, he declined the voyage.[4] The Council

---

[1] R.S. Council Minutes, 15 February 1768.

[2] Admiralty secretary to Royal Society, 1 April 1768, Adm 2/541.

[3] Kippis, 16, makes the delicate comment that Hawke 'possessed more of the spirit of his profession that either of education or science'.

[4] Dalrymple, in his later reminiscences, says that offers were made to him 'that the instructions for the voyage should be entrusted to him, and the Officer commanding the vessel be positively ordered to follow his opinion, on the compliance with which his promotion was to depend'; but Dalrymple still refused to go, since his *Cuddalore* experience had taught him 'that a divided command was incompatible with the public service in such voyages.'—'Memoirs of Alexander Dalrymple', *European Magazine*, 42 (1802), 325. It is hard to know what to make of this, except that it is most unlikely that the Admiralty or anyone connected with it, would have made the 'offers' he refers to. He may have been referring to his discussions with the Royal Society.

was prepared to be philosophic; it resolved to think of someone else.

All this is traditionally considered part of the biography of Cook. The history of Pacific exploration is part of the biography of Cook; the fact that Cook became an observer of the Transit is part of his biography; the fact that Dalrymple became a sort of natural and perpetual critic of Cook's proceedings is perhaps part of the biography of Cook, though much more of that of Dalrymple. In relation to Cook's command of the Transit voyage, however, Dalrymple's cultivation of the Royal Society, Dalrymple's vision of himself as the new Columbus, Dalrymple's conditions of command, were quite irrelevant. To the Lords of the Admiralty Dalrymple was irrelevant. For Cook, in due course, his geographical learning was both relevant and important, even though Cook was forced into becoming the most destructive critic of Dalrymple. It is difficult not to see them as antagonists. But in 1768 there was not the slightest question of rivalry. So far as we can see from the documents, the Admiralty, having bought a ship to carry the astronomers to the South Seas, some time between 5 April and 12 April decided to take Cook temporarily from the Newfoundland survey and appoint him to her command. We may ask, why Cook?—and answer with another question:—Considering Cook's capacities and equipment, and that the voyage was also to be a voyage of discovery, was not that the most natural thing in the world? This is to rely too heavily on hindsight. Cook's capacities as a marine surveyor were known, but no one was persuaded that he was one of the principal geniuses of the age. No one could put a finger on him, and say, Here is a great sailor, here is the greatest of discoverers by sea. We do not even know that at the moment when he was appointed, the Admiralty had decided to add discovery to the more limited scientific purpose of the voyage —though with a ship in the Pacific, a further attempt at discovery would seem logical enough. Wallis had not yet returned. Had he had any success? And as this ship was to be sent into the Pacific, a considerable voyage, was it not a little strange to select for her command a mere master, whose most important previous command had been a sixty-ton schooner, or brig, with a crew of twenty? Of his predecessors, Byron was a commodore, the second son of a nobleman, had commanded line-of-battle ships; Wallis was a post-captain of eight years seniority. There were plenty of meritorious and experienced half-pay officers who would have been glad of employment: it could not be said that Mr Cook was the only man in the market. Scientific leanings, however advantageous, were not strictly necessary. It is possible, indeed, that to begin with the voyage did not rate very highly with the Lords of the Admiralty, as long as a naval officer of some sort was in charge of a naval vessel. It is possible that there were many commanders eligible. Philip Stephens, the secretary, solved the problem. A large part of his business was to know men. Certainly by now he knew Cook, and his knowledge was not confined to a paper acquaintance. He made the suggestion to the Lords; he referred them to Palliser for a supporting opinion. Palliser was prepared to lose his surveyor, glad to enlarge on his merits.[1] Mr Cook was appointed. It was a remarkable event indeed.

We may look once more at its context, not merely naval. A voyage to the Pacific was a voyage to an ocean that had been criss-crossed repeatedly for two centuries—in certain directions only, and within certain limits. For certain persons it had always been the abode of an illimitable hope. As the eighteenth century moved on the hope was not less; the age of enlightenment had its own romance. But the light that was growing was a clear one, dry, wide. It would dissipate the ancient hope. It would not destroy romance for the romantic. To say that in this decade of the 1760s science had taken control of geography and navigation would be absurd. None the less, we are at the beginning of an era in which a man gifted enough in practical ways could add the clarity of science to his own clarity of mind. For geography and navigation that meant a change of method and a change of hope.

[1] Kippis, 17, note: 'From the information of Philip Stephens, Esq: communicated by Sir Joseph Banks.' We can probably rely on this.

VI

Preparations

THE SHIP for the command of which Cook had been selected, early in April 1768, was the *Endeavour*. Just bought into the navy, she was not yet fitted out. More than one person later claimed the credit of selecting her: Dalrymple, springing to another conclusion, said he did so; Palliser, possibly the victim of defective memory, said that he and Cook did so. It is not likely that either claim could be justified.[1] The Admiralty took its first step as early as 5 March, when it ordered the Navy Board, the body concerned with supply and oversight of ships, 'to propose a proper vessel'. The Navy Board proposed the *Tryal* sloop, lately taken into dock at Deptford for repair; she would need sheathing with wood or copper as a protection against the ship-worm, and would not be ready before the end of May, but there was no suitable vessel at home that could be sooner fitted. A sloop in naval parlance was any small vessel with a small number of guns; the *Tryal*, built in 1749, carried fourteen. The Admiralty agreed, with direction that the shipwrights should work overtime if necessary; and then had the idea that the *Rose* might be considered, because the ship should sail early in the spring. The *Rose* was a 24-gun frigate of 1740, even then ready to receive men. This was 10 March. The Navy Board replied eleven days later: the *Rose* was 'the best there was at home in good condition', but she could not stow a sufficient quantity of provisions for the contemplated voyage; why not buy a cat-built vessel, which would be roomy enough? One of about 350 tons could be picked up in the Thames. Now a cat-built vessel, or cat, was exactly the east-coast collier, or her type, strongly built, of shallow draught, certainly without the lines or the speed of a frigate, as different from the *Dolphin* of Byron and Wallis as could

[1] Dalrymple, in the memoir he wrote of himself, said that the Royal Society appointed him to observe the Transit, and, 'the Admiralty approving of his being employed for this service, as well as for prosecuting discoveries in that quarter, Alexander Dalrymple accompanied the Surveyor of the Navy to examine two vessels that were thought fit for the purpose.'—*European Magazine*, 42, 325. This statement is not entirely accurate otherwise. Palliser's claim is reported by Kippis, 17. The relevant documents (Admiralty, Navy Board, Deptford Yard Officers) are calendared in *Journals*, I, 605–6.

be—and no doubt the sort of vessel Cook would have picked, if he had known anything about the sort of service he was to go on. Of that he certainly knew nothing. It was some years later, speaking of a ship for his second voyage, when he might, if he had been less of an honest man, have claimed some credit, that he wrote, 'of all that was said and offered to the Admiralty's consideration on this subject as far as has come to my knowledge, what in my opinion was most to the purpose was suggested by the Navy Board'.[1] The properties on which the Navy Board then laid stress were, briefly, strength and capacity. It does not seem that the Navy Board would have been less acute in 1768 when, precisely because of those properties (as Cook tells us) a particular vessel was chosen. If credit were due to him, he might, in all modesty, with the lightest of assertions, or even of implications, have said so. He does not. Who first had the heaven-sent idea—perhaps even some officer of the Deptford yard—is another of the things we do not know. Fortunately the Admiralty was receptive, and ordered the Board, informally, at once, leaving formality till later, to have two vessels surveyed which were then lying close to Shadwell docks, the *Valentine* and the *Earl of Pembroke*, both about the suggested size. The Deptford yard officers acted with zeal, surveyed even a third vessel, the *Ann and Elizabeth*; and on 27 March reported in favour of the second-named.

She was bought. 'The *Earl of Pembroke*,' ran the Yard report, 'Mr Thos. Milner, owner, was built at Whitby, her age three years nine months, square stern back, single bottom, full built and comes nearest to the tonnage mentioned in your warrant and not so old by fourteen months, is a promising ship for sailing of this kind and fit to stow provisions and stores as may be put on board her.'[2] She was not large: 106 feet long overall, 97 feet 7 inches on her lower deck, an inch short of her gun or upper deck; of extreme breadth 29 feet 3 inches; the length of her forecastle 18 feet 8 inches, only 4 feet 4 inches longer than her great cabin; her burthen in tons $368\frac{71}{94}$. Fully laden, she drew about 14 feet. She came from the yard of the redoubtable builders Messrs Fishburn: the scene of her building is now covered by different yards, those of British Railways. She was exactly the vessel the Navy Board had desiderated: her value, said the report, was £2307 5s 6d, of which £2212 15s 6d stood for her hull, and £94 10s for her masts and yards. The Board paid £2800.

Even an excellently built, comparatively new collier had to go into dock; and by the time the work on her was done and all hope of a

[1] Draft introduction to *Voyage towards the South Pole*, Dixson Library, MS. F1.
[2] Deptford Yard Officers to Navy Board, 27 March 1768, Adm 106/3315.

departure early in the spring long lost there may have been those
who looked back with some regret to the *Tryal* sloop. How was the
ship to be fitted?—the Navy Board enquired on 29 March, in reporting the purchase to the Admiralty. By what name was she to be
known? She was to be 'sheathed, filled, and fitted in all respects
proper' for the service she was to be engaged on, replied the Admiralty on 5 April, to receive six carriage guns of four pounds each
and eight swivel guns, and to be registered on the list of the Royal
Navy as a Bark, by the name of the *Endeavour*.[1] So do that famous
vessel, and that famous name, come into the history of exploration.
We have, in the extant records and plans—her sheer draught, her
deck plans, as well as journal references—as detailed evidence as we
can wish on the state of the ship and the alterations made to fit her
for her mission; there is no ship we can know more exactly than this
one. She was taken from 'Mr Bird's Ways' on the last day of March
and docked at Deptford on 2 April, and the carpenters began immediately the orders reached them. 'Sheathing and filling' entailed
the addition of another skin, outside her planks, of thinner boards,
over a lining of tarred felt; and to give further protection from the
'worm', the ruinous *Teredo navalis* of tropical seas, the sheathing was
filled with nails with large flat heads. Unlike the experimental
Dolphin, the *Endeavour* was not sheathed with copper, which presented
a problem in repair far from home and had led to corrosion of
ironwork. On 18 April the Yard officers were reporting that several
of the masts and yards were defective, reducing their value to £56
17s; in the end practically all these had to be renewed. Next day,
for 'quicker dispatch', they proposed that certain joiners' work
should be done 'by task'; on the 25th they announced that the ship
would be ready to receive men the following week. Then, though
matters had been pushed so hard for a month, came a severe interruption. An anonymous fragment of journal tells us something:
'The Ship had been bought into the Service and an order from the
Admiralty directed that she should be fitted for the intended Service
with the greatest dispatch—Every other business in the Dockyard
was laid aside till this order was fulfilled—But she was suffered to lay
in the Dock during three weeks afterwards of very hot weather and
receiv'd much damage from it—the Expedition seemed now to be
totally forgot; owing it was thought to the tumults and riots of the
Seamen in the River. . . .'[2] Tumults and riots there were in plenty in
that violent century, and from January to August 1768 there was a

---

[1] Admiralty to Navy Board, 5 April 1768, ADM/A/2606; entered Adm 2/237.
[2] ATL, Miscellaneous material relating to Cook's voyages.

spate of mass-meetings and petitions among not merely sailors, but coalheavers, the Spitalfields weavers and other sections of the depressed, mainly because of low and reduced wages in face of high prices for food. At the beginning of May seamen left their ships, vessels were unrigged and the quieter spirits among their crews carried off, and the Thames waterside was plastered with bills announcing that the men would not work till their wages were raised. We have no specific mention of the Deptford yards, but they can hardly have been unaffected, and it was not until 18 May that the Yard officers reported that the ship was out of dry dock—where no doubt her seams had opened in the heat—and into the Basin.

Meanwhile, at the beginning of April, as we have seen, the Admiralty had communicated with the Royal Society, Dalrymple had made his great refusal, the Society was looking round for a second observer —for it already had Mr Green, though it was not inclined to accept Mr Green's terms of £300 per annum—the Admiralty had decided to appoint Cook to the command, and for some weeks after 12 April Cook disappears from the records. Very possibly, in view of the length of the voyage that awaited him, he was on leave, and his Elizabeth could make the most of his presence at Mile End. He comes back at a council meeting of the Society on 5 May. The Society had been informed that he was to be the commander and would be a competent observer; no doubt Dr Bevis, if no one else, pointed out that he had already appeared in the *Transactions*; he was introduced by Captain John Campbell and agreed to accept the office in return for £120 a year for victualling himself and the other observer (an agreeable addition to naval rations) and whatever gratuity the Society should think fit. At the same meeting Mr Green, an astronomer by profession, agreed to accept a fee of 200 guineas for the voyage, and 100 guineas a year if it lasted more than two years.[1] At the meeting of 19 May Cook attended again, and agreed to his own gratuity of one hundred guineas.[2] The Society could do without Dalrymple. The day after that the *Dolphin*, Captain Samuel Wallis, anchored in the Downs at the end of her second circumnavigation. It was not long before the elements of her story got about.

Wallis, though a good commander, was not a gifted explorer, and for a large part of the time that he was in the South Seas he had the ill luck to suffer from sickness; but he had one piece of amazing good luck in discovery which would mark out his voyage forever, and was

[1] Royal Society Council Minutes, 5 May 1768.
[2] Royal Society Council Minutes, 19 May 1768.

of the utmost significance, not for that voyage alone, nor alone for the great voyages that succeeded it, but for the whole history of the western mind. That discovery came about half way through his voyage. He had sailed from England in August 1766 with two vessels besides the *Dolphin*: a sloop misnamed the *Swallow*, so aged, badly fitted out and painfully slow that her commander, Philip Carteret, could hardly believe her intended to make the whole voyage, and a store-ship which was in fact designed to return from the Strait of Magellan. She did so while the *Swallow* followed the *Dolphin* in a four months' passage of the Strait which was one of the longest and most agonising on record. At the western entrance, as difficult weather blew up, they parted company—the *Dolphin* into the ocean, the *Swallow* forced back into the Strait. They did not meet again. Wallis's instructions were to look for the continent west of Cape Horn, where he might pick up its coast in longitude 100° or 120° W; having found it, he might return round the Horn, or if driven too far north, by way of the East Indies. If he had not found it, he was to search north-west to latitude 20° S, and then refit in China or the East Indies for his homeward passage. The writers of instructions were all too hopeful of making a westing from the Horn or the Strait, and by the time Wallis, driven north-west from the start, crossed the hundredth meridian he was at about latitude 38°. Early June brought him into the Tuamotus, slightly north of 20°, a succession of atolls and islets he named with proper feeling after the royal dukes—until, on the 18th of the month, he came to an island such as dreams and enchantments are made of, real land though it was: an island of long beaches and lofty mountains, romantic in the pure ocean air, of noble trees and deep valleys, of bright falling waters. Man in his cool dwellings there was not vile—after one skirmish with a large canoe fleet in the bay where the *Dolphin* anchored—nor woman neither; welcoming and tender were the brown beautiful girls, with tattooed thighs and chaplets of sweet-smelling flowers, though a little mercenary it is true—so that the ship almost fell to pieces as ardent spirits in her company wrenched out the nails that were the price of love. There was a Queen, one Oborea, all dignity, tall and strong, who lifted the ailing Wallis like a child over bad places in the road, yet wept when he announced his departure. Grief indeed was then general. There was abundance of food produced in a delightful climate; the climate itself almost made sick sailors well. This spot it was that Wallis called King George the Third's Island, annexing it to the dominions of that monarch, this bay of his anchorage Port Royal Bay. It was the island of Tahiti, famous name, the heart of

Polynesia: on the day that Wallis discovered it the knell of Polynesia began to sound.

Five weeks later he departed westward. He picked up other islets in no way comparable to his great discovery, including the two northernmost of the Tongan archipelago, whence he changed course north-west, to refresh again at Tinian, one of the Marianas; he sailed round north of the Philippines, south to Batavia, refitted at the Cape, and brought home his news. Not merely did that news include the announcement of King George's Island, but also an exact position for it, astronomically ascertained at Port Royal Bay by John Harrison, the purser of the *Dolphin*—latitude 17° 30′ S, longitude 150° W. This unusual purser had arrived at the longitude by— to use his captain's words—'taking the Distance of the Sun from the Moon and Working it according to Dr Masculines Method which we did not understand.'[1] The position was almost in the centre of the area prescribed by Maskelyne as the most favourable for observations of the Transit of Venus south of the line; and, as a place of observation, it would not have to be rediscovered before it could be utilised, as the Marquesas or the islands of Rotterdam or Amsterdam would have to be. There was another piece of news brought by Wallis, not bruited abroad, and of less interest at that moment to the Royal Society, though it would have electrified Dalrymple—and perhaps, at that moment, have driven him almost mad with frustration. On the day Wallis had turned in to the actual Tahiti, some at least of his men were sure they saw to the south at sunset the mountain tops of the southern continent, 'often talkd of, but neaver before seen by any Europeans.'[2] Perennial and brilliant visions!—those sunset continents on the vast Pacific horizon. But, though the Royal Society's interest was in worlds beyond this one, there were people besides Dalrymple who grasped at sailors' stories. In the journal kept by the *Dolphin*'s master's mate some person from whom the news could not be kept—perhaps Lord Egmont himself?—scribbled a note on Wallis's discoveries, not only those mentioned in this journal, 'but others 20 leagues to the south of Georges Island, which are hitherto kept secret. . . . But Capt Wallis and his First Lieutenant being both exceedingly ill when at George's Island, in an unknown part of the world, at this immense distance from any possible assistance, & having only one single ship, it was too hazardous under these circumstances, to coast the Continent (which they had then actually in view) and afterwards thought most prudent on their return, not to

[1] ATL, note by Wallis in a copy of his journal, 20 August 1766.
[2] George Robertson, *The Discovery of Tahiti* (London, 1948), 135.

take notice that they had ever seen it at all.'[1] The Admiralty, not with quite such faith, also took note; for obviously a voyage to the South Sea could have more than one purpose. However that might be, when the Royal Society made known its desire to have the forthcoming expedition go to Tahiti there could hardly be a desire contrary: there lay the land.

That was one necessary decision. There were earlier ones, as we have seen, on the command and naming of the ship, and her furnishing with stores and provisions (it is fairly clear that the Admiralty was thinking of a two years' voyage). The command: there was still a point to settle. Cook was to command, and in nautical parlance he would be the captain, but the captain of a ship might not necessarily be a captain in a navy list. This one was a master, taken only for the time being—so it seems—from the Newfoundland survey, and it may be that the Lords had no intention initially of giving him a higher rank; for a commission instead of a warrant might simply, on a long view, limit his usefulness. Why commission a man who was so exceedingly useful as a master, and one who—be it added—might very well lose and not gain income by the change? This seems to be the deduction from the remark that 'It was once proposed that C. Cook should only have a Mate as the second in Command, with 35 Seamen',[2] which would even then have been about twice the complement of the ship as a North Sea collier. It was Mr Cook who waited on the Council of the Royal Society on 5 May. Discussion went on, raising the complement to seventy, which included forty able seamen—the Lords no doubt contemplated a considerable amount of disease and death—though no marines. Either for this reason of for some other it was decided to elevate the commander's rank: on 25 May it was 'Resolved that Mʳ James Cook 2ᵈ be appointed first Lieutenant of the Endeavour Bark.'[3] He had caught up with Mr James Cook the first, lieutenant of the *Gosport*; that namesake, however meritorious an officer, becomes merely a curiosity for a footnote. The new lieutenant was commissioned the same day, 'required and directed to use the utmost dispatch in getting' the ship 'ready for the sea accordingly, and then falling down to Gallions Reach take in her guns and gunners' stores at that place and proceed to the Nore for further orders.' He went to work with energy; orders and warrants and his own communications followed thick and fast. Another officer was immediately appointed, Mr Zachary

[1] B.M., Add. MS 47106, quoted by Carrington in Robertson, xxvii–xxviii.
[2] *Journals*, I, cxxvi.
[3] Admiralty Minutes, 25 May 1768, Adm 3/76.

Hicks, promoted second lieutenant from acting lieutenant in a sloop, and no doubt had his hands full too.

The supplies kept pouring into that capacious hold:[1] twelve months of all species of provisions at whole allowance except beer, of which one month, and brandy in lieu of the remainder, for seventy men, for foreign service, water, eight tons of iron ballast, coals to be used as ballast, more iron ballast, additional stores and provisions as she could stow, mustard seed, a green baize floor cloth for the great cabin (Cook's request: 'if there be not painted Canvas in store', agreed the Navy Board), four additional swivel guns, additional salt, one hundred gallons of arrack additional to the spirits already supplied, puncheons, hogsheads and barrels for wine and water, twenty cork jackets, stationery, 'a Machine for sweetening foul water', surgeon's necessaries. The admiralty and its sub-departments —Navy Board, Sick and Hurt Board, Victualling Board—were in an experimenting mood with provisions, and this sort of voyage gave an excellent opportunity to experiment. We are not to think that the original impulse to reform came from Cook. Scurvy, the great enemy, was known to be a dietary disease, and sailors enough knew pragmatically that fresh food would prevent or cure it. Yet how on some long passage without sight of land, how on some tedious blockade, with a ship's company half-starved at the very beginning to provide or simulate the fresh food that meant salvation simply because it broke the awful succession of salt beef, salt pork, salt fat, of 'bread'— the hard-baked biscuit that yet was penetrable to every variety of noxious insect that haunted a ship—of dried pease, oil and vinegar? True, there were raisins and sugar, to go with the suet into the duff. Some hope was now being entertained of 'sour krout', the German sauerkraut, a preparation of fermented cabbage: a supply of two pounds per week for seventy men for twelve months was supplied, and Cook was to report to the Victualling Board on his return 'how he had found the same to answer.' He was given 1000 lb of 'portable soup', cakes of a sort of glue or meat essence, that could be boiled with pease or oatmeal on the three banyan or meatless days of the week Mondays, Wednesdays and Fridays, and would not anyhow spoil whatever nutritive value the pease and oatmeal had. There were robs of lemons and oranges, syrups preserved with sugar, the invaluable juices being deprived of their virtues in the boiling down process. There was a wort or decoction of malt held by the Irish physician Dr David MacBride to be 'of great benefit to seamen in scorbutic and other putrid diseases' (it is the Admiralty secretary writing), and

[1] The relevant documents are calendared in *Journals*, I, 610 ff.

that was to be tried. Copies of Dr MacBride's *Experimental Essays*, which had reached a second edition in the previous year, were supplied also. Saloup, that popular drink, was thought worth taking. There was going to be a good deal of reporting to be done. Wallis's surgeon, John Hutchinson, was reporting already on some of these things. It is odd that the Admiralty could ignore so completely the work on citrus fruits of Dr James Lind, whose *Treatise of the Scurvy* of 1753 might have saved the lives of innumerable sailors. There is no indication that Cook ever heard of it. This again is odd, because Palliser, advised by Lind, had had striking experience of the value of lemon juice on a voyage to India and back in 1748, and a rob was no substitute for the fresh fruit. There was, of course, the difficulty of keeping the fruit in a fresh state.

Cook himself with particularity applied for scientific instruments; and as he wrote out his applications at the Admiralty Office and received immediate replies from the secretary it appears that he was perfecting his technique of explaining on the spot what he wanted and losing no time over paper pleas. 'In order to make surveys of such parts as His Majesty's Bark the Endeavour under my command may touch at, it will be necessary to be provided with a set of Instruments for that purpose.'[1] He is told by Stephens to buy them and send in the account, as once before. He wants a 'Theodolite compleate', a plane table, a brass scale two feet long, a double concave glass, a 'Glass for traceing Plans from the light', a parallel ruler, 'A Pair of Proportional Compass's', stationery and colours. They cost £48 10s.[2] Then there is a compass of a different sort: 'Admiralty Office. Doctor Knight hath got an Azimuth Compass of an Improve'd construction which may prove to be of more general use than the old ones; please to move my Lords Commissioners of the Admiralty to order the Endeavour Bark under my command to be supplyed with it.'[3] And a micrometer: 'Admiralty Office. The Navy Board have been please'd to supply His Majesty's Bark the Endeavour under my command with the Reflecting Telescope that was on board the Grenville Schooner for makeing Astronomical Observations at Newfoundland; in order to make it of more general use I have got made a Micrometer for measuring the apparent magnitudes of the Heavenly Bodies, which will be of great service in the observation of the Transit [of] Vinus, the Bill for which I here inclose. . . .'[4]

[1] Cook to Stephens, 8 July 1768, Adm 1/1609.
[2] ibid., and Cook to Stephens, 20 July 1768, Adm 1/1609; Admiralty to Navy Board, 21 July 1768, ADM/A/2609, Adm 2/238.
[3] Cook to Stephens, 25 July 1768, Adm 1/1609.
[4] Cook to Stephens, 27 July 1768, Adm 1/1609. The micrometer cost £13 18s.— Admiralty Minutes, 27 July, Adm 3/76.

The Lords made no difficulty. It was now almost the end of July, and the Royal Society had long arranged for the instruments that it was providing: '2 Reflecting Telescopes of two feet focus, with a Dollond's micrometer to one of them and moveable wires for the other, now at Mr Shorts, 2 Wooden Stands for the Telescopes with polar axes, suited to the Equator. . . . An astronomical quadrant of one foot radius, made by Mr Bird. . . . An astronomical Clock and alarum Clock, now at the Royal Observatory. A Brass Hadley's sextant, bespoke by Mr Maskelyne of Mr Ramsden. A Barometer bespoke of Mr Ramsden. 1 Journeyman Clock, bespoke of Mr Shelton. 2 Thermometers of Mr Bird. 1 Stand for Bird's Quadrant, now at the house of the Society. A Dipping Needle, bespoke of Mr Ramsden.'[1] Dollond Short, Bird, Shelton, Ramsden—famous names; they are the great instrument-makers. The Astronomer Royal lent the Society an admirable watch of his own. A portable wood and canvas observatory, designed by Smeaton of the Eddystone lighthouse, was constructed, overseen by Maskelyne and Cook. In the products of technology the expedition could not have been better equipped.

Then there was the miscellany of trifles for winning the friendship of islanders and carrying on trade with them—nails, mirrors, fishhooks, hatchets, red and blue beads, scissors, even a few dolls.

An expedition is not merely a ship or technology or trade-goods, it is men. The men who served with Cook over the next ten or eleven years provide an interesting study in human nature and capacity, and some of those who joined the *Endeavour* were with him till the end. Officers naturally stand out with more prominence, though now and again a ray of light makes vivid, for good or ill, one of the able seamen or other inhabitants of the vessel whom casual fate in that century picked up and turned into circumnavigators. Of Zachary Hicks, commissioned as second lieutenant, it would be agreeable to know more. He was a Londoner, born at Stepney in 1739, and carried on board the seeds of tuberculosis—how acquired we do not know, but it was a plague to which seamen were not immune. He entered the navy at Ripon, which is some distance from Stepney, whether as a volunteer or a pressed man, and when, again we do not know—probably not pressed, as the records refer to him as a midshipman; he was in sloops as A.B., master's mate, and acting lieutenant from 1766 to 1768, and in March of the latter year was given a lieutenant's pay, two months before his appointment to the *Endeavour*

[1] Royal Society Council Minutes, 5 May 1768, Vol. V, 315–16.

on 26 May. It was an appointment which he held for precisely three years. At the age of 29 it seems that he was experienced and mature, a good sailor and officer, a man with a good eye when it came to discriminating between land and cloud-banks, one of forethought and independent judgment. He was one of those men who take responsibility without the chance to shine, the men who look after the ship; obviously thoroughly equal to his duties. What else might have happened to him one cannot guess; for he was doomed. When July was two-thirds past, the Admiralty concluded that another lieutenant would be an advantage, and appointed John Gore. He comes before us in the end much more clearly than does Hicks, because in the end we see and read more of him. Certainly neither was a ready writer. Gore was—probably—in his late thirties. He was American-born, had gone to sea in 1755 and served for five years as a midshipman in larger vessels than Hicks's sloops, in the Atlantic, the West Indies and the Mediterranean. He was a master's mate in the *Dolphin* under both Byron and Wallis, so that he knew already more about the Pacific and its islands than anybody else in the ship. Under Wallis he was one of the men who had taken over the chief responsibilities of the voyage, and he was indeed an excellent subordinate. He is a particular type of sailor—perhaps, if he were not an American, a particular type of Englishman; in eleven years more to be a captain through sheer force of survival, never an admiral; a man of commonsense, able practice, and ceaseless activity, without scientific learning, with some dogmatic fancies but no real imagination; a great sportsman who has gone after wild cattle on Tinian to provide fresh beef for the *Dolphin*, who will go after the wild duck in Tahiti, the kangaroo and the stingray in Australia; who is ready for any expedition into any country anywhere, of pleasure or of duty. A third man, quite different from these two, a lieutenant before the voyage was out, but for most of it indifferently A.B., midshipman or master's mate—the lines are indifferently drawn—was Charles Clerke. A farmer's son from Weathersfield in Essex, entering the navy in 1755 at the age of twelve, captain's servant and midshipman to be, he was now 25 and looking forward to a commission. A young fellow ripe for every sort of excitement, he was bound to be on the mizen-top of the *Bellona* when the mast was shot away in a celebrated action with the *Courageux* in 1761, bound to survive and crawl half-drowned up the chains. He too was in the *Dolphin* with Byron, but served in the West Indies during Wallis's voyage. He had enough mathematical ability to become a good scientific navigator, and was a good observer of natural phenomena. Brave as well as experienced, he was also, beneath a rattling exterior, a man with a profound sense of duty. What made him invaluable was his high spirits. Clerke was always cheerful, talkative, amusing, with some of the rollicking vices as well as the rollicking virtues; a generous spirit who made friends easily; tall, long-nosed, with an eye both roving and sparkling. He was with Cook on all the voyages; the development of his personality is remarkably interesting. The survival of a handful of his letters, in addition to his journals, gives one a certain sense of intimacy with him; it must be a difficult soul who, when all is over, does not feel some affection for him as well.

Other men came with Gore from the *Dolphin*, joining their new ship after only three or four weeks on shore—Robert Molyneux, Richard Pickersgill, Francis Wilkinson. They were young, nevertheless the first two, who had both been master's mates, were good hands at drawing a chart, and were to add something to the surveying strength of the *Endeavour*. Molyneux became master, Pickersgill and Wilkinson his mates. Molyneux undoubtedly had intelligence, though Cook was never to trust him completely; he was, like so many of his fellows, intemperate with drink, which was a defect in a master. Wilkinson was to keep an unusually articulate journal. Pickersgill was the most interesting of the three. Another Yorkshireman, not twenty when the voyage began, he ended it as master; a good observer, able and amiable, a natural romantic, a little oversensitive, a little given to the grandiose concept and the swelling word, yet a successful subordinate, he was to do good work for Cook. At some latter stage he also went down before intemperance; and then, taken away into independent command, was struck by disaster. The bottle played havoc with too many of these young men, and we have to remember again what century it was. William Brougham Monkhouse, the surgeon, was another, though here one may possibly overstate the addiction. A Cumberland man, not without professional merit, he had been surgeon in the *Niger* for some years from 1763, and thus had been on the Newfoundland station; he was literate and accurate in observation, and one regrets that only a small portion of his journal has survived. He had a conscientious surgeon's mate in William Perry, who was to earn Cook's high regard. Whether we shall regard midshipmen—the 'young gentlemen'—as officers is a moot point. They were petty officers, and in due course they would be able to take their lieutenant's examination, and under Cook they would get a very good training indeed. They would have to serve a good deal of their time as able seamen, if they were old enough. If not, they got to know the sea, like Isaac Manley, aged 12, son of a bencher of the Middle Temple, who appears first as the master's servant, is classed as a midshipman in February 1771, when vacancies exist; and long after his voyages with Cook becomes an admiral, and the last survivor of this voyage of the *Endeavour*. There are some more responsible and experienced young fellows, like Jonathan Monkhouse, the surgeon's brother; and Isaac Smith, Mrs Cook's cousin, aged 16, who had been for a season in the *Grenville*, and now is a 'very expert' help in surveying; and there are some rather odd young fellows as well.

There is not much that can be said collectively about the crew. It was a young crew: few of them had passed their thirtieth year, very few were as old as their captain. Few of them achieved any particular distinction, except of being black or parti-coloured, sheep; many got drunk, and stole liquor whenever they could; practically all went after women; a few tried to desert, more talked about deserting; some were rash, quarrelsome, disobedient or 'mutinuous'—that is, they swore at the master; some were flogged. Granting the custom of flogging, and the regulations of the navy, they were not flogged excessively. Cook would have no scenes in the *Endeavour* like those he had witnessed in Halifax harbour. We may regard it as a triumph of administration that in that overcrowded ship there were so few unpleasant scenes avoidable by any human agency. On the whole that crew was to win the captain's respect in most of the situations to which destiny had called them from their separate corners of England, Wales, Scotland and Ireland. There were two or three from farther afield, like James Maria Magra from New York, and Antonio Ponto from Venice, and John Dozey from 'the Brazils'. The British navy took what it could get; Cook, on this voyage, took what he was given. He did struggle over one matter: that was the ship's cook (there were other cooks: the captain had a cook, the lieutenants had a cook). 'Honble Gentlemen,' he expostulated to the Navy Board on 13 June, 'The man you have been pleased to appoint Cook of His Majestys Bark the Endeavour, is a lame infirm man, and incapable of doing his Duty without the assistance of others; and as he doth not seem to like his appointment, beg you will be pleased to appoint another.'[1] The Board, at once agreeable, appointed John Thompson. Cook wrote again three days later, having inspected the newcomer: 'as this man hath had the misfortune to loose his right hand, I am of opinion that he will be of little Service; and as I am very desirous of having no one on board but what is fully able to do their duty in their respective stations I hope the Board will not be displeased at my

[1] Cook to Navy Board, 13 June 1768, Adm 106/1163.

objecting to this man also, and at the same time to recommend Jn°
Pritchard to be appointed, who (tho' a Pensioner of the Chest at
Chatham) is a very able Man.'[1] This suggestion the Board would
not accept: there was no other ship for John Thompson. If the new
lieutenant had cared to go back in history, he might have found an
Admiralty order of 1704, calling on the Navy Board, in the future
appointment of cooks, 'to give the preference to such cripples and
maimed persons as are pensioners of the chest on Chatham';[2] but
his candidate was too able. John Thompson seems to have been
successful enough, or at least no worse than other cooks.

At the beginning of August, the Admiralty, which had started off
with a total complement of seventy, decided to raise it to 85, including a dozen marines—a sergeant, corporal, drummer, and nine
privates. This meant more provisions; wonder and admiration grow
at the infinite capacity of Messrs Fishburn's collier. Cook might have
felt disconcerted at this, particularly since it was only twelve days
since he had heard, officially, that he was to take a scientific party
with him, as well as Mr Green and his servant; if so, he made no
recorded sign. We may feel disconcerted ourselves, reading through
the ship's muster-books, to find rising out of the Pacific Ocean, as it
were, in April 1769 a James Cook who becomes Hicks's servant, and
then in September 1769 a Nathaniel Cook, A.B. In May 1771 the
first becomes the servant of Clerke, on his promotion to third lieutenant, and the second becomes the carpenter's servant. Who were
these two persons thus listed, without details of origin or age? They
were the sons of Lieutenant James Cook, aged six years and five
years respectively, and were then comfortably at home at 7 Assembly
Row. Their names were on the ship's books 'earning time', so that,
if they should enter the navy, they could sit their lieutenant's
examination in the shortest period practically possible, irrespective
of the letter of the regulations. This was chicanery, but accepted
naval custom. It is interesting to see Cook ambitious for his family,
interesting to see that his ambitions for his young sons were centred
on the navy, and that he wanted them to be lieutenants before they
were forty; interesting that for their advancement he was willing to
follow the example of post-captains and admirals innumerable, in
flagrant defiance of an act of parliament which threatened the
penalty of permanent dismissal from the service.[3]

[1] Cook to Navy Board, 16 June 1768, Adm 106/1163; Navy Board to Cook, 17 June,
CLB.
[2] Michael Lewis, *England's Sea-Officers*, (London, 1948), 239.
[3] The Act was 22 Geo. II. Section XXXI reads, 'Every Officer, or other Person in the
Fleet, who shall knowingly make or sign a false Muster or Muster-book, or who shall

One comes to the civilians, and first to Mr Green, who has already appeared before the Council of the Royal Society, and may be regarded for practical purposes as a civilian.[1] He was a Yorkshire farmer's son, born in 1735, who had become an accomplished astronomer; he had been assistant to two astronomers royal at Greenwich, Bradley and Bliss, and in Bliss's incumbency had done most of the work; in 1763 he made the voyage to Barbados with Maskelyne to test John Harrison's chronometer. As a reward for his services then he had, on the recommendation of the Board of Longitude, been appointed a purser in the navy, in the fifth-rate *Aurora*. A purser was not incited, but was expected, to do better for himself than his pay would indicate. At Barbados he had fallen out with Maskelyne, who nevertheless had a high enough professional opinion of him to insist on his appointment by the Royal Society, and he was now granted leave of absence from his ship, 'upon his finding a sufficient Deputy'—which he must have done. He was indefatigable in making and calculating from observations, because his functions went far beyond the stated one of observing the Transit, and he was a good teacher of others. He, alas, was another of those whose life was inadequately regulated, a matter which was to be remarked upon later. He, and Cook as observer, might be regarded as the ship's most important passengers—if we can separate Cook the Royal Society's man from Cook the captain. But the Royal Society was willing to do more for philosophical pursuits, at no expense to itself, than its duty to the Transit implied; and the consequence for Cook and for the *Endeavour* was Mr Joseph Banks. This implied a great deal.

Mr Joseph Banks is the young gentleman we have already encountered so briefly in the harbour of St John's, two years before, at the end of his summer's holiday, in the *Niger*, about to attend the Governor's ball. He is now twenty-five years old, since 1766 a Fellow of the Royal Society, and bent on greater things in the way of travel. He is one of those fortunate beings, an eighteenth-century English landed proprietor, with an ample income that would continue to rise, partly, and largely, through his own good management of his estates, partly through family bequests. The issue of some generations of Lincolnshire land-owners, seated at Revesby Abbey

---

command, counsel or procure the Making or Signing thereof, or who shall aid or abet any other Person in the Making or Signing thereof, shall, upon Proof of any such Offence being made before a Court-martial, be cashiered, and rendered incapable of further Employment in His Majesty's Naval Service.'

[1] William Wales, the astronomer of the second voyage, contributed a short memoir of Green, his brother-in-law, to Kippis, 176–8, note.

near Boston, men of a fair level of intelligence and public spirit, he
had been educated both at Harrow and Eton, and then, almost, both
at Oxford and Cambridge—for, finding no instruction at Oxford
in the science of botany, he had made nothing of going over to
Cambridge, picking up a botanist there, and bringing him back to
lecture at Oxford. Joseph Banks's love at this time—indeed, always
one of his loves—was botany. He never became, he could never have
become, a scholar in the ordinary sense. He remained, in terms of the
eighteenth-century conventions, uneducated. A more intimate
acquaintance with the classics would merely have dragged him from
his own original passion, pursued as a child in the fields and lanes
outside school, nourished on Gerard's *Herbal*, extended to the other
phenomena of schoolboys' natural history, butterflies and beetles and
shells, extended with time to all the branches of natural history; and
his own original passion, as things turned out, was important for the
the science of his time. Not Homer, not Virgil or Ovid, but Linnaeus
was the god of his idolatry. A few semi-philosophical ideas he accumulated; but what he was really after was the detail of the natural
world. There was no limit to Banks's curiosity, within limits—if one
may put it in this way—laid down by himself. His father died when
he was eighteen. He was virtually his own master from that time. As
soon as he came of age he bought a house in London. His good looks,
his charm, his enthusiasm, his interests, brought him excellent
friends, from John Montagu, fourth Earl of Sandwich, his senior by
twenty-five years, who had been First Lord of the Admiralty and
was to be so again, to a wide circle of natural historians and antiquarians. It was no wonder that, instead of travelling in Europe and
inspecting the ruins of Rome, he should elect to travel to Newfoundland with his friend Lieutenant Constantine John Phipps and inspect
the works of Nature there, collecting plants and insects instead of
dubious Old Masters and heavily-restored marbles. It was no wonder
that, after his return and two or three tours of curiosity about
England, he should think of a journey to Sweden to salute the great
Linnaeus, even of one to Lapland in Linnaeus's footsteps. It was no
wonder that, in a stroke of something like genius, he should discard
this idea in favour of shipping himself in the *Endeavour*. When he first
put the notion to the Royal Society is uncertain, but quite early in
April, even before the decision to appoint Cook had been made
public, a friend seemed to think that his influence might be useful
in the appointment of a midshipman.[1] A great deal seemed to be

---

[1] Thomas Pennant to Banks, 10 April 1768; Warren R. Dawson, *The Banks Letters*
(London, 1958), 662.

assumed about Mr Banks, not least by Mr Banks himself. When, one asks in vain, was Cook first apprised of the plan? It was not put formally to the Admiralty till 9 June, by which time Banks had certainly made all his arrangements—except one. The Society's secretary, announcing the appointment of Green and Cook as observers, supplemented his letter thus:

> Joseph Banks Esqr Fellow of this Society, a Gentleman of large fortune, who is well versed in natural history, being Desirous of undertaking the same voyage the Council very earnestly request their Lordships, that in regard to Mr Banks's great personal merit, and for the Advancement of useful knowledge, He also, together with his Suite, being seven persons more, that is, eight persons in all, together with their baggage, be received on board of the Ship, under the Command of Captain Cook.[1]

The Admiralty may have taken a little time to digest this, and perhaps consider it with Cook; for not till 22 July was Cook formally ordered to receive Green and his servant and baggage, and Banks and all his people and baggage, 'bearing them as supernumeries for Victuals only, and Victualling them as the Barks Company during their Continuance on Board'.[2] However great Mr Banks's personal merit, their Lordships had no thought of preferential treatment. It meant some rearrangement of cabin space, and lieutenants and warrant officers can not have been immediately pleased (the date was that on which the Admiralty announced the addition of a third lieutenant, with servant). Then there was the decision to add the marines. And then Banks wanted someone else, and got him. He got Dr Solander.

Everybody liked Solander—Dr by courtesy, not right; how could a learned Swede not be Dr? Ten years older than Banks, five years younger than Cook, Daniel Carl (the second name assumed to distinguish him from another Daniel) Solander was one of the favourite pupils of Linnaeus, and when the London natural historians urged the master to send some one to England to spread the Linnaean gospel, he was the chosen man. He arrived in 1760. Acute and encyclopaedic in his knowledge, yet an ever-diligent and unostentatious student, modest, cheerful and friendly to all his acquaintance, his popularity among the scientists and the collectors was great. He was a sort of touchstone. He liked London. He refused to go to the St Petersburg Academy of Sciences as its professor of botany. London was charmed. In 1763 he became an assistant at the British Museum, organising the vast Sloane collection, and

---

[1] Royal Society Council Minutes, 9 June 1768.
[2] Stephens to Cook, 22 July 1768, Adm 2/94, CLB.

in 1764 a Fellow of the Royal Society. It was about this time that Banks, just down from Oxford, got to know the brilliant and amiable man, and was introduced by him to a wider scientific world. Solander, not exactly the type of which heroes are made, had not chosen the role of 'apostle', as Linnaeus called the young men his students at Uppsala who went forth to study and collect in the far and perilous places of the world, the victims of pirates and plague, hunger, thirst and poverty, who every so often died on their travels—the young men in the Americas, the Atlas mountains and Palestine, the East Indies, China and Japan: unless it be apostleship to survey the Duchess of Portland's numerous cabinets and work at the British Museum. Nevertheless the role claimed him. This was the arrangement, if one's reading of the evidence is correct, that Banks had not made. It happened at dinner at the house of Lady Anne Monson, the daughter of an earl, and a hostess of standing. The conversation ran on about the intended voyage, Banks no doubt enlarging upon his own intentions; Solander took fire, leapt to his feet and proposed himself as a travelling companion. Banks was enraptured. Next day he talked the Admiralty into acquiescence. Solander was the only person of note who did not take a servant.

Banks, as we have seen, took a 'suite': two artists, a secretary, four servants, and—for he was an Englishman—two dogs. The first of the artists was Sydney Parkinson, the young son of a Quaker brewer of Edinburgh. Apprenticed to a woollen-draper after his father's death, his talent for drawing would out, and he came to London, where his flowers and fruits attracted the attention of the natural historians. Banks employed him, had been going to take him on his abandoned northern journey, and found him an indispensable choice for this larger one, in which botanical investigation, he intended, would bulk so greatly. Parkinson was indeed to find much to do. His talent did not stop with the pencil or the brush; he was intelligent, highly observant, sensible, sensitive, serious, with ever-expanding interests in the new, so un-Quaker world where his life was now cast; a slight dark wisp of a young man, long-nosed, with long thin fingers, a rather prim little mouth; a young man of the highest moral standards. His fellow-draughtsman, Alexander Buchan, comes alive much less; pleasant, with some talent, but also an epileptic, whether Banks knew that at the outset of the voyage or not, and epileptic fits were no sort of equipment for a travelling artist. He was engaged to draw the figure and 'landskip'. The secretary was Herman Diedrich Spöring, another Swede, in between Solander and Cook in age, the son of a professor of medicine at the University of Åbo in Finland; after taking a course in surgery at Stockholm he had sought his fortune in London. He had not found it; he made his living for eleven years as a watchmaker, and was then employed for two years by Solander as a clerk.[1] Here no doubt came first the link with Banks. Spöring had probably a leaning to natural history, like so many other men trained in medicine; his watch-maker's fingers were potentially very useful, while both his eye and his fingers made him a very useful supplementary draughtsman; 'a grave thinking man', as Banks called him, he was no mere copyist. The four servants were two countrymen from Banks's Lincolnshire estate, James Roberts and Peter Briscoe, and two negroes, Thomas Richmond and George Dorlton. And Banks's baggage was no trifle. What it was, in part, we get some indication of in a well-known, though not totally accurate, letter from the natural historian John Ellis to his admired correspondent Linnaeus. How delightful was scientific gossip! Banks and Solander, he writes, would collect all the natural curiosities of 'the new discovered country in the South Sea', and after the completion of the observations of the Transit,

they are to proceed under the direction of Mr. Banks, by order of the Lords of the Admiralty, on further discoveries of the great Southern continent, and from thence proceed to England by the Cape of good Hope. . . . No people ever went to sea better fitted out for the purpose of Natural History, nor more elegantly. They have got a fine library of Natural History; they have all sorts of machines for catching and preserving insects; all kinds of nets, trawls, drags and hooks for coral fishing; they have even a curious contrivance of a telescope, by which, put into the water, you can see the bottom to a great depth, where it is clear. They have many cases of bottles with ground stoppers, of several sizes, to preserve animals in spirits. They have the several sorts of salt to surround the seeds; and wax, both beeswax and that of the *Myrica*; besides there are many people whose sole business it is to attend them for this very purpose. They have two painters and draughtsmen, several volunteers who have a tolerable notion of Natural History; in short Solander assured me this expedition would cost Mr. Banks ten thousand pounds.[2]

'All this', concluded Ellis, 'is owing to you and your writings.' That may be true. It is fairly clear that Banks, however lavish he was in expenditure over equipment—and one could easily add to the list that Ellis gives—could not have spent £10,000. It is quite clear that neither the Admiralty nor Cook had the idea that any part of

---

[1] Solander to Linnaeus, 1 December 1768, in Arvid H. J. Uggla, 'Daniel Solander och Linné', in *Svenska Linné-Sallskapets Arrskrift*, xxxvii–xxxviii (1954–5), 64.
[2] Ellis to Linnaeus, 19 August 1768; J. E. Smith, *A Selection of the Correspondence of Linnaeus, and other Naturalists* (London, 1821), I, 230–2.

the voyage should be conducted under the direction of Mr Banks. It is interesting to note however that some part, at least, of the scientific world was already impressed with an elevated opinion of the part that Banks was supposed to play in it. Perhaps because of this was he able to take with him something he could not buy, an addition to the useful small library of voyages and travels with which the ship was already endowed. This was a copy of Dalrymple's pamphlet of 1767, with its map of Pacific discoveries pricked with explorers' tracks, presented to him by the author; and perhaps Dalrymple felt able to give it to him as one fellow of the Royal Society to another, when Cook, as a recipient, would have been altogether ruled out. It is obvious that a great deal of the happiness of the voyage would depend on the relations that developed between the civilians thus embarked and the sailors whom they dispossessed of their quarters— and, in particular, between the gentleman of large fortune and large assumption of his rights, and Cook, the master so recently given his first commission, in social standing so remarkably below this new and surprising shipmate. It would have occurred to no seaman that the presence of Banks could be a positive advantage.

There was also among the ship's company a goat. This animal had already contributed to Pacific history. Sailing in the *Dolphin* with Wallis, on the first morning at Tahiti she had cleared the deck of all visitors by butting one of them unexpectedly on the behind. She had supplied milk for the officers, and this was to be her function again.

On 30 July the Lords of the Admiralty signed Cook's instructions.[1] They were denoted secret. They were in two parts. The first part pertained to the passage to King George's Island and the observation of the Transit. Cook, then in Gallions Reach, was to put in at Plymouth, where his men were to be paid two months' wages in advance. After sailing he was to call first at Madeira, to take in wine; having done so, he was to 'proceed round Cape Horn to Port Royal Harbour in King Georges Island', touching if he thought necessary on the coast of Brazil or at Port Egmont, the British settlement in the Falklands, for water and refreshments. The plan to go round the Horn, no doubt, was the result of the fearful passage of the Strait of Magellan that Wallis had had, though the previous naval expedition

---

[1] Cook's original copy of his instructions has disappeared. They were regarded as lost until the 1920's when they were found in the Public Record Office, Adm 2/1332, with other 'secret' instructions of the period. They were first printed in the Navy Records Society's *Naval Miscellany*, III (1928), 343–50. Another copy was found in CLB. In the *Journals* they will be found in I, cclxxix–cclxxxiv.

to venture the Horn, Anson's, had been shattered in the process: what knowledge there was of the winds was reflected in the injunction to stand well to the southward (Anson's advice),[1] in order to make a good westing, but to fall into the parallel of the island at least 120 leagues to the eastward of it. The ship would arrive at Tahiti a month or six weeks before the critical date, 3 June, to allow of proper preparations. Cook received copies of the *Dolphin* surveys, plans and 'views'; and he was to record all the additional things of the sort he could. He was 'to endeavour by all proper means to cultivate a friendship with the Natives, presenting them such Trifles as may be acceptable to them, exchanging with them for Provisions (of which there is great Plenty) such of the Merchandize you have been directed to Provide, as they may value, and shewing them every kind of Civility and regard. But as Captn Wallis has represented the Island to be very populous, and the Natives (as well there as at the other Islands which he visited) to be rather treacherous than otherwise you are to be Cautious not to let yourself be surprized by them, but to be Constantly on your guard against any accident.' If he was not able to make a landing, he was to find some other place for the observation within the limits of latitude and longitude laid down by the Royal Society. 'When this Service is perform'd you are to put to Sea without Loss of Time, and carry into execution the Additional Instructions contained in the inclosed Sealed Packet.'

These additional instructions were devoted mainly to the Southern Continent.

Whereas the making Discoverys of Countries hitherto unknown, and the Attaining a Knowledge of distant Parts which though formerly discover'd have yet been but imperfectly explored, will redound greatly to the Honour of this Nation as a Maritime Power, as well as to the Dignity of the Crown of Great Britain, and may tend greatly to the advancement of the Trade and Navigation thereof; and Whereas there is reason to imagine that a Continent or Land of great extent, may be found to the Southward of the Tract lately made by Captn Wallis in His Majesty's Ship the Dolphin (of which you will herewith receive a Copy) or of the Tract of any former Navigators in Pursuits of the like kind. . . . [on leaving Tahiti] You are to proceed to the southward in order to make discovery of the Continent abovementioned until you arrive in the Latitude of 40°, unless you sooner fall in with it. But not having discover'd it or any evident signs of it in that Run, you are to proceed in search of it to the Westward between the Latitude before mentioned and the Latitude of 35° until you discover it,

---

[1] Chapter IX of Anson's *Voyage* is devoted to 'Observations and directions for facilitating the passage of our future Cruisers round Cape Horn'. By standing a good distance south, argued Anson, 'in all probability the violence of the currents will be hereby avoided, and the weather will prove less tempestuous and uncertain'.

or fall in with the Eastern side of the Land discover'd by Tasman and now called New Zeland.

These, it may be remarked, are excellent instructions, drafted by someone—whoever it was—who knew the extent of geographical conjecture. If the continent was where it was said to be, this course would infallibly reveal it; and to sail south from Tahiti (if there was anything in the *Dolphin*'s view of the cloud banks) was a much more economical procedure than to try to sail west from Cape Horn. Then, as a second-best, New Zealand anyhow must exist—a distant part which though formerly discovered had yet been but imperfectly explored: all being well it could hardly elude the search. If he should discover the continent, then Cook was to explore as much of the coast as he could, and bring back all possible observations, charts, views and hydrographic details—a list almost as inclusive as if he were setting out on a season's work in Newfoundland. That was not all: the Lords wished to know about the nature of the soil and its products, beasts, birds, fishes and minerals; they wanted seeds of trees, fruits and grains, and an account of the native inhabitants, if any, and friendship, alliance and trade with them; the discoverer was 'with the Consent of the Natives to take possession of Convenient Situations in the Country in the Name of the King of Great Britain; or, if you find the Country uninhabited take Possession for His Majesty by setting up Proper Marks and Inscriptions, as first discoverers and possessors.'

'But if you should fail of discovering the Continent before mention'd, you will upon falling in with New Zealand'—New Zealand, we see, was taken for granted—ascertain its latitude and longitude; and—the demands are fewer than for the continent—'explore as much of the Coast as the Condition of the Bark, the health of her Crew, and the State of your Provisions will admit of'; reserving provisions sufficient to reach a known port where enough could be obtained for a passage to England, either round the Cape of Good Hope or Cape Horn, whichever should be judged the better. The situation of newly-discovered islands too should be ascertained, and those that seemed to be of consequence should be surveyed and taken possession of, though Cook was never to be diverted from the grand object, the discovery of the Southern Continent. In emergencies he was to consult with his officers. The closing paragraph dealt with reports to the Royal Society and the Admiralty, the confiscation of logs and journals of officers and petty officers, and the 'enjoyning them, and the whole Crew, not to divulge where they have been until they shall have Permission so to do.'

With all this was provided a note for Cook to display to any of his superior officers in the navy he might encounter, safeguarding the secrecy of the instructions, and ordering that he should be given any assistance he stood in need of.

These were the official instructions. It seems likely that the Lieutenant may have read with great attention also a paper of '*Hints* offered to the consideration of Captain Cooke, Mr Bankes, Doctor Solander, and the other Gentlemen who go upon the Expedition on Board the *Endeavour*', prepared by the Earl of Morton, President of the Royal Society, who was not to live to see the expedition return.[1] He was a humane man, in an age when humanity was becoming less uncommon, and no other humane man could read his hints without sympathy, even if they were not entirely original. But, remembering the general nature of the century, and the blood that was shed on the immediately preceding voyages, we cannot deem them pointless. Lord Morton reminded the gentlemen 'To exercise the utmost patience and forebearance with respect to the Natives of the several Lands where the Ship may touch. To check the petulance of the Sailors, and restrain the wanton use of Fire Arms. To have it still in view that sheding the blood of those people is a crime of the highest nature. . . . They are the natural, and in the strictest sense of the word, the legal possessors of the several Regions they inhabit. . . . They may naturally and justly attempt to repell intruders, whom they may apprehend are come to disturb them in the quiet possession of their country, whether that apprehension be well or ill founded.' Therefore every effort should be made to avoid violence: if it became inevitable, then 'the Natives when brought under should be treated with distinguished humanity, and made sensible that the Crew still considers them as Lords of the Country.' So much by way of illustration of the President's moral precepts, in the application of which he himself provided illustrations. He had another piece of advice to give in this sphere, or rather in the allied but even higher sphere of religion: 'Ships of so small a rate, not being furnished with Chaplains, it were to be wished that the Captain himself would sometimes perform that Office, and read prayers, especially on sundays, to the Crew; that they may be suitably impressed with a sense of their continual dependance upon their *Maker,* and all who are able on board, Passangers and others should be obliged to attend upon those occasions.'

---

[1] These 'Hints' are preserved in manuscript in the National Library of Australia, Canberra. They are printed in *Journals* I, 514–19. James Douglas, 14th Earl of Morton (1702–68) was president of the Royal Society from 1764 till his death, a few weeks after Cook's departure. He was active in the preparations for the voyage.

A large part of this paper, not unnaturally, was devoted to matters of scientific observation—first the Transit, then the Continent ('A Continent in the higher Latitudes, or in a rigorous climate, could be of little or no advantage to this nation'), then the people of any continent that was found, on whom Lord Morton suggested what would be, in modern terms, a comprehensive study in social anthropology; then its Animal, Vegetable and Mineral Systems. 'These open so vast a field,' as he justly remarked, 'that there is no room in this place for descending to particulars'. If we look ahead, as at this stage we may, we shall find that Lord Morton's *Hints*, 'hastily put together' as they were, no less than Cook's instructions from the Admiralty, provide an analysis of the journal and other reports which, after three years, he was to hand in to his astonished masters. We must allow for the non-appearance of a continent.

What discussion led up to the second part of Cook's instructions nowhere seems to be recorded. Nothing, however, could have been more logical. It would have been foolish not to take advantage of having a ship at Tahiti, if Wallis's men had actually sighted a continent—almost, as it seemed, from Tahiti. If they were deceived, but the shore of a continent came anything like as far north as Dalrymple made it, then a trip to 40° south—more than 20 degrees of latitude south of Tahiti—must infallibly pick it up. As to the secrecy of the instructions, they were probably only conventionally secret, an aid to fobbing off possible inconvenient enquiries from Spain. The details were not known; but everybody at all interested knew about the Transit of Venus. There was the usual amount of government mystery; the usual balloons were flown by the press—the *Gazetteer*, the *Public Advertiser*. 'It is said' that two sloops of war were to go in quest of the missing *Swallow*, to rendezvous at the newly discovered island, and from there to attempt the discovery of the Southern Continent. 'On the other hand, we are told that no further discoveries in the South Seas will be attempted for the present.'— 'We are informed' that the principal and almost sole national advantage of George's Land is, 'its Situation for exploring the Terra Incognita of the Southern Hemisphere.'—'The gentlemen, who are to sail in a few days for George's Land, the new discovered island in the Pacific ocean, with an intention to observe the Transit of Venus, are likewise, we are credibly informed, to attempt some new discoveries in that vast unknown tract, above the latitude 40.'[1]

[1] The quotations are from the *Gazetteer*, 13 June; ibid., and *Public Advertiser*, 20 June; *Gazetteer*, 18 August 1768.

There were wilder statements. There was Ellis's more particular communication to Linnaeus, which suggests that the Banks–Solander circle had talked things over. Everybody assumed that a voyage round the world, apart from anything else, was in prospect.

VII

Passage to Tahiti

AT HOME there were arrangements. Cook collected his final pay as master of the *Grenville*, and no doubt turned it over to Mrs Cook. Before he left he seems to have sold to Jefferys his rights in his published Newfoundland charts.[1] Elizabeth was to have during the years of absence the company of a cousin of her husband's, a Yorkshire girl called Frances Wardale, who was already living with them.[2] She probably needed company. She was close to the birth of her fourth child: a young Joseph was baptised on 5 September, and dead within the month. His father by then was well out in the Atlantic. On 30 July, the day the instructions were signed, the *Endeavour* had weighed from Gallions Reach for a leisurely passage to Plymouth. Thence on 14 August Cook sent for Banks and Solander, who were still enjoying their London farewells; and there after arriving they had a ten days' wait, while the shipwrights completed their cabins and the wrong winds blew. The ship's company were paid their two months' wages in advance, and warned not to expect any additional pay at the end of the voyage—despite which they were well satisfied, reports Cook, 'and express'd great chearfullness and readyness to prosecute the Voyage.'[3] On 25 August in the afternoon he got under sail and put to sea. Mr Banks, also, registered in his journal a proper degree of good temper: 'all', he said, were 'in excellent health and spirits perfectly prepard (in Mind at least) to undergo with Chearfullness any fatigues or dangers that may occur in our intended Voyage';[4] and the very next day, struggling against his sea-sickness, he began to note down his observations in natural history. The wind turned to hard westerly gales at the end of the month—Biscayan weather—which carried overboard a small boat of the boatswain's and—much worse—three or four dozen poultry. In another day or

---

[1] Skelton and Tooley, *Marine Surveys*, 8–9.
[2] We get this information from much later correspondence, John McAllister of Philadelphia, Frances Wardale's son, to J. L. Bennett, Mrs Cook's executor, 17 October 1851; National Library of Australia, NK 9528.
[3] *Journals* I, 3, and n. 2 on that page. [4] Banks, I, 153.

two the ship was off Cape Finisterre and Cook was entering in his journal his first longitudes of the voyage by lunar observation. One presumes, on no positive evidence, that they were his, but they may have been Green's, or arrived at with the assistance of Green. If we are to take literally what Green wrote to the Royal Society from Rio de Janeiro, the captain was new to the process: 'I thought it a little odd when I found that no person in the ship could either make an observation of the Moon or Calculate one when made.'[1] He must have familiarised himself with it as rapidly as possible: before reaching Rio he was to record observations, and longitudes reckoned from them, of the moon and the stars Arietis and Aldebaran as well as of the moon and the sun. On 12 September he was at Funchal, where Banks and Solander, guests of the British consul, plunged happily into botanical investigation, and entertainment at a local convent while Cook was busy over maritime matters. Some trifling misunderstanding appears to have occurred here with the authorities, so trifling that Cook does not mention it in his journal; it would not be worth mentioning at all had not a later critic magnified it into a bombardment of the Loo fort by the *Endeavour* and an English frigate, and accused the historian of the voyage of deliberate concealment.[2] In truth Cook had enough trouble without bombarding the Portuguese. In manœuvring the stream anchor Alexander Weir, a master's mate, carried overboard by the buoy-rope and down to the bottom with the anchor, was drowned; he was replaced by a man impressed from a New York sloop. A seaman and a marine who refused their allowance of fresh beef were deemed guilty of mutiny and given a dozen lashes each. This is interesting, both because it seems to show determination on Cook's part from the very beginning to insist on good health through diet—was anybody flogged on the American station for refusing fresh food?—and because, for the only time, he uses corporal punishment as a persuader. He was to think of better ways of making his point. Next day he issued to the whole ship's company twenty pounds of onions a man—for which he had

[1] Green to the Secretary, R.S., 28 November 1768.
[2] George Forster, *A Voyage round the World* (London, 1777), I, x. 'The same authority which blew off M. de Bougainville from the island of Juan Fernandez, could hush to silence the British guns, whilst the Endeavour cannonaded the Portuguese fort at Madeira.'—And footnote: 'The two circumstances here alluded to, are well known facts, though suppressed in the published narratives. M. de Bougainville spent some time at Juan Fernandez, and completely refreshed his crew there, though he wishes to have it understood, that contrary winds prevented his touching at that island. Captain Cook in the Endeavour, battered the Loo-fort at Madeira, in conjunction with an English frigate, thus resenting an affront which had been offered to the British flag.' Bougainville's course took him far west of Juan Fernandez, his first landfall after leaving the Strait of Magellan was Vahitahi, one of the Tuamotus.

later to make special explanation to the Victualling Board. The Board was not in the habit of paying for onions. Wine was a different matter: after all one came to Madeira for wine, and 3032 gallons were not too much. Green vegetables and a live bullock were legitimate. At midnight of 18 September the ship sailed again, and in the morning every man got ten pounds more onions.

The next five or six weeks were pleasant ones, an Atlantic passage in the north-east trade winds, with intervals of sunny calm in which Banks went out in a boat with gun or net, collecting birds and fish and floating shells, exclaiming at the beauty of Portuguese men-of-war, while Solander busily described, and Parkinson equally busily drew. There were glimpses of Tenerife and Boa Vista, in the Cape Verde islands. Cook early put the men to three watches instead of two—a humane idea officially inculcated, not always adopted—which gave them eight hours continuous rest off duty instead of four. Hooks and lines, pipes and tobacco, were distributed. Green worked at the education of his shipmates in scientific navigation: 'The Obs^ns of this Day are pretty good', he wrote in his journal not long after leaving Madeira, 'the Air being very Clear, but might have made more, and better, if *Proper Assistance* could have been had from the Young Gentlemen on board';[1] but he persevered, and in the end his perseverance, and Cook's, bore fruit. The big fish chased the flying-fish, the flying-fish came on board; sharks were caught. The men were kept busy at shipboard routine. The mates and midshipmen were exercised at small arms, and Green laughed at their gaucherie; when they were told to scrape and clean between decks, Pickersgill refused, and was sent before the mast. The captain was curious about the current, and had a boat out day after day observing it; was assiduous with his lunars; noted down regularly the variation of the compass. On 25 October came the crossing of the line, with due ceremony according to the 'Ancient Custom of the Sea'. Cook and the gentlemen, who had never passed the Equator, ransomed themselves with rum, as did a number of others more potentially victims (Banks even had to compound for his dogs), while about a score were plunged in the ocean on a sort of chair falling abruptly from the mainyard. The passage of the south-east trades was most agreeable, no untoward incident marred the approach to the coast of Brazil; a Portuguese fishing boat was spoken on 8 November and enough fresh fish bought for the whole ship's company; on 13 November she was in the harbour of Rio de Janeiro. Then came an episode which in the perspective of two hundred

[1] *Journals* I, 9, n. 2.

years has certain elements of comedy, but at the time infuriated Cook extremely.

He could have called at Port Egmont in the Falkland Islands and got water. He wanted more than water, however, he wanted live stock and all the fresh food he could get, he wanted to heel and clean his ship, and Rio de Janeiro had a good reputation with the English; Byron, indeed, had met with a flattering reception there. Were not England and Portugal allies of more than fifty years? Since Byron's visit Bougainville had been treated with incivility, which Cook did not know; if he had known, he would probably have reflected that Bougainville was French. His own expectations were rudely dashed. He sent Lieutenant Hicks to explain his presence to the Viceroy and to ask for a pilot. Hicks was detained until Cook should appear himself, instead of a pilot came a customs officer and a guard boat. When Cook went on shore he was informed that none but himself and his boat's crew would be allowed on shore, and certainly no passengers. When Banks and Solander dressed up in their best to call on the Viceroy they were turned back. When Cook went on shore again a guard was put in his boat and he was accompanied everywhere by an officer. He was to be allowed to buy provisions, but only through an agent appointed for the purpose. Rather than suffer such restrictions he refused to go on shore at all, and proceeded to argue with the Viceroy by way of 'memorials', which Don Antonio Rolim de Moura, Conde de Azambuja, was not behindhand in replying to. This argument had hardly begun when a boat's crew was flung into gaol for a night and the boat seized, because Hicks refused to have a guard in her. Naturally misunderstandings multiplied. Banks took a hand, both on his own account—he and Solander desperately wanted to get on shore—and in helping Cook with draft protestations. 'Tantalus coud never have been more tantalised', wrote Solander to Lord Morton.[1] There is a sort of magnificent futility about all this paper, with its exasperated and elaborate politeness, its invocations of his Britannick Majesty, 'the King my Master', and his most Faithful Majesty, and Science and Duty and Honour and Candour and Surprise; for its total effect was frustration on Cook's side, stubbornness on the Viceroy's. Not that there was total frustration: there was no want of supplies, which the surgeon was allowed to buy every day in the town; some of the necessary work on the ship could be carried out ashore, though there was great inconvenience in heeling her with most of her company (in-

[1] Banks, II, 311, 1 December 1768. Banks wrote very indignantly to Morton also on the same date, ibid., 313-15.

cluding the baffled gentlemen) on board; Solander managed to get ashore in the watering boat, masquerading as surgeon's mate on the errand of buying drugs, and seeing a good deal under the escort of a good-humoured sergeant; Banks, stealing once to land before dawn, was able to spend a whole day there till dark night, busily inspecting the town and collecting plants in the country; his servants were ashore collecting for him more than once. Parkinson got ashore. Some specimens too were picked up in the greenstuff brought out to the ship. But what might have been done!

The fact of the matter was that the Viceroy could not bring himself to believe that the *Endeavour* was a ship of the royal navy; certainly no ship ever looked less like the royal navy than the *Endeavour*. What was she then? He very much suspected she was a merchant-man, and if a merchantman, a smuggler. Naval practice could be imitated, commissions could be forged. British seamen had a leading reputation on the South American coast as smugglers; dishonest papers were a commonplace of their trade. The Viceroy was a soldier, not a sailor; his many years of distinguished frontier service had not brought him well acquainted with science. It was very well for Cook to tell him about the Transit of Venus, but was not that a cock-and-bull story, a patent blind? If it was true that, as Cook reported, 'he could form no other Idea of that Phenomenon (after I had explained it to him) than the North Star passing thro the South Pole', that did not brand him as a complete fool, administratively speaking. If the ship were indeed a naval one, and Mr Banks, with his talk about the use of scientific researches to mankind, were indeed a philosopher and not an engineer come to spy on the land, what was a philosopher doing in a naval vessel? Men were slipping ashore, that was certain, whether as smugglers or spies. 'Those That like it may Take a Trip in disguise', said Gore.[1] It may be that the Viceroy, when he referred to orders from his most Faithful Majesty which Cook could not believe were orders, did have orders that put the amiable Portuguese treatment of Byron out of date. If Cook were really a naval officer, it might be even worse than if he were a smuggler or a forger. The Portuguese were nervous, and their forts, over which Cook was casting a critical eye from the sea, had not been built without a purpose. In the eighteenth century Rio de Janeiro had been twice attacked; it had been sacked in 1711. In Portugal the reforming minister Pombal had become convinced that Portuguese prosperity had been drained away by English trade-privileges; and he had not received much sympathy from London

[1] *Journals* I, 27, n. 2.

when in 1764, fearing a dangerous international crisis, he had called for his ally's aid. Thereupon he turned away from England to France and Spain in the great campaign he was fighting to have the Jesuit order suppressed. He had expelled the Jesuits from Brazil in 1759. Now he persuaded himself of something extremely unlikely—that the Society of Jesus was strongly supported by England. This fantastic obsession drove him in June 1767 to declare in a despatch to the then Viceroy of Brazil that the Jesuits had promised to admit the English into the Portuguese colonies, and that therefore no British ship could desirably appear in Brazilian waters. Five months later the Conde de Azambuja became Viceroy, and he may have read the despatches. It may be significant that a Spanish packet-ship, coming in some time later than Cook, was subject to no restrictions; and that a Lieutenant Thomas Forster, an Englishman in the Portuguese service who tendered his good offices in the imbroglio, was cast into prison as a reward, though without formal charge. Yet the Viceroy was not entirely unfeeling; when the *Endeavour*'s longboat was carried away in an unusual storm of wind and rain, he lent help without question to reclaim her; and he must have turned a blind eye on a good deal of surreptitious invasion of the shore. And he patiently answered all Cook's, and Banks's, memorials.

As for Cook, one is glad that the episode lasted no longer. He did not shine in this sort of pointless diplomacy. Never had he written so much, so ineffectually, nor come so close to pomposity.[1] It was not the pomposity, or the near-pomposity, of James Cook in person; even confined on shipboard, he found enough to think about to exclude the cultivation of his own ego. But reading between the lines, as one must read between his lines so often, one can make a reasonable guess at Lieutenant James Cook, with his six-months-old commission, feeling his responsibility and his position a little as an officer and a gentleman, even *vis-à-vis* the representative of the sovereign of Portugal; feeling it incumbent upon him to state that tame acquiescence in the proceedings of that potentate would render him 'unworthy of the rank in His Britannick Majesty's Service which I now have the honour to bear'; considering that 'my Court', as well as 'the King my Master', was a phrase that might have a useful part in his protests. It is a far cry from the log of the Newfoundland surveyor, or even from the daily entries in his *Endeavour* journal. He did, in the time at his disposal, compose a truly immense letter to the King his Master, or at least the secretary of the Admiralty, detailing with solemnity the whole history of the encounter,

[1] The correspondence is all printed in *Journals* I, 487–97.

which he forwarded by the Spanish packet, with copies of all the memorials he had written to the Viceroy, as well as the Viceroy's in reply. He does not seem to have thought it ever worth referring to again, and the Admiralty does not seem to have treated his plaint with great attention. He did also collect a good deal of information about Rio de Janeiro, its resources and fortifications, wrote sailing directions for entering the harbour, and—no doubt as much from force of habit as to outwit 'Count Rolim'—drew 'a Plot or Sketch of great part of the bay'. He is duly modest: 'the strict watch that was kept over us during our whole stay hinderd me from takeing so accurate a Survey as I wished to have done and as all the observations I could make was taken from on board the Ship, the Plan hath no pretentions to accuracy, yet it will give a very good Idea of the place, difering not much from the truth in what is essential'.[1] This was something that would have caused the Viceroy unrest if he had been aware of it, and it, much more than the exchanges with the Count, is the essential Cook.

There were some punishments while the ship lay here, which may indicate that dissatisfaction was not confined to the captain and the gentlemen. John Thurman, pressed at Madeira, got a dozen for refusing to assist the sailmaker; so did another seaman, who tried to desert, and a marine who abused the officer of the watch; so did John Reading, the boatswain's mate, for being remiss in carrying out execution on the previous two. A more serious matter was the drowning of a man who had been with Cook ever since the beginning of the Newfoundland survey, Peter Flower, who fell overboard as the ship turned down the bay on sailing and could not be rescued —'a good hardy seaman & had saild with me above five years'. He was replaced by a Portuguese. In spite of all the difficulties, the three weeks' stay had been well worth while in supplies and work on the ship, cleaning, caulking, rigging, minor repairs. She was ready for her next two thousand miles, to the Strait of Le Maire, a passage that could have its own difficulties of variable winds and squalls and currents. She was a week getting out of the bay and to sea. 'This Morn thank god we have got all we want from these illiterate impolite gentry', wrote Banks on 2 December; but they were still to get a surprisingly polite letter from the Viceroy wishing them a good voyage. On 7 December they were free of the pilot and the guard boat and were turned south.

It was five and a half weeks before they were securely in the Strait, weeks of good seamanship for Cook, with some moments of great

[1] ibid., 29.

technical interest for him and Green, as they compared their lunar observations and calculations of the longitude, and Cook compared with them his own dead reckoning. He was beginning to be pleased with the results, though sometimes a little puzzled by evident errors, suspecting the influence of currents. The editor of the *Astronomical Observations* later published could have a different explanation: one error of nearly a degree, of Tierra del Fuego, he found 'not at all surprising, if we consider, that although the air was extremely clear when these observations were made, yet the sea ran so high that it filled the quarter deck three times while they were observing; and the motion of the ship was so great the Captain Cook did not attempt to observe'.[1] A violent pitching bout this was, thought Banks—not the only one who thought so, for they had all sorts of weather, from calms to heavy gales with hail and lightning. Only two days out, in fine weather and gentle breezes, the swell was so great that the fore topgallant mast carried away; there was much reefing of sails; more than once they had to lie to, with cots hitting on the sides and tops of the cabins all night and not a little discomfort. The ship was proving her virtue however: during a gale of early January, writes Banks, she 'has shewn her excellence in laying too remarkably well, shipping scarce any water tho it blew at times vastly strong; the seamen in general say that they never knew a ship lay too so well as this does, so lively and at the same time so easy';[2] and then they said she went all the better for it, with her joints loosened. Early in the passage Cook put his men to two watches again, a third of them not being adequate for working the ship in these latitudes. Fortunately Christmas Day brought nothing worse than a fresh breeze: 'the People were none of the Soberest', remarks the captain; or, to quote Banks, 'all good Christians that is to say all hands get abominably drunk so that at night there was scarce a sober man in the ship, wind thank god very moderate or the lord knows what would have become of us'.[3] It was another 'Ancient Custom of the Sea'. Cook, though he was a disciplinarian, never bothered to struggle against the inevitable: Banks might have considered it possible that his captain had a close enough eye on the weather. As cold grew, early in the new year, fearnought or 'Magellan' jackets and trousers were issued, thick woollen articles excellent in use. Meanwhile the natural historians had their eyes, and hands, full. At first a turtle, then innumerable sea-birds, petrels, the first

[1] The editor was William Wales, astronomer on Cook's second voyage: *Astronomical Observations* . . . (1788), 95.
[2] Banks, I, 213.   [3] Banks, I, 207.

albatross, red lobster krill staining the water, penguins and seals raised their excitement. About latitude 42°, thirty leagues off the land, swarms of butterflies, moths and other insects blown out to sea settled on the deck or floated past the ship; four hours on end Banks fished them up in a net and had the sailors gathering them up from the deck, profitable work for these volunteers with a bottle of rum at the end. On 11 January 1769 Tierra del Fuego was sighted, smoke—perhaps the smoke of signals—rising above it; and Banks, who had been disappointed of inspecting the natural history of the Falkland Islands, was rejoiced by Cook's decision to look for a convenient harbour and let him land.

Cook had difficulty getting into the Strait of Le Maire. The weather was boisterous; he was driven back past Cape St Diego, the western entrance point, three times by the force of the tide-race; at one point indeed the ship was pitching her bowsprit under water. At length the wind and sea moderated. He was able to send Banks and Solander ashore in a little cove outside the strait, Thetis Bay, while the ship plyed off and on: 'At 9 they return'd on board bringing with them several Plants Flowers &cᵃ most of them unknown in Europe and in that alone consisted their whole Value'[1]—a judgment that may indicate a little testiness or else a little humour, but certainly no appreciation of botanical science. The scientists were very pleased: besides the plants they recognised they had found about a hundred others, every one new and entirely different from anything either had seen before. Sydney Parkinson was going to have difficulty in keeping up. As soon as they returned Cook entered the strait, anchored for the tide outside another, not very promising, cove, 'Port Maurice'; then, the afternoon of 15 January, anchored again in the Bay of Good Success. Here he was to stay for five days.

It was a commodious bay, about half-way through the strait on the Tierra del Fuego side, good holding-ground everywhere, with plenty of wood and fresh water, and large quantities of edible greenstuff, a sort of wild celery and one of the varieties of 'scurvy grass', berries, few birds, few fish except shellfish, a few seals and sea-lions swimming in the bay, a few primitive people. The last were encountered when Cook and the gentlemen went on shore, while the ship was mooring, to look for a watering place. Cook thought them 'perhaps as miserable a set of People as are this day upon Earth'. The men were naked, the women wore a small apron of animal skin, unless for warmth they flung the skin of a guanaco or a seal over their shoulders; their dark copper colour was varied with streaks of

[1] *Journals* I, 44.

red and black paint, their long black hair unadorned, their necks hung with strings of small shells or bones; they seemed to live chiefly on shellfish, though they had bows and arrows, and their only shelter was rough open beehive huts; they had no boats. They had had earlier European contacts, because some of their arrows were pointed with bits of glass and they knew the use of fire-arms; they showed no particular shyness, accepted· the gift of beads eagerly, while three quite willingly came on board the ship. Thus the *Endeavour's* first introduction to primitive man: this the natural history that Banks studied on his first afternoon. Next morning early, the seamen being busy wooding and watering, and Cook beginning to survey the bay, he started out on a larger expedition. The morning was one for high spirits, the sun shining as on a fine day of May at home: Banks, Solander, Buchan, the four servants were accompanied by Monkhouse the surgeon, Green the astronomer, and two sailors to help carry the baggage. Their intention was to get as far as possible into the country behind the harbour, ascending a ridge of hills where spots showed clear of trees.

They pushed up through thick woods till mid-afternoon, when they arrived at a clear spot—what they had taken for turf, which now turned out to be a sort of waist-high bed of birch, growing in ankle-deep bog, about a mile across. They kept on across two-thirds of this, when Buchan was seized by a fit. With some difficulty lighting a fire, where the servants and sailors stayed with him, Banks, Solander, Monkhouse and Green pressed on to the top and the alpine plants they sought. The temperature went down, the antarctic wind brought blasts of snow; the idea of returning to the ship that night was abandoned, in favour of finding a sheltered spot where another fire and a 'wigwam' could be built. The cold seemed infinitely worse, and Solander insisted, to Banks's horror, on lying down to rest in the snow for a quarter of an hour; Richmond, one of the black servants, was almost in the same state. Somehow they got Solander to the fire. Richmond would not move, so his fellow-black, Dorlton, and a sailor, the least affected by cold, were left to guard him under the promise of early relief. The relief was sent, but the three could not be found: they had discovered a bottle of rum and drunk themselves stupid. The sailor turned up about midnight. Banks and four men went out again and found where he had left the negroes, but not even the whole party could get them to the fire through the darkness and the snow and the birch, nor was it possible to light another fire on the spot: they were therefore left covered with branches, and the others set themselves to outlast the snow. In the morning the two unfortunates were found dead, though Banks's greyhound, who had stayed with them all night, had come to no harm; the snow stopped, the sun came out; a vulture which had been shot the previous day was divided up and roasted for breakfast. A march of three hours brought the party to the ship, to which they were much nearer than they thought; for instead of making directly into the country, they had gone round the hills in a half-circle. Their exhaustion was no doubt due, not to starvation nor even the cold, but to the large and incautious amount of exercise they embarked on after so many shipboard weeks. Banks himself remained lively: he immediately got a boat and went out for the afternoon to haul the seine—unsuccessfully.

Meanwhile Cook had finished surveying the bay before the weather again deteriorated, when strong southerly winds, with snow, hail and rain brought in such a swell and surf on the shore that no boat could land. In this gale he lost a kedge anchor, which was used to aid the longboat in watering. The ship proved her quality by 'riding very easey' broad side to the swell. 'I never knew the Ship to roll more at sea', said Molyneux the master,[1] who had the awkward task of striking six guns down into the hold for the Horn passage. Wooding and watering completed on the 20th, the boats were hoisted in; early next morning they put to sea.

Cook had now to pass the Horn—or rather, as a Horn passage involved much more than merely sailing from one side of a particular point of land to the other, he may be said to have come to a critical period in his passage from off the east coast of South America, in a latitude of about 50° S (he reckoned it himself from his first sighting of Tierra del Fuego on 11 January, for which date his latitude was 54°20′), to a corresponding position off the west coast. This was a passage of something like 1500 miles. He passed Cape Horn only twice in his life, making westward on the present voyage, eastward as he drew towards the end of his second one. The westward passage was in general more difficult technically than the reverse, because it meant sailing into the teeth of the prevailing winds, and when Cook came to plan a second voyage, he planned on the basis of sailing with the westerlies. The traditional entrance into the Pacific, however, was from its south-east corner, whether through the Strait of Magellan or round the cape. Late January could be regarded as the height of summer. Summer off the Horn did not guarantee an easy time for the sailor: although Cook did not expect

[1] *Journals I*, 46, and n. 4 on that page.

the sort of fearful autumnal tempest that Anson had had before him and Bligh was to have after him, although his seamanship from day to day was admirable, he undoubtedly had good luck. The coast, once the Strait of Le Maire had been left behind, was not a coast the seaman stood close in to by preference; but Cook wanted to have a good look at it, and certainly he wanted to fix the position of the cape as accurately as possible. Was he bound to Tahiti to observe the Transit of Venus? He also felt himself bound, in a different sense, as no sailor had felt himself bound before, to these works of supererogation.

The immediate object was to get south-west. The first day or so brought rain and squalls, then there were a few hours of calm and clear weather in which the ship drove fast to the north-east in a current, so that when a light northerly breeze sprang up, Cook loosed all his reefs and set his studding-sails to make up the lost ground. Not often did a captain carry full sail in those parts, and most of the weather Cook had for five weeks was far from encouraging it. 'Fore part fresh gales and squally with hail and rain remainder moderate and clowdy', Cook would give a fairly regular report in his journal; or 'Former part fresh gales, latter light airs and clowdy'; or 'Fore and middle parts little wind and dark clowdy weather . . . . hazey rainy cold weather. . . . Clowdy and sometimes drizling rain. . . . Fresh gales with heavy squalls. . . . in the night hard squalls with rain and afterwards hazey rainy weather.' It was under these conditions that he at first worked his way along the coast, within islands (charting a new one), until he could be certain of Cape Horn; having satisfied himself, the comments he sets down in his journal are very characteristic.

It appeared not unlike an Island with a very high round hummock upon it: this I believe to be Cape Horn for after we had stood to the Southward about 3 Leagues the weather clear'd up for about a $\frac{1}{4}$ of an hour, which gave us a sight of this land bearing then WSW but we could see no land either to the Southward or westward of it, and therefore conclude that it must be the Cape, but whether it be an Island of it self, a part of the Southermost of Hermites Islands or a part of Terra del Fuego I am not able to determine. However this is of very little concequence to Navigation, I only wished to have been certain whether or no it was the Southermost land on or near to Terra del Fuego, but the thick Foggy weather, and the westerly winds which carried us from the land prevented me from satisfying My curiosity in this point; but from its Latitude and the reasons before given I think it must, and if so it must be Cape Horn and lies in the Latitude of 55°59' South and Longitude 68°13' West from the Meridian of Greenwich, beeing the mean result of Several Observ^{ns} of the Sun and

Moon made the day after we left the land and which agree'd with those made at Straits Le Maire, allowing for the distance between one place and the other, which I found means very accuratly to determine.[1]

This position, considering the conditions under which Cook and Green made their observations—the weather, the heaving platform on which they stood—is remarkable. Cape Horn is indeed the extremity of an island. The latitude given is, according to the most modern computation, exactly correct; the longitude a little less than a degree too far west—in that latitude less than forty miles. Cook, being now about to take his departure from the land, goes on in his journal to an excellent succinct description of the coast he has seen, from the northern entrance of Le Maire Strait, and refers to his chart. The appearance of Cape Horn and Hermites Islands, he says,

is represented in the last View in the Chart which I have drawn of this coast from our first making land unto Cape Horn in which is included Strait Le Maire and part of Staten land. In this Chart I have laid down no land nor figure'd out any shore but what I saw my self, and thus far the Chart may be depented upon, the Bay[s] and inlets are left void the openings of which we only see from the Ship . . . . [because of short and imperfect accounts] it is no wonder that the Charts hitherto published should be found incorrect, not only in laying down the land but in the Latitude and Longitude of the places they contain; but I can now venter to assert that the Longitude of few places in the World are better ascertain'd than that of Strait Le Maire and Cape Horn being determined by several observations of the Sun and Moon, made both by my self and Mr Green the Astronomer.[2]

There was no trivial boasting about this. It was a careful statement of fact.

Cook, always attentive to his instructions, stood well to the southward, 'in order to make a good Westing', though not as far as Anson had recommended, to 61° or 62° 'before any endeavour is made to get to the westward'—and he had reflections on this. So far as possible, he stood south-west, until the evening of 30 January, when he found himself in latitude 60°10′ and longitude 74°30′; a calm followed, then the wind backed. 'At 3 am wind at ESE a Moderate breeze, set the Studding sails, and soon after 2 birds like Penguins were seen by the mate of the watch.' Studding-sails again, to astonish later Cape Horn seamen: and it was not till the afternoon of the following day that he took them in and took a reef in his topsails.

---

[1] *Journals* I, 49. Cape Horn is the southernmost extremity of Horn Island, the most southerly of the Hermite or Cape Horn group. Its position, as given in the South American Pilot (14th ed., 1956) is 55°59′ S, 67°16′ W.

[2] *Journals* I, 52–3.

There were calm periods in the next few days, in which Banks could get out in a small boat under the gloomy sky and shoot sea-birds for his collection, albatrosses and petrels and whale-birds, without ill effect and without remorse; indeed albatross carefully cooked and served up with savoury sauce made a highly commendable dish. There were a great many about the ship. On 13 February Cook and Green observed carefully the sun and moon. The ship was in longitude 90°13′ W, latitude at the time about 49° S, and Cook again thought it worth while to write down some of the thoughts he had.

From the foregoing observations it will appear that we are now advanced about 12° to the westward of the Strait of Magellan and 3½° to the northward of it, having been 33 days in doubbling Cape Horn or the land of Terra del Fuego, and arriving into the degree of Latitude and Longitude we are now in without ever being brought once under our close reefe'd Topsails since we left strait la Maire, a circumstance that perhaps never happen'd before to any Ship in those seas so much dreaded for hard gales of wind, insomuch that the doubling of Cape Horn is thought by some to be a mighty thing and others to this Day prefer the Straits of Magellan.[1]

Reasoning from the ships' journals he had read, particularly those of the *Dolphin*, Cook found himself 'no advocate' for the Strait passage; he found himself differing also from the advice of Anson to avoid the Strait of Le Maire and run down to latitude 61° or 62°. That, he said,

is what I think no man will ever do that can avoide it, for it cannot be suppose'd that any one will Stear South mearly to get into a high Latitude when at that time he can steer West, for it is not Southing but Westing thats wanting, but this way you cannot steer because the winds blow almost constantly from that quarter, so that you have no other choise but to stand to the Southward close upon a wind, and by keeping upon that Tack you not only make southing but westing also and sometimes not a little when the wind Varies to the northward of west, and the farther you advance to the South[rd] the better chance you have of having the winds from that quarter or easterly and likewise of meeting with finer weather, both of which we ourselves experience'd. Prudence will direct every man when in these high Latitudes to make sure of Sufficient westing to double all the lands before he thinks of Standing to the Northward.[2]

---

[1] *Journals* I, 57–8. Also, a different line of argument, 'The Longitude by account [dead reckoning] is less then that by Obser[n] 37′ which is about 20 Miles in these high latitudes, and nearly equal to the Error of the Logg Line before mentioned: this near agreement of the two Longitudes proves to a demonstration that we have had no Western current sence we left land.' It proves as well his skill in dead reckoning. We learn from Pickersgill that the observers were also using the star Regulus and the occultation of the planet Saturn.—*Journals* I, 57, n. 4.

[2] *Journals* I, 59.

It may be argued that Cook has come to a conclusion not very different from Anson's; but there is a difference, he has thought the matter out for himself on the basis of his own experience as well as his scrutiny of the experience of others, and he has expounded it with lucidity.

For the next few weeks the winds had a good deal of south in them as well as west, and Cook was able to make a fairly consistent north-west course, except once or twice when north-westerlies set him south by west. He was still to have some strong gales or squalls, gloom and rain: on 16 February he shipped a sea which carried away his driver boom, and next day the main topsail split; observations on the 23rd were impeded by the rolling of the ship as seas broke over the quarterdeck; but next day, wrote Banks, the wind had 'settled at NE; this morn found studding Sails set and the ship going at the rate of 7 knots, no very usual thing with Mrs Endeavour.'[1] Those easterlies did not last more than a day or two. On the 23rd the distance sailed was only 13 miles; a fortnight before, in a southerly, Mrs Endeavour had logged 130 miles; on 17 and 18 February, in south-westerlies, 132 and 140 miles. There were also calms, when the slaughter of sea-birds continued. As March came on the temperature rose—'pleasantly warm', noted Banks at first, 'and the Barnacles upon the ships bottom seemd to be regenerate'.[2] Cook, a good deal farther west in the ocean in his longitude than anybody had been before, began to consider the continent. A large south-west swell at the end of February, that kept up thirty hours after a gale, proved to him that there was no land in that quarter. Then the agreement of dead reckoning and observation in fixing the longitude, 100°33′ W, 560 leagues west of the coast of Chile, argued the absence of currents, to be expected near a continent, and therefore the absence of a continent where it was supposed to be. And day after day the great Pacific swell continued.

Ten days into March the winds turned easterly. It was fine pleasant weather, and Cook returned his men to three watches. The guns that had been struck down to the hold for the Horn passage were mounted again. Tropic birds began to appear. After a week came westerlies for a while, which pushed the course to the north, taking the ship a little more quickly across the Tropic of Capricorn. Men-of-war birds and 'egg birds' or terns joined the tropic life in the sky, both thought not to fly far from land, but there was no land.

[1] Banks, I, 235. [2] Banks, I, 237.

It was Banks's turn to discuss the question. The nearest land they knew of just then was Pitcairn Island; a little to the north and to the west. 'I cannot help wondering that we have not yet seen land. It is however some pleasure to be able to disprove that which does not exist but in the opinions of Theoretical writers. . . .'[1] Dalrymple had laid down reported land many degrees to the eastward of the *Endeavour*'s track. As for the theorists of balance, 'The number of square degrees of their land which we have already chang'd into water sufficiently disproves this, and teaches me at least that till we know how this globe is fixd in that place which has been since its creation assignd to it in the general system, we need not be anxious to give reasons how any one part of it counterbalances the rest'[2]—a passage that persuades one that Banks knew less of Newton than he should have done. The month advanced and very early on the 24th a log of wood passed by the ship—a sign of land? At daylight there was no appearance of any, 'I did not think myself at liberty to spend time in searching for what I was not sure to find',[3] says Cook, although he thought he could not be far from the islands discovered by Quiros in 1606. He was right on both counts: a few days more would bring him up with the Tuamotu archipelago, simply by pursuing the course he was on already, and he could have wasted a great deal of time by allowing himself to be put off his prime object. Meanwhile the boats could be repaired and painted, the cables strengthened.

As the ship sailed into warmer waters there happened a poignant and needless episode that reminds us how desolation can oppress the human heart even in a crowded company. A quiet young marine, William Greenslade, asked on sentry duty by a companion to look after a piece of sealskin, had taken a piece of it to make a tobacco pouch; being immediately found out he was so persecuted by his fellow marines as betraying the honour of their corps that when in the evening the sergeant was about to take him to the captain to complain, overcome by the blackness of despair he slipped overboard. Poor William Greenslade may have been forgotten in a few days by these over-righteous men, because excitement was at hand. In the first days of April, latitude about 19° S, a succession of easterly winds drove the ship ahead rapidly; and on the 4th in the morning land was sighted to the southward, 'by Peter Briscoe servent to Mr Banks (to ye Honour of ye 2d watch which was then upon deck)', we are told by Pickersgill, also probably a member of the second

---

[1] Banks, I. 239.
[2] Banks, I, 240.
[3] *Journals* I, 66.

watch.[1] This first island of all the Pacific islands discovered by Cook was an atoll—'an Island of about 2 Leagues in circuit and of an Oval form with a Lagoon in the Middle for which I named it *Lagoon Island*.'[2] The Polynesians called it Vahitahi. The thread of land round this lagoon was low and narrow, but it supported people, who marched along the shore abreast of the ship; above them the great fronds of coconut trees streamed out in the trade wind like flags. In the afternoon, a few miles to the west, appeared another island, small, round and shaggy with wood and bushes, whence Cook's name for it, Thrum Cap;[3] it was Aki Aki. Next afternoon came Bow Island, so called from its shape, or Hao, first discovered (as Cook deduced) by Quiros in 1606 and by him called San Pablo; the next afternoon again, 65 miles to the westward, the Two Groups, islets strung together by the same reefs, the one group Marokau, the other Ravahere; then the uninhabited small Bird Island, or Reitoru; then—after a day without islands—Chain Island or Anaa, a set of islets again strung together by reefs round a lagoon. On 10 April was sighted in the north-west the high round island called Osnaburg by Wallis, who first discovered it—Mehetia; and at six o'clock next morning, full ahead, the high peaks of King George's Island. The winds were variable and light, the weather sultry; the ship sailed only eighteen miles in twenty-four hours. A few people came out in canoes with coconuts and the green boughs of friendship, and were given some beads: *Taio, taio!* they called—Friend, friend!—but would not come on board. The wind settled in the east; clouds, squalls and rain were followed by gentle breezes and a clear sky; the *Endeavour* ran under an easy sail all that last night, in the morning the pinnace was hoisted out to lie over a reef which the *Dolphin* had hit at the entrance to Royal Bay, and at 7 a.m. the anchor went down in 13 fathom. It was Thursday, 13 April. There lay the beach, the river, the valley, the green romantic heights. It was Matavai Bay, it was Tahiti.

This passage from Plymouth to Tahiti must be reckoned a remarkable piece of seamanship, and one is to remember that it was Cook's first long ocean passage. However one may estimate the element of luck, it is clear already that he could wring every advantage out of luck. Without looking for a continent, he had already, by working his way farther west in the higher latitudes of the Pacific than anyone

[1] ibid., 69, n. 4.   [2] ibid., 69.
[3] ibid., 70. Thrums or ends of thread all over a piece of cloth would give it a shaggy appearance. Thrum caps were worn by sailors. Cook found the name useful: there was a Thrum Cap in Halifax harbour, and he used it for small islands both in Newfoundland and in Dusky Sound, New Zealand, as well as here.

had gone before,[1] pushed back its possible eastern limits. He had, while his mind had played freely over some of the problems of navigation and geography, shown that it was possible to comply literally with instructions. He had been advised to come into the parallel of King George's Island at least 120 leagues to the eastward of it, and entering the Tuamotu archipelago from the south-east at exactly the right time, that was what he had done: allowing a few miles either side, he had been running down the latitude for almost a week. He was to use his best endeavours to arrive at Tahiti a month or six weeks before the date of the Transit. He had done better. He had seven weeks and one day ahead of him before the designated moment. His men and his passengers were in good health.

They were in good health, almost eight months after they had left England. Four men had died through accident, one by suicide; none from sickness. This would have seemed to the generality of captains and ships' surgeons a remarkable fact. True, there were a few men —very few—upon the sick list with slight complaints. Banks, at the end of March, had suspected himself of scurvy, and dosed himself successfully with lemon juice. Cook, his pen at the page in his journal devoted to 'remarkable occurrences', paused to meditate, not on winds and currents, or longitude, or the variation of the compass, but on this matter of good health. He put it down to the regular serving of sauerkraut and portable soup to all 'the people', and of wort—the decoction of malt—to every man who showed the least symptom of scurvy; 'by this Means and the care and Vigilance of Mr Munkhous the Surgeon this disease was prevented from geting a footing in the Ship.' He did not think earnestly of the onions of Madeira, the wild celery and scurvy grass and fresh water of Tierra del Fuego. He did write words which show that he had got beyond flogging as an inducement to dietary change, and could consider the sailor's mind rather than his back as the effective area of persuasion.

The Sour Krout the Men at first would not eate untill I put in practice a Method I never once knew to fail with seamen, and this was to have some of it dress'd every Day for the Cabbin Table, and permitted all the Officers without exception to make use of it and left it to the option of the Men

---

[1] To do justice to predecessors, one may however compare him with Roggeveen. Cook went south to lat. 60°4′, when his longitude was 74°10′ W; Roggeveen south to lat. 60°44′, long. 67°56′ W (of Greenwich, translating from E of Tenerife, and accepting his calculations as more or less correct). Roggeveen went as far west as 86°38′, in lat. 53°11′; Cook was not as far west as that until he was in lat. 51°16′. But Cook kept on a north-westerly course from the time he rounded the Horn, so that in lat. 34° (approximately) he was in long. 120°54′ W. But Roggeveen, from his long. 86°38′, had made in for the South American coast, altering course westerly only about lat. 34°, when he was in long. 74°52′. Cook, on the other hand, had increased his longitude steadily from the time he rounded the Horn, so that when he was in lat. 34° his longitude was 120°54′ W.

either to take as much as they pleased or none atall; but this practice was not continued above a week before I found it necessary to put every one on board to an Allowance, for such are the Tempers and disposissions of Seamen in general that whatever you give them out of the Common way, altho it be ever so much for their good yet it will not go down with them and you will hear nothing but murmurings gainest the man that first invented it; but the Moment they see their Superiors set a Value upon it, it becomes the finest stuff in the World and the inventer a damn'd honest fellow.[1]

Cook was not the first to put his finger on this characteristic conservatism. The significant thing is that he began to find means of counteracting it.

[1] *Journals* I, 74. 'A damn'd honest fellow': I give this phrase as Cook originally wrote it. Both in his MS journal and in the Mitchell copy he deleted the word 'damn'd'—in obedience, one supposes, to polite convention, because he can hardly be thought to have feared to outrage the tender minds of the Admiralty, or to be considering the rhythm of his prose. In the later Admiralty copy of the journal, which did not include the objectionable expression, he inserted other words, to make the passage run, 'the inventer according to their phras an honest fellow'. We get a little, amusing, light on Cook as well as on his men.

VIII

Tahiti

THERE IS no general agreement that Tahiti is the most beautiful island in the Pacific; but it is generally agreed that it is a beautiful island, and to its first discoverers it seemed paradisal. Coming to it after so many atolls, lagoons encircled by a broken rim of sand and coral, islet-studded, they saw a great volcanic upthrust high in the sea, rising from mere hilly slopes to five thousand, six thousand, seven thousand feet, forested and green till the final peaks; a land also of deep valleys and quick rivers. Almost round the slashed mountainous mass runs a narrow band of level fertile ground, widest at the north-west end, in places failing altogether, so that the steep hillside falls straight to the rocks of the sea;[1] on the north are sandy beaches, on the south fewer beaches but much rough coral strand; at the south-east curve are coastal cliffs. The whole outline is a sort of irregular figure-of-eight; the larger, north-west, loftier section was, and is, known as Tahiti-nui, or Great Tahiti; the smaller, south-east, one as Tahiti-iti, or Little Tahiti—or more commonly in Cook's day as Taiarapu; between them lies the narrow flat isthmus of Taravao. A barrier reef, on which the swell drums and roars incessantly, girdles the island, half a mile to two miles off, though there is a break in it on the north, while a number of passes give canoes entrance to the lagoon. A larger one of these opened from the northern point of Matavai Bay, where the fresh water of a river discouraged coral growth, and it was here that Wallis had found his way into a harbour, and Cook followed him.

Matavai Bay, except for north-west and westerly winds, provides excellent shelter, and in the months when Wallis and Cook were there, those winds hardly blow. It is a superb bay, its long line of black volcanic sand backed by the tall innumerable pillars of coconut trees with their wild crowns, immobile and sculptured in a hot still noon or moon-charmed night, streaming like vast bunches of pennants on a rising wind; given sobriety by the deep green of the sand-

---

[1] Strictly speaking, this statement should be modified now, because of the motor-road that has been cut right round the island.

haunting casuarinas, drooping and myriad-fingered; absorbing into a general pattern the splay-limbed untidy pandanus; backed with the splendid bread fruit and ancient-buttressed *mape* or chestnut, their arms extending in benedictions of plenty. If one stands on the flat sandy point that is the extremity of the bay, in fine weather, with gentle impulses of water from east and west meeting and mingling at one's feet, their level hardly altered by the tide, and gazes inwards, one sees a perfect curve, beyond and above it the cleft uneven lines of the nearer ridges—'uneven as a piece of crumpled paper' as Sidney Parkinson said; beyond them again, the great form of the mountain, its shoulders and steep flanks falling away still hung with green, the peak of Orofena. It is a view paralleled elsewhere in Tahiti, eye rising from beach and sea over forest and shadowed valley to the heights, but it does not lose its enchantment. Behind the beach flows out no longer to the point the lively river, the Vaipopoo, thirty feet wide, where Wallis and Cook filled their casks with fresh water— its course has changed, it is largely swamp that remains. The warm air remains, in bright day or soft night; the green of spontaneous growth, the smell of earth and blossom; enough remains to show why the eighteenth-century sailor should think himself imparadised, even without considering man or woman. There were defects, of course: there were flies, there were some of the characteristics of man and woman.

Cook had followed Wallis to the heart, the centre of Polynesia, geographically speaking. In the next ten years he was to find how far the Polynesian people had spread upon the ocean, was to remark differences between their different branches, was to account for differences as best he could, while he recognised certain things as fundamentally the same. Of certain preconceptions he could not rid himself: with island business to do, he needed some authority with whom to bargain; he felt, like other discoverers from Europe, that every considerable island or island-group should have a king; he felt that social and individual morality in relation to property rights should be the same as European morality. Wherever he got his own ideas from, he was inclined to fancy vague feudal systems before him; but how could a man, however perceptive, in a few weeks understand a language that was simple yet subtle, understand all the institutions and relations of chiefship, understand the implications and the indications of *tapu*, the sacred, the forbidden, the penalty-ridden; understand the structure of society and its classes; apprehend courtesies and obligations; separate the ritual of sex from orgiastic displays, or an island freedom from the commercial libertinage of the sea-shore? Observation of canoes and houses, weapons and domestic artifacts, was a simpler thing. Cook and Banks were eager observers of everything their eyes rested on, and they did their best to understand, their journals are the foundation of Polynesian anthropology and of some Polynesian history. They register an honest, but a gradual, process of discovery; and the very queries with which Cook was left, his half-statements, his own implications, have been starting-points for later investigators. It now began to be fortunate that he had Banks with him: the young man, with plenty of time at his disposal while Solander worked on plants and fishes, revealed a universal interest and the happiest gift for getting on with people, whether men or women; and his susceptibility to the latter—who can forget 'the very pretty girl with a fire in her eyes'?—was welcomed and echoed by them. As a coadjutor, as a junior manager, he was invaluable; as an observer he was excellent; he was excited but not often thoughtless—he could, even, be more cautious than Cook; he was sympathetic, amused, accurate. It is obvious that his journal and Cook's lay open before each other; obvious that he was baffled by some things as much as Cook was. It is obvious that neither was sentimental enough at that time to nourish the thought of Noble Savages.

The name the island was known by to its inhabitants was learnt soon enough—Otaheite, *O Tahiti*, 'It is Tahiti'.[1] Its population of 'Indians' may be guessed, without confidence, as upwards of 50,000; and perhaps that of its near neighbours should be taken into this total. It was not settled in villages, but scattered visibly in single huts and small groups all round the verge of flat land, less visibly throughout the valleys and over the uplands. The high valleys also gave refuge to the fugitive and to the oppressed; for there was a class-structure and varying degrees of prosperity, there could be oppression; and, though desperate warfare was rare, it was not unknown, briefly. The coming of Europeans was almost coincidental with one of these brief periods, and, not unnaturally, led on to another and longer one. The remains, however, of Tahitian building are not those of forts but of *marae*—the coral-stone structures of courtyard and 'altar', small or large, that almost innumerably dotted the land, the centres of religious ceremonial for families or communities or craft-groups; highly important when they belonged to chiefly families, the importance of whose members themselves might be measured by

---

[1] The 'O' is really untranslatable. It is an article prefixed to proper names when in the nominative case. *O Tahiti* might equally well be rendered 'The Tahiti'. Other examples are the personal names 'Oborea' and 'Otoo' for O Purea, O Too; or the name of the district, Oparre for O Pare.

their seats on the *marae*, immensely *tapu* or sacred, surrounded with sacred trees, ministered to by a priesthood the very language of whose invocations was an esoteric thing; less important as social rank declined, yet, whether the centre of human sacrifice or of a more ordinary ritual, the abode of awe and the visiting-places of gods. Tahitian society, that is—as was to become apparent to the European mind only gradually—Polynesian society in general, was in its own terms a profoundly religious society. The secular also was sacred. Chiefs—the *ari'i*—were sacred in their degrees; most sacred of all were the *ari'i rahi*, particularly the three great heads of clans who might in some sort present to men from a different world the quality of 'kings'. The *ari'i* commanded and was obeyed; he was addressed in special forms; his person, his clothing, his possessions were protected by *tapu*; he had, as we have seen, his *marae*; he had his mountain and his promontory, his symbols of authority, his staff and spear; his authority extended even to the *rahui*, the laying of a prohibition in his district on the use of the produce of land or sea or industry, for his own convenience or that of the community—to anticipate a festival, to conserve maturing breadfruit, or fish in the spawning season. The sanctity of the *ari'i rahi* extended even beyond all this, to the ground on which he trod, his very presence; when he came men stripped off their clothing to the waist, women below their shoulders, as they did when passing by houses that belonged to him, or the sacred images connected with his *tapu*. He himself could never appear in public on foot, nor enter the house of a subject, and consequently was carried on men's shoulders, staying only in houses set aside for the purpose; and there was protection in this for the subject, to whom the ground was indispensable, who did not wish his dwelling to become in an instant the property of his chief. The commoner who infringed any of the chiefly *tapu* would, it was believed, either die or be afflicted by *o'ovi ari'i*, 'chief's leprosy'. An *ari'i* first-born was regarded with a particular veneration, all the more if male: he was recognised immediately as the head of the family, and his father, or his mother, took on the role of regent. A regent of course may exercise considerable power. But the power of the *ari'i rahi* or his regent was not equal to his privilege, his social consequence; he could not command the obedience of other chiefs, even in his own district; there was great scope for personality. Hence Wallis's acceptance of Oborea, or Purea, as a queen, the magic of her name in England; hence Cook's bafflement, sometimes, as his experience continued, over who might be the really great man with whom he should deal.

We need pay little attention to sub-orders of chiefdom: the great bulk of the population were *manahune*, or commoners, the fishermen, the cultivators of taro or yam, the gatherers of coconuts and breadfruit and bananas and the wild upland plantains, the labourers of house-building and canoe-building and stone-carrying. They looked after the pigs and fowls and dogs that marked the island animal economy; they included the hereditary retainers of *ari'i*, called *teuteu*—taken by Cook, quite wrongly, for slaves. There were skilled handicraftmen, able artists who could tattoo buttocks and thighs. Their women beat out and stained the fabric of bark cloth, *tapa*, which was the substance of clothing—the loin-cloth or *maro*, the skirt or *pareu*, cloaks and mantles—and was bestowed in ceremonial gifts; wove mats and sails; pounded food. There were differences enough in personality among them, as among chiefs, though few among them could resist the temptation proffered by European goods, whether useful to them or useless, but particularly nails and edged tools; commoners as well as chiefs were highly curious; islanders generally turned out to be 'prodigious expert' as thieves. It was the less restrained young women of this social order who provided seamen with such advantageous entertainment, the lithe and laughing girls who were always ready to dance, whose impromptu dances on the beach seemed to the graver mind so often lascivious. Island sexual morals took on a delightful simplicity to the first visitors; and although it was not quite simple, there is reason to think this Central Polynesian culture as profoundly permeated with sex as it was with religion. Certainly there was a great deal made of the sexual relation in the institution of the *arioi*, the people whom Cook could not otherwise describe than as 'strolling players'; and to the uninstructed view, their 'libertinage' and their practice of infanticide might seem much more impressive than their secular and religious functions in the social pattern. They were a trained and graded society, celebrating in dance the seasonal festivals and those that marked the great events of communal life—like the birth, marriage or inauguration of *ari'i*—and providing a great part of the mime, drama and wrestling that were favourite social diversions. They toured the island group in fleets of consecrated canoes, were met with gifts and with joy; their god was the god of peace and fertility. It is probable that Cook was entertained by *arioi* more often than he knew.

It is probable that, more often than he knew, some simple, well-intentioned action of his own, some effort to impose order, was entangled in a web of island preconceptions, understandings, etiquette, mores not morals. It is probable that his hosts were baffled as often as he was.

Cook had obviously given some thought to his instructions and to Lord Morton's hints; he was anxious to regularise trade, keep up the value of his trade goods, and obviate the confusion and quarrels that would arise from lack of direction. Immediately he arrived in Matavai Bay, therefore, he issued his carefully drafted 'Rules to be observe'd by every person in or belonging to His Majestys Bark the Endevour, for the better establishing a regular and uniform Trade for Provisions &c^e with the Inhabitants of Georges Island'; and the first of these rules was 'To endeavour by every fair means to cultivate a friendship with the Natives and to treat them with all imaginable humanity'. Secondly, trade for provisions was to be carried on only through a properly appointed person, except with the captain's special leave. Thirdly, 'Every person employ'd a Shore on any duty what soever is strictly to attend to the same, and if by neglect he looseth any of his Arms or woorking tools, or sufters them to be stole, the full Value thereof will be charge'd against his pay according to the Custom of the Navy in such cases, and he shall recive such farther punishment as the nature of the offence may deserve.' Fourthly, 'the same penalty' would be inflicted for private trading with ship's stores. Fifthly, 'No Sort of Iron, or any thing that is made of Iron, or any sort of Cloth or other usefull or necessary articles are to be given in exchange for any thing but provisions.'[1] Obviously Cook had also paid attention to Wallis's journal. How far these excellent regulations could keep sailors from losing their tools, or from trading stolen nails or their own shirts for the delights of the flesh, how far they could impose an invariable humanity towards the islanders, remained to be seen.

People came off to the ship with fruit, upon which a great value was set, and when Cook and a party landed, they saw no evidence of plenty. Those who had been there before, indeed, were astonished at the depopulation of that part of the bay: where were the hogs and fowls, where was 'the Queen's house' (the great house for *arioi* performances), where was the Queen? Next day it became plain that population had moved to the west, whence came many canoes and whither Cook went to look for a larger harbour and to 'try the disposission of the Natives'. Their disposition was hospitable and friendly, apart from their tendency to pick pockets—Solander lost

[1] *Journals* I, 75-6; and I print a draft on pp. 520-1.

his spy-glass and Monkhouse the surgeon his snuff-box, though an
obviously great chief got them returned. A better harbour not being
found, Cook resolved to settle down where he was, and there the
people flocked in increasing numbers. Near the north-east point of
the bay he would fix a spot for his observatory, building a little fort
to protect it, the tents and all the domestic arrangements. With one
tent pitched, on the afternoon of the third day, he left a midshipman
and the marines to guard it, while he and a small party took a walk
over the river into the near country, accompanied by a great number
of Tahitians. The sensation when Banks brought down three ducks
with one shot was gratifying; but then came the sound of other shots.
Cook, hastening back, found that the people at the tent had been
troublesome, one of them had knocked down a marine, snatched his
musket and run off, and the other marines had fired and killed him.
The musket was clean gone; so were most of the people. This was
exactly the sort of thing Cook was anxious to prevent, and it did little
good to confine the sentry afterwards. With some pains he collected
together a number of the fled, and managed to reconcile them. But
he warped the ship nearer the shore so as to command with his guns
all that part of the bay, particularly the site for the fort. Then the
unfortunate Buchan had another fit, and died, and to avoid any
possible infringement of native susceptibilities his body was taken out
to sea for burial. An ingenious and good young man he was, wrote
Banks, and his loss was irretrievable: who now would portray scenes
and men? The answer that came was poor Sydney Parkinson, who
had to draw everything; and life for Sydney Parkinson was not
rendered easier by the swarms of flies that settled on him and his
colours. The same morning, the first Monday at the island, a number
of chiefs from the west visited the ship with plantain branches, their
emblems of peace, in hand; among them were two men whose
friendship was important, one whom Banks christened Lycurgus, the
other Hercules. Lycurgus was a great *ari'i*'s eldest son—Tepau i
Ahurai Tamaiti;[1] Hercules was Tuteha, a chief extremely influential
over a large part of Tahiti-nui. They brought with them two of
the scarce hogs as a present, and when Tuteha later in the week
put up his house and put his family to live in it near the growing fort friendly relations seemed to be sealed. Cook would not
even cut down a tree without permission. He and Green were the
first to spend a night on shore, in an attempt to determine the
longitude by astronomical means—vain, because of cloud; and

[1] The father was Vaetua i Ahurai, chief of Tefana or Faaa; *tamaiti* means 'the son'.
For convenience I refer to him as Tepau.

a little later Banks and Solander took up their residence in the tents.

By the end of a week all was going well. Banks and Solander were the principal managers of trade, exchanging beads for coconuts and breadfruit: nails in this traffic at first seemed to have lost their value.[1] Cook was determined to live off the land so far as possible, to conserve the ship's provisions. The gentlemen began to study the Tahitian language. Individual friendships were formed: every man had his *taio*, who exploited him to the best advantage: 'this might be productive of good Consequences', wrote Molyneux the master, 'but the women begin to have a share in our Freindship which is by no means Platonick.'[2] On the second Sunday Cook gave his men a half-holiday, with certain restrictions, 'Viz:'—it is Molyneux again—'that they should not go over one tree Hill', a prominent hill at the other end of the beach, 'that they should not molest or offer Violence to any of the Natives, that they should in all things behave as if he himself were present acquainting them also that no Viloence could be committed without his Knowlidge & that he was resolv'd to punish all Offenders severely & debar them of Liberty for the Future.'[3] Henry Jeffs, the butcher, who a few days later did offer violence to a woman from whom he wanted a stone hatchet, was the first to suffer in this cause, in spite of the tears of Tahitians who were not used to the sight of flogging. Sunday liberty became fairly regular, but it was not till half-way through May that Cook could find time for a holier observance, in which the service was read not by himself, but by Monkhouse the surgeon. After a few Sundays we lose sight of this. The captain may have been more interested in his secular concerns. In the first fortnight his fort was finished, with a bank of earth and a ditch at each end; on the side facing the river a double row of casks with two four-pounders mounted on them; on that facing the sea, built at high water-mark, another bank of earth surmounted by palisades; six swivel guns flanking the walls. It was to accommodate about 45 men with small arms, including the officers and gentlemen, as well as the observatory, the armourer's forge and a cook's oven; outside was a tent for the cooper and sailmaker. Thus Fort Venus on Point Venus. 'I now', says the captain,

---

[1] Values fluctuated; see *Journals* I, 82 and n. 4 on that page, and Banks, 275, on the price of coconuts, '6 for an amber coloured bead, 10 for a white one, and 20 for a forty-penny nail'. Hatchets and axes were also on the scene.

[2] *Journals* I, 553; cf. Wilkinson the master's mate, 'we find the woman of this Island to be very Kind In all Respects as Usal when we were here in the Dolphin.'

[3] Molyneux, ibid. Wilkinson has the proviso that the men were 'to Take Care to be upon their guard for there own Safty as the Indians are very Tracherous.'— p. 84, n. 2.

'thought my self perfectly secure from any thing these people could attempt.' With all this, and the other four-pounders commanding the beach from the ship, he may well have thought so; but he was mistaken.

Meanwhile the old hands of the *Dolphin* had rediscovered their Queen—a Queen in adversity. Her rank was not less, her appearance was still distinguished, but obviously she was less regarded. Moly-neux found her in Banks's tent and took her on board, where Cook made much of her, his most successful present being a child's doll, which—he says with an unexpected stroke of humour—'I made her understand was the Picter of my Wife.' This she paraded about the shore till she made that great man Tuteha so jealous that he had to have a doll too. She had a husband, Amo; a 'bed-fellow', one 'Obadee', that did not prevent her from angling for Banks; and a principal attendant, whom Cook knew as Tobia—Tupaia, a priest and adviser of importance. What had happened to lower her dignity and raise Tuteha's could not at this time be disentangled. Tuteha's very prominence, however, brought him into difficulties, the first of which arose from the affair of the quadrant. No sooner was the fort completed than the observatory was set up inside and the astronomical quadrant taken ashore in its box. Next morning it was gone. In spite of walls and sentries some nimble fellow had slipped in, stolen the heavy and precious article and made off with it— information soon came—to the eastward. A reward was announced for its recover. Banks and Green rushed to pick up Tepau, found that he knew the instrument had been unpacked and who the thief was, and through the whole of a sweltering day, with the chief and a pair of pocket pistols for protection, were bent on the chase, uphill and down. Finally they got back every essential piece, and on the way home met Cook coming up with a party of marines in support. Cook's first impulse had been to seize all the large canoes in the bay, in addition to the persons of Tuteha and others, until the quadrant was returned; later, learning that Tuteha was certainly quite innocent, he left orders that the chief should not be molested. By some mistake he was, when a canoe that put off from the shore was stopped, and was sent from the ship to the fort, where he was de-tained expecting death. On Cook's return he was immediately freed. The situation was a little difficult, because, although he gave Cook two hogs before he left, he was clearly displeased. Next day he demanded by messenger an axe and a shirt in return for the hogs; pending their delivery the supply of provisions stopped. Reconcilia-tion came, however, in two more days: Cook, Banks and Solander themselves went with the axe and shirt, and for good measure a broadcloth gown,[1] to the chief in his district of Pare, were received with honour amid a suffocating crowd, entertained with a display of wrestling before the *arioi* house, and the supply of provisions was resumed. The impression of this chief's power was strengthened when Molyneux and Green took the pinnace twenty miles to the eastward in search of hogs and fowls; after nearly losing their boat in the surf, they were told that nothing could change hands without Tuteha's permission. 'I can foresee that it will be a hard matter for us to keep up a freindship with Tootaha his demands being too exorbitant for us to comply with', writes Cook in his log;[2] but he managed to surmount the difficulty.

The days moved on from that point without great untoward incident. There were minor thefts—even Banks's particular friend Tepau stole nails—and attempted thefts; at one stage water casks seemed attractive booty; iron and iron tools were always tempting. There were ceremonial occasions of display, occasional minor quarrels. Banks noted down the native name of the island, and the Tahitian versions of English names—Tooté for Cook, Tapáne for Banks, Torano for Solander, and so on. The long-boat was found honey-combed with teredo. Cook had a plot of ground turned up and planted English seeds there. There was an overnight visit to Tuteha and Purea in the chief's district on the west coast, in the hope of securing a supply of hogs; the hope was illusory, Cook had his stockings stolen from under his head while still awake, Banks lost his jacket and waistcoat,[3] and would have lost all his other clothes had it not been for the good offices of Tupaia, two midshipmen lost their jackets. There was little consolation to derive from the music which followed, in the middle of the night, an hour of drums and flutes and singing. They were more entertained on the way back, by the sight of Tahitians riding the surf on the stern of an old canoe. The weather varied: as May came almost to an end it was reasonably fair, but not so fair that there was no anxiety for the day of the Transit. There was great diligence in looking to the instruments, and now no impediment from the surrounding people. Cook had determined to take Lord Morton's advice and send out other parties to observe, one to the west, the other to the east; their members had to be carefully instructed.

[1] The 'gown' was in the form of the native *tiputa*, an upper garment slipped over the head, through a hole like the South American poncho.
[2] B.M. Add. MS 27955, 8 May 1769.
[3] Parkinson (*Journal*, 31) writes that 'Mr Banks lost his white jacket and waistcoat, with silver frogs'—so that Banks cut an elegant figure even in Tahiti.

The preparations at Fort Venus he describes in his report to the Royal Society.

The astronomical clock, made by Shelton and furnished with a gridiron pendulum, was set up in the middle of one end of a large tent, in a frame of wood made for the purpose at Greenwich, fixed firm and as low in the ground as the door of the clock-case would admit, and to prevent its being disturbed by any accident, another framing of wood was made round this, at the distance of one foot from it. The pendulum was adjusted to exactly the same length as it had been at Greenwich. Without the end of the tent facing the clock, and 12 feet from it, stood the observatory, in which were set up the journeyman clock and astronomical quadrant: this last, made by Mr. Bird, of one foot radius, stood upon the head of a large cask fixed firm in the ground, and well filled with wet heavy sand. A centinel was placed continually over the tent and observatory, with orders to suffer no one to enter either the one or the other, but those whose business it was. The telescopes made use of in the observations were—Two reflecting ones of two feet focus each, made by the late Mr. James Short, one of which was furnished with an object glass micrometer.[1]

On Friday, 2 June, writes Molyneux, a useful supplement here to Cook, the winds and weather were not very promising: 'the Captain and Mr Green is entirely employ'd getting every thing compleatly ready. I was order'd to prepare for Observation & had a Telescope ready accordingly, every thing very quiet & all Hands anxious for Tomorrow.'[2] Evidently, and not unnaturally, there was a little tension. Solander made a fourth observer, and that very competent man, Satterley the carpenter, was to attend the clock and the thermometer. No apprehension about the weather, however, was needed; Saturday the 3rd dawned bright and faultless, and went on through a calm perfection. To avoid any possible disturbance, no Tahitian was allowed to come near. It was hot: the thermometer in the sun, about the middle of the day, rose to 119°, hotter than it had ever been before. But something was wrong. The critical hours were from nine in the morning to about half-past three in the afternoon. The journal entry runs:

This day prov'd as favourable to our purpose as we could wish, not a Clowd was to be seen the whole day and the Air was perfectly clear,.so that we had every advantage we could desire in Observing the whole of the passage of the Planet Venus over the Suns disk: we very distinctly saw an Atmosphere or dusky shade round the body of the Planet which very much disturbed the times of the Contacts particularly the two internal ones. Dr Solander observed as well as Mr Green and my self, and we differ'd

---

[1] *Phil. Trans.* LXI (1771), 397–8. [2] *Journals* I, 559.

from one another in observeing the times of the Contacts much more than could be expected. Mr Greens Telescope and mine were of the same Magnifying power but that of the Dr was greater then ours.[1]

The 'Atmosphere or dusky shade', or what he calls also the penumbra, was visible during the whole transit, Cook says elsewhere, and appeared to him to be 'nearly equal to ⅛th of Venus's semidiameter', and the 'first visible appearance' of Venus on the sun's rim, very faint, was that of the penumbra, at 21 minutes 50 seconds past 9; while after 3 p.m., when the transit was completing, Cook found the limb of Venus difficult to distinguish from the penumbra, and 'the precise time that the penumbra left the Sun could not be observed to any great degree of certainty, at least not by me.'[2] In the six hours' interval anybody could have seen the little black spot crawling across the sun, but that was a quite different matter; and if there was not a great degree of certainty about precise times on the part of some reliable observer, then the observation had failed. The possibility of such a phenomenon had not oppressed the mind of Halley. Almost two years after this day Cook wrote that 'there were some other appearances beside the above not more favourable to the observations'—without specifying what these were.[3] Green at least had some figures written down. The question of their precision did not arise till later.

It remained to collate the results of the other two parties. Hicks, Clerke, Pickersgill, and Saunders, a midshipman, had gone in the pinnace round to the eastward, and observed from an islet on the reef they called 'Lord Mortons Island'—Taaupiri or Isle Nansouty. Pickersgill returned highly pleased with every circumstance, 'so that if the Observation is not well made it is intirely owing to the Observers.'[4] The western party also reported success. This was Gore, Surgeon Monkhouse and Dr Spöring; they had gone farther, rowing the long-boat across the nine or ten miles of water to the island of Aimeo or Moorea, Wallis's York Island. Banks went with them, not as an observer, and while they made their preparations on a large flat rock called Irioa, between the reef and the shore, and next day carried out their scientific business, he went on shore to trade for provisions and look at the country and the people. Some of these he had already seen at Matavai, though the chief, and '3 hansome girls' he got to spend the night in the tent on the rock, were new to him.

[1] ibid., 97–8.
[2] *Phil. Trans.* LXI (1771), 410–11.
[3] Cook to Maskelyne, 9 May 1771, Royal Society Council Minutes, 11 July 1771; *Journals* I (2nd ed.), 692–3.
[4] *Journals* I, 98 n. 1.

The island did not seem as fertile as Tahiti. The only irritation arising on the great day was the theft by seamen of a large quantity of spike nails from the ship's stores; for which Archibald Wolf, found with some of the booty on him, was punished with two dozen lashes, the greatest number meted out on this voyage.

One might have thought that Cook would now be ready to leave Tahiti, the purpose of his visit being carried out; but in fact the observation of the Transit marks only a half-way point. The delayed celebration at a banquet on 5 June of the King's Birthday, which drew from the chiefs the toast of Kihiargo—they could come no nearer to King George—and made Tupaia particularly drunk, was but an episode of entertainment on the British side. There were many observations that Cook was still to make, in different spheres, some of them among his most valuable ones, and Banks was a very busy man. Cook himself wanted to overhaul his ship and his stores thoroughly before he went continent-hunting in higher latitudes; he also, his first responsibility off his shoulders, wanted to become more closely acquainted with the geography of the island and to chart it properly. Work about the ship was going on all the while: she was careened, says Cook—not dragged on shore, but heeled over where she lay, and 'boot-topped', that is her foul bottom was cleaned off to as near the keel as possible and coated with a mixture of pitch and brimstone, she was caulked and painted, her rigging closely inspected and repaired, spars varnished, cables restored, powder dried, provisions inspected. It was slow work, one reason being that the men were divided between the ship and the shore.

The longer the ship stayed, the more could be learnt about Tahitian life—or at least could be seen or experienced, without always being understood. The surgeon was forcibly assailed for picking a flower from a sacred tree on a *marae*, an infringement of *tapu* no native person would have been guilty of. Gore, finding that bows and arrows were in use, challenged Tepau to an archery contest, which broke down when it was found that in this exclusively chiefly diversion the Tahitians shot only for distance and not at a mark. There was further entertainment by 'travelling musicians', *arioi*, flutes and drums and voices again. The Indians, says Banks, asked in return for an English song, which was so enthusiastically received that one of them desired a passage to England to learn to sing. Banks was so greatly interested in custom and so friendly with Tepau that he was able to enlist himself in a mourning ceremony, in which Tepau, fantastically attired in shells and a feathered mask, was 'chief mourner', and Banks, stripped to a fragment of *tapa* or native cloth round his waist and blackened with charcoal, in the company of two women and a boy similarly decked, rushed about and terrorised anybody they met: it was all very inspiriting. Banks, too, recorded carefully the process of tattooing as he saw it carried out on a young girl, until she could bear it no longer. Some of the visitors, much taken with this sort of adornment, had their own arms marked before they left. There was from time to time a native dish to try, pork or a pudding from the Polynesian 'earth-oven', steamed between layers of hot stones and green leaves. A culminating point was the dog presented by Purea, a diplomatic return for some theft in which she had been implicated, at first to her surprise rejected; but similarly cooked it proved very sweet meat—'few were there of us but what allowe'd that a South Sea Dog was next to an English Lamb', says Cook. The South Sea dogs were vegetable fed. So were the South Sea rats, which Tahitians did not eat but British seamen did, as we learn from Molyneux: 'shooting of rats is not only a pleasant but a profitable amusement as they are also good eating & it is Easy to Kill 1000 in a day as the ground swarms & the Inhabitants never disturb them.'[1] Cook highly approved the local pork. Though it was in short supply, he managed to give it to his men for most of their Sunday dinners, not from a Tahitian oven.

One morning, as June advanced, there was a stir among the natives at the fort, among whom was Purea, and stripping their garments from their shoulders, like all the standers-by, they went out to meet some new arrivals. These were a chief called Oamo or Amo, with a boy about seven years old, carried on a man's back, 'altho he was as able to walk as the Man who carried him', and a girl of perhaps 15 or 16. Neither young person was allowed by the Tahitians to enter within the fort. This Amo must be a very extraordinary person to be received with such ceremony, thought Cook, who was none the less puzzled to see so little notice taken of him after the ceremony. But it was not Amo who was the really extraordinary person, it was the boy: 'we was inform'd that the Boy was Heir apparent to the Sovereignty of the Island and the young woman was his sister and as such the respect was paid them, which was due to no one else except the *Arreedehi* which was not Tootaha from what we could learn, but some other person who we had not seen, or like to do, for they say he is no friend of ours and therefore will not come near us.'[2] Such Cook's valiant effort to get at the truth. He did learn, truly enough, that the boy was the son of Amo and Purea. If there had

---

[1] *Journals* I, 559. [2] ibid., 104.

only been present two or three other people whom he had met, and
two whom he had not, he would have had at once together before
him the principal notables of Tahiti-nui; and if his knowledge of
the language, which is so ambiguous on personal relationships, had
only been adequate, he could have disentangled a curious piece of
history. He never did disentangle it, or the family relations that
underlay it; but it explains some of the jealousies and strains of the
island situation to which, all blind, he had brought himself—in
which, by his very presence in a particular part of the island, and his
friendship with particular people, he was already playing an unconscious part. Amo was certainly a person of distinction. He had
been until his son, Teri'irere, was born, the high chief or *ari'i rahi*
of Papara, on the south of Tahiti-nui, and he was now that son's
regent. He himself was also the eldest son of the daughter of the chief
of Haapape, in which district lay Matavai; he was therefore distinguished there. He married Purea, the daughter of the chief of
Faaa, an important district in the north-west corner of the island.
Tepau, an eldest child, was her brother. The family had a marriage
connection with the family of Tuteha, the chief of Paea, the district
abutting on Papara—a man whose other connections, and his
personal force, gave him power from thence northwards round to
Haapape. One of these connections was with Tu, the *ari'i rahi* of
Pare, or of a rather larger district, the Porionu'u, between Faaa and
Haapape. (So often was the name of this district heard that it
appears, as 'opooreonoo, on Cook's chart, given to the whole of
Tahiti-nui. He was Tu's great-uncle, and Tu was the 'some other
person who we had not seen', not because he was no friend, but
because he was a timid young man completely under Tuteha's
thumb, and Tuteha thought he was better out of the way. Cook was
to see enough of him on later visits. The girl who came with
Teri'irere was not his sister but Tu's sister, also a first-born child,
and she was the designated wife of Teri'irere.[1] These chiefly families
were not merely related (which explains Purea's seeming primacy
in Wallis's eyes), but at times bitterly divided; and it was the result
of bitter family dissension and war, caused by Purea's overweening
ambitions for her young son, that as a defeated person she now took
a subordinate role to that of Tuteha, the organiser of victory.[2] Cook
learnt a little of this, and was to learn a little more on the tour of the
island which he made with Banks in the last days of June.

Meanwhile the stealing of attractive articles went on. Cook's

[1] See the 'Note on Polynesian History', *Journals* I, clxxxii, and also p. 104, n. 1.
[2] *Journals* I, clxxxii–clxxxiv.

patience gave way in the middle of the month when an iron oven rake was neatly abstracted from the fort. He seized every canoe he could find of any value and impounded them in the river behind the fort, and threatened to burn every one of them unless the principal stolen articles were returned—'not that I ever intend to put this in execution'. It was a misconceived tactic, because the owners of the canoes were not the thieves, the fish in the canoes stank the fort out, little was regained beyond the rake; and as for the 'principal' articles—musket, pistols, and so on—some people said that Tuteha, his friends that Purea, had them. After a week Cook had to hand the canoes back thwarted. To be thus thwarted was a serious matter. As a humane man, who took Lord Morton seriously, he did not want to shoot, he felt that one death was enough: 'contrary to the opinion of everybody', he writes, 'I would not suffer them to be fired upon, for this would have been puting it in the power of the Centinals to have fired upon them upon the most slightest occasions as I had before experienced, and I have a great objection to fireing with powder only amongest people who know not the difference; for by this they would learn to dispise fire arms and think their own arms superior and if ever such an Opinion prevail'd they would certainly attack you the event of which might prove as unfavourable to you as them.'[1] As a humane man and a thwarted man he could only go on applying, so far as possible, his policy of even-handed justice, punishing his own men for offences against the native people, and securing what reparation he could from the latter for their own offences. One return his men got in full measure from their hosts, and that was venereal disease. Cook would have been puzzled by this also, had it not been for information given at about the same time.

It was a thing which weighed on the humane man for the rest of his life, and on humane men among his officers, this question of the transmission of the evil to the people of the South Sea; and where there were so many islands, innocence in one case was not necessarily innocence in another. The mutual attraction of the sexes—his men, the island women—Cook did not have to read Wallis's journal to foresee. He may even have foreseen, in general terms, episodes so ridiculous as the rivalry and the 'éclaircissement' between Banks and the surgeon over young women; and it would certainly have been most unfortunate if either of these had shot the other.[2] Before Wallis let a man land in 1767 he had the whole of his crew inspected by his surgeon and declared free of any sign of the disease. Similarly Cook:

[1] ibid., 101.   [2] ibid., 102, n. 1, and Parkinson, 32.

'I had taken the greatest pains to discover if any of the Ships Company had the disorder upon him for above a month before our arrival here and ordered the Surgeon to examine every man the least suspected who declar'd to me that only one man in the Ship was the least affected with it and his complaint was a carious shin bone; this man has not had connection with one woman in the Island.' None of the *Dolphin*'s men had contracted it at the island, as far as he knew; yet by early May some of his own men had— 'sad work among the People', to quote the master[1]—so that he 'had reason (notwithstanding the improbability of the thing) to think that we had brought it along with us which gave me no small uneasiness and did all in my power to prevent its progress, but all I could do was to little purpose for I may safely say that I was not assisted by any one person in ye Ship . . . this distemper very soon spread it self over the greatest part of the Ships Compney but now I have the satisfaction to find that the Natives all agree that we did not bring it here.'[2] If the ship's records are correct then Cook has overstated the extent of the contagion, which was confined to about a third of her company, but that was bad enough. Nor did he, or any ship's surgeon, or any surgeon anywhere, then know enough to be able to make dogmatic statements, except on a basis of the most clear and obvious proof—as Cook himself concluded after some years' more experience. Not enough was known about the varieties of the disease, nor the possibilities of quiescence and renewal, nor about carriers; so that Cook, getting now the information already referred to, was happy to feel that both the *Dolphin* and the *Endeavour* were free of the unpleasant responsibility. There had been two other ships visiting the island, ten or fifteen months earlier, at a harbour to the eastward called 'Ohidea' or Hitiaa; they had had a woman on board, and had carried away the brother of the chief of that place. Thus was accounted for various old pieces of iron, at first supposedly but not certainly from the *Dolphin*, which had been seen about, and an axe of strange pattern which Purea had brought to be sharpened. Also, said the Tahitians, these ships 'brought the Venerial distemper to this Island where it is now as common as in any part of the world and which the people bear with as little concern as if they had been accustomed to it for ages past.'[3] Information thus phrased indicates that the ailment was not syphilis, to which the endemic island disease of yaws gave immunity, but gonorrhea; and to that the British seaman was no more immune than the islander. Cook and Banks took Tepau on board the ship and showed him a coloured print of

[1] *Journals* I, 556.   [2] ibid., 99.   [3] ibid., 98–9.

the flags of different nations: he at once picked out the Spanish flag as the one flown by these unexpected vessels; and had not jackets and shirts such as those usually worn by Spanish seamen been lately seen? It was proved beyond doubt, thought Cook, that the ships were Spanish, from some South American port.

Early on the morning of 26 June he set off eastward in the pinnace with Banks to make the circuit of the island. For about ten miles there was no reef. At 8 o'clock they landed and walked while the boat rowed along the shore sounding, a rough walk at times between the sharply rising hills and the beach, encountering nothing very remarkable till they came to Hitiaa, where they were shown where the ships had lain—Spanish ships, as Cook thought them—and where their men had camped on shore. They kept on walking, found they could not in that way reach the bottom of the great bay between Tahiti-nui and Taiarapu, and called in the boat for the last stage, so that they were able to lodge the night with friends on the northern side of the Taravao peninsula. Cook inspected this muddy canoe-portage next morning; beyond it, he was told, was enemy's country, subject not to Tuteha but to 'King Waheatua'. Although the people encountered as the travellers walked on were strangers they proved as friendly as anybody else, not least the magnate Vehiatua, the *ari'i rahi* of Taiarapu, 'a thin old man with very white hair and beard', says Banks, found sitting with his daughter 'near some pretty Canoe awnings' on the shore of the beautiful Vaitepiha Bay. To reach his side of the bay they had been ferried across a large river in a canoe; now they walked again, accompanied by his young son, along the edge of fine cultivated country, with a *marae* on every point and others inland, and almost innumerable large double canoes drawn up on the beach—until tiredness drove them into the boat. They rowed till dark, when they put into a little creek and spent (surprisingly, as they thought) a supperless night in a deserted *arioi* house. Nor could they get provisions next morning, although they met friends, until, after rowing with a native pilot round the south-east point of the island, the steep Pari or cliffs above them and the broken dangerous reef outside, they came to a flat called Ahui and a plentiful harbour. Here they saw a fat goose and turkey-cock, left by Wallis at Matavai Bay. A less grateful sight, at one end of a house, was a semi-circular board to which were fastened fifteen human jaw-bones. For what purpose? Cook could not find out.

The tour continued, all this day in the boat, inside the reef, past a fruitful and populous coastal fringe, to a halting-place for the night—the night of the 28th—in the district of Vaiuru, within the large bay on the southern side of the peninsula. It was here that an important chief unsuccessfully attempted to decamp in the dark with a cloak lent to keep him warm, amid great excitement; and here that some alarm was caused towards morning by the absence of the boat. She had only drifted from her grapling. At daylight the gentlemen set off again in her, still inside the reef, landing for a short time and walking at Vaiari, round the bend of the bay, and noting down some remarkable signs of the Tahitian religious cult. They designed to spend the next night in the Papara district, with Purea; she being not at home, they nevertheless stayed. Here, on a low point of land, about a hundred yards from the sea, they found the most remarkable product of human hands in Tahiti, 'a wonder-full peice of Indian architecture and far exceeds every thing of its kind upon the whole Island', and indeed in the whole of Polynesia. It was the colossal *marae*, built of worked coral stone and basalt, which Purea and Amo, in their colossal pride, had raised to the honour of their infant son Teri'irere[1]—which, with all the attendant circumstances of reckless vanity, had so outraged the other *ari'i* that Tuteha and Vehiatua had joined to overthrow the pretensions of the Papara family. There were smaller *marae* near by, and many large altars, or *fata*, bearing the remains of sacrificial food set out for the gods; and the beach between them and the sea was thickly strewn with human bones—the bones of the Papara men killed six months before. The jaw-bones of Ahui were trophies of this battle. Cook and Banks measured the prodigious thing, before they went to rest in Purea's house, and learnt something of the fate which had descended on its makers. The next day, the last of June, they rowed up the west coast, a slow passage through reefs and shoals, to some part of Tuteha's domain, visited him the following morning and by evening had trodden their path back to Matavai Bay and the fort. They had been out on their circuit for six days and five nights; something more than thirty leagues, was the estimate; and the 'Plan or Sketch' which Cook had drawn, 'altho it cannot be very accurate yet it will be found sufficient to point out the Situations of the different Bays and harbours and the figure of the Island and I believe is without any material error.' Later comers found it remarkably accurate.

It was time, the captain thought, to depart. With the advance of the season provisions were growing short, the only breadfruit was a small late harvest brought down from the hills, and the natives were using a 'sour paste' made from it earlier, preserved in pits. The fort

[1] *Journals* I, 112–13; also Banks, I, 303–5.

was dismantled for firewood. The preparations took another week. Banks improved one fine day by exploring the river valley till he was stopped by great cliffs shining with water, and another by planting a variety of fruit seeds—of Cook's planting only mustard had come up. Cook was on the point of bringing his men on board when two of them deserted. They were marines, Clement Webb and Samuel Gibson. Nothing at this juncture could be more irritating. Since the ship's arrival discipline had been on the whole satisfactory, though it could not be expected that all rules would be obeyed. There had quite early been some 'mutinous' talk; but Molyneux, whom the captain evidently trusted, had intervened to secure pardon for the delinquents. 'I had many reasons for doing this', he says darkly, 'as I well knew the Spring that caus'd these commotions';[1] and even earlier there had been 'great murmurings' because of the scarcity of pork, 'which begun in a quarter least expected & serves to shew that People may be Guilty of the Highest Ingratitude'.[2] There was a vague story told to Banks twenty years later by one who had been a midshipman on the voyage, about desertion planned both by 'most of the People of the Endeavour', and by two or three 'gentlemen' who relinquished their intentions on learning of the men's.[3] Nothing is more likely than that men discussed mutiny or the delights of desertion, in that balmy air, in the abstract, as an irresponsible dream. When a man was first suspected of desertion, however, it appeared that he had been briefly kidnapped; and it does not seem likely that mutiny, in the more serious sense, was ever seriously considered. Webb and Gibson did desert, irresponsibly, for a dream of love; they had 'strongly attache'd themselves' to two girls;[4] they may even have fancied they could succeed. They should have known their captain better. They had gone to the mountains, said the Tahitians, who were certainly able to return them. The seizing of canoes earlier had not persuaded these people to act: Cook therefore resolved to seize chiefs and took half a dozen for hostages, including Purea, Tuteha and Tepau. This brought the return of Webb, though Jonathan Monkhouse and the corporal of marines, sent to bring in the fugitives, had been seized in their turn. Cook thereupon despatched Hicks with a strong party and orders from Tuteha, which combination was effective, and the chiefs were released. Though not maltreated, they had been affronted—from the Tahitian point of

---

[1] *Journals* I, 556 (7 May).   [2] ibid., 555 (5 May).
[3] ibid., cxlvi. The midshipman was J. M. Magra or Matra, later British consul at Tangier, whence (in 1790) he wrote to Banks on the subject of the *Bounty* mutiny, and then adverted to the *Endeavour*.
[4] *Journals* I, 116.

view very considerably so. It was not the happiest note on which to conclude a visit. The night before the ship sailed, therefore, Cook, Banks and Solander paid a visit to Pare and patched up a reconciliation.

The last job about the ship was renewing the stocks of both bower anchors, which had been eaten away to destruction by the worm. And then there were two additions to her company. More than one Tahitian had wished to join her. Cook was reluctant to take away anyone whose return he could not foresee, but Banks was eager. Tupaia the priest, Purea's adviser, had been much with them; he was a man of intelligence, of encyclopaedic local knowledge, came of a family of famous seamen, and had already provided a long list of islands from which it was possible to construct some sort of map, so that Cook agreed that he might be a help in discovery. Banks the collector, the man of fortune, overbore Cook: 'Thank heaven I have a sufficiency and I do not know why I may not keep him as a curiosity, as well as some of my neighbours do lions and tygers at a larger expence than he will probably ever put me to; the amusement I shall have in his future conversation and the benefit he will be of to this ship, as well as what he may be if another should be sent into these seas, will I think fully repay me.'[1] So Tupaia, natural history specimen and prospective pilot, was embarked, together with a small boy his servant, Taiata. Just before noon on Thursday, 13 July, in a light easterly breeze, the *Endeavour* sailed from Matavai Bay.

Cook did not at once turn south in pursuit of his instructions. He thought it better first to look at the nearby islands of which he had heard. He did not land at Moorea, nor at Tetiaroa, some eight leagues north-west of Point Venus, a low uninhabited island where the Tahitians went for fish and refreshment, but after taking a nearer view of the latter and noting the position of Tubuai Manu, forty miles to the west of Moorea, bore away farther westward for Huahine, about a hundred miles distant from Tahiti. Webb and Gibson both got their two dozen and were returned to duty. Gentle breezes led Tupaia to pray to his god Tane for wind (when he thought a wind was coming, said Banks), and whether or not with his assistance the ship, passing round the north of the island, was anchored on the afternoon of 16 July within the reef on its western side, in a fine deep harbour called Fare. It was here that Tupaia really began to prove his mettle. As the ship manœuvred he made a man dive down to

[1] Banks, I, 312–13.

the heel of the rudder and report the depth she drew, 'after which', says Banks, 'he has never sufferd her to go in less than 5 fathom water without being much alarmd.'[1] People had come on board at once when they saw Tupaia, among them their chief Ori. Ori and Cook struck up an immediate friendship, exchanging names—a thing in itself of no particular significance, perhaps, in the annals of explorers, but singular so far in Cook's experience, and though the two men's encounter was fleeting, the mark of a permanent regard. When a party landed, Tupaia, now priest rather than pilot, went through a lengthy propitiation ceremony to avert the anger of the local gods at the coming of strangers, and a hog and some coconuts were presented to signify their approval; but trade was not brisk, nor were these islanders. They were well-built, fairer than the Tahitians, rather incurious, and did not steal; according to Pickersgill, they 'Expres'd a great Desire of our going to Kill the Bollobollo Men'. Cook surveyed the island; Banks went up the hills and found the whole place much like Tahiti. Before Cook sailed on the 19th he gave Ori a few medals as testimony of his discovery, but more particularly a small pewter plate inscribed with the words *His Britannick Maj. Ship Endeavour, Lieut Cook Commander 16th July 1769. Huaheine.* The chief promised never to part with it, and he did not.

Leaving this harbour, Cook crossed over to another on the near side of Raiatea, twenty miles west: Teava Moa, the 'sacred harbour' of the Opoa district, where stood the most revered *marae* of all Polynesia, Taputapuatea, an inmost heart. Tupaia went through his propitiation ceremony again, though this was his own native island; Cook, faithful to his instructions, hoisted the English flag and took possession of the island and its neighbours. Next day sounding and coastal surveying went busily on, while Banks inspected boat-houses and canoes and measured a great canoe under construction— the Raiateans were famous canoe-builders—and the surgeon managed trade, much to the disgust of some on board, who wanted to acquire curiosities; instead they got fresh pork and as much fruit as they could eat.[2] The weather turned bad. It was not till the 24th that it seemed safe to leave shelter and haul to the north to look at Tahaa, an island within the same reef as Raiatea and divided from

[1] Banks, I, 323.

[2] *Journals* I, 144, n. 2. Pickersgill was very indignant: 'This day Trade Oligopoliz'd on Shore by the Surgeon &c whilst the most Trifling Thing was not admitted to be Purchas'd on board even by the Petty Officers a Centinal being Putt on each ganway on Purpus while the 2d Lieutn (Mr Gore) stay'd on the Qr Deck all day.' Wilkinson, the other master's mate (also a petty officer) remarks about the pork and fruit that it was 'the Captains Chief Steady [Study] to get for them.'

it only by a narrow channel; not till after beating about for four days that a boat could go in to sound a harbour and land Banks and Solander for provisions. Nor was the wind favourable for a landing on Borabora, though after leaving Tahaa Cook was close in with it. Fresh south-east gales forced him to ply for two days off the west side of Tahaa and Raiatea, so that it was the morning of 2 August by the time he could warp the ship into the harbour of Rautoanui on that side of Raiatea, where he wanted particularly both to stop a leak in the powder room and to pick up stones for ballast—and of course to resume his survey; and, for full measure, to fill his water casks. All this was done, and fresh provisions received; Banks and Solander explored the country, with or without Cook, met delightful people, were interested by their dances, and witnessed a number of 'interludes' or dramatic performances. Puni, the great warrior chief of Borabora, was then on Raiatea, most of which he had subjected to himself. He sent a present to Cook, who called on him with his own gift; the chief, in spite of his all-conquering reputation, seemed surprisingly decrepit and stupid, and not at all generous. Cook was more interested in the island and in sketching another harbour. After returning to the ship he was wind-bound for a day, the last day of a week at this place, where the supply of hogs and vegetables was so pleasing. There were, for an observant man, many impressions to assemble.

Among the islands neighbouring Raiatea which Cook had annexed for his royal master were two inconsiderable ones he had merely sighted, the atoll Tupai or Motu Iti a few miles north of Borabora, and Maurua or Maupiti, a high island rather more to the west: to these, with Huahine, Raiatea-Tahaa and Borabora he gave the collective name Society Isles, 'as they lay contiguous to one a nother.' The three main ones were worth having, in point of beauty. Anciently dead and shattered volcanoes, they were striking objects from the sea; Raiatea the largest and highest though by no means as high as Tahiti, Borabora the smallest and most fantastically dramatic. They had smooth and secure harbours. So much like Tahiti in general character and produce, they gave the naturalists little that was new; although without Tahiti's superabundance of breadfruit, their cultivated plantains and yams called forth the admiration of the seamen. The people seemed more open and free. The number of human jawbones hung up as trophies certainly argued a good deal of free and open violence.

In the morning of 9 August the wind, coming round to the east and steadying, carried the ship through the reef, and Cook made sail to the southward. Considering the mission on which he was now engaged, the words of Banks were perhaps too casual: 'Launchd out into the Ocean in search of what chance and Tupia might direct us to.'[1]

[1] Banks, I, 329.

IX

New Zealand

FOR THE first few days it was possible to hold a fairly direct southerly course, while Tupaia expatiated upon islands, and the captain himself and Banks, one imagines, began to compose their immensely valuable descriptions of the life of Tahiti and the neighbouring island group. The weather was agreeable. Four days from Raiatea, in latitude 22°26', an island was sighted to the east, and this one at least was prophesied by Tupaia—'Ohetiroa', Hiti-roa or Rurutu— a high island, dark-green with the *toa* or casuarina on its more level parts close to the shore, without barrier reef but fringed all round with a coral bank. As the ship could not get in close and Cook had no wish to stay he sent off the pinnace with Gore, Banks and Tupaia, to see if they could land and acquire any knowledge from the inhabitants of what lay to the southward. These inhabitants, in their bright red or yellow stained *tapa* garments, with their lances and spears of *toa* wood, proved a little belligerent, trying to seize the boat; so that, after the harmless discharge of a musket or two and some inconsiderable trade, Cook, having made the circuit of the island, hoisted her in again and made sail. He ignored Tupaia's pleas to turn west: not in that direction lay his instructions. Within the next week the weather began to deteriorate: as it got colder the island hogs and fowls, taken for a sea stock, unused to any diet but their native vegetables, began to sicken and die; neither did the store of those vegetables, other than yams and plantains, last well. Sea birds were abundant, albatrosses, petrels, shearwaters. The great Pacific swell discouraged any thought of land, though as early as 16 August a line of cloud in the east tempted the ship off her course for part of the morning. August 25 was the anniversary of her departure from England. The gentlemen brought out a piece of Cheshire cheese and tapped a cask of porter, and 'livd like English men', said Banks. There had been too much tapping of other casks, he thought, by surreptitious persons without need to celebrate, but at least they had not filled them up again with salt water, as he was told was the habit. Within a few days of this, died unexpectedly the boatswain's mate,

John Reading, who was fond of being drunk—for some unexplained reason carried off by three half-pints of rum, neat, which the boatswain had given him 'out of mere good nature'.

At the end of the month a comet was seen, a phenomenon observed also at Greenwich and Paris. September came in with squalls and gales and rain, high seas and cold, and more than once Cook brought to. On the first day of the month, in the afternoon, he found he was beyond the parallel to which his orders took him, in latitude 40°22', and longitude 145°39' W. He decided, with some regret, that he had come far enough: 'I did intend to have stood to the Southward if the winds had been moderate so long as they continued westerly notwithstanding we had no prospect of meeting with land, rather then stand back to ye northrd on the same track as we came; but as the weather was so very tempestuous I laid a side this design, thought it more advisable to stand to the Northward into better weather least we should receive such damages in our sails & rigging as might hinder the further prosecutions of the Voyage.'[1] So, in rather better weather, on a north-westerly course, he sailed up to latitude 29°, on 19 September briefly misled one day by a fog bank which looked like land, and sounding without finding bottom in a paler-coloured sea; then south-west to 38°30', ten days later. In those days seaweed had begun to float by, and one or two pieces of barnacle-covered wood, and everyone noticed the seal asleep in the water, and reflected that seals do not go far from land. The collectors never finished collecting: October brought one or two calms, in which Banks was off in a boat, shooting birds and netting jelly-fish. Cook altered course, as he made west, to a little north, then a little south. Expectation was rising. There was a gallon of rum promised to the first person who should sight land, despite John Reading's fate, with the further promise that his name should be given to some part of the coast. 'Now', wrote Banks for 30 October,

do I wish that our friends in England could by the assistance of some magical spying glass take a peep at our situation: Dr Solander setts at the Cabbin table describing, myself at my Bureau Journalizing, between us hangs a large bunch of sea weed, upon the table lays the wood and barnacles; they would see that notwisthstanding our different occupations our lips move very often, and without being conjurors might guess that we were talking about what we should see upon the land which there is now no doubt we shall see very soon.[2]

If friends of Cook could have invoked this magical glass they might have wondered whether he retained any rights in his own cabin.

[1] *Journals* I, 161.　　　　　　　　　[2] Banks, I, 396.

'Our old enemy Cape fly away entertaind us for three hours this morn': it is Banks again, 5 October, about latitude 38°, and some were sure the clouds were land. A paler sea had for some days again caused frequent sounding, without bottom. The 6th came with settled weather and gentle easterly breezes, before which the ship sailed slowly, making once more a little northing. At 2 p.m. a boy at the masthead, Nicholas Young, shouted Land!—and by sunset the line, no bank of cloud or fog, could be seen from the deck. At noon next day it was still about 8 leagues away, high land; below the heights smoke was rising; the weather was still clear; before nightfall a bay was descried, and the inland ranges appeared higher than ever. 'Much difference of opinion and many conjectures about Islands, rivers, inlets &c. but all hands seem to agree that this is certainly the Continent we are in search of', are the words Banks commits to his journal that night.[1] In the morning Cook stood in for the bay, where canoes, people, and houses could be seen; the sail-makers were busy making covers for the 'blunderbusses'—presumably the swivel guns—for boat service, so that he was taking no chances with these potentially difficult inhabitants; in the afternoon he anchored on the north-east side of the bay before the entrance of a small river, and immediately went ashore with Banks, Solander, and a party in the yawl and pinnace. They landed on the east side of the river.

'Certainly the Continent we are in search of'? Were these, then, the first steps, or the first European steps, on that fabled shore? Banks might think so. Others, even if not all hands, thought so. The titling of a number of Pickersgill's charts begins, 'A Chart of Part of the So Continent . . .'.[2] There is nothing to indicate that Cook thought so. Not having discovered it or any evident signs of it in his run south—and he had found 'no prospect' at all then of meeting with land—he was to turn west until he discovered either it or the eastern side of Tasman's 'New Zeland'. He does not mention Tasman in his journal until the end of the year; but his longitude differed only some half-dozen degrees from Tasman's reported longitudes on the west coast, and it would be hard for him not to think he had come to New Zeland. What then was Tasman's New Zeland? Cartographically, it was a scratch on the map. Tasman, who had certainly seen its north-western point, which he had called Cape

---

[1] Banks, I, 399.
[2] *Journals* I, 262, n. 5. His chart of the coast between Poverty Bay and the Court of Aldermen has the note '(N.B. This chart was taken before this country was found to be an island).'

Maria van Diemen, had rightly deduced open ocean to the east: at the same time, he thought it not impossible that the coast ran south-east to join Le Maire's Staten Land, and he gave his discovery the same name. Wherever it went, it did not join Staten Land, as was immediately proved by the Dutch Captain who sailed round Staten Land and saw no sign of a continent. Also, Cook had just proved, it could be no part of the continent hypothetically outlined by Alexander Dalrymple. That did not prove it could be no part of a southern continent. It might be the northern projection of some mass that lay, perhaps, far to the south. There might, again, be an open passage through this projection leading to the ocean that lapped South America and its Spanish wealth—the great bay, *Zeehaens bocht*, where Tasman had ridden out the stormy Christmas of 1642. Obviously the only thing for Cook to do was to obey his instructions, and to explore as much of the coast as the condition of the bark, the health of the crew, and the state of his provisions would admit of. This, large as was the sum total of his observations on mankind—on the 'Indians' of this country—obviously was his leading and immovable thought over the next six months; and whereas his Tahitian experience was so much in the discovery of men, this one was in the discovery, quite remarkably rounded and complete, of a country.

A discovery, none the less, immediately concerned with men; for he had landed. The first two days were disastrous, all that Cook deplored and Lord Morton had warned him against, all with the best intentions. These Indians, clearly, did not regard the stranger as someone automatically to be welcomed. Cook, seeing a number of them on the west side of the river, crossed over in the yawl to meet them, leaving the pinnace at the river entrance. When they made off he and his party walked two or three hundred yards to look at some huts; at this four men rushed out from the trees on the eastern side to seize the yawl, which, warned by shouts from the pinnace, dropped downstream closely pursued; the pinnace fired, first over the pursuers' heads, then directly at them, and one fell dead. His three companions stopped, startled by this novelty in killing. Cook went back to the ship. He landed again next morning, this time with the marines, on the river's west bank, to face a body of hostile people on the other side, flourishing their weapons and leaping in a war dance. He managed to bring them to a parley; to his surprise, they understood Tupaia perfectly; twenty or thirty of them swam over to him. In spite of presents given them they remained truculent, snatching at the English weapons, Tupaia was full of warnings; when one of them fled with Green's hanger Cook felt forced to have him fired at, first with small shot, then with ball; and he fell fatally wounded. The others retreated with his arms and a few wounds from further small shot. Cook, baffled of friendly contact and finding the river salt, decided to row round the bay, both to look for fresh water and if possible to surprise and secure some persons, who might then be convinced that his intentions were friendly. Heavy surf prevented his landing a second time this day, but seeing two canoes coming in from fishing he intercepted one of them. Tupaia's invitations failed to attract its occupants, and a shot fired over their heads, instead of stopping them, caused them to attack the boat with every weapon and missile they had. Cook, on the defensive, ordered his men to fire again: two or three of these uncomprehending savages were killed, and three more, all young, who jumped into the water were taken up. On board the ship these young fellows, who were inured to hazardous chances, turned at once 'as cheerful and as merry as if they had been with their own friends'; they 'seem'd much less concerned at what had happen'd then I was myself.'[1] Cheerful and merry Cook could not be. He had meant well and his well meaning had broken down. He had to accuse himself in his journal; but could he accuse himself unreservedly?

I can by no means justify my conduct in attacking and killing the people in this boat who had given me no just provication and was wholy igernorant of my design and had I had the least thought of their making any resistance I would not so much as have looked at them but when we was once a long side of them we must either have stud to be knockd on the head or else retire and let them gone off in triumph and this last they would of Course have attributed to thier own bravery and our timorousness.[2]

That did not seem quite right and he tried again, beginning, 'I am aware that most humane men who have not experienced things of this nature will cencure my conduct', and omitting those last miserable phrases with which, after all, he had tried to buttress self-justification, 'and let them gone off in triumph . . .'.[3] He did not deny the bravery: his men recorded it with admiration. As for Banks, who had been the first to fire that morning, he had his own sorrow to set down: 'Thus ended the most disagreable day My life has yet seen, black be the mark for it and heaven send that such may never return to embitter future reflection.'[4] The reader may himself care to reflect that this was a rather new note in the literature of discovery.

[1] *Journals* I, ccxi, 171.
[2] ibid., ccxi, printed from a fragment in the Mitchell Library.
[3] For Cook's final version of his account see *Journals* I, 171.   [4] Banks, I, 403.

The following day some wood was cut and the three youths, full of ship's food and reluctant to leave, were put ashore. Out of some two hundred armed natives who assembled only one man seemed conversable, crossing the river to receive presents; Cook therefore to avoid a further clash, took his men back to the ship. Early next morning, 11 October, he stood out of the bay. What would he call it: Endeavour Bay? He thought so, then changed to Poverty Bay, 'because it afforded us no one thing we wanted' except a little wood, in spite of the obvious population and the smokes that spread far up the inland valleys. The name of the boy Nicholas Young was used, true to promise—the south-west point of the bay became Young Nick's Head. Cook turned down the coast intending to go as far as 40° or 41° and then, if the prospect was not encouraging, to sail north again. In this way he employed a week of running survey and sporadic contact with the New Zealanders, often enough hostile, who came off in their canoes to inspect the wonder.

On the first afternoon, in a calm, several canoes came along-side and some men even on board, to trade their paddles for Tahitian cloth. Three stayed overnight, and reassured more cautious visitors in the morning that their hosts did not eat men. The three captured youths, when first put on shore, had seemed afraid of being killed and eaten by their enemies. Were these savages then cannibals? There was then no further evidence, and the men departed. This was off the flat headland Cook called Cape Table, whence the land trended south-south-west on the outside of a peninsula to the Isle of Portland, much like its namesake in the English Channel; and hauling round the south end of this island he found himself in a large bay. It was large enough to contain subsidiary bays; behind its white cliffs, sandy beaches and houses, a well-wooded interior ran back to hills and mountains patched with snow; but as Cook slowly followed its coast, he could find no harbour or watering place, while more than once he had to disperse hostile canoes with shots fired wide from his four-pounders. On the 15th, abreast of a point which was the south-west limit of the bay, there was a more serious incident. Several canoes came out to the ship and sold her some 'stinking'—that is, smoked or dried—fish; 'however, it was such as they had, and we were glad to enter into traffick with them upon any terms.' Then a man cheated the captain of a piece of red cloth, offered in exchange for a dog-skin cloak, and the canoes all put off, only to return with more of the fish. Bargaining went on during which Tupaia's servant-boy, Taiata, was over the side; he was suddenly snatched into a canoe, the canoe fled, the ship opened fire, in the confusion the boy leapt from the canoe into the water and was rescued, and the natives retreated to the shore with two or three more dead. To the bay Cook gave the name of Sir Edward Hawke, the First Lord; the cape he called Kidnappers. He continued in fine weather slowly down the coast, which did not alter its direction, past houses and canoes by day and fires by night; until on the 17th, having come to his limit, 'Seeing no likelyhood of meeting with a harbour, and the face of the Country Vissibly altering for the worse', he 'thought that the standing farther to the South would not be attended with any Valuable discovery, but would be loosing of time which might be better employ'd and with a greater probabillity of Success in examining the Coast to the Northward'. It was off Cape Turnagain, which he put in latitude 40°34′, that he reversed his course; and his instinct was quite sound.

Sailing north at first further out at sea, he was off the peninsula—Mahia—two days later, and the natives began to come out to the ship continually. They were now very friendly. Past the 'remarkable head' he called Gable End Foreland he sighted two promising bays, in which he determined to try for water and see a little of the country. The more southerly one he could not fetch, but in the other, 'Tegadoo'[1] or Anaura, he was able to land, carry on a little trade for sweet potatoes, collect wild celery, and get a little water—though Banks and Solander also got a thorough dowsing in the surf from an overturned canoe. Leaving this bay, he found a contrary wind, and learning that there was a good supply of water in the other, put in there, anchoring a mile outside a small cove just within its south point. The name of the bay he got incorrectly as Tolaga, perhaps from the native tauranga, an anchorage: it was correctly Uawa. The cove, at the bottom of a great green amphitheatre, we know now as Cook's Cove. Wood and water abounded, wild celery and 'scurvy grass';[2] the trees, plants and birds sent the natural historians into an ecstasy. Cook could sound the bay, settle the latitude and longitude by exact observation, climb hills and look at the country, he admired the native gardens, noticed no sign of animals except dogs and rats, established most amicable relations with the people. There was good trade: fish, sweet potatoes or curiosities on the one side, cloth, beads

---

[1] Parkinson uses the form Te Karu. 'Tegadoo' illustrates the difficulty Cook had sometimes in reducing a native word to English, as well as in determining a place name. It may be derived from Te ngaru, breakers or the heavy surf his informant thought he was referring to. See Journals I, 183, n. 1.

[2] Wild celery was a genuine celery, Apium prostratum. The 'scurvy grass', Maori nau, botanical Lepidium oleraceum, was once very common on New Zealand coasts, but few living eyes have seen it, except in a herbarium, as it has been eaten out of existence by sheep and cattle.

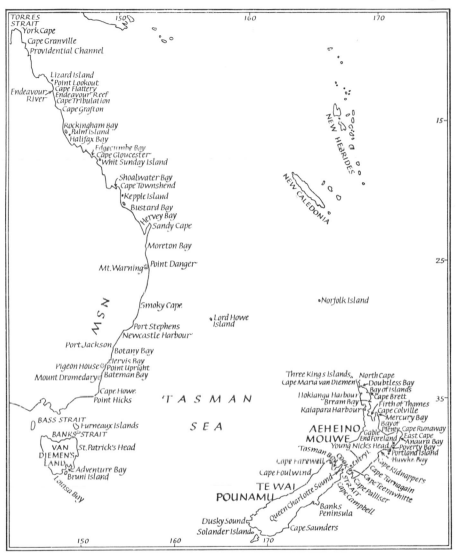

New Zealand and the East Coast of Australia

and nails on the other. Cook let trade be general. These people valued the *tapa* cloth from Tahiti and Raiatea more highly than anything else, everybody in the ship had some; so 'I suffer'd every body to purchase what ever they pleased without limitation, for by this means I knew that the natives would not only sell, but get a good price for every thing they brought'—and would bring to market whatever the country afforded. There were not the fruits of Tahiti, though the wild celery, gathered free, 'a great Antiscorbutick', could be boiled every morning with portable soup and oatmeal for breakfast. Banks measured a great canoe; Parkinson and Spöring sketched the cove, the bay, the romantic natural arch through the hillside.; Tupaia talked. It was a useful five days, and on the morning of 29 October Cook was at sea again heading north.

Next day he rounded East Cape, which he had 'great reason to think . . . the Eastermost land on this whole Coast', passed Hicks Bay (Lieutenant Hicks being the first to sight it), and Cape Runaway, off which a number of suspiciously heavily armed canoes were sent hurrying off to shore by a round shot fired over their heads; and was in the large opening in the coast he was to call the Bay of Plenty. He called it so not from any improvement in his own fortunes, but from the fertile, cultivated and well-populated appearance of the land. Off one island he saw a large double canoe full of people, one of the few of these canoes seen since Tasman. Visiting canoes tended to disregard European ethics of trade, paddling off without return for what they were given: it did not strike Cook—how could it?—that here might be current different rules of exchange, and that if he waited he might get a handsome equivalent later on as a present; indeed, if it had struck him, he could not afford to wait. Nor could he afford the linen, towing over the side to wash, which was carried off without ceremony, nor did volleys of stones seem the mark of a generous spirit; so that his own friendly efforts were varied with an occasional musket shot or four-pounder. There were a number of islands in the bay, rocks, some shoal water, all to go down on the chart. Further west the country changed its appearance: 'Continent appeard this morn barren and rocky', noted Banks on 3 November, noting also the cluster of rocks and islets that was called the Court of Aldermen from their resemblance, 'thick and squat or lank and tall, to some one or other of those respectable citizens' of London. In the afternoon three canoes came alongside, unornamented, simply hollowed out of large trees, with naked paddlers, 'yet these few despicable gentry sang their song of defiance and promisd us as heartily as the most respectable of their countrey men that they would kill us all'.[1] When Cook turned into an inlet that appeared an hour later the ship was accompanied by a small truculent fleet, which went away with the further promise to attack her on the morrow—a promise which led to nothing beyond a visit by night, some 'parading about', trade and 'trickery' in the morning, and the discharge of a few firearms; after which the people became extremely friendly. Cook found a good anchorage a mile inside the south entrance point of the inlet, off a smooth sandy half-moon beach and a river into which the boats could go at low water. Here was the harbour he had wanted; here also a convenient place for observing the transit of Mercury, due on 9 November, which if well done would give him an accurate longitude. Here, in Mercury Bay,[2] he was to remain for eleven days, observing, wooding and watering, recruiting his men, cleaning the ship, surveying (one of his own most elaborate coastal profiles takes in the whole circuit of the bay), and giving much study to the life of the people of the district.

The weather was clear for the observation. Unfortunately while Cook and Hicks were on shore attending to it a man in a visiting canoe cheated Gore, on board the ship, of a woven cloak he had agreed to exchange for a piece of cloth; and as the canoe moved off, with paddles shaken defiantly, the furious Gore seized a musket and shot the man dead. 'I must own', says Cook, that this 'did not meet with my approbation because I thought the punishment a little too severe for the Crime, and we had now been long enough acquainted with these People to know how to chastise trifling faults like this without taking away their lives.'[3] There were no more lives taken away. In this bay there was no more truculence. The people did not seem highly prosperous, nor their country cultivated; probably, as they slept under trees and temporary shelters, they were seasonal visitors, eaters of fern root, who came to the coast for the fishing;[4] and up the river, as Cook's men found, there were boat-loads of delectable rock-oysters, as well as wild fowl in the country and the wild celery on which the captain set such store. There were certainly, on the other hand, many fortified villages, pa, on promontories and

---

[1] Banks, I, 425.
[2] On the name see *Journals* I, 202, n. 3. It was a second choice; he at first intended to use a native name, probably 'Opoorage', from Purangi, the name of the stream he called 'Oyster River'.
[3] *Journals* I, 196.
[4] And probably to assert land-claims, which was a matter Cook could not guess at. To quote later Maori reminiscence: 'Our tribe was living there at that time. We did not live there as our permanent home, but were there according to our custom of living for some time on each of our blocks of land, to keep our claim to each, and that our fire might be kept alight on each block, so that it might not be taken from us by some other tribe.'—Beaglehole, *The Discovery of New Zealand*, 89.

rocks, built with ditches, palisades and fighting stages, most admirable pieces of engineering; Cook was hardly less impressed by the
native weapons, lances, truncheons, and darts, though the bow and
arrow was unknown. An ingenious as well as warlike people he
thought they must be; and they confirmed his impression that they
ate their enemies.

He and Banks were not the only curious observers. The people
were tenacious of memory; more than eighty years later, when
Cook's countrymen had come to New Zealand as settlers, an
ancient chief, Te Horeta, a man of blood in many wars, told them of
the great happening of his childhood. The ship had come, it seemed
a supernatural thing, and its men supernatural beings, for they
pulled their boats with their backs to the shore where they were to
land—had they eyes at the backs of their heads? They pointed a
stick at a shag, there was thunder and lightning and the shag fell
dead; the children were terrified and ran with the women into the
trees. But these *tupua*, goblins or demons, were kind, and gave food:
something hard like pumice-stone but sweet, something else that was
fat, perhaps whale-blubber or flesh of man, though it was salt and
nipped the throat—ships bread, or biscuit, salt beef or pork. There
was one who collected shells, flowers, tree-blossoms and stones.
They invited the boys to go on board the ship with the warriors, and
little Te Horeta went, and saw the warriors exchange their cloaks
for other goods, and saw the one who was clearly the lord, the leader
of the tupua. He spoke seldom, but felt the cloaks and handled the
weapons, and patted the children's cheeks and gently touched their
heads. The boys did not walk about, they were afraid lest they should
be bewitched, they sat still and looked; and the great lord gave Te
Horeta a nail, and Te Horeta said *Ka pai*, which is 'very good', and
people laughed. Te Horeta used this nail on his spear, and to make
holes in the side boards of canoes; he had it for a god but one day his
canoe capsized and he lost it, and though he dived for it he could not
find it. And this lord, the leader, gave Te Horeta's people two hand-
fuls of potatoes, which they planted and tended; they were the first
people to have potatoes in this country. There are other traditions,
brief lights: none as circumstantial as this.[1]

Delayed two days beyond his intentions by foul weather and
easterly winds Cook did not sail till early on 15 November. Before he
left he cut the ship's name and the date on a tree near the watering

[1] Te Horeta Taniwha told his story to numerous people. It is now most easily to be
consulted in Beaglehole, *Discovery of New Zealand*, 88 ff., reprinted from John White,
Ancient History of the Maori, V (Wellington, 1889), 121–8.

place, displayed the colours and took formal possession of the place for his royal master—though he does not indicate that he had 'the consent of the natives' for this proceeding.[1] Three days later he was off a cape he called after his old commodore Colville, with land both to the north-west and the south-west; turning the cape he found himself in a deep gulf. He was in fact on the inner side of the hilly peninsula of which Mercury Bay is an indentation on the east, and after sailing south twelve or thirteen leagues and anchoring for a night, had to anchor again because of shoal water. Though the water shoaled, however, it did not come to an end. Cook thought he might now be able to see some of the interior of the country: taking to the boats with Banks, he rowed nine miles to the bottom of the gulf, then twelve or fourteen miles up a river that flowed into it, landing at noon to examine the magnificent forest trees about them, trees standing tall and straight as an arrow. He called the river the Thames, from some resemblance he saw to the English river—perhaps its marshy banks where there were no trees, its breadth (and he included in the name the whole of what we call the Hauraki gulf, as if it were an estuary), and its strong tides. The natives encountered were all very friendly. On the return journey the wind and the flood compelled the boats themselves to anchor for the night; after they had regained their ship a combination of tide, calms, and then stormy rainy weather kept her in the gulf until 23 November. Many islands were to be seen—perhaps there were harbours behind them? The weather made it impossible to lay down the western main with confidence, when it was again relatively clear the ship was off Bream Bay, with the fantastic peaks of its northern head, and the fishing was excellent. A little further north canoes were troublesome: 'in order to get rid of them we were at the expence of 2 or 3 Musquet Balls and one 4 pound shot but as no harm was intended them none they received unless they happend to over heat themselves in pulling a shore'.[2] The Cook who gave the doll, his wife's 'Picter', to Purea is evident again here; things were going cheerfully, he was not above the humour of the Court of Aldermen, or, a little later, of Cape Brett—because off the cape lay a high rock with a hole pierced through it, and the distinguished admiral after whom he named it was Sir Piercy. That cape stood outside another deep bay, which at first he passed by; but losing ground steadily before a strong westerly wind, he bore away for it again and anchored in shoal water before one

[1] It is to be noted that Cook did not here, or anywhere else in New Zealand, take possession of the whole country, as many New Zealanders fancy he did. On the 'consent of the Natives', see his instructions, *Journals* I, cclxxxiii.
[2] *Journals* I, 212.

the many islands within its entrance, Motu Arohia. The day was 29 November.

The familiar pattern of native behaviour was repeated, this time with more danger. A crowd assembled in their canoes, from which a few persons were allowed on board and given presents; then others tried to carry off the buoy of the anchor, the muskets and a gun were fired, the people fled, it took Tupaia's good offices to bring them back. Cook moved the ship farther out, and, with Banks and Solander landed on the island. Almost at once they were surrounded by two or three hundred armed and jostling men, some of whom broke into a war dance while others tried unsuccessfully to seize the boats; pushed back by small shot beyond a line drawn on the sand they rallied more than once, until the attentive Hicks, swinging the ship round, fired her guns over their heads. This dispersed the mob, and they became 'meek as lambs'. Cook could peaceably load the boats with celery, intending to sail next morning. But next morning the wind fell calm, thereafter turning to the north. He flogged three sailors for robbing sweet potato plantations during the night, and settled down to some days of trafficking, mainly for fish, filling his casks, gathering greens, sounding the harbour, and visiting as much of the country as possible. It was more thickly populated than those parts further south, the people more elaborately tattoed, some of their canoes more elaborately carved; the bay itself beautiful, with many good anchorages, the hills and valleys round it, forests and cultivations, beautiful also. Cook called it the Bay of Islands. Early on 5 December he weighed anchor with a favourable wind, which changed in the afternoon and then faded away altogether, so that shortly before midnight the ship was almost carried on shore by a current; escaping that the ship struck a sunken rock, from which she fortunately went clear without damage. In the morning she was once more safely at sea.

Cook now had ahead of him an extremely difficult period. It displays his temper and his patience at their best. He had to undergo a month of weather that varied from contrary winds of no great strength to furious gales, in which he was determined to abandon neither the land nor his purpose of fixing its position. For the first ten days he tacked off and on up the last hundred miles of the eastern coast, past bays and promontories and a long straight 'desart shore' that he religiously described and charted with an accuracy which would have given lesser men pride under the most favourable conditions. A few canoes came out once or twice; from them he learnt that the land would soon turn west to a point that could only, he thought, be Tasman's Cape Maria van Diemen. On the morning of 13 December, after a rainy night, the gales began, and he was driven out of sight of land for the first time since coming upon the coast. A squall split the main topsail—the outset of many days' hard work for the sailmaker over sorely-tried and torn canvas. There were, luckily, some intervals of clear weather. At noon on the 14th the ship was north-east of a point already seen, now judged by Cook to be the northern extremity of the country, as a great swell rolling in from the west argued against any covering of land: its position must certainly be fixed. Forced east and then north-west, Cook was close enough to it to do so, describe it minutely, and even to see a few people upon it, by the 18th—in spite of the winds and a strong current from the west. He had 'not gained one Inch to windward this last 24 hours'. He called the point North Cape.[1] He was driven northwards out of sight of land again, though with intervals of clear and even a short one of pleasant weather; on the 24th the island or little cluster called Three Kings by Tasman, seen from the masthead the previous day, was recognised. It was well that the weather cleared; 'Christmas day', wrote Banks, who had been improving a calm by shooting gannets or 'Solan Geese', 'our Goose pye was eat with great approbation and in the Evening all hands were as Drunk as our forefathers used to be upon the like occasion'—or as they themselves had been in the Atlantic twelve months before. On the 26th Cook reckoned that standing south, they were in the latitude of the Bay of Islands and only about thirty leagues west of the longitude of North Cape, yet they could see no land; so the northern part of the country must indeed be narrow. In the afternoon they had a fresh gale which in thirty-six hours rose to a hurricane, with rain and a 'prodigious high' sea. Twice the ship was brought to, the gale abated only to renew itself; she was blown to the west, then got to the north-east, crossing her previous course; then the wind veering south-west, the sea ran so high that she went bodily to leeward. But whatever course was forced upon him, Cook was determined to fix the position of Cape Maria van Diemen. In the end he had it in sight for three days —on one day North Cape as well—and the position he fixed was astonishing: two minutes out in latitude, four minutes in longitude.[2] His reflection, having done that, and as he began the new year, was a

[1] Cook's position for the North Cape was 34°22′ S, 186°55′ W, or 173°5′ E. The position as now accepted is 34°26′ S, 173°4′ E. The most northerly point of the country is in fact Kerr Point (a slight bulge rather than a point) just west of North Cape, a little less than 34°25′ S in latitude.

[2] Cook's reckoning was 34°30′ S, 187°25′ W (172°42′ E); the modern position is 34°28′ S, 172°38′ E. His North Cape is just as accurate—even more so, with an error of only one minute in longitude.

sober one: 'I cannot help thinking but what will appear a little strange that at this season of the year we should be three weeks in geting 10 Leagues to the westward and five weeks in geting 50 Leagues for so long it is sence we pass'd C Brett but it will hardly be credited that in the midest of summer and in the Latitude of 35° such a gale of wind as we have had could have happen'd, which for its strength and continuence was such as I hardly was ever in before. Fortunately at this time we were at a good distance from land otherwise it might have proved fatal to us.'[1]

Nor was the gale yet over, nor the struggle to keep the coast in view without running on to it, nor sober reflections. On 2 January 1770 there was no land in sight, and a wind blowing right on shore and 'a high rowling sea' from the west made dangerous any closer approach. Until the 6th south-westerlies continued. Beating against them, Cook by the 4th was as far south as the Kaipara harbour (his False Bay): he had missed a good deal of the land, though standing north-west again he could judge its direction. What he could see struck him, like that on the other side, as desolate and inhospitable, another 'desart coast' and obviously dangerous: 'this I am so fully sencible of that was we once clear of it I am determind not to come so near again if I can possible avoide it unless we have a very favourable wind indeed'.[2] On the 6th the wind dropped and the weather cleared; next day variable winds gave way to gentle north-east breezes. The storm was over. Cape Maria van Diemen was again in sight to the north, but there was a turtle upon the water, and the ship could sail south comfortably along the line of the shore, a good stretch every day. The aspect of the land improved; the shore turned the great bulge where Taranaki, the mountain to which Cook gave the name of Egmont, that earl not so long before so deep in Pacific plans, thrust up its noble snow-topped height; and on the 14th he found himself in what seemed a 'very broad and deep Bay', its westward limit beyond sight, its south-west side high and broken. On that side were visible a number of inlets. It was the *Zeehaens bocht* of Tasman. Into one of these inlets Cook determined to go. The ship was foul; she needed small repairs, wood and water, as well as cleaning; her men needed another taste of the land. After plying on and off for the night he passed a ledge of rocks, keeping clear, with the help of the boats, of the north-west shore towards which a strong current drew him; saw a startled sea-lion rise up, a canoe cross the

---

[1] *Journals* I, 228.
[2] ibid., 230. Admiral Wharton, in a footnote to his edition of Cook's first journal, p. 178, remarks, 'The mingled audacity and caution of Cook's navigation off this coast must awake the admiration of every seaman.'

bay, a village standing on the south-west point of an island a few miles within it, inhabitants all under arms. The weather was clear and settled with hardly any wind, and hauling round this point, towed by his boats, at two o'clock in the afternoon of 15 January 1770 Cook anchored in 'a very snug Cove' facing it, on the north-west side of the inlet. The precision with which one writes is justified; for the captain had come to the beautiful spot which, though at that moment he was unknowing of the future, was to be a centre of rest and strategy in all his ocean campaigns. It was Ship Cove, in Queen Charlotte's Sound.

At that moment he would have been surprised to learn something else he did not know. He was not the only European sailor to have been on the northern shores he had lately left. Jean François Marie de Surville, one of a French syndicate who had come by garbled reports of an immensely rich Pacific island seven hundred leagues west of Peru—there were elements of Tahiti in this—had sailed from Pondicherry in June 1769 to beat the English to it, just as Cook was taking a last precautionary look at his telescopes in preparation for the Transit. Surville had determined to sail through the Eastern Archipelago; after unwittingly encountering the Solomon Islands he found his men so sick that he determined to strike south and try to pick up Tasman's Staten Land for refreshment; he went to 35° and then changed his course to the east, so that he sighted the New Zealand coast on 12 December, in latitude 35°37′, just south of the bar harbour Hokianga. On that day Cook was nearly opposite him, on the other side of the island, half a league from shore. Surville, no more than Cook later, was tempted to make a landing here, and resolved to double Cape Maria van Diemen. This he did, not without some danger as he made his way north. The westerly gale that blew Cook out of sight of land, and out of possible sight of the French vessel, was kinder to Surville; on 16 December he rounded North Cape, with Cook fifty miles to the north, next day anchoring his *Saint Jean Baptiste* within an opening somewhat to the south which Cook had called, without entering, Doubtless Bay. Unlike Cook, he had a ship's company in dreadful state—sixty men dead, and the rest so enfeebled by scurvy that they could hardly handle the boats. The land, fresh food and water rapidly improved the state of these; but the easterly storm which fell on Cook at sea on the 27th imperilled Surville frighteningly in harbour and he lost anchors, cables and a dinghy. He suspected the local people of stealing his dinghy, alienated them by using force, though unsuccessfully, to recover it, and was compelled to sail away to further disaster, off the coast of

Peru, where he was drowned in attempting to land. A good seaman, he was an adventurer rather than an explorer. One has difficulty in picturing the scene had he and Cook met.

The deep inlet to which Cook had come is a precipitous place, and only at its southern end, so far down that Cook never had time to explore it, does any real expanse of flat country begin; but the steep high hills were clothed in dark green, the land was 'one intire forest'. Into the cove ran an abundant stream of sweet fresh water; the waters of the sound rendered up god's plenty of fish, its shores illimitable quantities of the wild celery and scurvy grass that were the delight of Cook's heart. He had come in the season of fair weather; for though the winds can tear down in fury from the heights and rain fall heavily, for the first fortnight of his three weeks' stay there was little to record but gentle breezes and a clear sky. There was much work to do: 'rest', for Cook's men, tended to be the refreshment they got from change of labours and change of diet, but refreshment they certainly got, and they had their hours of wandering. Few of them were immune to the sound of bird song across the water, so charmingly recorded by Banks two days after the ship anchored. 'This morn', he wrote, 'I was awakd by the singing of the birds ashore from whence we are distant not a quarter of a mile, the numbers of them were certainly very great who seemd to strain their throats with emulation perhaps; their voices were certainly the most melodious wild musick I have ever heard, almost imitating small bells but with the most tuneable silver sound imaginable to which maybe the distance was no small addition. On enquiring of our people I was told that they had observd them ever since we have been here, and that they begin to sing at about 1 or 2 in the morn and continue till sunrise, after which they are silent all day like our nightingales.'[1] So does the bell-bird, the Maori *korimako*, enter the literature of New Zealand, though doubtless his notes were accompanied by those of other victims of the collectors' gun; for Banks and Solander had arrived in another natural historian's paradise. It was plants rather than birds, however, that filled their bags; it was mankind, also the study of the natural historian, that for a moment appalled their minds. For a moment, because in spite of the horror that cannibalism inspires, one must admit that in its discussion there is a certain element of the agreeable.

Like a number of other New Zealanders, the people of the sound introduced themselves with a shower of stones, but in general they

[1] Banks, I, 455–6.

were friendly enough. They seemed poorer than those in the north, and Cook reckoned their number at only three or four hundred; their canoes were mean and unornamented, they had no plantations nor anything to exchange but fish and their weapons. He thought they had more commonsense than their more prosperous fellows, because they took nails as payment for fish, and were eager to acquire English cloth rather than paper or Tahitian *tapa*. Their savagery was more directly visible. The day following the ship's arrival Cook, Banks, and Tupaia visited a cove not far away, where, with a dog then cooking, were bones obviously human and not entirely picked, about which Tupaia got all the information that native mime did not convey. Next morning, alongside the ship, another bone was handed over, 'and to shew us that they had eat the flesh they bit and naw'd the bone and draw'd it thro' their mouth and this in such a manner as plainly shew'd that the flesh was to them a dainty bit.'[1] Other bones were found lying around, some near a native oven; Banks was able to buy the preserved head of one of the persons who had constituted the recent feast. 'I suppose they live intirely upon fish dogs and enemies', he said in remarking upon the absence of cultivation. He had forgotten the fern-roots he saw in Mercury Bay.

Cook's primary interest, however—to repeat—was geographical, and while work on the ship went on he had the boats out, exploring and surveying in every direction. The inlet must, he thought, be not far from the Murderers' Bay where Tasman had lost four of his men: Tasman's bay was in fact distant about seventy miles, and Tasman was unknown to the tradition of the tribe he was now meeting. He made two excursions towards the sea along this western shore and found a good harbour but nothing else except forested hills. Then came a more remarkable expedition. On 22 January he set out in the pinnace in the opposite direction, towards the end of the inlet. After rowing twelve or fifteen miles against the wind he could neither reach nor see it; so at noon he landed on the eastern side and, leaving Banks and Solander to botanise, climbed with a sailor up the steep flank of a hill—part of a ridge the highest point of which is called Kaitapeha[2]—to take a view. Even from twelve hundred feet he could not see what happened to the inlet; but he was 'abundantly recompenced' otherwise. To the east, under his eye lay the ocean; and from it an open strait ran to the 'Western Sea' which he had sailed from Cape Maria van Diemen to the very broad and deep bay off which

[1] *Journals* I, 236–7.
[2] The point has been most accurately identified by Charles and Neil Begg, and is now known as Cook's Lookout. See their *James Cook and New Zealand* (Wellington, 1969), 62–5.

ran his inlet. Tasman's *bocht* was then a strait after all, as the wind-baffled Tasman had thought possible, and Cook was standing on one of the narrow ridges on its south-west side. On the other side was the land he had been coasting; the eastward limit of which he could not see. It was one of the dramatic moments of the voyage, but the journal-page remains sober. Cook returned to the ship examining islands, bays and coves, and four days later made another 'excursion' to the eastern side of the inlet, closer to the entrance. He climbed another hill, 'very high', this time with Banks and Solander, and saw the strait stretching full before them with the opposite shore (he thought) about twelve miles away, though to the south-east haze blocked the view. 'However', writes the cautious man, 'I had now seen enough of this passage to convence me that there was the greatest probability in the world of its runing into the Eastern Sea as the distance of that Sea from this place cannot exceed 20 Leagues even to where we were, upon this I resolve'd after puting to sea to search this passage with the Ship.'[1] Whereupon, placing in a pyramid built of loose stones some musket balls and other odds and ends likely to last they went down the hill to find Tupaia and the boat's crew in amiable converse with some of the native inhabitants. Tupaia was proving exceedingly useful.

The last expedition was to the mouth of the inlet, where Cook landed on the western point and once more climbed a hill, this time 'pretty high', he raised another pile of stones, with a silver coin, a few musket balls and beads inside it, and a piece of an old pendant flying from the top. This hill gave him a view of the coast to the north-west and an island about ten leagues off which he called after Philip Stephens, the Admiralty secretary with whom he had most to do. For the eastern point he was able to obtain the native name, and put it on the chart, Cape Koamaru. There was little more to do, either in producing the sort of survey, somewhat short of perfection, which he thought then necessary, or in work on the ship; so he had the carpenter prepare two posts with the ship's name and the date cut on them. One of these was set up at the watering place and the Union flag hoisted on it. The next day, the last of the month, the other was taken over to the island opposite the cove, Motuara; its purpose was explained to the people, to be a mark to show any other ship that came to the inlet that the *Endeavour* had already been there; they promised not to pull it down, and received presents of silver threepenny pieces and spike nails stamped with the broad arrow, things likely to be preserved. The post was planted on the highest

[1] *Journals* I, 240.

part of the island, at its southern end, the flag hoisted, the inlet 'dignified' with the name of Queen Charlotte, and it and the adjacent lands taken possession of for King George III. The health of his Queen was then drunk in a bottle of wine, and the empty bottle given to a much-gratified old man. This was the last time that Cook took possession of any part of New Zealand, and how he would have defined 'the adjacent lands' may be left in obscurity. The weather for this ceremony was fair, though it had previously shown signs of breaking; but February came in with such a storm of wind and rain from the north-west that the hawser mooring the ship to the shore broke, the overflowing stream carried away and lost ten water casks, and—noted Banks—'our poor little wild musicians were totally disturbed by it.' Happily this did not last long, though the wind was still in the north, for Cook was now ready to leave. As he collected his last celery and traded for his last dried fish the people made it clear that they were ready to see him leave. The depredations of a hundred men for three weeks on the food supplies of that haphazard community cannot indeed have been small.

On the afternoon of 5 February the ship was warped out of the cove and got under sail, but in faint and variable winds, falling to a calm all night, had to anchor until the following morning, when a renewed light breeze took her out of the sound and round Cape Koamaru into the strait. Cook's first purpose was to pass the strait. He does not give it a name: Banks is the man who tells us it is to bear the captain's own name, and we may suspect Banks of insisting on the point. When the captain had passed it, what then? We learn his intentions from his actions and from a conversation he had with the old man on Motuara, on the day he took possession. He had 'some conjectures that the lands to the SW of this strait (which we are now at) was an Island and not part of a continent'; and the old man said that there were 'two *Wannuaes*, that is two lands or islands that might be circumnavigated in a few days, even in four.' These two 'wannuaes' or *whenua* he called 'Tovy-poenammu', or *Te Wai Pounamu*, and it was the short circumnavigation of these that Cook thought he was engaged upon even while he was in the strait. There was a third land, a large one, which could be sailed round only in many moons, on the east side of the strait, and obviously Cook had been on its coasts already. Its name was 'Aeheino mouwe'.[1] About this third land the only doubt is how to transliterate the name Cook came

[1] The name Cook got may have been *He hi no Maui*, 'a thing fished up by Maui'. See *Journals* I, 243, n. 3; and also Edward Shortland, *The Southern Districts of New Zealand* (London, 1851), 155–6, and Johannes C. Andersen, *Maori Place-Names* (Wellington, 1942), 89–91.

by; for it does not easily fit into the traditional name of that island, *Te Ika no Maui*, 'the fish of Maui'. As for the other two, clearly there was misunderstanding on Cook's part, perhaps on the old man's, perhaps on Tupaia's. One of them must have been Arapawa, the island that formed the north-east side of the sound, and this could be circumnavigated in a few days, even by canoes; the second was *Te Wai Pounamu*, 'the Water of Greenstone', so called because of the river-beds of its west coast where the green stone or nephrite was found of which weapons and ornaments were made—not, as Cook supposed, the 'green Talk or stone' itself. To circumnavigate this land, or *whenua*, would take moons also not days; it is not improbable that, as Pickersgill said, Cook's informants 'had but a very Imperfect knolledge' of it.[1]

Cook passed the strait. It has its dangers, as he found. He was scarcely into it, in the early evening, four miles off the two small islands he called the Brothers, when the wind fell calm again and the ebb tide drove him almost on to the rocks about one of them; he was saved by his anchor in 75 fathoms with 150 fathoms of cable out and by a small change in the direction of the tide as it met the island, roaring past the ship like a mill-race. It took three hours to weigh the anchor again, after which he could make over for the eastern shore, where the wind and the tide combined swept him through the narrowest part of the passage, and he could stand away south by west for the most southerly point of land in sight. This he called Cape Campbell, after the eminent officer who had introduced him to the Royal Society; the southernmost point of the northern island, to the east and about twelve miles north, he called Cape Palliser. He spent some hours steering along the coast south from Cape Campbell; the wind died away; then, a south-west breeze springing up, he put the ship right before it and retraced his course. The officers had just started the notion that Aeheinomouwe was not an island at all. They had not inspected the coast between Cape Turnagain and Cape Palliser, twelve or fifteen leagues about: might there not be a swing away to the south-east, a continent after all? Cook did not think so, but he was being challenged on his own ground of accuracy, and we may be glad that he was forced to fill in this piece of his chart. He came in sight of Cape Turnagain, his officers allowed their satisfaction, there was possibly some quiet amusement on both sides, and on

---

[1] *Journals* I, 243, n. 2. Pickersgill's report, quoted in that note, is more easily understood than Cook's—'3 lands', one to the north (three months to circumnavigate); a second, 'which we was upon' (the island Arapawa, on the eastern side of Queen Charlotte Sound—four days to circumnavigate); and the third 'Towie poe namou' ('very Imperfect knolledge').

14 February he had passed Cape Campbell again and was abreast of a high snowy mountain—Tapuaenuku—the highest of a high double ridge that ran parallel with the shore. A few canoes had paddled out to the ship from the Aeheinomouwe coast; four double ones now came to a stone's throw to gaze, but could be induced to come no nearer, hence the name 'Lookers on' Cook gave to the peninsula—Kaikoura—he was then passing. In the night he ran eleven leagues to the south-east, because some persons thought they had seen land in that direction. At daylight on the 16th as he edged in for the land, he saw what appeared to be an island detached from the main; at the same time Gore thought he saw land in the south-east. Cook was certain this was clouds, but Gore was not a very persuadable man; and after convincing himself, from the lie of the land, that the island was a reality, and calling it Banks's Island—Banks is this time too modest to mention the matter—he devoted the whole of the 17th to sailing after this latest figment.[1] There was nothing, and nothing on a southerly course during the night; so in the morning he hauled to the west, thinking, on the information he had from the people in Queen Charlotte's Sound, that he must now be far enough south to weather the main island. After another twenty-four hours he presumed he must be westward of it, and bore away north-west for two hours more, when it appeared running from south-west to north-west. He reckoned that Banks's Island was thirty leagues distant; he had missed forty or fifty miles of close observation of the coast-line, and he did not realise that the 'island' was a peninsula.

Ten very trying days followed, in weather that swung between calms and hard gales from the south, dark and gloomy, with a head sea, carrying away small spars, splitting sails. Cook clung to the coast desperately, tacking off and on, for a time losing ground, sometimes in a fair interval seeing it distinctly, but not certain that it was continuous; making a good stretch one day in a temporary favourable wind till he was off the high bluff he called Cape Saunders (another admiral remembered), about which the land appeared green and woody and hilly, and there were two or three inviting bays. He was anxious not to lose time, however, and resisted the temptation to land—only to be driven by the last day of February a hundred and twenty miles to the south, and even farther to the east. Next day in heavy weather from the west he stood north again from latitude 48°, a large south-west swell persuading him there was no land in that

[1] 'Mr Gore notwithstanding Yesterdays run was of opinion that what he saw yesterday morning might be land, so he declard on the Quarter deck: on which the Captn who resolved that nobody should say he had left land behind unsought for orderd the ship to be steerd SE.'—Banks, I, 468.

quarter; and on 3 March, the wind having gone to the north, made all the sail he could to the west. There were whales and seals about. He once more sighted Cape Saunders, where the land trended south-west, and seeing none directly south, thought that this side of Tovy Poenammu must be reaching its limit—still inhabited, to judge from a large fire ashore at night. We learn from Banks that there were two parties on board the ship, those who 'begin to sigh for roast beef', who wanted an island so that they could finish with it and go home, and a small minority, including himself, who wanted a continent. The swell gave great spirits to the no-continent party; but in the evening of the 5th, as the weather cleared, 'we Continents had the pleasure to see more land to the Southward.' Their pleasure was doomed. By this time there was a larger mass of land to the north, and Cook could not tell whether there was a strait between them, a large bay, or simply low land. The ship was making slow progress— the whole of the 7th was calm; still she kept south-west and west for the next day and a moonlit night, escaping two dangerous ledges of rock on which the sea broke high—the Traps—and next day again fixing the position of the southernmost point of all the land, South Cape. 'Blew fresh all day', wrote Banks for 10 March, 'but carried us round the Point to the total demolition of our aerial fabrick calld continent.'[1]

As Cook turned north in the south-west swell so indicative of an empty ocean, to get in touch with the land, and passed the small rocky Solander's Isle, he looked east. He still asked himself whether he had sailed outside a strait a week before, because now when he looked there appeared an open channel, about which his officers had no doubt; but, he says, when he came to lay down the most southerly land upon paper from the bearings he had taken he hardly had a doubt that this was joined to the rest of the country, with a large bay on either side of the connection. We are given a curious instance, in Cook, of the evidence of the eyes being overthrown by a more abstract reasoning;[2] for the open channel is there. He seems to have caught a glimpse of its rugged northern coast, the sombre snow-patched inland heights. Meanwhile gales forced him south again, as far as 47°40'. He was back in sight of very high land on the morning of the 13th, not far from a south-west point, and in the afternoon hauled in for a wide-mouthed bay, inside which a line of islands promised good anchorage and shelter; he could not, however, get in

---

[1] The Banks quotations are from I, 470, 471, 472.

[2] For discussion of this point see *Journals* I, 263, n. 2. If Cook had been deceived by his eyes, looking from the western end of the strait, it would have seemed natural—anyhow under certain conditions of cloud and atmosphere.

before dark, the wind was too strong for him to risk either a night entrance or keeping to windward, and he bore away along shore. He called it Dusky Bay, and it lodged in his memory. Not far north of this another possible harbour appeared, a narrow opening with an island in the middle, flanked by high perpendicular cliffs, with mountain-summits behind covered with snow. 'Very romantic' was the land hereabouts, thought Sidney Parkinson, who knew the right language, its 'mountains piled on mountains to an amazing height'. Romantic himself, he cannot be accused of exaggeration. Banks wanted Cook to go in here for botanical exploration, and maintained a permanent grievance that he would not: what was a day or two's fair wind against the interests of science?[1] The captain had reason enough, and knew a great deal more about winds than Banks did. He was responsible for his ship and her company including the philosopher. 'I saw clearly that no winds could blow there but what was either right in or right out. This is Westerly or Easterly, and it certainly would have been highly imprudent in me to have put into a place where we could not have got out but with a wind that we have lately found does not blow but one day in a month: I mention this because there were some on board who wanted me to harbour at any rate without in the least considering either the present or future consequences.'[2] There had evidently been some argument. He had another argument against delay which he quite obviously did not bring forward at the time. It finds no place in his journal. We shall see its force a few weeks later. Doubtful Harbour was left unvisited.

There was a generally favouring wind, and the chart delineates this westerly shore without a break. For some days the great mountain chain was still white; even some of the valleys seemed covered with snow—glaciers, inching their way down through forest to the sea. The ship was coming up with Tasman's coast. On the 20th the wind veered to the north-west, with hazy weather, rain and squalls. Cook, forced to stand for a while to the west, gave the name Cape Foulwind to the prominent point he sighted on coming back to the land; and hereabouts and further up to the north one may note that Tasman, closer in, provides a better rendering of its outline than he does. Like Tasman, he remarked on the great, the 'prodigious', swell; on the 22nd, when he was no more than three or four miles off a bluff and rocky head, he was 'under a good deal of apprehension' that he might be obliged to anchor, but good seamanship kept the vessel from driving nearer the shore. By noon on the 23rd she was off

[1] Banks, I, 473, and n. 3 on that page; *Journals* I, 266, n. 1.
[2] *Journals* I, 265–6.

another point which he was afterwards to call Cape Farewell. Then the wind turned east and a day's tacking brought no advance—'an excellent school for patience', certainly, the sea, remarked Banks; then a northerly arose, an east-south-east course was set, at daylight on the 26th land was visible in the south-east, and fifteen miles distant rose Stephens Island. At the beginning of this run, Cook had sailed outside a long low finger of land (he could not see to the other side because of haze and rain). If he had only had a better account of Tasman's voyage, he would have realised that within this finger lay that seaman's Murderers' Bay; but the thick misty weather, and night, concealed from him not only that but the whole extent of the indentation between it and Stephens Island, a large expanse which he gave to Tasman and called on his chart Blind Bay. From Stephens Island the north-west head of Queen Charlotte's Sound was full in view; the circumnavigation was accomplished. Intervening was a bay where must be shelter and convenient water. There he anchored, and for the next four days, in overcast rainy weather, his men were busy watering, cutting wood, and fishing. This bay, which took in a great many smaller bays and openings he had not time to investigate, he called Admiralty Bay; its outer points he named after the secretary and the second secretary to the august body—the north-west one, within the island, Cape Stephens; that to the south-east (which was also the north-west head of the sound, where he had stood eight weeks before), Point Jackson.

Cook described in his journal, with brevity but feeling, the western coast he had sailed up. There must, he thought, be a continuous chain of mountains from one end of the country to the other. As he was not read in polite literature he did not use the word romantic, but spoke of prodigious heights, barren rocks, snow that perhaps had lain since the creation; no country upon earth could appear with a more rugged and barren aspect; or it is mountains standing back behind wooded hills and valleys; always hills rising from the sea, and forest. Such broad statements come easily enough from the pen. One would like a closer impression than we have of the process by which Cook produced his whole chart of the country's coastline—2400 miles in less than three months. No drafts or trial scraps of paper have been preserved, no pages of calculation, no reference anywhere to work spread out in the great cabin—and one must assume that sometimes the captain had the use of his own quarters. It was almost entirely a running survey from the sea, with a constant eye on compass bearings and sextant angles, though when in harbour for as long as he was in Queen Charlotte Sound he could use triangulation.[1] Whenever he could he climbed hills and took bearings—on his last afternoon we have him on an 'eminency' upon the west side of Admiralty Bay; but he could not climb hills at sea. He was scrupulous in fixing the positions of his leading points of reference—'points of reference' a phrase that little enough conveys the settled determination of his seamanship off the North Cape. He gives us his own summary of the work that had been done, his own critical estimate of his chart's value. Of the work: 'This country, which before now was thought to be a part of the imaginary southern continent'— significant words, for one who would know Cook's mind—'consists of Two large Islands. . . . Situated between the Latitudes of 34° and 48° S and between the Longitude of 181° and 194° West from the Meridion of Greenw^h. The situation of few parts of the world are better determined than these Islands are being settled by some hundred of Observations of the Sun and Moon and one of the transit of Mercury made by Mr Green who was sent out by the Roy^l Society to observe the Transit of Venus.'[2] That told the truth; and it gave Green his due.

Of the chart—and the passage should be quoted in full, because these words too are part of the portrait of Cook, with his anxious regard for the fact, his awareness of some merit, his denial of a claim too great:

The Chart which I have drawn will best point out the figure and extent of these Islands, the situation of the Bays and harbours they contain and the lesser Islands lay[ing] about them. And now I have mentioned the Chart I shall point out such places as are drawn with sufficient accuracy to be depended upon and such as are not, beginning at *Cape Pallisser* and proceed round *Aehei no mouwe* by the East Cape &c^a. The Coast between

---

[1] Wales, working later over the records of the voyage, and puzzled by the lack of evidence, concluded that Cook 'determined the ship's place from time to time by means of a series of triangles, which he carried on all round the island, and which formed a continued connection of the situations of the ship with remarkable objects inland, and the principal points of the coast; and he made no farther use of the log than to connect those points of the track which the ship was in when he took his angles and bearings.'— Wales, *Astronomical Observations* . . . (1788), 108.

[2] *Journals* I, 274. We may compare with Cook's own words those of Lieutenant Julien Crozet, second in command of Marion du Fresne's *Mascarin*, which was on the northern New Zealand coast in 1772: 'As soon as I obtained information of the voyage of the Englishman, I carefully compared the chart I had prepared of that part of the coast of New Zealand along which we had coasted with that prepared by Captain Cook and his officers. I found it of an exactitude and of a thoroughness of detail which astonished me beyond all powers of expression, and I doubt much whether the charts of our own French coasts are laid down with greater precision. I think therefore that I cannot do better than to lay down our track off New Zealand on the chart prepared by this celebrated navigator.'—H. Ling Roth, *Crozet's Voyage to Tasmania* . . . (London, 1891), 22.

these two Capes I believe to be laid down pretty accurate both in its figure and the Course and distance from point to point. The oppertunities I had and the methods I made use on to obtain these requesites were such as could hardly admit of an error; from the *East Cape* to *Cape Maria Vandiemen* altho it cannot be perfectly true yet it is without any very material error, some few places however must be excepted and these are very doubtfull and are not only here but in every other part of the chart pointed out by a prick'd or broken line. From *Cape Maria Vandiemen* up as high as the Latitude of 36°15′ we seldom were nearer the Shore than from 5 to 8 Leagues and therefore the line of the Sea Coast may in some places be erroneous; from the above latitude to nearly the length of Entry Island we run along and near the shore all the way and no circumstance occur'd that made me liable to commit any material error. Excepting Cape Teerawhitte we never came near the shore between Entry Island and Cape Pallisser and therefore this part of the Coast may be found to differ something from the truth. In short I believe that this Island will never be found to differ materialy from the figure I have given it and that the coast affords few or no harbours but what are either taken notice of in this Journal or in some measure point[ed] out in the Chart; but I cannot say so much for *Tovy-poenammu,* the Season of the year and circumstance of the Voyage would not permit me to spend so much time about this Island as I had done at the other and the blowing weather we frequently met with made it both dangerous and difficult to keep upon the Coast. However I shall point out the places that may be erroneous in this as I have done in the other. From Queen Charlottes Sound to Cape Campbel and as far to the SW as the Latitude 43° will be found to be pretty accurate, between this Latitude and the Latitude 44°20′ the coast is very doubtfully discribed, a part of which we hardly if att all saw. From this last mentioned Latitude to *Cape Saunders* we were generally at too great a distance to be particular and the weather at the same time was unfavourable. The Coast as it is laid down from Cape Saunders to Cape South and even to Cape West is no doubt in many places very erroneous as we hardly ever were able to keep near the shore and were some times blown off altogether. From the *West Cape* down to *Cape Fare-well* and even to *Queen Charlottes Sound* will in most places be found to differ not much from the truth.[1]

Moderate as this statement is, we may think it still goes a little too far in its claims, unless we remember that Cook is thinking of the general line of the coast. His Banks's Island is a peninsula; but unless it is examined close to, it looks very like an island. What we now call Stewart Island is a peninsula; but the isthmus connecting it with Tovy Poenammu, or the South Island, is very conjecturally delineated. The coast-line from Cape Farewell to Point Jackson, and on the western side of the Hauraki Gulf, is not, we may think again,

[1] *Journals* I, 275–6.

well done; but we may remember the weather, and the time that could be disposed of, and the complexity of those pieces of coast, and the fact that the line shows deliberate gaps; and we may conclude not only that the statement is a candid as well as moderate one, but that the chart as a whole is one of the very remarkable things in the history of cartography. There was one defect in it, as a whole, which Cook did not suspect until his second voyage; and for that Green, as much as himself, perhaps more than himself, was responsible. It was a matter of longitude. The greater part of the South Island was laid down about 40′ too far east, the greater part of the North Island, 30′. This was a fact that he found a little painful; but it was a fact, and he swallowed it.[1]

As for the interior of the country, that must be left to future generations—it was, after all, the size of the United Kingdom. Cook had landed at six places on the North Island and two on the South Island, and had spent altogether about seven weeks ashore. In that time an extraordinary amount of information had been collected, and the journals, within their limits, are encyclopaedic. Admittedly, Banks was with Cook, but could ever discoverer have more literally obeyed instructions to observe and describe the place and people of his discovery? Banks and Solander sailed away with four hundred new plants; Cook with admiration not merely for the face of the country—its timber, its evident fertility, its promise for settlement— but for its inhabitants. He had found no king or 'great prince', but a people evidently divided, and of differing degrees of prosperity; a people strong, well made, active, ingenious, artistic, brave, open, warlike, void of treachery. On the whole, after a bad beginning, he had managed to get on well with them. The only trouble in Queen Charlotte Sound had arisen from a minor affray in which a boat's crew of his own men had gone out of bounds fishing and had fired on two canoes coming (as was fancied) to attack them; they had concealed the affair from Cook, who learnt later, first that one New Zealander had been killed, and then that he had not. All New Zealanders were liars, said Tupaia, who had a meaner opinion of this people than Cook had, and objected to cannibalism. Cook himself, in time, though he never lost his fundamental sympathy for them, was compelled to recognise some less amiable characteristics than those he now catalogued. To the enquiring mind their evident likeness to the South Sea people he had met already posed a problem. They had 'the same Notions of the Creation of the World Mankind &cᵃ. . . indeed many of there Notions and Customs are the

[1] *Journals* II, 173–4, 579–80.

very same, but nothing is so great a proff of they all having had one Source as their Language which differs but in a very few words the one from the other': then what was that source? Neither to the eastward nor to the southward, thought Cook, 'for I cannot preswaid my self that ever they came from America and as to a Southern Continent I do not believe any such thing exists'—unless in a high latitude. The problem of the Polynesian origin and diffusion would recur to him for as long as he lived.

The two explicit parts of the instructions, the Transit, and (failing the continent) New Zealand, had been dealt with: the captain could go home. What did the instructions say about that?—'either round the Cape of Good Hope, or Cape Horn, as from Circumstances you may judge the Most Eligible way'. And in unforeseen emergencies, 'you are . . . to proceed, as upon advice with your Officers you shall judge most advantageous to the Service on which you are employed'. Coming back to the ship on the evening of 30 March, after looking at Admiralty Bay, Cook decided to consult his officers. Was he faced with an emergency? Hardly: and it is difficult to think that he had not already quite made up his mind. Nevertheless it would be good to carry other minds with his. He put the possibilities to them. They could go east round the Horn, as he would most like to do, because that route, by striking right across the area of the southern continent of the geographers, would either prove or disprove its existence; but that would mean keeping in a high latitude in the depth of winter, which—it was agreed—the condition of the ship would not permit. They could go west directly for the Cape of Good Hope; but the same objection applied, in addition to which on that route 'no discovery of any moment' could be hoped for. We begin to see the inward workings of Cook's mind. They could go to the Cape of Good Hope by way of the East Indies, like everybody else; but as there were provisions more than enough for the passage to the East Indies it was resolved to get there 'by the following rout: upon leaving this coast to steer to the westward untill we fall in with the East Coast of New Holland and than to follow the deriction of that Coast to the northward or what other direction it may take untill we arrive at its northern extremity, and if this should be found impractical than to endeavour to fall in with the lands or Islands discover'd by Quiros.'[1] There was a diplomatist in Cook. He had not wished to push his idea too soon. He may have been turning it over for a long time. The unstated argument off Doubtful Sound becomes clear, though still not

[1] *Journals* I, 272–3.

stated for another three years, in the journal of another voyage. Then he gives his clinching reason for not landing on that west coast: 'I had other and more greater objects in view, viz. the discovery of the whole Eastern Coast of New Holland.'[1] Had he already discarded the possibility of going east round the Horn? This new route, certainly—this addendum to original plans—should provide some discovery of moment, as a matter of geographical logic. What Cook did not foresee, as he wrote his sober unornamented words, was that it would dazzle the world. He wasted no further space enlarging on reasons, the thing was settled. 'With this view at daylight in the morning we got under sail and put to sea having the advantage of a fresh gale at SE and clear weather.' It was 31 March. In the afternoon he took his departure from Cape Farewell; next morning New Zealand was lost in rain and cloud.

[1] *Journals* II, 112, n. 2, from P.R.O., Adm 55/108.

X

New South Wales

TASMAN, IN November 1642, had picked up the western coast of
Tasmania, or Van Diemen's Land, had rounded the island to the
south, and left the eastern coast in the latitude of about 41°34′ somewhere near St Patrick Head, where a wind in his teeth stopped him
from following the north-west trend of the shore. Sailing east, he
discovered New Zealand. Cook, sailing west from New Zealand, and
from Cape Farewell in latitude 40°30′, hoped to pick up the coast of
Van Diemen's Land where Tasman had left it, and trace the coast
of New Holland northwards from that point. What he should expect
to find it was impossible to say, whether a continuous coast or a
congeries of islands, or a coast broken by a strait leading through to
some inlet on the north coast, or whether in due course he would
arrive plump on the coast of New Guinea as a part of New Holland,
or would be guided into some certainty about the discoveries of
Quiros. On board the *Endeavour* were at least two pieces of evidence
which cast some light on the New Guinea question, arguing—or, as
Cook might say, 'conjecturing'—that there was a clear passage between it and New Holland. One of these was the 'Chart of the South
Pacifick Ocean', in Dalrymple's pamphlet of 1767, the copy of which
he had presented to Banks. It had a number of strongly individual
features, the existence of some of which, to a person able to check,
would have cast doubt on the credibility of others; but it did show,
clearly enough, a strait south of New Guinea, and a track for Torres
marked through it. The other piece of evidence was the strait shown
in the maps provided by Robert de Vaugondy for the volumes of de
Brosses: from these maps Cook deduced 'that the Spaniards and
Dutch' had 'at one time or a nother circumnavigated the whole of
the island of *New Guinea* as the most of the names are in these two
Languages'; which was all the more curious because 'I allways
understood before I had a sight of these Maps that it was unknown
whether or no New-Holland and New-Guinea was not one continued

226

land and so it is said in the very History of Voyages these Maps are bound up in'.[1] So he had at once in his hands conjecture, assertion, and contradiction. All he knew for certain was that New Holland, like New Zealand, must have an east coast, and that if he sailed west far enough he would come to it.

In a day or two the wind turned to southerlies; then in a few days more to a week's gentle breezes from the north that sometimes dropped to light airs or a calm, so that Banks could go out shooting birds in the warm weather, and the crew were on a not unpleasant routine of picking oakum and working up junk, while the carpenters repaired the yawl and the sailmaker took the spritsail topsail, worn to pieces, and mended the topgallant sails with it.[2] Then, as the land-haunting sea birds began to appear, after the first fortnight, the Tasman Sea shook itself, as it were, and considered its true character; on 16 April the wind went round to the south and turned to hard gales, squalls and rain with a great sea. This drove the ship farther to the north than Cook had intended, to 38°. All night between the 17th and 18th he was running under his foresail and mizen, sounding every two hours. The birds in the morning seemed certain signs of the nearness of land; indeed by this time, according to his own longitude he was a degree to the westward of the east coast of Van Diemen's Land according to Tasman's longitude—which was about 3° too far east. The wretched weather continued throughout the 18th and the following night, and at 1 a.m. Cook brought to; at 5 he set close-reefed topsails and at 6 Hicks saw the land, extending from north-east to west five or six leagues off. The ship had been heading towards Bass Strait; she was held on this western course for two hours more, and then Cook bore away for the easternmost land in sight, calling the southernmost point of land he could at that time see Point Hicks. It is now known as Cape Everard, a little west of the south-east extremity of Australia. Further south was nothing, where, 'due south from us', ought to have been Van Diemen's Land. It was indeed there, though not due south but west of south, and well below the horizon: 'from the soon falling of the Sea after the wind abated' Cook had reason to think it was there, but taking that into account together with the westward trend of the coast he was on, did it not

---

[1] *Journals* I, 410–11. De Brosses's plate V might well seem conclusive.

[2] The spritsail topsail, according to Alan Villiers, was of no use anyway. It was 'a sort of hangover from the days when a small mast was stepped cumbrously on the end of the bowsprit and a sail set from a light yard which hoisted on it. . . . Its successor in Cook's time, this sprits'l-tops'l, was little if any better, except that being set from a light yard (or "sprit") hauled out along the jib-boom and sheeted to the arms of the spritsail-yard inboard of it on the bowsprit, it did not strain the headgear so much.'—*Captain Cook, the Seamen's Seaman* (London, 1967), 133.

merely exist but exist independently of New Holland? He had to leave his last query unanswered.

The long procedure of coasting began, in which two thousand miles of shore, brought out of the shades, were placed in a firm line on the chart. If Cook could have prefigured exactly the four months that lay ahead of him, until he should round the northern tip of New Holland, he might have paced his deck uneasily; as it was, the weather cleared, the winds were manageable, he had a good view of the coast as he sailed, sometimes two or three miles off it, sometimes increasing his distance to three or four leagues. As he advanced past promontories and bays the names of admirals and captains and other naval persons advanced with him, interspersed with metaphor and experience and reminiscence, plain characteristics, and—later— his own emotions. There were few resources for nomenclature his chart did not illustrate in the end: even in the first few days he had Ram Head, Cape Howe, Mount Dromedary, Bateman Bay, Point Upright, the Pigeon House, Long Nose, Red Point. He turned the south-east corner of the land at Cape Howe and steered north, bring- ing to not infrequently at night, sometimes tacking off shore and in again in the morning: for there was a high surf beating on the shore all along. Beyond the surf the appearance of the country, in those first days, was agreeable enough, moderately high with gentle slopes, grass-grown here and there though mainly covered with trees. Banks, in a week, expressed himself differently: 'The countrey tho in general well enough clothd appeard in some places bare; it resembled in my imagination the back of a lean Cow, covered in general with long hair, but nevertheless where her scraggy hip bones have stuck out farther than they ought accidental rubbs and knocks have entirely bard them of their share of covering.'[1] It was not possible, unfortun- ately, to investigate every potential harbour. The name Long Nose was given to the north point of a bay, itself unnamed that seemed sheltered from the north-east, Cook had then an unfavourable wind, 'and the appearance was not favourable enough to induce me to loose time in beating up to it.' Thus he passed by that fine haven Jervis Bay, when he was thinking the time had come for a landing; but it was not the only fine haven that his fate caused him to pass by. There were a few people seen on the beach, and a fire or two.

On the afternoon of the 27th Cook put off in the yawl with Banks, Solander and Tupaia to see if he could land. The surf made it im- possible.[2] Next morning at daylight a bay was discovered, well

[1] Banks, II, 51. He is describing the country about Jervis Bay.
[2] This seems to have been between Bulli and Bellambi Point, about nine miles north of Red Point (Port Kembla). See Edgar Beale, 'Cook's First Landing Attempt in New

sheltered to appearance, into which he resolved to take the ship. In the afternoon he did so, anchoring off the south shore under the eyes of a few natives, some painted over with broad white stripes and armed with pikes and shorter weapons of wood. A few others, striking fish from canoes almost in the surf, seemed to take little notice of the passing ship. As the landing party approached the shore the natives there made off, save for two men who remained to repel the invaders. They were darker-skinned than the men of the islands or New Zealand. This time there was no understanding between aborigines and Tupaia, they were not conciliated by nails or beads thrown to them, nor at first deterred by small shot from defending their country. 'Isaac, you shall land first', said Cook to his wife's young cousin, and Isaac Smith and Europe leapt ashore. Cook was deterred from following the natives, now in retreat, too fast or too far by Banks's fear that their darts might be poisoned. A few bark huts were found, lying about them a number of these darts, more like fish spears than weapons of war, which were taken; in one of them were four or five small children, hiding behind a shield, with whom were left some strings of beads. Canoes on the beach were made of bark. Fresh water seemed scarce. With this introduction to New Holland Cook returned to the ship for the night.

In the morning enough water was found for the ship's needs in a small stream and in holes dug in the sand. There was plenty of wood, there was plenty of fish. Having come into a harbour, Cook surveyed it thoroughly and explored the country round about it as far as he could in the week he stayed there—and the wind kept him longer than he had intended. He wrote a favourable account of it, perhaps too favourable; for though it was 'capacious safe and commodious', a good deal of it was also shallow. Green made the latitude 34°. The land was low and level, its soil in general poor sandy stuff, though some of it was rich, some mere swamp; shrubs, palm trees, mangroves grew, with greater trees, heavy and hard—probably black-beans and casuarinas. The sand and mud flats fostered pelicans and other waterfowl, the oysters, mussels, and cockles which formed a large part of the native provision; parrots and cockatoos were beautiful. Banks describes animals that may have been bandicoots, dingos, native cats, and the dung of something—could it have been a stag? he wondered—that must have been a kangaroo. Gore the sportsman went out over the shallows at high water and struck a number of huge

South Wales', in Royal Australian Historical Society *Journal and Proceedings*, Vol. 50 (1964), 191–204. The landing attempt and the ship's movements can be pictured quite clearly from the flat land above the beach.

stingrays. Banks and Solander collected so many new plants that their preservation became a large problem, and the drying paper had to be carried on shore into the sun to hasten the process. The 'Indians', in no great number around the bay, were shy, dark-skinned, as Cook had already noticed, lean and active, quite naked, with black lank hair, some with bushy beards, certainly not negroes; they threw a dart or two but generally behaved on the principle of live and let live. Small parties of them visited the watering place, unattracted by presents, 'all they seem'd to want was for us to be gone'. To learn anything of their customs, beyond their use of bark and shellfish, their lack of acquaintance with clothing and their painting of themselves, was impossible. Cook's own men remained healthy, except for one young seaman from the Orkneys called Forby Sutherland, who here died of tuberculosis seemingly acquired at the Strait of Le Maire. Cook named the inner south point of the bay after him. What name, however, would he give to the harbour itself, where he had displayed the English colours ashore every day, and cut upon a tree near the watering place, as at Mercury Bay, the ship's name and the date? He made no patriotic choice. He wrote in his log, after the last catch of stingrays, 'The great quantity of these sort of fish found in this place occasioned my giving it the name of *Sting ray's harbour.*' On this he had second, third and fourth thoughts, as he considered in his journal another kingdom of nature and its princes: 'The great quantity of New Plants &cᵃ Mʳ Banks and Dʳ Solander collected in this place occasioned my giving it the name of' —Botanist Harbour? Botanist Bay? The famous name at last was written—'*Botany Bay*';[1] the heads at its entrance Points Solander and Cape Banks. When the name emerged he had long left the place. He sailed out with his rejoicing natural historians, who had spent the whole of their last day collecting specimens, on the morning of 6 May, in a light north-west breeze that immediately went round to the south, as if a benediction were being laid upon him.

The wind was all important. The southerly continued for two and a half pleasant days, then began to hesitate; on 8 May it turned for a day or so to northerlies and briefly to the west, so that at night Cook stood off, except when it was north-west or west, when with a light moon he made the best of his way along shore to the northward. It went again to the north on the 13th for a day, and thereafter to the south; until, on the 21st, when in about latitude 24° the coast changed direction to north-west, the south-easterlies began, gentle breezes with 'clear weather' or 'serene weather' or 'fair weather'. Now he

[1] For the process of naming see *Journals*, I, ccix and 310, n. 4.

seems to have run at full sail during the day, taking in his studding sails and perhaps others during the night. Few indeed were the unpleasant intervals; never had the trade wind been more equable. Dangers and awkward moments there were; it was no period of gentle wafting up an unbrokenly benevolent coast; but at least that summer gave its best. The fatality that pursued the captain, however, where harbours were concerned, was with him still. Botany Bay, though it provided satisfactory anchorage for a small vessel, could not truthfully be called a good harbour; but at noon on the day he left it he was two or three miles off the entrance of a 'Bay or Harbour' —could, in fact, see right up it—where appeared to be safe anchorage. He called it Port Jackson: it was to be one of the most distinguished harbours in the southern hemisphere. Four days later he passed unsuspectingly by another entrance the opening of Newcastle harbour, a fine port with a fine river and a fertile valley within it; only to note and name, a few hours later, being much closer to the land, the much inferior Port Stephens. Smoke was seen inland from time to time, which argued habitation: a good quantity of it on one point brought the name Smoky Cape. This was in latitude 30°51′, a week after Botany Bay was left. People were seen occasionally too; they, so far as the sight of them through the glasses could indicate, showed no sign of interest in the ship. The land was becoming higher, still 'diversified with an agreeable variety of hils ridges Valleys and large planes all cloathed with wood', rising from a low and sandy shore with rocky points.[1] Every day had its observations and its inches added to the chart. The sailors were not the only ones with a routine. Sydney Parkinson was catching up with his work: 'This evening', wrote Banks for 12 May, 'we finished Drawing the plants got in the last harbour, which had been kept fresh till this time by means of tin chests and wet cloths. In 14 days just, one draughtsman has made 94 sketch drawings, so quick a hand has he acquird by use.'[2]

With Smoky Bay behind, there was a day of thunder, squalls and rain—even hail, as the wind changed finally to settle in the south; and then came the first tricky piece of navigation. A pattern was beginning to be imposed. At sunset on the 15th breakers were seen ahead, on the larboard bow, though the ship was five miles from land and in twenty fathoms. Cook hauled off to the east and brought to. A strong southerly blew all night: nevertheless in the morning he

[1] ibid., 316. He is describing the country as the coast ran northwards from Botany Bay towards Cape Byron.
[2] Banks, II, 62.

found that he had drifted to the south. He passed a league outside the breakers, which stretched two leagues east over a shoal running out from the point he called Point Danger; a high peak a few miles inland, south-west, he called Mount Warning. He stood past Point Lookout (look out, he advised the future, for more breakers) and the wide, not deep indentation he called Morton Bay—a name transferred, mis-spelt, to the vast opening on the inside of the islands that formed the outline of his bay.[1] The land, now becoming lower, even when it was of a moderate height presented a barren sandy aspect; and the distance Cook was from it, whether a few miles or a few leagues, made difficult for him the separation of islands from the mainland. So he did not perceive that Sandy Cape, itself high enough to be visible for thirty or forty miles, was the northern end of a long island. It had a thirty mile shoal extension, Break Sea Spit, over the tail of which he crossed with a boat ahead sounding, the sea 'so clear that we could distinctly see the bottom',[2] into the smooth sheltered water outside Hervey Bay, steering west till he picked up the land again and found it had changed its direction to west-north-west. It now once more seemed well-wooded and fertile. After spending a night at anchor because of shoal water he sailed on for a day; and then—the evening of 22 May—hauled in for an inviting bay where he intended both to anchor and to land. It is at this moment in his journal that he bursts into a passage of indignation that in its first uninhibited utterance by word of mouth may well have made the whole ship tremble.

There had been on the previous night, while the ship lay at anchor, a grave breach of discipline, 'a very extraordinary affair' which came upon Richard Orton the captain's clerk. He had gone to bed drunk— and again we are left amazed that these men could so often find the wherewithal for the purpose: was it by careful saving, or by robbing the ship's stores, or private casks?

Some Malicious person or persons in the Ship took the advantage of his being drunk and cut off all the cloaths from off his back, not being satisfied with this they some time after went into his Cabbin and cut off part of both his Ears as he lay asleep in his bed.

The furious captain went into the matter.

The person whome he suspected to have done this was Mr Magra one of the Midshipmen, but this did not appear to me upon inquirey. However as I Know'd Magra had once or twice before this in their drunken frolicks cut of his Cloaths and had been heard to say (as I was told) that if it was

---

[1] *Journals* I, 318, n. 3.   [2] Banks, II, 64.

not for the Law he would Murder him, these things consider'd induce'd me to think that Magra was not altogether innocent. I therefore, for the present dismiss'd him the quarter deck and susspended him from doing any duty in the Ship, he being one of those gentlemen, frequently found on board Kings Ships, that can very well be spared, or to speake more planer good for nothing. Besides it was necessary in me to show my immediate resentment against the person on whome the suspicion fell least they should not have stoped here.

Yet it was puzzling. Orton was a man not without faults, but he had not designedly injured any man in the ship.

Some reasons might however be given why this misfortune came upon him in which he himself was in some measure to blame, but as this is only conjector and would tend to fix it upon some people in the Ship whome I would fain believe would hardly be guilty of such an action, I shall say nothing about it unless I shall hereafter discover the Offenders which I shall take every method in my power to do, for I look upon such proceedings as highly dangerous in such Voyages as this and the greatest insult that could be offer'd to my authority in this Ship, as I have always been ready to hear and redress every complaint that have been made against any Person in the Ship.[1]

The thing is more than a storm in a teacup, and one would like to have Cook's earlier drafts of these passages, as well as the modifications we do have; for it casts some light, of which we have too little, an odd and dubious light, on the human nature and strains of the voyage. In what ways was Mr Orton to blame? Who were the persons Cook would fain believe innocent? The allusions make for curiosity. And do we not begin to see, not merely the indiscipline of the age, not merely 'resentment', but a little of the interior of the captain's mind—his sense of justice, here defeated; his regard for evidence, in other matters than marine surveying; his picture of himself as a commander?

Meanwhile he landed to inspect the country, finding a channel strewn with shoals, leading to a lagoon skirted with mangroves and pandanus, sparse woods growing in a dry and sandy soil, eucalypts and grey birch; no people, but clear signs of them in smoke and fires that they had just left, and small bark shelters against the wind. Banks remarked the ants' nests, the green hairy stinging caterpillars drawn up in rows, a 'wrathful militia', on the mangroves, and the great variety of plants—some of them known from the islands and the East Indies, not all new as at Botany Bay. The Botany Bay birds were there, and ducks, and shy pelicans; a large bustard was shot

[1] *Journals* I, 323–4, and the notes to those pages, on Cook's deletions and rewriting.

(subsequently eaten with great pleasure), whence the name given to the place, Bustard Bay. They sailed again in early morning, brought to for the following night, passed Cape Capricorn, anchored in a calm on the 25th, 'having the Main Land and Islands in a manner all round us'—small high barren islands, the main land hilly, its shore rocky, the prospect generally indifferent. Next afternoon, when the *Endeavour* was between Great Keppel island and the main, the shoals became embarrassing: Cook was forced to anchor in sixteen feet of water, a bare two feet more than the ship's draught, while the master, sounding ahead, found only $2\frac{1}{2}$ fathoms. Luckily the wind veered for a short time to a north-easterly, so that he could stretch back a few miles and anchor in 6 fathoms for the night; in the morning the boats found a passage out through the islands. He not unnaturally thought it wise to shorten sail and bring to the following night. Next day, as he came round Cape Townshend into Shoalwater Bay, there seemed to be islands everywhere before him, islands out at sea. He had to tack suddenly to avoid shoal water, then sent a boat ahead. The difficulties are reflected clearly enough in the journal, without excitement.

A little before noon the boat made the Signal for meeting with Shoal water, upon this we hauld close upon a wind to the Eastward but suddenly fell into $3\frac{1}{4}$ fathom water, upon which we immidiatly let go an Anchor and brought the Ship up with all sails standing and had then 4 fathom course sandy bottom; we found here a Strong tide seting to the NWBW$\frac{1}{2}$W at the rate of between 2 and 3 Miles an hour which was what carried us so quickly upon the Shoal. . . . Having sounded about the Ship and found that there was sufficient water for her over the Shoal we at 3 oClock weigh'd and came to sail and stood to the westward as the land lay having first sent a boat ahead to sound. At 6 o'Clock we Anchord in 10 fathom water a sandy bottom about 2 Miles from the Main land. . . .[1]

Opposite the anchored ship appeared the mouth of an inlet. Cook, as if drawing breath, decided to put in here for a few days, to wait until the moon increased while he examined the country; and judging the inlet, when he got inside, to be a tidal river with a considerable ebb and flow, he thought he might lay his ship ashore to clean her bottom. There were spots suitable, he and Molyneux found; but the whole neighbourhood had one decisive defect—not a single drop of fresh water could be found. He therefore stayed only two days at this place that he called Thirsty Sound. It was not a river, it was a long channel separating islands from the main. Cook took bearings from a hill at the entrance, and went in a boat through

[1] *Journals* I, 330.

to the great spread of water at the other end, Broad Sound. The
country seemed infertile: the red clay uplands grew eucalypts but
no underwood, the swampy salt low land grew mangroves; where it
was rather higher it was gashed by the torrents of the rainy season.
For the naturalists there were a few new plants, as well as the sharp-
speared sand burrs which joined with innumerable mosquitoes to
torture their skins, and with mud and mangroves to make walking
almost intolerable; there were ants and billowing clouds of butterflies, beautiful loriquets, shells, and one 'very singular Phenomenon', the little fish we call the mud-skipper, seemingly as much
at home on the land as in the water, leaping from stone to stone as
nimbly as a frog; mankind signified his presence by smoke and burnt-
out fires. The weather turned dirty for a day, then fortunately cleared,
because there were enough discomforts for a sailor without rain and
haze. Cook left this unrewarding spot on the last morning of May.

A boat was ahead sounding. Just after noon there was a repetition
of the episode of a few days before: the boat signalled shoal water,
'we hauld our wind to the NE having at that time 7 fathom, the next
cast 5 and than 3 upon which we let go an Anchor and brought the
Ship up.'[1] Round about the shoal there was deep water. Cook got
under sail and anchored for the night in the lee of a nearby island.
How much more of this was there to be? he must have asked himself; and now, if ever, he must have blessed the nature of his cat,
her broad bottom and stout timbers, the comparative lightness of
her spars that made for quick manoeuvring. Now was he remarking
with care the rise and fall and set of tides. Islands of various sizes
lay parallel with the coast all the way along it, a fair distance in the
offing, other smaller ones were close to the land. Islands can be
avoided, can even be a convenience; but only the most consummate
seamanship, with a little good luck added to it, can explain how
Cook kept his ship off the ground in the next few days. His chart is
no less good than it was; it, and his journal pages, are soon thick
with the names he gave to every notable feature; his descriptions are
no less lucid. One long fair afternoon, that of 3 June, was spent
steering through Whitsunday Passage, between the Cumberland
Islands and the main, in deep water, with pleasant bays and coves
on either side, hills and valleys, woods and green levels. On a beach
were seen two men with an out-rigger canoe, very different from
the crude bark contrivances further south. So, past Cape Gloucester
and Edgcumbe Bay, Cape Upstart springing from its level base,
'*Magnetical head* or *Isle* as it had much the appearance of an Island'—

_____
[1] ibid., 333.

which it is—'and the Compass would not travis well when near it';
a mainland rugged, rocky and barren, but still with the smoke of
habitation; Halifax Bay, Rockingham Bay; continuing the course
at night in the bright moonlight under reduced sail. On an islet out
of Halifax Bay what were thought to be coconut trees were seen,
and Hicks with Banks and Solander was sent for a supply of the
nuts, only to find cabbage palms. Even on this Palm Island were
found new plants, as a few more still were found two days later on
Cape Grafton, in latitude 16°55', within which Cook anchored briefly
in the hope of convenient fresh water. Fresh water there was, but
not convenient. Why therefore stay? Cook 'thought it would be
only spending time and looseing so much of a light moon to little
purpose, and therefore at 12 oClock at night we weigh'd and stood
away to the NW, having at this time but little wind attended with
showers of rain.'[1] This was the midnight that began Trinity Sunday,
10 June. Just off Cape Grafton lay a low islet that Cook called Green
Island. Banks describes it rather more at length, 'a small sandy
Island laying upon a large Coral shoal, much resembling the low
Islands to the eastward of us but the first of the kind we had met with
in this part of the South Sea.'[2] Looking to the shore as he ran northwards from Cape Grafton that morning, Cook named a flattish
trend of the coast, which included one or two minor indentations,
Trinity Bay; its northern point, looking at it on the chart later, he
called Cape Tribulation, 'because here begun all our troubles.'

There was something the captain was unaware of. It was the
Great Barrier Reef. It is a reef that lies not parallel but at an angle
with the Australian coast, and it is not a single line. It is farthest
from the coast at its southernmost point, rather beyond latitude 22°,
and when Cook turned Cape Townshend, which he put in 22°13',
and brought up standing in Shoalwater Bay over a sandy bottom,
he had come within its influence though not yet where the shoals
had a bottom of coral. To run aground on coarse sand would have
been highly inconvenient, not fatal. But as the latitude becomes
lower and the reef approaches closer to the shore, the area between
becomes at once smaller and more dangerous; the insects have built
in outcrops which run in all directions, the shoals have risen in every
direction in the sheltered water; until, within a few degrees of the
northern tip of the country, it is almost a confusion of coast and reef
and shoal. Cook's position, on that Sunday of June, was not as bad
as this; but the sides of the great funnel into which, all unaware,

---

[1] *Journals* I, 342.   [2] Banks, II, 77.

he had been sailing were drawing together, and Banks's small sandy island on a large coral shoal looks, to hindsight, like a dark and fearful scrawl of intimation. The ship throughout the day was steering along shore three or four leagues off, in 10, 12, or 14 fathom water; the wind was east-south-east. At 6 o'clock, about which time the tropic dusk would fall, the northernmost part of the mainland bore NBW$\frac{1}{2}$W, and two low woody islands, which could be taken for mere rocks above the water, N$\frac{1}{2}$W. 'At this time', says Cook, 'we shortend sail and hauld off shore ENE and NEBE close upon a wind.' There were those who, after his story appeared, accused him of rashness and argued that he should have anchored. He could have answered that he was not on the edge of a shoal, or in a bay preparing to land. His intention was not to risk danger but 'to stretch off all night as well to avoid the dangers we saw ahead'—the dubious island-rocks, and according to Banks, shoals—'as to see if any Islands lay in the offing, especialy as we now begin to draw near the Latitude of those discover'd by Quiros which some Geographers, for what reason I know not have thought proper to tack to this land, having the advantage of a fine breeze of wind and a clear moonlight night.' That is, he had the ideal conditions for night sailing that he had exploited before. He had a man heaving the lead continuously, and the ship being under way was in the best state for manoeuvring. 'In standing off from 6 untill near 9 oClock we deepen'd our water from 14 to 21 fathom when all at once we fell into 12, 10 and 8 fathom. At this time I had every body at their stations to put about and come too an anchor but in this I was not so fortunate for meeting again with deep water I thought there could be no danger in stand^g on.' The gentlemen were at supper: they must, they concluded in Banks's words, have passed over 'the tail of the Sholes we had seen at sunset and therefore went to bed in perfect security';[1] the sea was calm, the moon continued her radiance, in it the *Endeavour* stole along under double-reefed topsails. 'Before 10 o'Clock' (we return to Cook) 'we had 20 and 21 fathom and continued in that depth untill a few Minutes before a 11 when we had 17 and before the Man at the lead could heave another cast the Ship Struck and stuck fast.'[2] They were on a coral reef, at high tide.

[1] ibid.
[2] *Journals* I, 343–4. The ship had been here passing just northward of Pickersgill Reef, which is about three miles long north-west and south-east. Four and a half miles north of it the next—Endeavour—reef stretched for five miles east and west. This reef is in two sections. It appears from the work done in reclaiming the ship's guns in January-February 1969 that she struck at a point three-quarters of the way from the eastern end of the eastern section; not the main reef, but a small detached upthrusting 'bornie' just in front of it. This is now marked by a steel peg.

Within an instant Cook was on deck; sails were taken in, boats sounding round the ship, yards and topmasts struck, anchors carried out for heaving her off. In some places about here were three or four fathoms, in others 'not quite as many feet' of water, a ship's length from the starboard side as much as twelve fathoms, even more astern. She would not budge under any strain, but was making little or no water, while the horrible sound was heard of her bottom scraping on the coral underneath. Everything heavy that could be thought of was thrown overboard—the six guns and their carriages, half a ton each, iron and stone ballast, casks, decayed stores, a general miscellany of fifty tons and more. She had struck at high water at night; at high water twelve hours later, with all this lightening, she still would not move. Fortunately there was a flat calm, the grating of her bottom ceased; but as the tide went down again she heeled to starboard and began to make water. Everybody, including the gentlemen, took to the pumps in quarter-hour reliefs; there were four pumps, but one of them had rotted and would not work. Banks admired the coolness of the officers; he was surprised at the unusual absence of oaths among the men; he had understood that under such circumstances sailors generally ran riot and plundered the ship. Some hope was now born from the old belief that night tides rose higher than day tides, and while the pumps worked Cook got all ready for another attempt at heaving off. The leak was gaining: if the ship did come off into deep water she might go straight down. This risk had to be taken: what alternative was there? The tide rose high and higher, she floated; she was hauled off, after twenty-three hours. While the leak still gained a mistake happened 'which for the first time caused fear to operate upon every man in the Ship.' A new man measuring the depth of water in the ship took it from a different level and reported a terrifying increase. Realisation of the mistake caused an equal reaction; vigorous pumping gained upon the leak. The anchors were brought in, except the small bower, which had to be cut away with the cable; the stream anchor cable also was lost. The foretopmast was sent up, the ship was got under sail, and she edged in for the land, six or seven leagues distant. If she could not make it there were the two low woody islands seen at dusk two days before, still visible—Hope Islands—surely they could be reached? While she sailed she was fothered—that is, a sail sewn with tufts of wool and oakum and spread with sheep's dung was dragged over the place of the leak, which was thus partially plugged by the force of the water itself. Jonathan Monkhouse, who had had some experience of this, was in charge of the operation, and 'exicuted

it very much to my satisfaction', says Cook; high praise indeed for
the midshipman from that measured pen. The leak could now be
kept down with one pump. As for the ship's company all through the
crisis—the captain gives judgment again—no men ever behaved
better. At night between the 12th and 13th she was anchored; next
day she was again edged in with boats ahead sounding and looking
for a harbour. The first that was examined—Weary Bay, as Cook
significantly called it—had not enough water, and another night
was spent at anchor, among shoals, two miles off shore. The pinnace
then reported a good one, the ship ran down to it, by which time it
had begun to blow, she would not work and missed stays twice;
still entangled among shoals Cook again anchored, and went and
buoyed the narrow channel into the harbour himself. It was in the
midst of these anxieties that the captain found time for an act of
justice: 'This day I restore'd Mr Magra to his Duty as I did not find
him guilty of the crimes laid to his Charge.'[1] The weather turned to
gales and rain. He could not move. He got in spars to lighten the
ship forward; and at last, after two more days, he ran in, grounding
first on the bar, then inside. It was 16 June: he was not free of that
harbour until 4 August.

He was in a river-mouth, the banks well suited to laying a vessel
ashore. Cook lost no time in emptying the hold and adjusting the
ship's trim so that the carpenter could get at her forepart. The few
sick were installed in a tent: of these only Tupaia and Green were
at all serious cases, the first undoubtedly with bad symptoms of
scurvy, the second with some illness unspecified. Tupaia went
fishing and rapidly cured himself, Green recovered a little more
slowly. Banks and Solander were out plant-hunting. The armourers
were busy making nails and bolts. Cook climbed the highest accessible hill to look at the country, 'a very indifferent prospect',
mangroves on the low lands, higher land barren and stony. By the
22nd the bow of the ship was ashore. At low tide, the damage could
be inspected. The coral rock had gone right through her bottom on
the starboard side in a clean cut, but by a most extraordinary piece
of good fortune a lump of the rock had come away and stuck in the
hole: this, with the fother and other bits of rubbish, had stopped a
fatal inrush of water. The close and heavy build of the floor timbers
had prevented more widespread damage of the severer kind; nevertheless, part of the sheathing under the larboard bow was gone, with
part of the false keel, 'and the remainder in such a shatter'd condition
that we should be much better of, was it gone also;' the fore foot and

---

[1] This is a marginal note in one copy of the journal.—*Journals* I, 347, n. 5.

part of the main keel were also damaged, not materially it was thought. The loss of the sheathing might be serious, because it would open the way to 'the worm'. To repair the main damage did not take many days, but in spite of all the ingenuity employed it was impossible to come at the part further aft, because there was no way of heaving the ship down. Cook, however, respected the opinion of his carpenter: Mr Satterley thought she would do, and he resolved to worry no more. It was now 6 July.

Parties sent into the country to forage brought back a few pigeons, palm cabbages, wild plantains and taro. All these ate pretty well, as long as the taro experiments were confined to the leaves; 'the roots were so Acrid that few besides my self could eat them', says Cook. What was there that he could not eat? Fishing with the seine, which began badly, improved so as to provide fresh food for the whole ship's company. There seemed to be no game animal on land, unless the animal of which fleeting glances were several times caught (once by Cook himself)—about the size of a greyhound, slender, mouse-coloured, swift, with a long tail, jumping like a hare—was a game animal. Banks began to refer to it as 'the' animal. Then there were one or two 'wolves', probably dingos or native dogs; and the thing so oddly described by a seaman, 'about as large and much like a one gallon cagg as black as the Devil and had 2 horns on its head, it went but slowly but I dard not touch it'[1]—which may have been a flying-fox. Banks and Gore, the naturalist and the hunter, were determined to secure specimens of 'the' animal; they went up the river until they had to drag their boat, saw some which easily outdistanced Banks's greyhound by bounding over the long grass, and returned with only a few ducks and the additional sight of an alligator. Gore was a determined man; a week later he shot a small one, a fortnight after that a second, much larger. They were kangaroos, grateful both to the curiosity and to the stomachs of those who dined on them, and a capital contribution to knowledge of the world's fauna. Purslane and wild beans were added to the diet. The master came back from examining the shoals with quantities of large clams; then, to general jubilation, with hundredweights of turtle. Cook's policy was settled: 'Whatever refreshment we got that would bear a division I caused to be equally divided amongest the whole compney generally by weight, the meanest person in the Ship had an equal share with my self or any one on board, and this method every commander of a Ship on such a Voyage as this ought ever to observe.'[2]

[1] Banks, II, 84.　　　　　　　　　　[2] *Journals* II, 366.

Turtle led to what might have been a highly embarrassing episode. Traces had been seen of the native people by the hunters and naturalists. It was not till after three weeks had gone by that a few of them, shy and suspicious like those of Botany Bay, naked, nimble, painted in the same way, but of smaller size, began to approach the ship—even then leaving their women at a distance, for glasses to scrutinise. They did not seem interested in gifts. They let their weapons be examined; Banks was allowed by one of them to experiment with a wet finger and get below the layers of smoke and dirt to the brown chocolate skin underneath. They chattered somehow to Tupaia, and a few of their words were picked up. When they saw turtles lying on the deck of the ship they showed real animation and prepared to go off with two of them, as their own property; resentful at being stopped, no sooner were they on shore than one seized a handful of dry grass, lighted it at a fire that was burning and in an instant had the whole place in flames; immediately after which they set fire to the grass surrounding some fishing nets and linen laid out to dry. Luckily the ship's powder had been returned on board, and only that morning her tents; there was nothing lost but a piglet, and nobody hurt but an aboriginal grazed by small shot. Reconciliation was soon effected. They fired the woods on the hills round about, however, perhaps as a warning—the first bush fire seen by Europeans in that inflammable country.

Before the end of June Cook had his young gentlemen surveying the harbour. At 3 o'clock on the morning of the 29th he himself and Green observed an emersion of Jupiter's first satellite, which gave them a remarkably accurate longitude for the place;[1] then, as Satterley was getting on so well with his work, he turned his attention to leaving it. On the last day of the month, at morning low water, he climbed the 500 foot hill above its south point. From what he saw he derived 'no small uneasiness'. Sandbanks or shoals lay all along the coast, the innermost three or four miles from the shore, the outermost as far off to sea as his glass would reach, some just appearing above water. Only to the north could he hope to get clear of them: to return south would be difficult if not impracticable because of the constant south-east wind. He sent Molyneux to sound and search. Molyneux came back reporting a passage out to sea between coral reefs; at five leagues distance he was outside all the dangers. This Cook did not believe. After a week he sent the master

[1] His result was $214°42'30''$ W—i.e. $145°17'30''$ E, the now accepted longitude being $145°15'$. He made another observation of the emersion on 16 July, which gave him $145°6'15''$ E, not quite so good, with a mean of $145°11'52\frac{1}{4}''$.

out again. Molyneux came back this time to say he had been seven leagues off the coast, there were still shoals beyond, and there was no getting to sea that way. At least he brought the turtle. On the 17th he was sent to the north. He was away for two and a half days. Cook and Banks also went to the northwards, walking six or eight miles and climbing another high hill, 'whence we had an extensive view of the Sea Coast to leward; which afforded us a Meloncholy prospect of the difficultys we are to incounter, for in what ever direction we turn'd our eys Shoals innumerable were to be seen'; and 'no such thing', adds Banks, 'as any passage to sea but through the winding channels between them, dangerous to the last degree.'[1] Molyneux's report from sea-level was equally gloomy.

In any case, would the ship ever get out of that narrow-mouthed harbour? The wind, the wind! Day after day it blew from the south-east, in gentle breezes, fresh breezes, strong breezes, very fresh gales. Was the blessing become a curse? There had been a few hours of a land breeze once only, very early, while repairs were still in progress, and much as an enforced stay might profit natural history, how long could this harbour-bound existence go on without imperilling the voyage itself? If, in the end, the ship survived the reefs and shoals, would she be pinned down by the monsoonal change? Reefs and shoals would have to be risked. By 19 July everything was on board, there was nothing to do but work on the boats and the decayed pumps, or try to strike turtle or gather greens or hunt the animal, or fish. At last, on the 29th, there was a calm, followed by a light breeze from the land. Cook hove up the anchor and sent a boat to the bar. The tide was on the ebb, there was already six inches less water than the ship drew. The wind went back to south-east, gales and squalls with rain. Cook determined to warp out. At first it blew too fresh. August came. On the 3rd he tried. The ship tailed up on the sand on the north side of the river, and he had to moor her just inside the bar. He laid his coasting anchor and cable outside, to be ready for the flood. Early next morning it fell calm again, and in two hours he was off the harbour's mouth and under sail, farewell bade to the Endeavour River, the pinnace ahead of him. He anchored a mile from Molyneux's turtle reef, until he could view the shoals at low water from the mast head, and determine whether to beat back to the southward, or try for a passage to the east or the north, 'all of which appear'd to be equally difficult and danger-

---

[1] *Journals* I, 361; Banks, II, 95. The different copies of Cook's journal show more than one version of Cook's own words: in the holograph he has improved on himself by copying Banks.

ous.' While the boats fished he decided to try the north-east, where it seemed fairly clear, made sail next afternoon, and by the end of it was forced to anchor again. He was in twenty fathoms; a mile farther on the pinnace was in four or five feet over a reef. Morning showed him breakers all the way from the south round by the east to the north-west. The journal becomes a detailed description of shoals and reefs, their direction and their nature. The weather turned to strong gales with cloudy weather. Molyneux was all for turning back. Cook recorded his desperate quandary: 'I was quite at a loss which way to steer when the weather would permit us to get under sail; for to beat back to the SE the way we came as the Master would have had me done would be an endless peice of work, as the winds blow now constantly strong from that quarter without hardly any intermission—on the other hand if we do not find a passage to the north^d we shall have to come back at last.'[1] The ship began to drive towards a reef astern; he gave her more cable and another anchor, struck topgallant masts and topmasts and yards, and at last she rode fast. She stayed thus for three days, the last of which was spent wrestling to get up the anchors again.

He would try sailing northward closer to the land. It was now 10 August. He crept back past shoals and reefs and islets till he was between a headland on the main and three high islands lying outside it. There now seemed a clear open sea ahead, all danger past. Illusion: the headland became Cape Flattery. To the north, from the mast head appeared more land, more breakers, a great reef. Cook hauled in for the land and anchored under another headland, his Point Lookout, which he climbed for the view—to the west a flat sandy plain running in ten or twelve miles to the higher country, with its smokes and fires; to the north broad sand and mud flats running out from the mangrove belt to sea, a group of small low islands, shoals smaller and larger, and the three high islands; to the east the dangers he had come in from. He determined to visit one of the high islands and scrutinise the scene from there, sending Molyneux to the north again in the yawl. Next day he went with Banks in the pinnace to the northernmost and largest island—Lizard Island, so called from the only animal inhabitants—and looked out from the bare 1100 foot top. Two or three leagues distant was the reef, stretching north-west to south-east till it was lost in the haze. Mortification, however, was mixed with hope: on this reef the sea from the east broke high, as if on outermost defences; through it were 'breaks or Partitions'; between it and the islands was deep

---

[1] *Journals* I, 370.

water. After staying all night on the island and sending the pinnace to verify the depth of water Cook returned to the ship, sounding on the way. There was a clear passage. Molyneux had also found a passage, between the main and the low islands,[1] but narrow and he thought dangerous. Cook agreed about the danger, and the risk of being at last 'locke'd in' by the main reef and having to seek a way back: 'an accident of this kind or any other that might happen to the Ship would infallibly loose our passage to the East Indies this season and might prove the ruin of the Voyage,' for little more than three months provisions were left. He put it to his officers, they agreed. 'I therefore resolved to weigh in the morning and endeavour to quet the coast altogether untill we could approach it with less danger.' Accordingly at daylight on 13 August he got under sail, had a clear course to Lizard Island and out to the reef, sent the pinnace ahead through one of the channels he had seen from the island,[2] and followed in the ship. She was free.

A 'well growen Sea' was rolling in from the south-east and breaking on the reef, with 150 fathoms under the ship without bottom. In that sea she leaked more, but not more than one pump could deal with, and the danger seemed trifling. Cook brought a greatly relieved mind to consider his position. Obviously there was nothing to fear from the direction of the sea, and he was outside the 'Shoals &c^a—after having been intangled among them more or less ever sence the 26th of May, in which time we have saild 360 Leagues without ever having a Man out of the cheans heaving the Lead when the Ship was under way, a circumstance that I dare say never happen'd to any ship before and yet here it was absolutely necessary. It was with great regret I was obliged to quit this coast unexplored to its Northern extremity which I think we were not far off, for I firmly believe that it doth not join to *New Guinea*, however this I hope yet to clear up being resolved to get in with the land again as soon as I can do it with safety and the reasons I have before assigned will I presume be thought sufficient for my haveing left it at this time.'[3]—Sufficient reasons indeed! As if the man had to stamp down, at the bottom of his mind, a little suspicion that after all he had been guilty of some derogation of duty. He does not here explain the firm belief he had that New Holland did not join New Guinea—whether it was from the trend of the coast combined with his speculative maps, or from other hydrographic compulsions that bore on his mind.—He stood off and on all night, and next day, the 14th,

---

[1] These islands were the Howick group.   [2] The Cook Passage.
[3] *Journals* I, 375–6.

steered a north-westerly course. At noon there was no land in sight.
He brought to for the following night. At morning of the 15th he
steered west in order to make the land, 'being fearfull of over
shooting the Passage supposing there to be one between this land and
New Guinea.' Shortly after noon the land appeared, and shortly
after that breakers between it and the ship, from one end of the
horizon to the other.

The wind was at ESE and then changed to EBN, which was right
upon the reef where the sea was breaking, 'and of course made our
clearing of it doubtful'. Cook stood north with all the sail he could
set for the rest of the day and till midnight, then tacked and stood
to the SSE. He had run two miles when the wind fell quite calm, and
he was left to the mercy of the waves. To anchor in that vast deep
was impossible. Before dawn the roaring of the surf could be heard;
when the day came it could be seen, only too clearly, not a mile
away; and towards it the ship was being resistlessly impelled. Her
men by now knew the nature of the reef, a perpendicular wall standing up from unfathomable depths, at which the whole ocean hurled
itself, flooding over the top in a chaos of smashed water and foam,
or withdrawing, infinite force all reversed, for another ruinous blow.
In that tremendous surge the heavy-timbered *Endeavour* might have
been a cork: except that the cork would have gone over with the
foam, or back with the retreat, while the *Endeavour* would smash and
sink in a moment. Yet men will struggle: if there was no wind to
fill the sails the boats must tow; the pinnace was under repair but
the yawl and the longboat were hoisted out, and with the help of
sweeps from the aft ports got the ship's head round to the northward; the carpenter got another strake on the pinnace and she was
sent down too. At this time the ship was perhaps eighty yards from
the breakers; one sea washed her and then fell into the trough
before its final rise and descent; a seaman was heaving the lead;
and on the deck Green, helped by Clerke and Forwood the gunner,
with what was either the last refinement of professional coolness or
stark insensibility, was taking a lunar. Suddenly a little breath of
air moved, blew for a few minutes, faded, the merest cat's-paw;
the ship moved with it about two hundred yards; it blew again as
briefly and again she moved outwards. About a quarter of a mile
distant a narrow opening appeared in the reef; the boats and the
sweeps together got her abreast of this, when the force of the ebb
tide, gushing out, carried her a quarter of a mile off. By the end of
the morning the boats had made the gap something between a mile
and a half and two miles. Then the struggle became one with the

flood. There was still no wind, and how long could the human arm endure? Another narrow opening was seen in the reef, the ship's head was pulled round again, a light breeze at last sprang up, at ENE, with which the boats and the tide now combined in her favour, the tide hurried her through this 'Providential Channell'; and Cook anchored in smooth water.

It has been 'the narrowest Escape we ever had and had it not been for the immeadate help of Providence we must Inavatably have Perishd', said Pickersgill; and he was not the only one to heave a sigh. Cook's own words at last show signs of strain, as of a man dropped suddenly from extremest peril, the climax of unremitted effort, into exhausted reaction. His mind, so self-contained, suddenly opens. It would be wrong not to quote him again at length.

It is but a few days ago that I rejoiced at having got without the Reef, but that joy was nothing when Compared to what I now felt at being safe at an Anchor within it, such is the Visissitudes attending this kind of Service & must always attend an unknown Navigation where one steers wholly in the dark without any manner of Guide whatever. Was it not for the Pleasure which Naturly results to a man from his being the first discoverer even was it nothing more than Sand or Shoals this kind of Service would be insupportable especially in far distant parts like this, Short of Provisions & almost every other necessary. People will hardly admit of an excuse for a man leaving a Coast unexplored he has once discover'd, if dangers are his excuse he is then charged with Timerousness & want of Perseverance, & at once pronounced the most unfit man in the world to be employ'd as a discoverer, if on the other hand he boldly encounters all the dangers & Obstacles he meets with & is unfortunate enough not to succeed he is then Charged with Temerity & perhaps want of Conduct, the former of these Aspersions I am confident can never be laid to my Charge, & if I am fortunate to Surmount all the Dangers we meet with the latter will never be brot in Question, altho' I must own that I have engaged more among the Islands & Shoals upon this Coast than Perhaps in prudence I ought to have done with a single Ship, & every other thing considered, but if I had not I should not have been able to give any better account of the one half of it, than if I had never seen it, at best I should not have been able to say wether it was Main land or Islands & as to its produce, that we should have been totally ignorant of as being inseparable with the other & in this case it would have been far more satisfaction to me never to have discover'd it, but it is time I should have done with this Subject wch at best is but disagreeable & which I was lead into on reflecting on our late Danger.[1]

<hr/>

[1] This extract is from the Mitchell Library copy of the journal, printed in *Journals* I, 546-7, a version a little closer to Cook's original thoughts, before he had had the advantage of scrutinising Banks's more elevated account of the whole episode. The danger

This, we may guess, is hardly Cook composing a public statement—
hardly even, with its reminiscences of his instructions, a commander
justifying himself to the Lords of the Admiralty; it is a man, not
unduly nervous but emerging from one of the dark places of the
soul, communing with himself, passing judgment on himself.

For a short time he considered returning outside the reef through
Providential Channel. That, however, would have meant waiting
indefinitely for the right wind; and once outside, the reefs might
force him so far from the land that he could not answer the question
that now filled his mind. What the alternative to a strait beyond
New Holland might mean for him in practical terms—what long
cast round New Guinea—he does not, curiously enough, ever discuss; as if the question, anxiously as he felt it, could really meet with
only one answer. He therefore settled to keep close to the main, then
eight or nine leagues within, whatever risks that might entail, first
staying a day at anchor while the pinnace was properly repaired.
The other boats were sent to the reef, then dry, to see what provision
they could find, and regained the ship loaded down with the meat
of the great cockle or *Tridacna*. In the morning—18 August—he
stood north-west towards the land, two boats ahead, sounding
constantly over a most irregular bottom. The only way to follow
with accuracy the next three days' sailing is to follow it on a chart
tracing with attentive patience the course described line by line in
the journal. Cook anchored from sunset to daylight. When daylight
came he resumed his struggle through a sort of insane labyrinth[1]
of islands and islets, shoals and reefs and keys, with those violently
fluctuating depths below him. It was the 'threading the needle'
navigation of which an admiring successor spoke; let no man not of
strong nerves, said Flinders, embark upon it. At noon on the 19th
Cook summed up his position: latitude 12°, just short of the latitude
of Cape Grenville, having passed round the outside of an island
seven or eight miles from the main coast; to the north-west of this
island 'are several small low Islands and Keys which lay not far
from the Main, and to the northward and Eastward lay several
other Islands and shoals so that we were now incompass'd on every

was then so vivid in his mind that in his entry for the 16th he wrote, 'It pleased GOD at
this very juncture to send us a light air of wind'; but later consideration of the chances
apparently led him to dismiss the Deity as a likely agent of salvation. He nevertheless
preserved the name Providential Channel. His later version of the passage quoted
(*Journals* I, 380) is shorter.

[1] Over all the reefs and shoals noted down by Cook on his chart north of the Endeavour
Reef he spaced out in capital letters the word LABYRINTH.

side by one or the other, but so much does great danger Swallow up
lesser ones that those once so dreaded Shoals were now looked at
with less concearn';[1] in the previous twenty-four hours course and
distance made good, N29°W 32 miles. Some of the islands were inhabited. His latitude next noon was 11°23'; course and distance
sailed N22°W 40 miles. The main land was low, flat and sandy. He
had had a good channel that day, soundings 14 to 23 fathoms, 'but
these are best seen upon the Chart as Likewise the Islands shoals
&c[a] which are too numerous to be mentioned singly'.[2] Journal or
chart, or journal and chart together: to study them, and then let
the mind go back to the masterly advantage taken of every minutest
favouring incident in the struggle for the ship a few days before—
go farther back, to the previous December and the clinging through
the long gale to the North Cape, or still farther to the passage of the
Horn—to do this is to begin to comprehend how great could be
seamanship.

At daylight on 21 August, after another night at anchor, seeing
for once no danger ahead, Cook made all the sail he could towards
the northernmost land in sight. In two hours the shoals appeared
again, but the northernmost land revealed itself as islands, separated
from the main by a passage sown with shoals, through which, however, with boats ahead on each bow and a man at the masthead, he
made his way on a strong flood tide. At noon he was through. The
nearest part of the main, 'and which we soon after found to be the
Northermost', bore west a little south. It was the end of the land,
'the Northern Promontary of this country', and Cook named it York
Cape.[3] He had come through what we know as the Adolphus Channel, and at once stood along shore to the west, boats still ahead.
There seemed here too an open channel. At four in the afternoon
he anchored off a small island, 'in great hopes that we had at last
found a Passage into the Indian Seas'; landed, Banks and Solander
in company, to the fright of a few people who were seen, and climbed
the highest hill. It was no great height; 'but I could see from it no
land between SW and WSW so that I did not doubt but what
there was a passage.' To the north-west, as far as sight could carry,
was nothing but islands. Just before sunset on that day Cook carried
out his final act of annexation. His words have become classic.

[1] *Journals* I, 382.
[2] ibid., 384.
[3] He gave it the latitude of 10°37' S for the north point, corrected in the Admiralty
copy of his journal by himself to 10°42', and 10°41' S for the east point; and the longitude
of 218°24' W—i.e. 141°36' E. The position as now received is lat. 10°41' S (presumably
the north point), longitude 142° 32' E.

Having satisfied my self of the great Probabillity of a Passage, thro' which I intend going with the Ship, and therefore may land no more upon this Eastern coast of New Holland, and on the Western side I can make no new discovery the honour of which belongs to the Dutch Navigators; but the Eastern Coast from the Latitude of 38° South down to this place I am confident was never seen or viseted by any European before us, and Notwithstand[ing] I had in the Name of His Majesty taken posession of several places upon this coast, I now once more hoisted English Coulers and in the Name of His Majesty King George the Third took posession of the whole Eastern Coast from the above Latitude down to this place by the name of *New South Wales*, together with all the Bays, Harbours Rivers and Islands situate upon the said coast, after which we fired three Volleys of small Arms which were Answerd by the like number from the Ship.[1]

Classic words: but what did they mean, or what did Cook intend them to mean? In the first place, we may note that, however the present page of his journal runs, in taking possession of this eastern coast (without the agreement of the aboriginal inhabitants) Cook did not give it the name of New South Wales, or any name at all, though when he found a name he may have called it New Wales by analogy with Dampier's New Britain, earlier detached from New Guinea. New South Wales was a name that emerged later, certainly not before he despatched a copy of the journal to the Admiralty. In the second place, we are unaware what proportion of the country Cook thought he was annexing under the head of 'coast': how far into the interior did the 'coast' run? Did the 'Rivers . . . situate upon the said coast' include river systems back to their sources? We may conclude that the resounding statement meant no more than a vague assertion of authority over a quite vague area, a gesture which the discoverer thought he was bound to make. The island on which he made the gesture was called Possession Island.

Time spent sailing next day was rather short, as Cook advanced into his passage, his *Endeavours Straight*. From 10 a.m. to noon he stood south-west, past the islands in the north; from noon for three or four hours north-westerly, till at the signal for shoal water from the boats he anchored, over a bank where the depths fell next morning, 23 August, on the same course, from eight to three fathoms.[2] This course took him by noon to a small bare island where, the wind falling, he and Banks briefly landed. There was now no part of the New Holland coast in sight. They shot a few of the sea-

[1] *Journals* I, 387–8.
[2] He was anchored on the Rothsay Banks, extending sixteen miles west from the southern point of Prince of Wales Island, which forms the northern coast of Endeavour Strait. To the south of these banks are Red and Wallis Banks; between them and Rothsay Banks is deep water, but Cook, standing north-west, had put that behind him.

birds called boobies; Banks found a few plants; Cook called the place Booby Island. They returned to the ship. That brief landing was like the point that a writer puts down at the end of some long and difficult chapter. Booby Island, for the sailor, still signifies the end of Endeavour Strait, or its western approach, the end of danger or its announcement. One must again quote Cook. While he was on the island the wind had gone to the south-west, 'and altho it blowed but very faint yet it was accompaned with a swell from the same quarter; this together with other concuring circumstances left me no room to doubt but we were got to the Westward of *Carpentaria* or the Northern extremety of *New-Holland* and had now an open Sea to the westward, which gave me no small satisfaction not only because the dangers and fatigues of the Voyage was drawing near to an end, but by being able to prove that New-Holland and New-Guinea are two Seperate Lands or Islands, which untill this day hath been a doubtfull point with Geographers.'[1] He describes the strait: probably, he thinks, there are as good ones, or better, among the congeries of islands to the north, if safer access from the east could be found: 'the Northern extent or the Main or outer Reef which limets or bounds the Shoals to the Eastward seems to be the only thing wanting to clear up this point, and this was a thing I had neither time nor inclination to go about, having been already sufficiently harrass'd with dangers without going to look for more.'[2]

Those shoals! He cannot but recur to them. He had done his best with his chart; but as a conscientious hydrographer he must say to seamen who might come after him that he did not believe he had one half of them laid down; and how could he lay down every island, 'especially between the Latitude of 20° and 22°, where we saw Islands out at Sea as far as we could distinguish any thing'? He could not deny that his work had some value, that it was solidly founded.

However take the Chart in general and I beleive it will be found to contain as few errors as most Sea Charts which have not under gone a thorough correction, the Latitude and Longitude of all or most of the principal head lands, Bays &cᵃ may be relied on, for we seldom faild of geting an Observation every day to correct our Latitude by, and the observation for Settleing the Longitude were no less numberous and made as often as the Sun and Moon came in play, so that it was impossible for any material error to creep into our reckoning in the intermidiate times. In justice to Mʳ Green

---

[1] *Journals* I, 390. Cf. 411, on the 'two Seperate Lands or Islands': 'however we have now put this wholy out of dispute, but as I beleive it was known before tho' not publickly [a reference to Dalrymple?] I clame no other merit than the clearing up of a doubtfull point.' The best channel through Torres Strait is the Prince of Wales Channel discovered by Flinders in the *Investigator* in 1802.
[2] ibid., 391.

I must say that he was Indefatigable in making and calculating these observations which otherwise must have taken up a great deal of my time, which I could not at all times very well spare. Not only this, but by his Instructions several of the Petty officers can make and Calculate these observations almost as well as himself. . . .[1]

He is carried away by his fervour to recommend the lunar method to all sea officers; to assert his hope for the extended publication of the Ephemeris.

Before the journal proceeds with the voyage it devotes some pages, as was proper, to the description of this eastern side of New Holland. They do not convey the idea that the captain admired the country greatly, apart from its bays and harbours. In the south low and level, more to the north of no great height, indifferently well watered, indifferently fertile, with no great variety of trees and most of the large ones too hard and ponderous to apply to many uses, the land by nature produces hardly anything fit for man to eat, though a great variety of plants hitherto unknown. Land animals are scarce; kangaroos are good eating. Some of the birds are beautiful. The sea is indifferently well stocked with fish, though the various sorts are excellent in their kind; on the reefs are cockles and clams of a prodigious size, and in the waters nearby great numbers of the finest green turtle in the world. Botanical things, says Cook, are wholly out of his way to describe, 'nor will this be of any loss sence not only Plants but everything that can be of use to the Learn'd World will be very accuratly described by Mr Banks and Dr Solander.' At the end of his description he remembers that his New Holland is not as barren and miserable as Dampier and the Dutch found the western coast; it is in the pure state of Nature; grains, fruits and roots would flourish here, there is provender for more cattle than ever could be brought into the country. He finds the naked people not unattractive, straight-bodied, slender-limbed, with features far from disagreeable, voices soft and tunable; ornamented simply, some of the men with a bone three or four inches long run through the bridge of the nose —what the seamen called a spritsail yard—some on Possession Island with breastplates of pearl shell (though these were a different people); with few weapons, but adept in the use of dart and throwing stick; with shelters of sticks and bark, canoes of bark or dugout logs; a primitive race indeed. Yet Cook bursts into a panegyric that almost persuades one that he had spent the voyage reading Rousseau: 'From what I have said of the Natives of New-Holland they may appear to some to be the most wretched people

[1] ibid., 392.

upon Earth, but in reality they are far more happier than we Europeans; being wholy unacquainted not only with the superfluous but the necessary Conveniencies so much sought after in Europe, they are happy in not knowing the use of them. They live in a Tranquillity which is not disturb'd by the Inequality of Condition:'— and so on.[1] There are simplicities still in this sailor, one perceives. Has he been listening to some oration of Banks, while the ship lay at anchor in the night; or read through some piece of paper adorned with the Banks version of the fashionable intellectual indiscretions? We return to the clear head, the hydrographer, with 'a few observations on the Currents and Tides upon the Coast'—five hundred words of reality and close argument, which tell us again that it is James Cook we are dealing with.

The dangers and fatigues of the voyage were not quite over. Cook wanted to touch on the coast of New Guinea and accordingly stood away north-west. From Booby Island he had a short afternoon's sailing before the wind fell calm and he anchored for the night. While the anchor was being weighed the following morning the cable parted and the ship drove. A day of frustrating work did not recover the anchor; it was not till the morning of the 25th that he had it and could resume his course. In the afternoon the water began to shoal rapidly again, and again the ship was brought up with sails standing, in six fathoms, with hardly two fathoms over a rocky bottom all round her except the way she had come—and it was almost high water, with 'a short cockling sea'. A fortunate escape, thought Cook, from the most dangerous sort of shoal, which did not show till you were almost on it—and then the water looked merely as if shadowed by a dark cloud.[2] He was still in the western approaches to Torres Strait. By nightfall he was out of danger, to the south and west. His persistency did not fail, however: after finding deeper water he turned once more north-west, then north, and made the land on the 28th. He was in a bight not far from the southwest point of the island, a low shore fringed for miles out to sea with a mud-bank shoal. Stretching off again to haul round this point, he found himself continuously rebuffed; not until 3 September had he rounded the further Frederik Hendrik Island, and, a short distance north of it, got close enough in to land; even then, in three

---

[1] He repeats this nonsense in a letter to John Walker after he got home, 13 September 1771 (*Journals* I, 508–9), so one must presume that he was rather taken with it.
[2] He was on the Cook Shoal. 'This was one of the many fortunate escapes we have had from shipwreck for it was near high-water and there run a short cockling sea that would soon have bulged the Ship had she struck. . . .'—ibid., 403.

fathoms, he was three or four miles from shore over the same bank of mud. He landed, wading from a boat to the beach, with Banks and Solander, just for the sake of landing, determined then to quit altogether a part of the earth where he was merely wasting time. There were traces of men and their voices, but the bush was so thick that he was deterred from doing more than take a walk along the beach. Three or four natives, looking much like New Hollanders, rushed out hurling their darts, retreating at the fire of the muskets; while Cook, to avoid gratuitous trouble, retreated to the boat himself, as a larger number came towards him. He was puzzled by a sort of noiseless fire-arm these people had—strips of hollow cane in which they carried only burning tinder. It was an encounter therefore without harm on either side; and he refused the advice of some of his officers, to send a party on shore to cut down coconut trees for the nuts—no way to get refreshments, but a certain way to court disaster. Instead he made sail to the westward. There was general satisfaction. The greatest part of the ship's company, says Banks, were now much afflicted with that longing for home 'which the Physicians have gone so far as to esteem a disease under the name of Nostalgia; indeed I can find hardly any body in the ship clear of its effects but the Captⁿ Dr Solander and myself, indeed we three have pretty constant employment for our minds which I beleive to be the best if not the only remedy for it.'[1]

Home was still half the world away. Cook was bound first for Batavia, which he wanted to reach as soon and as safely as he could. He knew it was a port well equipped for the repair of ships, and his leaky *Endeavour* might well need heaving down; so he would sail to the south of Java and through the Strait of Sunda. It would have been agreeable to settle the question whether, as New Holland and New Guinea were different countries, their inhabitants were different peoples, still the point was of very little if any consequence (he is almost apologetic over mentioning it), and there was no other discovery to be made in these seas; to Batavia therefore. A rather tedious passage it was to be, of just over five weeks, with one break only. The water soon deepened, and though Cook sounded constantly to begin with he felt himself released from the necessity of anchoring at night. He steered west of south-west and south-west, sometimes a little puzzled by the charts he had, irritated by faulty compilers and dishonest publishers, but unable to delay himself for the sake of correcting them, and unwilling to jeopardise his ship in more shoal water, over more foul ground. He sighted the most

---

[1] Banks, II, 145.

southerly of the Aroe islands, then Timorlaut or the Tanimbar group (where he would have landed had he identified it soon enough), and on 11 September was off Timor, which interested him for Dampier's sake. Westerly winds now imposed delay, he crept along the coast for four days till they went back to the north-east and blew him through the strait between the southern end of Timor and the island of Rotte. Some of his officers, again anxious to advise, 'strongly importune'd' him to go to Concordia (the modern Kupang), the Dutch settlement and fort at this end of Timor. He would not, 'knowing that the Dutch look upon all Europeans with a jealous eye that come a mong these Islands, and our necessities were not so great to oblige me to put into a place where I might expect to be but indifferently treated.'[1] There was depression. Steering west from the strait, clear of the islands as he thought, he was surprised a day later, 17 September, by one in the south-west, certainly not laid down in its proper place on any chart. On its north side were houses, coconut trees, herds of grazing cattle, the green not of savage nature but of human cultivation. Considering the feeling in the ship since his refusal to touch at Timor, and tempted himself, Cook decided to try for refreshment here. Gore was sent ashore. It was the island of Savu; and here he learnt that the Dutch did indeed look with a jealous eye.

Gore returning with a hopeful report, was sent back with money and goods, only to return again with news of a bay to leeward where both anchorage and provisions could be obtained. While the ship was being moved there Dutch colours were hoisted on shore, as they were next morning on the beach at the anchorage. Gore, despatched still again, was taken to the 'king' of the island, the local rajah, who explained somehow that he could supply nothing without the permission of the Dutch governor or factor. Early in the afternoon this person and the king came on board, were entertained to dinner, liberally liquored, given presents, and in return promised as liberally to provide all the supplies Cook wanted. Both Solander and Spöring had enough Dutch to make the factor, one Lange, a German, know what they were. But when Cook himself landed next morning with Banks and a party to return the rajah's visit, he found the promises so far hollow: there were on the beach none of the buffaloes that he wanted to buy, or sign whatever of preparations for trade; instead Lange talked of a letter he had just had from Concordia (from which the ship had been seen) on the subject of trade and presents to the natives; and though there was dinner with the rajah, little could be

[1] *Journals* I, 417.

obtained except palm wine and more promises. On the morrow it became fairly plain that Lange was interfering with trade through his influence over the rajah, though the people were anxious for it and he himself was not immune to bribery, which pushed up extravagantly the price of the first buffaloes bought. Matters were made no better when Sydney Parkinson innocently enquired of the natives whether they had spices on the island, an enquiry immediately reported to Lange, who as immediately suspected some inroad on that sacred Dutch monopoly—a circumstance unknown to Cook, who, trade having at last begun, certainly wished to stay no longer than the one day he was now allowed. He got his buffaloes, disappointing beasts, a few sheep and hogs, a large quantity of poultry, and enough 'syrop'—boiled down palm wine—said Banks, 'for futurity'. In the three days' visit Banks accumulated a vast amount of information about the island's social and political arrangements, something about the Dutch commercial régime; for the much abused Mr Lange was quite talkative.

It was 21 September when Cook sailed. It was 1 October when he came in sight of Java Head, the south-west extremity of the island of which Batavia, that great centre of Dutch commercial activity, was the capital and the port. He had had good weather most of the time, on this due west then more northerly course, but either no time to make observations—he may have been busy writing up his journal—or Green had ceased to work on them; for his longitudes were strangely erroneous during almost the whole period—almost four degrees too far west by 30 September, almost three on 1 October. A strong westerly current ran, as he realised, and he allowed 20′ a day for it: 'this allowance I find Answers', but it did not answer at all, and there was some worry lest he had overshot the entrance to the Strait of Sunda. We have an excellent illustration of the fallibility of dead reckoning, even with the best of navigators. The weather turned squally on the last day and the main topsail was badly split. After two years the voyage was having its effect: 'many of our sails are now so bad that they will hardly stand the least puff of wind.'[1] One of the passengers too was sick—Tupaia, and Cook sent on shore to get some fruit for him as well as grass for the remaining cattle, not with much success. Next day in the strait a Dutch ship was encountered. Hicks went on board her for news. Some of it was agreeable: Carteret's *Swallow*, last seen by Wallis in the Strait of Magellan in April 1767, had called at Batavia 'about two years ago', and so she had survived the Pacific; some was what might be

[1] ibid., 427.

called the normal news of civilisation, as that the English were rioting, the Americans refusing to pay their taxes, the Russians besieging Constantinople. It was all very different from the news that Cook brought with him. His, however, was not for general distribution. He had already, on the last day of September, collected the log books and journals of his officers and men, according to his instructions, and enjoined them not to divulge where they had been—which may be taken as a counsel of perfection; now, when Dutch officers boarded him with official enquiries, he would tell them no more than that his ship was English, her name *Endeavour*, and that he was bound for England; Hicks, a little more communicative, went so far as to say she came from Europe.

This was off Bantam Point, the north-eastern extreme of the strait; thence four days of slow and painful sailing, labouring against strong currents, past almost as many islands, reefs and shoals as were met within the Great Barrier, anchoring and weighing with light winds from the land, brought her into Batavia road. There, on the afternoon of 10 October, by Cook's time, he found an English East Indiaman, and learnt that it was 11 October. Another boat came on board him, to enquire who he was. Both its officer and his people, notes Banks, 'were almost as Spectres, no good omen of the healthyness of the countrey we were arrivd at; our people however who truly might be called rosy and plump, for we had not a sick man among us, jeerd and flouted much at their brother sea mens white faces.'[1] Cook sent Hicks ashore to announce his arrival to the governor, and to apologise for not saluting, as he had not enough guns to do it properly.

[1] Banks, II, 184.

6. Joseph Banks, after Benjamin West, 1773
Mezzotint engraving by J. R. Smith

7a. 'A View of part of the West Side of Georges Island' (Tahiti)
Drawing by Cook

7b. 'The West Elevation of the Fort' (at Point Venus, Matavai Bay)
Drawing by Cook

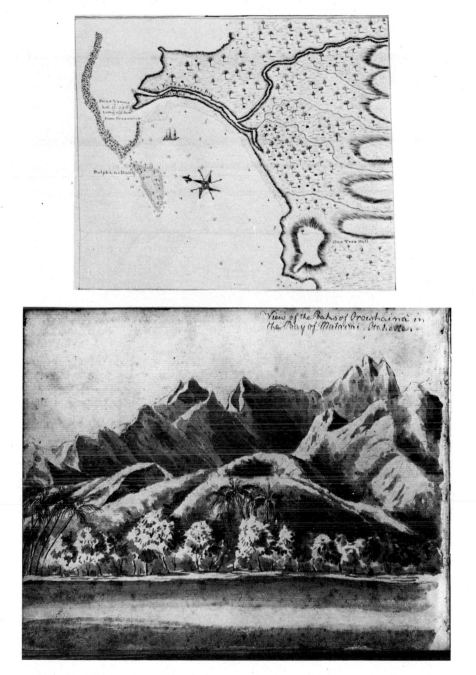

8a. 'A Plan of Royal or Matavie Bay in Georges Island' (Tahiti)
Drawing by Cook

8b. Peaks of Matavai Bay
Pen and wash drawing by Parkinson

11*a*. The *Endeavour* at sea
Drawing by Parkinson

11*b*. The hull of the *Endeavour*
Drawing by Parkinson

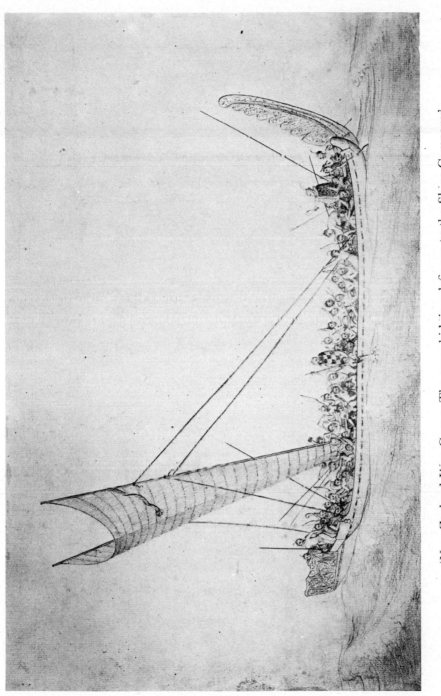

12. 'New Zealand War Canoe. The crew bidding defiance to the Ships Company'
Drawing by Spöring

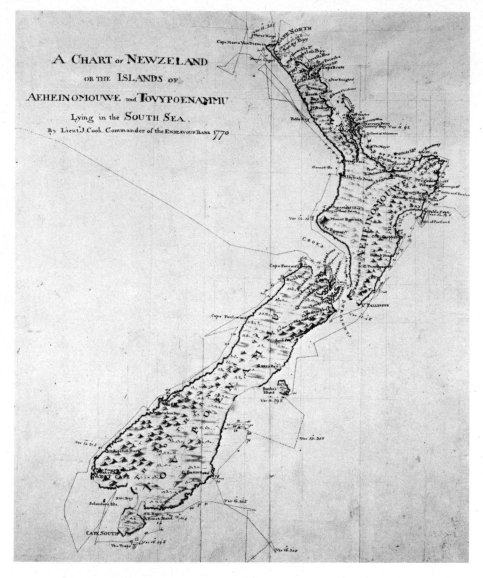

13. 'A Chart of New Zealand or the Islands of Aeheinomouwe and
Tovypoenammu lying in the South Sea'
By Cook

the small assistance our boats could give us to trust
to, the Pinnace was under a repair and could not
immidiatly be hoisted out, the yawl was put into
the water and the Long-boat hoisted out and both
sent a head to tow which together with the help of
our sweeps abaft got the Ships head round to
the northward which seem'd to be the only way to
get her off the reef or at least to delay time. before
this was effected it was 6 oClock and we were not above
80 or 100 yards from the breakers. the same sea
that dashed the sides of the Ship rose in a breaker
prodigeously high the very next time it did rise
so that between us and distruction was only a dismal
valley the breadth of one wave and even now no ground
could be felt with 120 fathom. the Pinnace by
this time was patched up and hoisted out and sent
a head to tow. little did we had hardly any hopes of saving
the Ship and full as little our lives as we were full
10 Leagues from the nearest land and the boats
not sufficient to carry the whole of us yet in this
truly terrible situation not one man ceased to
do his utmost and that with as much calmness
as if no danger had been near. all the dangers
we had escaped were little in comparison of
being thrown from this reef where the Ship must
be dashed to pieces in a moment, a reef such a one
as is here spoke of is scarcely known in Europe
it is a wall of coral rock rising all most perpendicular
out of the unfathomable ocean always overflowen
at high-water generally 7 or 8 feet and dry in
places at low-water. the large waves of the vast
ocean meeting with so sudden a resistance makes
a most terrible surf breaking mountains high
especially as in our case when the general trade

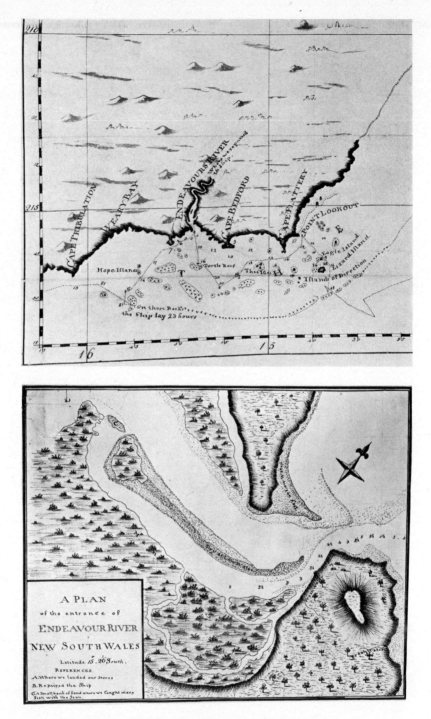

15a. The reef where the *Endeavour* struck, 11 June 1770
Detail from 'Chart of Part of the Sea Coast of New South Wales'. By Cook

15b. 'A Plan of the entrance of Endeavour River'
By Cook

16. The *Endeavour* being careened
Engraving by W. Byrne after Parkinson

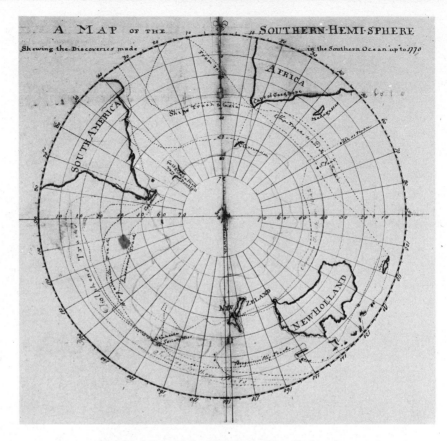

17. 'A Map of the Southern Hemisphere'
By Cook; showing his proposed route by a strong continuous line (yellow in the original)

XI

Batavia to England

BATAVIA, SAID Cook, was certainly a place that Europeans need not covet to go to. Founded by the Dutch on the ruins of Jakarta in the early seventeenth century, it had been instrumental in extending their empire through the East Indies, had sent vast riches to the Netherlands, seen the coming and going of fleets, had provisioned and loaded and mended them; gained a reputation as 'Queen of the Eastern Seas'. It was a queen that stank to heaven, corrupt and filthy. At the end of the century an earthquake choked the streams with mud and turned the surrounding country into a swamp, the tree-lined canals which the Dutch built, on the pattern of home, became torpid ordure-choked tanks of disease. Both in the city and out of it mosquitoes bred infinitely; the fresh food for which the sailor pined betrayed him. In the eighteenth century, with a mortality of something like fifty thousand a year, the place was one of the deadliest on earth. Little wonder that the seamen who greeted the *Endeavour* had a spectral look. Even then, Cook might have got away from the East Indies with relatively little damage, had it not been for a call he made later. Meanwhile, Batavia had its efficiency as well as its fevers.

Preliminary to Cook's application to the authorities for their help in repair, he called on the carpenter for a report. Mr Satterley gave a faithful one, within his competence; for he could not see everything.

The Ship very Leakey (as she makes from twelve to six Inches pᵣ Hour) Occationd by her Main Keel being wounded in many places and the Scarph of her stern being very open. The False Keel gone beyond the Midships (from forward and perhaps farther) as I had no opportunity of seeing for the water when haul'd a shore for repair). Wounded on her Larboard side under the Main Channel where I immagine the greatest Leak is (but could not come at it for the water). One Pump on the Larboard side useless the others decay'd within $1\frac{1}{2}$ Inch of the bore. Otherwise Masts, Yards, Boats & Hull in prety good condition.[1]

[1] *Journals* I, 432.

Satterley and all the other officers were agreed that the ship must be hove down and her bottom inspected before she could safely leave for Europe. Her safety was further ensured in that thunderous climate by fixing an 'electrical chain' to the top of the main mast: this, on her second night in harbour, warded off a thunderbolt which shattered and carried away the main mast of a Dutch Indiaman lying a quarter of a mile off, with only an iron spindle rigged. Cook, making formal application to the governor-general and council for assistance, was granted everything he asked for; then, after making proper calculations, found he would have to apply also to this exalted body for a loan of money—5000 rix dollars—wherewith to meet the expense; and then found his business would be delayed because someone had translated the English expression 'heave down' wrongly. Nevertheless, on 18 October he took the ship from her anchorage in the road across to the outlying Cooper's or Kuyper Island, where, and at its companion Onrust, the Dutch had their equipment, and the crew were put to clearing her of all her stores and ballast. Cook was rather nettled that his own men were not allowed to do the actual work of repair, of which they were quite capable, according to naval regulations; but the Dutch had their regulations also. It was not till 6 November that the officers of the yard at Onrust took the ship in hand.

Three days after Cook's arrival at Batavia a Dutch ship sailed for home. He just had time to write the Admiralty secretary a few lines by her to say where he was. Ten days later, he learnt, a fleet would sail; and to its commodore, Captain Kelger of the *Kronenburg*, he entrusted a very precious packet—a letter to Mr Stephens, a shorter one to the Royal Society, both dated 23 October, a copy of his journal,[1] a chart of the 'South Sea', another of New Zealand, and another of the coast of New South Wales. The letter to the Royal Society merely announced that the mission on which he had been sent had been successfully completed, and was accompanied by one from Green with some details of the observations; that to Stephens, in the usual form, 'Please to acquaint my Lords Commissioners of the Admiralty', must unless Stephens read it very slowly, have made his head turn—and subsequently, when they were acquainted, the heads of the Lords Commissioners. In six hundred and fifty words it distilled the captain's journal, from the day he left Rio de Janeiro to the moment at Onrust, 'where we have

---

[1] This was pretty clearly the copy in the hand of Richard Orton, the clerk, that I have called the Mitchell MS, known earlier as the Corner copy. It was this that was printed by Admiral Wharton in 1893. Its nature is discussed in *Journals* I, ccxviii–ccxxi.

but just got a long side of the warfe in order to take out stores &c^a'
They were words much more heavily laden than those which the
Lords were accustomed to hear read out, and as a flat record of fact
they may still take one's breath away. They included one puzzling
statement about the mishap on the reef: 'this prove'd a fatal stroke
to the remainder of the Voyage', because of the time taken up in
repairing the damage. There are other brief paragraphs, a mixture
of plain satisfaction, modesty, and even apology—which one can
say reflect very accurately certain aspects of the captain's character,
both his professional pride and his sense that he himself is a man
under command. The journal that he now sends has been kept 'in
the best Manner I was capable off'; the 'whole transactions of the
Voyage' are set down in it 'with undisguised truth and without
gloss'. The charts and plans have been made with all the care and
accuracy that time and circumstances would admit of: 'Thus far I
am certain that the Latitude & Longitude of few parts of the world
are better settled than these.' Mr Green's assistance has been very
great. The 'many Valuable discoverys made by Mr Banks & D^r
Solander in Natural History and other things usefull to the learn'd
World cannot fail of contributing very much to the Success of the
Voyage.' As for the ship's company, 'In Justice to the officers and
the whole crew I must say that they have gone through the fatigues
and dangers of the whole voyage with that cheerfullness and allert-
ness that will always do honour to British Seamen, and I have the
satisfaction to say that I have not lost one man by sickness during
the whole Voyage' (he must have forgotten Forby Sutherland, or
did sickness mean only scurvy?). Then, after the breath-taking
summary of work done (and the Lords may have had their breath
equally taken by the statement that not one man had been lost
through sickness in two years), there is another summary:

Altho' the discoveries made in this Voyage are not great, yet I flatter my
self that they are such as may merit the attention of their Lordships, and
altho' I have faild in discovering the so much talk'd of southern Continent
(which perhaps do not exist) and which I my self had much at heart, yet
I am confident that no part of the failure of such discovery Can be laid to
my Charge. . . . Had we been so fortunate not to have run a shore much
more would have been done in the latter part of the Voyage than what
was, but, as it is I presume this Voyage will be found as Compleat as any
before made to the South Seas, on the same account.[1]

[1] The whole letter is printed in *Journals* I, 499–501. The last sentence of the quotation
runs in Cook's draft, 'I presume that this Voyage will be thought as great and as compleat
if not more so than any Voyage before made in the South Seas on the same account.'
He may have thought that the phrase 'if not more so' looked like boasting.

We are left wondering what precisely this writer meant by the remark that if the ship had not run on the reef, that 'fatal stroke', much more 'would have been done in the latter part of the Voyage than what was'. What limit had he put to the voyage? In the terms of his instructions his presence on the eastern coast of New Holland and its charting were already an addendum, a sort of large work of supererogation. Even after all the strokes of fate the part of his chart he had had to leave conjectural was only a quite small part.[1] He had done what he set out to do when he left New Zealand, sailed from his landfall to the northern extremity of the country; he had verified the strait that his maps asserted to exist. If he had not run on the reef and been forced to spend all those weeks in the Endeavour River he would still have had a sound and relatively well-provided ship. Did he think that, being 'morally certain' that Quiros never was upon any part of the New Holland coast, he might have gone on to pin down the Austrialia del Espiritu Santo, so cardinal in the theory of the southern continent, which was said to lie in the parallel of the Endeavour River?[2] Or would he have gone on to chart the islands of Torres Strait, or attempted a more scientific rendering of the southern side of New Guinea, which he had designed anyhow 'if Possible to touch upon'? Carteret, although he did not know it,

[1] From the first settlement of Sydney to the end of the eighteenth century there was minor coastal exploration that corrected or clarified Cook's chart. The position at the beginning of 1801, in relation to Cook, is thus summarised by Flinders, in the lucid and admirable introduction to his *Voyage to Terra Australis* (1814), I, cciii: 'On the east coast of New South Wales from Bass' Strait to Bustard Bay in latitude 24°, the shore might be said to be well explored; but from thence northward to Cape York, there were several portions which had either been passed by captain Cook in the night, or at such a distance in the day time, as to render their formation doubtful: The coast from 15°30′ to 14°30′ was totally unknown.

'The following openings or bights had been seen and named by captain Cook, but were yet unexamined: *Keppel* and *Shoal-water Bays*; *Broad Sound*; *Repulse*, *Edgecumbe*, *Cleveland*, *Halifax*, *Rockingham*, and *Weary Bays*. To the northward of these were *Weymouth*, *Temple*, *Shelburne*, and *Newcastle Bays*; and perhaps many others which distance did not permit our great navigator to notice. There was also a numerous list of islands, of which a few only had been examined; and several were merely indicated from a distant view.'

Then there were the reefs. When Flinders came to work carefully north from Hervey Bay, he found Cook's longitudes fairly constantly and progressively in error, due initially to an overcalculation of the width of Hervey Bay by sixteen miles, and then to the trend of the coast to the west. He thought Cook was out at York Cape by 35 miles. But the authority of Cook was so great, even for a precisian like Flinders, that he wrote, of one point in his Prince of Wales Channel, 'the position of almost every island in this neighbourhood is so different in his chart to what I make them, that it has occasioned me much perplexity and uneasiness.'—*Voyage*, I, 349.

[2] 'The Islands discover'd by Quiros call'd by him Astralia del Espiritu Santo lays in this parallel but how far to the East is hard to say, most charts place them as far to the west as this Country, but we are morally certain that he never was upon any part of this coast.'—*Journals* I, 376. De Brosses's plate IV places 'Terre du St Esprit' in New Holland, on the coast of a sort of bulging Queensland. The map in Harris, Vol. I, has nothing of this sort.

had already done something there. We are left to guess, and to guess how long he could have maintained the cheerfulness and alertness of that excellent crew—the behaviour of every member of which, we recollect if we read the captain's journal, had not been entirely impeccable.

As soon as the ship anchored Banks went ashore with Solander to live, tried a hotel and then hired a house next door to it, sending for Tupaia and his boy Taiata also. These two were transported with the sights of the town. Tupaia brought in some fresh South Sea news; for while he was walking in the street with Banks a man ran from a house and asked had he not been there before? No: but it appeared that a compatriot of his had, the man who had been taken away from Tahiti by those predecessors of Cook, not Spaniards as had been concluded, but the French expedition of the Sieur de Bougainville. Any Spanish iron could easily have been brought by Bougainville's store ship from the River Plate. Carteret's visit to Batavia had been followed by Bougainville's. So here were the French in the Pacific, hard on the heels of the British, the French at King George the Third's Island! Cook ruminated a little on that. He had to wait some time to get a full account of Bougainville's adventure, and when he did he found it extremely interesting. In the meantime there was plenty to do, both for him and the natural historians. Banks was as busy as he had been at Tahiti in the pursuit of miscellaneous experience and information. One little piece of experience he never acquired, and nor did Cook. They were both experimental eaters. Banks, in his later years, boasted of his catholicity to a friend: 'I believe I have eaten my way into the Animal Kingdom farther than any other man'—a claim that Cook could well have contested. Certainly they had both tried dog in Tahiti, shags in New Zealand, kangaroo in New South Wales. It might be useless in the light of that belief, said the friend, to ask what he had eaten, 'but allow me to inquire what you have not eaten?' Banks's answer, after a short pause, skipped the years.

I never have eaten Monkey although when at Batavia Capt Cooke Dr Solander and my self had determined to make the experiment, but on the morning of our intended feast I happened to cross the yard of the House in which we resided and observed half a dozen of those poor little Devils with their arms tied upon cross sticks laying on their backs preparatory to their being killed, Now as I love all sorts of Animals I walked up to them and in consequence of their plaintive chattering and piteous looks I could not resist cutting the Strings by which they were bound and they immediately scampered off so that we lost our Monkey dinner.[1]

This was an episode that did not come into any journal, and it might well disappear under the dark cloud that now descended upon the voyage. Men began to fall sick. When the ship arrived in Batavia, three people were more or less indisposed—Tupaia, who had never got used to ship food; Green, suffering from the effects of his own intemperance; and Hicks. Cook, perhaps, did not know how fatally stricken the last was, because he thought none of them qualified for a sick list; Monkhouse, the surgeon, must have been of the same opinion. By the time the letter went away to Stephens, reporting that remarkable record of health, the tents set up to take the crew while the ship was under repair became hospital as well as lodging —'owing as I suppose to the extreem hot weather', said Cook at first, bringing in 'fever' and other diseases later. The swooping enemy was malaria. Tupaia and Taiata early went down with it, apart from the sailors; then Banks and his servants, Solander and the surgeon, all severe cases. Monkhouse died on 5 November, succeeded as surgeon by his mate, William Perry, an able person who had immediately to buy more medical stores. The young Taiata died, and a few days later Tupaia, inconsolable. Of him Cook writes a short notice which indicates that Banks's tiger-substitute had not been entirely a success: 'He was a Shrewd, Sensible, Ingenious Man, but proud and obstinate which often made his situation on board both disagreable to himself and those about him, and tended much to promote the deceases which put a period to his life.'[2] Green's servant John Reynolds died, three sailors died. Banks took a house in the country for himself and Solander, where they were surrounded with servants and nurses; Cook sent his own servant to him, and, a sick captain, stayed by his ship, while Banks returned the servant. Every man in the ship fell sick except one, the sail-maker John Ravenhill, regarded as an old man, more or less drunk every day. By the time the carpenters at Onrust had begun to look at the ship Cook congratulated himself on Dutch obstinacy—so far from his own men being able to do the work he had then only about twenty officers and men fit for any duty at all; by the time it was finished he had twelve or fourteen.

The ship was in as bad condition as her crew. What Mr Satterley had not been able to see was indeed disastrous. It was true that almost

---

[1] This story is from a sheaf of reminiscences of Banks collected by Dawson Turner, his projected biographer. The MS was generously lent to me by the late Kenneth A. Webster. Banks does not ever seem to have eaten penguin or walrus.

[2] *Journals* I, 442.

all the false keel was gone, the damage to the main keel was severe, a great deal of sheathing lost; but also on the larboard side (which he had suspected) near the keel, 'two planks and a half near 6 feet in length were within $\frac{1}{8}$ of a Inch of being cut through, and here the worms had made their way quite into the Timbers, so that it was a Matter of Surprise to every one who saw her bottom how we had kept her above water; and yet in this condition we had saild some hundreds of Leagues in as dangerous a Navigation as is in any part of the world, happy in being ignorant of the continual danger we were in.'[1] There was naturally a great amount of caulking to do. The Dutch had skilled labour in abundance, as well as a method of careening that Cook admired much, and he was highly pleased with the repairs. On 15 November the *Endeavour* could be moved from the yard at Onrust back to Kuyper, where his men were painfully employed for the next three weeks in getting on board stores, provisions and water, rigging the ship, and repairing and bending the sails. Thunderstorms and rain, as the westerly monsoon set in, did not add to comfort; nor was there amusement for sick or convalescent men when at three o'clock one morning the hawsers parted in hard squalls and the ship had to be warped back to the wharf. On 8 December, with all the sick brought back on board, she ran across to Batavia road, to take in more provisions, to scrape and paint, and complete the other details of getting ready for sea. Cook acquired a new pump. He strengthened his crew with nineteen more men, mainly British, that he found at the place: one of these John Marra, a young Irishman of Cork, was the cause of some trouble, because he had deserted from a Dutch ship and the Dutch wanted him back. They said he was Jan Marre, a Dane, from Elsinore; he was certainly one of those seamen who embarked as the spirit moved them, and was probably no more particular about his origin than he was about his destination. Cook was satisfied that he was a British subject, and refused to give him up; and the Dutch, though disapproving—they thought the Captain's behaviour was 'ungrateful and discourteous'—had to acquiesce.[2] This, as a closing scene, was a little regrettable; for the Dutch officials had done everything for Cook he wanted, and he had been the rounds to thank them. In due course Marra was to present him too with problems. While he gained these men, he lost another. This was Patrick Saunders, a

---

[1] ibid., 437–8.
[2] The Dutch blamed Cook for not giving a straight answer. Their minutes of their dealings with him will be found in the Algemeen Rijksarchief at the Hague, Kol. Arch. Inv. No. 700, 438–40.

midshipman, who deserted. Saunders seems to have been under some suspicion at the time of the episode of Orton's ears, because Cook then sent him before the mast. The episode still rankled with Cook, who at Batavia, with the officers, held out a reward of fifteen guineas and fifteen gallons of arrack to anyone who would discover the guilty person or persons. No impeachment followed, but Saunders's disappearance at that place and time was held to make the case against him black.[1]

On 26 December 1770 the restored *Endeavour* weighed and came to sail. She was to have eleven days of the same frustrating sort of passage she had had through the Strait of Sunda three months before, in reverse, with unpleasant squally rainy weather for the last part of it. She was like a hospital ship, said Cook, upwards of forty of her company sick, the rest in a weakly condition except for the sail-maker, more or less drunk; yet the Dutch captains congratulated him on his good luck in not seeing half his people die. What Solander saw was the mosquitoes breeding on the surface of the ship's very scuttle-butt. On the eleventh day, by which time the general health had deteriorated badly, he anchored off Princes Island or Panaitan, at the southern entrance of the strait, to see if he could get wood and water, and fresh food for the sick. He had just had the first salt meat day since Savu, but now there was turtle again. During a week at Princes Island he did get fresh food, fish, flesh, fowl and fruit, and water, but he soon concluded the water was bad, and put lime into the casks as a purifier. It was 16 January 1771 when he could at last get away from the island, to head in sultry weather with variable light winds and calms towards the Indian Ocean. Then the real martyrdom descended: upon the weakened malaria-stricken company came dysentery, whether caused by the Princes Island water or its death-laden fruit—the 'bloody flux'. In the next six weeks twenty-three men were to die. Banks, afflicted again, 'endurd the pains of the Damnd almost'; by the end of January not more than eight or nine men could keep the deck, and the watches were reduced to four men each. It was not of much use to 'clean between the decks and wash with vinegar'. Cook's journal is little more than notes of the weather and a list of deaths, here and there a brief obituary phrase or a few words on the waxing or waning of disease. The first who went, on 24 January, was John Truslove, corporal of marines, 'a Man much esteem'd by every one on board'. Then Spöring died, and Sydney Parkinson, and Ravenhill the sail-maker, whom drink could preserve no longer;

<hr>

[1] Parkinson, *Journal*, 138 n., 207.

and Green—'he had long been in a bad state of hilth, which he took no care to repair but on the contrary lived in such a manner as greatly promoted the disorders he had had long upon him, this brought on the Flux which put a period to his life.'[1] Cook found his papers in distressing confusion. Two of the carpenter's crew died; then, as January came to an end, one-handed John Thompson the cook, and three other men—in one week eleven deaths: 'A Melancholy proff of the Calamitous Situation we are at present in, having hardly well men enough to tend the Sails and look after the Sick, many of the latter are so ill that we have not the least hopes of their recovery.'[2] About this time the south-east trade wind began to blow steadily, a wholesome air, and Cook thought the worst was perhaps over, though the lives of several men were despaired of. Five died in the second week of February, including Jonathan Monkhouse, that valuable midshipman; then in the third week 'Mr John Satterly, Carpenter, a Man much Esteem'd by me and every Gentleman on board',[3] a seaman, and a marine; in the fourth week 'Alexr Simpson a very good Seaman'; in the fifth, on 27 February, three more seamen, of whom one was sick when he entered at Batavia and never recovered, and the others had clearly long been doomed, 'so that the death of these three men in one day did not in the least alarm us; on the contrary we are in hopes that they will be the last that will fall a Sacrefice to this fatal desorder, for such as are now ill of it are in a fair way to recovering.'[4] It was no wonder that one or two men, who did not die, were affected with a sort of hysteria.[5] The terrible period, however, was over.

Luckily there was, over those weeks, no heavy weather; not till the last day of February did a south-west squall split the fore topsail all over, forcing the ship to bring to, and consequently, even with her enfeebled crew, she could be kept in fair order. She made a dubious landfall on the evening of 4 March, when Cook was not on deck or informed, and a certain one at daylight next morning, when he found he was about two leagues from the land, steering full towards it in a fresh south-east breeze. It seemed that an increasing

---

[1] *Journals* I, 448.   [2] ibid.
[3] ibid., 450.   [4] ibid., 452.
[5] 'I shall mention what effect only the imagery approach of this disorder had upon one man. He had long tended upon the Sick and injoy'd a tolerable good state of hilth: one morning coming upon deck he found himself a little griped and immidiatly began to stamp with his feet and exclaim I have got the Gripes, I have got the Gripes, I shall die, I shall die!—in this manner he continued untill he threw himself into a fit and was carried off the deck in a manner dead, however he soon recover'd and did very well.'— ibid., 458. This seems to have been the trouble also with Thomas Rossiter, drummer of the marines, who was punished with twelve lashes on 21 February for getting drunk, grossly assaulting the officer of the watch; 'and beating some of the sick.'—ibid., 451.

westerly current must have been affecting him: when he worked out his observations this day, he found that his longitude thus determined was between six or seven degrees west of dead reckoning; and he was again lucky that daylight came that morning no later. He wore and stood to the east for a day, at the end of which he found himself not merely ninety miles more south than he should have been 'by account', but also the same distance more to the west and closer to the land. He was, in fact, in the Agulhas current; his dangerous landfall had been the coast of Natal. He now had the land in sight every day, with Cape L'Agulhas, the most southerly point of Africa, west of him on 11 March; on the 15th, having rounded the capes and lain outside Table Bay for a day and a half because of a south-easterly gale, he was anchored in the road of Cape Town. The governor was obliging, and quarters were at once hired ashore for the twenty-nine sick. One of them died while still on board; Solander had hardly gone into lodgings before he fell once more violently ill. As a homeward bound East Indiaman was just sailing Cook des-patched in her letters to the Admiralty and the Royal Society announcing his arrival.

Another Indiaman, from Bengal, the *Holton*, arrived and departed in the next few days—indeed Dutch and English vessels were coming constantly into Table Bay, one of the great refreshing points of the world for shipping. Cape Town, says Cook, after this visit, 'may be consider'd as one great Inn fited up for the reception of all comers and goers', and its inhabitants were correspondingly civil and polite. He studied these vessels with interest, as he had those at Batavia, and the *Holton* sent him into a train of thought which forms an interesting appendix to his reflections within the Barrier Reef, after that swift passage through Providential Channel.

This Ship during her stay in India lost by sickness between 30 and 40 Men and had at this time a good many down with the scurvy, other Ships suffer'd in the same proportion, thus we find that Ships which have been little more than Twelve Months from England have suffer'd as much or more by Sickness than we have done who have been out near three times as long. Yet their sufferings will hardly if atall be mentioned or known in England when on the other hand those of the Endeavour, because the Voyage is uncommon, will very probable be mentioned in every News paper, and what is not unlikely with many additional hardships we never experienced; for such are the disposission of men in general in these Voyages that they are seldom content with the hardships and dangers which will naturaly occur, but they must add others which hardly ever had existence but in their imaginations, by magnifying the most trifling accidents and Circumstances to the greatest hardships, and unsurmountable dangers without the imidiate interposion of Providence, as if the whole Merit of the Voyage consisted in the dangers and hardships they underwent, or that real ones did not happen often enough to give the mind sufficient anxiety; thus posteriety are taught to look upon these Voyages as hazardous to the highest degree.[1]

This is an interesting passage, or—one might call it—piece of rambling—and addressed to whom? To some vague public in his mind, to the Admiralty, to himself? Does it begin as apologetic justification, as he thinks of his dead sailors, a third of his original ship's company? It is not altogether good prophecy, for the newspapers were not to enlarge on the sufferings of the *Endeavour*'s men. It is accurate enough about the natural leaning of men to imagination; in its reference to the immediate interposition of Providence it foreshadows one of the controversies arising from this voyage—or rather supplied with fresh fuel thereby; but does Cook want posterity —he has come a long way from the *Holton*'s sickness—to think that voyages such as his are not particularly hazardous? He is no doubt writing as a professional sailor, a responsible person; but also as James Cook, this time in no crisis of the spirit, with a constitutional distaste for fanfaronade, reluctant (as he was in his letter to Mr Stephens from Batavia) to make extreme claims. So we get this kind of interim statement, by implication, of some of the principles of a particular explorer's mind.

The stay at the Cape was recuperative. Though in appearance the place was barren, the weather was pleasant, except for one storm. Under the care of Perry, all but three of the sick recovered. The well were allowed time off to entertain themselves. Gore climbed Table Mountain. Refreshments were ample, Cape prices low— except for naval stores, the monopoly of the Dutch East India Company. Banks collected his usual miscellany of information and watched over Solander. More information was picked up about Bougainville's voyage; Banks, hearing that the islander, Ahutoru, was to be returned to Tahiti by a French ship from Mauritius, was much exercised by the probability of the French laying claim to British discoveries. How important to publish as soon as possible an account of the *Endeavour*'s! News came in from Europe—war was daily expected between England and Spain; but Cook, who could not wait for the arrival of an English ship said to be in the offing, entered ten more men, got his sick on board (some of them still badly off) and on 14 April weighed anchor. He anchored again for the night off Robben Island, at the mouth of the bay, and next

[1] *Journals* I, 460-1.

morning in a calm, sent a boat to the shore to buy a few odds and ends he had forgotten at the town. The boat was not allowed to land. The Dutch sent criminals to labour at the island, Cook understood —also English seamen they did not wish to lose from their own service to English vessels short of hands; a boat might abstract either sort of person. It was not a matter worth worrying about.

In the afternoon of 15 April the calm turned to a south-east breeze, and he put the Cape behind him. That afternoon died Robert Molyneux the master, who should, if Cook is correct, have allowed himself a better fate—'a young man of good parts but had unfortunately given himself up to extravecancy and intemperance which brought on disorders that put a pirod to his life.'[1] Pickersgill was promoted in his place. With a wind generally favourable, the ship made St Helena in a fortnight, crossing the meridian of Greenwich and thus completing her circumnavigation on 29 April. At St Helena she found the 50-gun *Portland*, Captain Elliot, with the sloop *Swallow* and a convoy of twelve Indiamen homeward bound. But the convoy did not mean war; the news at the Cape was wrong; the *Swallow* had brought out reassuring news. Cook stayed only long enough to take in a few stores, repair sails and overhaul rigging, while Banks as usual explored, botanised, conversed. They sailed with the fleet on 4 May. Cook would have liked to have kept with it for the rest of the passage home, but he doubted the *Endeavour*'s sailing capabilities, especially with her sails and rigging in so bad a condition; after a few days, therefore, and as an insurance against accident, he turned over to Elliot another letter for the Admiralty, with a box of log books and officers' journals, that the Lords might have as soon as possible information supplementary to that sent from Batavia. By this means also he told Maskelyne of the discrepancies he had found in Green's papers relating to the Transit, sending copies of the papers themselves for Maskelyne to study before they were submitted to the Royal Society—and adding some remarks of his own on the distressing penumbra.[2] On that day, 10 May, they were in sight of the island of Ascension. Banks, of course, was full of curiosity: 'Our Captn however did not chuse to anchor unwilling to give the fleet so much start of him.' There was little to do. Cook observed an eclipse of the sun 'meerly for the sake of Observing'. He took lunars for longitude, remarked the variation of the compass, all with ample time. Hicks was clearly sinking, and an

[1] *Journals* I, 466.
[2] Cook to Maskelyne, 9 May 1771; Royal Society Council Minutes, VI, 107–10. I have printed this in *Journals* I (2nd ed., 1968), 692–3.

Indiaman's surgeon was brought on board to look at him. On 21 May in a calm, while boats were out to tow, Cook's interest was much excited by a 'machine' for warping which the *Portland* used instead, a sort of large canvas umbrella against which a hundred and fifty men could haul; Cook would have made one at once if his forge had been in working order. On the 23rd the fleet, outsailing him disappeared into haze—notwithstanding which Elliot reached home only three days before he did. On the 25th died Zachary Hicks, that useful man, of whom we know so little apart from his quiet observant eye: 'in the evening his body was commited to the Sea with the usual ceremonies; he died of a Consumption which he was not free from when we saild from England so that it may be truly said that he hath been dieing ever sence, tho he held out tollerable well untill we got to Batavia.'[1] There are no more obituaries. There is another promotion: Gore moves up, and to the vacant lieutenancy is ordered Charles Clerke, 'he being a young Man extremely well quallified for that station'.

The passage continued without much incident. Two or three times a sail was sighted or a vessel spoken. On 19 June, in the middle of the North Atlantic, west of the Azores, Cook sent a boat on board a schooner out from Rhode Island on the whale fishery, heard that all was peace in Europe, disputes between Britain and her American colonies made up; there were other whaling vessels; on the 21st and 22nd he seemed to have caught up with the East India fleet. But his sails were splitting; in the morning of the 22nd the carpenter reported the main topmast sprung in the cap, 'which we supposed happen'd in the PM when both the weather backstays broke, our Rigging and Sails are now so bad that some thing or another is giving way every day.'[2] The East Indiamen sailed out of sight again. Banks's surviving dog, his greyhound bitch, the chaser of kangaroos, died suddenly. The goat seemed immortal. Early in July ships were seen or spoken every day. From a London brig bound to the West Indies it was learnt on 7 July that no account having been received in England of the *Endeavour*, wagers had been laid that she was lost; which seemed strange to Cook, because the Dutch fleet with his packet had sailed from the Cape five months before. There had certainly been news manufactured at home, when the newspapers recollected the ship, in the context of threatened war with Spain. For example:

It is surmised, that one ground of the present preparations for war, is some secret intelligence received by the Ministry, that the Endeavour man of

[1] *Journals* I, 471.   [2] ibid., 475.

war, which was sent into the South Sea with the astronomers, to make observations, and afterwards to go into a new track to make discoveries, has been sunk, with all her people, by order of a jealous Court, who has committed other hostilities against us in the Southern hemisphere. Mr. Banks, and the famous Dr. Solander, were on board the above vessel, and are feared to have shared the common fate with the rest of the ship's company.

So *Bingley's Journal* for Friday, 28 September 1770, which at least confirms our feeling that Cook's secret instructions for his behaviour after he should leave Tahiti were not altogether secret. The Banks family had its correspondents, and in October Miss Sarah Banks was informing the naturalist and traveller over England, Thomas Pennant, that there was not the least foundation for such alarming reports, though 'we begin to fear we shall not see them till spring, upon account of their having missed the Trade Wind. . . .'[1] Then rumour swung the other way: early in January 1771 it was printed that the ship was 'safely arrived at the island of Batavia', on the authority of 'the last Ships from India'.[2] In May there is at last something authentic: 'Certain Advices came yesterday to the India house, that the ship Endeavour . . . arrived the 10th of October last at Batavia, all well on board'; a little later an abstract is given of a letter from Mr Sydney Parkinson, 'principal drawer to Mr. Banks'.[3] The East India Company had in fact passed on its information to the Admiralty before it did so to the press: the Lords' minutes for 7 May include the message, and the resolution that the Secretary of State be acquainted therewith, 'for the King's information, as it was feared the said Vessel was lost.'[4] A natural fear, perhaps, even in the Admiralty. Byron's Pacific voyage had lasted twenty-three months, Wallis's twenty-one months; even Carteret, in his dreadful ship, and monsoon-bound in the East Indies for five months, had reached home, however unexpectedly, in thirty-three months. Cook had certainly been at Rio de Janeiro at the end of November 1768, presumably had departed from it within a few days; after that, what? What the Lords had not understood, when they put Cook into the *Endeavour*, was that they had inaugurated a new dispensation.

Our minds, however, are with Cook, not with the newspapers nor even with the Admiralty. On 10 July at 6 a.m. he sounded, and judged from his depth and bottom—was this not his old naval cruis-

---

[1] S.S. (Sarah) Banks to Thomas Pennant, 6 October 1770; ATL, MS Papers 155:20.
[2] *General Evening Post*, 8 January 1771, and other papers of same date.
[3] *London Evening Post*, 9 May, 16 May 1771. For these notices see *Journals* I, 642–3.
[4] Adm 3/78.

ing ground, when he was master's mate of the *Eagle*?—that he was
the length of the Scilly islands. At noon that day Young Nick at the
mast head sighted land, 'which we judged to be about the Lands
end.' The wind was fresh, the weather clear, the ship ran briskly
(which was remarkable, considering the state of her bottom) up
Channel; at noon on 12 July she passed Dover, at 3 o'clock in the
afternoon anchored in the Downs. Cook had been writing busily.
Soon after the anchor went down he landed at Deal: there was still
one of his instructions to carry out . . . 'upon your Arrival in
England you are immediately to repair to this Office in order to lay
before us a full account of your Proceedings in the whole Course of
your Voyage . . . '. The Office was the Admiralty Office, and he carried a letter to Mr Stephens, dated from the Downs on that day.

Sir,
It is with pleasure I have to request that you will be pleased to acquaint
my Lords Commiss^{rs} of the Admiralty with the Arrival of His Majesty's
Bark under my Command at this place, where I shall leave her to wait
until' further Orders. And In Obedience to their Lordships orders
immediately, & with this Letter, repair to their Office, in order to lay
before them a full acco^t of the proceedings of the whole Voyage. . . .

He made no doubt that his communications from Batavia and by
way of the *Portland* had been received, since when nothing material
had happened beyond the death of Hicks and the promotion of
Clerke,

a Young Man well worthy of it, & as such must beg leave to recommend
him to their Lordships, this as well as all other appointments made in the
Bark Vacant by the Death of former Officers, agreeable to the inclosed
List, will, I hope meet their approbation.
    You will herewith receive my Journals containing an Account of the
Proceedings of the whole voyage, together with all the Charts, Plans &
drawings, I have made of the respective places we have touched at, which
you will be pleased to lay before their Lordships. I flatter my self that the
Latter will be found sufficient to convey a Tolerable knowledge of the
places they are intended to illustrate, & that the discoveries we have made,
tho' not great, will Apologize for the length of the Voyage.[1]

Stephens, whose acquaintance with naval officers was not small,
might well have been pardoned if he had thought this man's obedience to orders almost painfully literal; and, as he took a preliminary
glance through the Charts, Plans and drawings, this unwillingness

---

[1] *Journals* I, 504-5.

to claim more than minimal credit incomprehensible. Insistent modesty, it is true, may serve to screen a large measure of vanity, but all the indications are that in dealing with Cook's modesty we must ourselves be literal.

XII

England 1771–1772

BANKS WAS a happy man. When he stepped into London he stepped into glory. The newspapers were all Mr Banks, and Mr Banks's voyage, Mr Banks and Dr Solander, once or twice Dr Solander and Mr Banks; they had touched at near forty undiscovered islands, they had brought back over a thousand different species of plants, unknown in Europe before, they had brought back seventeen thousand plants, never before seen in this kingdom; Mr Banks was presented to the King by Lord Beauchamp at St James's Palace; Dr Solander and Mr Banks, accompanied by Sir John Pringle, the president of the Royal Society, had the honour of a conference with His Majesty at Richmond, on the discoveries they had made on their late voyage; they presented His Majesty with a coronet of gold, set round with feathers, which had been given them by a chief on the coast of Chile; Lady Mary Coke saw them at Court, they were the most talked of people at present; the celebrated Mr Banks was to have two ships from Government to pursue his discoveries in the South Seas, and would sail next March; the celebrated Mr Banks would shortly make another voyage to St George's Island, in the South Seas, and it was said, that Government would allow him three ships, with men, arms, and provisions, in order to plant and settle a colony there. Such talk went on throughout August, but when the nonsense died down the gentlemen did not cease to be objects of interest. Banks did not need to bring back a lion or tiger or a Tupaia; he was a lion himself. The nobility called at his house to see his curiosities. In November he and his friend were called to Oxford to become doctors of civil law. Their friend Ellis of course wrote to Linnaeus, and Linnaeus touched extravagant heights of excitement: New South Wales, he thought, should be named *Banksia*, botanists should raise a statue to the 'immortal Banks' more enduring than the Pyramids. It was intoxicating. It was not entire happiness, even in that wonderful August. There was Miss Harriet Blosset, and there was Stanfield Parkinson. Miss Blosset was the young woman to whom Banks had betrothed himself shortly before he left England, whom he did not hasten to meet when he set foot in England again, from whom his efforts to extricate himself did not seem to his friends to be altogether gentlemanly. He managed it.[1] Stanfield Parkinson was the brother of Sydney Parkinson, and his executor, an upholsterer to whom Banks immediately gave employment, with whom he almost as soon came at loggerheads over Sydney's possessions. Stanfield was unbalanced and badly advised, Banks was cavalier and dilatory, though generous; the quarrel blew up to the publication the following year by Stanfield of his brother's 'journal', and its absorption in public policy.[2]

Meanwhile Cook, who remained attached to Mrs Cook, was not still in his twenties, had not a place in society or a house in New Burlington Street frequented by the nobility, nor plants to present to the Dowager Princess of Wales, pursued a more sober course. Certainly he must have sped to Mile End, to his Elizabeth—and probably with some anxious thoughts about his family; for it was not a time when children could be confidently expected to survive any given three years. James and Nathaniel, those able-bodied seamen, were flourishing, the first rising eight years old, the second between six and seven; but the little Elizabeth had died three months before her father's return, at the age of four, and the baby Joseph must be ever a shade. This home-coming we can only imagine. The official side is plainer. Cook had made further reports to the Admiralty, on the ship, on Dr Knight's azimuth compasses, on the health of the ship's company, their diet and the precautions taken against scurvy; had tendered a special report to the Victualling Board, in terms of high praise, on 'Sour Krautt'. He was anxious to get promotion for some of his men. There were the 'Curiosity's' he had collected on the voyage to sort and pack and send to the Admiralty, accounts to pass, no doubt Royal Society officials to communicate with in person as well as by letter. There was a great deal for the Society to print in its *Philosophical Transactions* for 1771—much more than a simple account of the Transit. He would write to Maskelyne in the following year about the South Sea tides, and that communication would be printed too.[3] There were other letters to write, like that to George Monkhouse of Cumberland on the affairs of his two dead sons.

He bade goodbye to his ship, which before the end of July, her

---

[1] Banks, I, 54–6; to that documentation may be added the letter from J. R. Forster to Thomas Pennant, 13 August 1771, 'But Mr *Banks*, I have heard, undertakes already a new Expedition to Africa: the Marriage with Miss *Harriet Blosset* is not to take place. & she is to have 5000£: this Dr Bosworth told me.'

[2] ibid., 56–61; *Journals* I, ccliii–cclv.

[3] *Phil. Trans.* LXI (1771), 397–432; LXII (1772) 357–8.

company dispersed, was docked at Woolwich, to be resheathed and fitted to carry stores to the Falkland Islands. The Lords were a little slower in dealing with her commander. They met on 1 August. The next day the Secretary wrote Cook a letter, 'sent to him at his house at Mile End'. His own letters had been received, 'with the several Journals and Charts to which you therein refer me. And having laid the same before my Lords Commissioners of the Admiralty I have the pleasure to acquaint you that their Lordships extremely well approve of the whole of your proceedings and that they have great satisfaction in the account you have given them of the good behaviour of your Officers and Men and of the chearfulness and alertness with which they went through the fatigues and dangers of their late voyage.'[1] The promotions he had made were confirmed. Those he had asked for were made. Then, a little late, perhaps, a month after his return, he was himself promoted. To judge from the terms of a letter to Banks, it does not seem probable that, as his first biographer states, he asked to be made a post-captain,[2] and was refused. If it had been so, we might have been more surprised by the request— so quite out of character—than by the refusal; for the Admiralty had no ships for post-captains just then. It also had no precedent for rewarding brilliance in Cook's line of duty; and we need not suspect that either it or Cook thought it was being less than just in merely moving him one step up the ladder. Nor need we be surprised that Cook got the news first from Banks, a friend of the Earl of Sandwich, who had been First Lord since January of that year, 1771. He writes to Banks on a Sunday morning from Will's Coffee-house at Charing Cross, having, it seems, just received a missive from him.

Your very obliging letter was the first Messenger that conveyed to me Lord Sandwich's intentions. Promotion unsolicited to a man of my station in life must convey a satisfaction to the mind that is better conceived than described—I had this morning the honour to wait upon his Lordship who renewed his promises to me, and in so obliging and polite a manner as convinced me that he approved of the Voyage. The reputation I may have acquired on this account by which I shall receive promotion calls to my mind the very great assistance I received therein from you, which will ever be remembered with most gratefull Acknowledgments. . . .[3]

[1] Stephens to Cook, 2 August 1771, Adm 2/731.
[2] Kippis, 182: 'Mr. Cook, on this occasion, from a certain consciousness of his own merit, wished to have been appointed a Post Captain.' This would 'have been inconsistent with the order of the naval service. The difference was in point of rank only, and not of advantage. A Commander has the same pay as a Post Captain, and his authority is the same when he is in actual employment.'—Kippis notes that he writes 'From the information of the Right Honourable the Earl of Sandwich'.
[3] Cook to Banks, 11 August (?) 1771, British Museum (Natural History), Dawson Turner Transcripts of Banks Correspondence (D.T.C.), I, 32; printed in *Journals* I, 637-8.

Why Lord Sandwich could not himself convey his intentions to Cook, that Sunday morning, we do not know: perhaps he had deputed the pleasing office to Banks as one of friendship. We do not know either what the promises were that he renewed so obligingly: perhaps they included promotion, perhaps they included something to which Cook had given a great deal more thought, another voyage. He did something which Banks certainly could not do when on 14 August he introduced Cook in his turn to the King at St James's, so that the monarch could have the voyage and the charts explained to him at first hand; and George in his turn handed Cook his commission as a commander. At the end of the month this was particularised; he was to command the *Scorpion* sloop, a converted fire-ship, which was to take part in a large campaign for correcting the charts of the English coast.[1] This was a natural ship for his talents, if his talents were to be employed at home. It is possible, however, that the appointment was only a formal one, to safeguard his pay; for there was much more in the wind than the charts of the English coasts. With him to the *Scorpion* went Pickersgill, promoted lieutenant, Perry the surgeon, young Isaac Smith, Nowell the carpenter and Forwood the gunner.

John Walker of Whitby wrote to Cook, and Cook wrote two letters to him, a short and a long one, which gave him a conspectus of the voyage. The first, of 17 August, is interesting because it shows Cook, somewhat in the presence of his old master and a familiar friend, divesting himself of a little of the modesty he more habitually wore.

Your very obliging letter came safe to hand for which and your kind enquiry after my health I return you my most sincere thanks—I should have wrote much sooner but have been in expectation for several days past of an Order to make my Voyage Publick after which I could have wrote with freedom; as this point is not yet determined upon I lay under some restraint I may however venter to inform you that the Voyage has fully Answered the expectation of my Superiors I had the Honour of a hours Conference with the King the other day who was pleased to express his Approbation of my Conduct in Terms that were extremely pleasing to me —I however have made no very great Discoveries yet I have exploar'd more of the Great South Sea than all that have gone before me so much that little remains now to be done to have a thorough knowledge of that part of the Globe I sayled from England as well provided for such a voyage as possible and a better ship for such a Service I never would wish for.

[1] The *Scorpion* carried a complement of 120 men, 14 carriage guns and 14 swivels. See *Journals* II, 898–9 (Calendar of Documents).

A few lines take him round the Horn 'without ever being once brought under our close reefed Topsails, however we had no want of Wind'; at Tahiti he had 'an Extraordinary good Observation of the Transit of Venus'; up to his visit to the neighbouring islands the voyage was 'very agreeable and pleasent, the remainder was What I must refer to some other oppertunity to enter upon. Should I come into the North I shall certainly call upon you and am with great respect' Mr Walker's most obliged humble servant.[1]

The other oppertunity he made on 13 September, skimming from his journal the cream of his descriptions of the islands—'Was I to give a full discription of those Islands the Manners and Customs of the Inhabitants &c^a it would far exceed the bounds of a letter, I must therefore quit these Terrestrial Paridises in order to follow the Course of our Voyage'—New Zealand and New South Wales, including the perils of the reef and the aboriginal Eden-dwellers, 'far more happier than we Europeans'; and then Batavia, 'all in good hilth and high spirits', and the dreadful reversal. The interest of the Whitby circle, to which this circumnavigator had so intimately belonged, must have been highly aroused. Then some things further for discussion:

If any intresting circumstance's should occur to me that I have omited, will here after acquaint you with it, I however expect that my Lords commissioners of the Admiralty will very soon publish the whole Voyage, Charts &c^a. Another Voyage is thought of, with two Ships which if it takes place I beleive the command will be confer'd upon me.[2]

There can be no doubt that Cook hoped there would be another voyage, and that he would command it. Indeed, he had sketched out its scope even before he handed over his journal to the Admiralty. There can be no doubt that the continental possibility had been a good deal discussed in the great cabin of the *Endeavour*, both Banks and Cook discuss it in their journals. Banks, after scouting most of the arguments advanced for its existence, found himself still attracted by the idea of ice as an exclusively fresh water phenomenon, which must therefore have a land origin, taken, too, by the 'signs of land'—seaweed, and a seal—that had been encountered in August and September 1769; he confesses that his reasons are weak, 'yet I have a prepossession', and concludes, 'That a Southern Continent exists, I firmly beleive . . .' But it must be situated in very high latitudes.[3] Cook is negative where Banks is positive, but does allow a

[1] Cook to Walker, 17 August 1771, Mitchell Library, MS A 1713-2; *Journals* I, 505–6.
[2] Cook to Walker, 13 September 1771, Dixson Library, MS Q 140; *Journals* I, 506–9.
[3] Banks's discussion is in his '*Endeavour*' *Journal*, II, 38–40.

little: 'as to a Southern Continent I do not beleive any such thing exists unless in a high latitude.' He pursues his argument particularly after his circumnavigation of New Zealand had proved that it, at any rate, provided no support for the great hypothesis. He considers the critical voyages of Quiros and Roggeveen: neither do they shore it up, however much Dalrymple may build on Quiros—'hanging Clowds and a thick horizon are certainly no known Signs of a Continent, I have had many proofs to the contrary in the Course of this Voyage'. True, between his own tracks north from the Horn, and south from the Society Islands, was unexplored ocean enough to accommodate a pretty large extent of northward-thrusting land —though not very much northward of 40°. But on what foundation might one suppose that it was there?—'none that I know of but this that it must be either here or nowhere'. Well: what followed about the grand Object? 'I think it would be a great pitty that this thing which at times has been the object of many ages and Nations should not now be wholy clear'd up, which might very easily be done in one Voyage without either much trouble or danger or fear of misscarrying as the Navigator would know where to go to look for it'; and if no continent was found, south of the equator waited a multitude of tropical islands to be discovered. Unless the ship were ordered to search in a high latitude (that is, south of 40°), she would not need to go west of longitude 145°, because between that longitude and New Zealand Cook had already been. Therefore she would always be within reach of Tahiti for refreshment. If she went in Tupaia's lifetime and took him she would always be assured of friendly reception and direction; 'this would inable the Navigator to make his discoveries the more perfect and compleat', because he would not be obliged to hurry for fear of wanting provisions.[1]

That last point is interesting: it shows Cook with a plan for discovery in which an essential part was played by a base, Tahiti—or at least by places of call which would fill the functions of a base. By the time he came to write the postscript to his journal, perhaps drafted at the Cape, he had had further thought, and his projected discoveries by no means envisage any possible confinement to a segment of ocean north of latitude 40° S and east of longitude 145° W. Like Banks, he has discussed the French interest in Tahiti, and the importance of fixing by publication the British prior right. He continues and concludes with an important paragraph:

Now I am upon the subject of discoveries I hope it will not be taken a Miss if I give it as my opinion that the most feasable Method of making

[1] Cook's discussion is in *Journals* I, 288–90.

further discoveries in the South Sea is to enter it by the way of New Zeland, first touching and refreshing at the Cape of Good Hope, from thence proceed to the Southward of New Holland for Queen Charlottes Sound where again refresh Wood and Water, takeing care to be ready to leave that place by the latter end of September or beginning of October at farthest, when you would have the whole summer before you and after geting through the Straight might, with the prevailing Westerly winds, run to the Eastward in as high a Latitude as you please and, if you met with no lands, would have time enough to get round Cape Horne before the summer was too far spent, but if after meeting with no Continent & you had other Objects in View, than haul to the northward and after visiting some of the Islands already discover'd, after which proceed with the trade wind back to the Westward in search of those before Mintioned thus the discoveries in the South Sea would be compleat.[1]

This clearly was an advance, towards both a larger scope in the amount of ocean to be covered, and economy of effort in taking advantage of the winds that were now known to prevail. If anything like the traditional continent did exist, this would hit it in the middle, and naturally there would be some enforced modification or elaboration of the plan. If it did not, then the plan need not be modified, but could be elaborated by as many other 'Objects in View' as came into the mind of the discoverer. One of these might be Tahiti, though Cook does not now specifically name it; others might be the islands 'before Mintioned' by Tupaia. The base whence the spring into the Pacific is now to be taken is New Zealand, more pointedly Queen Charlotte's Sound. To this plan Banks, who gives a version of it something, though not quite, the same, adds a little appendix of his own. Such a voyage, he thinks, 'as a Voyage of Mere Curiosity, should be promoted by the Royal Society to whoom I doubt not but his majesty would upon a proper application grant a ship, as the subject of such a voyage seems at least as interesting to Science in general and the increase of knowledge' as the observation of the transit of Venus.[2] If Cook nourished that sentiment, he did not utter it. He continued to develop inwardly the plan of a voyage; but the voyage which on 13 September he told Walker was being thought of was probably the voyage as adumbrated by himself, with the addition of a second ship. The memory of the Barrier Reef was still with him. The voyage, in fact, was not merely being thought of, it was determined on, and on 25 September the Admiralty instructed the Navy Board to purchase two proper vessels, of about 400 tons, for service in remote parts.[3]

[1] *Journals* I, 479.   [2] Banks, II, 41.   [3] ADM/A/2647.

Cook was henceforth a busy man. He might have been even busier if he had had to defend himself in an action brought against him by Matthew Cox, one of the men he had punished at the Bay of Islands in New Zealand for robbing native gardens. Cox—hardly old enough to be complete sea-lawyer, perhaps the victim of some London land lawyer—evidently still resented his irons and lashes. The Admiralty solicitor took the matter in hand, and it drops from the records.[1]

Cook's immediate business therefore was with shipping; for the Navy Board, in pursuance of the Admiralty's instructions, asked him to see what could be bought. Bought: because of the sort of ship required, no navy ship. He would have been willing to sail in the *Endeavour* again, but she was otherwise intended. Something as much like the *Endeavour* as possible, therefore, must be obtained, for the same reasons which urged the selection of the *Endeavour*; and as he went over the Pool of London he had a clear picture in his mind. He knew the arguments for larger ships, or faster-sailing ships, East Indiamen, three-decked West Indiamen, frigates, and he knew that they were all wrong. The great danger in voyages of discovery was running aground on an unknown coast: the great desideratum was to keep the sea for long periods of time. The ship must therefore be of burden and capacity enough to carry a large quantity of provisions and stores, without drawing a great amount of water; she must be strongly enough constructed to take the ground, and not too large to be laid on shore for repair. Ships of this sort were those built in the north country for the coal trade: there were no others. It was unfit ships, not unfit men, that before the *Endeavour* stood in the way of progress in discovery. 'It was upon these considerations', says Cook, that the *Endeavour* was chosen for her enterprise.[2] 'It was to these Properties in her, those onboard owe their Preservation. Hence I was enabled to prosecute Discoveries in those Seas so much longer than any other Man ever did or could do. And altho' discovery was not the first object of that Voyage, I could venture, to traverse a far greater space of Sea, before then unnavigated; to discover greater Tracks of Country in high and low South Latitudes; and even to explore and Survey the extensive Coasts of those new discover'd Countries, than was ever performed before during one Voyage.'[3] So, again, he comes a little through his modesty, but only to exalt his ship. So, naturally, without hurry, he picked on three colliers or barks, and of these the Navy Board early in November bought two,

[1] Stephens to Cook, 20 September 1771; P.R.O. Adm 2/731; *Journals* I, 640.
[2] He adds, in B.M. Add. MS 27889, 'being the first ship of the kind so imploy'd'.
[3] Dixson Library, MS F 1, draft introduction to printed account of the second voyage.

the *Marquis of Granby* and the *Marquis of Rockingham*.[1] The first was 462 tons (so a larger ship than the *Endeavour* by almost 100 tons), the second 340 tons; the lower deck length of the first was 111 feet, her beam 35 feet; those measurements for the second 97 feet and 28 feet; in both the hold had a depth of 13 feet.[2] Both came from the Fishburn yard at Whitby, like the *Endeavour*; the first was fourteen months old, the second eighteen, and they were, in Cook's opinion, as well adapted for their intended purpose as if they had been built for it. They were bought from Captain William Hammond of Hull, who may have been known to Cook already; certainly the men were on friendly terms later. On 27 November the Admiralty decided that they should be registered as sloops under the names *Drake* and *Raleigh*, sheathed and filled as the *Endeavour* had been, the *Drake* to carry twelve guns and 120 men, the *Raleigh* ten guns and 80 men and, indicating that thought had been proceeding for some time already, simultaneously the principal officers and warrant officers were named. Cook went to the *Drake*, with Robert Palliser Cooper and Charles Clerke, first and second lieutenants; Tobias Furneaux, commander, to the *Raleigh*, with Joseph Shank, first lieutenant. These commissions and warrants were signed on 28 November; next day another was made out for Pickersgill to be third lieutenant *Drake*.[3] Manifestly, it was not only the purchase of ships that had been going on.

The commander *Drake* was instructed in the usual formula. His ship was in dry dock at Deptford; he was 'hereby required and directed to use the utmost dispatch in getting her ready for the Sea accordingly, and then falling down to Gallions Reach take in her Guns and Gunners Stores at that place and then proceed to the Nore' for further orders.[4] It was hoped that this 'voyage to remote parts' might start in March, which allowed upwards of four months for getting the ship ready under Cook's direction. After that first voyage, his standing with the Admiralty and its departments was as high as any man's ever was, and his direction was almost sovereign. He was perhaps fortunate in the men who now presided over the Lords Commissioners and the Navy Board—though it is hard to think that any other men would not have been as agreeable. But John Montagu, fourth Earl of Sandwich, whatever might be said against his personal and political morals—his enemies said a great

[1] Navy Board to Admiralty, 15 November 1771, ADM/B/185. The tonnage of the ships is in this letter given as 450 and 336 tons.
[2] *Journals* II, xxv, gives more precise measurements.
[3] Admiralty Minutes, 27 November, 29 November 1771, Adm 3/79.
[4] Admiralty to Cook, 30 November 1771, CLB.

deal endlessly—was a perceptive and able man, of knowledge and charm, who rapidly became Cook's friend as well as admirer. It was one thing for Sandwich to entertain his young friend Banks at Hinchinbrook, his Huntingdonshire seat; it was another thing for a First Sea Lord to treat a commander on such terms of familiarity. It may seem less surprising that Captain Palliser, who had become Comptroller of the Navy, or head of the Navy Board, in the previous year, was as firm a friend; for this was the Palliser of the *Eagle* and the Newfoundland command. Professionally he knew Cook as well as anyone did; officially, as general manager of naval ships, their equipment and supply, he was the key to the commander's happiness at this moment; and he was on excellent terms with Sandwich. We may add among friends, as Cook added, Sir John Williams, the Surveyor of the Navy; we may give Cook's own summary of the process now begun: 'the Victualling Board was also very attentive in procuring the very best of every kind of Provisions in short every department seem'd to vie with each other in equiping these two Sloops: every standing Rule and order in the Navy was dispenced with, every alteration, every necessary and usefull article was granted as soon as ask'd for.'[1]

To illustrate this, one need only glance over the correspondence of the next month or so. Cook perfects his technique of calling at offices, explaining what he wanted, writing his letter on the spot, and getting an immediate answer. The day the Navy Board reports to the Admiralty the purchase of the ships, the Victualling Board seeks authority to supply the salted cabbage Cook has already asked for—additional to the sauerkraut he was to get, and as he thought, equally good. Extra wheat, extra portable soup, extra oatmeal and spirits, sugar instead of perishable currants and almonds, rob of oranges and lemons, stockfish, extra tools, ice-anchors and hatchets, extra anchors, better quality seine nets, deck-awnings, patent medicines—a great quantity of Dr James's Fever Powders, that astonishing eighteenth-century remedy for everything, officially recommended in the naval regulations—better compasses (this time one of 'Mr Gregorys Azimuth Compass's of an improved construction'), 'warping machines' such as Cook had seen in use by the *Portland*: all and more were furnished—even the warping machines which the Navy Board could not at first comprehend. One thing was denied him, in spite of the total compliance for which he thanked the departments: he wanted brass in place of iron for the metal furnishings in his great cabin, which seems a reasonable enough request

[1] *Journals* II, 3.

considering the prospects of rust before him; but here regulations stood firm, iron it must be except for locks, and he had to pay for brass door-hinges himself. On the Admiralty side, the voyage was regarded as an excellent opportunity for experiment, particularly in antiscorbutics, and correspondents from outside were positively encouraged to send in their recipes. The Baron Storsch, of Berlin, was particularly enthusiastic about a marmalade of yellow carrots he had invented, and a quantity was made; Dr Priestley, the eminent chemist, had a device for sweetening water by applying 'fixed air' or carbon dioxode to it, and the papers were passed on to Cook. Mr Irving's apparatus for rendering salt water fresh, and Lieutenant Orsbridge's machines for rendering stinking water sweet, were fitted; Mr Irving's improved fire-hearth was tried and rejected by Cook as unimproved before the ship was out of dock. Mr Pelham, secretary to the Victualling Board, had a recipe for experimental beer, based on a wort of boiled-down malt: that, too, was to be tried. There was the usual supply of trade goods. Cook, as usual, had his 'mathematical instruments' repaired or renewed.[1]

In the midst of all this there were social obligations. We may wish we knew more about them. One sort is witnessed by a stray letter, proof of amiability, that has somehow survived from Cook to Mr Joseph Cockfield, not a man, evidently, interested in voyages to remote parts. 'Sir,' it runs,

M[r] Colier at Deptford Victualling Office acquented me some time ago with your desire of seeing some of M[r] Banks's rare Plants &c[a]—If you will please to let me know on what morn[g] you can go to M[r] Banks's and I will engage that gentleman or D[r] Solander to be at home and will at the same time attend you my self I can meet you any where between Mile end and Newburlington Street. . . . P.S. Next Monday or Tuesday I believe will suit M[r] Banks.

This letter gives a more detailed address for Cook than he usually supplies—'Next Door to Curtis's Wine Vaults Mile end 10th Dec[r] 1771'.[2] A letter which casts more significant light on his movements is one of 14 December to the Admiralty Secretary. This was his application for three weeks' leave of absence, 'Having some business to transact down in Yorkshire as well as to see an Aged Father'.[3] What the business can have been it is impossible to guess, unless it were connected with his father's small affairs. Cook's mother had

---

[1] For all this I refer the reader to the Calendar of Documents in *Journals* II, 899 ff.
[2] Mitchell Library MS, Safe (1/80), Autograph Papers of Captain James Cook, 11.
[3] Cook to Stephens, 14 December 1771, Adm 1/1609, from the Admiralty Office. It is formally answered on 17 December, Adm 2/731.

died in 1765,[1] and it may have been now that his father, aged 77, left the cottage he had built at Ayton in 1755 to live with his daughter Margaret Fleck, the fisherman's wife, on the coast not far away at Redcar. Elizabeth, the Londoner, went the journey with her husband, probably to make the acquaintance for the first time of her relatives by marriage. Cook himself made at least one new acquaintance, who became a firm friend. This was Commodore William Wilson, late of the East India Company's service, the discoverer in 1758 of the Pitt Passage between the Moluccas and New Guinea to China, who had retired to live at Great Ayton. His wife was the sister of George Jackson, the Admiralty secretary. It was a long time since Cook had been the apprentice seaman at Whitby, but the progress of the commander in the royal navy had been well enough noted there, and his circumnavigation, and the eminence of Whitby-built ships; and when on the last day of the year he rode over from Ayton to see Walker and his other friends the gentlemen of Whitby rode out to meet him at Swarthowe Cross, on the edge of the moor.[2] In Walker's house old Mary Prowd, the housekeeper who had given a candle to light his earliest mathematical studies, forgot all instruction on the respect due to personages and officers, threw her arms round him and cried, 'Oh honey James! How glad I is to see thee!'[3] One hopes he was wearing his uniform. From Ayton after this warming visit, he wrote to Captain Hammond at Hull.

I am sorry to acquaint you that it is now out of my power to meet you at Whitby nor will it be convenient to return by way of Hull as I had resolved upon but three days ago Mrs Cook being but a bad traveler I was prevailed upon to lay that rout aside on account of the reported badness of the roads and therefore took horse on Tuesday Morn^g and road over to Whitby and returned yesterday. Your friends at that place expect to see you every day. I have only my self to blame for not having the pleasure of meeting you there. I am inform'd by letter from Lieut^t Cooper that the Admiralty have altered the names of the Ships from Drake to Resolution and Raleigh to Adventurer which, in my opinion are much properer than the former. I set out for London to morrow morning, shall only stop a day or two at York.[4]

Within a few days more he was back supervising his ship, and could learn the reason for the change of names.

[1] The precise date was 18 February 1765.
[2] The story is given by Young, but the detail about the meeting at the Cross, authentic or not, appears in H. P. Kendall, *Captain James Cook* (Whitby Literary and Philosophical Society, 1951), 10.
[3] Young, 121.
[4] Cook to Hammond, 3 January 1772; endorsed 'from my friend Capt Cook the great Navigator'; Whitby Museum.

It was a matter of the international amenities, and a little caution. Lord Rochford, one of the secretaries of state, considered that the names *Drake* and *Raleigh* would give great offence to the Spaniards, irritated enough already by the idea of British ships in the Pacific, with whom the quarrel over British settlement on the Falkland Islands had been patched up for less than a year; for they were names detested in Spain. Rochford had consulted the king, and at his wish wrote privately a 'hint' to Sandwich. 'What do you think of the Aurora and the Hisperus which two names are just come into my head?'[1] Sandwich evidently did not think much of them, though he was not wedded to those originally given. He wrote back on Christmas Day, 'My Dear Lord/The names pitched upon for the two Discovery ships are the Resolution & Adventure';[2] and so, whoever chose them, those two famous names came into the history of the ocean. New commissions and warrants were issued to the officers.

The *Resolution*—how inevitable it now sounds!—was being fitted out at Deptford, the *Adventure* at Woolwich, and on 6 February the former came out of dry dock. Cook, brooding still over his 'present intended voyage', and how he intended it—and perhaps thinking that, in spite of delays now only too apparent, he might within a few weeks be at sea; thinking anyhow of the drawing up of his instructions, on that day addressed himself to Sandwich. 'My Lord/I beg leave to lay before your Lordship a Map of the Southern Hemisphere Shewing the Discoveries that have been made up to 1770, to which is subjoined my opinion respecting the rout to be pursued by the Resolution and Adventure All which are humbly submitted to Your Lordships Consideration. . . .'[3] His opinion had, as it were, taken a step further south from the Postscript he had written six months before, and another step further east. His intention expanded by a sort of geographical logic. For, in the first place, even if the continent stretched north at about longitude 140° west, its greater extent might be in a really high latitude; and in the second place, to come home from the Horn would leave a regrettable hiatus, with the southern Atlantic unexplored, where a continental mass might equally lie. The problem was not simply a Pacific problem. He had, we may be certain, since his return to England been enquiring more deeply into the history of exploration. No doubt he had read

[1] Rochford to Sandwich, 20 December 1771; Sandwich Papers, Hinchingbrooke.
[2] Sandwich to Rochford, from the Admiralty, 25 December 1771; P.R.O., S.P. 42/48, No. 51.
[3] Cook to Sandwich, 6 February 1772, Mitchell Library MS, Safe 1/82. The map is reproduced in *Charts and Views*, Chart XXV.

Carteret's journal, and he must have studied exhaustively Dalrymple's *Historical Collection*, which became a continual point of reference for him; but those were Pacific documents. He had also in mind the French Lozier Bouvet, a man he admired, who, looking for some coast which might provide a way-station for French voyages to the East Indies, had found it south-east of the Cape of Good Hope in a Cape Circumcision—icy, forbidding, hardly sighted before it was lost in cloud and fog; nevertheless, Bouvet felt, a cape indeed, the projection of a shore along which he had subsequently run for some distance. This was in 1739. He could never get a second voyage. Then Dalrymple had turned his attention to the Atlantic, publishing in 1769 a South Atlantic chart, which showed, fifteen degrees east of the Horn, land and a huge opening to stretch far below the sixtieth parallel, the 'Gulf of St Sebastian'. The accompanying memoir displayed his method. He had taken his continent, with astounding faith, from the 1587 world map of Abraham Ortelius, incorporating it with such more reliable features as the tracks of Bouvet, and of Halley's *Paramour* Pink in 1700. Cook, composing his map for Sandwich, marked on it Cape Circumcision, and also, less trustingly, 'Gulf of St Sebastian Very Doub[t]full'. They signified work to be done. So, in the memorandum he composed to go with it, the arguments of his Postscript are not merely repeated but enlarged: the possible break north before passing the Horn becomes compulsory, another base for recruitment is added in Tahiti, and the port at which discovery finishes is to be the Cape. He writes:

Upon due consideration of the discoveries that have been made in the Southern Ocean, and the tracks of the Ships which have made these discoveries; it appears that no Southern lands of great extent can extend to the Northward of 40° of Latitude, except about the Meridian of 140° West, every other part of the Southern Ocean have at different times been explored to the northward of the above parallel. Therefore to make new discoveries the Navigator must Traverse or Circumnavigate the Globe in a higher parallel than has hitherto been done, and this will be best accomplished by an Easterly Course on account of the prevailing westerly winds in all high Latitudes. The principle thing to be attended to is the proper Seasons of Year, for Winter is by no means favourable for discoveries in these Latitudes; for which reason it is humbly proposed that the Ships may not leave the Cape of Good Hope before the latter end of September or beginning of October, when having the whole summer before them may safely Steer to the Southward and make their way to New Zealand, between the parallels of 45° and 60° or in as high a Latitude as the weather and other circumstances will admit. If no land is discoveried in this rout the Ships will be obliged to touch at New Zealand to recrute their water.

From New Zealand the same rout must be continued to Cape Horn, but before this can be accomplished they will be overtaken by Winter, and must seek Shelter in the more Hospitable Latitudes, for which purpose Otahieta will probably be found to be the most convenient, at, and in its Neighbourhood the Winter Months may be spent, after which they must steer to the Southward and continue their rout for Cape Horn in the Neighbourhood of which they may again recrute their water, and afterwards proceed for the Cape of Good Hope.

On the map the tracks laid down were those of Tasman, Wallis, Bougainville and the *Endeavour*, with the routes of the East Indiamen on their regular voyages; added to them was a broad yellow ribbon round the Pole, weaving in and out of the sixtieth parallel.

The yellow line on the Map shews the track I would propose the Ships to make, Supposeing no land to intervene, for if land is discovered the track will be altered according to the directing of the land, but the general rout must be pursued otherwise some part of the Southern Ocean will remain unexplored.[1]

Sandwich was too intelligent a man to need all this, but he may have asked for it, and it may have been useful with colleagues.

This grand strategy, this main theme, was to be adopted. Set in it there was to be another, which had not hitherto interested Cook —the proving of the chronometer, as a mode of determining longitude. His devotion to the lunar method, by the end of his first voyage, is clear. He did not see why the generality of sea officers should not master this. He paid them too high a compliment; a more direct method was still needed. It was presented by the fourth chronometer John Harrison made, the model that was tested first on a voyage to Jamaica, and then, by Maskelyne himself, on the Barbados voyage of 1764, when it gave so remarkable a result. In spite of its accuracy, the Board of Longitude, not noted for rashness, settled down to make difficulties over paying the reward; but Harrison, who had difficulty explaining clearly in words what he could put together so beautifully in practice, did, in 1765, get half, £10,000, on condition of handing over all four of his models.[2] Of the fourth, a very large flat watch in appearance, an exact duplicate was made by Larcum Kendall, an excellent craftsman of Furnival's Inn Court, London; and it was with this, and with other chronometers made by John Arnold of the Adelphi, on principles of his own,

[1] Cook to Sandwich, 6 February 1772, Mitchell Library MS, Safe 1/82. The map is reproduced in *Charts and Views*, Chart XXV.
[2] He got the rest in 1773, after the king had taken a personal interest in the matter.

that the Board was now concerned. The man chiefly concerned, as organiser, was the Astronomer Royal. Maskelyne, as we have seen, dominated both the Board of Longitude and, on astronomical matters, the Council of the Royal Society, which came into the plans for this voyage only by giving its advice when asked; there is no doubt that if machinery was to be vindicated against his own lunar method, its performance was to be most stringently tested. Kendall's duplicate would go the voyage; so would three of Arnold's machines—one that had been under trial at the Royal Observatory for a year, two that had been rather hurriedly ordered and most inadequately tried.[1] Stringent testing would mean constant astronomical observation and calculation. There were other matters, physical and hydrographical, on which the Board wanted regular observation; by the time Maskelyne had finished with the instructions it was obvious that the observers would have their hands full. Maskelyne put his basic proposals to Sandwich as early as October 1771; the Board deliberated and decided from November 1771 to May 1772, borrowed instruments from the Royal Society, made over its own, including a great many specially bought, took into account the Royal Society's (that is, Maskelyne's) thoughts on instructions. Its chosen observers, on the proposal of Maskelyne 'and the other professors' (those of astronomy at the universities) were Mr William Wales and Mr William Bayly, at £400 per annmu each.[2] Mr Bayly contrived a portable observatory that was later highly spoken of by Wales, and they were supplied with one each. The Admiralty was asked to direct the commanders of the sloops to give the gentlemen assistance and support whenever they might stand in need of it.

There must have been more social life for Cook in London than we know of, as well as some disagreeables. He seems to have been on good terms with the gentlemen of the Royal Society. He met at Hinchinbrook the gregarious and friendly Dr Charles Burney, the musician, who knew practically everybody, and Burney took the chance to put in a word for his twenty-one-year-old son James, who had been in the navy since the age of ten.[3] The Doctor was successful, and the Burney family was raised to a high pitch of excitement at the prospect of their James sailing with the great navigator. Cook

[1] For a detailed, expert, and fascinating history of these instruments see Derek Howse and Beresford Hutchinson, *The Clocks and Watches of Captain James Cook 1769–1969* (reprinted from *Antiquarian Horology*, London 1969).
[2] The relevant Board of Longitude minutes are printed in *Journals* II, 719 ff., Appendix III.
[3] Frances Burney, *Early Diary*, I, 138–9.

apparently became a visitor, and there was one dinner at least at Queen Square in February 1773 when Burney drew him out over a copy of Bougainville's *Voyage autour du Monde* which was lying on a table. Burney wanted to know how Cook's track round the world compared with the other; and 'Captain Cooke instantly took a pencil from his pocket-book, and said he would trace the route; which he did in so clear and scientific a manner, that I would not take fifty pounds for the book. The pencil marks having been fixed by skin milk, will always be visible.'[1] Presumably it was the Cook of this period, perhaps even of this visit, that Fanny (or rather, Madame d'Arblay) went on to describe in the Burney *Memoirs*: 'This truly great man appeared to be full of sense and thought; well-mannered, and perfectly unpretending; but studiously wrapped up in his own purposes and pursuits; and apparently under a pressure of mental fatigue when called upon to speak, or stimulated to deliberate, upon any other.'[2] There may be no more here than that Cook was less volatile than nineteen-year-old Fanny, not so ready on the newest novel or opera. Burney had already played a small but not negligible part in the story; for much earlier, in September 1771, he had met Sandwich at Lord Orford's Houghton, when the First Lord was casting round for someone to 'write the voyage'—that is, to take Cook's journal and put it into a form suitable for the reading of the polite world; and not only Cook's journal, but those of the three other circumnavigators, Byron, Wallis and Carteret. Cook and Banks, we remember, were patriotically anxious that this should be done as soon as possible, and it was all the more important to get something authentic on the market because of the temptation put by the booksellers in the way of anyone who could provide a connected narrative of a hundred pages or so. Burney recommended his friend Dr John Hawkesworth, who had time and could do with the money; even as he did so Messrs Becket and de Hondt, of the Strand, were rushing forward their anonymous *Journal of a Voyage*

---

[1] Frances Burney, *Memoirs of Doctor Burney* (1832), I, 270–1. Burney's story, often quoted, runs, 'Observing upon a table Bougainville's *Voyage autour du Monde*, he turned it over, and made some curious remarks on the illiberal conduct of that circum-navigator towards himself, when they met, and crossed each other; which made me desirous to know, in examining the chart of M. de Bougainville, the several tracks of the two navigators; and exactly where they had crossed or approached each other.' But Cook and Bougainville never met: Burney must have been thinking of the occasion when Bougainville, in the *Boudeuse*, caught up Carteret, in the *Swallow* in the Atlantic, 20 February 1769. The two captains did not meet then, either; Carteret thought Bougainville's conduct was 'neither liberal nor just', according to Hawkesworth, I, 668; which Burney would later read. See also Helen Wallis, *Carteret's Voyage Round the World* (Cambridge, 1965), I, 94–7, 266–73. Burney's copy of Bougainville, with Cook's pencilled track on Map 1, is now in the British Museum Library.

[2] *Memoirs*, I, 271.

round the World . . . containing All the various Occurrences of the Voyage,
which appeared before the end of this same September.[1] 'As to Mr
Becket, and his Catch-penny, the subject is so interesting that there
is no putting the book down,' wrote a naval correspondent of
Banks's, Captain Bentinck, 'at the same time that the inaccuracy
with which it is wrote makes it most tiresome and indeed the most
provoking reading I ever met with.'[2] Hawkesworth was an experienced journalist, who imitated Dr Johnson's style with some success;
when Sandwich accepted his nomination a considerable responsibility, therefore, rested on him to be accurate as well as interesting.
He was the envy of all his fellow-practitioners. Sandwich made over
all the captains' journals to him, and got Banks to lend his journal
too for the writer to use at will.[3] Hawkesworth was left to make his
own bargain with the booksellers, and made a very satisfactory one.
They were convinced that he would anyhow be interesting. Garrick,
who also claimed to have recommended Hawkesworth to Sandwich,
was annoyed that he did not arrange publication with his own bookseller and friend Becket, of the anonymous journal. But Becket,
explained Hawkesworth, would not give him more than £2000 for
the copyright, and, 'having had applications from half the Booksellers in London, none of whom offered me more than five thousand
pounds without allowing me a single Copy, Mr Strahan offered me
six thousand, & to furnish me with all the Copies that I had engaged
to give away, which, being five & twenty, amounted to seventy five
pounds. . . .'[4] Strahan, that is, swept everybody else aside; and
though he had some second thoughts, he had them too late. The
amount of £6075 compares very favourably with the wages of Cook,
or even the combined wages of the four commanders who made
the voyages; it was a great deal more than was paid for some of the
most famous and successful books of the century; Hawkesworth
would have to work hard to destroy interest. As to accuracy, the
different accounts were to be subject to the perusal and emendation
of all the commanders concerned. Because of Cook's expected early
departure, the voyage of the *Endeavour* was first prepared, two

[1] The author may have been J. M. Magra, the midshipman, but the charge cannot
be confidently made. See *Journals* I, cclvi–cclix.
[2] 10 October 1771; Dawson Turner Transcripts, I, 27. John Albert Bentinck (1737–75)
was captain of the guardship *Centaur*, 74, then at Spithead.
[3] Hawkesworth to Sandwich, 19 November 1771; Sandwich Papers, Hinchingbrooke;
Banks, I, 47 n.
[4] Hawkesworth to Garrick, n.d. 'Wed. Evening'. B.M. Add. MS 28104, ff. 45–6.
There is in the Osborn collection, Yale University Library, a copy of a letter from
Hawkesworth to 'My dear Madam', undated (? August, 1773) which gives a circumstantial account of the whole affair. I am indebted for a copy of this copy to Professor
John L. Abbott, of the University of Connecticut.

volumes out of Hawkesworth's three, in little more than four months. If Cook expected to read them, or hear them read, he was disappointed; indeed, he had now to deal with the disagreeable consequences of Mr Joseph Banks.

They were not all disagreeable. It was indeed a pleasant consequence that Banks should meet Dr Johnson and extract from him the famous distich for the collar of the famous goat, now browsing at Mile End in honourable retirement from naval service:

> Perpetui, ambitâ bis terrâ, praemia lactis
> Haec habet, altrici Capra secunda Jovis.

'The globe twice circled, this the Goat, the second to the nurse of Jove, is thus rewarded for her never-failing milk.'[1] It was a pleasantry that might have had to be explained to Cook. There were more serious things that Banks could do. As soon as the second voyage had been resolved upon, Sandwich had asked him if he would care to sail again. Certainly he would, and Dr Solander as well. He at once proceeded to make himself highly useful. He dealt, for example, with the order to Matthew Boulton for the striking of a medal to be distributed throughout the Pacific as a sign of British presence—the medal with the presentment of the two ships and the premature wording 'Sailed from England March MDCCLXXII'. He was prepared to be a general scientific manager and consultant, to spend his own money as liberally as he had done on the first voyage, to recommend, recruit, expatiate. He was, unfortunately, prepared to go further; and having read the newspapers so much, talked in society so much, seen and heard the name 'Mr Banks' and the phrase 'Mr Banks's voyage' so often, had come to conceive of himself as a sort of presiding genius of exploration. From the moment it was known that he was to go on a second voyage communications descended upon him as if he were another department of state—in English, French, Latin, from London and the counties, France, Holland, Germany, Switzerland, making suggestions on every conceivable matter, asking for anything from the command of a ship to the essential parts of a whale; asking, the great majority of them, to go too. For some of them ruin, even suicide, is the alternative;

[1] Johnson to Banks, 27 February 1772; D.T.C., I, 30, printed by Boswell and in Chapman's edition (1052) of Johnson's *Letters*. She had, alas, few days to live, and died on 28 March 1772, at Mile End.—*General Evening Post*, 3 April. Robert Chambers, *Book of Days*, for 28 April (I, 559–60), giving that as the anniversary, says the Admiralty had just before signed a warrant admitting her to the privileges of an inpensioner of Greenwich Hospital. One hopes that this information at least was true. The collar was of silver.

they 'pant' to go with Banks. It is not merely civilians, a little un-hinged, who seek his patronage; seamen in the royal navy (including some from the *Endeavour*) write to him rather than adopt a less dramatic mode of volunteering. They acknowledged his fame; they prophesied his immortality. Banks kept their letters.[1]

He knew it was to be a southern voyage. 'O how Glorious would it be to set my heel upon the Pole! and turn myself round 360 degrees in a second', he wrote to his French friend the Comte de Lauraguais. From what we can gather from his papers that was the extent of his geographical interest, though no doubt he would have been pleased to come upon the continent. But he was getting ready for most other things in the scientific line, and collecting what might be called a staff. He collected fifteen people in all, starting with the scientific Dr James Lind from Edinburgh and the painter Zoffany, and going on to lesser draughtsmen, secretaries, servants—even two horn-players; which, with Solander and himself, made a super-numerary party of seventeen to be accommodated. The great catch was Lind. Banks had first made an offer to the more celebrated Joseph Priestley, and then withdrawn it, on the ground that the professorial establishment of the Universities would veto a Unitarian minister.[2] Solander was set to write to Lind, a pleasant young Scots physician and amateur astronomer, with general scientific interests, something of an inventer. He did so in high excitement. 'Will You my Dear Doctor give us leave to propose You, to the Board of Longitude, as willing to go out as an Astronomer. Your well known character makes us all beg, pray & long for your affirmative answer. . . . Good God, we shall do wonders if you only will come and assist us.'[3] The matter did not move quite as fast as Banks wanted, and it was February before the Council of the Royal Society recommended Lind to the Board of Longitude as a person who would be extremely useful, 'on account of his skill and experience in his profession, and from his great Knowledge in Mineralogy, Chemistry, Mechanics, and various branches of Natural Philosophy; and also from his having spent several years in different climates, in the Indies.'[4] The Board, having appointed its own men, paid no attention to this. Then Parliament was prevailed on to make a special grant of £4000 for the benefit of Dr Lind, 'but what the discoveries were, the

[1] They are all bound up in the volume of Banks papers in the Mitchell Library, Safe 1/11, lettered 'Voluntiers, Instructions, Provision for 2d. Voyage.'
[2] Priestley wrote a rather cutting reply to Banks, 1 December 1771, 'Voluntiers', 597–8, and Banks, I, 72, n. 1.
[3] Solander to Lind, n.d.; Dixson Library, MS Q 161. The whole letter is printed in *Journals* II, 901–3.
[4] Royal Society Council Minutes, VI, 131, 8 February 1772; *Journals* II, 913.

Parliament meant he was to make, and for which they made so liberal a Vote, I know not',[1] said Cook, who had not read the minutes of the Council, and was less certain of the mineralogy of the South Pole. Banks kept on talking and heaping up baggage. We are brought back to the *Resolution,* in which almost all these persons were to sail.

The ship, we remember, was selected by Cook: 'she was the ship of my choice and as I thought the fitest for the Service she was going upon of any I had ever seen.'[2] That service was geographical discovery. She was not chosen as a passenger ship or a floating laboratory or an artist's studio, but precisely because she was what she was —a soundly-built collier, with adequate room for her crew and her stores. When Banks first saw her, he did not like her. Though she was larger than the *Endeavour,* he feared she was not large enough for him and his entourage, and he must already have begun to picture an entourage larger than his earlier one. 'Mr Banks's voyage', he could not forget, was a social and international sensation: he pictured a second Mr Banks's voyage which would be more sensational still, as well as even more scientifically valuable. Nor, it is to be feared, could he cease to take for granted his position as an English landed gentleman of very considerable estate; nor forget that the First Lord was his friend. While he remained scientifically disinterested, he had, a little prematurely, 'given pledges to all Europe', and he meant to astound all Europe. As the voyage was to be 'his' voyage, so—though it is improbable that he began by making too large claims—he was to be its real commander, Cook his executive officer, the ship's master rather than its captain. Mr Banks, we must conclude, had come by an unusually swelled head.

He was even prepared to dogmatise on nautical concerns; and he must have the vessel altered. Some adaptation was called for, as a matter of course. On some things it was indispensable to consult Banks. He thought he should be consulted on everything. From the start there was one firm obstacle in his way—Palliser. The Comptroller of the Navy was a good judge of ships, and he agreed entirely with Cook about the type of ship needed on this occasion; and beyond necessary details he did not want the ship altered at all. Banks removed that obstacle by going to Sandwich. The Navy Board—Palliser was not alone in his objection—was overruled. Cook's sentiments at the large reconstruction that followed can be established with a good deal of certainty. He disapproved, he was anxious to oblige Banks, he hoped for the best; he forced himself,

[1] *Journals* II, 4.   [2] B.M. Add. MS 27888, f. 5; *Journals* II, xxvii.

against all reasonable expectation and in spite of all naval experience, to think it might do. In the end the vessel got a heightened waist and an additional upper deck, necessarily solidly built, and a raised poop or 'round-house' on top to accommodate the captain, who had relinquished his own quarters—including the 'great cabin' —to Banks. There could hardly be a greater sacrifice to friendship. Banks accepted it without hesitation, and complained about the cabin's size. The extra space otherwise provided, or its equivalent, was to be occupied by Banks's followers, and the staggering amount of impedimenta, useful or useless, which for months he was accumulating. This programme made the *Resolution* the sight of the river: she was visited not merely by those whose business it was, but, as Cook remarked, by 'many of all ranks . . . Ladies as well as gentlemen, for scarce a day past on which she was not crowded with Strangers who came on board for no other purpose but to see the Ship in which Mr Banks was to sail round the world.'[1] Whenever there was a hitch in the work, by which some little set-back to Banks seemed possible, he brought out his sovereign argument—he threatened not to go.

There would certainly be no March departure. By the end of April Cook was feeling alarm; at Long Reach the ship's draught, with guns and ordnance stores on board, was seventeen feet, but overbuilt as she was, she still looked as if she would prove crank; nevertheless he restrained himself till she had a full trial, and even had twenty tons of ballast taken out. Sandwich had been down to look at the work several times, 'a laudable tho rare thing in a first Lord of the Admiralty',[2] and on 2 May he, the French ambassador, and other 'persons of distinction' were entertained on board by Banks. Twelve days later came the crisis. Ordered to the Downs, the ship moved on the 10th. At the Nore, on the 14th, the pilot gave up. She was so top-heavy that she could hardly carry sail without capsizing. Cooper, the first lieutenant, in charge of her, gave Cook his opinion that she was 'an exceeding dangerous and unsafe ship'; and the more ebullient Clerke gave his to Banks: 'By God I'll go to Sea in a Grog Tub, if desir'd, or in the Resolution as soon as you please; but must say I think her by far the most unsafe Ship I ever saw or heard of.'[3] Cook's error of judgment in hoping that all might be well stared at him, and he immediately told the Admiralty secretary that the upper works would have to be cut down again. A day of rapid com-

---

[1] B.M. Add. MS 27888, f. 4-4v.   [2] *Journals* II, 6.
[3] Cooper to Cook, 13 May 1772, encl. in Admiralty Secretary to Navy Board, 14 May, ADM/A/2655. Clerke to Banks, 15 May, Mitchell Library, Banks Papers, 2, f. 1. Both letters are printed in *Journals* II, 929-31.

munications between Admiralty and Navy Board settled the matter: the *Resolution* was to go back to Sheerness, the round-house and new upper deck to be removed, the guns reduced in weight; within a week it was resolved to shorten the masts as well. The passengers would have to fit the ship, not the ship the passengers. The effect on Banks, when he saw what was in train, was staggering. To quote the memoirs of the then young midshipman John Elliott, 'Mr Banks came to Sheerness and when he saw the ship, and the Alterations that were made, He swore and stamp'd upon the Warfe, like a Mad Man; and instantly order'd his servants, and all his things out of the Ship.'[1] Or if that summarises too much, the result was no other. This time the Admiralty took Banks at his word.

Rumours and counter-rumours flew, about the ship's behaviour in the merchant service. While the remedial work was going forward, Cook wrote from Sheerness to Hammond, whom he thought was in London, on 28 May, in terms of urgent intimacy: 'Dear Sir

As you cannot be Ignorant [*sic*] of what is said in Town for and against the Resolution, I beg you will sit down and give me a full detail thereof, and if you suspect her to be, or ever thought her a tender ship let me find so much friendship from you as to trust me with the secret, as I can now Load and trim her accordingly; for my own part I am in no doubt of her Answering now she is striped of her Superfluous top hamper—Believe me to be Dr Sir Your most Affectionate friend & Humble Servt. . . .[2]

He could have got only a reassuring reply. Banks himself was busy in composition before he quite gave up hope. He wrote a long letter of passionate self-justification to Sandwich.[3] It was unwise to present the First Lord with a lecture on naval construction, or to complain that the Navy Board had purchased the ship 'without ever consulting me'; and the side-blow at Cook, that there were many commanders of ability and experience, ambitious of showing the world that success depended more on a captain's prudence and perseverance than on any particular build of ship, was the least generous and most foolish thing that Banks ever said. The Navy Board and Palliser made their own remarks on this outburst; Sandwich entertained

---

[1] 'Memoirs of the early life, of John Elliott . . .', B. M. Add. MS 42714, ff. 10-11. Cf. *Journals* II, xxx, n. 1. We have to allow for the fact that Elliott wrote later in life, and as a youth had not taken to Banks.

[2] Cook to Hammond, 28 May 1772, Dixson Library, MS Q 140. Hammond must have been in London, as Cook first addressed him at Batsons Coffee House / Roy^l Exchange / London, and then substituted Hull.

[3] 30 May 1772, Sandwich Papers, Hinchingbrooke, endorsed 'No. 93'. I have printed it, with a note on other copies and printings, in *Journals* II, 704-7; and, from Banks' draft, in Banks, II, 335-8. In the latter volume I have printed also the draft of another letter to Sandwich, not sent, probably a trial run for that of 30 May.

himself by composing in his turn a detailed and crushing rejoinder, for use in case Banks rushed into print.[1] The man retained enough sanity not to do so, though the press was active enough on his behalf, there were questions in the Commons, and some confidential political consultation. Lord Sandwich, for the time being, had had enough of his young friend. There was to be no Banks on the second voyage, no Solander, no Zoffany, there were to be no horn-players in scarlet and silver, performing to the brown girls, flower-garlanded, on far shores. Cook may sum the unhappy matter up.

To many it will no doubt appear strange that Mr Banks should attempt to over rule the opinions of the two great Boards who have the sole management of the whole Navy of Great Britain and likewise the opinions of the principal sea officers concern'd in the expedition; for a Gentleman of Mr Banks's Fortune and Abilities to engage in these kind of Voyages is as uncommon as it is meritorious and the great additions he made last Voyage to the Systems of Botany and Natural History gain'd him great reputation which was increased by his imbarking in this. This, together with a desire in every one to make things as convenient to him as possible, made him to be consulted on every occasion and his influence was so great that his opinion was generally followed, was it ever so inconsistent, in preference to those who from their long experience in Sea affairs might be supposed better judges, till at length the Sloop was rendered unfit for any service whatever. . . .

Mr Banks unfortunate for himself set out upon too large a Plan a Plan that was incompatible with a Scheme of discovery at the Antipodes; had he confined himself to the same plan as he set out upon last Voyage, attended only to his own persutes and not interfered with the choice, equipmint and even Direction of the Ships things that he was not a competent judge of, he would have found every one concerned in the expedition ever ready to oblige him, for my self I can declare it: instead of finding fault with the Ship he ought to have considered that the Endeavour Bark was just such another, whose good quallities . . . gave him an oppertunity to acquire that reputation the Publick has so liberally and with great justice bestowed upon him.[2]

There had been no need, and no attempt, to alter the *Adventure*, and about her no controversy ever centred. She shared the virtues of her build; she was to serve her purpose admirably. She was not

---

[1] The Navy Board memorandum, 'Observations upon Mr Banks's Letter to the Earl of Sandwich', and Sandwich's letter are both in the Sandwich Papers, Hinchingbrooke, endorsed 'No. 93'; similarly Palliser's 'Thoughts upon the Kind of Ships proper to be employed on Discoveries in distant parts of the Globe', endorsed 'No. 98', and Sandwich's draft of his rejoinder to Banks, endorsed 'No. 94', I have printed all three in *Journals* II, 707 ff., where I have noticed other printings, and, with some other relevant papers, in Banks, II, 342 ff.
[2] B.M. Add. MS 27888, ff. 5–5v; *Journals* II, 718.

18. The *Resolution*
Water-colour drawing by Henry Roberts

letters[1]—the journal in particular gives us a personality enlarged and matured as well as lively; he is capable of systematic observation and recording, serious generalisation as well as lightness of touch; it is Clerke with whom we feel tedium and irritation as well as amusement, it is Clerke whom we should like to hear talking at the end of the voyage. Banks evidently tried to tempt him away from his ship: 'Am exceedingly oblig'd to you, my good Sir, for your kind concern on my account: but have stood too far on this tack to think of putting about with any kind of credit,'[2] he wrote. He is a first-class seaman, an excellent officer. Pickersgill is third lieutenant: 'a good officer and astronomer, but liking ye Grog',[3] said one of his juniors. There is something desperately serious about Pickersgill, as about so many of his fellow-romantics, something, in the end, of pathos. There are good intentions, never realised, the something beyond his grasp, whether because of lack of training or lack of mental stamina one does not know. When he amuses us, it is not of set purpose. A less striking figure than Clerke, he is a more complex one, less on good terms with the world; where Clerke writes down a jest, Pickersgill explains a grievance. Yet he is fit for responsible work, makes some notably good charts, and Cook finds him very useful. He seems to have got on well with the island peoples. Joseph Gilbert, the master, is the last of the senior officers, apart from the excellent Edgcumbe of the marines. Gilbert is old as ages go in that ship, about 40; one of the growing list of men from Lincolnshire who have to do with the Pacific, and one whose career, like Cook's, has been marked by his part in the Newfoundland–Labrador survey, when he was master of the *Guernsey*. He is a sound officer, in principal charge, underneath Cook, of the surveying work of the voyage. Cook says the right things about him, in due form, but even more indicative is the reason given for certain action, that 'Mr Gilbert the Master, on whose judgement I had a good opinion', was of a particular opinion himself. Gilbert was a good draughtsman, too: when it came to a 'view', a much better one than Cook, who had no large pretensions in that line.

We know more about the midshipmen, that rather vague class, than usual, largely through the reminiscences of John Elliott, himself one of the 'young gentlemen'; and we know how Cook trained them. They were not all a band of brothers. Some of them no doubt got their positions on their known merit, like the three who had been

---

[1] The letters are all to Banks, and are in the Banks Papers, 2, Mitchell Library. They are printed in *Journals* II, Calendar of Documents.
[2] Clerke to Banks, 31 May 1772; Banks Papers, 2, f. 2; *Journals* II, 936–7.
[3] Elliott, *Memoirs*.

out in the *Endeavour*, Manley, Harvey and Isaac Smith; some, like Elliott, through 'interest'; some perhaps through accident. It was thought, says Elliott, 'it would be quite a great feather, in a young man's Cap, to go with Captn Cook, and it requir'd much Intrest to get out with him; My Uncle therefore determin'd to send me out with him in the Resolution'—and took the boy to Palliser, who passed him on to Cooper, who introduced him to Cook, 'who promis'd to take care of me', and did. Elliott wrote brief characterisations of all the officers and civilians in his ship. Of most of them he thought highly. They were in general 'steady', some of them steady and clever as well. Henry Roberts indeed was a 'very clever young man', a skilful draughtsman and cartographer. Burney, 'Clever & Excentric', was outside the usual run—though what his eccentricity led him to in the *Resolution* we never learn. Then there was the small 'wild & drinking' set; in which was poor Charles Loggie, with the trepanned head, drinking 'from misfortune', who was a great trial to the captain. There were two whom our memoirist disliked—the 'Hypocritical canting fellow' Maxwell, who got Loggie into trouble; and the 'Jesuitical' Whitehouse, 'sensible but an insinuating litigious mischief making fellow'; with whom we may contrast one who was to rise to fame himself as an explorer, 'Mr Vancouver', aged 'about 13½' (in fact nearer 15), 'a Quiet inoffensive young man'. Inoffensive or offensive, steady or unsteady, they all had to knock down together, and Cook made the best of them he could. To quote Elliott again (and to anticipate), 'In the Early part of the Voyage, Captn Cook made all us young gentlemen, do the duty aloft the same as the Sailors, learning to hand, and reef the sails, and Steer the Ship, E[x]ercise Small Arms &c thereby making us good Sailors, as well as good Officers'; later on they were put to observing, surveying, and drawing. The training the young gentlemen got was to be highly regarded in important circles; it is difficult, indeed, to imagine a better education for a young seaman than three years in the *Resolution*. Lastly, not among the young gentlemen, but not very old, we must notice the surgeon and his mates, all three 'steady clever' men. James Patten, there can be no doubt, was good professionally: so far as any surgeon could, he was to save Cook's life. William Anderson, his first mate, was an extremely intelligent person, with a mind agreeably wide-ranging, interested in all the peculiarities of mankind, all the branches of natural history: his journals are the great loss from the records of this voyage. Benjamin Drawwater, the junior mate, apart from his steadiness and cleverness, remains but a name.

Those in the *Adventure*, with not many exceptions, are more shadowy. Tobias Furneaux, the commander, is plain enough.[1] One of a Devon-Cornish connection, which included Samuel Wallis, he had become a midshipman rather late, at the age of twenty, in 1755; on the Jamaica station had been promoted master's mate; for his gallantry in a sloop action further promoted lieutenant. He served on the coast of Africa and again in the West Indies; after the war was on half-pay for three years; appointed to the *Dolphin* as second lieutenant under Wallis, he was virtually in command during the long periods when Wallis and his first lieutenant were both sick men, while his conduct in charge of landing parties was considerate and wise. Experience and character alike, then, seemed to mark him out as an excellent second in command to Cook. But the face in his portrait, with its rather large nose, full eyes and lips, conveys vigour rather than a sense of thought; Furneaux, however humane, was indeed an executive rather than a ruminative officer. He was certainly a good seaman. As long as he was close to Cook, watched over by Cook, one finds no criticism to make. Separate them: and one feels immediately that he was not really an explorer. There was an incuriosity about him, a lack of imagination, a limitation to the mind, that would always prevent anything he touched from turning to the gold of discovery. His first lieutenant, Joseph Shank, departs early, smitten by gout, at the Cape. Arthur Kempe, there promoted from second to first, seems to have been the parallel of Cooper, educated, competent, without frills; he had some Pacific experience, having been a midshipman with Byron. He followed Cooper later up the ladder of promotion but out-topped him, because longevity (it is to be presumed) was to make him an admiral. Burney, transplanted at the Cape from the *Resolution*, as second lieutenant, is our personality on board the *Adventure*, and a man we know a good deal about. We have seen his father speaking for him at Hinchingbrooke; when he sails he is of age, on paper still only an A.B., but one who has passed his lieutenant's examination; owing to a hint from Sandwich to Cook, he now sees promotion reasonably near. It comes, and it is clear by the end of his voyage that he has made the most of it. Burney, though he sailed very little with Cook himself, is one of the most interesting of Cook's officers; a thorough seaman, certainly one of the mainstays of the *Adventure*'s company; lively, observant, and (like all the Burneys) articulate. He was to become the great

[1] His biography has been written: *Tobias Furneaux*, by Rupert Furneaux, London, 1960. His portrait was painted by Northcote. He did not have a long life; after his voyage with Cook he had a period on the North American station as a frigate captain, then three years on half-pay, and died in 1781.

scholar of Pacific exploration; some of his other activities might have been regarded by Mr Elliott as further proof of eccentricity. Peter Fannin, the master, was a good professional man, a talented chart-maker hardly visible as a person otherwise. In the journals, from time to time, are glimpsed his fellows, their horse-play or melancholy or quarrelling; evidently in the case of James Scott, lieutenant of marines, a quite real derangement of the mind, which made him a difficult shipmate.

We must consider the astronomers. William Wales, assigned to the *Resolution*, was a Yorkshireman in his late thirties, the brother-in-law of Green. He had observed the Transit of Venus for the Royal Society at Hudson Bay and helped Maskelyne with the *Nautical Almanac*. William Bayly, a few years younger, a Wiltshire farm-boy who had shown a talent for arithmetic and been an usher in schools, had gone to the North Cape for the Transit and been an assistant at the Royal Observatory. Both had published papers on their observations. Both were later to have a part in mathematical and naval education. Wales was the man who did the more varied work, had the more civilised, wide, and at the same time incisive, mind. It may have been a sort of luck that after the voyage he taught the Mathematical School at Christ's Hospital, so that, having Charles Lamb and Coleridge and Leigh Hunt among his pupils, he became enshrined in English literature, and we can remember, like Lamb, his Yorkshire accent, his 'constant glee', his severities that were without sting. To read his journal is to be impressed by a man devoted to a quite austere and fine sense of duty; to read his letters is to find him severe enough towards inadequate intellectual standards. He noted, with resignation, the rule of thumb conservatism of the sailors, the meddling of midshipmen with his belongings; registered his amusement at the behaviour of pretentious persons. His close scientific eye fronted a head that also carried poetry—he knew his Thomson and Shakespeare and Milton—and he was humane. With all this richness Bayly hardly compares, he was of a lesser order altogether; yet he knew his job, kept a hold on it, was at the same time aware of what was passing round him. We must consider also that rather late appointment, William Hodges the young artist, sent on board the *Resolution* by the Admiralty influenced by Lord Palmerston, while the ships lay at Plymouth at the end of June. He was a quite different thing in painters from Zoffany—or Sydney Parkinson: a pupil of Richard Wilson, his interest was landscape, and, more and more as he developed his own individuality in foreign climates, light. On the voyage he was to work hard, and we are happily in his debt: we should be still happier had he had any talent for the figure. His landscapes, his seascapes, his wave-worn ice, his rapid wash drawings or oil sketches, his careful panoramic renderings of island cliffs and shores, on the other hand, are exactly what was desired; to Cook, an unsophisticated critic of art, they were masterly. Cook and Wales both liked him: likeable, gifted, making the most of his chances, he seems a rather enviable person.

But who is going to envy John Reinhold Forster? We have come to one of the awkward beings of the age,[1] who walked on board the *Resolution* because Banks and his friends walked off. Let us admit at once the virtues of Forster, his learning, the width of his interests, his acuteness in some things; let us admit the lumbering geniality that was said to exist deep below the surface. Let us admit that the surface itself must have been, at first sight, sometimes impressive— or how else could he have taken in, temporarily, so many excellent persons? Let us concede, as a mitigating factor, that for ocean voyaging no man was ever by physical or mental constitution less fitted. Yet there is nothing that can make him other than one of the Admiralty's vast mistakes. One does not wish to draw a caricature; but how is one to deny that he was dogmatic, humourless, suspicious, censorious, pretentious, contentious, demanding? To deal with such a man is a problem anywhere, a desperate problem at sea. Cook is forced to conclude one interview by turning him out of the cabin, Clerke threatens to put him under arrest; the master's mate, whom he has called a liar, knocks him down; the seas break over him, men grow tired of listening to him; he says too often that he will complain to the king, the crew mimic him. He is exasperating, but not to be ignored.

Forster was one of those unsettled men who so often, in the eighteenth century, came to England in search of prosperity. Born in 1729 in Polish Prussia of a family originally Scottish, he grew up with a large amount of learning, not scientific, and became a solidly old-fashioned orthodox minister near Danzig. In 1754 his son George was born.[2] It was George, a clever boy interested in natural history, who turned his father's mind in the same direction, while, with a growing family, an inadequate living, and a total lack of economy,

---

[1] The best account so far of J. R. Forster is that by Alfred Dove in *Allgemeine Deutsche Biographie*, VII (1878); but much light is thrown on his character by his letters, even the English ones in the Banks Papers and the Sandwich Papers. The brief note here given is enlarged upon a little in *Journals* II, xliii–xlviii.

[2] Recent German writers and editors insist on giving his name as Georg. It was natural enough to make him George in England. George, however, is the form as given by Dove, and seems likely to have been his baptismal name—in full, Johann George Adam.

Reinhold used up his inheritances, and plunged into the debts that became his way of life. With a year's leave of absence from his church, he went with George to try his fortune in Russia, had poor fortune, overstayed his leave, lost his church; sold his library to maintain his family, went with George to England in 1766, spent a period of provincial teaching in languages and natural history, (though not the art of war, which he also proposed to teach), quarrelling with his acquaintances. Another man of large hopes, Alexander Dalrymple, invited him to London, to take a post with the East India Company, which was not Dalrymple's to give away. He came—always with George—and Dalrymple was himself dismissed by the Company. For two years he drudged in poverty, producing pamphlets on botany, zoology, mineralogy, geography, while George drudged at translation; getting himself known in scientific circles and picking up patrons—picking up, even, an F.R.S. Then came his chance. Banks, Solander, Lind—Science, as it were—deserted Cook. What would happen to Lind's £4000? At that moment Daines Barrington stepped in, that 'worthy and learned gentleman', lawyer, antiquary, naturalist, scientific hobbyist, with important and useful connections; a friend, if ever there was one, to the improvident and persistent Forster. He was successful at the Admiralty; the £4000 descended upon Forster, and Forster descended upon the *Resolution*. He descended with George, as natural history assistant and artist. George, brilliantly gifted, serious, intellectually alive, romantic, not yet eighteen, with difficult times behind him, a difficult parent beside him, a place in history, yet unguessed at, ahead of him, was for the next three years to have the difficult task of making the name of Forster tolerable.

It was three weeks through June before work on the *Resolution*, and her subsequent stowage,[1] were completed. On the 8th Sandwich had to implore Lord North, the prime minister, not to consider the possibility of Banks's changing his mind again;[2] on the 15th, Cook had to see to the accommodation of the Forsters by the rebuilding of cabins already taken down—'two fore mast Cabbins under the Quarter Deck',[3] supplies were still being prepared or requested, the Baron von Storsch's marmalade, stockfish, spirits in which to

[1] 'Captain Cooke never explain'd his scheme of Stowage to any of us. We were all very desirous of knowing, for it must have been upon a new plan intirely: know he kept whatever scheme he had quite a secret: for Cooper ask'd my opinion, and repeatedly declar'd he cou'd form no idea how it was possible to bring it about.'—Clerke to Banks, 31 May 1772, Mitchell Library, Banks Papers, 2, f. 2; *Journals* II, 936.
[2] Sandwich to North, 8 June 1772; Sandwich Papers, Hinchingbrooke.
[3] Cook to Navy Board, 15 June 1772; Adm 106/1208.

preserve specimens. On Sunday the 21st, at the end of his last leave, he said good-bye to his family, and with Wales joined the ship at Sheerness. She sailed next day for Plymouth, arriving after some delay from the wind on 3 July. The previous evening, between the Start and Plymouth Sound, she had met the Admiralty yacht *Augusta*, bearing Sandwich and Palliser on their return from a dock-yard inspection. The two came on board for a final report on the *Resolution*—which, says Cook, 'I was now well able to give them and so much in her favour that I had not one fault to alledge against her. . . . It is owing to the perseverance of these two persons that the expedition is in so much forwardness, had they given way to the general Clamour and not steadily adhered to their own better judgement the Voyage in all probabillity would have been laid aside.'[1] As soon as he arrived at Plymouth he wrote officially to Stephens to assure him of the recovered virtue of the vessel: 'a doubt of a contrary Nature does not, I am persuaded, remain in the breast of any one person on board'; next day he similarly informed the Navy Board.[2] What doubts, if any, were harboured in Banks's breast about the wisdom of his behaviour we do not know; he thought, quite mistakenly, that the East India Company might give him a ship for a South Sea voyage in the following year, and, with a large train left on his hands, he had just chartered a brig for a voyage to Iceland.

The *Adventure* had been waiting at Plymouth since the middle of May. There the ships' companies, as the result of unprecedented generosity on the Admiralty's part, received most of their arrears of pay and two months' advance, to provide themselves with what they deemed necessities for the voyage (they can have had few dependants to provide for);[3] and there Cook received his instructions. They were dated 25 June, and they told him nothing he did not know already: 'indeed I was consulted at the time they were drawn up and nothing was inserted that I did not fully comprehend and approve of'[4]— in other words, they put into formal words the plan he had himself matured. The ships had been fitted out to proceed upon farther discoveries towards the South Pole. He was to call at Madeira for

[1] *Journals* II, 9.
[2] Cook to Stephens, 3 July 1772; Adm 1/1610, CLB. Cook to Navy Board, 4 July; B.M. Add. MS 37425, f. 134; *Journals* II, 943–4. He tells the Navy Board, 'I beg leave to inform you that the fault she formerly had in being crank is now entirely removed and that from the little tryal we have had of her sailing and working she promises to answer very well in these respects.'
[3] According to Midshipman Harvey, the Admiralty generosity had to be stimulated by a petition to Sandwich from the *Resolution's* crew,—*Journals* II, 10, n. 3.
[4] *Journals* II, 10. The Instructions are entered in Adm 2/1332 and CLB, and printed in *Journals* II, clxvii–clxx.

wine, at the Cape of Good Hope for refreshment and supplies. He was to leave the Cape by the end of October or beginning of November and search for Cape Circumcision; if he found it, and it proved to be part of the continent, he was to explore as much of the continent as was possible and report on it as fully as possible (the instructions on this theme are virtually a transcript of those for his first voyage); then, if possible, to carry on discovery either to the east or west, as near to the South Pole as possible. If Cape Circumcision should prove to be part of an island only, he should, after examining this (or from its reported position if it was undiscoverable) stand on south so long as there seemed a likelihood of falling in with the continent, then eastward to circumnavigate the globe; after which the Cape of Good Hope, and home. When the season made continuance in high latitudes unsafe, he should retire to 'some known place' northwards to refresh and refit. Islands were to be surveyed, charted, taken possession of, if consequential enough; such instructions presented nothing new. The explorer had what he wanted. The chronometers were all taken ashore at Drake's Island, checked in the portable observatories, and got going by Wales and Arnold. The *Resolution* would take the Kendall instrument and one of Arnold's; the *Adventure* the other two of Arnold's. At 6 a.m. on 13 July 1772 he sailed from Plymouth, the *Adventure* in company, and stood south-west. 'Farewell Old England', wrote Lieutenant Pickersgill in his journal, very large, and scribbled a not very ornamental border round the words.

XIII

England to New Zealand

THE FIRST spot of large importance in Cook's plan was the Cape. It was to be more than three months before he arrived there, after a passage generally agreeable; and that passage, a sort of prologue to the great story that was about to unfold, itself contains not merely minor incident, but indications sufficient of the administrative control and scientific detail of the voyage. Cook's journal at once fills with observation. Sighting the Spanish coast on 20 July, he picked up the north-east trade wind unusually early off Cape Finisterre. Two days later the ships were stopped by a Spanish squadron, a scene which Forster found 'humiliating to the masters of the sea', though to Cook it was quite unimportant, and the Spaniards, having identified them, merely wished them a good voyage. In the interval, in a calm, Wales had been across to the *Adventure* to compare the chronometers' rates of going. On the 29th they were at Madeira, anchored in Funchal Road. Here they were well received: Cook got his wine, water, fresh beef and fruit, and a thousand bunches of onions to distribute among his people for a sea store—'a Custom I observed last Voyage and had reason to think that they received great benifit therefrom.'[1] He also, for whatever reason, collected statistics of the island. From Madeira he reported on the behaviour of his ship:

... the Resolution answers in every respect as well, nay even better than we could expect, she steers, works, sails well and is remarkably stiff and seems to promise to be a dry and very easy ship in the Sea; In our passage from Plymouth we were once under our Courses but it was not wind that obliged the Resolution to take in her Topsails tho' it blow'd hard, but because the Adventure could not carry hers, in point of sailing the two Sloops are well match'd what difference there is is in favour of the Resolution.[2]

In the same letter he reported on a person who had been waiting three months at the island for Mr Banks's arrival, and left three

---

[1] *Journals* II, 21.
[2] 1 March 1772; the person addressed is not apparent, but was possibly Stephens.—ibid., 685.

days before Cook's. The person, who had spent much time botanising, had arrived as a gentleman who was to join the ship, but no one entertained a doubt that his sex was wrongly defined. It is fairly clear that the thoughtful young philosopher, in providing so many amenities for himself, before the explosion over the *Resolution*, had provided also for the companionship of a lady. Cook was amused; there is amusement still in the vision of Banks trying to persuade the captain to accept this new addition to the scientific staff.[1]

With the new month Cook steered for Porto Praya, in San Tiago, one of the Cape Verde islands, to take in more water; for he did not want his people to be on an allowance. We find in the logs and journals—not Cook's only—evidence of the regimen he applied— the bilge pumped out regularly with fresh sea-water, the ship cleaned, aired, and dried with charcoal fires; the brewing of Pelham's 'experimental beer'; the men compelled to air their bedding, to wash and dry their clothes properly and frequently. This in the *Resolution*: there is no sign that Furneaux imposed such rules in his ship. The two vessels were tried against each other deliberately in sailing qualities: this first time the *Resolution* was the better, but more trials and experience made it hard to award a preference. At Porto Praya, 12–14 August, the water was tolerable, though not good, bullocks were unobtainable, hogs, goats, fowls, fruit were in plenty, the Forsters did some useful botanical collecting, Cook and Wales made a useful survey of the bay, the sailors bought monkeys. These poor animals dirtied the ship, and before long Cook had to have them thrown overboard.[2]

Five days after the departure from Porto Praya a carpenter's mate, Henry Smock, who was working over the side fitting a scuttle, fell into the sea and sank almost before he was seen. His loss might be regarded as a normal accident in the sailor's life, and Cook was not startled; but when a week later he learnt from Furneaux that one of the *Adventure*'s midshipmen was dead he might well have felt some alarm—and even more, less than three weeks after that, when another died. They both, said Furneaux, died of a fever 'caught at St Iago by bathing and making too free with the water in the heat of the day'. Neither Dr James's Powders nor Dr Norris's Drops availed to save.[3] Others who had fallen sick had recovered; nevertheless, one may ask, why should men fall sick so soon after leaving

---

[1] ibid., and xxix, n. 4.

[2] Forster, I, 41, was censorious. Cf. Wales, *Remarks on Mr. Forster's Account of Captain Cook's last Voyage* (1778), 20: 'the captain paid more attention to the health of his people, than to the lives of a few monkies.'

[3] *Journals* II, 33, n. 3; 37, n. 4.

England? The *Resolution* had no sick, even from drenching in tropical rain. On 8 September the ships crossed the equator, with appropriate horseplay in the *Resolution*, none in the *Adventure*—for Furneaux thought it dangerous. Cook continued to experiment in one way or another, hoisting out a boat to try the current, trying the temperature of the sea with his submersible thermometer seventy fathoms below—Furneaux refused to allow Bayly a boat for the same purpose; trying the effect of his patent still in converting salt water to fresh, and getting a much better result, with no expenditure of fuel, from collecting rain-water; trying the effect of his experimental beer on his sailors, conservative men some of whom declared they would rather drink water. On 30 October the ships were anchored in Table Bay. The first thing noted, not only by Cook but by his officers, was the absence of sickness in the *Resolution*: to quote Clerke, 'Our people all in perfect Health and spirits, owing I believe in a great measure to the strict attention of Captain Cook to their cleanliness and every other article that respects their Welfare.'[1] The *Adventure* too was doing well at this time, her only invalid being Lieutenant Shank, who for some weeks had been suffering badly from gout. This was in marked contrast to two outward bound Dutch Indiamen arriving a few days later, where the ravages of scurvy had been frightful; between them they had lost almost two hundred men.

Cook liked the Cape as a port of call, except for its inevitable delays. The acting-governor, the Baron van Plettenburg, and one of the leading merchants, Mr Brand, made themselves very agreeable and helpful. There was delay over the baking of bread and the making up of the quantity of spirits deemed necessary: it did not matter, however, very much, as the men got every day all the fresh bread, meat and greens they could eat, and shore leave in batches for air and exercise. Wales and Bayly took their instruments on shore, for ordinary astronomical observations and to check the chronometers. Of these, the Kendall one in the *Resolution* had been behaving remarkably well, the Arnold one not at all well. The latter suffered when Wales was bringing it off from the shore; jarred to a stop as the long-boat struck the ship's side, it was started again, but continued to go badly for the rest of its life. The first Arnold instrument in the *Adventure*—that which had been tested at Greenwich— was 'not to be complained on', though it lost at an increasing rate; the second, having gone most imperfectly on the passage to the Cape, there stopped entirely. Cook had not yet begun to regard his Kendall

[1] *Journals* II, 46, n. 1.

chronometer with affection, but as early as the beginning of September, in noting a noon longitude by lunar, and contrasting this with the result by log, or dead reckoning, he had remarked, 'Such is the effect the Currants must have had on the Sloop, and which Mr Kendalls Watch tought us to expect.'[1] While the astronomers worked, Hodges painted an excellent picture of Capetown and its harbour, and Cook acquired information about two French voyages that interested him. The information was not very precise. The first voyage was one of two ships which had anticipated him in the south, discovering land in latitude 48° and losing a boat and its crew (this last item was not in fact true, though it could well have been so from the commander's behaviour). It was the first voyage of Kerguelen, in early 1772, which resulted in that nobleman's extravagant announcements of 'La France Australe' and its annexation. The second was the expedition of Marion du Fresne, to return Bougainville's 'Aotourou' to his native Tahiti, as well as to embark on more extended exploration. Cook learnt neither commander's name, though he did hear that poor Ahutoru had died of smallpox. Travel, it seemed, was dangerous for Tahitians.

There were a few changes in the ships' companies. In the *Adventure* the unfortunate Shank felt obliged to relinquish the voyage; his second, Arthur Kempe, was promoted in his place, and James Burney, in compliance with Sandwich's promise to his father of early advancement, was sent across from the *Resolution* to be second lieutenant. When Forster was on shore he met a young Swedish doctor, Anders Sparrman, who was studying the natural history of the place; nothing would content him but that, at his charge, Sparrman should join the expedition as his assistant. He persuaded Cook that there was room for one more. Sparrman was a sedate, discreet young man, a late student of Linnaeus, a good ethnographical collector as well as natural historian, destined for his own distinction—'endowed with a heart capable of the warmest feelings, and worthy of a philosopher'.[2] Cook never quite learned to spell his name. There was little more for the captain to do than to write letters, to report to the Admiralty on the experimental beer and on happenings at the Cape; to be conciliatory towards Banks; to bid farewell to Walker. These last two letters cast some light on his own character. 'Dear Sir', he wrote to Banks, 'Some Cross circumstances which happened at the latter part of the equipment of the Resolution created, I have reason to think, a coolness betwixt you and I, but I can by no means think it was sufficient to me to break off all

[1] ibid, 35 (2 September).   [2] Forster, I, 68.

corrispondance with a Man I am under many obligations too'. He tells him of a collection Brand has got together for him and of the two French expeditions: he thinks of Banks's own talk of a South Sea voyage, as one explorer considers a fellow in the trade.

I am in your debt for the Pickled and dryed Salmon which you left on board, which a little time ago was most excellant, but the eight Casks of Pickled salted fish I kept for my self proved so bad that even the Hoggs would not eat it; these hints may be of use to you in providg for your intinded expedition, in which I wish you all the Success you can wish your self. . . .[1]

In this there may have been some deliberate generosity—he certainly did not refer to Mr, or Mrs, or Miss Burnett; in the letter to Walker there is certainly real warmth and regard for the Quaker mind.

Having nothing new to communicate I should hardly have troubled you with a letter was it not customary for Men to take leave of their friends before they go out of the World, for I can hardly think my self in it so long as I am deprived from having any Connections with the civilized part of it, and this will soon be my case for two years at least. When I think of the Inhospitable parts I am going to, I think the Voyage dangerous, I however enter upon it with great cheerfullness, providence has been very kind to me on many occasions, and I trust in the continuation of the divine protection; I have two good Ships well provided and well Man'd. You must have heard of the Clamour raised against the Resolution before I left England, I can assure you I never set foot in a finer Ship. Please to make my best respects to all Friends at Whitby. . . .

Thus one 'Most affectionate Friend' to another.[2] After which, on the afternoon of 22 November, Cook weighed anchor, and having got clear of the land directed his course for Cape Circumcision— for 'new and awful scenes'.[3]

He was three weeks late, in terms of his instructions. It did not matter: it was even probably an advantage, because it gave the pack-ice a chance to break up, and though this might provide dangers of a particular sort, it also provided an opportunity to penetrate farther south than would otherwise have been given. Cook could not take full enough advantage of this; for knowledge of the antarctic ice had to be built up over a long period, and he was the pioneer—a pioneer, furthermore, with no previous experience of ice-navigation. Cer-

[1] Cook to Banks, 18 November 1772; *Journals* II, 688.
[2] Cook to Walker, 20 November 1772; General Assembly Library, Wellington, ibid., 689.
[3] The phrase is Forster's, I, 88.

tainly he had experience enough of fogs, in the North Sea, off the coasts of Newfoundland and Nova Scotia; he had seen ice, even been entrapped in it for a day, on a passage from Halifax to the St Lawrence; but what was that? Nor were his men more deeply acquainted: two had served in the Greenland whale-fishery, Wales had had a summer month or two in Hudson Bay. There were certain dogmas to unlearn: that ice, for example, was a fresh-water pheno-menon, and hence argued the neighbourhood of land, that some sorts of bird did not go far from land—hence the careful noting and description of birds in more than one journal; there was the dis-covery that in the higher latitudes, beyond 60° S, the prevailing wind is not westerly but easterly, so that the grand strategy of the west to east voyage was not necessarily, all the time, the best. There were problems set up by the currents that were consequent on those winds, the 'west wind drift' and the 'east wind drift,' to which Cook could give only very tentative answers. On the other hand, if he could have accounted for his fogs through knowledge of the Antarctic Convergence—the converging of layers of cold water from the south and the less cold of lower latitudes—he might have felt scientific satisfaction, but it would not have reduced his practical difficulties in navigation. He simply, for four months, had to keep a good look-out, and his men prepared to act instantly. This was the first, and the longest, of what have been called his three ice-edge cruises. How long he would be out of sight of land he could not guess: he began by announcing limits, not ungenerous but strict, on the use of fresh water.

Cape Circumcision was said in the English documents to lie approximately in latitude 54° south and longitude 11°20′ east of Greenwich. Cook had his chart of the Southern Ocean published by Dalrymple in 1769, which showed Bouvet's track.[1] Bouvet's point of departure, when he struck south, was Santa Catarina, an island on the coast of Brazil, and for a start his longitude for this island was 4°20′ too far east. The ice was unusually far north in the summer of 1738–9, so that when on 1 January, the Feast of the Circumcision, Bouvet descried out of the fog his high, rocky, desolate cape, flanked by glaciers, surmounted by a massive ice-cap, with ice stretching away to the east, he might be forgiven for thinking that he was on the edge of a considerable extent of land. Ice, seaweed, seals, penguins, all testified. His chief pilot was convinced that the cape,

---

[1] There was a brief account, translated from De Brosses, in Callander's *Terra Australis Cognita* (1768), III, 641–4. Dalrymple's production was his 'Chart of the Ocean between South America and Africa. With the Tracks of Dr Edmund Halley in 1700 and Monsr Lozier Bouvet in 1738.' There was an accompanying *Memoir*, also published in 1769.

though indubitably cape, was part of only a very small island, and he was right: it is an island only five miles long and less across, the most remote spot in the world, if one measures distance from other land, and it was only by a most remarkable chance that Bouvet sighted it.[1] He could not get ashore; after making south to 57° he coasted the ice-edge eastwards for four hundred leagues, turned north-east to about 38°, and thence steered for home. The latitude he gave for his cape was 54°10'–15'S—which, considering the difficulty of accurate observation, was not badly astray from the correct one, 54°26'S. His longitude was between 27° and 28° east of Tenerife—that is, close to the Admiralty's 11°20'. Even with the correction for the Santa Catarina error it would have worked out at 5°17' east of Greenwich—still nearly two degrees from the truth of 3°24' E. Cook had no correction. He was well aware of the un-reliability of any figure for a longitude, but he was bound to begin by going as near as he could to a position given to him; was bound to begin, that is, by searching for Bouvet's discovery where he was certain not to find it. Bouvet's ice-field retreated; his fogs, in the midst of them his hard crumb of rock, remained.

Cook plunged straight south, a course he maintained, inclining a little east, for the next three weeks. On the second day out he issued to each man a jacket and trousers of the thick warm material called fearnought; later on he had the skimped sleeves of these lengthened and red baize caps provided in addition. Without this extra clothing it is difficult to fancy the ships' companies surviving at all as they went farther south, as the cold pinched, sleet and snow fell, ice stuck to the sails and rigging. November went out; December came in with hard westerly gales, rain and hail, the ships hove to, Wales put Dr Lind's wind-gauge to trial: 'the Adventure', noted Clerke, 'we find to be the most weatherly Ship in a Gale tho' this is as good a Sea Boat as can possibly swim.'[2] Oakum worked out of the seams and the ship began to leak, the men got colds, Cook lost hope under the succession of westerlies of reaching Cape Circumcision, the stock brought from the Cape died fast, and was eaten. On 10 December— latitude almost 51°—an 'Island of Ice' was sighted, twice as high as the topgallant masthead, at first mistaken for land; then ice islands

---

[1] Bouvet Island, lat. 54°26' S, long. 3°24' E. 'It is possible to draw, round Bouvet island, a circle with a radius of 1000 miles . . . which contains no other land at all. It is the only spot on the earth's surface possessing this peculiarity.'—R. T. Gould, *Captain Cook* (1935), 111. In 1808 it was found again by the Enderby whalers *Swan* and *Otter*; no landing was possible. Sealers visited it in 1822 and in 1825; in the latter year they managed to land. Its position was finally settled by the German Deep Sea Explora-tion Expedition in the *Valdivia* in 1898, which did not succeed in landing.

[2] *Journals*, II, 53, n. 2.

came thick. Pickersgill registered some excitement: 'We being Now across M. Bouvets track to ye Eastwd of Cape Circumcision, expect to find land hourerly, tho' sailing here is render'd very Dangerous ... such is the dispossion of ye Crew that every Man seems to try who shall be foremost in ye readest performance of his duty which calls for ye loudest acknowledgemts under such rigorous circumstances.'[1] Cook was not yet ready for such enthusiasm. The thermometer went below freezing point, he counted the icebergs—brought up, one must think, from the ice shelf of the Weddell Sea—many of them two hundred feet high; remarked on 13 December that he was in latitude 54°, but 118 leagues east of Bouvet's cape; and next morning was stopped by the pack ice, in 54°55′. This was a good deal farther north than the mean for December, though even then not so far as Bouvet's pack—'an immence field of Ice to which we could see no end, over it to the SWBS we thought we saw high land, but can by no means assert it.'[2] He bore away south-east close along the ice-edge, noting the whales, the penguins and other ice-haunting birds; had Furneaux on board to arrange rendezvous in case of separation; and trying some pieces of ice found that, rather surprisingly—though why surprising if it came from a river?—it yielded fresh water.

On 14 December the ships turned a point of the ice-field and hauled SSW, as there appeared to be clear water in that direction. Soon embayed, however, they were forced away to the north and east to clear the ice. Fog was so thick next morning that it was impossible to see the length of the ship; the jolly boat, out with the master, Wales and Forster to try the current and the temperature of the sea, was for two hours uncomfortably lost. They recorded a surface temperature of 30″ F. The ship could do nothing but tack briefly one way and the other, because of the fog and snow; the rigging and sails, hung with icicles, grew difficult to handle; whales played about the ship. On the 17th Cook, once more steering south, was once more stopped by heavy pack ice. The pack had begun to break up, and the process would be fast. Many bergs and much loose ice were found to seaward of the main body—very hampering obstacles to navigation they were; but the main body of ice to the south was still impenetrable, and how could Cook foretell its behaviour? If he had had the experience that no one had, he could have expected this main body to break effectively by the end of December, giving him three months of clear water. He considered the two evils, bergs and 'field ice'; he preferred the bergs. 'Dangerous as it is

[1] ibid., 57, n. 3.   [2] ibid., 59.

sailing a mongest the floating Rocks in a thick Fog and unknown Sea,' he says, 'yet it is preferable to being intangled with Field Ice under the same circumstances.' He had heard of a Greenland ship lying a whole nine weeks caught in that sort of ice. He could not risk it. He still watched for land, where in bays and rivers ice might form. By 18 December the ships had sailed some ninety miles eastward along the great edge, which lay nearly east and west except for its own bays—and they provided no way south. Cook, like Bouvet under the same circumstances, thought it reasonable 'to suppose that this Ice either joins to or that there is land behind it and the appearence we had of land the day we fell in with it serves to increase the probabillity, we however could see nothing like land either last night or this Morn, altho' the Weather was clearer than it has been for many days past.'[1] He would not abandon his general plan: after getting a few miles farther north, he would 'run 30 or 40 Leagues to the East before I haul again to the South, for here nothing can be done.'[2] He did, however, modify it: from no farther north than 54°, he at once made south as well as east. At this time there were a few signs of scurvy, and wort was made from malt for those affected. In a calm the current was tried; the boat found none, but Forster was able to shoot a few prions or 'whale birds'. Next day Cook sent the master to see if fresh water could be collected in the Greenland fashion, as it ran from an iceberg; there was not a drop. The day after that was 25 December. The captain knew when to humour his crew. They had been hoarding their liquor. 'At Noon seeing that the People were inclinable to celebrate Christmas Day in their own way, I brought the Sloops under a very snug sail least I should be surprised with a gale of wind with a drunken crew'— and he added somewhat to the rum. He filled the great cabin at dinner with all the officers and petty officers who could get in, entertained the others in the gunroom; 'mirth and good humor reigned throughout the whole Ship; the Crew of our consort seem'd to have kept Christmas day with the same festivity, for in the evening they rainged alongside of us and gave us three Cheers.'[3] There were those who were disdainful, or shocked: the 'savage noise and drunkenness' were not to Forster's taste, any more than to Sparrman's the passionate barbarities of English shipboard boxing. Indeed bloody noses and oaths may have consorted ill with the silent dignity of ice islands.

The ships were passing through fields of loose ice, rotten, honey-

[1] 18 December; ibid., 63.   [2] ibid.
[3] ibid., 66. This is from the Admiralty MS of the journal, P.R.O., Adm 55/108.

combed lumps sculptured into every variety of fantastic animal shape, or pieces heaped one upon another, the 'rafted ice' of modern terminology. On 27 December they were 240 miles almost due south of their position a week before. There seems little doubt that Cook had worked them round the end of a wide tongue or belt of pack ice, that in the early summer of most years stretches out in an unbroken mass far to the east from the Weddell Sea. His longitude was about 17° E. Not improbably—if again he could have known— he could then have pushed his way south through the loose ice to clear water in about latitude 60°; indeed he might have gone far enough to have sighted, perhaps even to have reached, the antarctic continent. He decided, as he had a clear sea and a favourable wind, to run as far west as the meridian of Cape Circumcision. This was on 29 December, a day when he tried unsuccessfully to pick up ice for water, but was instead regaled by the military behaviour of penguins on an iceberg: to quote Pickersgill, 'they Seemd to perform their Evolutions so well that they only wanted the use of Arms to cut a figure on Whimbleton Common.'[1] Two days later, steering 'direct' for Cape Circumcision, he had to haul a few points to the north to avoid loose ice, only to discover an immense field to the north; and the wind turning to a south-east gale, with a dangerous sea, he had to stand back to the south—in retreat, that is, from the southern edge of the tongue of ice around which he had worked his way. He resumed his western course till 3 January 1773. At that moment, in latitude 59°18' and longitude 11°9', he had a well defined conviction. He was now west and south of the position assigned to the cape; the weather had been clear for a few hours and the horizon empty.

In short, I am of opinion that what M. Bouvet took for Land and named Cape Circumcision was nothing but Mountains of Ice surrounded by field Ice. We our selves were undoubtedly deceived by the Ice Hills the Day we first fell in with the field Ice and many were of opinion that the Ice we run along join'd to land to the Southward, indeed this was a very probable supposission, the probabillity is however now very much lessened if not intirely set a side for the Distance betwixt the Northern edge of that Ice and our Track to the West, South of it, hath no where exceeded 100 Leagues and in some places not Sixty, from this it is plain that if there is land it can have no great extent North and South, but I am so fully of opinion that there is none that I shall not go in search of it, being now

[1] Pickersgill more at length: 'Saw on the Island a Number of those live things which we found to be Penguins, they set errect on their Leggs ranged in regular lines, which with their Breast's forms a very Whimsical appearance we fire two 4 Pounders at them but Mist them after which they wheeld off three deep and March down to yᵉ water in a rank. . . .'—ibid., 69, n. 1.

determined to make the best of my way to the East in the Latitude of 60°
or upwards, and am only sorry that in searching after those imaginary
Lands, I have spent so much time, which will become the more valuable as
the season advanceth. It is a general recieved opinion that Ice is formed
near land, if so than there must be land in the Neighbourhood of this Ice,
that is either to the Southward or Westward. I think it most probable that
it lies to the West and the Ice is brought from it by the prevailing Westerly
Winds and Sea. I however have no inclination to go any farther West in
search of it, having a greater desire to proceed to the East in Search of the
land said to have been lately discovered by the French in the Latitude of
48½° South and in about the Longitude of 57° or 58° East.[1]

This is a passage of interest, because it shows us the reasoning
Cook. He had been attentive to the ice, its appearance and movement, since he first encountered it. He was still prepared to admit—
wrongly, though in accord with the philosophers—that sea ice
invariably implied land. He was right in thinking that the pack
moves in an easterly direction, though it comes with the current
rather than with the wind. (It is true that the current—the west
wind drift—is itself engendered by the wind.) The course he had
sailed quite certainly disposed of the cape as a projection of any large
extent of land. The effect of the great bergs upon his mind, and of
the pack, is evident from his conclusion that Bouvet, with the best
will in the world, had been deceived by the ice. What is curious
is that he does not weigh the possibility of an island, not of ice but
of earth and rock—unless it is weighing a possibility to say that 'if
there is land it can have no great extent North and South, but I am
so fully of opinion that there is none that I shall not go in search of
it.' It is all the more curious in that his instructions raise the possibility, and he had virtually written the instructions. The only person
who talks in terms of an island is Lieutenant Kempe of the *Adventure*:
'Standing now to the Eastward having given up our Searches after
Cape Circumcision concluding if any such place, a small spot extending it self near East and West may be supposed from the Track we
run down.'[2] This was an accurate supposition. It may be that at
this time Cook was not prepared to class such a phenomenon as land,
especially against the other supposition that in the east he might find
something more validly reported, also by the French, Kerguelen's
land; and sailing eastwards he would be resuming his own fundamental strategy. As he changed course, in most unpleasant weather,

---

[1] *Journals* II, 71-2, 3 January 1773.
[2] Kempe, 5 January 1773; ibid., 72, n. 1. Cf. Alan Villiers: 'looking for such a place
down there was like groping for a pinhead on a fogged-in airport.'—*Captain Cook* (1967),
167.

strong gales, thick fog, sleet and snow, with ice-covered rigging, he may even have felt a sense of relief. The crew were standing up to the conditions 'tolerable well', with their warm clothing and an extra glass of brandy every morning.

On 4 January 1773 the ships were running to the east, some eighteen miles north of the position where there had been an impenetrable field of ice four days earlier. Cook infers correctly that such a large body of ice could not have melted in four days, that it must have drifted northward; once more, not for the last time, his journal-page receives his reflections on the current, as he makes east and somewhat south. It was the 9th that saw an important and triumphant experiment, the taking in of loose ice from round a berg for water—arduous and freezing, as well as picturesque, work (Hodges's drawing struck every fancy); but, with the coppers melting down the stuff and the boats on deck stacked high with it, the ships after another day's effort had more, and sweeter, water than when they left Cape Town. A few days later, while trying the current, Cook sank a thermometer to 100 fathoms, finding the temperature there 32°. That stimulated further cogitations, wherein the accepted physical and geographical principles are questioned. 'Some curious and interesting experiments are wanting to know what effect cold has on Sea Water in some of the following instances: does it freeze or does it not, if it does, what degree of cold is necessary and what becomes of the Salt brine? for all the Ice we meet with yeilds Water perfectly sweet and fresh.'[1] By this time he had abandoned his predominantly easterly course, with some southing in it, to steer sharp south, and a few days later, on 17 January, shortly before noon, he crossed the Antarctic Circle for the first time in history. His position for that day was latitude 66°36½'—four and a half miles south of the circle—and longitude 39°35' E. Icebergs had become scarce; he was hoping that he had reached a clear sea. There were too many antarctic petrels and snow petrels about, lovers of the pack; in the afternoon this appeared, loose pieces so strewn about it 'that we were obliged to loof for one and bear up for another'—a constant process of dodging; right across the bows stretched a long line of bergs. In latitude 67°15' he was to tack and stand away. Apart from the bergs and 'smaller pieces packed close together', to the southeast could be seen an endless mass, sixteen or eighteen feet high, of

[1] *Journals*, II, 77. In Cook's later version of his journal, B.M., Add. MS 27888, he writes, 'if it does freeze (of which I make no doubt)'; but we do not know precisely when he made this addition—probably after his other ice observations. J. R. Forster discussed the problem at some length, concluding that the sea did freeze, and thus produce pack-ice.—*Observations*, 76–102.

what the Greenland men called 'field ice'. Cook did not think it prudent to try to get round this ice field. He was wise. He thought of his ships and remembered that the summer was half spent; but if he had known that he was then only 75 miles from the continent he might have hesitated a little longer.

He stood north-east for the rest of the month, spreading the sloops four miles apart on favourable occasions to widen the field of vision. Only on one day were no icebergs seen—the only day since they were first met with, and Cook amused himself calculating how many square miles of ocean would be occupied altogether by the islands of ice. A great deal of the weather was disagreeable. At the beginning of February the ships were in the reported latitude of the land they were searching for, prevented by the wind from being as far west as Cook had planned to be. Furneaux reported seeing rock weed and diving petrels, 'a great sign of the vicinity of land': was it to the west or the east? If to the west that was bad luck, because with the wind where it was the only direction to go was east. He was, in reality, about ten degrees west of the land, though east of the meridian of Mauritius, on which it was supposed to lie. He tried east for a day or two; then the wind changed and he tried west. On 6 February the wind went round again. 'Indeed', says Cook, 'I had no sort of incouragement to proceed farther to the West as we have had continualy a long heavy Swell from that quarter which made it very improbable that any large land lay to the West.'[1] He bore away east and south, all sails set. Clerke summed up the facts: 'We've been for these 6 or 7 days past cruizing for the Land the Frenchman gave intelligence of at the Cape of Good Hope—if my friend Monsieur found any Land, he's been confoundedly out in the Latitude & Longitude of it, for we've search'd the spot he represented it in and its Environs too pretty narrowly and the devil an Inch of Land is there.'[2] So the nearest Cook came to Monsieur's discovery, as he steered his new course, was to have the land on his larboard quarter, about five degrees off. Then, on 8 February, the ships parted company.

It was in the morning, in a thick fog,[3] in latitude 49°53′ S, longitude 63°39′ E. Penguins and diving petrels made men think that land might not be far away, and in the fog Cook made short tacks rather than carry blindly on his course; this, he later concluded, must have led to the separation, because the *Adventure* did

---

[1] *Journals* II, 89.   [2] ibid., 89, n. 2.
[3] The previous day, 'Having fair and clear weather', Cook 'had all the peoples Bedding &c^a upon deck to air a thing that was absolutely necessary.'—ibid., 90.

not answer his signal guns, so far as he could hear. He cruised about the position where he had last seen her, or lay hove to, for two days out of the three stipulated for such happenings; after which he judged that she, like his own ship, had been driven to leeward, and could not regain position. If that was so, he would do no good waiting a third day, and he resumed the course that he had broken off. He had no fear for his consort's safety, and a rendezvous had long been arranged at Queen Charlotte Sound. Three days later penguins about the ship in increased numbers made him consider again the question of land, and 'various were the oppinions among the officers of its situation.'

Some said we should find it to East others to the North, but it was remarkable that not one gave it as his opinion that any was to be found to the South which served to convince me that they had no inclination to proceed any farther that way. I however was resolved to get as far to the South as I conveniently could without looseing too much easting altho I must confess I had little hopes of meeting with land, for the high swell or Sea which we have had for some time from the West came now gradually round to SSE so that it was not probable any land was near between these two points and it is less probable that land of any extent can lie to the North. . . .[1]

Why not? Because to the north lay Tasman's track of 1642, and Tasman had met with no land till he altered course even more to the north and discovered Van Diemen's land. The intervening space, Cook rightly guessed, would be traversed by Furneaux, who was more of a free agent than his own officers, with their eyes fixed in the wrong direction. But these officers were somewhat justified. Only about forty miles to the north-east, on that 13 February, lay Heard Island, a great breeding-ground of penguins—not very great in extent, true, but still land; and the ship must have passed closer than Cook would have chosen, if he had had the choice, to the two small rocky islets lying off Heard Island to the west, the Mc-Donald islands. The captain had another, allied, meditation: 'it is now impossible for us to look upon Penguins to be certain signs of the vicinity of land or in short any other Aquatick birds which frequent high latitudes.' This is true of penguins, though not of all 'Aquatick birds'. Still, another dogma had gone.

Two days after Cook's determination to go on further south, we come on another characteristic episode. There had been in the *Resolution* an outbreak of petty pilfering. Justice demanded, and was granted, some flogging—after which (we learn from the

[1] ibid., 93.

midshipman Bowles Mitchel) 'examin'd the peoples hands—those who had dirty where punish'd by stopping their daily allowance of Grog'.[1] We have the same scrutiny recorded a fortnight later, and (says Mr Mitchel) 'the usual punishment'—which may have been regarded as a heavy one by the dirty-handed. And here we have Clerke testifying to the régime: 'Captain Cook having Observ'd many of the People in rather a ragged condition, this forenoon he gave them some Needles thread and Buttons, that they may have no excuse for their tatter'd [condition]—they also have every Saturday to themselves to wash &c—that they may likewise have no excuse for a dirty, or improper appearance.'[2] This was in addition to drying and airing the bedding, with anything else that could be dried and aired, in fine weather. Some of the tars may have felt put upon. No matter: the captain was going to see that they survived. It was as important for him as the sight of the Aurora Australis, now seen flooding the heavens, as trials of the electricity of the air, were important to Wales; almost as important, perhaps, as the constant replenishment of water from the broken pieces of icebergs. The voyage may sometimes seem to us to have been a mixture of trivialities and terrors. As the ship pushed south the number of icebergs increased—in a space of twenty-four hours more than a hundred were seen. Against one she just escaped being carried violently by a sort of indraught; another, three or four hundred feet high, toppled almost bottom up while she was close to it and the boats were picking up ice; another burst silently in pieces as she passed by —at least no noise could be heard above that of the waves and the wind. The gales, their heavy squalls and high seas, haze, snow and sleet, fell off only to return furiously; there was constant reefing of sails—in that cold!—and striking of topgallant yards; yet there were less unpleasant intervals, even gentle breezes. On 24 February, having gone as far as 61°52′ S, about longitude 95°15′ E, Cook decided he must go no farther. The weather was as bad as it could be, except that it did not blow quite a tempest. The captain's journal must be quoted again, both for the reasons he gives and for the glimpse we are allowed, among the trivialities and terrors, of a strange beauty. The night had been unpleasant.

Under these circumstances and surrounded on every side with huge pieces of Ice equally as dangerous as so many rocks, it was natural for us to wish for day-light which when it came was so far from lessening the danger that

---

[1] *Journals* II, 94, n. 3.
[2] ibid., 102, n. 4. On 14 March, Mitchel recorded, 'Mustered the People and found them very clean.'—ibid., 105, n.

it served to increase our apprehensions thereof by exhibiting to our view those mountains of ice which in the night would have passed unseen. These obstacles together with dark nights and the advanced season of the year, discouraged me from carrying into execution a resolution I had taken of crossing the Antarctick Circle once more, according at 4 oClock in the AM we Tacked and Stood to the North under our two Courses and double reefed Topsails, stormy Weather still continuing which together with a great Sea from the East, made great distruction among the Islands of Ice. This was so far from being of any advantage to us that it served only to increase the number of pieces we had to avoide, for the pieces which break from the large Islands are more dangerous then the Islands themselves, the latter are generally seen at a sufficient distance to give time to steer clear of them, whereas the others cannot be seen in the night or thick weather till they are under the Bows: great as these dangers are, they are now become so very familiar to us that the apprehensions they cause are never of long duration and are in some measure compencated by the very curious and romantick Views many of these Islands exhibit and which are greatly heightned by the foaming and dashing of the waves against them and into the several holes and caverns which are formed in the most of them, in short the whole exhibits a View which can only be discribed by the pencle of an able painter and at once fills the mind with admiration and horror, the first is occasioned by the beautifullniss of the Picture and the latter by the danger attending it, for was a ship to fall aboard one of these large pieces of ice she would be dashed to pieces in a moment.[1]

The pencil of Hodges was able enough, and there is hardly a journal of the voyage that does not attempt somehow to render the romantic fantasy. It may be added that if Cook had managed to cross the Antarctic Circle once more he would probably have found himself ashore, perhaps some miles inland on that part of the continent that is now the Australian Antarctic Territory; for in his longitude of 95°15′, and for about fifty degrees to the east, the circle runs either a very short distance from the coast or within it.

Although he stood to the north, he did so very half-heartedly. On 6 March he was still in latitude 60°4′ S, and it was not till the next day that he got to 59°59′. He sailed east in 58° or 59° another ten days, for the most part in gales, on one day covering 155 miles, on another 163, though generally only half or a third of those distances. The *Resolution* shipped no water to speak of, he observed: 'Upon the whole she goes as dry over the Sea as any ship I ever met with.'[2] Poor Mr Forster, however, thought he was always getting wet. At first the icebergs still abounded; at the end of February there were few—probably, Cook thought, broken up by 'the late

[1] ibid., 98–9.   [2] ibid., 103, 9 March.

gale', but more probably because the main body had been moved
away quickly to the north-east by wind and current. He saw the last
of them on 8 March. As late as the 14th of that month, having had
some milder weather, he was hankering after a higher latitude. He
soon changed his mind: next day the decks and rigging were covered
with snow and ice, and he had to admit that the time was approaching 'when these Seas were not to be navigated without induring
intense cold, which however'—even then he must not overstate—
'by the by we were pretty well used to'.[1] The Southern Lights could
not make it any warmer. On 17 March he gave way to prudence;
and from latitude 59°7' S, longitude 146°53', some nine hundred
miles south of Van Diemen's Land or Tasmania, bore away north-
east and north inclining to east, resolving to make the best of his
way either to New Holland or New Zealand. New Holland was
something new in his plan, but he might find out whether or no
Van Diemen's Land formed part of it. In the same journal-entry in
which he declares this motive he records his pleasure ('I was not a
little pleased') at determining the point of no variation of the
compass.[2] And he thinks fit to offer his potential reader a sort of
apology for thus breaking off his antarctic cruise, to lessen, perhaps,
any sense of shock that might be felt:

If the reader of this Journal desires to know my reasons for taking the
resolution just mentioned I desire he will only consider that after crusing
four months in these high Latitudes it must be natural for me to wish to
injoy some short repose in a harbour where I can procure some refreshments for my people of which they begin to stand in need of, to this point
too great attention could not be paid as the Voyage is but in its infancy.[3]

The reader is more likely to be baffled by the conscience that thinks
explanation necessary.

The wind was between north and west, and he put New Holland
aside. Penguins and rock weed, those ministers of deceit, were passed:
he did not know that Macquarie Island lay not far to his east. The
air grew agreeably warmer. There were seals, Port Egmont hens or
skuas, terns, weed which did say something, floating wood. At 10
in the morning of 25 March the masthead lookout sighted the coast
of New Zealand. Cook intended to put into the Dusky Bay of his
first voyage, or any other convenient port in the neighbourhood,

[1] *Journals* II, 105, 14 March.
[2] ibid., 106. There was variation, in fact, of 0° 31' E, but he writes, 'I was not a little
pleased with being able to determine with so much precision this point of the line in
which the Compass hath no variation.' He adds, in Add. MS 27888, 'for I look upon half
a degree [as] next to nothing'.
[3] *Journals* II, 106.

because he had earlier examined none of it thoroughly. When in the afternoon he was before the mouth of a bay he mistakenly took for Dusky—the coast hereabouts is very deceptive, and this was probably Chalky Inlet—the weather turned thick and he stood out to sea. Coming in with the land again next day he recognised Dusky Bay and entered it about noon; there was a great swell rolling in from the south-west, and the soundings rapidly deepened beyond his line, 'we were however too far advanc^d to return and therefore pushed on not doubting but what we should find anchorage, for in this Bay we were all strangers. . . .'

Dusky Sound is one of the most remote and wildly magnificent spots in New Zealand. The great sheet of water, screened within its entrance from the ocean by an irregular line of islands, and extending into a number of long arms and a vast number of smaller indentations, lies over a bottom anciently gouged in the land by stupendous glaciers, so that its shores tend to stand up immediately from the sea. The water is almost uniformly deep; only at the head of subordinate stretches have shoals been built up by the quick detritus-laden streams. There is little flat land; the eye is ever carried to immense heights, whether close around or in far misty recession. Except where a prodigious cliff-face falls vertically to the depths, the steep slopes are covered from high water mark up to the limit of growth by forest dense, unbroken, sombre. The scale is so deceptive, as well as so vast, that a full-grown tree, taken as the measure of some less regarded height, becomes insignificant and lost; a tremendous white cataract seems to descend only a few yards, not hundreds of feet, before it plunges hidden under the dark green covering and changes its direction. Low islets are tree-clothed; a rock perhaps will jut out quite bare of earth. Rain falls heavily for days, thick cloud makes invisible the whole landscape; then the sun of an occasional clear day will render the scene sharp as well as heroic. Into this large frame entered the *Resolution*, no larger than she would have seemed amid the waste of the southern ocean. But now nature, however wild, was friendly. There was more than the immensities, there was a superabundance of refreshment, as Cook was soon to find.

He ran about two leagues up the bay and inside the island he called Anchor Island let go his anchor for the first time in four months.[1] He had one man sick with scurvy, two or three others with

[1] Cook writes (*Journals* II, 110), 'after having been 117 Days at Sea in which time we have Sailed Leagues without once having sight of land'. In the Admiralty and Palliser Hudson MSS he gives the distance as 3660 leagues. His calculation of days seem to be wrong: as a point of pedantry, I make it 122 days.

slight complaints;[1] a boat was immediately put to fishing, and returned with supper for all hands. Meanwhile, not liking his anchorage, he sent Pickersgill to the southern side of the sound to look for better, going himself in the opposite direction. He was not as successful as his lieutenant, so that in the morning the ship was taken through a narrow passage between an island and the shore to the entrancing Pickersgill Harbour, 'full as safe and convenient as he had reported'. There she was moored head and stern to the trees—so close indeed that one tree growing out horizontally formed a natural bridge from shore to ship. Not far astern was a liberal stream of fresh water, above her stem rose a small bluff about fifty feet high which could be cleared for Wales's observations, and was called Observatory Point. The moss- and fern-covered stumps of a number of the largest trees then felled still stand amid the growth of two hundred years; the totara does not soon decay, even in that wet forest, and if the tangled cap of greenery be lifted, underneath in places can still be seen the straight cut of the seaman's axe.[2] Tents were pitched near the stream for the waterers, coopers, sailmakers, the forge was set up for the repair of iron-work; the fishermen were out every day; Cook began to brew 'spruce beer' on the Newfoundland model with the leaves and small branches of a tree which, he thought, 'resembles the Americo black Spruce'—the New Zealand rimu—together with those of the less astringent 'tea shrub' or manuka, his 'Inspissated Juce of Wort' and molasses. The majority of the crew took to it very well, and indeed they had to; for when the beer was started the spirits were stopped. Cook thought it was healthful, and a fair substitute for the green vegetables of which he could here find none; Sparrman, a connoisseur, liked mixing rum and brown sugar with it. The naturalists were busily employed, Forster at last removed from the reach of the waves and, if he cared to go far enough, other men's bad language; though the most devoted of naturalists found it hard to shoot a bird whose innocency led it to perch on the end of the gun-barrel. It was Forster who made his way up beside the stream, over the sodden foot-betraying ground, and found the enchanting small lake, a mirror of light and air, whence it flowed.

[1] Cf. Clerke, 28 March (ibid., III, n. 1), 'We've now arriv'd at a Port with a Ships Crew in the best Order that I believe ever was heard of after such a long Passage at Sea—particularly if we come to consult Climates; this happy state of Health was certainly owing to the Extraordinary indulgencies of Govern^t of Crowt, Wheat, Malt &c &c together with the strickt attention paid by Capt Cook to the Peoples Clenliness.'

[2] See the sketch map of the clearing on Astronomers Point with the stumps located, in A. Charles Begg & Neil C. Begg, *Dusky Bay* (Christchurch, 1966), 135; and pl. 4 in that volume.

Fresh provision was not confined to the daily catch of fish—'all large, firm, and exceedingly well tasted', says Clerke, with love enumerating them—'likewise great abundance of very large and very good Crawfish'. Seals found at Seal island or rock, not far within the entrance to the sound, were killed for food and lamp oil, 'whose Haslets are exceeding good, and some part of the Body properly manag'd make steaks very little inferior (some of our Gentry sware, far superior) to Beefsteak'. Cook is as rapturous as anyone over the wild fowl—'To day we had an excellent dinner on fish, seal, and wild fowl'—ducks of various sorts, wood hens or weka, oyster-catchers. There were sporting expeditions; the survey which was faithfully carried on (Pickersgill produced an admirable chart) might well finish for the day with a burst of firing. Some of the names inscribed upon the chart registered pleasant occasions of sport or its aftermath—Duck Cove, Luncheon Cove, Supper Cove. Goose Cove, however, was named not for slaughter, but because here Cook chose to leave the last of his Cape of Good Hope geese, rather than consume them, entertaining no doubt 'but what they will breed and may in time spread over the whole Country, which will answer the intent of the founder'.[1] Alas, it did not answer thus.

Were there people? If so, Cook was anxious to make their acquaintance. The morning after the ship was settled in harbour some of the officers took a boat on a shooting party into the next arm of the bay, the arm that Cook was soon to call Cascade Cove. Seeing inhabitants, they returned to inform the captain, thinking it unsafe to go on when the rain would make their fire-arms useless in case of need. The interested natives just appeared within sight of the ship, then retired behind a point of land in the heavy rain. When the rain lifted one canoe came again, closer, and those in it stared for half an hour before they retreated, untouched by demonstrations of friendship. After dinner Cook went to the cove in search of them; he found two poor huts, a canoe, fishing nets and a few fish, but no people; leaving a few medals, therefore, looking-glasses, beads and a hatchet, he himself retired in patience. Three days later these articles were still undisturbed. It was not until the evening of 6 April that Cook, on his way back with Hodges and the Forsters from ex-ploring the north side of the bay, met on a rock at the north-east point of a small island with an 'Indian' and two women who did not retreat when the boat drew near. Cook's approach is described by George Forster: he went to the head of the boat, called to the man in a friendly way, 'and threw him his own and some other handkerchiefs,

[1] *Journals* II, 126.

which he would not pick up. The captain then taking some sheets of white paper in his hand, landed on the rock unarmed, and held the paper out to the native. The man now trembled very visibly, and having exhibited strong marks of fear in his countenance took the paper: upon which captain Cook coming up to him, took hold of his hand, and embraced him, touching the man's nose with his own, which is their mode of salutation.'[1] Half an hour was spent in 'chitchat', uncomprehended on either side, the younger of the two women being the most voluble, 'which occasion'd one of the Seamen to say, that weomen did not want tongue in no part of the world'.[2] Next day Cook went twice to 'Indian Island', met the man and his whole family of seven, saw their huts and small double canoe, and exchanged gifts with them. Hodges drew them. It was then the turn of the natives to pay a visit, though nothing—not even bagpipes or fife and drum—would induce them to come on board the ship. They stayed three days nearby and after four more came back, when at last the man and the girl were tempted on board, to indulge a large curiosity and take the lead themselves in the exchange of presents with a valuable greenstone adze and feather cloak. The hatchets and spike nails the man got were a very considerable return in his eyes. The young lady was not 'kind'. Cook this time was anxious to be rid of them, because he was about to set off on a surveying expedition to the head of the most southerly arm of the sound. His early duck shooting roused more of the people, with two of whom, putting away his gun and advancing singly, he managed to get on friendly terms:

they retired but waited when I advanced alone and beckoned with their hands for the others to keep back as they had seen me do. At length one of them laid down his spear, pulled up a grass plant and came to me with it in his hand giving me hold of one end while he held the other, standing in this manner he made a speach not one word of which I understood, in it were some long pauses waiting as I thought for me to make answer, for when I spoke he proceeded; as soon as this ceremony was over, which was but short we saluted each other, he then took his hahou or coat from off his back and put it upon mine after which peace seemed firmly established. . . .[3]

---

[1] Forster, I, 137–8.   [2] *Journals* II, 116, n. 5.
[3] ibid., 124–5. This may be the occasion referred to by Midshipman Elliott in his *Memoirs*, ff. 16v–17: 'certainly no man could be better calculated to gain the confidence of Savages than Capt[n] Cook. He was Brave, uncommonly Cool, Humane and Patient. He would land alone unarm'd—or lay aside his Arms, and sit down, when they threaten'd with theirs, throwing them Beads, Knives, and other little presents, then by degrees advancing nearer, till by Patience, and forbearance, he gain'd their friendship, and an intercourse with them; which to people in our situation, was of the utmost consequence.' —Quoted ibid., 124, n. 3.

It is typical; and one would give much to have heard the voices and the words of those two men in that place. Cook could not stay to visit the habitations in the bush, up a tidal river. He arrived at the ship, with a good deal added to his chart, after two nights out, to find that his other friends had disappeared. The glimpses of these few men and women he gives us, the defeated and scattered remnant of the Mamoe people, driven from easier lands farther north, are the only glimpses we have; for even here their enemies pursued them and slew. Cook was at a loss to know why they lived apart.

Returning from this expedition he lacked the time to explore an arm of the sound that ran north. April was moving on, by the 25th there had been a week without rain, in which the ship had been put in a condition for sea, and he now determined to investigate this unexplored inlet. It was more than an inlet, it proved to supply a northern passage to the outer sea. Cook resolved to use it. He got everything on board and only waited for a wind to leave, spending a last few hours in digging a garden and sowing seeds, not with much hope of a successful outcome. On 29 April he weighed and stood up the sound with a light south-west breeze. It was 11 May before he was clear of the northern entrance and out at sea again. At first calms, then bad weather, then a baffling mixture of both delayed his progress; at times the boats towed, but this was slow work, and most of these days were spent at anchor, while the winter gales began to blow in from the Tasman Sea, and morning after a storm showed the heights covered with snow. It was still possible to manage shooting and exploring trips. Wales, the conscientious astronomer, went on one—'This is the first Days Amusement I have been able to take since I came to this Place.—I might with great Truth have said since I left England'; and added, 'About 9 oClock we returned on board the Ship with not a dry thread about us. I am right served for repining in the Morning.'[1] Happily the sport among the wild fowl had been good. Pickersgill, who had been sent with the Forsters in the pinnace to look into an arm which ran off east from the main passage, had a worse experience, being out for thirty-six hours in a most violent storm of snow, hail, thunder and lightning, with no fire—the wood being too thoroughly soaked to burn—and no food except a few mussels: it seemed 'as if all nature was hastening to a general catastrophe', runs the Forster record, and doubtful whether the ships would survive.[2] Cook, less dramatic, called this inlet

---

[1] 2–3 May; ibid., 783.
[2] '. . . our hearts sunk with apprehension lest the ship might be destroyed by the tempest or its concomitant aetherial fires, and ourselves left to perish in an unfrequented

Wetjacket Arm. He could not go on the little expedition himself because, he explains, he was 'confined on board by a Cold'. It is not surprising that he had a cold, after the previous five weeks' experiences; but balancing Forster's possible over-statement against Cook's under-statement, it is likely that he had more than a cold. The Forster version is 'a fever and violent pain in the groin, which terminated in a rheumatic swelling of the right foot, contracted probably by wading too frequently in the water, and sitting too long in the boat after it, without changing his cloaths'.[1] Cook, one is to remember, was now in his mid-forties, and may well have been fighting off, by denial, some rheumatic fever. It was one thing, on the day when he admits his cold, a day of fair weather, to get up the cables and everything else from between decks, clean the space and air it with fires; it was another to exert a scrupulous care over himself. He had done a good deal of forcing his way 'through the wet Woods up to the back side in Water'.

Nevertheless, no sooner did he have Pickersgill back on board than he was out himself, exploring another arm that ran eastwards, nearer the entrance, and was out for twelve hours, returning wet through, though with plenty of wild fowl. Meanwhile Gilbert the master had examined the passage to the sea. Next day Cook and all the officers were shooting again, 'for a Sea Stock'; then it was another strong westerly gale with heavy rain which kept the ship at anchor; as soon as this moderated he went to the rocks which lay off the entrance to gather in a supply of seals. At last, on the morning of 11 May, a breeze came from the south-east, and the *Resolution* got to sea in a 'prodigious' south-west swell. She left her name behind her attached to the lofty-peaked and much-indented island that forms a large part of the north shore of Dusky Sound, separated from the other heights by the passage up which Cook had just made his rain-soaked way.

He gives an appreciative account of the place, both for the 'curious reader' and for future navigators, 'for we can by no means till what use future ages may make of the discoveries made in the present'; and no port in New Zealand that he had been in, far remote as it was from the trading parts of the world, afforded such plenty of refreshments; a port of safe and easy access, with anchorages for fleets, with timber to mast them. As Mr Hodges has drawn the country very accurately, Cook will describe it only in general terms.

---

part of the world.—Forster, I, 185. It was this sort of thing that made Dr Johnson impatient of George Forster's book.

[1] Forster, I, 181.

We get more of its natural history than we should have done had this been his first voyage. His interests have widened since Banks hung over strange plants at Thetis Bay, just outside the Strait of Le Maire, almost five years gone. He may, contemplating John Reinhold Forster, have regretted a little the absence of Banks; for here was the part of the country where the young man whom he had had to rebuff was so anxious to land. Well: there is nothing to complain about apart from the rain and the constant plague of sandflies; nor has the rain done his people harm, they are all strong and vigorous. But perhaps the climate was less noxious to Englishmen than to any other nation, because it is analogous to their own, says Forster sourly. We may consult some of our other voyagers. Pickersgill and Gilbert climbed one of the heights above Cascade Cove, and reported that inland nothing could be seen but barren mountains with huge craggy precipices frightful to behold; Clerke talks of his gratitude to this 'good Bay', and its many good qualities, though frequent and heavy rains rendered it very disagreeable at times, but 'I do think that Dusky Bay, for a Set of Hungry fellows after a long passage at Sea is as good as any place I've ever yet met with'.[1] Wales, who was extremely busy the whole time with his professional observations, yet gives us a natural history résumé rivalling the Forsters'. He cannot help being a little testy by 10 May, he had not liked the weather: 'We are now (thank God) leaving this dirty, and, on that Account, disagreeable Place; after a stay of near Six Weeks, during the greater part of which I was continually troubled with severe Colds, attended with a fever owing to my being almost always wet, and sometimes so bad that it was with the utmost difficulty that I attended my bussiness.' Yet it was Wales who, after seeing a rainbow above a waterfall, 'one of Nature's most romantic Scenes', burst into quotation from *The Seasons*, adding a line or two of his own to adapt the bard to the New Zealand ambience.[2] We return to Cook, the master of these able, so divergent men, and his journal, as he turns up the coast from his Dusky Bay; we find little romance, no poetry, he does not seem to have had any really disagreeable experience; we do find him going thoroughly into the manufacture of spruce beer, a discussion of the chronometers, and sailing directions —diet, science, seamanship.

There was a mixture of weather as he made up the west coast, but nothing remarkable until 17 May. That morning the ship had

[1] *Journals* II, 755–6; and 'The Happy taughtness of my Jacket excites in me a gratitude to do some justice to this good Dusky Bay, Before I take my final departure from it.'— ibid., lxviii, quoted from B.M.' Add. MS 8951, 11 May 1773.

[2] *Journals* II, 782–3.

rounded Cape Farewell and was sailing towards Cook Strait; in the afternoon, in dark cloudy weather with the wind all round the compass, half a dozen waterspouts rose up about her, one whirling fifty yards or less from her stern. There was some perturbation in the ship as well as the sea. Cook wrote as minute an account of the phenomenon as he could. There was no casualty, the weather cleared, as he sailed on he was able to identify the bay where Tasman had had his fatal encounter with the New Zealanders; on the 18th in the morning they saw the flashes of signal guns from the *Adventure* in Ship Cove, by evening they were anchored, and next day moved further in and moored with a hawser to the shore.

XIV

The First Island Sweep

FURNEAUX CAME on board. His report interested Cook. When the ships parted company on 8 February he had done his best to carry out his instructions, but he could not regain position, and after waiting around three full days decided to bear away for the rendezvous in New Zealand. Although, as we can see from his log, he was anxious to make a landfall as soon as possible, he pursued the sensible course Cook thought he would. He knew that Cook had the Van Diemen's Land problem in his mind, he knew what course Tasman had sailed across the southern Indian Ocean, he had a fair idea what course Cook was intending to sail, and he therefore sailed roughly midway between them. In this way, though it would be possible to miss islands, the possibility of any large piece of land escaping notice could hardly arise. At the beginning of March, when his longitude was about 106° E, he began to decrease his latitude significantly in the direction of Van Diemen's Land. He had favouring winds though poor weather; no very remarkable events on board apart from signs of madness shown by his lieutenant of marines, and one mistaken cry of land just before he made north; and on 9 March did unmistakably see land—in modern terms, that around the South West Cape of Tasmania. He was not the first man on that coast since Tasman. Marion du Fresne had been there the year before; but Marion was not interested in the geography of the country, only in repairs to his ships and fresh water. The south coast was inviting to neither man. Furneaux, after getting a boat's crew ashore briefly at Louisa Bay, on the 11th anchored in a likeable spot further east that he called Adventure Bay, on the east side of Bruny island—which he mistook for the Tasman peninsula.[1] There was what he most needed, good water; the hillsides were thickly covered with eucalypts. He found few animated things, but he was no

[1] Furneaux, by beginning to identify from too far west the features Tasman had named —he thought, or was persuaded by Cook that his South West Cape was Tasman's South Cape—got them all wrong. He thought that the wide entrance to D'Entrecasteaux Channel was Tasman's Storm Bay. This latter however, was his own Adventure Bay.

naturalist; there were many signs of the native people, primitive huts, heaped mussel and scallop shells, fire-places, inland smoke, some large fires; none appeared, however, and having in four days got all the wood and water he needed, he left, intending to coast northwards till he came to Cook's landfall in New Holland and see if the two countries were joined. The weather was squally, there were islands and breakers closer in; Furneaux thought the coast generally dangerous. On 18 March, in latitude 40°50′, he was off a break in the land which he concluded, with little encouraging evidence, to be a deep bay, though his officers took it for a strait. On the morning of the 19th, in about 39° S, Bass Strait lay open before him. He had some shoal water. 'I should have stood further to the Northward', he writes, 'but the wind blowing strong at SSE and looking likely to haul round to the Eastward, which would have blown right on the land, I therefore thought it more prudent to leave the Coast and steer for New Zealand.' And the geographical query?—'it is my opinion that there is no Streights between New Holland and Van Dieman's Land, but a very deep bay.'[1] All his company, we learn from one of them, were looking forward to winter quarters, 'Spending a few Months in Ease & Quietness'.[2] The passage of the Tasman Sea threw up one storm. Early on 7 April the *Adventure* was moored in Ship Cove, and Furneaux celebrated by serving out an extra half-allowance of brandy.

Cook studied Furneaux's journal, possibly cross-examined him on it, and made his own analysis. Furneaux's consistent westerly winds were in contrast with the prevalent easterlies south of 58° or 60°: the southern oceanic wind system was obviously different from the simple pattern he had had in his mind at the outset of the voyage. He does not seem to have seen the journals of any of Furneaux's officers, or he might have hesitated longer over accepting Furneaux's verdict on the main point. A 'deep bay' and a 'very deep bay'? Curiously enough, those officers did not argue for a strait in the position of Bass Strait proper—the 'very deep bay'—or even raise its possibility. The 'deep bay' they took for a strait, however, was indeed a strait, Banks Strait, which communicates with Bass Strait between Tasmania and the Furneaux islands; and Bass Strait opens widely to the north of the Furneaux islands. Furneaux 'supposes' (perhaps under cross-examination) 'that there is a Strait or Passage behind' these islands; but neither he nor Cook supposes the possi-

---

[1] Furneaux's Narrative, B.M. Add. MS 27890, printed in *Journals* II, 736.
[2] *Journals* II, 153, n. 4: 'Every one being of Hopes to meet with our Concort, and Spending a Few Months in Ease & Quietness, After Beat^g the Seas For 4 Months without Intermission.'—Midshipman Wilby.

bility of this strait or passage joining a larger strait or passage. Cook considers the land seen and the distance estimated by Furneaux on 19 March: 'it is therefore highly probable that the whole is one continued land and that Van Diemens Land is a part of New Holland, the Similarity of the Countrys, Soil Produce Inhabitents &c^a all serve to increase the probabillity.'[1] Admittedly Furneaux had seen none of the inhabitants. One is left with the impression that Cook, who had himself turned *Zeehaens bocht*, another deep bay, into Cook's Strait, was persuading himself hard to agree with Furneaux, and that the man who had clung on through storm to the northern end of New Zealand and negotiated the shoals of New Holland would not have retired from Van Diemen's Land without proof one way or the other. We may remember also that Cook's own journal was a report to the Admiralty, and that all his journals indicate that he disliked acquainting his masters with a defect he might perceive in his subordinates.

He now formulated his plan for the immediate future. This entailed some disturbance of the expectation entertained by his second in command. Furneaux, like any orthodox naval captain, regarded the winter months as a time for winter quarters, for 'ease and quietness', and had stripped his ship and settled down accordingly. The first two or three weeks he divided between Ship Cove, in the usual work about the vessel, and the island Motuara, where he put up tents, moved his sick (he had some bad cases of scurvy), and planted vegetable gardens. On the rocky islet at its end Bayly had his observatory. The New Zealanders came daily both to ship and shore, trading freely their fish, and almost anything they had, for nails and old bottles and whatever else they could get: they would certainly not part with the freshly severed head they had in one of their canoes. They enquired about Tupaia. With some notable exceptions they were, thought Burney, 'Thieves and cursed lousy'. Towards the end of April Furneaux transferred the tents to Ship Cove, close to the watering place, and moored the ship closer in shore. Here it was that two severe shocks of an earthquake were felt, followed a week later by the possibly worse shock of Cook's arrival—though for the moment, after a separation of fourteen weeks, and a little despair of ever seeing the *Resolution* again, there was on both sides 'an uncommon joy'. Cook immediately had his men out, and went himself, to look for wild celery and scurvy grass; and, if his orders were obeyed, there was a radical revision of the *Adventure*'s diet. It is not clear that they were obeyed with a literal adherence

[1] ibid., 165.

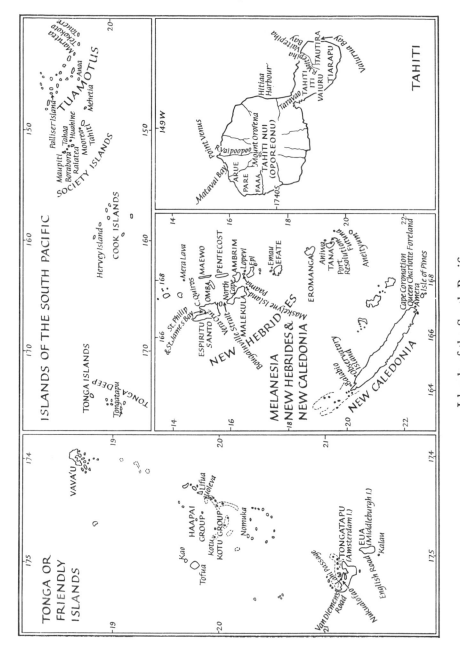

Islands of the South Pacific

Sadly enough, it was two members of the *Resolution*'s company that proved unequal to the land. These were a ram and a ewe, last of the sheep that Cook had brought from the Cape. At Dusky Sound they had tottered off the ship almost dead of scurvy; now, with herbage abundant, they survived a bare three days—the reason being 'some poisonous plant', thought Cook; 'thus all my fine hopes of stocking this Country with a breed of Sheep were blasted in a moment.'[1]

The shock of Cook's arrival arose from his announcement that there was to be no more ease and quietness, that winter quarters were over. Since Furneaux had 'in a great degree' cleared up the Van Diemen's Land question he would not go there himself; but he would not—to use his own uncompromising language—idle away the whole winter in port, he would explore the unknown parts of the sea to the east and north. This he 'proposed' to Furneaux; to this proposition Furneaux 'readily agreed'; really there was nothing else he could do, in the face of this overwhelming commander, and accordingly began to get his sloop ready for sea again, as he was 'disired', as quickly as possible. In the meantime Cook wasted few moments. He inspected the vegetable gardens, and encouraged the native people to look after them, cleared more ground on Motuara and planted wheat and peas, carrots, parsnips and strawberries; released a pair of goats, hoping, as Furneaux had already put a boar and sow on shore, that in time goats and hogs, even if not sheep would populate the country (he trusted too much in the fear that he thought the people had of these animals); he added to his observations of the New Zealanders' habits, their divisions, their unsettled nature, and noted that the visits of his own ships had done nothing to improve their morals. Alas, for wives and daughters; alas, for the 'happy tranquillity' enjoyed by this people and their forefathers before the arrival of civilised Christians—which he had so signally failed to notice himself when he first arrived three years before. There is a naïve oddity about these bursts of sentimental nonsense from Cook. Had the captain this time been too much exposed to the oratory of J. R. Forster? Well, he has a hard demand of us: 'tell me what the Natives of the whole extent of America have gained by the commerce they have had with Europeans.' Perhaps it was a useful diversion from these gloomy thoughts to be able to spend some of his royal master's birthday in festivity, with the officers of both ships to

[1] *Journals* II, 167. The poisonous plant theory is quite likely to have been correct. The sheep could very easily have come on the attractive, but deadly, Tutu (*Coriaria sarmentosa*)—the New Zealand farmers' 'Tute'—a bane of wandering stock.

dinner, and a jovial afternoon, a double allowance of rum to the seamen, and twenty-one guns echoing about the sides of the primitive hills and islands. Certainly (to leave both philosophy and commemorative joy) there was great interest in other observations, the scientific observations of Mr Bayly. There was no surprise in his latitude, his variation of the compass, dip of the needle, his tides; but his longitude, his 173°48′55½″ East of Greenwich? If that was correct then Cook had charted the whole country 1°20′ too far to the east. Were Cook and Green wrong in their 175°9′? Bayly's observations were borne out by Wales's at Dusky Bay, reduced to Queen Charlotte Sound by the Watches; it was—we can see from the way Cook recurs to it, in copy after copy of his journal, much more than from the words he employs—astounding. There is no doubt a little point of professional pride: 'errors as great as this will frequently be found in such nice observations as these,' he writes in his log, 'Errors I call them tho' in reality they may be None but only differences which cannot be avoided'. He had made a great number of observations himself; 'I cannot think the error so great as these two Astronomers have made it,' (he now writes his journal): 'but supposing it is it will not much effect either Geography or Navigation but for the benifit of both I thought proper to mention it though few I beleive will look upon it as capital error.'[1] Few indeed in that age would look on such an error as capital; and few would have been disturbed by the subtle line to be drawn between difference and error. The captain was right in thinking the astronomers had made the error too great. Cook had put Queen Charlotte Sound not 1°20′, but 40′, too far east; Bayly put it 40′ too far west. In the end Wales came to think less than well of Bayly; but Wales, for all his trouble, had not produced an impeccable result for Dusky Bay.[2]

By the beginning of June both ships were ready for sea. Cook summarised his programme anew and gave it to Furneaux in writing. He would sail east between the latitudes of 41° and 46° S until he came to longitude 140° or 135° W; then, if he had discovered no land, make for Tahiti to refresh: from Tahiti he would return 'by the Shortest rout' to his New Zealand base, whence he would plunge south for the completion of his instructions. That is, he would cross, first, a part of the ocean untouched on his previous voyage, when he had come down from Tahiti to latitude 40° and turned west to New Zealand; and second, another part where theoretically a

[1] *Journals* II, 174; and 579–80.
[2] Wales's own longitude for Dusky Sound was not quite accurate: he made it 166°2′46½″ E (*Journals* II, 138) compared with the correct 166°33′56″E.

continental peninsula might thrust upwards on the map, 'between his southerly track in August 1769 and the north-westerly one from the Horn to Tahiti in the earlier months of that year. He had not then considered land likely in this great sector, because of the run of the sea, but it must now certainly be explored to remove all doubt. We get another of Cook's little meditations as he considers the prospect:

It may be thought by some an extraordinary step in me to proceed on discoveries as far south as 46° in the very depth of Winter for it must be own'd that this is a Season by no means favourable for discoveries. It nevertheless appear'd to me necessary that something must be done in it, in order to lessen the work I am upon least I should not be able to finish the discovery of the Southern part of the South Pacifick Ocean the insuing Summer, besides if I should discover any land in my rout to the East I shall be ready to begin with the Summer to explore it; seting aside all these considerations I have little to fear, having two good Ships well provided and healthy crews.[1]

A dangerous expedition, thought Forster; a 'party of Pleasure', fancied others, their minds no doubt a little bemused with the notion of Tahiti. For two days a contrary wind kept the ships in harbour; on 7 June they were able to put to sea and next morning were clear of the strait. It was on this day, the 8th, that the Arnold chronometer on board the *Resolution* would not wind, and had to be let finally run down; the surviving *Adventure* one was still keeping reasonably good time. The Harrison-Kendall watch ticked steadily on.

The winter weather was unpleasant, though not intolerably so. There was no ice to coat the rigging and jam the blocks. There was some fog, a great deal of haze and rain, dark gloomy weather, a succession of southerly gales, fresh gales, strong gales, hard gales, squalls, high seas; when the wind went round to the north it generally blew a gale; topsails split; there was continual reefing and double reefing and striking of yards. There were a few calm, even pleasant, intervals, some gentle breezes. Once Cook was able to set his studding sails. The great swell continually came in from the south or southwest, with very few changes to the north. A little rockweed was seen, pretty clearly drifted from New Zealand. The *Resolution*'s wheel, bucking, carried two steersmen in succession right over it in opposite directions, one of them twice. A goat fell overboard, was rescued and died of the immersion. In the *Adventure*, said Bayly, there was very

[1] *Journals* II, 173.

little amusement save reading; but Bayly did not have to climb ropes and reef sails—if that can be called amusement. Cook, who was watching his longitudes narrowly, recorded them in relation to Cape Palliser as well as to Greenwich, noting that they were consistently farther east than they should have been had Bayly's Motuara observation been correct. Wales lost no chance of comparing the going of the two watches that remained in order. As for the track, the ships made southward to latitude 46°56', not far short of the latitude of the southernmost point of New Zealand, when they were according to reckoning in longitude 172°49', on 16 June, before Cook altered course north-east, then east inclining to north. June passed into July with moderately good weather. Cook gradually and irregularly lessened his latitude over almost forty degrees of longitude till he crossed the fortieth parallel at about 133°30' W, on 17 July, having run down the whole of the longitude he had intended—indeed, a degree and a half farther—and was nearly midway between his tracks north and south in 1769. Here he turned almost directly north, to bisect the unknown area, the last area possible in a temperate zone for the existence of a continent.

There was a flurry, not quite the last, of strong gales and squalls; after which the weather turned to gentle breezes and fair pleasant days, and sighs were heard for the trade wind. The temperature rose; lighter clothes were necessary. Then the *Adventure*'s men began to go down with scurvy. Her cook, a dirty indolent man, a natural prey, died of it on 23 July, though Cook learnt nothing of sickness for five days more. He was able to send a boat on board the day after that and was told of twenty men sick with scurvy and flux. He immediately despatched a new cook, and urged every method he could think of on Furneaux to stay the disease. A few of his own crew were showing slight symptoms but were already being specially dieted; a single man, a marine, was seriously ill, of dropsy—he had been ailing since the ship left England. Furneaux, it seems, was doing his best, too late: he could not, Cook thought, have insisted on a proper use of greens at Queen Charlotte Sound. Tropic birds appeared in the sky, the winds were uncertain, tending to go round to the north, the passage became tedious to many persons. Where was the trade wind? Furneaux on 6 August reported great improvement in his men, the flux gone; from that night the trade wind blew. But the improvement was temporary only: by the 10th more than a third of them were scurvy cases. His lieutenant Burney hit on one of the reasons, the ship's 'being greatly Lumber'd, the people have scarce room to stir below,' and they were depressed at the length of the passage; yet Cook's men, in equally crowded quarters, did not suffer from lack of exercise. It is true that one of his junior officers thought that it was 'd–d hard' to set this cruise down 'under the Article of Refreshment'.[1] The officer would find refreshment enough in Tahiti, if he could wait. Meanwhile Cook considered his progress again. He had crossed Carteret's track of 1767, in about latitude 25° S, on 1 August, looked out for Pitcairn Island in the east, and seen only two tropic birds: crossed his own track of 1769, in 19°, on 7 August: where was the continent? 'Circumstances seem to point out to us that there is none but this is too important a point to be left to conjector, facts must determine it'; there was sea still to be examined south of his present track. That could wait, now he must get to the north of his outward track in 1769; for something new might lie in the way to be discovered. But he could not press ahead recklessly in the now steady trade; there must be caution, he must bring to or shorten sail in the moonless nights; and thus delay the arrival of scurvy-stricken men at their salvation.

In the evening of 11 August, as the ships sailed almost west, an atoll was sighted to the southward—perhaps one of those discovered by Bougainville, vaguely placed by him? It was not, it was the islet Tauere; 'this Sea abounds in these little paltry Islands', says Clerke, islands producing nothing but coconuts and surrounded with dangerous coral reefs. In the evening there was another, Tekokota; and the following daybreak still another, right ahead not more than two miles distant, a large shoal or reef twenty leagues round, dotted with islets on its north side, a dreadful surf on the south—Marutea, one of the most dangerous atolls in the Tuamotus.[2] Well had Bougainville called this cluster the Dangerous Archipelago. There was another at daylight on the 13th: luckily, smooth as the sea was the ship had brought to for the night. That afternoon Anaa was visible, Chain Island of the first voyage; and Cook, reluctant to incur further delay by bringing to, met the night by sending his cutter ahead with a masthead light for signalling. By morning there

[1] The guess that it was a junior officer—a midshipman?—who delivered himself of this judgment may be wrong. We get it from Burney, Ferguson MS: 'One of the Resolution's gentlemen says Nothing hurts him more than this Cruize being mentioned as a party of Pleasure, if, says he, they had put it down to the account of hard services, I had been content & thought myself well off, but to have it set down under the Article of Refreshment is d–d hard.'—*Journals* II, 191, n. 4.

[2] *Journals* II, 194, 196. Tauere was not discovered by Bougainville, but by Don Domingo de Boenechea, in the *Aguila*, in 1772. The printed *Voyage* calls it Resolution Island. Cook was the first discoverer of Tekokota—the printed *Voyage* calls it Doubtful Island—and also of Marutea, called Furneaux in the printed *Voyage*. The atoll discovered on the 13th was Motu Tu'a. Cook tried various names, Stephens Isle, Sandwich Isle, Harveys Isle, and finally in the printed *Voyage* came down on Adventure Island. Wales called it The Devil's Girdle.

was a large swell from the south again, which convinced him that he was clear of danger from low islands, so he hoisted in the boat. He was right: the next island was the high Osnaburg, or Mehetia, the pointer to Tahiti. He had resolved to put in at once at Vaitepiha Bay at the east end of the island for refreshment before going on to Matavai Bay. As dusk began to fall on Sunday, 15 August, the Tahitian mountains stood clear in the west. The *Adventure* was so sickly that Furneaux had to borrow men from the *Resolution* to work the ship.

Cook estimated the shore to be about eight leagues off—some thirty miles. He sailed on till midnight, then brought to till 4 a.m., then stood in for the land. When he retired to bed he left directions for the steering of the ship; when he rose at dawn he found that 'by some mistake'—a dozing officer of the watch?—she was on a wrong course and not more than half a league from the reef. He immediately gave orders—no doubt delivered with some force—to haul off to the north. Had the breeze continued all would have been well: it flattened to a calm, and the set of the sea carried the ships closer and closer in. The boats were towing; for a short time it looked as if they might get them round the point of the island into the bay. Even then natives were on board and round them in canoes, busily trading fruit and fish for nails and beads. About two in the afternoon they were before an opening in the reef. The situation outside was becoming more and more dangerous. It was too deep to anchor. Perhaps they could get through that opening into safety? No, it was too shallow: worse, it caused such an indraught that both ships were carried towards the reef at an alarming rate. Cook held in readiness one of the warping-machines he had extorted from the Admiralty: now was the time to use it, and it was quite useless. He dropped a bower anchor; by the time the *Resolution* was brought up she was in less than three fathoms; the sea was breaking violently close under her stern, and at every fall of a wave her bottom struck. To add to this danger there was the other danger of collision; the *Adventure* was driving down on her, even with her own anchors let go. When Furneaux's anchors held, the ships were so close that a plank would have gone gunwale to gunwale. Cook sent out his kedge and coasting anchors; heaving on these, with the bower anchor cut away, sheer power of human muscle, saved the *Resolution*; when the current slackened all the boats towed, the anchors were hove up, and at that moment, as the day began to close in, a very light air came from the land. It was sufficient to help her to an offing of two miles by 7 o'clock, when all her boats were sent to the assistance of the

Adventure; but before they could reach her she was safely under sail, leaving behind her three anchors, a cable and two hawsers. It had been an uncomfortable twelve hours, of long strain for sailors and civilians both. At least the sailors had something to do. Mr Sparrman, even in his anxiety, watched his fellow-men, and was pleased to observe the celerity and orderliness with which all commands were carried out. He was a little wounded by the stream of 'Goddams' which poured from the officers, 'and particularly the Captain, who, while the danger lasted, stamped about the deck and grew hoarse with shouting'; and he distributed speaking-trumpets, he modestly adds, to those officers who appeared to him the most efficient in handling the vessel, for which they were grateful. He may be largely correct in what he says about Cook: 'As soon as the ship was once more afloat, I went down to the Ward Room with Captain Cook who, although he had from beginning to end of the incident appeared perfectly alert and able, was suffering so greatly from his stomach that he was in a great sweat and could scarcely stand. It was, indeed, hardly remarkable that, after so great a responsibility and so prodigious a strain on both his mental and physical capacities, he should be completely exhausted.' Sparrman prescribed 'an old Swedish remedy', a good dose of brandy. 'His aches vanished immediately, his fatigue a few minutes later and, after a good meal, we soon regained our accustomed energy.'[1] Cook himself, no chronicler of personal pains, does not mention this appendix to near-shipwreck; from him we learn that they spent the night, a rainy and squally one, making short boards, and next day anchored about noon in Vaitepiha Bay.

The purpose in coming first to this bay, in the Tautira district of Tahiti, was to get the *Adventure*'s sick men on shore, and fed with fresh food, as soon as possible. Cook's own sick man, the marine Isaac Taylor, died a short time after the ships arrived, from a complication of disorders in which scurvy had no part. He was taken out to sea for burial, like Buchan on the first voyage. The others, sent on shore in the morning and brought back at night, under the care of a surgeon's mate, rapidly recovered. There was a sufficient supply of fruit and roots, but hardly a hog for sale; those that were seen, it was explained, all belonged to the great chief Vehiatua, and Vehiatua was himself for some days nowhere to be seen. In the meantime Cook twice had boats out to look for the anchors left behind. They found the *Resolution*'s; the *Adventure*'s were lost beyond

[1] Sparrman's account is in his *Voyage Round the World* (London, 1953), 51–2.

recovery. Cook was philosophic: considering the danger they had been in, they might think themselves happy in coming off so well. The usual orders to regulate trade, such as it was, were published. Contretemps there were, none the less caused by nimble-fingered Tahitians; and the capacity of a whole community to disappear when a monitory gun was fired along the shore made justice difficult to impose. When an *ari'i* knocked down a thief and returned a stolen musket Cook was heartily glad; for as he said, he himself could not have got it back by gentle means, while other means would have cost him more than ten times the value of the musket, in interrupted trade and bad relations. He could think back to the experience of his first voyage; and the longer the experience he had, the deeper the embarrassment was borne in on him. This particular occasion was a minor one. His relations with the people were on the whole amicable, he did in the end manage to meet Vehiatua and get a few hogs. It was not Vehiatua the thin old man with a white beard that he had met on his island tour in 1769; it was the old man's son and recent successor, a pleasant youth with whom he now spent most of a day, sharing his *ari'i*'s stool, walking arm in arm with him, giving him news of Banks and others he remembered, giving him presents, explaining that he could not stay for some months. Pickersgill, left behind with a boat's crew to trade when the ships left, managed to obtain more hogs; managed to obtain also, after Cook's departure, a night's entertainment from the chief Reti, the friend of Bougainville, and some of his young ladies. 'The Hymeneal Songs being allready perform'd we retired to rest: untell the Blushing Morn told us it was time to depart'—how distinctly the lieutenant stands before his readers!

Cook sailed from Tautira on 24 August, after only a week's stay, in the hope that supplies would be greater at Matavai. He had in the week learnt more about island politics than the change in one great chieftainship, and was consequently prepared for further changes at Matavai and Pare, though he could not understand the innermost nature of chiefly rivalries. Just as the interval between Wallis's arrival and his own earlier one had humbled the proud Purea, so had the period since then cast down others of the mighty. It was a coalition between the great Tuteha and the great Vehiatua that had broken Purea: the success of the coalition had been its solvent, Tuteha had set out to crush his ally. He tried by sea, and the battle was drawn; he tried by land, and, overwhelmingly defeated by the old man, was himself killed together with that other notable whom Cook had known, Tepau-i-Ahurai Tamaiti. This was in March

1773, no more than five months before Cook's re-appearance. Vehiatua marched to the Porionuʻu—the Pare-Arue-Haapape district, which included Matavai Bay—laying waste the land, imposing mild terms on the conquered; then he too died. The principal surviving conquered chief, who had lived by fleeing to the mountains, was the *ariʻi rahi* Tu, or Tu-nui-ea-i-te-Atua, of Pare, personally unimpressive in spite of his name, 'Great Tu wondrous next to God'—of character even mean, but with advantageous family connections, ambitious, persistent. He was the young man sedulously kept out of sight by his dominant great-uncle Tuteha, during Cook's first visit; he was the person, his family was the family, to profit by the partiality for Matavai Bay as a port of call shown by Cook and Cook's English successors. If Cook had shown a preference for Vaitepiha Bay, for the Tautira district, it is possible that the later abode of power in Tahiti might have been different, because the presence of British ships meant prestige, alien goods, the musket. Those Europeans who came to the eastern part of the island made less impression because they traded less and broke off their visits too soon. Cook in 1769 had heard of Bougainville and took him to be Spanish; he now heard of a visit from Spaniards and took them to be French. Some of his men even said they had seen a Frenchman on shore.[1] A ship had come to Vaiurua harbour, commanded by one Opeppe, had taken away four young Tahitians, and left behind a sickness called 'Apa no Peppe'. It must, concluded Cook, have been one of the French vessels he had heard of at the Cape, which had intended to restore Ahutoru to his island. It was not: it was the Spanish frigate *Aguila* from Lima, sent on reconnaissance by the viceroy of Peru, Don Manuel de Amat, who was greatly alarmed by the news of English discovery of a large and fertile island in an ocean which he continued to regard as a preserve of Spain. His commander, indeed, called the place the Isla de Amat. The *Aguila* had remained for a month, in November and December 1772; the four

---

[1] The difficulty of communication, with other difficulties, is illustrated by Wales's longer account, 22 August: 'Several of our People being on shore to Day, told us on their return that they had seen an European who ran directly from them into the Woods, and that by his appearance they judged him to be a Frenchman: some Gentlemen who were then on shore endeavoured to enquire of the Natives concerning him and understood that a French Ship had come late here whose Capt had told them he would return in 5 Months and that the Person who had been seen was left behind untill his return.' 23 August: 'To day a more strict enquiry has been made into the Affair of the Frenchman by some who pretend to understand the language best. . . . The ship is now spanish; and the Capt, whilst here, hanged three or four of his People, and this escaped from him. . . . On the whole that there may have been a French or spanish Ship here since the Endeavour is very probable; but, in my opinion, all the rest of the story is a mere Fiction.'—*Journals* II, 792–3. Wales made a very accurate judgment. Cook paid very little attention to the story.

youths had been taken for instruction in Christian principles, so that they might be returned as the spearhead of a benevolent Spanish sovereignty; the disease, *e pohe no Pepe* (the name was one the islanders must have heard much), was perhaps some sort of gastric influenza, fatal to those without natural defence. The Spaniards came again more than once, always in intervals between Cook's visits; he was to keep on hearing about them, sometimes as being almost round the next corner; it must have seemed sometimes almost a game of hide and seek; he was never to meet them. It was they, however, who first met Tu, whom Cook thought 'now the Reigning Prince'.

Reigning prince he might be: what struck the visitors, for the week of their stay, apart from his fine stature (he was three inches over six feet) was that he was 'timorous'. He made no bones about it. He did not like the noise of guns, he disliked swords; his people did not hesitate to report, when he missed an appointment, that the *ari'i* was *matau*, or frightened. He liked presents, he liked the bag-pipes, he did not like others to get too much attention—not even the aged and sorrowing mother of Tuteha, whose tears on meeting Toote, her son's friend, almost reduced Cook to tears himself. Tu played his part reasonably well with reciprocal gifts of food and cloth, and the entertainment of a 'Dramatick Heava or Play' in which his own sister danced; yet here, as at Tautira, supplies were not plentiful. Pickersgill, sent along the coast, could get very little —all hogs belonged to the *ari'i*, he was told—and Purea, whom he encountered, seemed herself reduced to poverty. For a captain who wanted to lay in stocks, the island had not turned out well: twenty-five hogs, not large, and one fowl in a fortnight, was not much; and it was not the breadfruit season. Neither captain was backward in trying to please; some seamen and marines who had quarrelled riotously one night with the people on shore were duly punished. The shortage was, probably, due to the destruction of war; perhaps also to a *rahui*, a solemn embargo laid by an *ari'i rahi* on consumption, to build up resources, which only he could remove: thus it could be said that in one place all hogs belonged to Vehiatua, in the other to Tu. On the other hand, the sick had recovered, fresh water had been obtained, all necessary repairs completed, so that the stay could be considered valuable; while Wales had been able to take an observatory on shore and make observations on the very spot from which the Transit of Venus had been observed, astonished by the tractability of the four or five hundred Tahitians who always surrounded him, kept off only by a rope and four sentinels.

They were a happy four days for Wales. Cook decided to move on. A number of young men wanted to sail with him, undeterred by the failure of Ahutoru or Tupaia to return. Indeed there was here a remarkable lack of interest in the fate of those voyagers; it was not till Raiatea that people enquired after Tupaia. He consented to take one Porio, for the sake of his possible usefulness; and late on 1 September stood out of the bay. Porio wept as the land fell astern—'the Dear Isle', to quote Clerke: 'Poor Porio's are not the only tears I've seen rous'd upon leaving this good Isle by some hundreds, tho' I've been in a condition myself at the time not to see a great way.'[1]

There were to be calls at the leeward islands Huahine and Raiatea. It was not a long passage to Fare harbour, on the west side of Huahine, where the *Adventure* missed stays and went on the reef; but Cook was ready for this, with his launch in the water, and she was soon off again.[2] Supplies here were plentiful, even before Cook met his friend the 'brave old Chief', Ori, when there was an elaborate ceremonial exchange of plantain plants, accompanied on one side by pigs, a dog, and Ori's pewter plate—on the other by nails, beads, and medals. Ori fell on Cook's neck and embraced him; 'the tears which trinckled plentifully down his Cheeks sufficiently spoke the feelings of his heart.' Cook gave him the most valuable articles he had, 'for I regarded this old man as a father'; Ori on his part 'receiv'd me more like a son he had not seen these four years than a friend'.[3] Pork, yams and fruit abounded; the men were taken off ship's food entirely. Wales and Bayly went for a walk together across the island; they found it 'a perfect Orchard from one end to the Other, interspersed with the Houses of the Inhabitants who nowhere offered us the least incivillity unless picking our Pockets, unknown to us, may be thought so'.[4] Some of the inhabitants, however, lived up to their reputation for incivility: one bravo paraded on the beach in full war habit as if intending mischief, until Cook took his clubs and broke them; poor Sparrman, incautiously botanising alone, was set upon, assaulted, and stripped of all his clothes except his trousers. Ori insisted on going with Cook in search of the robbers —a vain search—and in spite of his people's expostulations placed

---

[1] *Journals* II, 211, n. 5. The cheerful Clerke had a very sentimental side.

[2] According to Wales, the *Adventure* went on the reef twice. The launch carried out an anchor for her, by which her men hove her off; 'but as they were going to carry out another, the first came home, and she fell again on the Reef where she lay untill we got to an Anchor, when the Master was sent with Hands to assist them farther, and by Noon they were clear of the Reef, & soon after safe at an Anchor.'—*Journals* II, 801.

[3] ibid., 217. Ori, according to Wales (ibid., 802), was 'a thin elderly man, very grave & seems to be much reverenced by his Subjects.'

[4] Wales, ibid., 801.

himself entirely in Cook's hands by going on board the ship to dinner. One or two of Sparrman's things were restored, with some other things stolen from an officers' shooting party, interrupted trade was resumed with vigour, and all was good fellowship. It was suggested to Cook that he should attack the Borabora men on behalf of Huahine—not by Ori, who felt quite capable of dealing with them himself, and in addition claimed their chief, the dreaded Puni, as a friend. Vastly richer in provisions after four days here than he had been after fourteen at Tahiti,[1] lesser as this island was, Cook presented his friend with a small copper plate engraved with a record of his visit, to add to the pewter one, and on 7 September made sail for Raiatea. Furneaux brought away a man who had haunted his ship from the moment she anchored. He expressed the greatest desire to go to 'Britania', said Furneaux; his name was Mae.

The passage to Raiatea was again a short one, round its southern end, where Cook corrected his chart, and up the west coast to Haamanino harbour by night—a dark night, wherein the lights of fishermen on the reef were sufficient signals of danger. Next morning, the 8th, with the wind blowing right out of the harbour, Cook proved his seamanship by 'borrowing' close to the reef on the south side of the channel, then shooting through it with all sails set to where a boat marked his chosen anchoring place. He warped further in and moored; the *Adventure* followed suit. It was the end of the day by the time both ships were settled, and long before then, crowded round with canoes offering the plantain plants of welcome, they were embarrassed at the quantity of hogs and piglets and fruit thrust on them, with nothing but beads and nails expected in return. To describe all that happened in the next week would be but to trace the details of a pattern. The hospitality was vast. The chief, Orio, though not so close to Cook's heart as Ori, put aside all ceremony, insisted on exchanging names with him, exchanged visits and dinners, brought along his young son for inspection and presents, had his beautiful daughter Poetua dance and act, arranged a 'Comedy or Dramatick Heava' every day when there was not a performance for the islanders as of course. The 'young Princess', slender and graceful, made an impression on more than one heart. It was remarked that a not infrequent theme of the drama in these islands was successful theft; and the people were as enthusiastic in stealing as they were in trade or in making presents. It would not

---

[1] '. . . during our short stay we procured not less than 300 Hogs to both Sloops, besides Fowls & Fruit . . .'—ibid., 221; and in Cook's log, 'we have got by purchase & presents in both sloops about 400 Hogs & half as many Cocks.'—ibid., n. 5. The men bought cocks for cock-fighting; Forster, *Voyage*, I, 458–9.

do: whenever one was caught red-handed, he was tied to the rigging, given a flogging and tossed overboard to swim ashore—as he
had to, because his self-righteous fellows would never pick him up.
Pickersgill was once again sent off on independent trading, to Tahaa
in the north, both for fruit and (so many were the hogs accumulated) for a sea-store of food for the stock. He had his own difficulties
with theft, triumphantly surmounted, and came back successful.
He was away two nights. What he says about his men on the first
of the subsequent mornings indicates a perennial possibility of conflict: 'I got up by times for to get a way as early as possible, but
enquireing for the people I found most of them absent and on a
further examination found them one in one house and one in an
other all stragled about the Woods each man with his Mistress.'[1] It
was therefore hardly surprising that, while he was still away, everybody suddenly decamped from the beach, though Cook was surprised. Getting a garbled account of an affray in which islanders had
been killed and wounded by muskets, he feared for Pickersgill's
party, so long away. It was all quite untrue, confidence was restored,
and Pickersgill himself picked up a story that, perhaps fortunately,
never came to Cook's ears—of the gunner and a midshipman out
shooting, followed, in the island fashion, by a pressing mob of curious
people who would not go away; so that, exasperated, one of the
sportsmen fired at them with a little gunpowder and sand, and this
doing no damage, both were indignantly seized and taken before
a chief. The chief painted a vivid picture of Cook's annoyance at
this seizure—he would come and kill them all—and sent the two
back in a canoe, while the people made for the hills. This perhaps
was behind the departure that puzzled Cook; and it may be put
beside the other story, of Forster, the panic stricken moralist, pepper-
ing an 'Indian' in the back with small shot, which led to some coolness between him and the captain.[2] Behind the general goodwill,
that is, there was always the chance of misunderstanding, which
might be converted to ill will, for a commander to bear in mind; he
must somehow be able to predict, or at least to avoid the unpredictable. Meanwhile the sociable meals went on; and whenever Orio
came to dinner he never failed to drink his glass of Madeira.

After eight days Cook was resolved to leave. There was no more
to be done; his decks were so heaped with supplies it was almost
impossible to move. The young Tahitian Porio had decided to

[1] *Journals* II, 772.
[2] Bayly has a brief account of the matter, ibid., 226, n. 3. See also Wales, *Remarks*,
97–8, and George Forster, *Reply to Mr. Wales's Remarks*, 36–8.

relinquish adventure for love; his place in the *Resolution* was taken by another youth called Hitihiti—or, as he was known to his ship-mates, Odiddy. Furneaux still had his Mae, the young person who was to figure on the stage of the world and for ages to come, as Omai. When would Cook return? asked Orio; let him bring his sons with him. The aging Ori had thought that he and Cook might not meet again; perhaps, in another four years, they would both be dead; but 'Let your sons come, they will be well received.' On 17 September in the morning the ships sailed. Cook had a good deal to commit to his journal as a result of this last month, in addition to the record of events. He had to modify or expand some of his earlier impressions; wherever he had gone he had tried to have the marine Gibson, the attempted deserter of the first voyage, with him, as the man best acquainted with the language; he had some pages of criticism of Bougainville's account of Tahiti, but with Gibson's help had verified Bougainville's assertion of human sacrifice there (only of *taata ino*, evil folk, he was told); at Raiatea he had tasted kava for the first time; he meditated once more—not improbably with the help of Wales, to judge from Wales's own journal—on the nature of island morals. 'One ought not to be too severe upon these people when they do commit a thieft sence we can hardly charge them with any other Vice, Incont[in]ency in the unmarried people can hardly be call'd a Vice sence neither the state or Individuals are the least injured by it.' Past criticism had undoubtedly gone too far. Were English-women to be judged from visitors to the ships of a naval port, or the commerce of Covent Garden or Drury Lane?[1] He suddenly, after some remarks on the latitude and longitude of Tahiti, breaks into a defence of Green against Maskelyne, forgetting that he himself had had something to say about the confusion of Green's papers; or perhaps, as Maskelyne had supposed 'a want of care and address in the observers'—a plural word—he took it that he himself was impli-cated.[2] But the important thing, immediately, were not interpola-tion or argument, it was the voyage.

He had modified his plan again. He had intended, when he left New Zealand, to return to it from Tahiti 'by the Shortest rout'. Now, leaving Raiatea, he steered a western course inclining to the south, not as the shortest route, but 'as well to avoid the tracks of former Navigators as to get into the Latitude of Amsterdam Island dis-covered by Tasman in 1643, my intention being to run as far west

---

[1] *Journals* II, 236, 238–9. Cook must undoubtedly have read Wales's journal, at an early stage; compare Cook, 238–9, and notes 1 and 2 on 239, with Wales, 796–7.
[2] ibid., 237–8.

as that Island and even to touch there if I found it convenient before I proceeded to the South.'[1] Thus, almost casually stated, we have the beginning of the programme of verification and co-ordination of earlier discoveries which was one of the great, and unexpected, works of this voyage. We begin to be treated to the curious sight of a sort of collaboration between Cook and Dalrymple—as Cook studies the *Historical Collection of Voyages* carried in the ship, and gives precision, and even reality, as it were, to island groups that were almost shadows from the past. So he pursued his chosen course through the rest of September, in generally good weather—generally shortening sail and bringing to at night. A week after his departure, the island plantains and bananas were exhausted; the people were on to 'Sea Bisket' again, but pork was still plentiful enough to give every man his fill. A day out peaked Maupiti, one of the most westerly of the Society Islands, was sighted; then nothing more than birds and sharks till 23 September and the atoll to which Cook gave successively the names of Sandwich, his Noble Patron, and, changing his mind, his friend the dashing Captain Augustus John Hervey—still called the Hervey islands, in the Lower Cook group. It lay much in the position that Dalrymple gave to Quiros's La Dezena, but Cook could not believe in Dalrymple's route for Quiros, and he was right.[2] On the first day of October he recognised Tasman's Middelburg, lying west-south-west, and next day, as he turned the southern point of this island, Amsterdam—or, as we should say, 'Eua and Tongatapu of the group called Tonga. He was to sail a good deal in and out of this group, coming in to it, as he did this time, always from the east.

The Tongan islands are like a narrow net flung irregularly over the ocean, 175 miles from north to south, falling more thickly in some places than in others, in places torn, so that we get a number of clusters or sub-groups—Tongatapu—'Eua in the south, Nomuka and Kotu as one moves north, then Ha'apai, then Vava'u; while beyond these limits, both north and south, are detached fragments that by settlement or nearest contiguity must be reckoned parts of the same system. The greater number of the more than hundred islands and islets, ranging from quite considerable pieces of land to specks almost awash, are coralline—Tongatapu itself is a raised atoll—and lie on the eastern side of the group; the waters that flow between them have a frightening floor of shoal and reef. To the west

---

[1] ibid., 239.

[2] Quiros's La Dezena or La Decena was most probably the Tuamotuan atoll of Tauere, lat. 17°23′ S, long. 141°30′ W, already seen by Cook, and a considerable distance from the Hervey Islands.—H. E. Maude, *Of Islands and Men* (Melbourne, 1968), 70.

of a ship's track northward through the whole group is a shorter volcanic line, the units of which are very scattered. In the eastern clusters only 'Eua, Tongatapu and Vava'u are of any height, but even the lowest and smallest bit of land is green with the vegetation of the islands, from the common beach hibiscus with its yellow blossom—one of the simplest and loveliest of flowers—to the tall close congregations of coconuts. On the windward side of these clusters the impeded ocean explodes infinitely in a long ribbon of white; it has worn away and undercut the low ledges of coral, the *liku*, which mark the raised island—low ledges, except the great cliffs of 'Eua, looking down on the thick leafy covering of a narrow strip of flat land, and beyond that to the vast surface of the sea, the plunging miles of the Tonga Deep. The defect of the islands for explorers, as Tasman found before Cook, is the scarcity of fresh water. Rain seeps away through the coral formation and the sea seeps in; ponds and wells are few and brackish, it is a brackish fluid that comes with digging. There is a little stream among the hills of 'Eua, which makes that island enviable; there is no other. For the islanders this mattered less; they drank from the coconut. In one respect, therefore, these islands were not profitable places of call— though it must be remembered that to seafarers sweetness of water could be a relative thing: in other respects they were highly profit- able, because they were well cultivated, fresh food abounded, and the people were friendly. Tasman had roughly indicated on his chart the main groups from south to centre; Schouten and Le Maire, a hundred and fifty years after them Wallis, had touched on or noted one or two of the most northerly outliers, without suspecting any larger archipelago beyond. Cook now began his exercise in con- nection and accuracy.

This first visit was confined to 'Eua and Tongatapu, the native names of which he was not long in finding out. Sailing up the western coast of 'Eua, inside an off-lying islet called Kalau, he anchored before a small opening in the rocks which led to the shore—the only anchorage the island provided on this side, as it turned out—in a place which he called English Road. Here the land rose immediately from the beach in a gentle grassy slope. The ships were surrounded by canoes; islanders, quite unarmed, eagerly clambered aboard, with tapa cloth to exchange for nails. A chief appeared, 'Tioonee', who took the two captains ashore with a party of others, through a crowd so thick they could hardly land, up the slope to his house. The situation was delightful, the people amiable, a performance on the ships' bagpipes was returned by a song from the young women;

there was kava to drink, fruit to eat, neatly fenced plantations to examine. In the afternoon the visit was repeated, the gentlemen walked out into the country botanising and admiring, enchanted by the perfumed airs and continued friendliness. Cook had his eye on the hogs and poultry he saw running about; but it soon became clear that these people had no interest in that sort of trade, and he decided to cross over to Tongatapu. He did so the next day, Sunday, 3 October, round the southern coast of the island and its western end, anchoring securely not far outside its north-west point, in what he took to be the Van Diemen's Road of Tasman. Even on the passage between one island and the other he had been met by canoes, and now great numbers of both men and women swam off to the ships in addition to the canoe-borne throngs. They brought cloth and 'curiosities' neither of which Cook wanted, though the seamen would barter away their clothes for them; he therefore issued stringent orders against the purchase of such things, with the result that provisions began to arrive in exchange for nails and pieces of English cloth. Inside the reef and the breakers, there was a good landing place; Cook was guided there in the morning by a young and useful man, one 'Otago' or Ataongo, a chiefly person whom we know to have been closely related to some of the island's ruling dignitaries. Cook could tell that this man had influence; it took much enquiry and repeated visits even to begin to get a preliminary idea of the complicated hierarchy of Tongan authority and respect. In the meanwhile it was enough to meet Ataongo half-way in his desire to be on good terms, so that Cook willingly exchanged names with him, willingly fell in with all his suggestions as a cicerone. The captain let himself be inspected as fully as he wished to inspect, viewed whatever he was shown with a certainly quite unforced attention—for the Tongan *fa'itoka*, or chiefly burial mount, was something quite new to him, he was glad to lay there his own offering of medals and nails, and to listen to what seemed to be the invocation of priests; was glad to meet and mark great men and to perambulate the 'delightfull Walks' of Tongatapu: 'I thought I was transported into one of the most fertile plains of Europe. . . . Nature, assisted by a little art, no where appears in a more florishing state than at this isle.'[1] Everybody—botanists, sportsmen out shooting, Hodges out drawing—was civilly treated; trade in bananas, coconuts, yams, pigs, fowls, was brisk. By the end of the following day so much had been obtained that Cook gave permission to his men to buy whatever they liked, whereon the foolish fellows sought curiosities with such

[1] *Journals* II, 252.

eagerness that humorous Tongans proceeded to offer them sticks and stones.

Cook stayed here four days, till the afternoon of 7 October. It could not be all paradise, the people could not all be irreproachably civil and cheerful. The chief to whom the greatest reverence was paid—he must certainly be the king, Cook thought wrongly—seemed a very dull stupid person indeed, though he did reciprocate gifts with generosity.[1] Wales, who considered the women of 'Eua to be 'the most lively laughing creatures I ever saw'—was charmed indeed with both sexes—at Tongatapu, when he first waded ashore, had his shoes snatched from behind him by another lively person, finding himself in a position 'ludicrous enough', with a thief to chase bare-footed over sharp coral rocks. Luckily he saw the captain with Ataongo, who reclaimed the shoes, and was rewarded with a large nail. That was trivial; Wales could laugh, and Cook could laugh at him. There were less trivial things, as when a boat's grapnel was spirited away, and next day an attempt was made to denude her of everything, oars and all; or when a man sprang out of the master's cabin of the *Resolution* with an armful of navigational books, as well as the master's sword and other sundries; at the landing place, said Wales, they 'several times attempted to take the Cloaths of our Back.' There was a little rough treatment in return, a few discharges of small shot—which, surprisingly enough, alarmed no one. Outside the ships, such things happened only at the landing place; in the country everyone, even if alone and unarmed, was perfectly safe. It was perhaps as well not to risk outwearing a welcome. The possibility did not, however, arise; Cook had his programme of work to keep up with.

The dozen or so pages of his journal which he devotes to the description of these two islands, after a stay of less than a week, summarise excellently what could be learnt by an assiduous observer in that time, and they seem to be founded almost entirely on his own observation. He is precise in latitude—between 21°29′ and 21°3′ S—and longitude, between 174°40′ and 175°15′ W, 'deduced from Observations of the Sun and Moon made on the spot. Mr Kendals Watch places them 34′ more westerly.' Others speak in admiration of visible aspects, the Forsters can in some ways be more professional as well

---

[1] His name was Latunipulu; he was a male *tamaha*, or 'sacred child'. The Tongan chiefly system was very complicated. The titular ruler was the *Tu'i Tonga* (Tu'i, a king or governor). His eldest daughter by his principal wife was the *Tu'i Tonga fefine*, the female Tu'i Tonga. She was so sacred that no Tongan could marry her, and her traditional mate was the Fijian chief the Tu'i Lakeba. Their first born was the *tamaha*, sacred child. Dullness did not make him any less sacred or reverenced.

as more personal, but Cook himself gives us an account which is objective, full and running over. He is once more taking literally those instructions to report. Everybody is agreed about the beauty, whether of the unevenly rising 'Eua or the uniformly flat Tongatapu. 'Eua, to Wales, 'affords, without exception, the most beautiful & varigated Prospect I ever beheld.' For Kempe it is 'the most delightfull prospect that can be seen, & which I shall leave to a more able pen to discribe what is due to that pleasing spott.' For Gilbert it seems 'one intire Garden'—an English country house's park and garden, perhaps; for, as Cook, more discriminating, points out, the interior parts were not cultivated, there was 'a beautiful disorder', in contrast to the wholly cultivated aspect of Tongatapu, where the plantations, with their houses and sweet-smelling shrubs, seemed to him extremely beautiful. Is there, after all his experience of wild and craggy lands, a lingering trace of the farm boy in Cook? The people are neither ugly nor handsome; the men are tattooed from the mid-thighs to the hips, the women only slightly on the arms and hands; both sexes are naked above the waist, wearing a sort of skirt of tapa that falls below the knees; some colour their hair red or blue, they dye their cloth; they wear handsome bracelets and necklaces of shell, and rather despise the English beads. Their teeth are perfect. Very many have lost a joint or two of the little fingers, which, after much shipboard discussion, is taken to be a sign of mourning. Many have had their checks burnt or otherwise wounded.[1] But they are a healthy race, and Cook has done his best to leave them so. 'As we had yet some Venereal complaints on board I took all possible means to prevent its being communicated to the Natives by not suffering a Man to go on shore on whom there was the least suspicion nor did I permit that any women should be allowed to come on board the Sloops.'[2] They drink much a beverage made of the 'pepper root' or *ava*, and their legs are sometimes unsteady as a result. Only Cook among the visitors would drink it, the others being put off by the preliminary chewing and spitting out of the root before its mixture with water. They have no towns or villages, living dispersed in their plantations. They have nose-flutes more elaborate than those of Tahiti, drums of hollowed logs of wood.

[1] The partial amputation of the little finger was not a sign of mourning but a propitiatory sacrifice to some god to secure the recovery from sickness of a relative superior in rank to the person concerned. The wounding of the cheeks was however done as mourning: they could be burnt, but might be beaten continually (hence the name for the mourning ceremony, *tuki*, a blow) or rubbed with coconut husk or some other harsh substance.

[2] *Journals* II, 268. According to Bayly, women could not be kept off the ship at 'Eua but the rest of the prohibition was put into effect.

Their large double canoes are extremely well made—Cook describes them with an attentive sailor's eye—accurately put together and sewn, so as not to need caulking, with platforms and little huts on top, and a sort of lateen sail; they are doubled-ended, so that they will sail easily either way. These people are not interested in edge-tools, but have an insatiable appetite for nails, of which they must have taken three or four hundredweight. Cook has added to the island fauna—birds, bats, pigs, fowls—a New Zealand dog and a Society Islands bitch, which the Tongans were exceedingly anxious to acquire. There is certainly property in land. For religion—here Cook, as in Tahiti, finds the matter dark. How otherwise, when language stood between? What was the language? Omai and Odiddy, who should have been of help, would have none of it, they could not understand a single sentence. They were not really very intelligent young men. Cook sighed for Tupaia. He himself, however, and others who knew a few Tahitian words, could both understand essentials and make themselves understood. They were faced with a 'Provincial dialect'. Consider, too, the vocabulary given in Dalrymple's *Collection*. Cook was back with a question he had asked himself when he had first met the Tahitians and New Zealanders. He could add other men's experience to his own, to reach the same answer as before: 'By carefully perusing the Voyages of former Navigators, I find such an affinity in the Language, Manners, and Customs of the different Islanders that I am led to believe they have all had one Origin.'[1]

With these things in his mind he made sail from Van Diemen's Road late on 8 October, bound for New Zealand. He lost an anchor in unmooring when the cable parted, and another cable was much damaged by the coral bottom. Just before he began to move, a canoe came alongside with a Tongan drum, for which he gave a piece of cloth and a nail, sending back also some wheat and vegetable seeds to Ataongo, additional to what he had already given him. Next day he had in sight the high island of 'Ata, Tasman's Pylstaert or Arrow-tail;[2] then for almost a fortnight there was open sea, the weather mainly pleasant, the winds easterly and south-easterly, going round to the north and west from the 17th. These latter winds kept the *Adventure* too far astern, and Cook had to shorten sail for her. On the

[1] *Journals* II, 275.
[2] Cook referred to the island as 'Pilstart'. Tasman called it 'hooge pijlsteerten eijlandt' —High Arrow-tail Tropic-bird Island. *Pÿlstaart* means 'arrow-tail', a sort of duck; he applied the name to the tropic-birds he saw flying about it, because of the two long feathers in this bird's tail.

night of the 20th a black rain cloud set up an alarm of land directly ahead; the night was so dark that guns were fired and false fires burnt to keep the ships in touch. Next morning New Zealand was in sight in the west, about Table Cape. Cook stretched in for the land. He wanted to give domestic animals and seeds to the inhabitants as far north as possible, regarding the people here as more civilised than those of Queen Charlotte Sound, and therefore more likely to care properly for such acquisitions. It was not till he was some distance down the coast from Cape Kidnappers, however, that canoes came off with a chief to whom he thought it safe to make presents; and what sent the chief into raptures was not pigs and fowls but a spike nail half the length of his arm. Nevertheless when he got his boars and sows, cocks and hens he eyed them jealously, promising not to kill any; he accepted also a large variety of vegetable seeds. Cook was hopeful of having done something to benefit the country; certainly his cabbage stocked the coast from that point south to Palliser Bay.

Not long after the canoes returned to shore the gale started: the afternoon of 22 October. It was one of those long wearing gales, mainly from the north and west, sometimes with a deceptive lull, sometimes with the wind switching round briefly to the opposite direction and then remorselessly back again, which can make so exacerbating the New Zealand spring, particularly in the region of Cook Strait. It began by carrying away the *Resolution*'s fore topgallant mast. Sails were split and torn; topsails were reefed and close-reefed, the gale abated, reefs were shaken out, the gale burst anew with heavy squalls, the men flew to the yards. To get into the strait was impossible. On the 25th, an hour before noon, says Cook, the storm 'came on in such fury as to oblige us to take in all our sails with the utmost expedition and to lay-to under our bare poles with our heads to the SW. . . . The Sea rose in proportion with the Wind so that we not only had a furious gale but a mountainous Sea also to incounter'; at least the sky stayed clear overhead, and they were not apprehensive of a lee shore. At this time they were eight or nine leagues SSE of Cape Palliser. The *Adventure* was carried to leeward but found again. Day after day the ships beat up and down or lay to; in the dark early morning of 30 October they parted company a second time, and finally. On the 31st the *Resolution* was off the Kaikoura mountains, in the South Island; in the morning the wind blew with great fury, in the evening 'with greater fury than ever, in so much that we were obleged to lie to under the Mizen Staysail.' At midnight it abated, a calm was succeeded by a wind from the south; on the afternoon of the first day of November the ship was under all the sail she could set, had passed Cape Campbell, was in the strait, would be in Queen Charlotte Sound the next flood tide: and the north-west gale rose yet again. Cook spent the night plying, losing ground continually. He was off Cloudy Bay. In the morning he could at least stretch over across the strait to the coast of 'Haeinomauwe'—the North Island; where, to the east of Cape Terawhiti, he discovered an inlet which looked as if it might be a good harbour. There was a large bay outside its entrance. Thoroughly tired of beating against the north-westerlies, he resolved to put into the inlet, or at least to anchor in the bay. Just as he reached the entrance the tide turned against him and he anchored a mile off a range of black rocks. Three canoes came out to the ship, a few of their not very attractive occupants came on board, accepting nails with enthusiasm, medals, cocks and hens with indifference. If Cook had had the *Adventure* with him, he would have investigated further. He was certain she must be already waiting in Queen Charlotte Sound, and that he should rejoin her as soon as possible; so, the wind shifting to the north-east, he weighed anchor again. It went round to the south, a fresh and increasing gale, in which he bore away for the Sound, leaving behind him unexplored the inlet, the superb harbour about which the capital city of Wellington now stands. As he tacked outside the Sound at dark the gale split most of his sails, and he anchored. In the morning there was a calm, then a breeze at north-west. He ran up to Ship Cove, moored, and unbent all his sails for repair. It was 3 November. There was no *Adventure*.

XV

The Antarctic Again

No TIME was lost in getting to work on the ship, cleaning her inside and out, repairing sails and ironwork, overhauling the spars and rigging, caulking, replenishing wood and water and fishing, examining the bread or ship's biscuit. A vast amount of this commodity, unappetising at the best of times, was rotten and had to be destroyed; another large quantity, not so far gone, was rebaked. Cook put the misfortune down to unseasoned timber in the casks, later to dampness in the hold caused by the storage of ice, followed by the heat of the island latitudes, which seems more likely. All the remaining coals were shifted and new ballast taken on board. The native people supplied plenty of fish, but here their utility ended: they stole anything they could lay hands on, one old chief while he was furiously berating his people for their sins even calmly picking Cook's pocket of his handkerchief, which the captain as calmly reclaimed. Clothes were stolen from the tents, but as Cook got most of these back he was not sorry, thinking his men needed the lesson in taking care of their belongings. There was some coming and going: at one time about a hundred and fifty canoes were about the place, though little trouble was suffered other than that caused by light fingers. The great trade, apart from fish, was now in greenstone or *pounamu*. Cook thought little of it. His men would give almost anything for a piece. We should like to see what they got. From what he could learn about the fate of the animals that had been left behind on the last visit, he was beginning to despair of any good result: goats and fowls had been killed and eaten; one sow was seen, lame, the other and the boar had been separated and taken to different parts of the country; the vegetable gardens, untended, had nevertheless done better. He did not quite give up hope, leaving another boar with three sows, and some cocks and hens, in a secluded part of the sound. If he could not, in the end, be effectively generous, he would show the example at least of justice: when the natives themselves complained about the stolen property and pointed to the man they held guilty, he got a dozen lashes. In recounting the episode Cook goes on to state explicitly some of his own principles in relation to savage races, which extend a little the thoughts he had had in Tahiti on pushing demands too far.

It has ever been a maxim with me to punish the least crimes any of my people have commited against these uncivilized Nations, their robing us with impunity is by no means a sufficient reason why we should treat them in the same manner, a conduct we see they themselves cannot justify, they found themselves injured and sought for redress in a legal way. The best method in my opinion to preserve a good understanding with such people is first to shew them the use of fire arms and to convince them of the Superiority they give you over them and to be always upon your guard; when once they are sencible of these things, a regard for their own safety will deter them from disturbing you or being unanimous in forming any plan to attack you, and Strict honisty and gentle treatment on your part will make it their intrest not to do it.[1]

Is this simply repetition of the advice given him by Lord Morton five years before, at the outset of his exploring career? Not quite; for the good Lord Morton's rather abstract statement of benevolence has put on the flesh of experience, and the first two or three lines of Cook's paragraph have something more intensive about them— sealed as they are with action—than the general exhortation 'to check the petulance of the Sailors'.

These 'uncivilised Nations': but what was civilisation? Cook was to be brought up against the question, without entirely solving it, before he left Queen Charlotte Sound. There had been rumours of a war expedition to Admiralty Bay, lately picked human bones had been found, when on 23 November, with Cook anxious to get to sea but prevented by the wind, some of the officers went on shore to amuse themselves and were confronted by the remainders of a cannibal feast. The broken head and the bowels of the victim were lying on the ground, his heart was stuck on a forked stick fixed to the head of a canoe. Pickersgill gave two nails for the head and took it on board, to the interest of a number of New Zealanders on board who had not participated in the banquet. Would one of them like a piece? asked Clerke, 'to which he very chearfully gave his assent'; Clerke cut a slice and broiled it in the galley, and the man devoured it ravenously. At that moment Cook, who had been absent, came on board with Wales, Forster and the young islander Odiddy, to find the quarter-deck crowded and excitement general. Revolted as he was, the spirit of science triumphed, he must be able to bear

1 *Journals* II, 292.

witness from his own eyes to a fact which many people had doubted on the first voyage reports; Clerke broiled another piece, it was similarly consumed before the whole ship's company. Some were sick; Odiddy, first motionless with horror, burst into tears and abused Clerke as well as the New Zealanders, up till then his friends; Wales and Cook thought it over. These people were cannibals because they liked to be cannibals, concluded Wales—from choice, not need: they had other animal food, dogs, birds, fish; were not merely carried away by frenzy, would run all the risks of war to obtain their end, were not particular even whether they ate enemy or friend. Cook went deeper in his attempt to understand; for the first time, in his little disquisitions on the people he met, we have the original, the mature Cook. He is far from the fantasy he had picked up, perhaps from Banks, of the innocent, care-free children of nature, so happy in their ignorance of all sophisticated wants.

. . . few considers what a savage man is in his original state and even after he is in some degree civilized; the New Zealanders are certainly in a state of civilization, their behavour to us has been Manly and Mild, shewing allways a readiness to oblige us; they have some arts a mong them which they execute with great judgement and unweared patience; they are far less addicted to thieving than the other Islanders and are I believe strictly honist among them-selves. This custom of eating their enimies slain in battle (for I firmly believe they eat the flesh of no others) has undoubtedly been handed down to them from the earliest times and we know that it is not an easy matter to break a nation of its ancient customs let them be ever so inhuman and savage, especially if that nation is void of all religious principles as I believe the new zealanders in general are and like them without any settled form of goverment; as they become more united they will of conccquence have fewer Enemies and become more civilized and then and not till then this custom may be forgot, at present they seem to have but little idea of treating other men as they themselves would wish to be treated, but treat them as they think they should be treated under the same circumstances.[1]

They had argued the point immovably with Tupaia, whom they respected; they merely laughed at the stripling Odiddy. It may be suggested that Cook, like Wales, wrote with inadequate knowledge of those he contemplated; but there is perceptiveness in this, of an unusual kind. Is not the tone, quite clearly, the tone of a new fashion of thought about man?

Meanwhile there was another, quite different, thing to think about—the *Adventure*. Cook tried every way of accounting for her

[1] ibid., 294.

continued absence, without finding a likely one. Halfway through his stay he had fancied she might be still in the Strait, and climbed a hill above East Bay (where in 1770 he raised the cairn, now gone) to look; even then he had despaired of seeing her again. He had no fear for her safety; the best conjecture he could make was that Furneaux, driven to leeward, tired of beating against the north-westerlies, had decided to run for the Cape of Good Hope. Yet he might still come. Cook (it was now 24 November) therefore put a message in a bottle, buried it at the foot of a large tree at the watering place, and carved on the trunk the words LOOK UNDER-NEATH. It was his intention, said the message, to spend a few days at the entrance of the Strait looking for his consort, after which he would proceed to the south and eastward. 'As Captain Cook has not the least hopes of meeting with Captain Furneaux he will not take upon him to name any place for a Rendezvous; he however thinks of retiring to Easter Island in Lat^d 27°6′ S Longitude 108°0′ West a Greenwich in about the latter end of next march, it is even probable that he may go to Otaheite or one of the society Isles but this will depend so much upon circumstances that nothing with any degree of certainty can be depended upon.'[1] Next day the *Resolution*, herself and her crew thoroughly fit for sea again, was under sail and outside the Sound.

She hauled over for Cape Terawhiti and ran along the North Island shore from point to point towards Cape Palliser, looking into the bays and firing half-hour guns. She brought to for the night half-way across Palliser Bay; rounded the cape in the morning still firing guns, and a few leagues to the north-east got a breeze from that quarter, which determined Cook to bear away for Cape Campbell, on the other side of the strait; a smoke inland then kept him plying till the end of the day, though it improbably had to do with the *Adventure*; and then, all his officers being unanimous that she could neither be stranded on the New Zealand coast nor spending time in a New Zealand port, resolved to make directly southward. Not a man was dejected, thought the captain, at the prospect of exploring that part of the Pacific Ocean without a consort; as for the captain, it is possible that after his experience of his consort, he preferred to be alone. He took his departure from Cape Palliser on the evening of 26 November, sailing rather to the east of south than directly south. The weather was variable, with a good deal of haze and fog

[1] The text of this message, which is called a memorandum, is from Furneaux's journal, Adm 55/1; printed *Journals* II, 297, n. 2.

and rain—the only regular phenomenon, indeed, being the great south-west swell witnessing against a continent in the direction whence it came. The only land that could lie south of New Zealand, concluded Cook, must lie far beyond the latitude of 60°: a valid conclusion, for apart from inconsiderable islands, it lay half a degree south of 70°. There were a few seals, penguins, albatrosses and petrels. On 7 December 'at half past 8 pm', the ship was directly opposite to London; toasts were drunk, Wales rejoiced in one piece of certainty: 'The good People of that City may *now* rest perfectly satisfied that they have no Antipodes besides Penguins and Peteralls, unless Seals can be admitted as such; for Fishes are absolutely out of the question.'[1]

As the latitude increased so did the gales. The early morning of 12 December brought the first iceberg, in latitude 62°10', which was $11\frac{1}{2}°$ farther south than the first ice seen after leaving the Cape of Good Hope. The longitude was something over 170° W. Cook illustrates the strategy of his seamanship with his journal-entry for 13 December: 'We stood to the SE with the Wind at SW and as the wind backed to the West we hauled more and more to the South, keeping the wind allways upon the beam till 9 am, when the wind veered to the North and being thick weather we hauled the wind to the Eastward under double reef'd Top-sails and Courses. By sailing with the Wind on the Beam we had it in our power to return back over that space of Sea we had in some measure made our selves acquainted with, in case we had met with any danger.'[2] Danger is a relative term. One would think that as the ship pushed steadily south—146 miles on 12 December, then on successive days 92 miles, 136 miles, 116 miles—it could hardly be avoided. On the 15th she was in a large field of loose ice, the summer break-up of the pack, with some leads and clear water beyond; the bergs were enlarging their number, there was a thick fog accompanied by snow and a strong wind. Cook thought it prudent to alter his course more to the east, then to the north-east, when he found himself embayed in the ice; forced back south-west to latitude 66°, he had the wind veer to the west and could stretch northward for a degree or two. Freedom from the loose ice did not mean freedom from the bergs: to turn from one of these was to run towards another, like the fearful mass which the ship barely weathered by her own length; 'had we not succeeded this circumstance could never have been related', says Cook with great moderation. The officer of the watch had been imprudent, relates Elliott in more detail, and when at last he called

[1] *Journals* II, 302, n. 1. [2] ibid., 303.

up all hands from dinner, horror sat on the captain's face no less than on others. Cook ordered the men to get light spars in readiness to fend the ship off—perhaps merely to give them something to do. She went clear with her stern 'just trailing within the Breakers from the Island', it was 'the most *Miraculous* escape from being every soul lost, that ever men had'.[1] A miss was as good as a mile, reflected Cook calmly, 'but our situation requires more misses than we can expect.' Land to the south seemed improbable; if any were found the ice would forbid its exploration. This 'feild or loose ice', was quite different from any he had encountered before—'not such as is usually formed in Bays or Rivers' (the old theories cling hard), 'but like such as is broken off from large Islands, round ill-shaped pieces from the size of a small Ship's Hull downwards'; it was often impossible to avoid running against large pieces, and no ship except one properly strengthened could long withstand such shocks. So did he summarise his reasons for hauling to the north. He made over a hundred miles in dark and gloomy weather, the sails and rigging encased in ice, before he brought to and hoisted out boats to take in ice for water; then he turned east and south-east again.

In such weather and conditions, sometimes worse, with rare clear intervals, he made his southing and slipped by the icebergs once more. On 20 December in the evening he crossed the Antarctic Circle for the second time—longitude about 148° W—and on the 22nd was in latitude 67°27'. He was now in a region of northerly winds, well south of the region where the westerlies prevailed, but made good easting for those days. On 23 December, his position being about latitude 67°19', longitude 138°15' W, he was again on the edge of the pack, a large field of thick close floes stretching from south to east over the whole sea; seizing the chance to take up some large pieces for water, he tried a westerly course a short while. At the same time he was taking careful note of new petrels seen about the ice. The conditions were as bad as they could be: ropes like wires, sails like boards or metal plates, sheaves frozen fast in the blocks 'so that it required our utmost effort to get a Top-sail down and up; the cold so intense as hardly to be endured, the whole Sea in a manner covered with ice, a hard gale and a thick fog . . . '. He must make north—well north, not merely because of the unwisdom of pushing farther east, but because of the unexplored space of twenty four degrees of latitude between his present position and his course eastwards from Cook Strait in the winter of 1773. He turned north-east therefore, on 24 December, and when just past the Ant-

[1] *Journals* II, 304, n. 5.

arctic Circle, between longitudes 135° and 134° W, more directly north. It was Christmas Day: fortunately, as in the preceding year, one of gentle wind turning to calm, clear all through the long daylight, as the ship drifted in the midst of a hundred icebergs like 'the wrecks of a shattered world'—to use George Forster's vivid words—and British drunkenness and British ribaldry made the cold scene as Christianlike as possible. There was none the less vigilance. Invitations had gone out to dinner for officers and petty officers; seamen and marines vowed that they would die happy on any ice island then attendant, as long as some rescued keg of brandy was in their arms. The next day upwards of two hundred and fifty of 'these divilish Ice Isles'—the phrase is now Clerke's—were counted, many of them standing more than two hundred feet out of the water.

The last day of the year provided some clear pleasant weather in which Cook aired his spare sails and 'cleaned and smoked' between decks. Then once more the snow and piercing cold: the northerlies had ceased to blow except very briefly. There could be no land in the north-west, Cook gave his opinion, 2 January 1774, because a swell still came from that quarter, even in the absence of a corresponding wind. He was then in latitude 57°58', some 560 miles north of his position on 24 December, his farthest point south, and about two degrees of longitude farther east. It was on 2 January that Cook at last lost patience in a matter of discipline and—a most unusual step—flogged a midshipman. This was one of the wild set, the unstable exasperating Loggie, who had already been sent before the mast and now, apparently in a drunken riot, had drawn his knife and cut two of the other young gentlemen. Cook excluded the story from his journal, as he excluded from that public document most other matters of a disciplinary sort. He does not exhibit the fury he had felt, once, over Mr Orton's ears; but we can go behind Cook.[1] It was anyhow a secondary matter, it was not geography or navigation. The wind went round to the west for two weeks successively. Cook, who had been trying to make some westing on his northern course, gave up and steered north-east. From day to day, studying the sea birds, he considered the chances of land. Albatrosses and most petrels were no indication, but the small diving petrels were supposed to be pointers—he saw a few, but not enough to be persuasive. The swell was more persuasive in the contrary sense. He would have to leave unexplored a space of sea 40° of longitude wide, 20° or 21° north to south: 'had the wind been favourable I intended

[1] ibid., 313, n. 1. Clerke and Elliott give us the fullest accounts.

to have run 15° or 20° of longitude to the west in the Latitude we are now in'—54'55'—'and back again to the East in the Latitude of 50° or near it, this rout would have so intersected the space above mentioned as to have hardly left room for the bare supposission of any large land lying there'.[1] He kept on his north-east course, logging good distances daily—161 miles for 9 January; noting the clear days, when by observation of the sun and moon the longitude could be determined 'beyond a doubt'. On this subject an interesting note is struck. 'Indeed our error can never be great so long as we have so good a guide as Mr Kendalls watch.'[2] On 11 January he was in west longitude 122°12' by 'reckoning', 122°17'30" by the watch—that is, over two-thirds of the distance from New Zealand to South America —latitude 47°51'. He changed course again. 'At Noon being little more than two hundred Leagues from my track to Otaheite in 1769 in which space it was not probable any thing was to be found, we therefore hauled up SE with a fresh gale at SWBW.'[3]

There was, we learn from Elliott, for a moment a 'buz' in the ship, and 'a very severe mortification'; for the simple sailors had taken it into their heads that they were sailing east for Cape Horn on their way home, and all their hopes were blasted in a minute. They should by that time have known their captain better. They thought he was a close and secret man, but they should not have thought the secret was so easily expounded. Nor had they the faintest idea what the message was for Furneaux in the bottle. Mr Forster, who was rather astonished that the captain had not consulted him more, was now dejected—and even more so when in a few days strong gales became 'excessive hard gales' (even Cook said that), the north-west sea ran 'prodigeous high', and he in his cabin was deluged with water. In addition, diet was no longer fresh. The men were back on salt beef and the decaying biscuit re-baked at Ship Cove, and only on a two-thirds allowance of that, so anxious was Cook to conserve. On the pleading of their spokesman, the master's mate, he at least restored the whole ration. He continued to plunge south, except for a few days of easting in southerly winds, with some dark weather, snow and sleet, though as the month advanced into its last week the weather was unusually mild, and there was a remarkable paucity of ice. There were few birds, a few whales. On 26 January he crossed the Antarctic Circle for the third time, in longitude 109°31' W, soon after which land appeared and transformed itself, as usual, into clouds or a fog-bank. Fog came down thicker. On the 28th loose ice was encountered, and some was taken up for water; the fog turned

[1] *Journals* II, 313–14.   [2] ibid., 315.   [3] ibid.

so thick that Cook made sail for a time to the north-west, not daring to stand south when he could not see the extent of the ice about him. Next morning the sky and the sea were clear again, except for some large bergs; to general surprise the weather could be called pleasant, and for a day it was not cold. In latitude 70°00′ the ship was still making south. A berg not less than three miles in circuit, with others visible ahead till thick fog hid them, made it advisable to tack to the north for the hour and a half the fog lasted, after which the SSE course was resumed. Then, on 30 January, the sea closed. Cook himself must here speak.

A little after 4 AM we precieved the Clowds to the South near the horizon to be of an unusual Snow white brightness which denounced our approach to field ice, soon after it was seen from the Mast-head and at 8 o'Clock we were close to the edge of it which extended East and West in a streight line far beyond our sight; as appear'd by the brightness of the horizon; in the Situation we were now in just the Southern half of the horizon was enlightned by the Reflected rays of the Ice to a considerable height. The Clowds near the horizon were of a perfect Snow whiteness and were difficult to be distinguished from the Ice hills whose lofty summits reached the Clowds. The outer or Northern edge of this immence Ice field was composed of loose or broken ice so close packed together that nothing could enter it; about a Mile in began the firm ice, in one compact solid boddy and seemed to increase in height as you traced it to the South; In this field we counted Ninety Seven Ice Hills or Mountains, many of them vastly large. . . . I will not say it was impossible anywhere to get in among this Ice, but I will assert that the bare attempting of it would be a very dangerous enterprise and what I believe no man in my situation would have thought of. I whose ambition leads me not only farther than any other man has been before me, but as far as I think it possible for man to go, was not sorry at meeting with this interruption, as it in some measure relieved us from the dangers and hardships, inseparable with the Navigation of the Southern Polar regions. Sence therefore we could not proceed one Inch farther South, no other reason need be assigned for our Tacking and stretching back to the North, being at that time in the Latitude of 71°10′ South, Longitude 106°54′ W.[1]

[1] ibid., 321–2. There were two claimants later on for the distinction of having been farther south than anyone else. Vancouver was one. 'Captain Vancouver used to say, that he had been nearer the South Pole than any other Man for when the immortal Cook in latitude 72, was stopped in his progress by impenetrable mountains of ice, and was prepared to tack about, he went to the very end of the bowsprit, and waving his hat, exclaimed *Ne Plus Ultra!*'—*The Naval Chronicle*, I (1799), 125. The other was Sparrman: 'In order to avoid the bustle and crowd on the deck, usual in such operations, I went below to my cabin to watch more quietly through the scuttle the boundless expanses of Polar ice. Thus it happened, as my companions observed, that I went a trifle farther south than any of the others in the ship, because a ship, when going about, always has a little stern way before she can make way on the fresh tack when the sails fill.'—*Voyage round the World*, 112.

Soon after he had tacked, standing north by east, a heavy fog descended, snow fell, the air was piercing cold; before long the rigging was coated with ice almost an inch thick.

When Cook revised his journal he added a little to the passage he had thus written. It was his opinion, it was the general opinion, 'that this Ice extended quite to the Pole or perhaps joins to some land, to which it had been fixed from the creation;' and that it was in this enormous southern area that all the ice 'scatered up and down to the North' was formed, to be broken off and floated on the north-bound currents; if land was near, penguins, whose sad croaking Cook heard where none was seen, could have no better retreat there than they had on the ice—indeed, land must be covered with ice. In all this was a great deal of sense: he was at the margin of a permanent ice-belt. He had still something to learn about the origin of sea ice and of 'ice islands', and we might now prefer to talk in terms of vague millions of years rather than of the creation. If the ice did indeed join to some land, it was impossible to say, or even to guess, where the join took place. He had sailed much farther south than was needed to discover the Antarctic continent, if only he had been forty or fifty degrees of longitude farther east: when Edward Brans-field and William Smith first set eyes on the northern extremity of the Graham Land peninsula in 1819, it was in latitude 64° and longitude 60° W. As for ambition—'farther than any other man has been before me . . . as far as I think it possible for man to go'—he had realised it: no ship in or near that longitude would ever sail so far south again. Almost fifty years later James Weddell was to sail farther south, to 75°, in the sea named after him, a sea where the ice edge strangely retreated or advanced; almost twenty years after that James Clark Ross's enormously strong *Erebus* and *Terror* were to force their way through the pack to 78°9′30″, in the sea called after Ross; but the one was far to the east, the other far to the west of Cook's position. That position was off the Walgreen Coast of the Amundsen Sea; the nearest land behind the ice was Cape Flying Fish of the Thurston Peninsula, perhaps 140 or 150 miles distant.[1] Over the greater part of this Pacific sector of the Southern Ocean no person has yet penetrated to the continent by sea.

One is of course struck by Cook's words about his ambition,

[1] The nearest later approach to Cook's furthest south was by the 96-ton tender *Flying Fish* of the Wilkes expedition, on 23 March 1839, when her position was 70° S and 100°16′ W.—Wilkes, *Narrative*, I, 154. Almost a hundred years later, the R.R.S. *Discovery II*, a full-powered steamship, specially built for navigation in ice, on 6 January 1931, reached latitude 69°49½′ S in longitude 101°25½′ W, but was then forced to return. Possibly, as this was between three and four weeks earlier in the year than Cook's 30 January, the ice was farther north than he had it.

so different from the modest understatement habitually practised by him. They are significant as well as proud words, they stand as self-revelation with the weary passage he wrote after his second escape from the Great Barrier Reef, on the anguish and pleasures of discovery, and the attitude of 'the world'. This time he has forgotten the world, and it is not a theme that interests him again. But there are other significant words, and the fact that he uses them shows his indifference to the opinion of the world: he 'was not sorry at meeting this interruption' of the pack ice, 'as it in some measure relieved us from the dangers and hardships, inseparable with the Navigation of the Southern Polar Regions'. He almost says he was glad to have an excuse to stop exploring. He could not have correctly argued that on 30 January the summer was over. He could not get further south, true: nevertheless for a week after he turned back he had easterly winds, and with them, conceivably, without turning back he could have pushed westwards, in the direction of the Ross Sea—though it is morally certain he would have found nothing but the pack. A rash man might have done so. Cook, as we have seen, was not a timid man, but he was not rash. He now had enough accumulated experience to found a wise judgment on, whether he could trace every step in judgment with scientific exactitude or not. Faced with the decision which confronts every explorer, when to retreat, he did not hesitate to reckon candidly enough the risks of going on. The planned examination of the Southern Ocean was not over: there was still the western part of its Atlantic sector to investigate. He knew well enough the strains on his crew and his ship. When he says he 'was not sorry' at being interrupted in his course, we may once again give him literal belief. It is possible that he was beginning to realise the strains on himself.

For three weeks the ship made a course north by east, with only a few modifications. Except for a small number of bergs, and floating pieces of ice enough to replenish her water, the sea was clear. The fog vanished, though there was snow and sleet for some days. She crossed the Antarctic Circle again on 3 February, and on the 6th Cook did not think it too soon to formulate a plan of operations for the remainder of the year. In the note he had put into the bottle at Ship Cove he had said he might go to Easter Island, even to Tahiti or the Society Islands; and in his journal, as he wrote of his leaving the New Zealand coast in November, he had remarked that 'if I do not find a Continent or isle between this and Cape Horn in which we can Winter perhaps I may spend the Winter within the Tropicks or else proceed round Cape Horn to Faulkland Islands, such were my thoughts at this time. . . .'[1] He allowed for unforeseeable circumstances. The Falklands would give him a springboard for a South Atlantic cruise, but he does not seem ever to have considered them very seriously. Now he reconsiders the whole prospect. There is no continent to be found to the west of Cape Horn. He thinks it just as improbable that there is one on the other side, in spite of Dalrymple and Bouvet. Nevertheless he must look for it. If he is wrong, before he could reach either Dalrymple's or Bouvet's continent, the exploring season would be over, he would have to winter there, or else retire to the Falklands or the Cape of Good Hope; in either case, six or seven months would be wasted. If he is right, and there is no continent, then he would be at the Cape by April, and the expedition, regarded as a continent-discovering expedition, would be over. But there is still a great deal to do in the Pacific: there is room for very large islands, and many of the islands already discovered are imperfectly explored, their situations imperfectly known. Cook has a good ship 'expressly sent out on discoveries', a healthy crew, no want of stores and provisions; to ignore these facts would betray want of judgment as well as of perseverance. Discoveries might not be 'valuable', none the less they would result in improvement to the sciences, especially Navigation and Geography.

These were not altogether new thoughts with Cook, as we have seen; he had more than once, he tells us, communicated them to Furneaux—perhaps at Queen Charlotte Sound, perhaps at Tahiti—and Furneaux had not been very receptive; whatever the state of the ships or men, he wanted to get to the Cape and, obviously, go home as soon as possible, though 'afterwards he seem'd to come into my opinion'. Cook could not have been highly confident that his second-in-command would remain so placed; now he could be ignored, except for the faint possibility of finding him at Tahiti. The *Resolution* could now embark on this vast parenthesis in the voyage as it was originally planned, without further need of argument or persuasion; it is even possible that Cook, the 'Main Object' of the voyage attained, as he concluded, and Dalrymple's *Historical Collection* open before him, had in his mind an unspoken reason, in addition to those he articulated, for wasting no time dangerously about the ice-edge. So he would now make north in search of the land said to have been discovered by Juan Fernandez in latitude 38° S; if that search was of no avail, he would look for Easter Island 'or Davis's land', which Carteret and Bougainville had failed to find;

[1] *Journals* II, 299.

then, reaching the tropics, proceed west, touching at and settling the positions of any island he might meet with as far as Tahiti, which he must visit to look for the *Adventure*; then, perhaps, if there was time, keep west farther still, to Quiros's Austrialia del Espiritu Santo, which Bougainville had called the Great Cyclades and been very vague about; and then get to the south and steer east to the Horn between the latitudes of 50° and 60°, arriving there in November, so that the best part of the summer could be spent in exploring the South Atlantic Ocean. 'This I must own is a great undertaking,' says the planner, 'and perhaps more than I shall be able to perform as various impediments may . . .'—he breaks off writing, we do not know for what nautical emergency (the weather was deteriorating), and when he resumes it is to redraft. 'Great as this design appeared to be, I however thought it was possible to be done and when I came to communicate it to the officers (who till now thought we were bound directly to the Cape of Good Hope) I had the satisfaction to find that they all heartily concur'd in it.' As for the seamen, 'they were so far from wishing the Voyage at an end that they rejoiced at the Prospect of its being prolonged a nother year and soon enjoying the benefits of a milder Climate.'[1] No one, officer, seaman, or civilian, contradicts this.

The weather over the greater part of those first three weeks of February was not pleasant, but at least when latitude 55° was left behind snow and sleet were exchanged for mist and rain. Generally there was the old south-west swell. One near-calm day allowed some of the officers to take a boat and attack the albatrosses and shear-waters, which provided a little feast after the awful monotony of salt beef and pork. From the 19th the days became fair, while the thermometer, $32\frac{1}{2}$° at the ice-edge, continued to rise steadily. On that day the ship was in latitude 42°5′, longitude 95°20′ W, nearly on the track of the *Dolphin* under Wallis; two days earlier Cook had crossed his own outward track in the *Endeavour* in 1769. A succession of westerlies had driven him farther to the east than he had wished to go; but on 22 February, latitude 36°10′, longitude 94°56′ W, a convenient change of wind allowed him to alter course to west-south-west for three days, to investigate the large land attributed to Juan Fernandez. When he compared the positions given this by Dalrymple and the French scientist Pingré with the courses steered by Wallis and his successors—let alone by the Spanish ships trading

[1] ibid., 326, 328. Also, 'I should not do my officers Justice if I did not take some oppertunity to declare that they allways shewed the utmost readiness to carry into execution in the most effectual manner every measure I thought proper to take.'—328.

between North and South America—and with the great swell, he was clear that it could be at best only a small island, perhaps as probably 'a fiction'. On the 25th he gave it up, to stretch away north-west for the next search on his list. The name of Juan Fernandez must be left to the island already familiar. He would try Easter Island. It was at this moment, or two or three days before, that Cook was taken dangerously ill.

Alarm and grief were general. Cook, who passes over the matter in a short paragraph, defines his ailment as 'the Billious colick and so Violent as to confine me to my bed'. It is not very likely that he had reckoned a failure in his health as a possible impediment to the carrying out of his great design, but it seems certain that a little more violence would have provided a very effective impediment indeed. Strong as the captain was, he had not been in unbroken good health throughout the voyage, though we must go elsewhere than his own journal to find this out: and careful as he was of his men's physical welfare, he does not seem to have given equal care to his own. George Forster, who remarks on the captain's indisposition at Dusky Sound in the previous May, indicates that this was not a normal rheumatism: 'The Captain was taken ill of a fever and violent pain in the groin, which terminated in a rheumatic swelling of the right foot'; and as the ship was standing north, in late December, her fresh food long exhausted, he remarks that Cook 'was pale and lean, entirely lost his appetite, and laboured under a perpetual costive-ness'. Unlike the elder Forster, however, who plunged at once into the Antarctic and the most intolerable rheumatism, in January he 'seemed to recover again as we advanced to the southward';[1] now, in gentle gales and fair weather, while others began to feel the sun in joints again loosened, he collapsed. If George's account is correct, Cook's recipe for his own treatment was to slight the trouble, conceal it from his fellows, and almost to stop eating. When Patten the sur-geon was at last allowed to take him in hand the purges and emetics, opiates and glysters, did no good; for almost twenty-four hours he was racked by a most dreadful hiccough. Finally, after some days of tension, Patten's hot baths and stomach plasters 'relaxed his body and intestines', and he began to recover. To speak in modern diag-nostic terms, it is likely that Cook was suffering from some acute ulceration or infection of the gall-bladder, complemented by a paralysis of the bowel—which would be quite adequate foundation for his unnatural look. Whatever the original strength of his constitu-tion, whatever his force of mind, the student of his career may be

[1] The three quotations are from George Forster, *Voyage*, I, 181, 538, 543.

grateful that James Patten was (to use his patient's words) both a skilful physician and a tender nurse. When he could again take nourishment, an island dog of Forster's provided it,[1] as broth or as more solid food. The crisis had lasted upwards of a week.

There was no island dog for anyone else. At the end of another week the light contrary winds went round to the east, remaining light; the ship ran north-west in pleasant weather. The thermometer was now in the mid-seventies, and well-dieted explorers would have been happy. Signs of scurvy, however, were manifest, against which sauerkraut was the only real specific; some men even grew weak from unwillingness to eat the ship's food. The breeze was sometimes too light. Wales heaved a sigh. 'Omnium rerum Vicissitudo, say my brother Star-gazers; and though they have worn the expression thread-bare, I am fully convinced by experience it is not a jot the less true, for it's scarcely 3 weeks ago we were miserable on acc° of ye cold: we are now wretched with ye heat: the latter is I think less supportable of ye two, as being attended with a sickly Appetite, but Salt Beef & pork, without vegetables for 14 weeks running, would probably cure a Glutton, even in England.'[2] Four albacores were caught one day, 'very acceptable', and there were plenty more for the catching, if a fisherman skilful enough had been on board, but there was not. Clerke scrutinised the birds for harbingers of land, sometimes with a little hope, sometimes with exasperation. 'For my own part, I do not believe there is one in the whole tribe that one can rely on. . .'. At last they became plentiful, tropic birds, man-of-war birds, noddies, terns and petrels: it was in the latitude of 'Davis's land or Easter Island': Cook turned almost due west, and on 11 March sighted the land. He was certain it was Easter Island. But was it also Davis's land? He had no doubt at first, then doubts arose: even after leaving it, he could never quite make up his mind. For it was in about the right position, as the position of Davis's land had been printed by Lionel Wafer, surgeon of the buccaneer Captain Edward Davis, who had sighted it in 1687, and

---

[1] This is the usual account, and seems to be that sanctified by Cook himself, *Journals* II, 333–4: 'Thus I received nourishment and strength from food which would have made most people in Europe sick, so true is it that necessity is govern'd by no law.' But according to George Forster, under the date 24 March, the dog was devoted to this purpose as an answer to Cook's relapse after leaving Easter Island: 'My father ordered his Taheitian dog, the only one which still remained alive after our departure from the Friendly Islands, to be killed; it was cut into quarters, which were served up to captain Cook during several days, and gave him some nourishment, as he could not venture to taste the ship's provisions. By such small helps we succeeded in preserving a life upon which the success of the voyage in a great measure depended.'—*Voyage*, II, 3. It is not likely that Forster made his sacrifice twice over, and Cook's need was greater the first time than the second.
[2] *Journals* II, 335, n. 1.

by Dampier. None of the geographers seemed to hesitate—certainly not Dalrymple, who reprinted Wafer in his *Collection*. Yet Davis's (David's, as the French and Spanish insisted on calling it) land was at least two islands, a small, low, sandy island, backed in the west by a range of high land; and though Roggeveen's Easter Island was certainly not large—thirteen miles in a straight line at its longest—it was equally certainly not low or sandy, it was high and rocky, and it was single. Carteret and Bougainville had both, independently, made what was probably the true identification;[1] if they were right, then Wafer's printed position was wrong. If they were wrong, then Cook would have to find a low sandy island. Meanwhile, at least, he could agree with Dalrymple over the accounts of Roggeveen's visit, the only ones discoverable, and most unsatisfactory; there was no account at all of the Spanish visit of 1770, traces of which survived in odd articles of clothing displayed by the islanders.

The ship was not in with the land, at its eastern end, until late on 12 March, when telescopes picked out both people 'and those Moniments or Idols mentioned by the Authors of Roggeweins Voyage which left us no room to doubt but it was Easter Island.'[2] Next day she ran along the south and west sides of the island in vain search for a harbour, then plyed back to an anchorage off the small sandy beach of Hanga-roa bay, about three miles north of the southern point. Two men came off to the ship in a canoe with a bunch of ripe plantains, happy with a medal each in return; a third, who swam out, insisted on staying. In the morning of the 14th Cook landed among a crowd of amiable natives, distributed medals, traded nails for sweet potatoes, plantains and sugar-cane, and found a small well of brackish water. He took a few casks of this water on board before deciding it was quite too bad to be of use, and was soon convinced by the small quantity of provisions brought to the beach that there would be little point in prolonging his visit. Nor was he happy about his anchorage. Nevertheless the island must be inspected. He was certainly not well enough to walk over it himself, so he sent a party

[1] The islands called Los Desventurados—San Felix and San Ambrosio—500 miles west of Copiapo, on the coast of Chile, latitude (as given by Wafer) 27°20′ S. Wafer and Dampier gave the longitude as about 500 *leagues* from Copiapo—Wafer indeed, as 500 leagues *east*, which is a patent slip. Easter Island is about 600 leagues west. 'Leagues' could be a slip for 'miles', or '500' could be a typographical error for '200'; but in either case it would be odd that Wafer and Dampier should both have the same errors. Roggeveen was clear enough that his Easter Island was not Davis's land and indeed, denounced Davis, Dampier and Wafer as all liars—*Journal*, ed. A. Sharp, (Oxford, 1970), 92–3, 102–4, 108. See also Helen Wallis (ed.), *Carteret's Voyage Round the World* (Cambridge, 1965), 50–3, 144–7; B. G. Corney, *The Voyage of Captain Don Felipe Gonzalez . . . to Easter Island* (Cambridge, 1908), 9, 20–2. Roggeveen's own journal was not printed till 1838, and Corney's translation of the Easter Island portion was the first in English.

[2] *Journals* II, 338.

out under the command of Pickersgill and Edgcumbe, accompanied by Wales, Forster, and others of the gentlemen. They trudged over to the south-east shore, along it a good distance, up a height whence they could see the northern coast, back over the stony hills—a good twenty miles of hot and thirsty going. The only relief was one spring of what would have been good sweet water if the natives had not combined drinking with bathing; some relief it was, however. Many of these people marched with the party, one going ahead with a sort of white flag, a mark of honour; friendly, they displayed few weapons, though some inclination to appropriate their visitors' belongings. Their island was certainly a treeless and infertile one; there seemed to be a fair number of sweet potato gardens and 'plantain walks', some sugar-cane; taro and yams were seen, a few gourds, but not a coconut, a few bushes four or five feet high, not a hog, not a dog, a few small specimens of domestic poultry, few other birds. The wonder, of course, was the monumental statues, the great ancestral torso figures brooding over the land with their melancholy gaze, their backs to the sea, grouped on the careful stone platforms or *ahu*, but many already toppled, prone and disregarded; some rising straight out of a grassy hillside slope. Wales measured one fallen giant, 27 feet long, eight across the shoulders; in the early afternoon shade of another stood the whole party of visitors, thirty strong. If anything was more astonishing than the carved figures themselves, it was the large red cylinders of a different stone which crowned their heads. Many of them had names, which were collected; but how to answer the other questions that arose? What did they signify? Were they solid stone or made of some ingenious composition? Who set them up and how? Cook could but register the astonishment and the interrogatory.

His account of Easter Island, considering the brevity of his stay, is remarkably full. He used his own eyes to good purpose about the beach, he had good eyes to rely on in the exploring party. Once again we find him working systematically through the demands his instructions imposed, as he commented on the nature of the people, their natural resources, their manufactures, their language, their polity and religion—even when he has to note sheer ignorance. As to the people, they were certainly of the same race as the New Zealanders and the other islanders, 'the affinity of the Language, Colour and some of thier customs all tend to prove it'; of moderate stature, slender, nimble, active, pleasant-featured, hospitable, thievish. Their number he could only estimate, and considerably underestimated, as perhaps six or seven hundred. Few women appeared, and those for a purpose deeply disapproved of by Forster; the others, Cook rightly guessed, had been stowed out of harm's way. The men were much tattooed. Their ears were their peculiar feature. They had enormous holes in them, distended very often by sugar-cane leaf rolled up like a spring, or bunches of feathers, so that the ear would hang down half-way to the shoulder. What clothing they wore was of the usual island bark cloth, but their cloth-trees were stunted plants. Their weapons were like some of the New Zealand ones. Their houses were 'low miserable huts', a frame-work of sticks thatched over with cane leaves; their utensils so few that they fell with joy on coconut shells in trade. Their canoes were few, small, mean, not very seaworthy, though skilfully patched together out of driftwood, or perhaps wood left behind by the Spaniard. Their stone, bone or shell tools were poor, but they carved ingeniously. Of government or religion Cook could not speak. There were certainly 'arreeke', or chiefs, and one who was said to be chief of the whole island. 'The Stupendous stone statues errected in different places along the Coast are certainly no representation of any Deity or places of worship; but most probable Burial Places for certain Tribes or Families.' Cook himself had seen a human skeleton lying in the platform of one, laid over with stones.[1] There seemed to be no general native name for the island. As Cook revised his journal-entry he came back to one of his chief problems: 'it is extraordinary that the same Nation should have spread themselves over all the isles in this Vast Ocean from New Zealand to this Island which is almost a fourth part of the circumference of the Globe, many of them at this time have no other knowledge of each other than what is recorded in antiquated tradition and have by length of time become as it were different Nations each having adopted some peculiar custom or habit &c[a] never the less a carefull observer will soon see the Affinity each has to the other.'[2]

On 16 March, a light breeze springing up, he got under sail and plyed to and fro while the boats made last visits to the shore to pick up what provisions they could; in the evening he made sail to the north-west. If he had found fresh water he would have spent some time seeking the low sandy isle: as he had not, was in want of refreshments—though the small quantity he had got at the island made an amazing difference to his men's health—and delay might have bad consequences, he left that problem unresolved. No nation would ever contend for the honour of discovering Easter Island, he reflected, so little would it profit shipping; and settled down for a long run in

[1] *Journals* II, 353.   [2] ibid., 354–5.

the trade wind to see what he could make of the Marquesas islands, last visited by Mendaña almost two hundred years before. If report were true, he would get there all he needed, to raise appetites jaded, spirits dulled, by so many months of salt junk. The ship made good distances daily, but the weather was sultry, and 'bilious' complaints began to recur, including almost at once Cook's own—because, it was thought, of his too great activity as a convalescent at Easter Island. He had to take to his bed again for a time. Patten himself fell sick. After that there was little to record during three weeks beyond agreeable weather, the daily position, the variation of the compass, birds seen; one or two punishments for dirtiness and insolence; caulking of the decks; the setting of the armourer's forge to repair ironwork and to make hatchets for trade at the expected islands. By the end of March the ship was in their reported latitude, 9°30′ S, and like any old-fashioned navigator Cook altered course and began to run down his longitude to the west. The first island—or rather the large rock, Fatu Huku—was sighted on 6 April by the sixteen year-old midshipman Alexander Hood, and called Hood's Island by the captain; then another, as the weather turned squally for the first time on the run. Next morning there were a third and a fourth, and Cook knew he had found what he was in search of.

They are among the most wildly romantic of islands, with high, jagged tops; black cliffs fall abruptly to the sea, precipitous ridges lead to deep valleys, valleys to new steeps and ridges. They are well-watered and fertile, lush even, where the windward heights and hollows take the rain; on the leeward side comparatively barren, as Cook thought Mendaña's Santa Christina was. They have no surrounding reefs, and the swell breaks formidably on the cliffs and beaches. They were not islands that a passing sailor could explore—though, had it not been for untoward circumstances, Cook might have stayed among them a little longer, and obtained there more refreshment, than he did. They are islands where the sailor needs to know his business; for, in the trade-wind season, down from the ridges tear violent squalls of wind which may put a ship in sudden desperate peril. Cook had early experience of this. The chart he carried showed Mendaña's four islands of San Pedro, La Dominica, Santa Christina, and, to the south-east, La Magdalena—as we should say, Motane, Hiva Oa, Tahuata and Fatu Hiva. It was the port that Mendaña had called Madre de Dios that he wanted, the bay of Vaitahu on the western side of Tahuata; and passing through the channel between Hiva Oa and Tahuata he ran along the shore of the latter south-westward. Canoes with lateen sails came out from several coves, where tolerable anchorage was offset by a great surf on the shore, until Mendaña's port or bay unmistakably appeared. As Cook was turning into it one of those violent squalls fell on the ship, so that she was within a few yards of going on the rocks to leeward. He stood out again, then prudently anchored in the entrance. Some rather hesitant canoes were alongside at sunset to trade, many more in the morning. Their occupants preferred to make no return for the nails they were given, until Cook fired a musket ball close: on this 'they observed a little more honisty', and some—indeed too many—came on board. The captain, preparing to warp the ship further into the bay, was going off in a boat to choose a mooring place; he had hardly told his officers to take care that nothing was stolen when the cry was raised that an iron stanchion was gone from the opposite gangway. Fire over the canoe! shouted Cook, and hurried round to intercept it; alas, they fired at those in it, and killed a man. There was another in the canoe, baling out blood and water 'in a kind of Hysteric Laugh', and a boy looking very dejected, apparently the dead man's son. The canoes all fled; Cook had much ado to get one to come back and take a present of nails. Nevertheless, a kedge anchor being carried out and buoyed to warp in by, they attempted to drag ashore either it or its buoy, on which shots had to be fired again, with no intent to kill. So much delay was caused by this that when squalls once more began to come down the bay Cook decided to remain where he was. Fear of muskets did not keep the people from stealing what they could, but Cook, thinking after looking at the place that it was not likely he would stay long, determined to put up with the trouble.

Canoes ventured cautiously off to the ship again, presents were given them, trade re-established. Cook went ashore, in spite of the surf, and got a load of water. On the appearance of a watering party with a guard in the afternoon, however, the people once more retreated in dread; next morning he himself went, but those that crowded round him were with difficulty kept from running from the guard. At last a chief arrived from the hills with many more people, presents this time were mutual, and trade for fruit and the very small pigs here found seemed to be stably set on foot. Cook was able to visit a different part of the bay where he was anxious to do some kindness to the son of the man who had been killed, to make plain that this had not been done 'from any bad design we had against the Nation'. Unfortunately, when he arrived the boy had fled. Next day, 10 April, trade still went on briskly. The following morning it stopped dead. The 'young gentlemen' had been foolish. They had broken the rules, handing over various novel articles which pleased the people more than nails or iron tools, 'but what ruined our Market the most was one of them giving for a Pig a very large quantity of Red feathers he had got at Amsterdam, which these people much value and which the other did not know, nor did I know at this time that Red feathers was what they wanted, and if I had I could not have supported this trade in the manner it was begun one day. Thus, was the fine prospect we had of geting a plentifull supply of refreshments of these people frustrated, and which will ever be the case so long as every one is allowed to make exchanges for what he pleaseth and in what manner he please's.'[1] Nothing could be more exasperating to a man who laid down rules, and was trying to re-provision a whole ship's company; his reproof, no doubt, was appropriate. And now there was nothing to do but leave, telling oneself truly enough that anyhow the place was not very convenient for bringing off wood and water or for carrying out repairs. Cook, the Forsters, and Sparrman embarked in the long boat, the sea got up, and only the most prodigious energies and skill on the part of the men at the oars saved her, like the ship a few days before, from being dashed on fatal rocks.

Before turning finally from these islands, Cook stood over to 'St Dominica' or Hiva Oa to look at its western coast, after which, on the morning of 12 April, he steered away southwards. He had in fact done what he principally came to do: he had verified Mendaña's discovery, though he saw Mendaña's fourth island, La Magdalena—Fatu Hiva—only from a distance as he sailed away; he had added a fifth, had corrected Mendaña's position, and fixed longitudes which were very accurate. He was not to know that there were further islands in the group out of sight to the northwest. Mendaña's port he named anew, Resolution Bay. As for supplies, in spite of the untoward he had not done badly. True, pigs were small and coconuts scarce; on the other hand he carried away a vast quantity of fine large breadfruit and plantains; the water was excellent. But what impressed him most, perhaps, and those others who kept journals, was the beauty of the islanders, not merely the most beautiful people in the South Seas, but the finest race ever beheld, all tall and well-proportioned, with good features, none with the extremes of fat or meagreness to be seen in Tahiti: Cook and Wales, Clerke and the Forsters, are united in admiration. It was an admiration, on the whole, of male beauty; for few women were seen. The men were tattooed in bold designs from

[1] *Journals* II, 369.

head to foot, and wore no more than a breech-clout—indeed, ten degrees south of the equator, needed no more. The women, like those of Tahiti, were clothed in *tapa* skirts and cloaks. There was also ornamental wear, such as the plaited fillets round many heads, fronted with shell, stuck with the long feathers of cocks and tropic birds, or a sort of wooden ruff decorated with red seeds. The favourite weapons appeared to be slings and clubs. The people who cooked and ate within the captain's observation were dirty in both employments: 'I know not if all are so, the actions of a few individuals are not sufficient to fix a Custom to a whole Nation.'[1] He saw nothing of their other conditions of life, except houses and strongholds high up on the ridges, and people passing the steep tracks, through his telescope. He had too much to do below, perhaps was not yet sufficiently restored to vigour, to go exploring on those paths. Wales did, and Clerke, and George Forster, and other gentlemen, and had no unpleasant experience; indeed Wales met no person, house or plantation, not even a single fruit tree. He would have had to toil a good deal farther for richness of cultivation. Cook would not let anyone go to the highest summits, for fear of attack. Clerke, who found it hard not to like people, thought they had passed the days 'very agreeably among these good Folks', and that want had been abundantly relieved. There was the usual 'affinity' noticed; Odiddy's conversation was understood and returned. Hodges had done his drawing. The captain directed his course for Tahiti, 'likewise with a view of falling in with Some of those isles discovered by former Navigators whose Situations are not well determined.'[2]

It was a course which would take him through the more northerly Tuamotus, where some of the isles touched on by Schouten and Le Maire, Roggeveen, Byron undoubtedly lay. For four days of fine weather he sailed, shortening sail at night, and on the fifth sighted the first atoll, another soon after. It rose from unfathomable depths, like most of the other low isles in this sea (to use Cook's words), a narrow string of islets lying in an oval connected together by a coral reef, the whole enclosing a lagoon or lake of salt water of eight or ten leagues round. Cook sent Gilbert the master to examine a small opening in the reef, followed, as the natives seemed not unfriendly, by two boats to make a landing and give Forster a chance to collect some plants. Neither he nor Cook had, it is to be remembered, looked at an atoll closely before. The islet beach was their limit: the people were not, after all, very friendly, though they exchanged a few dogs and coconuts for value received. Two or three

[1] *Journals* II, 375.   [2] ibid., 376.

guns were fired overhead from the ship, to indicate that the visitors had not been driven off by superior strength; next morning, after viewing briefly the neighbour atoll, Cook continued on his course. He had, as he made no doubt, just renewed a discovery previously made by Byron, in 1765, and by Roggeveen in 1722, which Byron had called King George's Islands; the first island was Takaroa, the second Takapoto. At the first Byron had found the people hostile, and in a skirmish several of them were killed, so it is hardly surprising that their attitude towards these new visitors was not quite one of welcome. Cook was pleased, however, to have excellent lunar observations for the longitude, which, checked against 'the watch' at Tahiti, would enable him to correct all Byron's positions. Smooth water persuaded him that he was not free yet of what he called 'drowned isles', and with a healthy respect for coral reefs he spent two successive nights plying under his topsails. In between them— it was 19 April—he discovered four more atolls, the group he called 'Palliser's Isles in honour of my worthy friend';[1] and then, finding a great swell rolling in from the south, he felt he was past his dangers. On 21 April he saw the high land of Tahiti, the following morning he was anchored in Matavai Bay.

[1] They were Apataki, Toau, Kaukura, and Arutua. They lie between latitudes approximately 15°20' and 16°02' S. and longitudes 145°56' and 146°40' W.

XVI

The Second Island Sweep

IT WAS with no thought of refreshment that Cook had come to Tahiti again, but merely to allow Wales to set up his instruments at a precisely known point and check the chronometer; he accordingly told his astronomer that there would be no more than two or three days for the purpose. 'As to Sick we had none.' In the end the stay lengthened to three weeks, with three weeks more spent at the neighbouring islands before the cruise was resumed. After his Tahitian experience of the previous August he expected little in the way of supplies, but now he was astonished at the recovery of the island, and the plenty and prosperity evident at both Matavai and Pare. Tu, with a large train of followers, at once brought a present of hogs. When—following on Marquesan experience—red feathers were produced as possible currency, excitement rapidly spread over the whole island. Vehiatua sent emissaries for them from Tautira. Polynesian trade might be an exchange of ceremonial gifts, or a less elevated sort of exchange, in the one case it was made plain that the mark of *taio*, or friendship, was *ura*, or red feathers; in the other *ura* simply commanded the greater return. As Cook's stock of trade goods was greatly depleted this was a boon. Tahiti produced few red feathers of its own; red was a royal and sacred colour; red feathers were potent aids to prayer and other exercises of religion; they conferred wealth and great distinction on their owners, ensured envy among chiefs as well as the favour of the gods. All things considered, Cook thought he would be as well off here as at any other island, and getting tents, casks, sails ashore, set on foot all the processes of overhaul and repair. The social Clerke surveyed everything with satisfaction: 'Tho' we ever found ourselves at Home among these good People, their reception this visit was if possible more social than ever. . . . Nothing in Nature cou'd exceed the unbounded civillity and friendship with which they now treated us. . . .' The only inconvenience in such abounding provision was to find room in which to stow it.[1] There were, however, before those three weeks were over, one or two causes for dissatisfaction evident as well as for pleasure.

One of these—though rather a thing that baffled the mind and could cause difficult relations—was the rivalry among chiefs, and the tender susceptibilities of chiefs. Steering a way through these without mishap was like steering a way through a cluster of atolls; without real knowledge of the language it was impossible, indeed, to make proper enquiry. Cook kept on thinking of Tu as a 'king', of other great chiefs as his 'subjects'—if they seemed to have influence with him, perhaps as his 'counsellors'; the renewed prosperity of the island he tended to put down to the 'policy' of Tu—who must be a wiser man than he had before thought him—or to measures advocated by these councillors. Again, he thought of an obviously great man, 'Towha' or To'ofa,[2] the paramount chief of the Oropa'a part of the Atehuru district, as Tu's 'admiral', and so in all innocency wounded feelings. Then how one day should Tu say frankly that the Admiral was not his friend, and the next day urge Cook to show him much respect; on another day both of them suggest that he should help them to make war against Taiarapu—which at the moment was, Cook gathered, in alliance with them to make war against Eimeo, or Moorea? True, such things were not unknown in European statecraft, but that was not a department with which the captain was intimately acquainted. Wounded feelings might mean a cessation in the supply of hogs or fruit. It was fortunate that such difficulties, ever inadequately understood, were resolved, and mutual presents sealed the renewal of friendship. Another complication arose from the readiness of chiefs, such as Tu or his father Teu, to be 'mataou-ed', or frightened, and consequently to cut off the supply of food, thus annoying their subjects as well as Cook. It might be that not only chiefs, but apparently the whole population, were *matau*, and would suddenly disappear; then Cook would know, before ever his own people had reported it, that something had been stolen, and that all Matavai had fled from his anticipated vengeance.

Not invariably was it so: once at least Cook was the first to move. A Tahitian who tried to steal a cask at night from the watering place was caught, sent on board the ship and put in irons. The captain decided to make a grand example. Early next morning Tu, To'ofa,

[1] Again, 'To say any thing of the properties of this good Isle after the publication of the Endeavours Voyage wou'd be tautology . . .'. *Journals* II, 385, n. 3.
[2] Cook sometimes spells the name of this great chief T'Towha. He was Te To'ofa or Teto'ofa: see Teuira Henry, *Ancient Tahiti* (Honolulu, 1928), 78; John Davies, *History of the Tahitian Mission* (ed. C. W. Newbury, Cambridge, 1961), xxxv, xxxvii, 102-3.

and several other 'grandees' came on a visit, bringing as gifts both provisions and what Cook thought were 'some of the most valuable curiosities in the island'. He exhibited his captive and recounted the crime. Tu begged for the man's liberty. Cook refused, took him ashore and had him tied to a post. He then addressed Tu at some length—and it must have been in some intelligible language, as To'ofa at least listened carefully—on the behaviour of the Tahitians and the British respectively, the merits of theft and fair payment, the punishment sailors received if they broke the rules; so that 'it was but right this man should be punished also, besides I told him it would be the means of saving the lives of some of his people by detering them from commiting crimes of this nature in which some would be kill'd at one time or a nother'. Tu, who seemed to understand, only desired the man might not be killed. Cook turning out the guard to keep off the now great crowd, thereupon had the unfortunate fellow flogged with two dozen lashes. To'ofa with great eloquence harangued the crowd on their sins, their duties and indebtedness to the visitors. The day was completed by Cook's carrying out a promise he had made earlier to have the marines put through their drill and firing practice, which caused great amazement, fright and pleasure. Barely more than a week after this display of potent force, a sentry went to sleep on shore in the night; his musket was stolen. This time Tu sent to inform Cook of the theft before fleeing to the hills, and apparently also sent men to get the musket back; it was brought back at the end of a day of the most troublesome and vexing complications, coming and going, swearing and counterswearing, seizure and freeing of canoes—followed by stoppage of supplies, interviews, the firing of the ship's guns to please Tu, an exhibition of fireworks to please everybody. Cook was compelled to think again over his relations with this people, without attaining final satisfaction. He had always respected their property, apart from detaining canoes for a while. He had ignored the fact that they were generally first aggressors. If he destroyed property he was sure to be the loser in the end; he might possibly make them sue for peace, but the honour he got from that would be empty. 'Three things made them our fast friends,' he concluded: 'Their own good Natured and benevolent disposition, gentle treatment on our part, and the dread of our fire Arms; by our ceaseing to observe the Second the first would have wore off of Course, and the too frequent use of the latter would have excited a spirit of revenge and perhaps have taught them that fire Arms were not such terrible things as they had imagined, they are very sencible of the superiority they have over us in numbers and no one knows what an enraged multitude might do.'[1] This is thinking rather deeper than Clerke did, 'social' as Clerke was and made his friends.

To balance such irritations were some things of new interest or deeper enquiry: most interesting of all for a sailor the great war fleet of over three hundred double canoes, large and small, with all their crews and equipment, which Cook unexpectedly found at Pare when he paid his first formal visit to Tu four days after his arrival—the Tahitian fleet, as he erroneously supposed, drawn up for inspection by its royal master. It was on this occasion that he was almost torn in two between To'ofa and his followers and those of Tu competing for his attention; bitterly did he regret his seeming neglect of To'ofa when he was told that Tu 'was gone into the Country Mataou' (because his people had stolen some of Cook's clothes in the wash). The canoes were magnificent, with flags and streamers, chiefs and principal officers splendid in their breast plates, helmets and plumes—'the whole made a grand and Noble appearence such as was never seen before in this Sea'. Cook, wanting much to go aboard, had lost his chance when he lost sight of To'ofa, and shortly after he started on his return to Matavai the whole fleet moved off to the west. Nor did he see that noble armament again, though he did see later a group of ten canoes, and later still one of forty rehearsing their manœuvre of landing on a beach, their crews engaging in mock battle. He gave To'ofa a pendant for his own canoe; Tu not merely a grapnel and rope which the chief begged of him, but a jack and pendant for a new double canoe almost ready to launch, the largest Cook had seen, 108 feet long—that is, almost as long as the *Resolution*—and Tu agreed to call it *Britannee* or *Britannia*. The purpose of the fleet, which was only a part of the total force in preparation, was, so it was gathered, to impose obedience on Aimeo, whose chief had revolted against Tu his lawful sovereign— or, alternatively, 'had thrown off the yoke of Otahiete and assumed an independency'. Neither interpretation was correct, however obscure the precise nature of the trouble. Certainly there was a struggle in progress on Aimeo, in which one of the chief contestants was related to Tu: but the last thing Tu wanted was to be engaged in warfare on his behalf. Some of the Aimeo chiefs may have been tributary to Tahitian chiefs: the one island was certainly not tributary to the other. To'ofa and that other important *ari'i*, Potatau, certainly eager for war, at this time were bringing pressure on Tu

---

[1] *Journals* II, 398. The sentence gives us a little foreshadowing of February 1779, in a different island.

to join them. He agreed, then drew back. Hence, no doubt, the combination of respect and fear in which he held To'ofa. Having failed to get Cook as an ally against Taiarapu, the chiefs thought he might lend his assistance in their actual war, but once again he was disobliging.

The sight of the fleet and computation of its strength in warriors and paddlers stimulated Cook to calculate also the population of the island. His statistical technique one cannot admire, his estimate must have been considerably too large.[1] He collected a little more information on the wide-spread family connections of Tu, and on the habits of the people; had a visit from Purea, who, he gallantly asserted, 'looked as well and as young as ever'; the ship's bread being inspected by the warrant officers, had to throw away three thousand pounds more of it as too rotten for consumption; noted the decline in the number of sheets and shirts on board the ship, as an index to payment by young gentlemen to young ladies for services rendered; considered the question of Odiddy. The youth, tractable and sweet-natured, without being either knowledgeable or highly intelligent, had become a favourite of all his ship-mates, had made something of a sensation in the island by his traveller's tales of white lands and snow, perpetual daylight, tempests and cannibals, and had been much patronised by Tu, who wanted him to stay at Tahiti. There were not wanting those among his new friends who urged him to take a further step in adventure and travel to England; there were not wanting volunteers who wanted to do likewise. Cook and Forster urged him to return to his own island of Raiatea. Forster was anxious to take a young person of his own and instruct him in mechanic arts. Cook, who had not much approved of Furneaux's embarking of Omai, said roundly he would take no one except Odiddy, if Odiddy really wished to go; told Odiddy that if he did, he must look on Cook as a father, but he would probably never return; Odiddy wept; Forster was offended. Tu suggested that Cook might take one or two of his entourage to Tonga to collect red feathers for him. Cook refused that request. Odiddy decided to go home to Raiatea. By the afternoon of 14 May all farewells had been made, Tu's with a last hog and a turtle, Cook's with a three-gun salute, the *Resolution* was under sail and under way, when the lieutenant of marines, idly looking out of a port, noticed a man swimming from the ship towards a canoe obviously in wait to pick him up. The cutter was launched and picked him up instead, he dived overboard and began swimming again, was taken up a

---

[1] *Journals* II, 409. His estimate was 204,000. Cf. Volume I of the *Journals*, clxxiv–clxxvii.

second time and put in irons. It was John Marra, gunner's mate, who made this attempt to desert; it was his second, because he had tried at Deptford, even before the voyage began. His intention, he explained to the world when he came to write a book, was anthropological study; he had been promised, Mr Elliott tells us, 'a House, Land and a Pretty Wife'. Cook now had him to reflect upon, and like Cook in his journal we may anticipate a little. After a night in irons he was let out at Huahine with a sentinel over him, at the more attractive Raiatea returned to irons. He no doubt expected a flogging.

I kept the Man in confinement till we were clear of the isles then dismiss'd him without any other punishment,' wrote the captain, 'for when I considered the situation of the Man in life I did not think him so culpable as it may at first appear, he was an Irishman by birth, a good Seaman and had Saild both in the English and Dutch Service. I pick'd him up at Batavi in my return home from my last Voyage and he had remained with me ever sence. I never learnt that he had either friends or connection to confine him to any particular part of the world, all Nations were alike to him, where than can Such a Man spend his days better than at one of these isles where he can injoy all the necessaries and some of the luxuries of life In ease and Plenty.[1]

He added, 'I know not if he might not have obtained my consent if he had applied for it in proper time.' This is an unusual mood for a person commanding one of the vessels of the royal navy.

The following day the ship was in Fare harbour at Huahine. The chief Ori was as welcoming as ever. His people were less so. The second day saw Forster's servant, Ernst Scholient, 'a feeble man', set on during a botanical excursion by a group of bravos who would have stripped him had he not been rescued by a companion, an assault all too reminiscent of that on Sparrman at the same place in the previous year; while two men in a canoe tried to cut away the anchor buoy. These two were chased off by a musket shot and the canoe destroyed by way of example. The other matter was not so easily dealt with. A council of chiefs, protesting their own innocence, which Cook had not doubted, advised him to kill the assailants: that was all very well, he answered, but who was going to produce them?—and the subject was dropped. In spite of this advice one party of officers had their trade goods stolen; another, themselves acting in some obscure way with reckless imprudence, were deprived of all their belongings, including their guns, by a mob from whom they had to be rescued by the interposition of the chiefs. The property was restored, but Cook complained to Ori

[1] *Journals* II, 403-4.

of 'repeated outrages'. The old chief invited him to take a force on shore and march inland with himself to chastise the 'banditti'. After some hesitation he agreed to do so, mainly as a demonstration of power. There was a long march, no banditti were found, Odiddy began to talk of an ambush, and when the party came into a deep valley very well suited for such an exercise Cook decided he had gone far enough. Two chiefs brought pigs and dogs and the young plantain trees of peace and ceremonially presented them; arriving back at the beach he fired several volleys of muskets to impress people who had seen them used before only by sportsmen missing two shots out of three; and for the last two days the supply of breadfruit and coconuts rose enormously. On the whole, thought Cook, the expedition had done good, though Wales was inclined to laugh at it; yet he was well aware of the carelessness of his sailors in their rambles and of his shortage of trade goods; nor were red feathers here of much value. His previous visit must have thinned out the island stock of hogs. He put his armourers to work to turn old iron into tools and nails. It was not really a very satisfactory visit. Once again he was led to contrast Ori, 'the good old chief', 'a good Man to the utmost sence of the word', with his people, too many of whom seemed to take advantage of his age. When they parted Cook said they would see each other no more, at which the old man wept, and said again, 'then let your sons come, we will treat them well'.

It took the whole of 23 May, with a light wind, to get from Huahine round the south end of Raiatea to its western side; another day and a half, when the eastern trade wind blew, to get the ship through the reef, where the sea broke with frightful violence, into the placid Haamanino harbour. While she was warping in, Orio, the chief, came off with his hospitable gift, and when Cook went on shore to return this visit he had an experience he had not had before. It was very Polynesian, and it denoted the reunion of friends. He was met by four or five lamentably weeping old women, cutting their heads with sharks' teeth, so that the blood poured down over their faces to their shoulders; they bloodily embraced him and Forster, after which they washed themselves (we learn nothing about the gentlemen) and were as cheerful as anybody. Orio came to dinner. The ship was surrounded with vast numbers of canoes and people, who remained two or three days in the neighbourhood feasting; for it appears that there was an additional excitement to the arrival of the *Resolution*—that of a party of the *arioi* society; which might account for an unusual succession of dramatic performances, though Cook had a different theory. There were two

'theatres'; there was very broad, and repetitive, comedy, there was
frequent allusion to the ship and Brittannee; there was only one actress,
Orio's beautiful daughter Poetua, 'at whose Shrine', writes the
admiring but discriminating captain, 'many pretty things were
offered by her numerous Votarists and I believe was one great inducement why her father gave us these entertainments so often'.[1]
Wales also, after a pleasant excursion into the country, finding that
'the Princess *Poydoa*' performed that evening: 'as these were my
favorite amusements, I made scarce more than a hop skip & Jump
to the Play-house where I found she could twist & distort a set of
very delicate features with as much dexterity as ever.'[2] Next day
Cook had the enchanting lady and her family to breakfast.

Provisions were plentiful at Raiatea; trade was brisk. There is
little theft recorded. There was one expedition along the shore
to reclaim property, and the iron tiller of the pinnace went
irreclaimably, but as among the number of articles returned were
some that Cook did not even know he had lost, he thought he had
done well, and the alarmed chief was restored to tranquillity. A
visit to what Odiddy said was his estate found his brother solidly in
possession; Cook got nothing here beyond a hog or two, together
with a detailed recipe, from his own observation, for the killing and
cooking of the animal. Odiddy got drunk. Cook made every enquiry
he could into the politics of the island and its neighbouring Borabora, where he would have gone had he not now all the supplies he
needed, and been anxious to proceed with his voyage. He met the
chiefs of Tahaa, almost a northern extension of Raiatea within the
same reef. His departure was delayed for a day by an astonishing
story brought him that two ships had arrived at Huahine, one
commanded by Banks, the other by Furneaux; the appearance of
these commanders was described to the life, the informant adding
with verisimilitude that on one of the ships he had been made drunk.
Cook almost sent a boat over at once with orders to Furneaux, and
did send Clerke to the farther part of Raiatea to make enquiry. By
the end of another day there was universal assertion that the man
was a liar, while he himself had disappeared. It was the first time
—it was not the last—that Cook encountered this singular species of
island practical joke; he was fortunate that it caused him no more
inconvenience than it did. He could address himself to taking a final
leave of 'these happy isles'. He had set off fireworks. There is indeed

---

[1] *Journals* II, 421.
[2] ibid., 842. There are many other tributes to the charms of this young woman, whose
portrait now hangs in the National Maritime Museum, Greenwich.

a valedictory air breathing over this last visit. Thinking upon bountiful Nature and its blessings, upon the benevolent disposition of Native mankind, upon the cheerful and generous response to the wants of the Navigator, Cook cannot find a hard word to say, among the last words of his journal, even about the less pleasing aspects of Huahine. He has become almost a sentimental man. When everything was in readiness to sail the chiefs came to the ship to make their farewells. 'Oreo's last request was for me to return and when he found I would not make him the Promise, he asked the name of my *Marai*'—a word to which the English gave the too exclusive significance of burial place. A strange question to ask a seaman, thought Cook; 'however I hesitated not one moment to tell him Stepney the Parish in which I lived when in London. I was made to repeat it several times over till they could well pronounce it, then Stepney Marai no Tootee was echoed through a hundred mouths at once.' They asked Forster the same question. 'What greater proof could we have of these people Esteeming and loving us as friends whom they wished to remember, they had been repeatedly told we should see them no more, they then wanted to know the name of the place were our bodies were to return to dust.'[1] They left, Poetua left, all weeping hard. Cook did his best to believe their sorrow was unfeigned. Odiddy was allowed to stay a little longer, till the ship was almost out of the harbour: he had the privilege of firing some of the guns which jointly rejoiced over the birthday of King George III and bade farewell to the island. Then, clutching the testimonial that Cook had written for him, he climbed slowly over the side into his canoe and burst into tears.

This day of grief and celebration was 4 June, a day also of gentle breezes and fine weather, which did not persist. John Marra, that devotee of freedom, was released from confinement. Cook directed his course a little south of west, as he resumed his purpose to visit Quiros's discoveries, the theme that remained so strongly in his mind from his cogitations when turning north from the ice. The course he steered indicates that he thought he would need further refreshment before he reached his goal, because it was not islets he was interested in, and the southerly inclination would bring him to Tonga. From there he would have to turn north. He followed his practice of bringing to for the night. On the 5th he recognised the

---

[1] *Journals* II, 425–6. Cook adds, 'I afterwards found that the same question was put to Mr F. by a Person a Shore but he gave a different and indeed more proper Answer by saying that no man who used the Sea could tell where he would be buried.'

atoll Wallis had called Lord Howe's Island, rightly identifying it
with one the Raiateans had told him of, Mopihaa, where they went
turtling; and after eleven days more encountered the man of war
and tropic birds which might or might not indicate land. This time
they did, another atoll, to which Cook gave the name of Palmerston,
a Lord of the Admiralty; he could not reconcile this with anything
Quiros had found. He could see no people; he might have landed
if he had descried a convenient place, because his breadfruit and
plantains had just run out and ship's bread was being served again,
but there being none he ran on. On the afternoon of the 20th still
another island was sighted, of a different sort. People were seen on
it next morning and he took two boats to examine its western coast.
To land on the rocky base of the shore was easy enough; to get any
farther up the shrub-covered cliffs was a different matter, nevertheless the naturalists began to collect plants while Cook explored the
way up. He displayed the colours and, according to Hodges, took
possession of the island—not very effectively, as advancing natives
were not at all friendly, hurling lumps of coral one of which struck
Sparrman on the arm. He fired his musket, as some other person did,[1]
to Cook's annoyance, and the islanders retired. So did Cook, looking
along the coast for another landing place, without much luck, till
he saw four canoes drawn up on a small stony bit of beach. He wished
to leave some nails and medals in them as a sign of friendship;
Hodges wished to sketch them. Within a very few minutes of their
landing the people rushed down on them through a sort of chasm
'with the ferocity of wild Boars', undeterred by the discharge of
muskets in the air, a spear whizzed close over Cook's shoulder, and
the armed guard Cook had placed on a flat rock let fly at another
party that had appeared above. Cook snapped his own musket at
his assailant, five paces off, but was glad afterwards that it had
missed fire; apart from Sparrman's bruise, no one on either side was
hurt. As it seemed pretty clear that the inhabitants did not wish
to encourage visitors, the captain rowed back to the ship and made
sail. He called the place Savage Island. It was Niue. He fixed its
position very accurately; considering the impediments to inspection,
he gave a good account of it.[2] Stout well-made men the people
appeared, almost naked, some of them painted black extensively.

[1] It was small shot that was fired, we gather from Sparrman, 129: 'The Captain,
however, perhaps with justification, was displeased at this shooting, for he believed that,
with more patience, some reconciliation could have been reached.'

[2] It is not very easy to see on the spot precisely where Cook landed: probably the first
time at a place called Tuapa, close to the principal village of the island, Uhomotu; and
the second time at Alofi, about the middle of the west coast. See the sketch map, *Journals*
II, 434.

Their canoes were much like those of Amsterdam. It was a raised coral island. 'To judge of the whole Garment by the skirts it cannot produce much, for so much as we saw of it consisted wholy of Coral rocks all overrun with trees Shrubs &cᵃ, not a bit of soil was to be seen, the rocks alone supplied the trees with humidity.' The loose rocks were coral; so were the cliffs of the coast. There was a consequent question. 'If these Coral rocks were first formed in the Sea by animals, how came they thrown up, to such a height? has this Island been raised by an Earth quake or has the Sea receded from it? Some Philosophers have attempted to account for the formation of low isles such as are in this Sea, but I do not know if any thing has been said of high Islands or such as I have been speaking of.' He left the question open for the philosophers.

The winds were still easterly; the course was WSW. At daylight on 25 June islands were again seen in the west, with a reef of rocks lying full ahead, as far too on either hand as the eye could reach. Cook bore up to the south to look for an opening; then, as the wind fell and an easterly swell continued, stood off to the south-east. When the day came again he saw the opening he wanted. Even before sighting land he had rightly judged himself not far from Rotterdam or 'Annamocka', Nomuka. He was now coming in to the Tongan archipelago about a degree of latitude farther north than he had done the previous year. The islands thickened ahead, but his passage was clear, just south of the 'Otu Tolu sub-division of the Nomuka group, with breakers further south. Canoes brought coconuts, shaddocks and the names of islands; by the end of the day on the 26th the ship was anchored off the north shore of Nomuka, where Tasman had been, and one of the people had already asked for Cook by name. Early in the morning the captain and the master went on shore to look for water. Courteously received, they were taken to a pond brackish but usable. Courtesy went further: Cook had no sooner returned to the beach than a man and an elderly dame presented to him an extremely personable young woman, who—he understood—was to be at his service. 'Miss, who probably had received her instructions, I found wanted by way of Handsel, a Shirt or a Nail, neither the one nor the other I had to give without giving her the Shirt on my back which I was not in a humour to do.' That did not settle the matter: we see for once the captain driven off a field of battle in utter rout.

I soon made them sencible of my Poverty and thought by that means to have come of with flying Colours but I was misstaken, for I was made to understand I might retire with her on credit, this not suteing me niether the old Lady began first to argue with me and when that fail'd she abused me, I understood very little of what she said, but her actions were expressive enough and shew'd that her words were to this effect, Sneering in my face and saying, what sort of a man are you thus to refuse the embraces of so fine a young Woman, for the girl certainly did not [want] beauty which I could however withstand, but the abuse of the old Woman I could not and therefore hastned into the Boat, they then would needs have me take the girl on board with me, but this could not be done as I had come to a Resolution not to suffer a Woman to come on board the Ship on any pretence what ever and had given strict orders to the officers to that purpose. . . .[1]

In the meanwhile the boat had been loaded with yams and shaddocks, which were plentiful as well as more welcome to Cook. Although the island had few pigs or fowls, a brisk trade went on till noon, both on shore and at the ship. The islanders helped to roll the casks to and from the pond, nails and beads changed hands amid mutual pleasure. Botanising and shooting parties (ducks were not lacking) were at large; it seemed a morning generally profitable. At noon all had returned to the beach except the surgeon; Cook could not wait for him, as the tide was ebbing fast. After dinner officers who landed again found the unhappy Patten bereft of his gun; Cook heard the news and hastened ashore 'for fear our people should take such steps to recover the gun as I might not approve'. They had taken no steps, and Cook refrained from taking any, because, he says, he was displeased with the occasion of its being lost—in other words, officers who were careless should suffer for it. He soon changed his mind: 'in this I was wrong and only added one fault to a nother; my Lenity in this affair and the easy manner they had obtained this gun which they thought secure in their possession incourag'd them to commit acts of greater Violence. . . .'[2] Next day Clerke and Gilbert went for more water, their men were jostled and got the casks filled with difficulty, Clerke's gun was snatched away, tools were carried off. One or two muskets were fired without intent to harm. Just as the loaded launch was ready to leave Cook arrived; this time he decided restitution must be made. He sent for the marines, and ordered guns to be fired to bring back Forster and his botanising party. His annoyance secured the return of Clerke's weapon at once. He was determined to have Patten's as well; as soon as the marines arrived he seized two large double sailing canoes and himself

1 *Journals* II, 444. Cf. Elliott's Memoirs quoted on that page, n. 2: 'It has always been suppos'd that Cook himself, never had any connection with any of our fair friends: I have often seen them jeer and laugh at him, calling him Old, and good for nothing.'
2 *Journals* II, 442.

peppered with small shot a man who made some resistance. At
this display of determination the people all fled, but some returned
when he called and brought the musket, when he immediately
restored the canoes. The other things he was willing to let go, except
an adze. The exhibition of the man he had shot, looking dead though
only slightly wounded, was at first regarded as a fair exchange for
this. Patten dressed his wounds; Cook, no doubt as an exercise of
charity, gave him a spike nail and a knife, of which he was immediately relieved by the owner of the canoe he had defended. The
adze was insisted on, and, after Cook had been berated for his
meanness by the same elderly woman who had denounced his lack
of gallantry the morning before, was at length returned. It had been
a troublesome morning. Both Cook and Lieutenant Cooper had been
kept on shore well beyond the usual hour of dinner, into the late
afternoon; in their absence Wales could not unlock the chronometer
to wind it up, for the first time on the voyage everybody forgot,
and it ran down. Fortunately, Wales's observations were enough to
set it running properly again.[1]

The ship being now plentifully supplied with provisions Cook
resolved to sail as soon as he got a wind. When he went ashore again
he found the people so very obliging that he was sure he could stay
longer without further trouble—in spite of what Clerke called 'their
great abilities and strict perseverance' as pilferers. He contented
himself with collecting all the information he could about the
islands to the northward, with observing all he could immediately
about him, and with giving (almost now his standard present) a
young dog and a bitch, animals of which the island had none, to
a man who had done his best to moderate the people's behaviour
in the morning. The island was roughly triangular, not large, by
no means fully populated or cultivated; its people seemed poorer
than those of the islands farther to the south; Cook could distinguish no particular chief or authority among them. They suffered
from some sort of 'leprous' complaint—probably it was yaws. He was
fairly certain that his visit had not added any venereal disease to
their ills. He noted the reefs, rocks, and anchorages, and many
names of islands and islets. He had not thought of giving a name to
the group as a whole, it seems, when he made sail at daylight on
29 June, with the intention of inspecting two high islands to the
north-west—a flat-topped one above which a continual column of

---

[1] *Journals* II, 847. No inconvenience could possibly arise from the accident, wrote Wales;
'however as I had now kept it going two years I had begun to flatter my self with the
hopes of carrying it home without anything of the sort happening'.

smoke argued a volcano, and another, with a high rounded peak.
With a contrary wind it was two days before he could come up with
these islands and pass between them—days during which canoes
kept bringing out provisions and 'curiosities' to the ship. When he
did reach them the level summit of the one, 'Amattafoa', or Tofua,
was covered with cloud, so that he could not tell whether it was
indeed a volcano (which it is) or was merely being burnt off; at least
he had a good view of the beautiful cone of 'Oghao', or Kao. They
were both inhabited. In the passage between these his seaman's eye
was fastened on a large sailing canoe—everybody admired the
Tongan canoe-building—to see whether, in tacking, it put about or
merely shifted its lateen sail and went the other end foremost. The
latter it did. Some of the largest canoes, nevertheless, were so rigged
as to have to go about, he noted; and the detailed description he
gives of spars, rigging and manœuvres shows that in matters of naval
architecture his seaman's eye was keen. Hodges was drawing hard.
Cook had considered touching at Amsterdam—Tongatapu—again,
but a fresh breeze from the south blew that idea away, the canoes
hastened to be gone, and he steered west with all sails set. Some time
in the days which followed he settled on a general island name: the
islets, sand-banks and breakers that surrounded Annamocka and
stretched off to the north, he thought, must also extend south to
Amsterdam, so that the whole, with Middleburg and Pylstaert, made
one group. He appears to have forgotten theft and violence: 'this
groupe I have named the Friendly Archipelago as a lasting friendship seems to subsist among the Inhabitants and their Courtesy to
Strangers intitles them to that Name.'[1] If this is a little romantic,
the speculation which follows is hard-headed and characteristic
enough. 'The Inhabitants of Boscawen and Keppels Isles, discovered
by Captain Wallis in 15°53' and nearly under the same Meridian as
this Archipelago, seem, from the little account I have had of them,
to be the same Sort of friendly people as these. The Latitude and
discriptions of these two isles point them out to be the same as Cocos
and Traitors discovered by Lemaire and Schouten, but if they are
the same Mr Dalrymple has placed them above 8° too far to the
west in his Chart.'[2] The two islands, Tafahi and Niuatoputapu, were
indeed discovered first in 1616 and rediscovered in 1767; their
people are very Tongan; though geographically a little remote from
Tonga, they have historically always been connected with it;
Dalrymple did err.
    Cook put his friendly islands behind him at the close of June. For

[1] ibid., 449.   [2] ibid.

the next few days he made west in about latitude 20°. If he had sailed a more northerly course he could hardly have avoided the large islands of Fiji, interest in examining which might certainly have diverted him from his pursuit of Quiros. The fearful choice did not arise: all he saw of the group was its southern outlier Vatoa (Turtle Island the name he gave, derived from some of the inhabitants) and a nearby reef. There were no turtles to be caught, and he sailed on. He went almost as far south as 21°, then, in unsettled weather, gradually decreased his latitude to 18°26', by which time, 11 July, he was in longitude 175° E, whence he steered north-west to get into the latitude of 'Quiros's Isles'. The weather became pleasant, he ran by day under all the sail he could set, lying to or plying under topsails at night lest he should pass land in the dark; man of war and tropic birds flew overhead again; on 15 July at noon, in longitude 171°16' E, he judged he was in the right latitude, 15°9' (he had Bougainville as well as Dalrymple to lean on) and turned directly west. The following morning brought south-easterly squalls, rain and thick haze—weather that, he reflected, in this ocean in the tropics generally indicated the vicinity of high land; in mid-afternoon, in the south-west, there was the land. He lost ground during the night, because of a great sea and a tremendous gale, which tore sails to pieces and worked ill to rigging, and lasted three days; but he had no doubt from the first that he was at Quiros's Austrialia del Espiritu Santo, the Great Cyclades of Bougainville, that the shore he saw through the haze was what Bougainville had called Aurora.

Quiros, coming from the north, saw islands that Cook did not see, and was convinced that he was on the fringe of a continent: to men who are already half-persuaded, the high ridges do rise up one behind another with a continental aspect. Bougainville, coming from the east, saw six islands and sailed right through the group. Cook, coming in a few miles to the south of Bougainville's track, missed that discoverer's northernmost islet, the volcanic Pic de l'Etoile or Mera Lava—an inconsiderable loss—but had a larger intention before him than merely verifying the existence of land. In the first place, he wanted to coast south from his landfall, to see how far the group extended in that direction. The south-east gale stopped him from doing this, and after tacking off Aurora, or Maewo, for twenty-four hours, he changed his mind, hauling round the northern end of the island into smoother water. His daily proceedings, his notes, for two-thirds of the next six weeks are so complicated, geographically speaking, that one must, as a preliminary, stand off and view them from a distance. The group is known by the name he himself gave it, the New Hebrides. As he sailed round it, it extends, roughly, over five degrees of latitude, from 14°35′ to 19°35′ S (there is another island farther south that he charted, without including it in his circumnavigation), and three degrees of longitude, from 166°30′ to 169°30′ E. To some angelic observer, poised high above the globe, to some cosmonaut speeding round it, the islands would seem flung out over the surface of the ocean in the form of a vast irregular letter Y. The upper right, or eastern, arm of this letter consists north to south of Maewo, Pentecost, and Ambrim, and inside the two former, Oba; the left or western arm of Espiritu Santo and Malekula. The long single leg or tail of the letter, pushed increasingly to the east from top to bottom, is formed by the islands Epi, Efate, Eromanga, Tana and Aneityum. There are smaller linking islands and islets in abundance, though the three bottom units stand more isolated than the others, and the course sailed by Cook, if dotted on the chart, serves to define the whole design. What he did, briefly, having turned the upper end of the right or eastern arm, was to sail down inside that arm, first between Maewo and Oba, then along Pentecost and through the channel between Ambrim and Malekula, where the two extended arms approach each other. That course brought him to the western side of Epi, at the top of the leg, having examined which he went through the leg, as it were, to its eastern side, down past Efate and Eromanga and round the bottom of Tana. He thus left Aneityum unenclosed. He then sailed up the leg and part of the arm on their western sides, and through Bougainville Strait—the passage between Malekula and Espiritu Santo—so that he was on the eastern coast of the latter, the largest island of the group. This he circumnavigated, to the north and down its west side; having arrived off the entrance to Bougainville Strait again, he departed to the south-west. He came round the northern end of Maewo on 18 July; he departed from Espiritu Santo on 31 August. Within this period he was anchored for two nights and the intervening day at Malekula, where he landed; for a night and a morning at Eromanga, where landing was abortive; for two weeks at Tana. For the rest of the time he was sailing, observing, and putting down on paper the remarkable chart that includes ten large islands, six or eight smaller ones, and three dozen or more islets and rocks. As an achievement in marine surveying that month's work ranks with his New Zealand of the first voyage.

Between Maewo and Omba (Bougainville's 'Isle of Lepers') the wind was still stormy, though the sea was smooth, and it was not till the morning of the 20th that Cook was finished with plying between the two islands and could stand over to Pentecost. All three islands were high and heavily wooded, cascades could be seen on the hills, the smokes of habitation above the forest, people on the shore; a canoe came out from Omba to reconnoitre. On the morning of the 21st land in the south-west detached itself from Pentecost as the separate island of Ambrim, where rose two heavier columns of smoke that Cook guessed to signify volcanoes—probably the two now called Marum and Benbow; volcanic eruptions have in fact much altered the western coast of Ambrim that Cook saw. Two other pieces of land appeared separately—the first itself really the two neighbouring small islands of Pa Uma and Lopevi; the second high, sharp-peaked Epi. To the west, however, was a larger mass. The wind had now sunk to a gentle breeze, the weather was fine. A creek or bay on this larger coast offered inviting anchorage, which Cook hoisted out the boats to inspect; while this was doing a throng of people armed with bows and arrows inspected the ship, and a current carried her two leagues to windward, in view of another and more promising harbour. Here the boats were sent instead. They signalled the ship in, and she anchored at sunset, 21 July. Cook had often sailed past good harbours, but this one was probably the best in the New Hebrides—Port Sandwich (the name he gave it), just above the south-east end of 'Mallecollo' or Malekula. Two natives were induced to come on board for a short time; others came off by moonlight, bringing torches to help in their scrutiny of the ship. They were not allowed on board, and went away after exchanging for pieces of cloth a few arrows, the green gummy bone points of which looked very much to suspicious eyes as if they had been poisoned.

Morning brought out many of these people again, some in canoes, some swimming. They came with nothing except their bows and arrows and curiosity, but Cook's welcome seemed to be leading on a friendly intercourse; they filled the deck and the rigging when suddenly all was changed. A man in a canoe, refused admittance into one of the ship's boats, drew an arrow on the boat-keeper, flung off a friend who tried to stop him, and aimed the arrow again; before he could loose it, Cook, running on deck, let go a charge of small shot. The canoes on that side of the ship paddled off fast; on the other side arrows began to fall. A musket discharged in the air and a four-pounder fired over the canoes sent everybody overboard from decks and rigging; some, in their anxiety to get ashore, even left their canoes behind, and drums began to beat. Perhaps this was not so bad a warning, thought Cook—doing nothing, when the confusion abated, to detain the canoes, even encouraging people to come alongside again; and, deciding the time had come to land, he took the marines as a guard; he would trade for provisions and a party cut wood. Leaping into the water with a green branch in his hand, he was presented with another in exchange, though behind the unarmed man who gave it stood a crowd of four or five hundred carrying bows and arrows, clubs and spears. Cook distributed medals and bits of cloth. There was no opposition to the cutting of wood. No one wanted to trade, there was only the handing over of a small pig, and in response to Cook's enquiries, the bringing of half a dozen small coconuts and a little fresh water. Was the pig a peace offering? Cook returned cloth for it; now and again an arrow, but never a bow, was exchanged for cloth. No one wanted nails or tools of iron; the people were most unwilling to let their visitors go beyond the beach —to do anything, in fact, but go away. Cook accordingly went, and set his men to work on the rigging for the afternoon. He went on shore a second time himself, with Forster and one or two others, when he saw a man bringing along the strand to the landing place a buoy (that object apparently of such sovereign desire all over the Pacific) that had been taken away from the kedge anchor during the night; the moment the boat landed the buoy was put into it by another man who walked off without a word. Cook and Forster— no one else—were allowed to go just within the skirt of the woods and look from the outside at a few oblong thatched houses, and small plantations; there were pigs and a few fowls running about, yams piled up on platforms. They were allowed to land briefly at two other points on the harbour shore, collected some island names, took some soundings, looked in vain for a stream of water, and went on board at nightfall. Not a single canoe had been out to the ship during the whole afternoon.

Next morning Cook sailed from this harbour where his reception had been so curious, and now the people seemed willing to trade with anything they had, even their bows. Certainly they were a different species from any he had hitherto met in the great ocean. They were small of stature, very dark; he thought them ugly and ill-proportioned; their lips were thick, their noses flat, their hair and beards crisp and curled, though not woolly. The men were naked, with a belt round the middle so tight it almost gave them two bellies, attached to this a penis case made of cloth or a leaf; they wore bracelets of shell-studded cord and hogs' tusks, curved cylindrical pieces of shell stuck through the nose, ear-rings of tortoise shell. The few women who

were seen, clothed somewhat more heavily in a sort of apron or
skirt to the knees, had their heads, faces and shoulders painted red
or yellow with turmeric; on the whole, there was nothing to choose
between the sexes in beauty. They seemed, in short, a rather 'Apish
Nation'; no fragment of language picked up elsewhere in the
Pacific served to communicate with them. Their only animal, so
far as could be seen, was the pig; Cook therefore left with them, as
with other beneficiaries, a dog and bitch from the Society Islands.
He thought, as he saw vast numbers of them picking up shellfish
on the reef at low tide, as he left, that he had not interfered with their
usual pursuits, and that therefore a longer stay would have ripened
a friendship. He did not know that you cannot make a ghost your
friend. He did not realise the truth about himself, that he was a
ghost. Some of his shipmates were in danger of becoming ghosts in a
more straightforward manner; for a pair of red fish rather like large
bream had been caught and served at dinner to the officers and
petty officers, with the most acute poisoning effects, while a pig and
a dog which had had a share died outright. It was a week or ten days
before everybody recovered, and Cook's mind was carried back to
Quiros, who with his whole company suffered painfully from fish-
poisoning at his Bay of St Philip and St James. On the other hand,
experiments with a poisoned arrow on a dog left the animal quite
unscathed.[1]

Off the southern point of Malekula was a group of small islands
which Cook failed to name; Wales therefore named them after the
Astronomer Royal, for he felt almost sentimentally indebted to
Maskelyne's help in his career. In the night, having run south again,
they fetched in close with the west side of Epi; by noon of the 24th
'we were not Able to distinguish the number of isles around us'.
Nevertheless Cook distinguished and charted them. He was in some
danger at this stage when a calm fell and he was at the mercy of the
currents, all too close to island shores, with no soundings at the end
of a 180 fathom line. Luckily a breeze sprang up, with which he was
able to pass inside these islands and stretch to the east for a short
time, into a clear sea. He gave to the ones he had escaped, off the
south-east end of Epi, the name of another astronomer, Dr Antony
Shepherd of Cambridge. Great columns of smoke could still be seen
rising from the mountain in the middle of Ambrim. Now outside the
islands, except for the remarkable peaked rock he called the Monu-

---

[1] The poisonous fish may have been the Red Bass, *Lutjanus coatesi*, or the Chinaman
Fish, *Paradicithys veneratus*. On 'Poisoned arrows' see, briefly, ibid., 465, n. 5; or more at
length, R. H. Codrington, *The Melanesians* (Oxford, 1891), 306-13.

ment, he steered for a large shape in the south. There were islets lying near it; currents in a dead calm carried him to the north-west for a while, then with a westerly breeze he got through a passage between one of these, his Montagu, and the larger mass that he called Sandwich. The First Lord was still much in his mind. Montagu was Emau. Sandwich was Efate; he could see no end to its shores, but thought its appearance, beyond a fringe of rocks and breakers, most delightful. He sailed on. It was 26 July; in the afternoon, the wind sinking again, and no bottom, he was again apprehensive of the effect of the currents. A south-west breeze relieved his mind, and he stretched south-east all night. At sunrise the high hills of another land appeared in the south. He came up with it slowly, partly because of the lightness of the airs and the ship's drift to leeward, partly because of his own caution in standing to the east one night. By the last day of the month he almost despaired of reaching it; meanwhile still more land had been sighted in the south and sunk beneath the horizon again. On 1 August however, close in, he could range from the northern point along the western side. Then the wind changed from south-east to north-west, he abandoned the thoughts he had of anchoring and continued south; in the night it fell, and he drove to the north with the current. The master was sent to examine a bay for anchorage: while he did so the ship still drove until, a south-west breeze springing up, Cook resolved to go back to the south, though down the island's east side. Just after sunrise on the 3rd, having rounded its north-east point, he was off a high bluff and inside a small island. He sent Clerke with two boats to see if he could cut wood on this island, but the surf stopped them even from landing; and the wind swinging round again, Cook went into a wide bay on the north-west side of the high bluff, where at the end of the day he anchored.

It was wood and water that he wanted. He looked for a landing place. The shore was rocky. Some men appeared who, in return for pieces of cloth and medals, were ready to haul the boats over the rocks, a procedure not fancied by Cook: as he rowed they ran, joined by many others, finally directing him to a sandy beach where he landed dry-shod, with nothing in his hands but a green branch he had somehow got from them. He was faced by a great multitude armed with clubs, darts, stones, and bows and arrows, but was received, he thought, 'very courteously'. They pressed near his boat; he motioned them back, and a chief made them form a sort of semi-circle round its bow. He distributed trinkets and made signs that he wanted water, hoping that he might see where they got it; the chief sent a man to a hut, who brought back a little in a bamboo. He asked similarly for food, and was brought a yam and a few coconuts. This was not getting very far. Then the chief, on his part, motioned Cook to haul the boat on shore. Cook was watching him narrowly, and he seemed to be giving directions among the crowd. It indicated no good: Cook stepped into the boat and ordered her off, signifying that he would come back later. At that the nearest of the crowd surged forward to drag the boat on shore by its gang-board and snatched some of the oars, others began to shoot arrows and hurl stones and darts: 'our own safety became now the only consideration' (writes Cook) 'and yet I was very loath to fire upon such a Multitude and resolved to make the chief a lone fall a Victim to his own treachery, but my Musquet at this critical Moment'—as at Niue—'refused to perform its part and made it absolutely neces-sary for me to give orders to fire'; the people thus thrown into confusion, a second discharge drove them off the beach, though they continued to throw stones and darts from the shelter of the bushes. Four lay seemingly dead on the shore—'happy for many of these poor people not half our Musquets would go of otherwise many more must have fallen'.[1] One man in Cook's boat had his cheek pierced by a dart; in the cutter thirty yards off Gilbert was struck on the breast by an arrow which fortunately did not penetrate. Back in the ship Cook fired a gun to show its effect: the ball fell short but the splash and the noise were sufficiently frightening. Still thinking he might stay, he hove up the anchor with the intention of moving the ship closer in. No sooner was it at the bows, however, than a northerly breeze springing up blew right into the bay, so he set his sails, plyed out, and steered for the south end of the island. An unprofitable morning: Cook remained unaware that he was a ghost.

We are fortunate to have not only his side of the story, but the other. It convinces us that when he gave to the high bluff at the entrance to the bay the name Traitors' Head he was not, in fact, quite just. Yet how could he be just? Both here and at Malekula he had encountered some of the deepest feelings, or beliefs, of mankind, and they were beliefs of which he knew nothing. He thought he had learnt something when at his next port of call he picked up the name of the place, 'Erromango' or Eromanga, which he applied to the whole island,[2] when he noted that the people were different from those of Malekula, were better looking, spoke a different language,

---

[1] *Journals* II, 479.
[2] Traitors' Head is one of the entrance points to Polenia Bay, where Cook had been anchored; his little island is now called Goat islet or island.

even while their garb, or absence of it, was much the same. Certainly they were both very different from the cheerful Polynesians; but he had had no chance to feel the sombre element in the human life of these lush islands. It is true that there was a darker side to Polynesian life than Cook had yet experienced; the prohibitions of all pervading *tapu* could be awful as well as inconvenient, the gods angry as well as generous; but Polynesian existence seems sunny while Melanesian does not, though the same sun shone on both. No European, however romantic, ever stepped on to a Melanesian island with the thought that he was stepping into the golden age. The Melanesian peoples nourished the immemorial and pardonable conviction that strangers were enemies; and there were other strangers, other enemies, besides ordinary men. They lived, like so many other savage peoples, on the narrow and terrible border of the unseen. They were very close to their dead; they feared the spirits of the dead, the menacing and maleficent ancestors who would not rest. The border could be burst, the invisible irruption become a visible one— in the forest, by night on a village path: why not from the sea? It was the part of wisdom to avoid or propitiate ghosts; but if the worst came to the worst they could be attacked with human weapons and driven away. Cook had broken through the border, but he had not disguised himself. Spirits, ghosts, were not the colour of human beings, they were white. Cook and his men were white. When he was at Port Sandwich, and the people, yet uncertain, crowded his rigging, Forster heard the word constantly repeated, 'Tomarr'. It may have been the Malekulan *damar*, peace; it was more probably *temar*, ancestors; possibly it was both. The single pig, the few coconuts, the small quantity of water offered the captain, the principal ghost, were propitiatory and symbolic; you did not offer ghosts great quantities of food. The people were anxious that he should depart. At Eromanga the boats were first seen rowing off from the small island, Goat Island, where Cook had gone for wood. This island, everybody knew, was the habitation of ghosts: no one else had ever landed there, or come from there. Again there was the symbolic offering of a little water, the yam, the coconuts; then the attack, the product of fear not bellicosity. Only the chief, Narom, was killed. So at least the tale handed down from generation to generation on Eromanga, and it is not an unlikely tale. Cook did not discover it.

By evening he had run right down the coast of Eromanga on his west, and had to the south in full view the island he had just glimpsed four days earlier. Shaping his course for its eastern end, he came up with it half-way through the night, guided by a large fire burning on it. In the morning this proved to be an exceedingly active volcano, the flames and smoke and rumbling of which were his constant companions for the next fortnight. To the north-east and south-west were the two small islands of Aniwa and Futuna. A small distance from the east end of the island he was steering for what was a promising inlet, and as his need of wood and water was now real he sent the boats to sound it; on a favourable signal followed them in, anchored, then warped in still farther. This was only the morning after the attack at Eromanga, and it was a question how the people would behave here: Cook did not want more flights of arrows, more musket-volleys. He looked at his harbour, his Port Resolution to be. It leads north and south; it is not large, from entrance to head less than a mile; a finger of fairly deep water runs up its middle, shoals spreading on each side; at the entrance on both sides is fairly high land, which continues all along the west side behind a shore of rocks; at the head and on most of the east side is beach. Gazing beyond the head he would have seen some flat land, behind it, standing up remarkably above the forested slopes, the almost 3,500 feet of Mount Merrin; close south-west, a bare 600 feet high, the volcano Yasua or Yasur, spreading its fine ash over the country for miles. No river ran into the harbour, but a pool of fresh water lay twenty yards from the beach at its head. It is a harbour that still speaks vividly of this eighteenth-century visit, although, raised by earthquake just over a hundred years after Cook, and partly silted up, with a population about it that has declined to a few score, it is not the harbour into which he came with hope and caution in that first week of August.

While the ship was warping in, large numbers of the people collected and gazed; many came off in canoes and some swam, not too near, while those in the canoes had their arms ready; growing bolder they came under the stern, exchanging coconuts for pieces of cloth; growing too bold, in the usual fashion tried to carry away the buoys, were frightened off with a few muskets and the noise of a gun; recovered themselves and came back for the buoys, finally retired when swivel-guns were fired over them. Only one pacific old man in a small canoe travelled backwards and forwards, bringing two or three coconuts or a yam each time: whatever feeling animated this elder in the first place, as long as the ship stayed his friendship was to be undeviating and useful. In the afternoon Cook landed with a strong party. He found the people assembled in two large groups, to his right and his left, all armed with their darts, clubs, slings, bows and arrows; he distributed to the senior among them presents of cloth and medals and boldly filled two casks at the pool. These people let go a few coconuts but nothing else; they pressed hard on the party, and would, he thought, have attacked had he not disconcerted them by re-embarking unexpectedly soon. Relations were thus still uncertain, the people difficult; as Clerke said, 'their behaviour upon this our first Visit was not the most friendly I've ever experienc'd among Indians—they did not insult us tis true but they did by no means seem reconcil'd to the liberty we took in landing upon their Coasts'; and this, though written with a tinge of humour, is probably an accurate observation. Cook now resolved to warp the ship in closer, to within two or three hundred yards of the shore, and moor her broadside on. This would make easier the labour of loading wood and water, it would give more protection to his working-parties, and it would, he thought, overawe the natives. The armed groups formed themselves on the beach again. A single canoe would come out from time to time with coconuts or plantains—never many—and invite the visitors on shore. Cook always saw that the occupants were recompensed; when the old man came he tried to make him understand the need to disarm. Then some bravoes cheated in the first little exchange they tried: 'this', says Cook, 'was what I expected and what I was not sorry for as I wanted a pretence to shew the Multitude on shore the effect of our firearms without materially hurting any of them',[1] so he let one of them have a barrel of small shot and fired off some musketoons or swivels. The crowd was unimpressed.

Cook decided to land; and this was the critical moment. If here again he was a ghost, there seems not to have been unanimity how to treat him. He took three boats with the marines and armed seamen. As he neared the shore he saw laid out in a clear space between the two large bodies of men a few bunches of plantains, a yam, and two roots of taro; leading to them from the water were four small reeds stuck in the sand. The old man with two other elders stood by and invited him on shore. The roots and the fruit, we perceive, were once again the propitiatory offering; the reeds were the usual means of indicating the *tapu* nature of an object. Cook was baffled, and suspected a trap; he did not want another Eromanga incident. He signed to the crowds, every moment growing larger, to move farther back; the three old men added their persuasions, without success.

In short every thing conspired to make us believe they intended to attack us as soon as we were on shore. The consequence of such a step was easily

[1] *Journals* II, 484.

seen, many of them must have been kill'd and wounded and we should hardly have escaped unhurt. Sence therefore they would not give us the room we required I thought it was best to frighten them away rather than oblige them by the deadly effect of our fire Arms and accordingly order a Musquet to be fired over the heads of the party on our right for this was by far the Strongest body, the alarm it gave them was only momentary, in an instant they recovered themselves and began to display their weapons, one fellow shewed us his back side in such a manner that it was not necessary to have an interpreter to explain his meaning; after this I ordered three or four more to be fired, this was the Signal for the Ship to fire a few four pound Shott over them which presently dispersed them and then we landed and marked out the limits on the right and [left] by a line.[1]

Only one person stood his ground, the old man, Paowang. Reasons for his self-possession in face of the supernatural can be conjectured, if not confirmed; if he was a natural sceptic, he made no instantaneous conquest of his fellows' minds. The space Cook wanted for a passage to the fresh water was roped off and guarded by the marines. No one had been hurt. The natives began to drift back in a friendly way, threw down coconuts without expecting a return, and seemed to have no notion of trade. Many, noted Cook—and the observation is not without significance—'were afraid to touch any thing which belonged to us'. There were marked differences, obviously, between these people and those in the islands of the more eastern groups. In the afternoon it was possible to work very peaceably, and haul the seine profitably; the following morning 'many of the younger sort were very daring and insolent and obliged us to stand with our Arms in hand', and Lieutenant Edgcumbe found it necessary to fire a slug at one; thereafter active opposition died down. There was toleration, even some amiability. The ancestor-spirits, one must suppose, when fully discussed were deemed not so maleficent after all. The only fury that arose was from the volcano.

Indeed, in a day or two more Cook ceased to protect with particularity his passage to the water, though he kept a guard on shore. He was scrupulous in cutting wood only after permission, and in making some return for any service rendered him. There was little food to be got, from plantations none the less flourishing; when fruit or roots were presented, in small quantities, or a single pig or a cock, it was usually done with a good deal of ceremony. Fishing was not good. The people seemed to form two clans, one on the eastern side of the harbour, one on the west—of whom the former seemed rather more open-hearted to wanderers. The naturalists managed to make

----

[1] *Journals* II, 485.

some useful expeditions, others had little excursions inland, but on the whole, visitors were discouraged from going far beyond the beach—or, for some days, even from walking along the shore. At last they were allowed to go shooting in the woods. It was never possible to explore the volcano. No objection, however, was made to the repeated investigation of steaming hot sulphurous patches on the western slope just above the beach, and the hot springs below high water mark which were first discovered when a sailor, one of a party gathering ballast, scalded his fingers. Wales and Cook went on a pleasant visit to an eastern village. The people themselves were scrupulous in bringing back any ship's property carelessly lost, if they found it; as the days went on a few, including Paowang and an old chief whom he introduced, were prevailed upon to dine on board. The usual dog and bitch were presented to Paowang. Cook's chief anxiety might seem to arise from his own men. One day two or three boys threw a few stones from behind a thicket at the wooding party; the petty officers replied with their muskets. Cook was extremely displeased at such wanton abuse of fire-arms, 'and took measures to prevent it for the future'. It may have been at this time that he gave the order that no man was to shoot until shot at. He maintained the guard, because he was not prepared to rely whole-heartedly on native good feeling: even after ten days, when the visit was drawing to an end—or perhaps because it had gone on so long—although most of the crowd about the landing place behaved with 'courtesy and friendship', others were 'a little troublesome, daring and insolent'. At that stage it seemed best to ignore such trespasses.

He was accumulating a good many useful observations of the people and the country, to which both Forster and Wales contributed. Forster reported that the island was called 'Tanna', which it has remained. This was an error: like other islands in the group, it had no name in the minds of its inhabitants; names were given from outside, and *Tana* merely meant the ground on which they stood.[1] As Cook had come further south, the islanders had grown more handsome: these were far different from the 'apish' Malekulans, better looking than the Eromangans. Had they, he wondered, not without cause, some mixture from the east? They spoke still another language—were there in it some traces of Tongan? They were as naked as their more northern fellows, wearing their hair, however, differently, in a multitude of odd queues. They were agile,

---

[1] 'Yesterday Mr Forster obtained from these people the Name of the Island (Tanna) and to day I got from them the names of those in the nieghbourhood.'—ibid., 489. Cf. the quotation in n. 4 of that page from C. B. Humphreys, *The Southern New Hebrides* (Cambridge, 1926).

handling their weapons well, and their style in throwing their spears reminded Wales of the Homeric heroes. His passage on this subject much struck Cook, who copied it out. Their canoes were clumsy. They were, he gathered, cannibals. They seemed to have no chiefs of great importance. They had no animals beyond pigs and fowls; their word *puaka*, for pig, served equally well for the novel dog, goat and cat. To island vegetable productions he could now add wild figs, nutmegs and a sort of inedible orange. The great natural wonders, of course, were the hot springs and the steaming 'pipeclay' on the slope above them, on the way up to the volcano. Now the position of this volcano led to thought, it controverted the opinion of the philosophers that all volcanoes must be at the summits of the highest hills: there were hills in this island higher by far, and he could see that the smoke on Ambrim came from a 'valley' between the hills rather than from the peaks: 'to these remarks must be added another which is that during wet or moist weather the Volcano was most vehement. Here seems to be a feild open for some Philosophical reasoning on these extraordinary Phenomenon's of nature, but as I have no tallant that way I must content my self with stateing facts as I found and leave the causes to men of more abilities.'[1]

He had further reflections, consistent with his intentions as a humane discoverer, not always consistent with facts. 'I cannot say what might be the true cause of these people shewing such a dislike to our makeing little excursions into their Country'—a naturally jealous disposition, hostile visits from their neighbours, quarrels amongst themselves? They seldom or never travelled unarmed. 'It is possible all this might be on our account, but I can hardly think it, we never gave them the least molestation, nor did we touch any part of their property, not even Wood and Water without first having obtained their consent.'[2] Some of that was true: his last request had been for permission to cut down a casuarina, a hard wood with which to repair his tiller, found to be sprung just as he was ready to put to sea. But there was the incident of the wooders firing on the boys; there was the fact that he had landed only after a show of force, whether that were justified or not. There was the fact that all his precautions could not control events. His last day, before he wrote those words, was marred by an incident that made him the volcano of fury. Some logs were being brought on board, the usual guard was on shore, the usual assembly pressing round the landing place. The sentry ordered them back, at which one of them presented his bow and arrow as if to shoot. Cook, who was near, thought

[1] *Journals* II, 498. [2] ibid., 501.

this was only a matter of form; he was astonished when the sentry fired, and with ball. The man was killed. Patten, for whom Cook sent at once, could do nothing; the people fled. It was an outrage, a crime, the sentry was flung into irons, and was to be flogged. The officers took his side; there was apparently an argument of much warmth between them and Cook, who finally remitted the flogging, but gave what he considered a faithful account in his journal.[1] Had he not set his face like stone against this sort of thing ever since Poverty Bay? He could turn back a page or two in his journal and find his own, cooler yet clear, comment:

thus we found these people Civil and good Natured when not prompted by jealousy to a contrary conduct, a conduct one cannot blame them for when one considers the light in which they must look upon us in, its impossible for them to know our real design, we enter their Ports without their daring to make opposition, we attempt to land in a peaceable manner, if this succeeds its well, if not we land nevertheless and mentain the footing we thus got by the Superiority of our fire arms, in what other light can they than at first look upon us but as invaders of their Country; time and some acquaintance with us can only convince them of their mistake.[2]

Only time and acquaintance: the captain had an inadequate view of the future. He did not conceive that invasion might follow after him. Meanwhile, the morning of 20 August having brought a favourable wind, he weighed anchor and put to sea, hoisted in his boats, and stretched to the east to take a nearer view of Futuna.

For the next eleven days he was viewing islands from the sea, close enough in to get a good idea of their characteristics, fixing the positions of their leading points with considerable accuracy. A remarkably clear morning on the 21st showed him no land to the east of the high flat-topped Futuna; he was equally convinced, as he ran back to coast the southern side of Tana, that to the south there was nothing in the group beyond Annatom or Aneityum. Next day he was past the western sides of Tana and Eromanga, steering for the same side of Efate, to finish its survey and that of the islands north-west of it. It was now, knowing that he could get no native name for it, that he called it Sandwich Island, in honour of 'My Noble Patron', and the two islets on its north-east side, Montagu and Hinchinbrook. He was much taken with the appearance of the

---

[1] ibid., 499. I have a long note on the matter beginning on that page, which there would be no point in now repeating. Young Elliott, who was not an eye-witness, thought that though Cook 'was a Most Brave, Just, Humane, and good Man', here 'He lost sight, of both justice, and Humanity'.—*Memoirs*, 32v. The sentry, William Wedgeborough, was not a man in whom Cook could place confidence.

[2] *Journals* II, 493.

island, its gentle slopes and luxuriant vegetation: Wales thought it
'one of the most beautiful & desirable Islands we have yet seen in
the South Seas'. He came up with Malekula on the 23rd—he was
lucky in his continuous south-east wind and fine weather, which let
him keep within two miles of the shore, so that in the night he could
hear the people assembled about a fire on the beach; and at morning
hauled round the northern end into the strait between Malekula and
Espiritu Santo that his predecessor had called Bougainville Passage.
So far Espiritu Santo was to him merely the 'northern land' or the
'northern isle'. There were islets, low and woody, off its southern
shore, including one larger quite high piece of land that because of
the day he called St Bartholomew—the first saint's name Cook had
ever given to an island. Islets stood off its eastern shore too: on the
night of 24 August he had run outside the most northerly of them,
on the morrow doubling both it and a bluff head to its west. Looking
south he saw 'a very large and deep bay', and he could see its
opposite shore running up to the north-west. He did not doubt that
this was Quiros's Bay of St Philip and St James, the famous bay. To
clinch his conviction he would have to explore it to its head. Variable
winds made this a little complicated: a north-east swell hurried him
over to the western side, the wind fell calm when he was two miles
from it in 120 fathoms, and 'we were apprehensive'—there is almost
an echo from that June of 1606—'we should be obliged to Anchor
in a great depth upon a lee shore'; rescue came with a breeze, and
next afternoon, after another calm, the ship was able to stand off
and on while Cooper and Gilbert reconnoitred the beach, and a few
canoes sailed out to reconnoitre in their turn, not bold enough to
come alongside. Their occupants seemed another people still, in
their differences from those of the group already encountered. The
sailors landed near a fine river, Quiros's Jordan; they noticed that
plants grew close to high water mark, an indication of the absence
of surf and easy access to the land. Cook was sure they had sounded
the anchorage that Quiros called the Port of Vera Cruz. He was
right. He had answered one of the main questions which had been
in his mind as he turned north from the ice in the previous February.
'Quiros describes this Land . . . as being very large, M. de Bougainville neither confirms nor refutes this account.' He could say accurately
where it was and what its limits were.

He wanted to spend no further time here. If he stayed, he could
not expect to find supplies, and he 'had no time to spend in amusements'—however he would define amusements. He steered for the
open sea. When night fell the country was alight with fires from the

shore to the hill-tops as the people burnt off the growth for their plantations; it must be a well-populated place, he thought, as well as a fertile one. He had been unable to find a native name for the whole of it: let it then be '*Tierra Del Espiritu Santo*, the only remains of Quiros's Continent'. Let the headland at the eastern entrance to the great bay be Cape Quiros; and let the north-western point— we are about to see more loyalty to the House of Hanover than sense of the fitness of things—be Cape Cumberland in honour of His Royal Highness the Duke. This cape he doubled on the afternoon of 27 August; in four days more, the wind being difficult,[1] he had coasted the island's western shore, doubled its south-western extremity and looked more closely at its southern end—when, 'haveing made the Circuit of the isle and with it finished the Survey of the whole Archipelago so that I had no more business there, besides the Season of the year made it necessary I should think of returning to the South', he put it behind him, hauled to the south-ward, and on the morning of 1 September was out of sight of land. There can be no doubt that, while he was anxious not to waste time, he found time to feel a sense of satisfaction in what he had done, which was not diminished as he worked over his journal and co-ordinated his impressions. He could not help looking back to Quiros, 'that great Navigator'; he could not help adding a phrase or two to his criticism of Bougainville. He himself—or rather 'we'—had not only ascertained the extent and situation of the islands already known to exist, but added to them several new ones and explored the whole: 'I think we have obtained a right to name them and shall for the future distinguish them under the name of'—certainly not the Great Cyclades; but what? It is unlikely that he hit on the New Hebrides until somewhat later, when he was finding a name for another country newly discovered. They had explored the whole, they had 'finished the Survey': but what did that mean? One must not claim too much. When he left the coast of Eromanga behind him and steered NNW for Sandwich Island, it was 'in order to finish the Survey'. He had later made the note, 'The word Survey, is not to be understood here, in its literal sence. Surveying a place, according to my Idea, is takeing a Geometrical Plan of it, in which every place is to have its true situation, which cannot be done in a work of this kind.'[2] He did not, that is, he carefully points out, profess to offer

[1] 'We've made but a poor hand of it these 3 days past; these light Airs and Calms detain us most confoundedly, and now begin to grow very tedious.'—Clerke, 30 August; ibid., 518, n. 4.
[2] For the quotations foregoing in this paragraph, ibid., 519, 521, and, on 'The word Survey', 509, n. 4. An Admiralty Hydrographer, 120 years later, was to make his comment

a Newfoundland. But he cannot refrain from pointing out, also, the care taken by Wales in calculating longitudes. The longitude of Port Sandwich was settled from the mean of 32 sets of observations, that of Port Resolution from the mean of 45 sets, either taken at those ports or reduced to them by 'the Watch'; and

It is necessary to observe, that each set of observations, consists, of between Six and ten observed distances of the Sun and Moon or Moon and Stars, so that the whole number amounts to several hundreds and these have been reduced by means of the Watch to all the islands, so that the Longitude of each is as well assertained as the two Ports above mentioned, as a proof of this I shall only observe that the difference of Longitude between the two Ports pointed out by the Watch, and by the observations did not differ from each other two miles.[1]

The Watch, indeed, had become 'our never failing guide'.

There was no further use for Alexander Dalrymple's *Historical Collection.* Cook, we may say, could now do with the Pacific Ocean as he liked. The season of the year made it necessary that he should think of returning to the south: not because wind and weather drove him from latitude 15°, but because he had designed, seven months before, to cross the ocean from west to east between the latitudes of 50° and 60° and be the length of Cape Horn in November, with the summer in front of him for the South Atlantic. It does not seem that at that time he had envisaged another call at his New Zealand base; but by the time he had got to Tana this was certainly his design. He was like an artist perfecting the formal construction of a picture as he works on it. At Port Resolution Wales bemoaned the difficulty of taking altitudes accurately to check the chronometer— 'Indeed I begin to despair of doing any thing to the Purpose here, and yet am so great a slave to it that I have scarce time to eat.' He would have ample opportunity at New Zealand, Cook told him;[2] in his own journal the captain explained necessity more at length. He must return to the south 'while I had yet some time left to explore

on this particular piece of work by Cook. 'His chart of the New Hebrides is still, for some of the islands, the only one; and wherever superseded by more recent surveys the general accuracy of his work, both in outline and position, is very remarkable. On several occasions up to the present year (1893) Cook's recorded positions have saved the adoption of so-called amendments reported by passing ships, which would have been anything but amendments in reality.'—Wharton, *Captain Cook's Journal* (London, 1893), xxxviii.

[1] *Journals* II, 524–5.

[2] ibid., 520. For Wales, 856; and his *Remarks on Mr. Forster's Account of Captain Cook's last Voyage* (1778), 89. The Forsters were apparently under the impression that Cook had meant to sail from the New Hebrides to Tierra del Fuego without any intermediate call. See George Forster, *Voyage,* II, 376; and *Journals* II, xcviii–xcix.

any lands I might meet with between this and New Zeland, where I intended to touch to refresh my people and recrute our stock of wood and Water, for another Southern Cruse'. He almost seemed to be working by some sort of instinct. He held his course for three days, and on the morning of the fourth, in latitude 20°, Midshipman Colnett sighted land. The first cape seen, in the south-east in the afternoon, was named after him.

It was a country, or rather a coast—for there was little seen of the country—that was to interest Cook a good deal, and place him in more continuous danger than he had yet been in. He had come to the north-eastern side of the fourth largest island in the Pacific, a comparatively narrow island running about three hundred miles from its south-east to north-west, barred all round by reef that hardly rose above the sea; an island breaking off at its northern end into shoals and a sort of continuation of islands within the same reef, at the south into a mass of low sandy islets, shoals and reefs, partly within the main reef, partly about a larger island standing out more independently. The wind blew from the east, south-east, fortunately not too often from the north-east—so that he would too frequently feel that he was on a lee shore, towards which the swell also tended; and too frequently the wind fell to a calm. A breeze off the land at the end of the day could sometimes be very welcome. Cook was on this coast from the time he sighted it till the end of September. Of those twenty-seven days, he spent eight at anchor inside the reef almost at the northern end of the island, and landed briefly on one of the sandy islets at the other end just before he sailed away. For the rest of the period he was under sail, charting and observing, more than once uncomfortable in mind, once in the most extreme peril; baffled in the end of his desire to circumnavigate the country, but leaving it not without conjecture as to its relation to the greater land-mass he had charted in the west. He found his mind turning much to New South Wales.

Cook was a day coming up with the land. At sunrise on 5 September he could see how it ran, and also the reef running parallel with it. Whether he coasted it in one direction or the other, south-east or north-west, seemed of no great importance: he chose the latter. After following the reef for a short distance, he came to an opening and sent in boats to sound, arming them because of the nearness of a dozen sailing canoes; he wanted to get ashore both to look at the land and to observe an approaching eclipse of the sun. The people in the canoes were friendly, the passage through the reef negotiable—there were no dangers but the steep-to reef itself—

through it, the ship anchored not far off a small sandy islet, the canoes followed and were joined by others, the ship was surrounded by a crowd of unarmed curious people whose shyness was so soon overset that several of them could be entertained to dinner. Here was another new language, as strange as the new friendliness, even if nothing to choose between the nakedness now found and that lately left; these people were ignorant not only of goats, dogs and cats but even of hogs; they immediately showed an inclination for large spike nails and red cloth, without inclination to appropriate them undirected. In the afternoon Cook landed on a pleasant sandy beach amid a still friendly crowd, distributed a few presents, and was the subject of what appeared to be celebratory speeches from the chiefs. One of these, called 'Teabooma', took charge of the search for a watering-place; he was, clearly, here the most striking personality. But though the captain could breathe freely this welcoming air, though friendship was so obvious, equally obvious did it quickly become that he could expect no supply of refreshment beyond water, that the people had nothing to spare in fact, 'but good Nature and Courtious treatment'. In these things, he adds, 'they exceeded all the nations we had yet met with, and although it did not fill our bellies it left our minds at ease'.[1] At the time this mattered the less, as he had New Zealand in view. He could relax the usual restrictions on trade; and 'such was the prevailing Passion for curiosities' that the native clubs and darts came to a good market. Contrary to what one might think, the ship was not a museum of ethnographical specimens; for the sailors would hand over at one island anything acquired at the last, destroy anything they had obtained when they were tired of looking at it. What riches, we reflect, were thrown away!

Next day Pickersgill found an excellent watering place nearly abreast of the ship; in the afternoon Wales, Clerke and Cook observed the eclipse, or at least the end of it (the first contact being obscured by clouds) from the sandy islet off which she was anchored. Their times, with telescopes by three different makers, varied by only four seconds.[2] In the evening came a third loss by death—Simon Monk the ship's butcher, a man highly thought of, who had fallen down the fore hatchway the previous night and injured him-

---

[1] *Journals* II, 531, and n. 5 on that page.
[2] 'Mr Wales measured the quantity eclipsed by a Hadlies Quad^t a method I believe never before thought of, I am of opinion it answers the purpose of a Micrometer to a great degree of accuracy and that it is a valuable discovery and will be a great addition to the use of that most usefull instrument.'—ibid., 532. This passage casts light both on Wales and on Cook's interest in scientific instruments.

self beyond recovery. Poor Simon Monk consigned to the deep, Cook went to the heights. Hills were for explorers to climb. He wanted, as usual, 'to take a View of the Country'. Up the path over the steep range behind the shore he was guided and accompanied by a numerous train. From the summit he gazed down into a large valley with a river winding through it; beyond the range on its other side appeared again the sea. The country then could not be very wide. The captain was rather taken by some at least of the prospect beneath him 'The plains along the Coast on the side we lay appeared from the hills to great advantage, the winding Streams which ran through them which had their direction from Nature, the lesser streames conveyed by art through the different plantations, the little Stragling Villages, the Variaty in the Woods, the Shoals on the Coast so variegated the Scene that the whole might afford a Picture for romance.'[1] This, however, was not the whole aspect of the country: much of it was scorched and rocky waste, the grass coarse, the trees sparse; where they stood more thickly they were eucalypts without undergrowth, or mangroves on the shore. 'No Land of Canaan', it seemed to Wales. Before Cook went away he could not fail to be impressed by a different sort of tree, the ever-present Niaouli or Leucadendron; and he recurs to the laboriously, the skilfully irrigated plantations of taro. This day of exploration was followed by a night in which Cook for the second time, with the Forsters, underwent the rigours of fish-poisoning. His clerk had bought from the natives a fish with a large ugly head—very likely a toadfish—against which, as food, they had given no warning. Although Cook ordered it for supper the scientists took so long over describing and drawing it that no more could be dressed—fortunately—than the liver and roe. The three victims just tasted of these, the suspicious Forster (according to his own account) only after being assured by Cook that he had eaten the fish before, on the coast of New Holland, and that it was perfectly innocuous. Rash confidence! Vomits and sweats relieved them; the dogs also, who had got ahead of the servants with what went from the table, were sick, and a pig which ate the entrails died. In the morning the natives who saw the fish hanging up were solemn in their warnings. All the evidence we have indicates that Cook was stubborn about food. After two days Forster was able to resume his botanising, not without a certain grievance.

While Cook was still suffering the ill effects of this supper Teabooma came with a small ceremonial present of yams and sugar-

[1] ibid., 533-4.

canes; Cook in return bestowed the usual dog and bitch,[1] which were joyfully received. A few days later he took a boar and sow ashore for the chief: the country, he thought, should be stocked. Teabooma he could not find, and it required much persuasion, and elaborate expatiation on the fecundity of pigs, before an assembly of courteous elders would accept these. Meanwhile he had sent Gilbert, of whose judgment he thought highly, and Pickersgill with the launch and the cutter to the north-west inside the reef, to see how far the coast was continuous. The expedition was not very successful. It reached an off-lying island, visible from the ship: Gilbert correctly concluded that the land ended opposite this island, but Pickersgill, no doubt misled by the glimpse of islets further north within the reef, differed; the cutter sprang a leak and nearly foundered; after three days they arrived back agreeing on the information, which Cook hardly needed, that there was no passage for the ship. There was not much more he could do here but set the carpenters to work on the cutter and complete his water. As first discoverer he did take possession, cutting an inscription testifying to the fact into a large tree close by, as he had done before elsewhere. He had been able to find no general name for the country, and as yet he gave it none; the district where he landed, where alone he met the people, was called, he learnt, Balade; the island along the coast to which Gilbert and Pickersgill had gone, was 'Balabea' or Balabio; the sandy islet of the eclipse he called Observatory Isle, for once ignoring a native name when he found it—this one being Pudiue. When he came to set down his impressions of the people themselves he found he had a good deal to say, in spite of the shortness of his visit. Like the Tanese in colour, they were taller and better built, with more agreeable features; their heads, covered with coarse black hair, needed frequent scratching, and their large, rather fan-shaped combs were ingeniously adapted to 'beat up the quarters of a hundred lice at a time'. He remarks upon the frequent elephantiasis, that common Melanesian disease of the generally naked men; the thick short petticoats of the women, the shell and tortoise shell ornaments, the sparse tattooing of both sexes, the men's peculiar cylindrical black caps. 'Was I to judge of the Origin of this Nation, I should take them to be a race between the people of Tanna and the Friendly isles or between Tanna and the New Zealanders or all three.' General affability, he remarks also, did not stretch to welcoming embraces from the

[1] The dog was red and white, the bitch 'all red or the Colour of an English fox'. He later adds the remark, 'I mention this because they may prove the Adam and Eve of their species in this Country.'—ibid., 535, and n. 6 on that page.

women. A race both chaste and honest: for seamen this was dumb-founding. Their weapons and tools, their beehive houses, hot and stifling, were all neatly made; they had earthenware pots for cooking, not much variety of food to cook in them. How like this sterile country was to New South Wales! Perhaps fish in the sea to some extent compensated; for he saw turtle nets, smaller nets, gigs for striking in shallow water on the reef; and canoes, heavy, clumsy structures of large tree-trunks hollowed out, two joined together by spars and a massive deck, laborious to paddle but going very well under their lateen sails. Cook notes their build and managemen with the attentive observation he had devoted to the canoes of Tonga and the other islands. As for the language, that was incomprehensible. Nevertheless he seemed to hear echoes of other tongues, and one word at least became clear, *tea* or *tia* for a chief; he himself was 'Tiacook'.

It was on the afternoon of 12 September that Cook performed his ceremony of annexation; next morning at sunrise he got under sail and, passing through the break in the reef by which he had entered, was soon at sea. The country must be an island, and he intended to circumnavigate it round by the south-east; Gilbert, however, strong in his conviction that he had seen its north-western end, persuaded his captain that the easier way was there. For two and a half days Cook tried this direction, outside the reef. He saw more land, and could not be certain whether this proved Gilbert wrong or was made up of detached islands—which indeed it was—but hesitated to move in for a closer view because he feared the wind might fall and the sea be too deep to anchor. Inside the reef further north were shoals: when he was certain he had passed the end of the land, on the morning of the 15th, the breakers still stretched illimitably north-wards. To explore shoals would entail altogether too much risk—a gale of wind or a calm would be equally fatal; he therefore determined to return to the south-east. The shoals gave him thought. They must end somewhere; they could not go farther north than 15° S, because in that latitude Bougainville had had a clear run west from his *Grandes Cyclades*, for a considerable distance:

but I think it not attall improbable but that they may extend to the west as far as the Coast of New South Wales, the Eastern extent of the isles and shoals off that Coast between the Latitude of 15° & 23° were not known and M. Bougainville meeting with the Shoal of Diana above 60 Leagues from the Coast, together with the signs he had of land to the SE[1] all

[1] Bougainville, meeting with the Shoal of Diana off the Great Barrier Reef, 4–6 June 1768, for this and other reasons decided to change course to the north. On p. 303 of the

conspire to increase the Probability. The semilarity of the two Countries might also be advanced as a nother argument. I must confess it is carrying conjectures a little too far to pretend to say what may lay in a space of 200 leagues, it is however in some degree necessary if it was only to put some future Navigator (if any should come into these parts) on his guard.[1]

It is an interesting example of Cook's geographical thought.

He tacked, with the wind blowing straight on to the reef. He weathered one of its points, and then the breeze began to fail. In the middle of the afternoon it failed altogether. We hear another echo from the first voyage: 'it fell Calm and we were left to the Mercy of a great swell which set directly upon the reef which was hardly one league from us, we Sounded but could find no ground with a line of 200 fathoms. I ordered the Pinnace and Cutter to be hoisted out and sent a head to tow, but they were of little use against so large a swell.'[2] The light breeze that sprang up this time fortunately lasted for some hours; from midnight the boats towed in a dead calm. The dawn might have been grim. When it came there was no reef in sight. The surprised Cook, when he got his latitude at noon on the 16th and found himself further south than he expected, concluded that a current or tide had come to his rescue all that anxious night. For the next ten days the wind was exasperating: light breezes, light airs and calm, variable light breezes and calms, winds faint and variable, run the journal entries, but at least, after the first two or three of those days, the weather was clear enough to give a good view of the land. It was mountainous. Balade over again. On the 22nd, the anniversary of George III's coronation, the coast was seen to change direction more southerly at a high promontory accordingly called Cape Coronation; on the 23rd another high point announced the south-easterly end of the land. This Cook named Queen Charlotte's Foreland. Three days earlier he had had his first sight of some peculiar 'elevated objects', one like a tower, others massed like the masts of a fleet of ships; now they began to appear on coast and islands in vast clusters. The coast was greener than it had been, and some, including Cook, thought they were trees. Opinions differed, bets were taken. Forster, convinced that smoke on shore

---

English translation of his book he has the passage, 'For twenty-four hours past, several pieces of wood, and some fruits which we did not know, came by the ship floating; the sea too was entirely falling, notwithstanding the very fresh S.E. wind that blew, and these circumstances together gave me room to believe that we had land pretty near us to the S.E.'

[1] *Journals* II, 548.
[2] ibid., 549.

meant a volcano, more convinced that these were pillars of basalt, like the Giant's Causeway in Ireland, was unwisely dogmatic, even dictatorial. There was no volcano: his other guess was not unreasonable, though its conversion into a certainty was unreasonable. The question had to wait a little, as Cook slowly and cautiously probed his way to the south and SSW, in his attempt to round the southern end of the land. Off that end stood a system, or semi-chaos, of islets, sand-banks and reefs, which gave him some difficult hours. A fine breeze at east was succeeded by a dead calm; 'our situation was now worse than ever, we were but a little way from the Shoals, which instead of turning to SW as we expected, they took a SE direction towards the SE land and seem'd wholy to shut up the Passage between the two'.[1] This 'SE land' was the larger island which Cook called the Isle of Pines. He would have to go round it by the south, if he could get away from the shoals—and a faint northerly breeze came in time to rescue him. It changed to south-west and then to fresh south-easterly gales, so that only on the fifth attempt was he able to weather the island and the dangers round about it. By now it was 28 September. Nevertheless this island, and the low islets, had their use. They all displayed a plenitude of the 'elevations' which had caused so much controversy. Everyone was satisfied they were trees, 'except our Philosophers', who still maintained they were stone pillars. Wales, to whom Forster was a constant source of mirth, admitted that 'nothing of the sort ever sure had so singular a form'; and their amazing size made all other vegetation look like so many bunches of reeds.

The night after this day brought the climax of danger. Cook wanted to fall in with the main coast a little to the south-west of Queen Charlotte's Foreland, so that he could continue his circumnavigation, and he steered NWBW. This brought him, as he began to find before long, into a sort of large triangular bay, the sides of which were formed not by mainland shore but by 'low isles', reefs and shoals. He tried to extricate himself by hauling off south-west: in vain, a continuous reef lay straight ahead. The wind still blew from the east, in what Cook called very fresh gales. At least the surrounding reefs kept the water smooth, except where the shattering breakers fell. He took a careful look at the main coast in the north, as the afternoon wore on, and addressed himself to the crisis. There was, he said later, a good lookout and the ship was managed very briskly. This is rather to file down the sharp edge of statement; but we can see that it is literally true, without quite doing justice to

[1] ibid., 553.

superb seamanship on the part both of the commander and of the men he commanded. Certainly he writes more at length.

After a short trip to the NNE we stood again to the south in order to have a nearer and better View of the shoals at Sun-set, we gained nothing by this but the Melancholy prospect of a sea strewed with Shoals: we were now about one mile from the reef to leeward of us and contrary to expectation had soundings . . . but Anchoring in a strong gale with a Chain of breakers to leeward was the last resource, it was thought safer to spend the night making short boards over that space we had in some masure made our selves acquainted with in the day. Proper persons were stationed to look out and each man held the rope in his hand he was to manage, to this we perhaps owe our safety, for as we were standing to the Northward the People on the Fore Castle and lee gang-way saw breakers under the lee-bow which we escaped by the expeditious manner the ship was tack'd. Thus we spent the night under the terrible apprehensions of every moment falling on some of the many dangers which surrounded us. Day-light shewed that our fears were not ilfounded and that we had spent the night in the most eminent danger havᵍ had shoals and breakers continually under our lee at a very little distance from us.[1]

It was an exceedingly dark night, Wales tells us; 'I realy think our situation was to be envyed by very few except the Thief who has got the Halter about his Neck.' That night, with its cries of *Breakers ahead*!, remained fast in Midshipman Elliott's memory: 'every way we stood for an Hour, the Roaring of Breakers was heard . . . a most anxious, and perilous Night, at last Daylight appear'd.'

Daylight appeared, and Cook found he had gained nothing to windward all night. He might have worked his way south out of that dangerous position as soon as possible. Scientific passion overcame him. He pushed instead into the apex of the near-fatal triangle:

I was now almost tired of a Coast I could no longer explore but at the risk of loosing the ship and ruining the whole Voyage, but I was determined not to leave it till I was satisfied what sort of trees those were which had been the subject of our speculation. With this view we stood to the north in hopes of finding anchorage under some of the isles on which they grow. . . .[2]

He was stopped by the shoals between the Isle of Pines and Queen Charlotte's Foreland. Yet to leeward were some low isles where the trees grew: and near one of these isles, not locked in by reefs, he anchored and immediately went ashore. He took the botanists. It was indeed a singular tree, 'a kind of spruce pine', thought Cook, 'very proper for Spars which we were in need of'; which was a bad judgment, though his carpenter agreed and a few were cut, because the timber was too heavy. There were trunks between sixty or seventy feet tall, but however tall they were, the branches were remarkably short, and the larger the tree, the shorter the branch. Trees a hundred feet high (for those that Cook now saw were by no means of the largest size) with branches shorter than six feet might well puzzle the mind. Thus was discovered the great *Araucaria columnaris* or *cooki*, the *pin colonnaire* or Cook pine. There were other things here to keep the naturalists busy—trees, shrubs, smaller plants, water-snakes, pigeons and doves; there was the hull of a wrecked canoe and the fire-places of native turtlers. Cook called the little expanse of prolific sand Botany Isle.[1] Meanwhile, at low water, Gilbert had reconnoitred from the mast-head; in spite of the encumbered sea he thought there might be a passage to the main coast and along it. Cook, balancing danger against advantages, determined not to risk his ship. His mind went to the little vessel he carried, stored in frame: if she were only set up, now she could be usefully employed, but he had certainly not the time both to put her together and send her away exploring. He had last considered fitting her up at Tahiti, but there too, so demanding was the work to be done on the ship, time lacked. He wrote out his reasons a little apologetically, so it seems; because he adds, 'After such an explanation few (I believe) will blame me for putting again to sea at daylight in the morning with a gentle breeze at EBN.'[2] It was the last day of September. The wind, deceitful to the last, fell again; swell and current combined to carry the ship still once more towards the breakers, from which she was rescued by a north-westerly breeze; that breeze went round to the south-west, turned to hard rainy squalls, the squalls to a hard gale with a great sea. But the shoals were astern; Cook could do nothing but stretch to the south-east and east, and hope the way was clear. By noon on 1 October the land was gone.

He could not get back in that gale even if he wanted to. He concluded that he did not want to. The southern summer, in which he had much to do, was coming on, the ship needed attention, he thought of 'the vast distance we were from any European Port where we could get supplies in case we should be detained by any accident in this Sea another year'. What did he mean by that? What sort of accident? Did he envisage calling at the cape before plunging into

[1] The islet now known as Améré.
[2] *Journals* II, 560. It is not likely that two hundred years later anyone will think he had reason to reproach himself.

the South Atlantic again? None the less he regretted that lost coast—
perhaps, except for New Zealand, the largest island in the whole
South Pacific: 'I was constrained as it were by necessity to leave it
sooner than otherwise I should have done.' He had discovered it, he
had left it only half-charted, and one should not leave unfinished
business. Well: he must find a name for it. He found New Caledonia.
He does not give his reasons, nor suggest why the world should not
be happy with existing Nova Scotia. It is possible that the lofty coast
reminded him of those sparsely covered hills of Scotland, as he, a
young master, had viewed them from the sea. It is more likely that
he considered the existence, not very far away, of a New Britain and
a New Ireland as well as of the New South Wales he himself had
added to the map, and thought of so often on this latest shore: then
was not a New Scotland demanded? If that was too like to Atlantic
Scotia, why not Pacific Caledonia? And then (it seems likely that
two problems were solved together) the name of Caledonia's off-
lying islands in the northern hemisphere could be taken for the
southern group he had a few weeks ago left behind, and the New
Hebrides would complete the circle.

The fresh gales continued for some days, fell calm, revived less
harshly from the south-east. Cook altered his course more to the
west, and sent off a boat in the calms to shoot sea-birds for the pot—
albatrosses 'were geese to us'. A harpooned dolphin was much admired by everyone who could get a slice of her. On 10 October,
about half-way to New Zealand, in latitude 29°, a small steep-sided
surf-beaten island was sighted and a landing made. It was uninhabited. The country this place reminded Cook of, from its trees
and plants—the flax-plant thick near the shore, the 'cabbage-palm'
—and birds was New Zealand; although he found growing everywhere, to a vast size, another spruce pine quite different from any
tree in New Zealand or that in New Caledonia.[1] The sailor's mind
at once turned to masts and yards. He took possession, conferring
the name Norfolk Isle, 'in honour of that noble family'. He sailed on.
The wind went to the north, and for five days more the weather was
pleasant. Then, at midnight of the 16th, the spring storm burst, in
heavy squalls, rain, thunder and lightning. He may have thought
of that fearful north-west gale of October the year before, which kept
him out of the strait so long and reft away his consort; but this time
he was off the west coast of New Zealand, approaching the northern
end of the strait, and the storm was to be a short one. Daybreak
showed him the snows of Mount Egmont; the following morning he

---

[1] The Norfolk Island Pine, *Araucaria excelsa.*

dropped anchor before Ship Cove, the strong flurries down from the hills stopping him short of his accustomed berth.

He landed, and at once went to see if his bottle remained where he had buried it. It was gone; and trees which were standing when he last left the place had been felled with axes and saws. A little later signs were found that an astronomer other than Wales had set up his equipment—no other surely than Bayly. So the *Adventure* had come into harbour, whatever had happened to her afterwards. That, at least, was reassuring. Next morning, the wind having fallen, the *Resolution* was warped in and moored. The crew needed refreshment, the ship needed wood and water; she badly needed some refitting. The sails had been much damaged in the gale, the main and fore sails had to be condemned as useless; the fore and main topmasts, urgently in want of attention, were struck; the whole hull was urgently in want of caulking. The forge, the observatory, the tents were set up on shore, orders given for the boiling of greens every day with oatmeal and portable soup for breakfast, with pease and portable soup for dinner. The regimen was unfailing. The vegetable gardens planted on Motuara, ignored by the local people and gone to waste, had some things flourishing. Those people themselves did not appear for a few days: when those who were old friends did there was general joy, they 'embraced us over and over and skiped about like Mad men'.[1] They were soon bringing plenty of fish; there were also strangers from further up the Sound, whose chief trade was in greenstone and women—'two articles which seldom came to a bad market'. Cook could have dispensed with them both. He noticed at first some nervousness, and there was some incomprehensible talk of killing.

The ship's work went on energetically, in spite of some bad weather. The more she was looked into, the more to be done was found. The longest job was caulking; for Cook had only two skilled men and had run out of proper material. At sea he had tried sealing the deck with varnish covered with sand. Now the seams were payed with a kind of putty made of fat from the galley and chalk from the gunner; pitch and tar had been exhausted for months and 'varnish of pine' too was all gone. He took in shingle ballast and struck down six of his guns into the hold. We are reminded of his preparations at the Bay of Good Success for his first passage of the Horn. He went about the Sound shooting for provender, taking Forster to botanise, and enquiring into the fate of the livestock left on previous visits;

[1] *Journals* II, 571.

the survival of some at least seemed probable, a sow was actually seen, but he placed still another boar and sow ashore to clinch the matter. He had been in harbour more than a fortnight when, on 5 November, he started out in the pinnace, with thoughts of getting to the end of the sound, or seeing if elsewhere it communicated with the sea outside; for this was a possibility he had suspected from his first hill-top view. Seventeen or eighteen miles from the ship the occupants of a canoe agreed with fishermen whom he had earlier met that the sound ended in land; on its east side, however, they said there was a passage to the sea. He made for the passage; found friendly people at a settlement inside its entrance who bore out the story; went down on a strong ebb tide till he could see through a narrow opening indubitably into the strait, and came back on the flood. Thus was discovered the way into Queen Charlotte Sound, now known as Tory Channel. It was a very satisfactory expedition.

Days were now few. The ship was the important thing; interruption to work on her a nuisance. John Marra again became prominent, for drunkenness and departing from her without leave. Desertion was naturally suspected; according to Elliott the captain declared that if he were not well assured the fellow would be killed and eaten before morning he would have let him go; but the only motive here, according to the fellow himself, was the pursuit of the fair. This time he got twelve lashes. So did John Keplin, 'for leaving the Boat when on duty and declareing he would go with the Indians',[1] even after he changed his mind and came back. More important to Cook, and not to be called an interruption, were his efforts to disentangle the truth about the *Adventure*. His informants concurred that she had returned and departed again, in safety. Then what was the other tale about a ship stranded on the coast, beaten to pieces on the rocks, her crew killed and eaten, some said on the other side of the strait, some on the other side of the sound?—all of which was also vehemently denied. Or a third story about a ship which had 'lately' been here and then crossed the strait? Cook felt easy, in the end, about the *Adventure*, but could not dismiss the possibility of disaster to some visitor unknown. The indefatigable Wales on his part had been conducting professional enquiry, and his results for the longitude of Ship Cove agreed with Bayly's. Cook bowed finally to the evidence, he accepted the mortification of having produced an inaccurate chart, and he went on to a wider statement:

[1] Keplin or Kepplin was a young A.B. Gilbert tells us of the incident.—*Journals* II, 576, n. 6.

it appears that the whole of *Tavai-poenammoo*, is laid down 40′ too far East in the said Chart, as well as in the Journal of the Voyage; but the error in *Eahei-no-mauwe* is not more than half a degree or 30′ because the distance between Queen Charlottes Sound and Cape Palliser has been found to be greater by 10′ of Longitude than it is laid down in the Chart. I mention these errors not from a supposition that they will much affect either Navigation or Geography, but because I have no doubt of their existance, for from the multitude of observations which Mr Wales took the situation of few parts of the world are better assertained than that of Queen Charlottes Sound. Indeed I might with equal truth say the same of all the other places where we have made any stay at. For Mr Wales, whose abilities is equal to his assiduity, lost no one observation that could possibly be obtained. Even the situation of such islands as we past without touching at are by means of Mr Kendalls Watch determined with almost equal accuracy.[1]

He is away from his own failing to a happier subject. Between his leaving Queen Charlotte Sound in November 1773 and returning to it in October 1774, 'which was near a year', the accumulated error of the watch was just over 19 minutes 31 seconds. 'This error can not be thought great if we consider the length of time and that we had gone over a space equal to upwards of three quarters of the Equatorial Circumference of the Earth and through all the Climates and Latitudes from 9° to 71°.'[2] Would that John Harrison could have seen those words as the pen wrote them out, somewhere in the southern ocean in a longitude east of New Zealand!

It was at daylight on 10 November that Cook weighed anchor and stood out of the Sound and through the strait. In the afternoon he passed Cape Campbell and steered south-east.

[1] ibid., 579 80.　　　　　　　　　　[2] ibid., 580.

XVII

From New Zealand to England

THE EXTRAORDINARY voyage proceeded. Cook had completed his parenthesis, which would have made a brilliant reputation for any other explorer; he could revert to the tracing of his main theme, as he had laid it down in early February, in latitude 64° S, longitude 99° W. Having steered south from Austrialia del Espiritu Santo as far as New Zealand, he must now steer still farther south to a latitude somewhere between 50° and 60°, and then east. He could not be the length of Cape Horn in November, because it was November already, and he could not cross the whole width of the Pacific in three weeks; but except for the most untoward happening he could still be at the Horn in time to explore, that summer, the southern part of the Atlantic Ocean. There was no untoward happening of great importance. Sails split and ropes gave way in gales that were generally favourable, there were few light airs or calms to slow the ship. It seemed to the captain an uninteresting passage; he strained himself, he thought, to record anything beyond the variation of the compass. Perhaps the period was one of those in which he rewrote— as he kept on rewriting and revising—his journal, until his secretary must have sighed at the prospect of yet another version to copy. Wales fixed a device to measure the roll of the ship. The *Resolution* sailed well: on 27 November Clerke registered the note, 'We've had a fine steady Gale and following Sea these 24 Hours, and run the greatest distance we've ever reach'd in this ship'—the distance being 183 miles. In the first twelve days Cook had steered south-east to latitude 55°48′, where he altered course to the east. On the day of the great run, convinced that he could abandon hope of finding more land in the Pacific Ocean, he resolved to make for the west entrance of the Strait of Magellan. He had no thought of passing through the Strait. He had modified his plan of action once more, quite otherwise, 'with a View of coasting the out, or South side of Terra del Fuego round Cape Horn to Strait La Maire. As the world has but a very imperfect knowlidge of this Coast, I thought the Coasting it would be of more advantage to both Navigation and Geography than any thing I could expect to find in a higher latitude.'[1] There was reason enough why the world's knowledge should be imperfect: it was a coast which, so far from inviting seamen to examine it, inspired in them a sort of horror. Cook, decreasing his latitude, made straight for it, meaning to fall in with Cape Deseado, the north-west extremity of Desolation Island, behind which is the entrance to the strait; and at midnight of 17 December he sighted land not far from the cape. He had made the first run across the South Pacific in a high latitude—unless Furneaux had preceded him, and who knew where Furneaux had gone?—and he was done with that ocean. 'I hope those who honoured me with this employ will not think . . .'— no, he could allow himself a little self-approval: 'I . . . flatter my self that no one will think that I have left it unexplor'd', or that more could have been done towards that end in one voyage than in this. Having said which, he did not enlarge on the matter. There was too much to say of the shore he had now to range.

Fortunate with the weather, he kept about two leagues off, concluding that it was by no means so dangerous as it had been pictured. His chart shows a much broken line, for his survey was swift: and indeed the line of coast is a very much broken one, with inlets, islands, islets, and rocks innumerable. Inland rose a mass of steeps and mountains, rocky and barren so far as he could see, except for dark scattered tufts of wood below the snow-patches. It could not be called inviting: Cook called it barren and savage. Known names were few, the result of accident rather than exploration. He began to add to them: Cape Desolation, 'because near it commenced the most desolate and barren Country I ever saw'; Gilbert Island after his master; a little later, on 19 December, the 'Wild rock' he called York Minster because of its two high towers, eight hundred feet almost perpendicular from the sea, the southernmost point of an island.[2] Both this day and the next, in a calm, the ship drove out to sea. Cook's mind fell to work: there must be a current, he thought, the melting of the snow must increase the inland waters and cause a stream to run out of the inlets. When an easterly breeze succeeded the calm on the 20th he put into a two-armed opening on the east side of York Minster, to 'take a view of the country' (familiar words) and recruit his wood and water. This course was not without danger —the danger that sprang at him in the most diverse places; for the breeze fell, a great swell rolled in and broke in 'a dreadful Surf' on all the shores about, boats towed in vain, and only a renewed breeze

[1] *Journals* II, 583.   [2] Waterman Island.

brought renewed control of the ship. Still standing in, he found after a short search excellent moorings, in a harbour that provided all he had come for, a harbour where he remained a week. To it and its neighbouring waters, explored by Pickersgill, Clerke and himself, he gave the name Christmas Sound; and, however 'awful' the surroundings, gloomy, savage, sterile—the adjectives are forbidding—the festival celebrated here was an agreeable one; for in addition to the excellent wild celery that was found, excellent mussels, a few ducks and shags, there was abundance of geese, and goose pie, roast geese, boiled geese made glad the day; some Madeira wine remained, 'the only Article of our provisions that was mended by keeping ... our friends in England did not perhaps, celebrate Christmas more cheerfully than we did'. Thus the third, and last, southern Christmas of the voyage. Signs of native habitation were not distant, and on Christmas Day native inhabitants appeared in their canoes, though they left before the great dinner—which was well, as their stench would have subdued all appetite. Cook thought they were of the same 'nation' as those he had met at the Bay of Good Success in 1769, and may be pardoned for thinking so, judging as he did mainly from the sealskin dress with which they varied their nakedness; but he was wrong. These were Alacaluf, a people distinct in language and their use of canoes from the Aush or Eastern Onas of his earlier acquaintance; they were little and ugly, he thought, though friendly enough, the most wretched of all beings he had encountered; they were pleased with the baize and old canvas he gave them to eke out their exiguous clothing. They were probably no more primitive and wretched than the drunken marine who fell overboard and was drowned the night after the ship got into harbour: William Wedgeborough, who had shot the man on Tana, fallen overboard once before, off Eromanga, had caused trouble enough. Probably his career was as valid a commentary on the English eighteenth century as was Cook's own. His death completed the tale of losses on this voyage.

On 28 December Cook stood out to sea to resume his eastward course. At the end of the day he was within sight of False Cape Horn, which may be regarded as the southern point of Tierra del Fuego, apart from the group of islands of which Cape Horn itself is the southernmost point; he shortened sail for the night, lest he should miss any of the coast, and next morning 'At half past 7 we passed this famous Cape and entered the *Southern Atlantick Ocean*'. Widespread haze prevented his verifying the charts that set down the cape as part of a small island, a matter which his imperfect view on his first voyage had made no clearer, and he could not stay to find out.[1] He altered course north-east for the Strait of Le Maire to look if there were trace of the *Adventure* in the Bay of Good Success, firing guns and sending Pickersgill ashore, while the ship stood off and on among the whales at play. Pickersgill found nothing; the only human beings he met were some of the native Aush. Cook thereupon determined to take a closer view of the coast of Staten Island. Haze and fog all over the strait urged caution; he hauled off to the north till he could get round a small off-lying island into smooth water. It was Observatory Island; on it could be seen a population of seals and birds—fresh provisions; Cook anchored in a favourable spot, the weather cleared, the campaign was on. The geese of Christmas Sound were nothing to this. Seals, sea lions, penguins, shags—they covered the interior as well as the shore.[2] Cook fancied a young shag: he was not so fond of penguin, but he put it well ahead of his salt beef and salt pork. A seal cub was very palatable; the older ones and the sea lions were useful chiefly for their blubber, boiled down for oil. During this renewal of supplies, Gilbert was despatched over to the main island to search for a harbour. He discovered a good one. The day was the first of January 1775; Cook called the place accordingly New Year's Harbour. He weighed on the 3rd and rounded the north-east point of the island, Cape St John, in a current so strong that he could hardly make head against it; then alternate calms and squalls, joined to the current, persuaded him that he had done enough here for the general needs of navigation; so that, leaving the land, he steered south-east. He set out with lucidity his observations on the coast he had ranged in the last fortnight, from Cape Deseado to Cape St John; the world's knowledge would be rather less imperfect. He did not wish to claim too much. Although it is clear that he had observed tides and currents acutely, he believed that 'the less I say on this subject the fewer Misstakes I shall make'. What he did say was cogent. His account of Observatory Island is highly interesting, even if 'very imperfect . . . written more with a view to assist my own memory than to give information to others; I am neither a

---

[1] 'In some Charts Cape Horn is laid down as belonging to a small island, this was neither verified nor contridicted by us . . .'.—*Journals* II, 602. It is the southern point of Horn Island, itself the most southern of the Hermite group of islands.

[2] 'It is wonderfull to see how the defferent Animals which inhabited this little spot are reconciled to each other, they seem to have entered into a league not to disturb each others tranquillity. The Sea lions occupy most of the Sea Coast, the Sea bears take up thier aboad in the isle; the Shags take post on the highest clifts, the Penguins fix their quarters where there is the most easiest communication to and from the sea and the other birds chuse more retired places. We have seen all these animals mix together like domesticated Cattle and Poultry in a farm yard, without the one attempting to disturb or molest the other . . .'.—*Journals* II, 614–15.

botanist nor a Naturalist and have not words to describe the productions of Nature either in the one Science or the other'.[1] This is not
quite the man who laughed at Banks for his plant-collecting devotion
in Le Maire Strait seven years before.

His general purpose, as he now put to sea, was plain enough. We
know it. Within it, however, there were two or three matters of
particular interest, joined, inevitably, to the leaping imagination
of Alexander Dalrymple. There was the Gulf of St Sebastian on
Dalrymple's Atlantic chart of 1769, for which the supporting evidence were two perfectly genuine though accidental discoveries
eastward of the Horn. The first of these was by Antoine de la Roche,
a London merchant, in 1675, the second by a Spanish merchant ship,
the *Léon*, in 1756; the first was perhaps one of the Falklands, the
second certainly a sighting of South Georgia.[2] They were persuasive
enough for Dalrymple, whose enthusiasm Forster thought laudable,
Cook's view was more tempered; indeed, setting a course which
would take him to the western point of the Gulf, he confesses he had
'some doubts of its existence'—doubts that he had already noted on
the map he had drawn for Lord Sandwich. Westerly gales carried
him in three days to the position of the non-existent; he was unwilling
to keep too far south lest he should lose the land reported (for he
took both reports to refer to the same land) by la Roche and the
Léon, and as he continued east he lessened his latitude a degree or
two. By the 12th, having sailed over the northern end of Dalrymple's
land, he had no doubt at all that it was another fiction. The air
turned colder, penguins appeared and petrels, then an island of
ice which in a few hours transformed itself into an island of land;
then, through an atmosphere of snow and sleet, stood up more land,
mountainous, rocky, almost wholly covered in snow, a land broken
by bays and inlets, with great masses of snow or ice inside them.
The first sighting was on the 14th, the latitude about 54°. Cook
worked his way cautiously round to the north and began to range
the coast. On the 17th he investigated one of the bays on this northern
coast: it had some sandy beaches, but at its head, and in other places,
he could see vast perpendicular cliffs of ice, exactly like the face of
an ice island, from which pieces were continually falling off. One
great mass came away with the noise of a cannon. He was looking
at glaciers, for which he had no word, and the birth of an iceberg.
As for what he could see otherwise, 'The inner parts of the Country
was not less savage and horrible: the Wild rocks raised their lofty

[1] *Journals* II, 615.
[2] I have discussed these discoveries more at length in *Journals* II, 615, n. 1; 617, n, 2.

summits till they were lost in the Clouds and the Vallies laid buried in everlasting Snow. Not a tree or shrub was to be seen, no not even big enough to make a tooth-pick.'[1] He had landed and scrutinised; he even took possession of the unpromising country for his royal master. Forster certainly found some tussock grass and one or two low creeping plants; the inhabitants otherwise were seals, penguins, other sea-birds, a duck, a pipit. Cook left Possession Bay with a load of the seals and penguins, 'an exceptable present for the Crew'—though, he hastens to write, the ship being in no want of provisions, for the last few days he had been able to add boiled wheat to the breakfast. He continued to range the coast, its glacier faces still in view, small islands and rocks in relief against it as he advanced.

At the eastern end of the land, he turned south-west. Beyond a projection he called Cape Disappointment he could see it stretching north-west, indubitably to join the main coast where he had first sighted it six days before. Disappointment: a coast line no more than seventy leagues in circuit, 'proved to a demonstration', says Cook; and Clerke, 'I did flatter myself . . . we had got hold of the Southern Continent, but alas these pleasing dreams are reduc'd to a small Isle . . .'. Well, his commander went on to reflect, if the continent were anything like this it would not be worth discovering. Frigid and gloomy as he found the place, he did not hesitate to confer royal and naval names—or, for the off-lying islets and rocks, those of his officers; and, upon the island in the mass, that of Georgia. It might not give lustre to George, considered the elder Forster (who made the suggestion) but George would give lustre to it. Cook put it behind him, and steered to the south-east. As he quitted it, his mind was both puzzled and enlightened. Puzzled: because how to explain, in a latitude no higher than 54° (the northern latitude of York) an island covered in the very height of summer with snow and ice? Enlightened: because if snow-covered land could exist thus in 54° in this longitude, then it could exist in the same latitude fifty degrees of longitude further east; so Cape Circumcision was not, as he had concluded, a vanished ice island but veritable land, and—Cook himself for once parts company with reality—he 'did not doubt but that I should find more land than I should have time to explore'.[2] He could not explain the—as it were—misplaced snow and ice because he had no knowledge of the course of the cold antarctic current, swinging northward to flow round both South Georgia and Circumcision Island, giving them their visages of despair, but he was

[1] ibid., 621–2.   [2] ibid., 626.

right in inferring one from the other. He was wrong in inferring that Bouvet's continent, as well as Bouvet's cape, must exist.

The two weeks that followed his departure, on 20 January, were weeks of prevailing fog or haze or thick mist, with some variety of drizzle or sleet, but also, fortunately, enough clear weather to make the period tolerable, and to reveal most of what there was to see. Cook began with circumnavigating, at some distance and owing to the conditions, over some days, a group of rocks, Clerke's Rocks, a short distance south and east of Georgia, to make sure that they were rocks only; after which he struck south to 60°, expecting to meet ice at any moment. Further south he would not go, unless he had quite certain signs of land. Cape Circumcision seemed now as likely as anything that might lie in that direction. The Gulf of St Sebastian had gone; he doubted whether la Roche or the *Léon* had ever seen the Isle of Georgia, but if they had, the charts placed it badly out of position; nevertheless, they had helped him to his own discovery, because except for these charts he would probably have sailed south of it. He would stand to the east. He cannot help making a significant admission: 'besides I was now tired of these high Southern Latitudes where nothing was to be found but ice and thick fogs'.[1] There were also penguins, snow petrels and whales.

On 27 January he met his first ice island of the season; next day the sea was thick with flat-topped bergs and loose ice—loose ice improbably fallen from these bergs, as Cook surmised it had done, more probably the edge of the pack, moving north-eastwards with the bergs from the Weddell Sea. For a short time he had to stand back to the west; on the 30th he was in the same longitude he had been in two days before, about 29°24′ W, now thirty miles further north. He made north-east through an ice-strewn sea and foggy air. The fog cleared enough next morning to show ahead three islets, the highest of which, a towering shaft of rock, went up 900 feet—Freezland Peak, so called after the man who first sighted it. Behind it appeared an elevated coast, marked by a point Cook named Cape Bristol; to the south another high coast, the most southern discovered, the limit, Southern Thule; between them, it seemed likely, the deep opening of Forster's Bay. He could not weather Thule; he stood to the north, when once again the wind dropped and left him to the mercy of the swell, falling as he thought 'upon the most horrible Coast in the World'; but the weather cleared, Cape Bristol was an island and he was beyond it, it belonged to no greater coast on which he could be driven. For three days more he was sporadically in sight

[1] *Journals* II, 629.

of land, as he made north with straining eyes, and the fog lifted, fell, lifted a brief moment, fell impenetrably. He could not tell exactly how far the land was connected, how much of it was islands: he was pretty sure of Saunders Island, quite sure of the Candlemas Isles, the last little group that he saw; for the rest, he was confused by fog, bergs and loose ice. There was, in fact, no coast between Bristol Island and Southern Thule, only the thirty miles of sea now known as Forster's Passage. Summits spired into the clouds, clouds exerted their usual deceptions 'I was sorry', writes Cook about the nature of the land, or his view of it, at one point, 'I could not determine this with greater certainty, but prudence would not permit me to venture near a Coast, subject to thick fogs, on which there was no anchorage', where ice and snow blocked off, obliterated, the lines of the whole country. 'The clifts alone was all which was to be seen like land.'[1] He wanted to return to the south to re-examine the coast he had left behind. By the time he was far enough south he was too far to the east, and Cape Circumcision called him. His new coast might be a group of islands; it might be a point of the Continent. He would name it Sandwich Land, and go on.

'A point of the Continent,' says Cook, 'for I firmly belcive that there is a tract of land near the Pole, which is the Source of most of the ice which is spread over this vast Southern Ocean:' and he goes on to the first of a series of extended considerations on this continent and on ice. In this first one he is more concerned with his own position as an explorer. There is an echo.

It is however true that the greatest part of this Southern Continent (supposeing there is one) must lay within the Polar Circile where the Sea is so pestered with ice, that the land is thereby inacessible. The risk one runs in exploreing a coast in these unknown and Icy Seas, is so very great, that I can be bold to say, that no man will ever venture farther than I have done and that the lands which may lie to the South will never be explored. Thick fogs, Snow storms, Intense Cold and every other thing that can render Navigation dangerous one has to encounter and these difficulties are greatly heightned by the enexpressable horrid aspect of the Country, a Country doomed by Nature never once to feel the warmth of the Suns rays, but to lie for ever buried under everlasting snow and ice. The Ports which may be on the Coast are in a manner wholy filled up with frozen Snow of a vast thickness, but if any should so far be open as to admit a ship in, it is even dangerous to go in, for she runs a risk of being fixed there for ever, or coming out in an ice island. The islands and floats of ice on the Coast, the great falls from the ice clifts in the Port, or a heavy snow storm attended with a sharp frost, would prove equally fatal. After

[1] ibid., 633.

such an explanation as this the reader must not expect to find me much farther to the South. It is however not for want of inclination but other reasons. It would have been rashness in me to have risked all which had been done in the Voyage, in finding out and exploaring a Coast which when done would have answerd no end whatever, or been of the least use either to Navigation or Geography or indeed any other Science; Bouvets Discovery was yet before us, the existence of which was to be cleared up and lastly we were now not in a condition to undertake great things, nor indeed was there time had we been ever so well provided.[1]

So he would resume his course to the east, in a northerly gale and a heavy fall of snow, so heavy that he was obliged every now and then to throw the ship up into the wind to shake it out of the sails, and rid both them and her of an insupportable weight. His latitude this day, 6 February, was 58°15′ S, his longitude 21°34′ W.

He kept much in that latitude for another eight days, of very variable weather and great cold. Icebergs were many but caused no danger. He crossed the meridian of Greenwich on the 14th, and next day turned north-east to get into the latitude of Cape Circumcision. On the 17th, in latitude 54°23′, longitude 6°33′ E, he steered east again. If he had only, against all logic, steered west! There was a 'prodigious high sea' from the south, so there could be no land near in that direction. The Cape—the evasive Cape!—could be only an island, of that he was certain in another twenty-four hours, but in that latitude he must see it if he only kept on sailing, and brought to at night. The only thing he saw like land was a fog bank. By the 21st he was in longitude 16°13′, which was five degrees to the east of the position he had been given. He tried another day: longitude 19°18′. He could not know that when he altered course for his final eastern run on the 17th, almost in the precise latitude of Bouvet Island, he was already three degrees eastward of it, and now for five days had been sailing away from it. He gave up hope. The rights and wrongs of geography! The Isle of Georgia, land that looked like ice, after all his scepticism, had convinced him that Bouvet was right. Now he was equally convinced that Bouvet, faced by an isle of ice that looked like land, was wrong. He was, however, now close to the position he had himself been in, in mid-December 1772, when for some hours there was a general persuasion of the presence of land: he ran over that position, the sky cleared, there was nothing, not an inch of ice, not a penguin. The sky thickened; storm, snow and sleet fell upon him. He turned north. It crossed his mind that he might look for that other French discovery of which he had heard at the Cape,

[1] *Journals* II, 637–8.

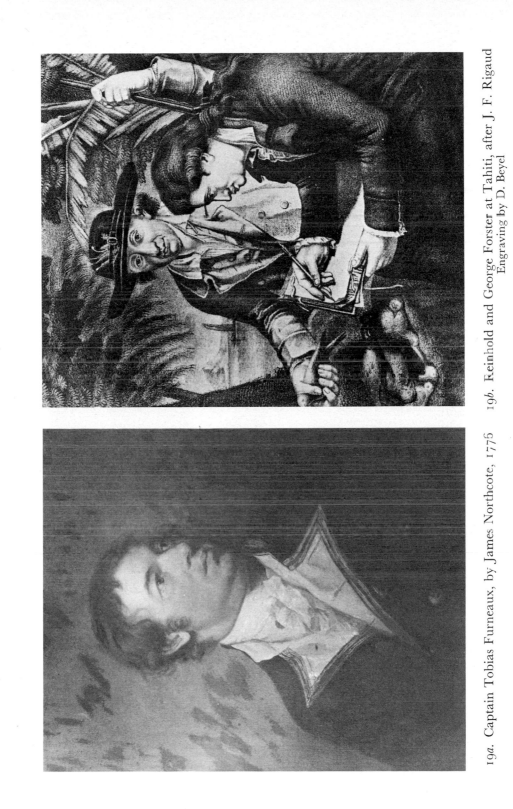

19*a*. Captain Tobias Furneaux, by James Northcote, 1775   19*b*. Reinhold and George Forster at Tahiti, after J. F. Rigaud
Engraving by D. Beyel

26. The *Resolution* off the South Sandwich Islands
Pen and wash drawing by Joseph Gilbert

on his outward passage—Kerguelen's; but why? If it was real it also must be only an island, not a fertile one; its rediscovery would mean two months longer at sea, which neither his ship nor his men could now support. He had to admire the patience and endurance of his men. He thought they were still healthy. On the other hand, his remaining provisions just kept life and soul together; sauerkraut was all gone, dried fruit was almost all gone; what if they were succeeded by scurvy? He could not continue fatigue and hardship gratuitously; he could not expose them to that enemy. To the Cape of Good Hope then: on the way he might at least pick up the two small islands of Denia and Marseveen, reported by the Dutch, laid down in Hallcy's chart, doubted even by Dalrymple.

On this passage to the Cape Cook had leisure to formulate some of the general conclusions to which he had been led—which he had begun to put into words, indeed, as he left the problematic coast of Sandwich Land. At first he seems to be commenting on the memorandum and the chart with which he had explained his purpose to the First Lord three years—or an age?—before, and on the various restatements and modifications of that plan he had made in the intervening time. There is accomplishment to record.

I had now made the circuit of the Southern Ocean in a high Latitude and traversed it in such a manner as to leave not the least room for the Possibility of there being a continent, unless near the Pole and out of the reach of Navigation; by twice visiting the Pacific Tropical Sea, I had not only settled the situation of some old discoveries but made there many new ones and left, I conceive, very little more to be done even in that part. Thus I flater my self that the intention of the Voyage has in every respect been fully Answered, the Southern Hemisphere sufficiently explored and a final end put to the scarching after a Southern Continent, which has at times ingrossed the attention of some of the Maritime Powers for near two Centuries past and the Geographers of all ages.[1]

This is the voice of authority and maturity; the change of tone from the letters with which he introduced his first journal to the notice of the Admiralty is marked and remarkable. Yet, beyond that initial statement, he must still deal in the probable and not the certain. His mind went again to Sandwich Land.

That there may be a Continent or large tract of land near the Pole, I will not deny, on the contrary I am of opinion there is, and it is probable that we have seen a part of it. The excessive cold, the many islands and vast floats of ice all tend to prove that there must be land to the South. . . .[2]

---

[1] ibid., 643.   [2] ibid.

It must, he argued, be irregular land, extending farthest to the north from opposite the southern Atlantic and Indian oceans—which is perfectly true: for in those parts he had encountered a greater quantity of ice farther north than elsewhere, and greater cold, and the greater part of those immense quantities of ice must originate with land. If there was no great extent of land, if ice did not need land for its formation, then there should be a belt of ice, and a belt of cold, right round the earth, at a more or less uniform distance from the Pole, say at the parallel of 60° or 70°. This was not so, and his conclusion followed. His argument was not unreasonable within the context of his own observation. But he knew too little of the oceanography of those regions; the movement of the great cold-water current, its effect on the movement of the ice, were notions as sealed from him as was the Pole. He was not, of course, dead to the drift of currents, and he had measured them.

There was more to say about ice, whether 'islands' or 'vast floats of low ice'—as we should say, bergs or the pack. The traditional theory, that as sea water did not freeze, all this ice must come from frozen rivers, would not do. Cook had never seen any earth or the products of earth, detritus, incorporated in it; he doubted the existence of rivers in a land too cold for water. No water ran on the coast of Georgia, no stream from any ice island. Vast ice cliffs he had seen at the edge of the sea (and he thought they might project a good way into the sea), valleys deep in snow; in Possession Bay he had seen the masses of ice breaking away. He arrived at his own theory, which, apart from the movement of glaciers, clearly accounted for the tabular, or flat-topped, bergs, with their sheer sides.

'It is here'—at the ice-cliffs—'where the Ice islands are formed, not from streames of Water, but from consolidated snow which is allmost continually falling or drifting down from the Mountains, especially in Winter when the frost must be intence. During that Season, these ice clifts must so accumulate as to fill up all the Bays be they ever so large, this is a fact which cannot be doubted as we have seen it so in summer; also during that season the Snow may fix and consolidate to ice to most of the other coasts and there also form Ice clifts. These clifts accumulate by continual falls of snow and what drifts from the Mountains till they are no longer able to support their own weight and then large pieces break off which we call Ice islands.'[1]

He was not so happy in accounting for the inequalities and extraordinary appearance of many of his ice islands. Although he knew well enough that bergs decay and disintegrate, he was not fully

[1] *Journals* II, 644.

acquainted with the facts of weathering, submarine erosion and capsize; and he had never seen the seracs of a glacier. Islands with 'a spired unequal surface', he thought,

must be formed on or under the side of a Coast, composed of spired Rocks and precepices, or some such uneven surface, for we cannot suppose that snow alone, as it falls, can form on a plain surface, such as the Sea, such a variety of high spired peaks and hills as we have seen on many of the Ice isles. It is certainly more reasonable to suppose that they are formed on a Coast whose surface is something similar to theirs.[1]

He appears to think of them, that is, as breaking away directly from the land, moulded to the land, carrying the land's impression with them. Yet they all, if of any extent, had a perpendicular side or sides of clear ice. 'This to me was a convincing proof that these, as well as the flat isles, must have broke off from a substance like themselves, that is from some large tract of ice'; so that subdivision went on all the while.

As for the pack or field ice, Cook has also his theory, built on his own observation. He has still to struggle with the dogma that sea water does not freeze, and fortunately he was never in water shallow enough to be able to watch it freezing around him. His observations are correct, though his initial doubt 'if ever the Wind is violent in the very high Latitudes', so violent, that is, as to keep the water in motion sufficient to stop freezing, is itself violently wrong-headed. He proceeds,

that the Sea will freeze over, or the snow which falls upon it, which amounts to the same thing, we have instances in the Northern Hemisphere; the Baltick sea, the Gulf of St Laurence, the Straits of Bell-isle and many other equally large Seas are frequently frozen over in Winter; nor is this attall extraordinary, for we have found the degree of cold at the surface of the sea, even in summer, to be two degrees below the freezing point, consequently nothing kept it from freezing but the Salts it contained and the agitation of its surface; when ever this last ceaseth in Winter, when the frost is set in and there comes a fall of Snow, it will freeze on the Surface as it falls and in a few days or perhaps in one night form such a sheet of ice as will not be easy broke up; thus a foundation will be laid for it to accumulate to any thickness by falls of snow, without it being attall necessary for the Sea Water to freeze. It may be by this means that these vast floats of low ice we find in the Spring of the Year are formed and after they break up are carried by the Currents to the North; for from all the observations I have been able to make, the Currents every where in the high Latitudes set to the North or to the NE or NW but we have very seldom found them considerable.[2]

[1] ibid., 645.   [2] ibid., 645–6.

This is, as he says, an imperfect account. The winter winds in the high latitudes are, in fact, violent; in the very low air temperatures of autumn the sea does itself freeze. But there are quiet periods; and, beginning with the freezing of the sea, the build-up of the winter pack-ice of Antarctica does proceed much as Cook here defines it. Once this build-up is well under way the blizzards of winter can do little to stop it, since the weight of frozen snow on the water inhibits the formation of waves. We may say, as we have said, that Cook knew too little of the oceanography of these regions. He was founding it.

He has a final word for the inexpressible, the 'horribleness' of the lands he had discovered, where these floating islands of ice were formed. What could be expected more to the south?—'for we may reasonably suppose that we have seen the best as lying most to the North, whoever has resolution and perseverance to clear up this point by proceding farther than I have done, I shall not envy him the honour of the discovery but I will be bold to say that the world will not be benefited by it'.[1] He had, he thought, gone as far as man could go. He now, by implication, withdraws this certainty. His prophecy was wrong. It would in his day have required too much imagination to be right.

Storms did not cease as the ship stood north, and contrary winds; sails and rigging continued to give way; but as February passed and March drew on the temperature rose, and sea-birds gave a little variety to the stale and tedious diet. Cook thought hard about winds and currents. Possibly it was at this time that the Muse overcame the otherwise able-bodied seaman, Thomas Perry, with the ballad beginning

> It is now my brave boys we are clear of the Ice
> And keep a good heart if you'll take my advice
> We are out of the cold my brave Boys do not fear
> For the Cape of good Hope with good hearts we do steer—

a conspectus of the voyage on which the captain was said to set a high value.[2] On 12 March in about latitude 40°, Cook was in the neighbourhood of the supposititious Denia and Marseveen. After

---

[1] *Journals* II, 646.

[2] These verses are in an album in the Dixson Library, MS F 1, called 'Captain James Cook Relics and MSS'. A note appended to them by Miss Louisa Jane Mackrell, great-niece of Isaac Smith, reads, 'This song composed by Thomas Perry one of the Sea Men that went round the world with Captain Cook and was very much valued by the Captain. Mrs Cook kept it with the Gold Medal till her death.' I have printed the whole thing in *Journals* II, 870–1.

another day he decided he could not afford the time to prove or disprove their existence. Everyone was impatient to get into port—possibly he himself shared in the 'general wish' to which he says he yielded. Those islands, at least, however they had impressed the Dutchmen, had unlike Bouvet's cape melted away into the ocean.[1] A gentle favouring breeze turned to a heavy north-westerly gale; it abated, and at daylight on 16 March two sail were seen in the north-west, one of them with Dutch colours. Cook collected the log-books and journals. In the evening he saw the land. Slow sailing it had become for all ships. On the 18th he sent a boat on board the Dutch vessel for news. Some of the news he got was startling. The *Adventure* had arrived at the Cape twelve months earlier. Furneaux had lost a boat's crew, killed and eaten by the New Zealanders. So the confused story gathered on that last visit to Queen Charlotte Sound, on which the people of the place had fallen so obstinately silent, was in substance true. It is obvious that Cook was shocked. He admired the New Zealanders. He stumbled for a comment. 'I shall make no reflections on this Melancholy affair untill I hear more about it. I shall only observe, in favour of these people, that I have found them no wickeder than other Men.'[2] While his boat was away three more sail came in sight. One of these spoke to him next morning. She was the *True Briton*, homeward bound from China without touching at the Cape. Her captain confirmed the story of the *Adventure*, sent fresh provisions and old newspapers, and took a note for the Admiralty. The *Resolution*, Cook briefly informed the secretary, was within two days' sail of the Cape, had met with no accident, her crew, 'thus far' had enjoyed a good state of health. Thomas Perry continued with his commentary,

> We were all hearty seamen no cold did we fear
> And we have from all sickness entirely kept clear
> Thanks be to the Captain he has proved so good
> Amongst all the Islands to give us fresh food
>
> And when to old England my Brave Boys we arrive
> We will tip off a Bottle to make us alive. . . .

The *Resolution* came through a final hard gale, and on 22 March anchored in Table Bay. But it was not Wednesday the 22nd, it was

[1] Nevertheless they appear solidified on Henry Roberts's General Chart that accompanied the official account of the third voyage, *A Voyage to the Pacific Ocean . . .* (1784), to the south of Africa, about latitude 41° S, longitude 21° E.

[2] This short passage appears to have been what Cook first wrote. For the second sentence, when revising his text he substituted, 'I must however observe in favour of the New Zealanders that I have allways found them of a Brave, Noble, Open and benevolent disposition, but they are a people that will never put up with an insult if they have an oppertunity to resent it.'—*Journals* II, 653 and n. 1 on that page.

Tuesday, the 21st; Cook's eastward circumnavigation, like his previous westward one, had thrown his dates awry.

Here he remained five weeks. The Dutch were welcoming, Cook reaffirmed his friendship with the merchant Christoffel Brand. There was much to do to the ship: her masts, spars and standing rigging had come through their trials extremely well, but running rigging and sails were in a desperate state, caulking was long overdue, the rudder had to be unshipped for repair. There was ample leave, ample refreshment for all officers and men, it is plain that the Brave Boys saw no reason to wait till old England to tip off a Bottle. Cook discharged from his company, 'by request', James and Nathaniel Cook; Forster parted with Mr Sparrman, who resumed his researches at the Cape. Wales took his instruments on shore. Some ten days after their arrival, another Indiaman, the *Ceres*, was leaving for England. Cook sent by her to the Admiralty copies of his journal and charts, a sheaf of Hodges's drawings, and a long letter summarising the voyage since he had parted with Furneaux. He praised his men. 'Mr Kendals Watch has exceeded the expectations of its most Zealous advocate.' How far his mission had been successful he submitted to their Lordships' better judgment.[1] He followed these up in April with two of the officers' journals. There was a letter waiting for himself to read, from Furneaux. It was true that that officer had reached Queen Charlotte Sound and lost ten of his best men there, together with a boat. He had not followed Cook to the Antarctic or the islands because of this, and because his bread was damaged. Between New Zealand and the Horn he had gone south beyond the latitude of 60°; on his passage to the Cape he had sailed over the place where Cape Circumcision was said to lie. (His track indicates that he narrowly missed sighting South Georgia, and passed just north of Bouvet Island.) Cook, revising his journal, perhaps at the Cape, perhaps later, found a few words more to say on the fatal event. He knew well the capacity of his own men for getting into trouble; he hesitated to accept it as simple murder. The New Zealanders, he reflected, with a certain idealisation, he had always found 'of a brave, Noble, Open and benevolent disposition, but they are a people that will never put up with an insult if they have an oppertunity to resent it'.[2] He had more to learn, on both sides.

Besides a letter to read, he found people to meet. One of these was to him of the very highest interest. He was Julien Marie Crozet, a

[1] P.R.O. Adm 1/1610. The letter is dated 22 March 1775. It is printed in full in *Journals* II, 691–3.
[2] Cf. p. 437, n. 2.

man of his own age, the captain of a French Indiaman in the Bay, who had been second in command to Marion du Fresne on the expedition Cook had heard of as leaving the Cape in March 1772. Crozet told him of that voyage, the discovery of islands south-east of the Cape, the visit to the Bay of Islands and the slaying of Marion with a number of his men—New Zealanders slayers again!—Crozet's route northwards to the Philippines and his return to Mauritius. The new islands were marked on a French chart that Crozet showed Cook. so was Kerguelen's discovery; so was the route of 'one Captain Surville', from the East Indies by way of the Philippines and New Britain, past land he had found in latitude 10° S,[1] south a few degrees to the west of Cook's own New Caledonia, and then to the northern part of New Zealand at the very time Cook was there; whence he had gone to Callao and been drowned. Cook's imagination of shoals between New Caledonia and New South Wales was therefore ill-founded; Surville had sailed over open sea. The Spaniards too had been in the Pacific: it was a vessel from New Spain, or Peru, not a French one, that had been at Tahiti, and she had charted new isles. Interesting indeed!—though Crozet was a little doubtful of the Spaniards. Cook was fired to a new ambition. 'Probably more authentick accounts may be got here after, but it will hardly be necessary to resume the Subject unless all the discoveries, both Ancient and Modern, are laid down in a Chart and then an explanatory Memoir will be necessary and such a Chart I intend to construct when I have time and the necessary materials.'[2] He would become a historian. The two captains were delighted with each other; they parted on terms of mutual admiration.

Something else Cook met with at the Cape. This was a copy of Hawkesworth's *Voyages*—the volumes in which Dr John Hawkesworth, according to arrangement, had adapted the journals of Byron, Wallis, Carteret and Cook, and, telling his tale always in the first person as the discoverer, had given them to the world. Cook read them, and was surprised beyond measure; worse, he was 'mortified'. He was mortified because he did not recognise himself—and could hardly do so when so much of Banks appeared as Cook, with original nautical blunders by Hawkesworth himself; he was surprised to learn from the introduction that the manuscript had been read to him at the Admiralty for his approval, after which it had been given to him to peruse, and such emendations as he had suggested had been made.

---

[1] The Solomon Islands. See John Dunmore, *French Explorers in the Pacific*, I (Oxford, 1965), 135–45; Colin Jack-Hinton, *The Search for the Islands of Solomon* (Oxford, 1969), 261–6.

[2] *Journals* II, 658.

Hawkesworth, no liar, seems to have been the victim of a vast misconception, but that did not make matters better for Cook. It made them no better for him, certainly, when he arrived at St Helena. He sailed from the Cape on 27 April, to the tune of a Danish band that played in his honour and the gunfire of salutes, in company with the Indiaman *Dutton*. 'Depending on the goodness of Mr Kendals Watch', he resolved to fetch St Helena, if he could, by a direct course. The watch did not deceive him, and he was there on 15 May—not without nervousness on the part of the *Dutton*, the day before, that they might miss it altogether. Cook had recovered his humour and, Elliott tells us, 'laugh'd at them, and told them that he would run their jibboom on the Island if they choose';[1] which was a pleasantry John Harrison would have heard with equal pleasure. John Skottowe, the governor of St Helena, was the son of Thomas Skottowe of Great Ayton, who had sent Cook to school; Mrs Skottowe, a woman of spirit, and her friends were acquainted with Hawkesworth's observations on their island. Cruelty to their slaves? No wheeled vehicles? Cook came in for a good deal of rallying, and at first was baffled by the sight of wheel-barrows and carts drawn up outside the house in which he was lodged. Mr Banks had been less than scientific in his enquiries. But hospitality was lavish and elegant, the matter was explained, and Cook committed sufficient admiration to his present journal—though the cultivation of vegetables as well as of livestock would, he thought, be of advantage to shipping.

Both ships put to sea on the evening of the 21st, keeping company till the 24th, when the *Dutton*, under orders to avoid the island of Ascension and its smuggling trade with the Americans, parted. Cook sent another letter by her, and more journals and charts, 'very accurate . . . executed by a Young man who has been bred to the Sea under my care and who has been a very great assistant to me in this way, both in this and my former Voyage.'[2] He was looking after Isaac Smith. At St Helena he had got from Captain Rice of the *Dutton* a specimen of Foxon's new hydrometer or patent log, with which he experimented: it did not behave well, and we have him reporting adversely on at least one contemporary appliance which might make life easier for seamen.[3] He steered for Ascension to take

---

[1] Elliott, *Memoirs*, f. 41v.

[2] Cook to the Admiralty secretary, 'Resolution at Sea / May 24th 1775 / Lat. 13° S / Long. 10° W^t'; P.R.O. Adm 1/1610; *Journals* II, 694.

[3] Foxon is a rather shadowy figure: even his Christian name appears to be unknown. His log was a self-recording device. Phipps also tried it, on his arctic voyage of 1773, but found it unsatisfactory, though he thought it would be useful in smooth water and fair weather.—E. G. R. Taylor, *Mathematical Practitioners of Hanoverian England* (Cambridge, 1966), 54, 55, 287.

in turtle, spent four days there, and gives a careful description of the not very attractive spot. He and Wales were still scrupulously settling the position of every place the ship touched at: leaving Ascension on the last day of the month he was anxious to do this for an island or St Matthew believed to lie two degrees south of the equator. As the island did not exist we may be the less concerned that the wind was against him. He turned his attention, after considering what might best be done, to fixing the longitude of Fernando de Noronha, off the coast of Brazil. His thoughts, at this moment, are extremely characteristic, and his words are words he has used before, as he balances his duties. 'The truth is I was unwilling to prolong the passage in searching for what I was not sure to find, nor was I willing to give up every object which might tend to the improvement of Navigation and Geography for the sake of geting home a Week or a fortnight sooner. It is but seldom that oppertunities of this kind offer and when they do they are but too often neglected.'[1] After this cogitation, and a pleasant run, on 9 June he and Wales settled the position of Fernando de Noronha without landing, by observation and watch, within a mile or two; he then struck north to Fayal, in the Azores, reaching it on 14 July. He set up again the apparatus he had been given for distilling fresh water—useful if one had the fuel but inadequate, last tried on his outward passage to the Cape: the fact that he was doing this only a second time as the voyage drew towards its end indicates, if nothing else did, that for him the aid was superfluous. Fayal's position was fixed, fresh beef given to the crew, water taken on board. Cook collected information about the little Portuguese place as if it had been a South Sea island. He stood away from the Azores on 19 July. On the 29th he made the land near Plymouth. Next morning he anchored at Spithead, 'Having been absent from England Three Years and Eighteen Days, in which time I lost but four men and one only of them by sickness.'

[1] *Journals* II, 669.

XVIII

England 1775–1776

SOLANDER WAS at the Admiralty on 31 July. 'Two oClock Monday', he wrote to Banks in high excitement, 'this moment Capt Cook is arrived. I have not yet had an oportunity of conversing with him, as he is still in the board-room—giving an account of himself & Co. He looks as well as ever. By and by, I shall be able to say a little more.'[1] Having conversed, he said a little more in the same letter. Cook, he now thought, looked rather better than when he left England; his expressions about Banks were the friendliest possible; nothing could add to his satisfaction in the voyage but having had Banks with him; only the length of time the Lords had kept him and his anxiety to see his wife prevented him from writing immediately to Banks. There were snippets of other news and a letter enclosed from Clerke: 'God bless you send me one line just to tell me you're alive and well . . . hope and flatter myself this will find you alive and happy. . . . my respects & every social wish to the good Doctor.'[2] If Banks were not immune to coals of fire he must have derived embarrassment, as well as pleasure, from these sentiments. It was necessary to write to him because he was away on a yachting trip down Channel with Lord Sandwich (all was cordial again between them), Miss Ray, the First Lord's mistress, Captain Phipps and other friends; we may conclude that he was embarrassed because although the news brought Sandwich and Miss Ray straight back to London, Banks remained away another month—looking, no doubt, rather a fool to those in the know, and feeling, no doubt, rather a fool himself. When he did at last return he found the process made easy for him: there was no recrimination anywhere, only friendship and natural history specimens, while he, still a sufficiently high-spirited young man, had in three years become more sober and responsible. He was a member of the Council of the Royal Society as well as of less solemn bodies; he managed Kew Gardens for the king and—with great

[1] Mitchell Library, MS As 24; *Journals* II, 957.
[2] Mitchell Library, MS 78-1; *Journals* II, 953.

acumen—his own estate in Lincolnshire; he had not yet become general manager of the reputation of Cook, but the way was open to him. It was to be a curious sequel to his great refusal.

Meanwhile there was plenty for Cook to do. His earlier communications from the Cape had come to the Admiralty in late June— 'Glorious Voyage', Solander had written to Banks—and the *Dutton* had preceded the *Resolution* at Portsmouth by ten or twelve days. He arrived with a final despatch in his hand—'The behaviour of my Officers & Crew during yᵉ whole Course of yᵉ Voyage merits from me the highest recommendations and I Shall be happy if my Conduct meets with their Lordships approbation'[1]— with reports on diet, his system of hygiene and the seamen's health, an armful of charts and drawings. While the captain was in attendance on the Lords, Wales had the trusty friend, the precious object, in hand: 'On Monday I brought the Watch up with me to London in a Post-Chaise and on Tuesday Carried it down to Greenwich in a Coach & delivered it to the Revᵈ Mr Maskelyne.'[2] Philosophers of all kinds, naval administrators, ocean-sailing mariners, had been presented with enough to talk about. One of the long chapters of human speculation had come to an end: simply as comment on the great classical hypotheses of geography—familiars through two millenia, on the maps that adorned the famous atlases—there is something magnificent in the amplitude and completeness of the voyage. There was something almost cruelly final about it, in relation to the myth that had gripped geographers with such tenacity; for it was in precisely this year, 1775, that Alexander Dalrymple published the collection of Atlantic voyages, the introduction to which detailed his transactions with Lord North of 1772.[3] Their subject was his desire to be sent at his own expense to colonise the island discovered by the Spanish *Léon* in 1756, where food might be grown for East Indian ships and West Indian slaves, whale and seal fisheries exploited, and a base set up for the exploration of the continent attached to Cape Circumcision and for the enlargement of British commerce. Lord North's aim, successfully accomplished, was to drop the subject. Cook's investigation of South Georgia showed that the prime ministerial inertia was well advised. No one could argue that Dalrymple had not rushed on fate; and fate had been swift. French dreams, as well as his, had gone. But the ocean of islands, of measurable distances, had taken on form. Wales, in his coach, carried down to Greenwich a proved revolution.

---

[1] Canberra Letter Book; *Journals* II, 694–5.
[2] *Journals* II, cxi, from Wales's journal.
[3] *A Collection of Voyages, chiefly in the Southern Atlantick Ocean.* London, 1775.

The *Resolution* was ordered up to Gallions Reach, whence it was intended she should go to Deptford to be paid off and laid up. Cook, home at Mile End, was on 9 August presented at St James's Palace, promoted post-captain and appointed to the *Kent*, a 74-gun ship built in 1762. The very next day this appointment was cancelled. The ship was to be laid up at Plymouth: the new post-captain was to go not to her, but to Greenwich Hospital, as Fourth Captain on that naval establishment: that is, he was to be very honourably pensioned, at £230 *per annum*, with free quarters, fire and light, and 1s 2d *per diem* table money. He did not think he was ripe for pensioning. We must suppose some discussions on the matter, and some arrangement about the exchange of letters between himself and the Admiralty secretary. There was to be a condition. Cook wrote, on 12 August,

The Death of Captain Clements one of the Captains in the Royal Hospital at Greenwich, making a Vacancy there, I humbly offer my self to my Lords Commiss^rs of the Admiralty as a Candidate for it, presuming if I am fortunate enough to merit their Lordships approbation, they will allow me to quit it when either the call of my Country for more active Service, or that my endeavours in any shape can be essential to the publick; as I would on no account be understood to withdraw from that line of service which their Lordships goodness has raised me to, knowing myself Capable of ingaging in any duty which they may be pleased to commit to my charge.[1]

Stephens's reply was one of immediate agreement. Cook would be employed whenever he asked to be. The decision was already made, obviously, to employ his ship again, immediately after the formal order to have her laid up. Solander acquainted the absent Banks with that in another letter, describing an expedition to see the *Resolution* at Gallions Reach, headed by Sandwich and Miss Ray. A glorious day: the First Lord had distributed happiness by announcing promotions; Clerke was promised command of the ship, to carry home the islander Omai; there were drawings of birds for Banks, and Forster had live birds for the Queen; Anderson the surgeon's mate had made a good botanical collection; with few exceptions, Solander believed, the whole ship's company would go out again; the marines made a fine appearance; Pickersgill had made the ladies sick by showing them, preserved in spirits, the New Zealand head where from broiled slices had been eaten on board the ship; Sandwich had asked the officers to dinner; all enquired after Banks.[2] One infers that

[1] P.R.O. Adm 1/1610 and 12/4806; *Journals* II, 958.
[2] Solander to Banks, 14 August 1775; Mitchell Library, Banks Papers, MS As 24; *Journals* II, 958–9.

Cook was present. Within a week he was writing a rather rueful letter to John Walker, in answer to the welcome his old master had hastened to send from Whitby directly on the news of the ship's return.

As I have not now time to draw up an account of such occurrences of the Voyage as I wish to communicate to you, I can only thank you for your obliging letter and kind enquiryes after me during my absence; I must however tell you that the Resolution was found to answer, on all occasions even beyond my expectation and is so little injured by the Voyage that she will soon be sent out again, but I shall not command her, my fate drives me from one extream to a nother a few Months ago the whole Southern hemisphere was hardly big enough for me and now I am going to be confined within the limits of Greenwich Hospital, which are far too small for an active mind like mine, I must however confess it is a fine retreat and a pretty income, but whether I can bring my self to like ease and retirement, time will shew. Mrs Cook joins with me in best respects to you and all your family. . . .[1]

He was Walker's most affectionate friend as well as humble servant, and a month later a long letter followed describing the voyage—'an imperfect outline', which he hoped Walker would excuse, 'as the multiplicity of business I have now on my hand will not admit of my being more particular or accurate. . . . I did expect and was in hopes that I had put an end to all Voyages of this kind to the Pacific Ocean . . . but the Sending home Omiah will occasion another voyage which I expect will soon be undertaken.'[2] He did not forget his compliments to 'Mr Ellerton', who had been master of the collier *Friendship* when Cook was her mate in 1753, 'if he is yet living'.

Another voyage for sending home Omiah: this was just what Cook could not imagine the possibility of when he was in the islands, strictly refusing to take away anyone himself, and not looking with much favour on Furneaux's willingness to carry off the young man properly called Mae—more commonly known in England, then and since, as Omai. He was part of Furneaux's history, so far, not Cook's; but he was to join Cook's, and there was a good deal to hear about him. Cook had things to hear about Furneaux, no doubt, beyond the information conveyed in that commander's letter at the Cape; his journal must be read. Furneaux had arrived home on 14 July 1774. After a year's leisure, he was about to be sent to the North American station, as captain of the *Syren* frigate. His journal was of more painful interest to Cook than this news; for it contained the history of the

---

[1] Cook to Walker, 19 August 1775; Phillips coll. Salem, Mass.; *Journals* II, 960.
[2] Cook to Walker, 14 September 1775; Dixson Library, MS Q 141; *Journals* II, 699. I print the whole letter, pp. 696–9.

massacre of his men by the New Zealanders. When the *Resolution* and *Adventure* parted company off the New Zealand coast at the end of October 1773, Furneaux's crank and leaking ship had a bad time, blown to leeward and almost unmanageable; she got near enough to Cape Palliser one day to buy crayfish from the natives, was blown off again and had to bring to, until, the wind switching to south-west, she bore away to take refuge on 9 November in Tolaga Bay. By then Cook had already been in Queen Charlotte Sound for six days. Three days later, with a supply of wood, water and fish, she left only to be driven back by the weather, so that it was the 16th before Furneaux was again at sea. He might still have made the rendezvous in time had not those fatal gales kept him beating backwards and forwards off the mouth of the strait, out to sea and out of sight when Cook sailed on the 25th. Not till 30 November did he come to an anchor in Ship Cove, when, seeing no *Resolution*, he in his turn began to fear for his consort's safety. Cook's bottle was found, and Furneaux immediately set to work on necessary repairs and preparations; these, he found, included the rebaking of a good deal of his bread, and thus delayed, he was not ready for sea till 17 December. The people of the place had been rather troublesome with their attempts on property, though in no way hostile. What happened now was totally unexpected. On the 17th Furneaux sent out the cutter for a final load of greenstuff, commanded by a master's mate, John Rowe, with a midshipman and eight other men in her. She was to go to a bay across the sound which bore the native name Whareunga—Grass Cove, as Cook called it. She did not return, and next morning Lieutenant Burney was sent in the launch to search for her, it being thought—no worse thought seemed possible—that somehow she had been stove on the rocks. What Burney found at a small beach next to Grass Cove in the afternoon was startling evidence of slaughter and cannibalism: baskets of cooked human flesh, scattered shoes, a piece or two of clothing, two hands (one of them Rowe's), and the head of the captain's negro servant. At Grass Cove itself—or Bloody Bay, to use the alternative name given by Peter Fannin the master[1]—when musket volleys sent off the exulting savages, he was confronted by 'Such a shocking scene of Carnage & Barbarity as can never be mentioned or thought of, but with horror.'[2] Behind the bay the slope was thronged with people; up the hill was a large fire. There was no

[1] The name comes on a chart of 'Cooks Straits' drawn by Fannin, in a volume of his MS charts and views now in the Navy Library, Vz 11/55, No. 1.

[2] *Journals* II, 751. I print the whole of the relevant portion of Burney's journal, 18 December 1773, pp. 749–52. There are MS copies of this, testifying to considerable interest.

sign of the cutter. Night fell, and rain; nothing could be done but destroy three canoes and return in gloom to the ship. Burney could not think the massacre premeditated: some of his speculation on its cause was sound enough, as Cook was later to find.

Indiscriminate revenge had no appeal to Furneaux. He was out of Ship Cove the following day, ran into his habitual bad luck with the wind and could not clear the strait till 23 December. He stood to the south-east, a month behind Cook. A more imaginative man might have given more serious consideration to the possibility, having plunged a great way to the south, of following Cook to the islands. Since Cook, however, had communicated only 'thoughts' and not orders, Furneaux, when he was in latitude 61° S, abreast of the Horn, after a month in the lonely ocean with a straining ship and a cold and wet crew, westerlies still blowing and provisions damaged, thought it most prudent to steer for the Cape of Good Hope. He was devoted enough to make another attempt on Cape Circumcision, amid the fog and the icebergs, rightly concluding that any land that did exist must be a very inconsiderable island. He was in Table Bay on 19 March; refitted and refreshed, and sailed for England on 16 April. An uneventful passage took him home in three months, with all this story, and with Omai.

Omai was, as it were, the British answer to Bougainville's Ahutoru, who had had marked success in Parisian society. He came from a different island, and his status there was a good deal lower. This did not interfere with his own social success in England. Beginning in the newspapers as 'the wild Indian, that was taken on an island in the South Seas, by Capt. Fonnereau of the Endeavour', he was soon advanced by Solander to the rôle of 'a private Gentleman of a small fortune' who had retired to Huahine after family misadventures in war and apprenticeship to a Tahitian priest.[1] He was apparently in his early twenties, personable if not handsome. The quality of his mind varied with the variety of observers. Neither Cook nor Burney, who both saw plenty of him, thought highly of it; but everybody was agreed about his amiability, cheerful imitativeness, and goodwill. Ravished by the process of finding Cook's message at Queen Charlotte Sound, he had at once declared he would learn to read and write; the amount of advice he got, however, rapidly put an end to this resolve. He was introduced to the king shortly after he arrived in England. 'How do, King Tosh!' he is alleged to have ejaculated, which was a fair rendering

[1] *Daily Advertiser*, 19 July 1774; Solander to a Scottish correspondent (Lind or Burnet?), 19 August 1774, ATL, *Holograph Letters and Documents*, 24. *Journals* II, 949–51. It was also said that Furneaux had introduced Omai at Cape Town as a 'priest of the Sun'.

of 'George' into Tahitian; but he never became an accomplished speaker of English. Fortunately for him at first, Banks, who had taken him in, and Solander were better at Tahitian; and when the king gave the sensible advice that he should be inoculated, they went with him into the country and looked after him. Returned to town, he became for a time the darling of the London scene; the king made him an allowance and he had his own lodgings in Warwick Street; at first got lost, and called out to be led to Mr Banks, but soon found his way through the streets; learnt to manage the sword the king gave him; was for some reason supplied with a suit of armour; visited the House of Lords, attended at St James's in a velvet suit, made a very good bow, was admired for his breeding by Dr Johnson. 'Indeed he seems to shame Education', wrote Miss Burney to her dear friend Samuel Crisp, 'for his manners are so extremely graceful, and he is so polite, attentive, and easy, that you would have thought he came from some foreign Court.'[1] He dined at the best tables; was remarkably complaisant to the Ladies, said Solander on his own observation; received a handkerchief from the Duchess of Gloucester, and kissed it; reproved the Duchess of Devonshire, walking dishabille in the Park, for letting her hair go. He stayed with Sandwich at Hinchinbrook. Banks took him to the Royal Society Club. Banks and Solander took him to the Burneys', and Fanny described him at length: not merely did she find him enchanting, but her adored brother Jem had a sort of proprietary interest in him. He went to the opera; he sang to the Burney family himself, barbarously. He learnt to skate—amazing exercise for a Pacific islander; could not learn to ride. The popular verse-satirists found him useful, unsophisticated nature in the midst of the sophistries of civilisation. He could himself annotate this theory on a social excursion to Mulgrave, the Phipps family home in Yorkshire, not long before Cook's return, when, while Phipps dug up ancient barrows and Banks botanised, he prepared luncheon in a Polynesian *umu*, or earth-oven; and, given a sporting gun, destroyed game-birds and barnyard fowl with equal enthusiasm. Hodges produced a picture of him. Nathaniel Dance made a drawing, which was engraved by Bartolozzi; Reynolds painted him, and the painting too was engraved. These were both rather romantic renderings. William Parry, a fourth-rate Welsh artist, just back from Italy, painted him with Banks and Solander, a stiff group which shows us a savage of not at all noble appearance, about whom the only romantic thing is his semi-Moorish gown. It was hard for an artist to discriminate between a Moor and a South Sea islander.

[1] *Early Diary* (London, 1913), I, 334.

All this was ridiculous, said the moralists, of whom Dr Forster was one; Omai should have been set to learn a trade, something that would have conduced to the advancement of his nation when he returned home; he should have been presented with tools, not trinkets. There is difficulty in thinking of any trade that would have adorned the life of the Society Islands, supposing this islander could have been brought to apply himself to it, and a few more axes and chisels would not have tended much to advancement. When he did fall into the hands of an educator it was Granville Sharp—in the early part of 1776 the humanities and not technical instruction formed the substance of his lessons: Sharp taught him the English letters and the sounds they made, and the meaning of adultery, which Omai could illustrate very happily from the example of Lord Sandwich. After a few weeks of irregular application, however, the pupil found himself so burdened with engagements that he had not the time to continue.[1] It was inevitable that in due course the excitement should die down, and King George and Lord Sandwich alike say, 'Omai, you go home'. Probably before that time came he did the best things for himself that he could have done, in enjoying himself hugely; for, though a child of nature, he was not one of nature's wise children. In the islands Cook had formed a low opinion of him, thinking Odiddy, or Hiti-hiti, also young and amiable, who had travelled in the *Resolution*, a person much to be preferred. In England he seems to have modified his condemnation somewhat, and he was probably far too busy to cast a cold eye on another's social amusements; after all, Omai's friendliness was undoubted, his gratitude for kindness unfeigned. On the other hand, by the time we are finished with him we may judge, with Cook, that he was at bottom a foolish inattentive fellow.

Cook's own social life shone with less refulgence. He seems to have been indifferent to duchesses' handkerchiefs. He had, after all, a wife and family, and the few pieces of evidence that exist indicate that he was not indifferent to them. Only two of his five children were alive in 1775, the boys—the premature able seamen—James and Nathaniel, the first of them twelve years old, the second eleven. James had been entered the year before in the Naval Academy at Portsmouth, the master of which was George Witchell, who had worked on Cook's observations of the eclipse in 1766. It was a somewhat dubious and undisciplined institution, but the only one that provided any

[1] Edward Lascelles, *Granville Sharp* (London, 1928), 108–11, tells the story as well as anyone.

systematic training as an introduction to naval life—and it did send out some youths who became men of note. Nathaniel also was about to enter the navy in this more formal fashion, though whether the father envisaged any career in the service for the sons other than the orthodox one we cannot tell. He now set about adding another to the family: Hugh, the youngest child and the fifth son, was born in May 1776.

Domestic life, however, was not all. In August 1775 Daniel Wray, F.R.S., an eminent antiquary, passing on news to his friend the Earl of Hardwicke, F.R.S., wrote, 'Cook is returned, and has resumed his seat at the Mitre. He is a right-headed unaffected man; and I have a great authority for calling him our best navigator.'[1] The Mitre was the tavern where the Royal Society Club dined. The implication is that he had been a familiar figure in the Club, but the probability is merely that the Mitre was a favourite place of refreshment with him. Certainly he dined twice with the Club this year, a sponsored guest, as he had been before—and more often in the first half of 1776; but in the latter year his status was above that of Omai, and he mingled as a Fellow among Fellows. It was an election to which the philosophers were more than usually attentive, and his nomination was a fitting one: 'Captain James Cook, of Mile-end a gentleman skilful in astronomy, & the successful conductor of two important voyages for the discovery of unknown countries, by which geography and natural history have been greatly advantaged & improved, being desirous of the honour of becoming a member of this Society, we whose names are underwritten, do, from our personal knowledge testify, that we believe him deserving of such honour, and that he will become a worthy & useful member.' The signatures that followed were a coruscation, twenty-five in number as against the more usual three to half-dozen that nominated, beginning with Banks, Solander and Mulgrave (Phipps having come into his peerage), going on to the great Cavendish and Hunter the anatomist, Morton the secretary, James Burrow an ex-president, Stephens the Admiralty secretary, James Stuart and Robert Mylne the architects, John Campbell, who had first introduced Cook to the Society, Wray, Maskelyne and his companion though less eminent astronomers Horsley, Shepherd, Aubert, Raper; and of course, among the others, John 'Reinold' Forster.[2] The nomination had its first reading on 23 November 1775, came up weekly until 29 February 1776, on which date it was bal-

---

[1] Wray to Hardwicke, 10 August 1775; John Nichols, *Illustrations of the Literary History of the Eighteenth Century*, I (London, 1817), 150.
[2] Royal Society Library. Royal Society Certificates 1767–78.

lotted and the election signified; and on 7 March Cook, having paid his admission fee of five guineas and signed his bond for future payments, was duly admitted. He had the happiness later in the year of adding his own name to that of Maskelyne's in the nomination to the fellowship of his shipmate William Wales. There were to be sequels to his own election; and in the month of the election he contributed to the *Philosophical Transactions* of the Society, in the form of a letter to its president, Sir John Pringle, a famous paper on the health of seamen.

There were resorts of conviviality of less distinction than the Royal Society Club, though equal fame, where Cook was known: there was the club at Young Slaughter's Coffee House, in St Martin's Lane, an establishment favoured by art and science, and hence by Banks; and another at Jack's Coffee House.[1] No doubt there were places of more nautical resort, close to the docks, where his figure was familiar. He also had the hospitality of Pringle, that great master of military hygiene and medicine, physician to the king (though a Whig), the benevolent elder who gave Boswell wise advice, a man to whom Cook's practice of naval hygiene was naturally of the greatest interest. It was dining at Pringle's house on 2 April 1776, that Boswell met the captain, 'the celebrated Circumnavigator, Captain Cooke, and his Wife', with other persons of distinction. 'Cooke, as Sir John had told me before, was a plain, sensible man with an uncommon attention to veracity. My metaphor was that he had a ballance in his mind for truth as nice as scales for weighing a guinea. Sir John gave me an instance.' The instance bore on the attempt of that notable Scottish judge Lord Monboddo, a man of great learning, to establish an unbroken 'chain' of existence between man and beings of a lower order; and the judge had caught on something in the reports of the second voyage. 'It was supposed that Cook had said he had seen a nation of men like monkeys, and Lord Monboddo had been very happy with this. Sir John happened to tell Cooke of this. "No", said he, "I did not say they were like Monkeys. I said their faces put me in mind of monkeys". There was a distinction very fine but sufficiently perceptible. I talked a good deal with him today, as he was very obliging and communicative.' And the severe Boswell came uppermost. 'He seemed to have no desire to make people stare, and being a man of good steady moral principles, as I thought, did not try to make theories out of what he had seen to confound virtue and vice.'[2]

---

[1] R. L. and M. Edgeworth, *Memoirs of Richard Lovell Edgeworth* (London, 1820), I, 188–9.

[2] *Private Papers of James Boswell*, ed. Geoffrey Scott and F. A. Pottle, XI, 217–18.

The next day Boswell called on Dr Johnson, to tell him all about Cook, and his own inclination, while he was with the captain, to go the next voyage; and was deflated.

A fortnight or more later there was another pleasant dinner, this time at the Mitre, with Pringle and some members of the Royal Society. 'I placed myself next to Captain Cooke,' says the diarist, 'and had a great deal of conversation with him; but I need not mark it, as his Book will tell it all.' Cook 'candidly confessed', however, that he and his companions, because of their ignorance of the South Sea language, could not be certain of any information they got, or supposed they got, 'except as to objects falling under the observation of the senses . . . any thing which they learnt about religion, government or traditions might be quite erroneous.' His account of New Zealand cannibalism was distinct enough. This did not repress Boswell's instinct to go voyaging, which rose again. His spirits were high:—'as the company was rising from table, and Sir John making an apology for our not having had a very good dinner, I made a tolerable pun. "I have had a feast", said I, (pointing to the Captain;) "I have had a good dinner, for I have had a good *Cook*." ' After this inevitable, this intolerable sally they drank coffee at Brown's Coffee House, and went on to the Royal Society for papers. A red letter day indeed for Boswell: he had conversed also with Solander and Banks.[1] Four days after this, on 22 April, he went down early to visit Cook at Mile End. He was not early enough for breakfast, but the captain gave him tea in the garden, where a blackbird sang; talked well, shook hands, and said, 'Much obliged for your visit.'[2] Quite pleasant, thought Boswell, thereupon making his way back to Westminster, to call upon the celebrated Mrs Rudd: he was piling up red letter days. Presumably it was about this time or a little later, and perhaps as one traveller to another, that he presented to Cook a copy of his *Account of Corsica*, inscribed fittingly on the fly-leaf: 'Presented to Captain Cooke by the Authour, as a small memorial of his admiration of that Gentleman's most renowned merit as a Navigator, of his esteem of the Captain's good sense and worth, and of the grateful sense which he shall ever entertain of the civil and communicative manner in which the Captain was pleased to treat him. James Boswell.' On the back of the frontispiece the recipient wrote his signature.[3]

About then, too, it must have been that Banks determined on another memorial of admiration, in the portrait of Cook that he

[1] *Private Papers of James Boswell*, XI, 256-7.   [2] ibid., 262.
[3] It was a copy of the 3rd edition, 1769; now in the Mitchell Library.

commissioned, not from Reynolds like his own, but from Dance. We have a letter from Cook to Banks—phrased, unusually, in the third person—that adverts to the subject: 'Cap. Cook intends to be at the west end of the Town tomorrow Morning, and thinks he could spare a few hours before dinner to sit for Mr Dance, and will call upon him for that purpose about 11 or 12 oClock.'[1] Dance, a lesser, was also a more literal, painter than Reynolds: there are no heroics, there is no drama, in this production; he was said to get a good likeness, and one who well knew Cook's face tells us that this was very like. It is a firm yet mobile face; in the strong, solidly yet easily sitting figure with the map before him there is nothing of the stiffness that so often makes Dance's portraits look like forced arrests. It is conventional, yet—and literally—unbuttoned; probably as good a portrait as we could hope to get of a man not self-conscious enough, or knowledgeable enough, to oversee his own depiction.[2]

The artist, no doubt, was trying for the face of a man considering deeply, and Cook was given diverse matters, official and unofficial, to consider, as we can see from the few bits of his unofficial correspondence that we have left to us. Not long after his return home he received a letter of congratulatory admiration from a young French naval officer called Latouche-Tréville, who was ardent to explore the Pacific. Cook was a little slow to reply, as he had first to get a friend to translate the letter; for 'je ne suis pas absolutement maître de la langue françoise'. The reply was graceful, as he thanked the young man and gave him what encouragement he could: he had not been working for his own people alone, but for all Europe: if he had French admiration he would not worry about the others. Latouche had defined his ambitions in an expansive way, and Cook, remarking on French achievement in the South Sea, at once provided some kindly flattery—the doing of great things there required men like his correspondent—and unlocked his own principle: a man would never accomplish much in discovery who only stuck to his orders.[3] Some months later, Latouche's hopes of commanding an expedition having risen, he was counselled on the likely areas for success. There was the southern coast of New Holland. Alternatively, if he went round the

[1] 24 May 1776; Mitchell Library, Safe 1/68, Brabourne Banks Papers; *Journals* III, 1498.

[2] 'It may not be amiss to observe, that the plate engraved by Sherwin, after a painting by Dance, is a most excellent likeness of Captain Cook; and more to be valued, as it is the only one I have seen that bears any resemblance to him.'—Samwell, *Narrative of the Death of Captain James Cook* (London, 1786), 23. The painting now hangs in the National Maritime Museum, Greenwich.

[3] 'Car je soutiens que celui qui ne fait qu'exécuter des ordres ne fera jamais grandes figures dans les découvertes.'—Cook to Latouche-Tréville, 6 September 1775; Bib. Nat., Paris, Nouv. Acq. Fr. 9439; *Journals* II, 695-6.

Horn, made for latitude 5° S, and in that latitude traversed a good part of the ocean—still very little known between 10° N and 10° S— he might find large islands; it would be relevant to examine with more exactitude the lands adjoining New Guinea that Surville and Bougainville had discovered. Geographers and sailors both differed about thè position of the Solomon Islands. The route thus suggested would clear up this point. And Cook, having missed the post for that day, went on to give his correspondent a generously long account of his own voyage.[1] He had, though the young Latouche was never to set forth, defined almost completely the scope of French exploration as it was carried on into the early years of the nineteenth century. He had also shown reason why he had not 'put an end to all Voyages of this kind to the Pacific Ocean'—to quote again his most recent letter to Walker.

There was a return to his earlier professional interest in the letter he wrote, possibly by request, to the chart-publisher Robert Sayer of Fleet Street, whose firm had taken over the plates of his Newfoundland charts after Jefferys' death in 1771. The letter was to recommend that famous volume *The North American Pilot*—so fundamental a part of which was formed by his own work and that of his mate and successor Michael Lane. He did not waste words.

                                        Mile End, Feb. 26, 1776.

Sir,

I am greatly obliged to you for the Perusal of the North American Pilot, for Newfoundland, Labradore &c. I am much pleased to see a Work, in which I have had some Hand, so likely to prove useful to Navigation.— From the Knowledge I have of these Parts (which is not a little,) I shall not hesitate to declare, that as much Faith may be put in the Charts, together with the Sailing Directions, as ought to be put in any Work of the Kind.[2]

This letter Sayer printed in the volume. If it was a puff, it was by no means a reckless one. Another letter, of a quite unprofessional nature, again reflects Cook's standing as a probably influential person; and reflects, too, both his own caution in an unfamiliar situation and his unwillingness to be used. His sister Margaret had married a fisherman

---

[1] Cook to Latouche-Tréville, 10 February 1776; Bib. Nat., Paris, Nouv. Acq. Fr. 9439; *Journals* II, 700–3.
[2] R. A. Skelton and R. V. Tooley, *The Marine Surveys of James Cook in North America* (London, 1967), 11, say that Cook was presented with a copy of the volume, first published in 1775, by the publishers, Sayer and Bennett; copies issued after the date of his letter had it printed on the verso of the introductory leaf bearing the dedication to Palliser.

of Redcar, on the Yorkshire coast, called James Fleck; and James
Fleck obviously had become implicated in one of the supplementary
activities of fishermen. Cook addresses 'Jn° Harrison Esqr Attorney
at Law' of Guisbrough.

Mile End, London 24th Feb. 1776

Sir

I have had some conversation with Mr Parks, on the subject of the letter
which you favoured me with. He seems to think, that my Brother in Law,
James Flick, cannot know neither the time nor place he Run the good[s]
for which he stands charged; as the officers of the Customs are very carefull to conceal these particulars. If so, he cannot know himself to be innocent, unless he never was concerned in such work; and this I suppose is
not the Case. Consequently he will in my opinion run no little risk in
standing a Trial. But this is a subject I have little knowledge of, Nor have
I time nor inclination to make my self acquainted with it. I am told that
the easiest way to get clear of such like affairs, is, after the Writ is served,
to Petition the Commissioners of the Customs or Excise, to which it may
belong; and to endeavour to make up the matter with the officers concerned. If this method is persued, I shall be ready to give any assistance
in my power, which cannot be much, as I know not a single Commissioners
[sic] at either the one Board or the other. This Method of proceeding,
supposes him Guilty the contrary of which he has not only asserted to you
but to me also in a letter which I have just recieved. The only thing he
seems to dread is the expence of a Trial, but in this I wish he does not
deceive himself, as well as you. If I should gain any further information
you shall be acquainted therewith. . . .[1]

One can see Mr Fleck's point quite clearly, once he had got into
trouble. What was the use of having a brother-in-law a post-captain
in the royal navy, if you could not make some profit out of the link.
Old John Walker, too, writing from Whitby with restrained affection,
wanted his 'Esteemed Friend' to interview an attorney, in a benevolent cause. 'I dare say thou must remember Alice Gill who was my
Servant at the Time thou was likewise one francis Sutton who belong'd
to the old friendship, and I think the Time of thy being Mate, who
Marry'd hir'; Francis had been pressed into the navy, and gone down
with the *Ramillies*, and their son Frank, an apprentice, had also been
lost with his ship; could Cook interview Mr Thomas Cotton of
Hackney and arrange for the payment to Alice of a legacy designed
for her son? No doubt Cook remembered Alice Gill and Francis
Sutton—he had a warm feeling for his associates of the Whitby days

---

[1] National Library of Australia, Canberra, MS 7. The MS is endorsed, 'The very
celebrated navigator, Capt. James Cook'.

—and he would do all he could to oblige the man who subscribed himself 'thy real friend'.[1]

By February 1776 he was deep in another task, for which he had had no more formal training than for the law; which did not come to his hand so naturally as the offices of friendship. This was the composition of the history of his voyage. There were other candidates for this task, some of whom had minimal qualifications; certainly the ambition to strike a bargain with the booksellers, in spite of the official confiscation of all logs and journals, stirred a little in a number of seamen's brains. It generally came to nothing: there were not many literate seamen, and even with Grub Street padding it was not so easy to produce a cohesive story of three years' adventure without a reasonably complete journal stowed away somewhere. But booksellers were avid; there was a public, it seems, for the most unsatisfactory account; anonymity could be preserved fairly well; and though the Admiralty was determined (with needless fears) that nothing would supplant an official account, something was bound to slip on to the market. Writing being a remarkable exercise among the crew, its practitioners and their secrets were known, like Richard Rollett the sailmaker, who 'Keept a Journal Interlin'd in his bible'; there were those who might have made a few guineas if anybody had been able to read what they had written. As early as mid-September, six weeks after the ship's return, Cook was tracking down an account said to be in the press, which proved to be by John Marra the gunner's mate, that vagrant Irishman. Marra had sold it to Francis Newbery, of St Paul's Churchyard, connected otherwise with the voyages by his supply of Dr James's Fever Powders. Cook did not think it would be worth regarding, and it duly appeared before the end of the year: a small book even when blown up by the editor, but interesting enough to be pirated in Dublin in 1776, and for a German translation to be published in that year, a French one in 1777. This at least was a measure of the captain's growing fame—which could be said also of a second anonymous English publication, quite worthless, of 1776.[2]

[1] Walker to Cook, 2 April 1776; Dixson Library MS Q 140. This MS is a draft on the back of Cook's letter to Walker of the preceding 14 February, and plunges straight into the amenities: 'I receiv'd thine of the 14 of february last which shou'd Acknowledgd before now, but waited for a favourable Opportunity to Send the Ale & a Ham which hope to meet with in a little Time . . .'.

[2] Cook's report to the Admiralty secretary on the matter, 18 September 1775, together with an enclosure addressed to himself by Anderson the *Resolution*'s gunner, who did the essential detective work (a very vivid piece of writing), is in P.R.O. Adm 1/1610; I have printed it in *Journals* II, 961–2. Marra's book has a long title, *Journal of the Resolution's Voyage . . . by which the Non-Existence of an undiscovered Continent, between the Equator and the 50th Degree of Southern Latitude, is demonstratively proved*, etc. The other publication

Meanwhile the preparation of the official account proceeded, not without difficulties.

The decision had been apparently quite early taken by the Admiralty, or Lord Sandwich, that there should be no more Hawkesworths. Hawkesworth's glory, so firmly founded, as it must have seemed to him, on £6000, had turned, if not to dust and ashes, at least to a good deal of unpleasantness. We have seen that Cook, when he read the volumes devoted to his own voyage, was 'mortified'; mortified also the commanders whose journals had been adapted in the first volume. Burney and Garrick, in nominating Hawkesworth to 'write the voyages', had not really made a good choice, though they had obliged a friend. Hawkesworth was not interested in geography, he knew nothing about nautical affairs; one rope, it could almost be said, or one compass-bearing, was as good as another to him. He wished to entertain. His use of the first person throughout, as he told the stories, may have brought the commanders and the reader closer together and made the stories more vivid; but it also made the commanders guilty of some strange statements. Writing for the polite world, he had laid down a condition that he should be free to intersperse his own sentiments when he thought fit, in addition to converting the seamen's language into his own, and Cook may well have been taken aback by some of the elevated speculations attributed to him, or to discover the close resemblance he had found between Diana and her nymphs and a party of Maori women feeling with their toes for shell-fish beneath the water at Tolaga Bay. There was more of this in the two Cook volumes than in the first; for by the time Hawkesworth came to compile the first volume he was running out of sentiments. Yet all might have been tolerable if the arrangement had been adhered to by which each commander was to read the text relating to himself. Hawkesworth, though reckless, thought it had been adhered to, and that he had done his duty; and he seems to have worked hard. 'My Lord', he writes to Sandwich on 19 November 1771 (with rather more feeling for Banks than for Cook),

I cannot help stealing a few minutes from the Work in which your Lordship is pleased to take an Interest so flattering to myself, and so favourable to the Undertaking, to acknowledge the Receipt of the first Volume of Mr Banks's Journal, and to assure your Lordship that as it is my highest Interest, it is also my earnest Desire to get my M.S. ready time enough to have the Sanction of Mr Banks and Capt Cook to what I shall relate after them. I am happy in your Lordship's powerfull Influence with Mr Banks

referred to was 'A Second Voyage round the World. . . . Drawn up from Authentic Papers . . .', was said to be 'Printed for the Editor', was obviously fake, and got a bad press.

for the use of his Journall; I flatter myself that I shall be able to prevent ill humour, and satisfy the utmost Delicacy of a Gentleman to whom I shall be so much obliged. I promise your Lordship that not an hour shall be bestowed upon any other Object, till the Account is finished, either of Business or Pleasure. your Lordship will judge that my Relaxations, however necessary must be short, from the time which was taken up by the mere reading of only part of my materials. . . .[1]

There is enough in these rather stilted lines to show us why Hawkesworth would never produce another Anson's Voyage; enough also to show that he was really anxious to have his text scrutinised, by Cook as well as by Banks. In his preface he said it had been. Cook, it can hardly be doubted, did see some of it. We have his conversation as reported by Boswell. 'He said it was not true that Mr. Banks and he had revised all the Book, and in what was revised Hawkesworth would make no alteration (I think he said this too.)'[2] What then had happened? One suspects some slipshod practice in the Admiralty office, perhaps on Sandwich's part—some careless break in the administrative process that left everybody in a false position, not least Hawkesworth. Banks also must have been careless, even if his own position with the Admiralty after May 1772 was not very secure.[3]

Cook, through Boswell, tells us a little more about his interpreter. 'He said Hawkesworth made in his Book a general conclusion from a particular fact, and would take as a fact what they had only heard. . . . He said that a disregard of chastity in unmarried women was by no means general at Otaheite, and he said that Hawkesworth's story of an *initiation* he had no reason to beleive. "Why, Sir," said I, "Hawkesworth has used your narrative as a London Tavern-keeper does wine. He has brewed it." '[4] One may interpose that this was the Cook of the second voyage, not of the first, speaking on Tahitian women, and that there was plenty in his own first journal, as in Banks's, to justify Hawkesworth. Unhappy Hawkesworth: with all

---

[1] Sandwich Papers.   [2] *Private Papers of James Boswell*, XI, 218.

[3] Rival advertisements reached a high tone. By the time Hawkesworth had sold out, Newbery had on the market the first numbers of a compilation in 48 weekly parts on all the English circumnavigations, up to Cook, taking in Sydney Parkinson and adding Bougainville for good measure.—*General Evening Post*, 2 August 1773. Strahan and Cadell, put on their metal, still in August did not fail to insist on the controverted point, 'That no doubt might remain of the fidelity with which the author has related the events recorded in his materials, the manuscript account of each voyage was read to the several Commanders, and to Mr Banks and Dr Solander, and afterwards lodged in their hands for a considerable time.'—*General Evening Post*, 21 August. On Hawkesworth in relation to the other voyagers see Robert E. Gallagher, *Byron's Journal of his Circumnavigation* (Cambridge, 1964), lxxvi ff., and Helen Wallis, *Carteret's Voyage Round the World* (Cambridge, 1965), 464 ff. and 499 ff. Dr Wallis has some useful remarks on the general problem.

[4] *Private Papers of James Boswell*, XI, 218.

his haste, his three volumes quarto at three guineas in boards were held up by the exigencies of printing and engraving until June 1773. They appeared on the 10th of that month, followed two days later by Sidney Parkinson's work, earlier held back by an injunction. In just over two months the edition was exhausted. There was a second edition published in August, broken down from the beginning of September into sixty weekly shilling parts—with the newspaper puff, 'The public are requested to observe, that the genuine voyages to the Southern hemisphere, undertaken by order of his present Majesty, and published by authority, from the journals of the several commanders, and from the papers of Joseph Banks Esq: and Dr Solander, are written by Dr Hawkesworth; and that all other publications are spurious, and calculated to mislead and impose upon the public.'[1] But again, unhappy Hawkesworth: expectation was too high, and he could not rise to meet it. To be attacked by Dalrymple was natural enough; to have the behaviour of his voyagers, through him, attacked, was natural enough. He shrugged off Dalrymple: Cook's reef navigation, Cook's sense of proportion in not pursuing the discovery of some inconsiderable island that seemed important to Dalrymple, were not matters in which he took interest. But to be a target for the arrows— or the reviewing swords and pistols, the indignant glances or the high-bred titters—of the polite world, was more than a man of vanity could take. His view of Providence, he knew, was unorthodox; but to have his other speculative opinions damned, to have even his dedication to the Sovereign damned, to be regarded as a foe to morality, was too much. It may be too much to say, as was commonly said at the time, that he died of chagrin. There are other wasting diseases of which a man may die: certainly, however, he fell victim to a 'slow fever', the nervous strain was acute, and he died, on 17 November 1773, two years almost to the day after his solemn declaration of intent to Sandwich, disappointed.

All this was directly to affect Cook. None of it, however, was his concern, as in those months he stood south-east from Cape Palliser, and then up through the islands and back to Queen Charlotte Sound. He was engaged in writing a new journal, of a different sort from that of his first voyage. He was not a born writer, with a natural gift of style. If we may regard the first voyage as his apprenticeship to discovery, we may regard the journal of that voyage as his apprenticeship to journal-keeping. Apart from the fact that he had a great deal to say, it followed the pattern of the journals he had kept before: that is, it abstracted the technical detail of a log under a few headings

1 *London Evening Post*, 18 August 1773.

such as winds, course, distance sailed, and so on, and, with some brief phrases on the weather, copied the daily entries in a log covered by the more general heading, 'remarkable occurrences'. Indeed, the first journal is entitled 'Remarkable Occurences on board His Majestys Bark Endeavour'. It followed the log, naturally enough, in its dating: that is, for the sailor the 'day', each unit of twenty-four hours with a number attached to it in the succession of the month, began at noon—not, as in civil time, at midnight; the afternoon of any date preceded its morning; when Cook wrote of the weather in 'the former part' of the day he was referring to what the landsman would have called yesterday afternoon. That, to a naïve landsman reading a journal, or thinking later about the events there recorded, could be confusing; and a writer like Hawkesworth, charged with describing a voyage for the public, would begin by adapting the dates. On the first voyage, while the ship was at Tahiti, Cook did go over to civil dating: because, as he explained, most of the events took place on land. These considerations become a key to the development of the journal on the second voyage, perhaps—it may be said—to the development of Cook's mind. Again he had a great deal to say, even more than when he was in the *Endeavour*. The commander of the *Resolution* encountered an extraordinary number of remarkable occurrences, and he found himself embarked on a constant need to theorise about them. One cannot say that Cook is becoming a reflective man, because there is evidence enough of reflectiveness in what he has written before; but the voyage kept his mind, as well as his technical ability as a sailor, continually on the stretch. It may have been, partly, because of this, that he wrote so much; another reason, probably, was that he had so much time to write in—as we have seen, for example, on the passage from New Zealand to Tierra del Fuego. For whatever reason, the voyage is marked by a vast amount of drafting and re-drafting of the journal—a journal different from that of the first voyage, in that the summary of the log, though faithfully adhered to for most of the time, is finally abandoned for more general statements; and these are the statements of a version, the last of four (if we accept the indications of copies made by the captain's clerk) which has also converted the dating, and hence the organisation, of the whole into civil time. He has also re-organised some of the information he has had from his subordinates, makes increasing use of the excellent Wales; now and again, as he improves, rubs off the fine point of a first vivid word or phrase. He is not writing, any more, simply a report to the Admiralty: the dating proves that. One is driven to guess, not exactly that Cook writes deliberately for publication—is composing a book, in fact—but that subconsciously he had the ambition to do so. He knew that there would certainly be a book about the voyage. He had seen something, at least, of what Hawkesworth had made of his *Endeavour* journal, although he did not know, until he met the printed product at the Cape, that his own emendations had been ignored. He himself may quite well have resolved that when another editor came to operate upon his pages the resulting statement would be Cook, not editorial. He had no illusion that he was a fine writer, or a master of spelling and punctuation; but he knew what he wanted to say about his voyage, and what needed to be said.

So, when the matter was first discussed in 1775, the situation was not quite the same as it was in 1771. What happened in the succeeding months can be disentangled reasonably well, and although it is part of the biography of John Reinhold Forster much more than of Cook it must be briefly traversed, because it made Cook formally into an author. Forster was convinced that from the very beginning, and all along, the intention was that he should write the history of the voyage; that he had laid this down as a condition before sailing; that it was accepted by the Admiralty, and that he had been assured by Daines Barrington, through whose friendly recommendation he had been given the place vacated by Lind, that that was one of the chief purposes of sending him out; that he should enjoy the sole profit and emolument accruing from that piece of history; and that after the voyage he should receive a pension sufficient to provide permanently for himself and his family: all this in addition to £4000. It is hardly conceivable that Daines Barrington made these extraordinary promises on behalf of the Admiralty. He may have expressed a moderate, even an encouraging, hope; and Forster lived in a world of fantasy. John Reinhold Forster was not invariably arrogant; very possibly, if he had had any judgment at all, he would have done quite well out of the Admiralty. Solander writes to Banks in early September 1775,

'Mr Forster overwhelms me with civilities upon your account. He is of all men I know either the most open or the greatest fool. He certainly has made some clever remarks during the Voyage; but he talks rather too much of them. You cannot imagine how much the Man is mended since he came home: the Officers say they hardly know the Man. He came home thinking himself very great—now he, like Bruce is reduced even in his own opinion.'[1]

[1] Solander to Banks, 5 September 1775; B. M. Natural History, Banks Correspondence, D.T.C., I, 98–9. James Bruce was the African traveller.

Lord Sandwich, the letter goes on, in its news of the voyagers, had asked him for a specimen of his writing, an account of the proceedings at Dusky Bay: if that was approved of, he was to do the whole voyage, sharing the profits equally with Cook. Sandwich, then, was willing to go some distance to meet Forster's expectations; and he was supplied with the relevant part of Cook's journal to combine with his own.

The specimen did not meet with approval. Obviously there was correspondence that has since disappeared. Much has survived, among Sandwich's papers, and poor Daines Barrington was deeply involved, as an intermediary who finally threw in his hand. 'By the letter I have received from you,' wrote Sandwich to him at the end of October, 'together with one from Mr Forster I begin to fear that there is no possibility of doing any thing with Mr Forster; and I am almost convinced that he is, what he has been represented to me to be, an utterly impracticable man.' As a proof that he was not a correct writer of English, his letter was enclosed; nevertheless Sandwich was prepared to keep him employed—'I am willing that his share of the emolument of that publication shou'd be considerable; & unless his vanity leads him to think he is entitled to more than his proportion, he will have no reason to complain'.[1] Vanity could take various forms, and when it was decided that Forster as sole author would not do, the man proceeded to refer to Cook in terms that the First Lord did not find tolerable. He wrote to Forster, while he still found it possible to write to him, 'You mention a satisfaction that you have in being eased from the trouble of methodizing & clearing Captain Cook's journal from its inaccuracies & vulgar expressions. I do not pretend to be a Critic; but I must say that I have met with very few vulgarisms or inaccuracies in that journal; but I have seen his journal misquoted, & vulgarisms introduced that were not in the Original.'[2] This was a decided blow, or would have been to anyone less encased in righteous self-approval.

It was thought, succeeding this experiment, that a joint work might be possible, Cook dealing with the navigation and Forster with the science. In the nature of things, this scheme could succeed no better. However it was couched, we have Cook, as the autumn of 1775 moved on, furiously busy over one of his own copies of the journal—operating on this creature of his mind with quite merciless determination: deleting, adding, interlining, incorporating footnotes in the text, filling up his margins, drafting sentences or paragraphs

[1] Sandwich to Daines Barrington, 28 October 1775; Sandwich Papers.
[2] Sandwich to J. R. Forster, 28 October 1775; Sandwich Papers.

on separate slips keyed in to his pages. Finally, when interlineations become confusing, or corrections are vital, he takes to the thing with red ink. He, the most unliterary of men, is the author in gestation. He is an author with his public in full view: why otherwise should he insert a phrase like 'which I shall endeavour to convey to the reader'? So far have we come since the strictly professional pages of August 1768. There was an adviser in the background. It was the Rev. John Douglas, canon of Windsor, a sociable man, no less than of quick and critical mind, who was asked by Sandwich to help in preparing the journal for the press. There was some secrecy, the king being in the secret, recorded Douglas.[1] Cook could do with help, in matters of 'style'—spelling and grammar, punctuation, division into sentences and paragraphs, the management of transitions; he showed skill in incorporating the substance of Wales into his writing, when he wanted to enlarge his own observations, but certainly he was a stranger to the niceties which Douglas understood so well. Douglas had tact as well as skill: the quarter-deck rapidity is slowed down a little, the breeze blows not quite so strongly; but Cook keeps a careful as well as grateful eye on his collaborator, he continues to command his own ship. The collaborator preserved the captain's letters.[2] The first of these introduced a new matter, which added to the complexity of the writer's life. It was dated from Mile End,

Thursday 4th of Jan^{ry} 1776.

Dear Sir / I have received your obliging favour, and am very sorry it is not in my power to except of your kind invitation to Windsor. For some time past, I have been looking out for a Ship to accompany the Resolution on her intended Voyage; I expect one will be purchased tomorrow, but then I shall have to attend to the alterations which will be necessary to be made in her. These things have retarded the copying my Journal; five Books are done which I shall send you by the machine tomorrow, and if you please you may return those you have gone through by the same Conveyance. I leave it intirely to you to make such alterations as you see necessary and even to strike out any part, or passage which you may think superfluous. By such time as you come to Town I hope to have the whole ready to put into your hands. I am with great esteem D^r S^r / your obliged Humble Servt / Jam^s Cook

He did inspect three ships the following day. Within a few days more

---

[1] B.M. Egerton MS 2181, f. 42 v; *Journals* II, cxliv.
[2] All Cook's extant letters to Douglas on this matter, probably all there were, are preserved together in the British Museum, Egerton MS 2180, except the first, f. 1–2, which is exhibited, Sal. A. 82. This reference may therefore serve all of them.

one of these was bought, and Cook was giving his advice on the necessary alterations to her.

The texture of his life was indeed thickening, and at this period we may suppose some inner tension too. Ever since the excited party to the *Resolution*, when promotions were announced, and Cook's appointment to Greenwich Hospital, and the ladies were sick, it was general knowledge that the ship would go out again; and Cook was to have employment whenever he should ask for it—or, at least, to use his own phrase, whenever his endeavours in any shape could 'be essential to the publick'. And, as he had written to Walker, whether he could bring himself to like ease and retirement, time would show. Association with John Reinhold Forster could hardly be called ease, but it did not occupy all existence. As advice was sought, and Cook learnt more about the voyage that was in prospect, and looked at ships with the dockyard people, it could hardly be that there were not stirrings within him. Some time, probably, in this month of January, and—it is possible—less dramatically than appeared to his first biographer, he made up his mind; for in a letter from Daines Barrington to Sandwich of 25 January, reporting on Forster's progress, there is reference to 'Captain Cook's destination', and the destination was a Pacific one. The background of further preparation of a book therefore is preparation of a voyage. This may not have been explicit with Cook's next extant letter to Douglas, wherein we find him steering clear of dangerous ground:

Mile End Jan^{ry} 10th 1776

I have recieved your letter of the 7th and also the Box with its contents. I have not had time to look over the corrections which you have made, but have not the least doubt but they were necessary, and that I shall be perfectly satisfied with them.

The remarks you have made on Bits of loose paper, I find are very just. With respect to the Amours of my People at Otaheite & other places; I think it will not be necessary to mention them attall, unless it be by way of throwing a light on the Characters, or Customs of the People we are then among; and even than I would have it done in such a manner as might be unexeptionable to the nicest readers. In short my desire is that nothing indecent may appear in the whole book, and you cannot oblige me more than by pointing out whatever may appear to you as such.

By the date of the following one all had been settled: he was captain of the *Resolution* once more. The amenities, however, come uppermost.

I beg your exceptance of 3 Doz^{n} Pints of Constantia Wine, White & Red, and $\frac{1}{2}$ a Doz^{n} of a different sort, which is pale coloured. I will not answer for them being packed in such a manner as to go safe to Windsor, tho' I think they will. You will herewith receive five Books more of my Manuscript, having kept the remaining three, as they want some alteration.

Mile End Friday Morn^g 8th March.

The 'Books' here referred to seem to be the separate blue paper-covered volumes in which Cook wrote out his copy, and to have no connection with the divisions of the narrative. In his note of the next day he is puzzled by a technical matter, that of the tense in which he should write.

As I intend to look over my whole Manuscript I shall have an oppertunity to make such alterations, as may appear necessary to bring it, either to the present, or past times. If you will be so obligeing as to give me your opinion on this matter. It was first written in the present time, but on find[ing] Dr Hawkesworth had mostly used the past, I set about altering it, but I find many places has escaped me.

Mile End 9th March 1776

Cook continued to wrestle. Meanwhile Forster also was busy. By April it seemed that the publication of the work, still conceived as in some sort a joint work, should be regulated, and on the 13th a meeting was held at the Admiralty of Sandwich, Cook, Forster, and Stephens the secretary. It was agreed, apparently without any consideration of the length at which the two authors were writing, that two volumes should be published, the first being Cook's journal, the second 'Doctor Forster's Observations upon Natural History, and upon the Manners, Customs, Genius, and Language of the natives of the several Islands, with his philosophical remarks in the course of the voyage, and a general introduction to his own work'. The authors were to bear equally the cost of paper and printing, and share equally the profit. The Admiralty would pay all the cost of engraving the plates, under the supervision of Cook, Forster and Hodges; the distribution of the plates between volumes was to be settled by the Admiralty, and they would afterwards become the property of the two authors. Forster was to get proofs of Cook's volume, as soon as convenient, so that he could translate the whole work into French and German, and likewise proofs of the plates, so that he could have others made from them for his translations.[1] The printer (though there was nothing about this in the agreement) was to be William Strahan, who had printed Hawkesworth and some of the greatest works of the age. Cook continued to labour, nearer to his

---

[1] George Forster, *Letter to the Earl of Sandwich* (London, 1778), Appendix.

end, not without a thought to the comforts of Windsor, as his next two missives to Douglas indicate.

Mile End Ap¹ 26ᵗʰ 1776

I have just drawn off a Hhd of Madeira which was round in the Resolution. I expected it to have been of the very best, but I think it does not prove so. Perhaps you are a better judge than I am, therefore must [beg] your permission to send you a few bottle[s] to taste. I wish to know whether you would have it sent to Windsor, or to your Town house if to the former, by what conveyance.

I have had a little Conversation with Mʳ Strahan about my Journal, he has promised to give it all the assistance in his Power. C. Campbell will look over the Nautical part & Sʳ Hugh Palliser has also promised to give his assistance.

I have divided it into Books and Chap. takeing the former Voyages and Lord Ansons for my guidance, but submit the whole to your better judgement, with full hopes that you will make such alterations, as you may see necessary.

Douglas, we find, was come to town, and invites Cook to call upon him.

[28 April]

Last night I was favoured with your agreeable letter, and have sent my servant for the Books as you disired. I am sorry Captain Furneaux's Journal has given you so much trouble, I am in some measure in fault for not looking over the Copy before it was put into your hands. If it is equally convenient to you I should be glad to put of waiting upon you till next Saturday, when I will bring the whole Manuscript with me, to let you see how I have divided it into Books & Chapters. By that time, I may have the Introduction ready for you to look over; I may also, know my Lord Sandwich's opinion on Mʳ Forsters work, a part of which I am told, by my friend Dʳ Shepherd,¹ is in his Lordships hands. These and some other reasons makes me wish to put of our meeting till that day. On your return to Windsor you will find a letter from me, requesting your permission to allow me to send you a little Madeira Wine, and to know whether you would have it sent to Windsor, or half moon Street. Without waiting for your answer, shall take the liberty to send it to the latter place tomorrow, if the Man who has it in charge is but in the way. Your acceptance of it will add to the many obligations confer'd on Dear Sir Your very obliged and Most Humble Servant Jamˢ Cook

Mile-End Sunday Mornᵍ

P.S. This Wine is part of [a] Cask that was round in the Resolution, it do's not turn out so good as I had a right to expect, but the Cooper tills

¹ The Rev. Dr Antony Shepherd (1721–96), F.R.S., Plumian professor of astronomy, Cambridge, from 1760. Cook named a group of small islands in the New Hebrides after him.

me it will mend in the Bottle. I have not tasted it, sence it was fined and bottled.

From this happy scene one must turn to a less happy one, that of Forster—with the preliminary remark that most of Forster's unhappiness was self-induced. His letters, and those of Daines Barrington, to Sandwich inform us what happened; Sandwich's own were fewer.[1] The evidence of a new specimen of Forster's writing was that he still conceived it his rôle to give a detailed account of the whole voyage; and Sandwich still believed the writing needed correction. The littérateur Richard Owen Cambridge was willing to do this ungrateful business, with Cook's journal by his side, both to avoid repetition and to ensure that the reader would learn all he wanted to know—'For example what is become of the Queen of Otaheitee'; but Barrington would assume all responsibility. Forster must leave plenty of room for corrections. The precaution was no doubt justified. On the other hand, Forster and not the Admiralty was bearing the cost of the book, except for the engravings; and such a clause had not come into the agreement of 13 April. Forster was outraged: he could not 'submit to that Indignity to have my performance treated like a theme of a Schoolboy'. No compromise seemed possible, though Forster, having railed at both Cook and Sandwich, for a time turned his rage against Banks, whom he accused of doing him ill offices with the First Lord. Then he seems to have made some agreement with Cook, which remains unclear. At this point, early in June, there was a royal command: unless he should submit to having his narrative corrected, the Admiralty was to have nothing further to do with him. This would mean that he would be deprived of all rights in the engraved plates. From the Admiralty point of view, and from Barrington's as a disinterested go-between, the April agreement had broken down—entirely through Forster's fault; from Forster's, he had been vilely and dishonourably treated. Barrington summarised: 'In short the poor Man is certainly out of his senses & hath rejected what your Lordship very kindly threw into his lap, & which would have amounted (I am persuaded) to £1500.'[2] At this stage we have further letters to Douglas from Cook, somewhat rudely made acquainted with the full import of what had been happening.

[1] The Sandwich Papers contain six letters from Barrington to Sandwich on the business, 25 January to 12 June 1776, and one from Forster to Barrington, which the latter enclosed in his own to Sandwich of 10 June. There are fifteen from Forster to Sandwich—two of August 1776, three of February 1777, one of June 1778, six of February 1779, two of November 1779 (both dated the 30th), and one of December 1779. There is one from Sandwich to Forster, 28 October 1775, and one to Barrington, 28 October 1775.
[2] Barrington to Sandwich, 12 June 1776; Sandwich Papers.

Mile-End June 11th 1776

Yesterday Mr Strahan & I went to the Admiralty in order to meet Mr Forster to settle about the Publication, but instead of finding him there, I found a letter from him to me couched in the following terms. That Lord Sandwich had thought proper to interpret the Agreemint between us, in such a manner, as he thought did not agree with its purport; and as his Lordship on that pretence had excluded him from all particip[a]tion of the Admiralty's assistance, our meeting was thereby rendered unnecessary. I afterwards saw Mr Barrington, who inform'd me the [*sic*] Mr Forster had absolutely refused to make the least alteration in his M.S. What steps my Lord Sandwich will now take I cannot say, but I apprehend I shall have to Publish alone. I do not expect to see his Lordship till Thursday Morning, and perhaps the next day I may leave Town, unless I was sure of seeing you on Saturday or Sunday in that case I would certainly wait a day or two at all events. What Mr Forster intends to do I have not heard, but suppose he will publish as soon as possible, and if so he will get the start of me. He has quite deceived me, I never though[t] he would have separated him self from the Admiralty, but it cannot hurt me & I am only sorry my Lord Sandwich has taken so much trouble to serve an undeserving man.

Sandwich, however, still seems to have nourished a little hope of accommodation when it had gone from Barrington and Cook—to judge from Cook's next letter.

Mile End 14th June 1776

Last night I received your favor, and as matters stand at present, your meeting me in Town can be of no use, nor did I wish it. Only if business had called you up, I meant to have waited upon you.

I was with my Lord Sandwich yester Morning, & found that he had not quite given up Dr Forster, but I believe he will be obliged to do it at last. I had some conversation with the D^r last night, and used all the arguments I was master of to persuade him to submit to his Lordship, but to no manner of purpose. The Charts are all finished, but the other Plates I am told, will not be done before Christmas. But if I am to have the whole, the Admiralty I know will forward them as much as possible. I have leave to remain in Town till this matter is settled, and at the desire of Lord Sandwich, shall join Mr Stuart with Mr Strahan to manage the Publication &c^a of my Book. It is now with Sr Hugh Palliser & Capt. Campbell for them to look over the Nautical part. As soon as they have done with it, it shall be put into Mr Strahans hands. My Lord Sandwich gave me a paper concerning Omai, which I have tack'd in its proper place in the 6th book. His Lordship desired that you might see it, & also the Introduction, this shall be sent you to morrow by the Stage, and as to the other, you can at any time look it over at Mr Strahans. I shall take care to get a Compleat list of all the Plates to leave with the Manuscript, &

have already made notes where the most of them are to be placed. I thank you for your kind wishes & hope that neither you nor my other worthy friends will be disappointed in their expectations of Dr Sir Your very obliged & most humble Servt Jam^s Cook

P.S. I do not expect to leave Town till about the Middle of next week, so that you may expect to hear from me again.

Ten days after writing this letter Cook left London. Within that period Sandwich made up his mind, irrevocably. Cook wrote once more, and for the last time, to Douglas the day before he left.

Mile-End June 23rd 1776

It is now Settled that I am to Publish without Mr Forster, and I have taken my measures accordingly. When Captain Campbell has looked over the M.S. it will be put into the hands of Mr Strahan & Mr Sturat [*sic*] to be printed, and I shall hope for the Continuation of your assistance in correcting the press. I know not how to recompence you for the trouble you have had, and will have in this Work. I can only beg you will except of as many Copies, after it is published, as will serve your self and friends, and I have given directions for you to be furnished with them. When you have done with the Introduction please to send it to Mr Strahan or bring it with you when you Come to Town, for there needs be no hurry about it. Tomorrow Morning I set out to join my ship at the Nore, & with her proceed to Plymouth, where my stay will be but short. Permit me to assure you that I shall always have a due sence of the favors you have done, and that I am with great esteem and regard, Dear Sir, Your Most Obliged and very Humble Servt Jam^s Cook.

On that note these two so dissimilar persons parted.

What the parting with Forster had been like we do not know. Forster certainly had convinced himself that he was the victim of injustice. Cook was willing that that part of the April agreement should stand which allowed Forster the use of his proof sheets for translation and proofs of the plates for copying, and Sandwich raised no objection. Cook, however, had come to distrust somewhat Forster's intentions, and left a note with Strahan that proofs should be handed over no earlier than ten days before publication; and Forster's protest to Cook, in his last moments at Plymouth before sailing, brought no reply. Nor would the printers deliver impressions of the plates without (according to Forster) being directly empowered by Sandwich to do so;[1] or (according to Stuart) a signed engagement by Forster that they would be made use of only to accompany the translations: 'This condition he refused, assuring us (myself & Strahan) that he had no intention to make such translation, but

[1] Forster to Sandwich, 2 August 1776; Sandwich Papers.

would publish his own account of the voyage'. He also attempted to get them in Stuart's name surreptitiously from Hodges. A troublesome business, thought Stuart.[1] Cook might have been 'actuated upon by the bookseller or some other mean thinking Man', but he had been guilty of 'a breech of honour & Integrity', Forster informed the First Lord, seeking an order that would rectify 'Capt Cooks mistakes (for I will not yet call them by a harsher but more just name)'.[2] This elicited no response—Sandwich being a master of inactivity when he so wished—and the complaints became dolorous as well as indignant. Having put himself into a position where no one would trust him, and interdicted from publishing any account of the voyage until after the official one had appeared, Forster fell back on his son George. George was a quick writer, and a better one than John Reinhold. He had taken part in no argument, was party to no agreement. By working hard, he could perhaps beat Cook on to the market, and gather in first profits for the Forster Family—plates or no plates. He did work hard: as he had no journal—for he had been far too busy on the voyage with his drawing to set down more than a few notes—he could but give a rendering of his father's, adding to it reminiscences and impressions of his own. When, therefore, he claimed originality for the book, except in so far as he had consulted John Reinhold's journals 'in every important circumstance', he was not strictly truthful. His first two chapters are almost a strict transcript of the second specimen of work which John Reinhold submitted to Sandwich. Or did John Reinhold submit to Sandwich not his own work, but George's? It may be noted that in the case of George there was no difficulty felt about revision by a different hand: Dr Hornsby, the Oxford professor of astronomy, scrutinised the manuscript for him. No delay being caused by engravings, it could be rushed through the press, and published in March 1777, six weeks before Cook's volumes. John Reinhold could proceed now more deliberately. His scientific and philosophical *Observations* did not appear until the following year.[3]

Cook's two volumes were given to the public by the booksellers

[1] Sandwich Papers, Memorandum by James Stuart, n.d., but beginning 'July, 9. Dr Forster wrote to Captain Cook as follows . . .', and going on to quote the letter referred to by Cook in his to Douglas of 11 June printed above. The second paragraph begins, 'After Captn Cook had left London Dr Forster applied to me . . .'. As Cook left London on 24 June, the internal evidence is that 9 July is the date of the memorandum—the date in fact, when, according to Forster (letter to Sandwich, 2 August 1776) he called on Stuart and Strahan; so Stuart lost no time in recording his impression.

[2] Forster to Sandwich, 2 August 1776; Sandwich Papers.

[3] George's book was *A Voyage round the World, in his Britannic Majesty's Sloop, Resolution, commanded by Capt. James Cook, during the Years 1772, 3, 4 and 5. By George Forster, F.R.S.*,

Strahan and Cadell in May 1777, under the title *A Voyage towards the South Pole, and Round the World. Performed in His Majesty's Ships the Resolution and Adventure, In the Years 1772, 1773, 1774 and 1775. Written by James Cook, Commander of the Resolution.* . . . Exclusive of appendices, they contained somewhat over seven hundred pages, and, as they had all the engravings, sixty-three plates, of which twelve were charts. The author explains to his readers the appearance he makes, in the last paragraph of his introduction, which may here be given not as Douglas laid on it a final polish, but as it came from his pen:

I shall conclude this preliminary discourse by publickly acknowlidging the Kind Assistance of some worthy friends, in whose hands I left the Manuscript, when I embarked on a third expedition, who were so obliging as to superintend the printing and make such corrections as they found necessary, without altering the stile. For it was judged that it would be more exceptable to the Public, in the Authors words, than in any other persons, and that the Candid and faithfull manner in which it is written would counterbalance the want of stile and dullness of the subject. It is a work for information and not for amusement, written by a man, who has not the advantage of Education, acquired, nor Natural abilities for writing; but by one who has been constantly at sea from his youth, and who, with the Assistance of a few good friends gone through all the Stations belonging to a Seaman, from a prentice boy in the Coal Trade to a Commander in the Navy. After such a Candid confession he hopes the Public will not consider him as an author, but a man Zealously employed in the Service of his Country and obliged to give the best account he is able of his proceedings.[1]

The publication of this book was, itself, one of the great events in the history of Pacific exploration.

Member of the Royal Academy of Madrid, and of the Society for promoting Natural Knowledge at Berlin. His father's *Observations made during a Voyage Round the World, on Physical Geography, Natural History and Ethic Philosophy.* . . . *By John Reinold Forster, LL.D. F.R.S. and S.A. And a Member of several Learned Academies in Europe.* (London, 1778). It was a quarto volume of 650 pages.

[1] Dixson Library, MS F. 1.

XIX

A Third Voyage

ONE WAY and another, the captain had had his hands full; and it is now necessary to turn from literary composition to the matter in which he felt himself more professionally engaged, we must look at the antecedents of this new voyage which had formed the background to his correspondence with Dr Douglas. We have seen that the *Resolution* had hardly arrived home before it was announced that she was to go out to the Pacific again, under the command—Solander reported—of Clerke; she had been put into dock to refit for that service; and, the *Adventure* having already been discarded, Cook was asked for his advice on a new consort. He had been looking about for some time, he had told Douglas on 4 January, and the next day he hit on the brig *Diligence*, 298 tons, a fourth Whitby built ship, eighteen months old. She was purchased at once; the Navy Board, acquainting the Admiralty with plans and dimensions for necessary alterations and rig, added, 'In all which Captain Cook who attended us thereon has been consulted'.[1] This was on 23 January; it was on 25 January that Daines Barrington, in his letter to Sandwich, referred to 'Captain Cook's destination'. When, then, did Cook find that the fine retreat, the ease and retirement of Greenwich Hospital, with its view of the ships in the river, but no ship beneath him, would be intolerable: when, as a man with domestic ties, who had been giving active and exhausting service to 'the publick' ever since he had formed them, did he feel the moment had come to quit shelter and the pretty income he got for doing nothing, and his wife and family, and take advantage of the Admiralty's promise to employ him whenever new service presented itself? It is unlikely that he made a sudden decision; for he was not a man of sudden decisions, though he could respond to emergency quickly enough. It is unlikely that he responded easily to indirect pressure. The pressure to which he did respond is likely to have been that of a whole set of circumstances, which his first biographer dramatised into one famous dinner party.

[2] For the official exchange of letters see *Journals* III, 1485.

There seems no reason to doubt that the party took place—though Kippis assigns no date for it—or that it consisted of four men: Sandwich the host, Palliser, Stephens and Cook. Its professed object was to consult with Cook on the command of the voyage in prospect. It was to be a voyage of large scope and possibly immense consequences, beyond comparison more important than merely returning Omai to his island. Indispensably necessary in its commander were great ability, skill and experience. 'That Captain Cook was of all men the best qualified for carrying it into execution,' continues Kippis, with a little heightening of his style, 'was a matter that could not be called in question. But however ardently it might be wished that he would take upon himself the command of the service, no one (not even his friend and patron, Lord Sandwich himself) presumed to solicit him upon the subject. The benefits he had already conferred on science and navigation, and the labours and dangers he had gone through, were so many and great, that it was not deemed reasonable to ask him to engage in fresh perils.' But to consult him constantly about it was natural; 'and his advice was particularly requested with regard to the properest person for conducting the voyage'. The dinner was held; the gentlemen held forth—upon the grandeur and dignity of the design, its consequences to navigation and science, the completion it would give to the whole system of discoveries. The charm worked. 'Captain Cook was so fired with the contemplation and representation of the object, that he started up, and declared that he himself would undertake the direction of the enterprise. It is easy to suppose, with what pleasure the noble lord and the other gentlemen received a proposal which was so agreeable to their secret wishes. . . .'[1] Sandwich hastened to the king.

It would be extremely innocent to believe that Cook was merely carried off his feet by a burst of eloquence from Lord Sandwich, Sir Hugh Palliser, and Mr Stephens. It is not impossible that they brought him to final, spoken, decision. He did not need eloquence. He was in a strong position, and external persuasion could hardly have affected him if he had already been strongly inclined to do what his friends wanted. He had been home five months or more; he had had ample time to hear and discuss what was being said in naval circles and in the Royal Society about the nature and direction of a new voyage; he could balance very well its interest against that of the sort of voyage he had recommended to young Latouche-Tréville. It may be that he was so free with Latouche because he assumed that his own interest in the South Pacific was finished. At any rate, he

[1] Kippis, 324–5.

volunteered. There seems to have been an interval before the final steps were taken, at the end of which, on 10 February, at the Admiralty office, Cook wrote out his application for employment, and on the same day received both Stephens' letter in reply and his commission. He wrote to the Secretary:

Having understood that their Lordships have ordered two Ships to be fitted out for the purpose of making further discoveries in the Pacific Ocean; I take the liberty, as their Lordships when they were pleased to appoint me a Captain in Greenwich Hospital were at the same time pleased also to say, it should not be in prejudice to any future offer which I might make of my Service, to submit my self to their directions, if they think fit to appoint me to the Command on the said intended Voyage; relying, if they condesend to except this offer, they will on my return, either restore me to my appointment in the Hospital, or procure for me such other mark of the Royal Favour as their Lordships upon the review of my past Services shall think me deserving of.[1]

The Secretary's reply left nothing to be desired. Obviously Cook was not unmindful of the future: perhaps Elizabeth Cook had had something to say. Sandwich's conversation with the king had been satisfactory. Matters proceeded briskly. On the date of the forementioned letters the Admiralty despatched five more to the Navy Board and the Ordnance Board on the fitting, stores, armament and manning of the ships. In the following weeks, while Cook wrestled with his book, the correspondence thickened, and Cook himself had a good many demands to make touching stores and provisions. His most significant letter, however, is the one he wrote to John Walker on 14 February.

I should have Answered your last favour sooner, but waited to know whether I should go to Greenwich Hospital, or the South Sea. The latter is now fixed upon; I expect to be ready to sail about the latter end of Ap[l] with my old ship the Resolution and the Discovery, the ship lately purchased of M[r] Herbert. I know not what your opinion may be on this step I have taken. It is certain I have quited an easy retirement, for an Active, and perhaps Dangerous Voyage. My present disposition is more favourable to the latter than the former, and I imbark on as fair a prospect as I can wish. If I am fortunate enough to get safe home, theres no doubt but it will be greatly to my advantage.

[1] P.R.O., Adm 1/1611: printed *Journals* III, 1486. The muster-book notes his joining the ship the same day, along with twenty-eight others, including Gore; Robert Anderson, Harvey, William Collett of both previous voyages; Ewin, Whelan, Cave, Henry Roberts of the *Resolution*, second voyage; and Dewar, Lanyon, Hergest of the *Adventure*, second voyage.

And there were best wishes to all the family, and the promise of a hearty welcome if any of them came to Mile End.[1]

What then was this voyage-to-be, this fair prospect, this enterprise of such grandeur and dignity, its design so pregnant of consequence both to human knowledge and to Cook? After that very agreeable dinner at Sir John Pringle's on 2 April, Boswell registered his sense of the extraordinary nature of things: 'It was curious to see Cook, a grave steady man, and his wife, a decent plump Englishwoman, and think that he was preparing to sail round the world.'[2] If, indeed, the voyage were successful it would entail sailing round the world. But sailing round the world, in itself, no longer demanded astonishment, or promised large consequences. This enterprise was the discovery of the North-west Passage, from its Pacific end.

Cook had destroyed one great illusion of the human mind, that of a habitable southern continent. He had destroyed it not so much as a sworn enemy to illusion—though he preferred facts—as a student solving a problem. He came now to a second cardinal problem of eighteenth-century geography, and to an illusion just as sedulously nurtured as that of *Terra australis*. The problem was more intractable than the first, because there was in fact a North-west Passage: the illusion did not lie there. It lay in the assumption that a passage had only to be discovered to be navigable; and it was allied with another illusion, the product of much pseudo-scientific thought and argument in the later eighteenth century, that of an ice-free arctic sea. Sea-water, it was argued, does not freeze because it cannot (the argument was carried on without the benefit of Cook's second voyage); ice is a product of fresh water and of the winter season; the ice of arctic rivers, floating at sea, will in the summer disperse, straits like rivers will be freed; a sea-passage from the Atlantic coast of North America to its Pacific coast there must be, for it is inconceivable that continuous land should exist to the Pole and beyond it; that passage must in the right season be navigable, and provide access to the rich trade of Asia incomparably more profitable than the tedious journey round the Cape of Good Hope. In the sixteenth century the vision was one of trade with the southern continent, the continent of Ortelius and Mercator. Their continent, Dalrymple's continent, had been swept away: no matter, a new route in the north would revolutionise the commerce of the world. There were still men of enormous faith, and men who could be persuaded by a logic founded on unhappy and

[1] Dixson Library, MS Q 140, pp. 79–82; printed *Journals* III, 1488.
[2] Boswell, *Private Papers*, XI, 218–19.

misleading premisses. They could not visualise the passage that did exist. It was not so much a passage as an impregnable fortress, defended by an unrelenting enemy. The enemy was ice.

The voyage which Cook found so fair a prospect would not be, of course, the first attempt to find that passage, even from the Pacific coast of America. It would be the latest in a series of something like fifty; and no part of their story is irrelevant to his story. The early shining names were those of Frobisher, Davis and Baffin, the tragic one that of Hudson, who it was hoped might sail to Cathay over the Pole. It was all discouraging: 'Wherefore I cannot but much admire the worke of the Almightie,' wrote Baffin in 1616, 'when I consider how vaine the best and chiefest hopes of men are in thinges un-certaine; and to speake of no other then of the hopeful passage to the North-West.'[1] The Hudson's Bay Company, when it was founded, was considered by some people to be a likely instrument of dis-covery; the Company, on the other hand, devoted itself to its very profitable fur monopoly, in the pursuit of which it was disturbed first by the French in the Spanish Succession War, then by one of its own governors, James Knight, then more effectively by an Ulster landowner, Arthur Dobbs. Knight planned to sail northwards up the west side of Hudson Bay until he met the high flood tide that he confidently expected would sweep through from the Pacific to that shore: there, where it emerged, would be the passage. He got two ships from the Company in 1719, certainly sailed into the Bay, and was seen no more. Observations of tidal directions in the northern part of the Bay were to become complicated, and arguments about them passionate. They were taken up by Arthur Dobbs, a man of large energies, who had never heard of Knight but was capable of considerable self-deception. Though a landowner, he was interested in trade, and widened his interest from the trade of Ireland to that of Britain and her colonies; this took him, as it took so many other publicists and commercial philosophers in that age, to colonial policy in North America and the thwarting of French ambitions, thence to exploration, and thence to the North-west Passage. He was convinced that it opened off a strait in the north-west corner of Hudson Bay; his elaborate though abstract study of the tides was buttressed by other observations somewhat dubious, as that of a clear sea in the north of the Bay while the south was frozen over, and of whales on the western side which could have come only from the Pacific; he was gullible over the printed word. He went back in his reading to *Purchas His Pilgrimes*, the vast seventeenth century ap-

[1] Quoted in C. R. Markham, *The Voyages of William Baffin* (London, 1881), 150.

pendix to Hakluyt, from which he took the story of the old Greek
pilot Juan de Fuca. According to this story, which transports us to
the other side of America, Juan de Fuca was sent by the viceroy of
Mexico in search of the Strait of Anian. In 1592, beyond California,
between latitudes 47° and 48°, he found a broad inlet, into which
he entered, sailing more than twenty days, passing by islands and
landing in divers places, seeing people clad in beasts' skins: a fruitful
land it was, 'rich of gold, Silver, Pearle, and other things'. In due
course he arrived at the Atlantic Ocean, and sailed back through his
passage to Acapulco, where he met with neither reward nor gratitude; for the Spaniards 'did understand very well, that the English
Nation had now given over all their voyages for discoverie of the
North-west passage, therefore they need not feare them any more
to come that way into the South Sea, and therefore they needed not
his service therein any more.'[1] To Dobbs this tale had the ring of
truth: he poured it with a large miscellany of data into a memorial
he composed in 1731, added a peroration on the short and easy way
to China, the advantages to be anticipated in either war or peace,
the new markets for manufactures and the employment of the poor,
and set off for London to see the Board of Trade, the Admiralty and
the Hudson's Bay Company.

He came to dislike the Company extremely. It would do little,
and misrepresented what it did do. After much persuasion, however,
he roused Admiralty interest: in 1740 (significantly enough, the
Anson year) royal consent was given to a naval expedition, and a
naval commission in 1741 to Captain Christopher Middleton, its
commander, an able person of scientific leanings who had been in
the Company's service. Dobbs had a hand in his instructions. Once
in the Bay, he would be led to the passage by the famous flood tide;
having penetrated it, he was to explore the western American coast,
form alliance with the inhabitants, take possession of the country,
winter on the coast or on some suitable island or return through the
passage, as he thought best, perhaps meet Anson off California—we
can see a sort of logical fantasy in it all granting only that the passage
was there and that Middleton was Cook. Middleton did what man
could do, found the flood tides all from the east and whales unreliable, and returned convinced that Dobbs was wrong. Dobbs
threw off Middleton with contumely; was energetic and ingenious
enough to organise a petition which brought an act of parliament

[1] Samuel Purchas, *Hakluytus Posthumus, or Purchas His Pilgrimes* (Glasgow, 1906), XIV,
416–17. See also Glyndwr Williams, *The British Search for the Northwest Passage in the
Eighteenth Century* (London, 1962), 273–6.

in 1745 offering a reward of £20,000 for the discovery of the passage; then, as the Admiralty had declined to try again, made one last effort, to beat down the monopolistic Company by enlisting the merchants of London in a speculative venture on his side. Once again an expedition returned with an icy answer. At least these abortive attempts had added to the knowledge of Hudson Bay, its inlets and rivers. At least a government had shown that it could take part in geographical investigation. But the North-west Passage, the merchants of London concluded, cutting their losses, could go hang. Was the case for the Passage, then, by the middle of the century, lost beyond redemption? It might seem so. If Hudson Bay were considered as the approach, it would have seemed even more so twenty years later, when the Company had begun to take exploration seriously—if the Company could have brought itself to believe that it had a duty to science as well as to itself, and would not lose by making public the results of exploration; for it was in July 1771 that the great journey of Samuel Hearne, one of its servants, northwards from Fort Churchill ended on the shore of the Arctic Ocean, a journey on which he had crossed no large river and no salt water, so that he had 'the pleasure to think' that he had 'put a final end to all disputes concerning a North West Passage through Hudson's Bay'.[1] The seventeenth century had abandoned all hope of Baffin Bay. What then was left?

Romantic geography was left; international commercial competition was left; the politics of trade and a not ignoble, a simple curiosity about the world were left. The triumphant end of the Seven Years' War had removed from the British mind the fear that the French, through brilliant exploration of a linked lake and river system, would be first over the North American continent to the Pacific and its trade. Although the continental hypothesis was dealt with effectively first, that priority was partly a personal accident—for no one could have planned the appearance of Cook; and the other hypothesis, of access to the northern Pacific by water through the American continent, was never entirely lost sight of. This was not necessarily the same as the Dobbs-Hudson Bay theory: the Juan de Fuca story, so pleasing to Dobbs, had nothing on its surface to do with Hudson Bay. There was a sort of English ancestry for the plan of discovery of the western entrance of a waterway in the sixteenth century Strait of Anian projects of Sir Humphrey Gilbert and Sir Richard Grenville, and in the Californian visit of Drake in 1579. Drake's New Albion, then added to the English crown, was a

[1] Hearne, *A Journey . . . to the Northern Ocean* (London, 1795), 303.

dubious gem, though it was to receive mention in exploring instructions in later centuries. There may have been something of de Fuca in the plans for the voyage of Sir John Narborough, sent into the Pacific by the Admiralty in 1669, with the double object of breaking the Spanish monopoly of trade and surveying the northwest coast of America beyond New Albion. The Hudson's Bay Company charter of 1670, we may remember, looked towards the other end of the passage. Narborough got no farther north than Valdivia, in Chile, whence the Spaniards sent him packing. Dampier the buccaneer carried on the thought. 'In my opinion', he wrote, describing his adventures off the coast of Mexico, 'here might be very advantageous Discoveries made by any that would attempt it: for the Spaniards have more than they can well manage.' The previous plans had been all wrong. 'But if I was to go on this Discovery, I would go first into the South Seas, bend my course from thence along by California, and that way seek a Passage back into the West Seas'[1]—or, as we should say, into the Western Atlantic. The Spaniards, added Dampier, were dogs in the manger—they would not look themselves, they objected to anybody else's looking. Yet the Spaniards had tried for the Strait of Anian more than thirty years before Drake, and their persistent and heroic exploration by land might well have left no energies to spare for maritime work. They devoted themselves to their trans-oceanic voyages to the Philippines and back until, no doubt stimulated by English and Dutch enterprises, they tried again in 1602 with Sebastian Vizcaino and his second-in-command, Martin de Aguilar. Vizcaino reached the latitude of 42° or 43° N, found no strait, but returned to Mexico with a theory that Upper and Lower California formed a great island, and that the strait opened up from the gulf inside. Here the matter rested for the Spaniards, until far on into the next century, and Dampier could make his comment.

Curiously enough, perhaps, the next piece of fantasy on the subject, appearing not long after Dampier, purported to be an account of a Spanish voyage. This was a 'Letter from Admiral Bartholomew de Fonte, then Admiral of New Spain and Peru, and now Prince of Chili', printed in 1708 in an English periodical called *The Monthly Miscellany or Memoirs for the Curious*. In that year the squib was sufficiently damp, and the periodical was short-lived. The Spanish admiral lived longer, the squib took fire. According to the letter, which did not lack circumstantial detail, in 1639 the Court of Spain, disturbed by advice that Hudson Bay–Strait of

[1] *Dampier's Voyages* (ed. Masefield, London 1906), I, 287.

Anian attempts were being undertaken by 'some Industrious Navigators from Boston in New England', commanded de Fonte to search the Pacific coast with four ships. The obedient admiral in 1640 sailed pleasantly from Callao to a river Los Reyes in 53°, inside an archipelago called St Lazarus. There he detached one of his captains, Pedro de Barnarda, up another river, leading to a large lake, with its end east-north-east in 77°. De Fonte himself, starting with the Los Reyes, went by rivers and lakes most of the way across the continent, until he met a ship that had come from the opposite direction, from Boston, commanded by a Captain Shapley. Though his orders were to seize any ship 'seeking a North West or West Passage into the South Sea', the generous Spaniard refrained at this time, saying that he 'would look upon them as Merchants trading with the Natives for Bevers, Otters, and other Furs and Skins'; among mutual courtesies, de Fonte gave Shapley a thousand pieces of eight for his fine charts and journals, sailed back down lakes and rivers to the South Sea, and so to Callao; 'having found that there was no Passage into the South Sea by that they call the North West Passage'—the way tried by Barnarda, one of whose seamen had had to go overland to Davis Strait—but, putting himself and Shapley together, nevertheless a clear waterway through the continent. A good deal of inviting circumstantial detail was supplied about fish ('excellent cod and ling, very large and well fed'), deer, berries, wild fowl, timber and honest Indians.

The thing was disinterred from defunct pages by Dobbs, equally eager as he had been over de Fuca, to have its great success after the publication in 1744 of his *Account of the Countries adjoining to Hudson's Bay*. Dobbs made no doubt of the genuineness of the story, though insisting on his own passage as well, which ran south of the de Fonte discoveries. The extraordinary part of the affair is the power it exerted over some of the leaders of French scientific geography and cartography—and in cartography the French were then the leaders of Europe—most notably over Joseph Nicholas Delisle and Philippe Buache. Rarely can disbelief have been so willingly suspended. They quarrelled between themselves over de Fonte's latitudes, and some other matters; but both, in their own maps, manage to include everything. Both, for example, have an immense expanse of water inland north of California, the 'Mer de L'Ouest', discovered in 1592 by de Fuca (says Delisle), with an opening from the ocean on each side of a large island—the northern one that of de Fuca, the southern that of Martin de Aguilar, Vizcaino's lieutenant. The two rash men were assailed by eminent compatriots, by English, Ger-

mans, and at least one Spaniard, the learned Jesuit historian Burriel
—who demonstrated that apart from anything else, Admiral de Fonte
had never existed. Unfortunately when in 1759 an English translation of his work appeared, as *A Natural and Civil History of California*,
the destructive pages were omitted; and the editor even argued that
it showed the discovery of a passage to be 'a very probable thing'.
Unfortunately the other translations made were from this English
version, not from the original. It became obvious that the only way
to settle the argument was to go and look.

Commodore Byron was the man the Admiralty in England selected
to go and look, in 1764, against the contemporary background of
commercial rivalry, British arrogance, French suspicion and Spanish
nervousness. There were other objects—rather too many—for Byron
to pursue, as we have already seen: the Falkland Islands were of
more importance than a North-west passage. Nevertheless the
planners had studied the current geographical controversies; for
the preamble to his instructions referred to the 'mariners of great
Experience who have thought it probable that a passage might be
found between the latitudes of 38° and 54° from that Coast into
Hudson's Bay'; and the instructions themselves directed him, after
his Atlantic business, to go to Drake's harbour in New Albion,
about latitude 38° or 38°30'. From this latitude he was 'to search the
said Coast with great care and diligence' as far to the northward as
he should find it practicable; 'And in case you shall find any probability of exploring a Passage from the said Coast of New Albion to
the Eastern side of North America through Hudson's Bay, you are
most diligently to pursue it and return to England that way, touching
at such place or places in North America, for the Refreshment of
your men, and for supplying the Ship and Frigate with Provisions,
Wood and Water, as you shall judge proper.'[1] Before even he entered
the Pacific, Byron thought his ships too much disabled for this
grandeur of programme, 'the California voyage'; the expedition, he
wrote to the Admiralty from Port Famine, had already gone through
an infinite deal of fatigue and many dangers; and he decided 'to
run over for India by a new Track',[2] which would lead to the rediscovery of the Solomon Islands. It was not a track absolutely new,
the Solomon Islands eluded him. When he arrived home he found
the British eye still fixed on the Pacific, but, for sufficient reason, on
the south Pacific; and Cook's two voyages there were of a magnitude
to dwarf, for the time being, any passage.

[1] P.R.O., Adm 2/1332, 99 ff.; printed Robert E. Gallagher, *Byron's Journal of his Circumnavigation* (Cambridge, 1964), 3 ff.
[2] Gallagher, 159.

For the time being only, and in England: we must remember the very lively European scientific scene, from England itself to St Petersburg. Mathematics and astronomy, chemistry, physics, half a dozen departments of natural history, medicine, all were being investigated with ardour, sometimes with fundamental thought; and of course geography. Even when perceptiveness was lacking— even when a woeful lack of scepticism prevailed—enterprise and ingenuity sometimes had practical effect. There was, among scientific men, a good deal of mutual stimulus in ideas. There was a good deal of scope for the ardent amateur. It was a time, too, when organised academies of science were eager to exert what influence they could over governments. We have seen the Royal Society stimulation of Cook's first voyage: its interest in the astronomical side of his second voyage was hardly less marked. Some of its Council, like Maskelyne, were men of real weight in influential positions. Others, without profundity or technical accomplishment, had wide interests and useful connections, like Daines Barrington, lawyer and antiquary, friend of Gilbert White and Banks and Lord Sandwich, misled and exasperated friend of John Reinhold Forster. Barrington had developed an interest in arctic exploration; he was almost inevitably the sort of man who would make large generalisations on an insufficiency of data, argue theories doomed to demolition by facts; and he became a correspondent of Samuel Engel, a Swiss of Geneva. Engel was one of those convinced that, as sea water did not freeze, the polar sea must be free of ice—or rather, free of ice that was not the product of rivers debouching on its coasts—ice therefore seasonal, avoidable by a ship that sailed at the right time in the right direction. He buttressed his theory, apart from his abstract meteorological and physical arguments, with testimonies, reliable or unreliable, from a variety of seamen and travellers who reported, or were alleged to report, ice-free waters in high latitudes. Barrington was smitten by Engel's enthusiasm and methods; and it was the strenuous advocacy of Barrington, on the Council of the Royal Society, a friend of the First Lord, that led in the summer of 1773 to the despatch into polar seas of the specially strengthened *Racehorse* and *Carcass*, under the command of another naval person in the Banks–Sandwich circle, Captain Constantine Phipps. Ice-pilots from the Greenland whaling fleet were taken. The hope was that the ships would work by way of Spitsbergen through an outer ring of ice, and then sail on smoothly to the pole. Phipps did reach a position far up the west coast of Spitsbergen, in latitude 80°37′; then, unable to move any farther north, extricated himself with difficulty from the ice-field that had closed round him, to arrive home, in spite of all precautions taken, in a rather battered state. Barrington should have been discouraged. He was not. He shifted his point of attack. He went over, and got the Royal Society to go over, to the North-west Passage.

Interest was not limited, however, to the North-west Passage and the Pole. There was also the North-east Passage to Asia, sought by the English and the Dutch in the sixteenth century, abandoned by them after the discovery of Spitsbergen, Novaya Zemlya and the Kara Sea, and the foundation of a profitable trade with Russia. Since then Russia had been expanding its power to the east, through Siberia; Russian statesmanship and the Imperial Academy of Sciences at St Petersburg began now to assume a large importance for geographers. Business men also in England, some with Russian connections, were not immune to excitement; Engel was not unknown among them and more than one of them gave advice to ministers on a north-east, or a north-west, passage, or a single expedition to search for both. The plan which Barrington matured, however, and put to the Council of the Royal Society in February 1774, was most convincing. This plan, with a consequential letter to the Admiralty, was approved by (among others) Banks, Solander, Henry Cavendish, Maskelyne, and Samuel Wegg, both a member of the Council and deputy-governor of the Hudson's Bay Company— who at some time had passed on to the Council his information about Hearne's journey. The letter was put solely in terms of science. It had one original point, in its suggestion of a western approach to the problem, rather than a preliminary passage round South America. An expedition fitted out in either Europe or the East Indies might be victualled finally at Canton in China: 'whence the run to the Northern parts of New Albion will not be, probably, longer than from England to Jamaica', and the American coastline could thus be investigated with a minimum of delay. If no passage should be found, then (the Russian advance has plainly become influential) 'the coast of the North Eastern parts of Asia, Kamshatska & Korea may be explored; with regard to which we are so imperfectly informed at present'; and the vessels might afterwards return in proper time to Canton.[1] The Admiralty response was the necessary first official one: that as no provision had been made for so expensive an undertaking, their Lordships did not think themselves at liberty to engage in it.[2] Real negotiations then started. Sir John Pringle was

[1] Royal Society Council Minutes, VI, 216–17, 17 February 1774; printed *Journals* III, 1483–4.
[2] R.S. Council Minutes, VI, 220–1, 7 March 1774; printed ibid., 1484.

to see the Speaker. Sandwich thought this meeting had better be deferred until he himself had talked with Barrington. Sandwich's inclination was clear: there would have to be, however, an additional vote for naval expenses if anything were to be done in 1774, and 'the leading friends of Administration in the House of Commons' would have to be sounded out. The leading friends did not agree: nevertheless there was triumph, and by the end of March Barrington could inform the Council that although 1774 was impossible, the voyage 'will be undertaken after the return of Capt Cook in 1775; when a similar expedition will be fitted out, which will in general follow the outline proposed by the Council of the Royal Society to the Board of Admiralty'.[1] Barrington did not leave the matter there: he could neither organise nor hasten the expedition, but he must have felt he could organise parliament, and certainly he had much to do with the bill introduced in the early part of 1775 to extend the terms of the 1745 act, which offered the great reward. The Royal Society's proposals were all science—'for the promotion of Science in general, and more particularly that of Geography'; the 1745 act was all trade—'of great benefit and advantage to the trade of this Kingdom'; it was now, in 1775, possible to bring science before a British parliament, and the bill was aimed at the 'many advantages both to commerce and science' that were promised by the discovery. The projected expedition was a naval one, and the inducement of the reward was no longer confined, as it had been, to private vessels. The 1745 act had specified that the passage should lie between the Pacific and Hudson Bay; in 1775 it must be north of latitude 52°, and Hudson Bay was unmentioned. Barrington had not forgotten the North Pole: he managed to get into the bill the promise of £5000 to the crew of the first ship to approach within a degree of it, since 'such approaches may greatly tend to the discovery of a communication between the Atlantic and Pacific oceans'. The bill passed finally in December 1775. By that time more practical preparations for the voyage were in train, and Admiralty thoughts were ranging more widely. The Royal Society influence diminishes; or, if that is unjust to the Royal Society, the persuasiveness of the Canton-based plan diminishes.

It diminished because of a new Russian geographical theory that became public in 1774, just as its force had rested on earlier Russian work. One must turn to Russia in the north Pacific, just because what her explorers did, or the scientific foreigners who manned her

[1] Sandwich to Barrington, 12 March 1774, Sandwich Papers; Barrington to Horsley, 30 March 1774, R.S. Council Minutes, VI, 232; printed ibid., 1484.

Academy did, was of fundamental importance for what Cook might do when he should find himself in that part of the world. The Strait of Anian is before us again, not as a passage through North America, but as a possible or probable division between North America and Asia; and quite apart from any north-west passage, the nature of the North American coast is before us. One may begin with the eastward Russian advance in the seventeenth century across Siberia. There were forays to its Arctic coast, some coastwise journeys on the ice; some, in favourable months, by sea; certainly no continuous accomplishment of a north-east passage. In 1648 Simeyon Ivanovich Dezhnev rounded the cape called after him, the north-east extreme of Asia, and arrived at the mouth of the Anadyr river, which flows through Kamchatka into the Bering Sea: passed through Bering Strait, that is, and answered one of the great geographical questions. Asia and America were not joined. But his answer was lost sight of. In 1724 Peter the Great formed a plan to deal with the same question, and in 1728 Vitus Bering, a Dane in the Russian service, sailed from the Kamchatka river and pushed north on the enquiry. Bering did in fact pass through the strait named after him and reached latitude 67°18′ north, but neither sailing north nor sailing south on his return did he see the fog-lost American shore. He might all the while have been in an enormous bay that swung round far in the north between Asia and America. He was convinced, however, that he had proved their separation. His lieutenant, Alexei Chirikov, did not think he had done so; nor did the Admiralty in St Petersburg.

He survived criticism, and took part in the planning, under the empresses Anne and Elizabeth, of a great campaign of geographic, scientific, and economic exploration of Siberia. The plans, indeed, stretched beyond Siberia, to include the Kurile islands and the northern islands of Japan, and the coast of America. Neither the islands nor the continent could be far from Kamchatka: both might provide profitable trade. Bering and Chirikov were to manage the American voyage. There were extraordinary delays. It was not until June 1741 that Bering, an ageing, badgered, and depressed man, and Chirikov, could sail from Petropavlovsk, with two ships, the *St Peter* and *St Paul*, late in the season and short of stores. They parted company after a fortnight, in bad weather, and did not meet again. On 16 July Bering sighted land between 58° and 59° north, a chain of snow-covered mountains, the highest of which he was to call after St Elias. He beat some distance up the coast north-west, anchoring once, but landing nowhere on the mainland, and on 21 July, disturbed over the chances of reaching home safely, left it. Contrary winds, storms, fogs, scurvy off the Aleutian islands, which he sighted from time to time, made frightful the passage; his ship was wrecked a hundred miles short of Kamchatka on one of the Komandorski islands, where Bering himself died; the survivors wintered there and reached Petropavlovsk the following summer in a small vessel put together from the *St Peter*'s timbers. Chirikov also met misfortune. He sighted America the day before Bering, about three degrees south of Bering's landfall. He anchored in a bay where he lost his boats and their crews in some unaccountable manner; unable to land and in want of water there was nothing he could do but return. He did not have so bad a passage as Bering's, though bad enough, and reached home a month before Bering was wrecked. Thus ended that effort. Curiously enough, nine years earlier, and four years after Bering's northern expedition, another Russian had sighted America, without knowing what he had done. This was the surveyor Gvozdev, who, incited by northern Kamchatkan reports of islands close to Bering Strait, and in particular of one they called 'the large country' (the Russian *bolshaya zemlya*), set off to investigate. He landed on one of the Diomede islands, in the middle of the strait, and gazing east-wards, quite surely saw *bolshaya zemlya*. His sailors refused to go fur-ther; he also, like Bering and Chirikov, never set foot on the continent.

How did all this story become public, and how does it fit into our principal story? Cook, or anyone else interested, could pick up an account of Bering's first voyage in Campbell's edition of Harris. For his second voyage and what he had to say of the American coast, there was no published journal and no adequate history. The best account was in the third volume of the Russian *History* of Gerhard Friedrich Müller, official historiographer of the Empire, a volume which appeared in 1758. Part of it was translated into English under the title of *Voyages from Asia to America* and published in 1761.[1] It gave to the world what could be said of Bering's first voyage of 1728 of Gvozdev, and of the American voyage of 1741–2. It also provided a map of great importance, which duly appeared in English guise. This map showed a firm coastline of northern Asia, fronting on the 'Icy Sea', from the Gulf of Ob and Novaya Zemlya right round to Kamchatka and the Kuriles, except for a conjectural magnified north-east point. It marked the ancient sea-route along this coast to the Sea of Anadyr, and referred to the Dezhnev voyage of 1648. Gvozdev's discovery was given a hard outline; so were the islands

---

[1] There were earlier maps that took in the Bering voyages—Le Rouge 1746, Delisle–Buache 1750/52, John Green 1753—but none of these has the relevance to Cook's voyage that Müller has. They are discussed in Lawrence C. Wroth, *Early Cartography of the Pacific* (New York, 1944), 136–40, and Glyndwr Williams, 142–53.

sighted by Bering, and the bits of Alaskan 'mainland' supposed to be sighted by him, with some of the names he gave, and one or two conferred, perhaps, by Müller. This was done also for the American sightings of Bering and Chirikov. South of Chirikov's discovery the coast was mere dots (including the de Fonte area), until it became a hard line again with the entrance to de Fuca's strait, and so past that of Martin de Aguilar, New Albion, and San Francisco Bay to what was then called California. The map had no truck with north-west passages: the nearest it came to a waterway across North America was a River of the West between Lake Winnipeg and (conjecturally) Martin de Aguilar's opening. This was a French, not the English conception. Courses were marked for Bering and Chirikov. But perhaps the most interesting thing, as we look back on it, was the suggested outline for the American coast opposite Kam-chatka and that part of Asia to its north. This took the form of a great blunt-ended peninsula, a continuous projection to the west of North America, its northern side running roughly parallel with the Asian coast, its southern side fringed with Bering's islands. Far to the north, after a large break, was conjectured another piece of coastline roughly parallel with Baffin Bay. If all this was soundly based— and Müller, reasonably hesitant, wrote, 'My work herein has been no more than to connect together, according to probability, by points, the coasts that had been seen in various places'—then it would seem fairly sensible, geographically speaking, to use the port of Canton for the start of a voyage into these northern waters, a voyage through Bering Strait to the sea that Hearne had found: to approach, that is, from the south-west. The map, then, was a by no means rash collation of the known and the unknown, and was for almost twenty years taken as standard, a document on which Barrington quite naturally assumed he could base his proposals.

On this assumption fell very heavily in 1774 a new book—a very small book—and a new map. Bering's men had brought back reports not merely of islands but of sea-otters, seals and foxes. A trading company, organised under imperial patronage, began a murderous onslaught upon the inhabitants of the Aleutian islands, both human and animal, which was to carry the Russians along the whole length of the islands to the Alaskan peninsula and at length to the main American continent, setting up storehouses and armed posts as they went. Traders and hunters were perforce discoverers. It is sometimes difficult, amid a confusion of names, to tell what they discovered, and there were naval officers who were abler explorers. The one of these, perhaps not the most meritorious, who nevertheless got the most attention, was Lieutenant Sindt. He did in 1767 touch on the continent, somewhere between latitudes 64° and 66°, though he made no survey; and he seems to have visited or seen a number of islands. He was enshrined in *An Account of the New Northern Archipelago, Lately Discovered by the Russians in the Seas of Kamtschatka and Anadir*, by a rather extravagant author, Jacob von Stählin, who was secretary of the Academy of Sciences. Published in its original German at Stuttgart, in 1774, it was brought before the Royal Society in June by Dr Maty, the secretary, and a translation into English at once put in hand, so that it was out in London before the end of the year. Obviously it caused some excitement among the geographically learned, and obviously it affected the Admiralty. The critical thing was the map, so very different from Müller's: what Stählin called 'the very accurate little Map of the new discovered Northern Archipelago here annexed, which is drawn up from the original accounts'. To name every one of the islands composing this new archipelago, said the author, was needless, as they were set down in the map with their situation and size; though he adds—with a moderate access of caution—'As to the absolute accuracy of the two first articles, namely, the true situation, as to geographical latitude and longitude, and their exact dimensions, I would not be answerable for them, till they can be ascertained by astronomical observations'.[1]

Stählin's 'very accurate little Map' looks as if some large fist has come down on the fragile surface of Müller's north-west American peninsula, shattered it into displaced fragments and sent some of it into thin air. The largest of the fragments is an island called Alaschka between what we may for convenience call East Cape or Cape Dezhnev and a bulge on the American shore—an island twice as far from America as it is from Asia. The bulge is labelled North America Great Continent, and 'Stachtan Nitada', which last form of words seems to be quite meaningless. Due south of Alaschka are a few small islands and a larger one, of uncompleted outline, called Unalaschka. From there a semi-circular fringe, a good deal of it named Aleutskia Isles, runs round towards Asia, straddling the 60th parallel and screening off the Sea of Anadir from the vast ocean. There is some truth of conception here, no sense of direction: a chain of Aleutskian or Aleutian islands, one of the larger of which is Unalaska, does actually extend from an Alaskan peninsula—though it was wise of Stählin, in this unwise piece of cartography, not to make himself answerable for the 'absolute accuracy' of his rendering. His unjustifiable rashness lay in the large passage he left between his Alaschka

[1] Stählin, *Account*, 15-17.

and his North America or 'Stachtan Nitada', because no one had looked there yet, and to argue that because some islands existed everything must be islands was not merely unwisdom but absurdity. Daines Barrington, sceptical for once, refused to give credit to the map at all; William Coxe, the first English historian of the Russian voyages, was after a critical examination equally condemnatory.[1] Coxe's book was not published till 1780, no help to voyagers who sailed in 1776; and there Stählin's Northern Archipelago was, with all the signs of confidence; and who could be blamed for hitting instantaneously on the admirable way, open, spacious and direct, thus presented of following the American coast from New Albion into the sea, not entirely frozen, on the shore of which Samuel Hearne had stood? Certainly that would be preferable to an approach from Canton.

Whatever might be thought of Canton, we can now see emerging the grand strategy of an actual voyage. Hearne, the Barrington–Engel ice theory, the Stählin island theory, are all there. During 1775 we must regard the mixture as settling down in the Admiralty mind: presumably in the Royal Society mind also. Some time or other Cook was brought into the discussion. To bring Cook in was to listen to Cook's ideas on strategy; and though Cook might know nothing about the Arctic, he knew a good deal about the Pacific, and had his own experience of bases. After his second voyage, he thought he knew the Pacific winds. The most advantageous, and therefore the most natural, way for him to get into the ocean and to the eastern side of it would be not by Magellan's strait or the Horn, like Byron or himself on his first voyage, but by the Cape of Good Hope. There he knew the possibilities of refreshment and had friends in the business; if nothing went wrong with his timing he would be able to look round a little on his eastward passage, south-east of the Cape, and verify the discoveries the French had made in that part, which the obliging Crozet had told him about in March 1775. Once within the Pacific his base would undoubtedly be the familiar Tahiti—though perhaps the Friendly Islands would be useful also—and Tahiti would not be too far south for recruitment during the arctic winter. This would fit in with the necessity of seeing Omai home. The passage from Tahiti to the north-west American coast could present no difficulty. We can descry at the back of Cook's mind one or two other thoughts: he could, on the long stretch from

[1] Barrington, *Summary Observations and Facts . . . to show the Practicability and good Prospect of Success in Enterprises to discover a Northern Passage* (London, 1776), 24; Coxe, *An Account of the Russian Discoveries between Asia and America* (London, 1780), 283–4, 300–2.

the Cape to Tahiti, look at Van Diemen's Land, omitted by him on two previous voyages, and if he called in at Queen Charlotte Sound he could certainly refill his water and collect greens; he might even pick up a more circumstantial knowledge about Furneaux's disaster in 1773.

At some moment, then, probably in the six months between 10 February 1776, when Cook formally volunteered for the service, and 6 July, when his instructions were signed, all these thoughts, from Royal Society to Cook, became co-ordinated, and the plan was given its final shape.[1] There would be two ships. Cook should go as directly as possible to the Cape, there to refresh and take in supplies. Leaving at the end of October or beginning of November (which might be deemed early summer) he should go south to latitude 48°, search for the islands of Marion du Fresne and Kerguelen, and if possible find a good harbour there, which 'may hereafter prove very useful, altho it should afford little or nothing more than shelter, wood & water'. Thence he was to proceed to Tahiti or the Society Islands, calling at New Zealand if he thought fit. Omai was to be landed. The islands should be left at the beginning of February 1777, or sooner if Cook judged it necessary. (Not much time is being left for contrary chances, but Cook must have approved the timing.) Then without delay, or looking deliberately for new lands, to New Albion, reaching its coast at about latitude 45° N: having thus a spring and summer for the real work of the voyage. He should coast northward to 'the Latitude of 65°, or farther, if you are not obstructed by Lands or Ice; taking care not to lose any time in exploring Rivers or Inlets, or upon any other account, until you get into the before-mentioned Latitude of 65°, where we could wish you to arrive in the Month of June', of 1777. Why 45°? Why 65°?—we may interpolate. Because, in the first place, the necessity of refreshing again, on the American coast, was foreseen; and secondly—one is justified in thinking—though there was no faith at all in Juan de Fuca in latitude 47°–48°, or de Fonte in latitude 53°, it would be useful to ascertain the lie of the coast north of 45°, and put into it, in proper relation, the discoveries of Bering and Chirikov. It was at about 65° that the Russian Great Continent or Stachtan Nitada bulged west; here it was that Gvozdev and Sindt had landed; it was about here, or farther north, that a passage leading to Hearne's sea must open, if one existed at all. It was here that Cook was 'very carefully to search for, and to explore, such Rivers or Inlets as may appear to be of a considerable extent, and pointing towards Hudsons or Baffins

---

[1] The Instructions, printed *Journals* III, ccxx–ccxxiv.

Bay': even now we cannot quite get rid of Hudson Bay. The injunction seems firm and exclusive enough; however, we have the usual elasticity—'nevertheless if you shall find it more eligible to pursue any other measures, than those above pointed out, in order to make a discovery of the beforementioned Passage (if any such there be) you are at liberty, and we leave it to your discretion, to pursue such measures accordingly.' If the passage should be found, sail through it; if not, winter at Petropavlovsk in Kamchatka, or somewhere better, and try again in the spring of 1778 for either a north-west, or a north-east, passage—because the latter, round Asia, between the Pacific and the North Sea, might after all be the answer. The general tenor of these instructions is, geographically, cautious: it is possible that Daines Barrington would have given a more confident ring to them; but they did give scope for triumph. If triumph was impossible, then Cook was to return to England by such route as he might think best 'for the improvement of Geography and Navigation'.

We do not know when the Admiralty was visited by a further thought on the improvement of geography and navigation; for its grand strategy was suddenly made even grander by an Atlantic addendum. Why not, some person seems to have asked, look for the passage at both ends?—and in this query Hudson Bay was excluded. Baffin Bay, however, had not been tried since Baffin himself came back defeated in 1616, 'having coasted all, or neere all the circumference thereof', and found it 'to be no other then a great bay'— not been tried, that is, in the sense of closely examined for a passage leading out of it. The whalers who realised the profit that Baffin had foreseen in their trade knew something about the more southern part. The time seemed ripe for re-examination. This should occupy two seasons. In 1776 a naval vessel would be going out to the Bay for the protection of British whalers against American ships of war: the American revolt had begun in 1775, one must remember, and if Barrington had not made his plea as early as he did, it is at least doubtful whether there would have been a third Cook voyage, or supplementary voyages, at all. When the safety of the whalers had been guaranteed, this vessel should make a preliminary examination of the coasts of the Bay, returning with nautical information, surveys and charts; on the basis of which another voyage should be made in the following year, specifically to explore its western shores. In the summer of 1777 Cook was expected to be at the other end of the passage—assuming there was one. Who could know what would happen after that? The documents expressed no wild hope; but was it impossible that the two explorers might meet in the middle? Thus, two hundred years after Sir Humphrey Gilbert and Sir Richard Grenville, the plan and its addendum stood complete.

Should one, after this discussion, enquire why Cook volunteered for the voyage? The enquiry may be needless. It may be enough to say that he preferred activity to quiescence, and that the activity of the mind was not enough for him. For a sailor in his forty-seventh year, with his mind at full stretch, the land was too stable. But could his mind be at full stretch, if his ship—and he in it—was not off some questionable coast? For him that was the fair prospect. There is more than one significant remark in the letter he wrote to Walker announcing his decision. There is the remark, 'If I am fortunate enough to get safe home, theres no doubt but it will be greatly to my advantage.' What promise had he? True enough, if he got home with a discovered North-west Passage, the commander's share of £20,000 would be advantageous. But if he merely got home from another difficult and arduous voyage, laden with charts, what then? The fourth captaincy in Greenwich Hospital would be no great reward. Some other 'mark of the Royal Favour'? Flag-rank? But a rear-admiral in Greenwich Hospital would be no more active than a post-captain. A red ribbon and star? We do not know what he thought of such things. Was there a revival, a transference, of his old ambition, to go 'as far as I think it possible for man to go'—a transference from the south to the north? But that might have nothing to do with the North-west Passage, if he found it. Possibly, to an extent unrealised by himself, he had given his heart away to the Pacific; or, if that is too fancifully romantic, possibly he merely saw, in professional terms, a highly complex problem, and could not resist it. In all his eagerness for activity, his lifting of spirit at the fair prospect, he does not appear to have guessed that, possibly, he was a tired man.

He expected to be ready to sail about the latter end of April, he had told Walker. He should have known better, even though men were joining and stores loading in February. There was time for a good many desertions from both ships, and men were still being taken in through June, some even later. Supply was no short process: butter and pickle, inspissated juice of malt, dried yeast, pressed hops, experimentally packed bread and meal, were still being supplied as June wore on, let alone a 'Draughtsman and Landskip Painter'. Cook, as we have seen, was busy over his book, and thrust into the running fight with Forster; at the end of May there was the business about his portrait. As with the previous voyage, the captain had his way with supply, and was willing to give oddments a trial: there were articles we have not met before, a sort of life-saving device for a man overboard, constructed of a wooden pole with a bell on the end and cork supports. It does not seem to have been highly practical. Each ship was also given 'an Apparatus for recovering Drowned persons', of undefined nature. With all this preparation and its supervision no fault could be found. There was, however, desperate fault in other preparation, and this concerned the *Resolution* herself.

No vessel, certainly, could have been more perfectly shaped to Cook's purpose than the *Resolution* on his second voyage. No vessel could have withstood harder usage from the elements for a longer time. Whitby never made a sounder ship, and at the end of that voyage she was still sound. She was of course in need of overhaul and refitting; but if there was to be another exploring voyage it is difficult to think of a sailor who would not automatically have taken her to make it in. The Admiralty had no doubt; Cook had no doubt. She was in the naval yard at Deptford in mid-September 1775; she was ready to receive men, the Navy Board reported, on 4 January 1776; she did not come out of dock till 10 March. In six months she should have been the subject of a thorough and honest job. That she was not is apparent from her history over the next—one does not need to say four years, because those four years would try any ship —few weeks, even, as soon as she put to sea. One may argue that Cook himself was at fault in not keeping a close eye on the work. Ordinarily that would be so. But during the three and a half months of the fundamental work Cook had no connection with the ship at all. Before the second voyage he did, it seems, have his eye on every detail. This time not only did he come late on to the administrative scene, but he still had a great deal to do on matters quite unconnected with getting the expedition away. One need not go into the subject of administrative corruption in the navy yards, or their state in general at the outset of the American war, after twelve years of peace. Palliser, when in due course he came on Cook's opinion of navy cordage, was scandalised at what he regarded as an unjustified attack; but Palliser, head of the Navy Board, which gave orders to Deptford Yard, was, one thinks, fobbing off a responsibility that was ultimately his. He did not need to read far in this journal of Cook's to suspect that the Yard had done a poor job. One may still feel some indignation that a fine ship, faithfully and, in terms of craftsmanship, nobly built in her home yard, strong enough to resist the battering of so many antarctic seas and sub-tropical storms, should on a new voyage begin to leak like a sieve when she was hardly out of the Channel, simply because her caulking had been scamped. One must not go too far: the *Resolution* was still good enough, with constant and tedious labour upon her, to see out a voyage of four years, which were to include some extremely arduous months; and as she had had no structural alteration, to outward appearance she was the ship that had sailed from England in 1772.

Her new consort, the *Discovery*, was the smallest of all Cook's vessels. She was built by the firm of G. and N. Langborn for Mr William Herbert, from whom she was bought: another collier, 'single bottom, full-built, is very roomly, and . . . appears a fit ship for the service'.[1] This was indeed so. She was converted from a brig to a 'ship'—that is, given three masts instead of two, though both she and the *Resolution* were classed in formal documents as sloops. She was 'sheathed and filled', in the regular manner, for protection against the teredo. Neither ship received extra protection against ice: the *Resolution* had not had it in the south, and if Barrington and Engel were right, there would be no great danger thence in the north. We have to reconcile this with the preparations for Phipps's voyage in 1773. His *Racehorse* and *Carcass* were 'bombs', heavily-built ships originally, and they were specially and very considerably strengthened, with double bottoms and reinforced bows. No whaler would have sailed for Baffin Bay in a ship like Cook's. On the other hand, whalers' voyages were then relatively short, and it is difficult to think that the Admiralty really envisaged a long voyage for Phipps. Extra weight would have much slowed down the *Resolution* and *Discovery*, not built for speed to begin with, and they had an enormous distance to cover. Their chief defence must be seamanship, as it had been the chief defence in the Antarctic. We know of no discussion on the point: if there was any, that reasoning may have been advanced. There may have been some blind fancy that ice on the western side of North America would be less dangerous than ice on the eastern side. As there was no knowledge, there may have been no thought.

The *Discovery* received a proper armament—eight four-pounders, eight swivel guns and eight musquetoons, against the twelve of each carried by the *Resolution*. In spite of the fact that on the previous

[1] Deptford Yard Officers to Navy Board, 5 January 1776; P.R.O. Adm 106/3318. She was of 298 $\frac{58}{94}$ tons burthen, with other dimensions, lower deck length 91′ 5″, extreme breadth 27′ 5″, depth in hold 11′ 5″, height between decks 5′ 7″–6′ 1″. The value of her hull was £1865, and necessary alterations were estimated to cost £550.

voyage the two small vessels 'in frame' had never been used, they were again supplied; it was thought that one of them might negotiate the passage, if it were found, and should prove impossible for the *Resolution* or *Discovery*. They might no doubt have been useful in case of wreck, presuming their survival; but for boat work in general the ships were well enough equipped. The *Discovery* was perhaps a little over-masted—though that criticism was by no means a general one. In sailing qualities the two ships were pretty well matched. Almost a year later, heading north from the Society Islands, the *Discovery*, for whatever reason, proved faster than the *Resolution*; she could also claw off a lee shore better, Cook was to say. We hear no murmurs from either ship over the behaviour of the other. They were, it is plain, excellent company-keepers.

The captain, the plan, the ships—and the men. The *Resolution*'s complement was, as before, 112; the *Discovery*'s 70. The two lieutenants of the last voyage had both been promoted commander. Cooper may have thought he had done his stint at exploration, and disappears from our story, though his fortunes did not suffer. Clerke was not to take Omai home in the *Resolution*; he was to command the *Discovery* instead, and it must have given him peculiar pleasure to sail as Cook's second, the one officer who was on all the three voyages. He was still only 33; but his natural high spirits, his capacity for general amusement, his leaning towards the facetious, had undergone some modification. On the first voyage he had improved his technical equipment; on the second shown himself a perceptive observer, with a marked gift for brief description; on the third he is a hard-working and devoted officer, a serious man, whatever the habitual humour of his phrase, with a sense of duty as deep as Cook's own; in administration Cook's disciple; with all Cook's knowledge of the sailor's mind; without any of Cook's ability—and certainly no training—as a surveyor. We have no chart from his hand, no coastal profile; but he was an excellent seaman. 'Social' —to use his own favourite word—convivial and genial he was always; generous but not weak in judgment or in act, the warmth of his feelings is illustrated by his letters to Banks, their depth by the last letter of all. Was he too generous in guaranteeing the debts of his brother Sir John Clerke? He had small resources of his own, and his action brought disaster on him. The affair is obscure in its details: he must have made himself security for these debts some time after his return from the second voyage, and then Sir John, a captain in the royal navy, sailed off to the East Indies. It may have been the announcement that Charles Clerke was himself to sail off in a different direction that brought the 'Israelites' down on him. Certainly he was committed for debt to the King's Bench prison, and lived for a time, anyhow, within the Rules of the Bench, thus far confined from activity in his profession; and if he could not get release he could not go the voyage. The efforts of his friends, however influential, were of little avail. Somehow he extricated himself, not without a grim gift from that unpleasant region, the seeds of tuberculosis, and not in time to sail with Cook. He was to catch up. Of a totally different order of mind from Cook, it is yet difficult to think of a man who complemented Cook better, or could more fitly stand behind him in command.[1]

From Clerke we pass to his old shipmate Gore, thrice also a circumnavigator, senior in years (the oldest officer on the voyage, indeed, next to Cook), in earlier time senior in rank, outdistanced in promotion—perhaps because of that absence from service on Banks's venture to Iceland, followed by half-pay—now first lieutenant in the *Resolution*. One would like to know what else had happened to Gore between voyages. Was it then that he met his 'Favourite Female Acquaintance' called Nancy, whoever she was? The phrase does not argue a wife, to be celebrated by the naming of a geographical feature; and who was the 'Young one' to whom Banks 'was so kind as to promise an attention' in case of Gore's death?[2] The different Gores are not easy to reconcile, one finds as one works through the voyage: the rather old-fashioned sound practical sailor, uninterested in technical advance, the rash speculator in imaginary shores and passages, the unromantic awkward journal-keeper who will suddenly for a few days, once only, burst into an almost Elizabethan romance of name-bestowing; the commander, in the end, a little uncertain of himself yet stubborn. One would never expect from him individual brilliance: within his limits, he was probably one of Cook's most useful men.

Certainly a highly useful man, in every other way a contrast, was James King the second lieutenant. Among the seamen, he was the intellectual of the voyage. In 1776 in his mid-twenties, the son of a Lancashire village parson, he had both naval and political connections. He had brothers intimate with the Burkes—Walker King was Edmund Burke's close associate in journalism and later Bishop

27. Captain Charles Clerke, by Nathaniel Dance, 1776

[1] For Samwell's criticism of Clerke, see *Journals* III, 1271–2; and for discussion of these criticisms, ibid., lxxiv–lxxv.
[2] Gore to Banks, 12 July 1776; ATL, *Miscellaneous material relating to Cook's Voyages*; printed *Journals* III, 1512. The reference to his 'Favourite Female Acquaintance' is in his log, ibid., 363 n.

of Rochester; he was himself well enough known to Burke to write to him from the Cape on the outward passage.[1] This was a circle that few young sailors moved in. Entering the navy in 1762, at the age of 12, and serving on the Newfoundland station under Palliser and in the Mediterranean, he was a lieutenant at 21; and then—an odd thing for a naval lieutenant—in 1774 went to Paris to study science, and from Paris to Oxford for a period with his brother Walker. At Oxford he met Hornsby the astronomer; on Hornsby's recommendation he was selected for the voyage. With enough sea service and his special training he was for Cook's purpose exceptionally well-equipped: he shared in the responsibility for the chronometer, and his presence, in association with Cook, obviated the need for a professional astronomer. In other ways than astronomy he was a helpful man: he had read all the books; he could think for himself; he could carry through a complicated geographical argument. He was a good observer, though when on shore his technical duties kept him from wandering as widely as some of his colleagues. This was made up for not merely by his quickness and literacy in recording what he did see, but also by the sympathetic attractiveness of his character, which more than once made him an invaluable delegate for Cook—so that in Hawaii he was even to be taken for Cook's son. There must have been an almost youthful charm about King, a certain refinement of mind and of body, a humanity, a kindness, a generosity and sensitivity of spirit without touch of the effeminate, unusual among seamen—or amongst men: the combination of qualities that led the ardent young midshipman Trevenen to write of him (we must allow for the idiom of the age), 'In short, as one of the best, he is one of the politest, genteelest, & best-bred men in the world'.[2]

When John Williamson the third lieutenant came on board, however, there came what we should call a psychological problem. His shipmates had a simpler attitude, and merely disliked or detested him—or perhaps tolerated: we come on no word of love. He seems to have been an Irishman, and presumably he was much of an age with the other lieutenants, but he had none of the warm feelings of youth. He could, it is true, fly into unpleasant rage and violence. A strange mixture of self-righteousness and acerbity, intelligence and intolerance, he was the wrong sort of person to have been appointed to a voyage of discovery; he could not have been a happy man, and

[1] *Journals* III, 1516. King was the only one remarked on as having an interest in politics, on which account Samwell admired him highly.—ibid., lxxvi, n. 3.
[2] Trevenen to his Mother, 9 September 1780; C. F. Penrose, *Memoirs of James Trevenen*, MS in ATL, Appendix 123–4.

he did not contribute to the happiness of others. Another curious mixture of qualities, to be studied much more closely by historians, was William Bligh. How this person became master of the *Resolution* at the age of 21, after only six years' service, is as much a mystery as how he had acquired his high competence as a surveyor and draughtsman. He will be mentioned a good deal in Cook's journal, never with dispraise; any journal he kept himself has disappeared. He must, one can see from the records, have conducted himself expertly. He was kind to his juniors like Trevenen. One gathers, however, from his later comments on the printed account of the voyage, that there were men to whom he did not wish to be kind, and dogmatic judgments which he felt himself entitled to make; he saw fools about him too easily, and the thin-skinned vanity that was his curse through life was already with him. King, whom he should have taken as his natural ally in his technical business, he regarded as a pretentious poseur. Bligh learnt a good deal from Cook: he never learnt that you do not make friends of men by insulting them. On this voyage his propensities must have been kept in check. There were three master's mates of some experience, all older than Bligh—Henry Roberts, who had already earned Cook's high opinion in the *Resolution*, a man with a charming talent for illustrating a journal with wash-drawings; William Harvey, the midshipman of both the *Resolution* and the *Endeavour*; and William Lanyon, who had been midshipman and master's mate in the *Adventure*.

Clerke's first lieutenant was James Burney. The Burney family was pleased and excited. Dr Burney had spoken to Lord Sandwich; but the young man's experience and merit were both now great, he was no mere favourite. After the *Adventure*'s return he had gone to the American station in the frigate *Cerberus*; and it was while he was there, in April 1775, that Fanny had written in a letter, 'There is much talk of an intended South Sea expedition: now you must [know] that there is nothing that Jem so earnestly desires as to be of the party; and my father has made great interest at the Admiralty to procure him that pleasure; and as it is not to be undertaken till Capt. Cooke's return, it is just possible that Jem may be returned in time from America. This intended expedition is to be *the last.* . . .'[1] Jem was ordered back in plenty of time, and then the question was, 'How will Jem like Clerke instead of his favourite Capt. Cook?'[2] Then, of course, there was the question, unasked by the Burneys, how would Clerke like Jem? They were to make a satisfactory partnership, and Burney's perceptive observation was to be useful.

[1] *Early Diary* (London, 1913), II, 38.   [2] ibid., I, 321.

Of the second lieutenant, John Rickman, we know nothing, except that he was to be involved without premeditation in later tragedy, and to publish an anonymous, and poor, account of the voyage. The master, Thomas Edgar, is a clearer figure, a busy journal-keeper and describer of harbours, careful with his charts; not highly educated though with considerable unbrilliant capacity; a little sentimental; a worthy conscientious hard-working man, one would conclude. Of his two mates, the more distinguished is the American-born Nathaniel Portlock, both in his capacity to record experience and for his experience a decade later; together with the *Discovery*'s armourer, George Dixon, he was to help open up the north-west American fur trade. The other, Alexander Home, is a good honest average master's mate, with an eye to humour, who will spend forty years of retirement fruitlessly pursuing a claim to a Scottish earldom.

Among the midshipmen, or young gentlemen in training for midshipmen, were three destined to high distinction: James Trevenen in the *Resolution*, Edward Riou and Vancouver in the *Discovery*. All midshipmen worked hard in Cook's ships; all came under his wrath and, no doubt, having leapt at the chance of sailing with him, looked at their calloused hands and with Trevenen called him despot; but it was Trevenen who elevated the captain above even King, in a class of his own, and referred to 'the sublime and soaring genius of a Cook';[1] and no doubt some of them at least would have agreed with that. Trevenen, a Cornish youth from the naval Royal Academy at Portsmouth, clever, high-spirited and warm-hearted, ready and vivid with his pen, gives us a number of brief invaluable glimpses of Cook. It was an unhappy fate that convinced him, after the voyage and the American war, that the only alternative to the inactive poverty of a married half-pay lieutenant was service with the Russians, which took him to his death at Viborg. Riou also was to die in battle, one of Nelson's captains at Copenhagen, 'poor dear Riou', with the reputation of the perfect naval officer, whose loss was irreparable. Vancouver, the veteran of the second voyage, was the only one whose work as a marine surveyor was to put him in the neighbourhood of his commander; to read his great book, with its constant recurrence to Cook, with Cook as its standard of value, is to realise alike the importance of a training under Cook and the admiration he evoked. When we pass from these seamen to the only marine officer, Lieutenant Molesworth Phillips of the *Resolution*, we pass to a different order. Just come of age, of an Irish family, he

[1] Trevenen to his Mother, 7 September 1780; Penrose, *Memoirs*, App. 119-20. The midshipman did not think much of Gore by comparison.

had tried the navy, but on Banks's advice went over to the marines. Without training himself, he could hardly train others, and the marines on this voyage cut no glorious figure. He had his hour of excitement, his moments of swelling honour; but his great luck was to make a friend of James Burney, and to be enshrined in a sentence of Charles Lamb's.[1]

The surgeons and their mates numbered six—an unusual provision. Three of these are of importance in the history for talents outside their medicine. The most important was William Anderson, the young Scotsman who had been Patten's mate in the *Resolution*, now promoted to surgeon in the same ship. He was clearly one of the best minds of all the three voyages—professionally competent, but with an interest in all the departments of natural history as they were known at that time, acute as well as wide-ranging, and with a linguistic talent both eager and careful. He took scientific equipment of his own. A pleasant and generous person, he thought independently and was capable of criticising even a course pursued by Cook; as a day-to-day chronicler he seemed to have an instinct, as he had the range of knowledge, for supplementing Cook; in scientific observation Cook could draw on him unhesitatingly. Everybody thought highly of him; Cook had an affection for him. Like Clerke, he carried within him a fatal germ. By his side, but darting away continually in observations of a very different nature, is his first mate the highly Welsh David Samwell. There is no question of his professional competence or seriousness: on the other hand, where Anderson's non-professional interests are scientific, Samwell's are social and literary, and as with many another parson's son, unholy. He was irreverent. He had a consuming interest in 'the Dear Girls'. He was a bard. He did his best to get Polynesian poetry down on paper. The journal he would write would convey, as did no other word, the more frivolous side of a voyage that had its frivolities as well as its moments of tragedy. Like Trevenen his friend, his admiration for Cook stopped only this side idolatry: Samwell 'gloried in him'.[2] The third of these exceptional young men was William Ellis, surgeon's second mate in the *Discovery*, a Cambridge man with a

---

[1] ' . . . the high-minded associate of Cook, the veteran Colonel, with his lusty heart still sending cartels of defiance to old Time.'—Lamb's 'Letter to Southey'. This is a rather romantic view of Phillips. He married James Burney's sister Susan, and did not treat her well.

[2] 'His great Qualities I admired beyond any thing I can express—I gloried in him— and my Heart bleeds to this Day whenever I think of his Fate.'—Samwell to Miss Anna Seward, 26 February 1781, ATL Miscellaneous material. He was a great admirer of Miss Seward's *Elegy* on Cook, and ventured to present her with a few South Sea curios as an expression of this.

patron in Banks, an amateur draughtsman whose water colours provide a charming and delicate appendix to the heaped-up record of the professional John Webber. Youth, good spirits, admiration for their captain, we find in most of these men, 'sea-officers' and others, and general self-approval: five years later Samwell would write of the happiness of their meeting again, 'We are perhaps somewhat partial to one another, for it is an article of Faith with every one of us that there never was such a Collection of fine Lads take us for all in all, got together as there was in the Resolution & Discovery.'[1]

There were also the supernumeraries: in the *Resolution* were Omai, lamenting at departure, excited at return, and Webber. Omai had a cargo of his own—port wine and gunpowder, the things he fancied most; some muskets to put the gunpowder in with some bullets, the suit of armour, a hand-organ, some tin soldiers, a globe of the world, crockery and kitchenware and a variety of fancy goods. Cook did not think it advantageous to conjoin Omai and fire-arms, but Cook's view did not prevail. He made his own prophecy that once Omai had thoroughly seen home again, his heart would turn to England. Cook was determined that by then no ships would be there to take him.[2] John Webber, aged 24, was the son of a Swiss sculptor settled in England, and had had his art education in Berne and Paris; he showed at the Royal Academy exhibition of 1776 a portrait of his brother, which was noticed by Solander, and this led to the offer of appointment by the Admiralty. Rapid, prolific, stylish, yet capable of a most un-stylish detail in botanical portraiture, he was to make this voyage the most fully illustrated of all. He lacked Hodges's interest in light and technical capacity in oil; but his landscapes show a sense of mass, his figure drawing is much more accomplished. He was a valuable man. In the *Discovery* was Bayly of the second voyage, again working for the Board of Longitude with a long list of instructions; and there was David Nelson, with no official appointment, a gardener from Kew sent out as a botanical collector by Banks, the first of a line of collectors despatched to various parts of the world in the service of that enterprising and well-off master. Nelson, Bayly, Anderson and King, and Ellis as a bird-painter, may be regarded as the scientific staff of the expedition.

It brings up an interesting point. What interested the Admiralty was exploration and navigation. It was prepared to give hospitality

---

[1] Samwell to Matthew Gregson, 20 November 1781; Liverpool Public Library, Gregson Correspondence, XVII.
[2] *Private Papers of James Boswell*, XI, 220–1.

on the first voyage to Banks and his party, blessed by the Royal Society, but the scientific impulse was private. On the second voyage science was impelled partly by the Board of Longitude, which certainly worked in close liaison with the Admiralty, and otherwise privately again, though private pressure brought the provision of the public £4000 for Lind—and then Forster. But this was a parliamentary, not an Admiralty, grant. On the third voyage there might, it seems, have been an official scientist. We do not know all the circumstances; but certainly, Lind being still favourably thought of, Maskelyne scouted him no later than January 1775, telling him in vague terms of the proposed voyage, and that he hoped Banks would be of the party, accompanied by Lind. That gentleman replied that nothing would give him more pleasure, provided that his friend, Mr Banks, went: 'But, I assure you, I shall not go to oblige Government after the ungracious treatment I received from them' over 'the late S. Sea expedition . . .'[1] There may have been some unfruitful enquiry of Banks; and 'Government', whom Lind would not oblige, may mean 'Admiralty'. We come on no more of the subject till we encounter a story told, curiously enough, by J. R. Forster, in the preface to a German edition, of 1781, of Rickman's dubious book. When King was appointed lieutenant in the *Resolution*, relates Forster, he called on Cook to pay his respects, and expressed his regret that no scientific person was going the voyage, as before. He came away rather shocked and had to be comforted next day by Forster, who explained that Cook's character was not so bad as it appeared, but his head had been turned by Lord Sandwich. That was the reason for his remark, 'Verflucht sind alle Gelehrten und alle Gelehrsamkeit oben drein'. This leaves us rather in doubt as to Cook's exact words. 'Curse all the scientists and all science into the bargain!' would be a modern equivalent. 'Scientists' was a noun, however, still uninvented. He may have used the words 'philosophers' and 'philosophy'; for nothing is more likely than that Forster's story is in substance true.[2] King was still not quite sophisticated, and he had experienced neither Banks between voyages nor Forster during or after a voyage. Neither had he known, we gather, that his captain could explode.

Finally, after these discernible—though not quite all discernible—

---

[1] Lind to Maskelyne, 30 January 1775; Banks Correspondence, D.T.C., I, 82–3, British Museum (Natural History), Botany Library.

[2] The story comes into the preface by Forster to the German translation (Berlin, 1781) of the anonymous English account of the voyage published by Newbery in the same year, *The Journal of Captain Cook's last Voyage to the Pacific Ocean*, the absurd production of (or founded on) Lieutenant John Rickman.

characters, 'the people', sailors and marines, the almost chance assemblage of men who carried out the orders. We cannot call them anonymous because we know their names; but there is little else we know about them. Nor is the assemblage entirely chance, because there are in it men who have sailed with Cook before—who, we must assume, even if we do not know, were willing or eager to sail with him again; though few, perhaps, would have insisted on following him out of a safe retirement, like William Watman of Greenwich Hospital. A dozen of these veterans were in the *Resolution*, half a dozen in the *Discovery*; and half a dozen of the total had been on both voyages. We may sympathise with the fifty or sixty deserters, while the ships' companies were building up: men who knew Cook by tavern-talk, and did not fancy long voyages, might well desert at prospect of a three years' sentence. It was one way of assuring a steady crew. Then, having before he sailed a slight overplus, he retained them until the last possible moment, so that he could discharge the least suitable. Those who remained could reflect that, while they would undergo discomfort, as long as they were with Cook their lives would be reasonably safe. They were, the majority of them, English, with a scattering of Irish, Welsh, Scots, American, and even Germans. Like their officers, they were nearly all young. We know something of character in the mass. We can see them ignorant, illiterate, irresponsible, blockishly conservative, prone to complaint when faced by novelty; drunken when opportunity offered, lecherous; capable of tears; capable of cruelty. Occasionally a head rises above the wave of oblivion; someone falls overboard, is rescued, or is not; another is punished for 'insolence and contempt', or drunkenness, or theft, or neglect of duty, or striking a native chief, or—faint hope—attempted desertion, and that unlucky or dishonourable head sinks again. They had the wit, some of them, to study their captain: they would play up to him at some anchorage by bringing a bunch of greens on board, prominently displayed, and one thinks one sees the surreptitious smirk. Some appear in a light more positively creditable, like Benjamin Lyon, the ex-watch-maker; or Heinrich Zimmermann, the jack-of-all-trades from the Palatine who liked to wander and wrote a little book about the voyage and the great captain; and Gibson, the marine who tried to desert at Tahiti on the first voyage but remained with Cook thereafter and became a sergeant, was liked by the Polynesians and (it seems) laid claim to having saved Cook's life; and Cleveley, the carpenter, with something of a talent for drawing. And there was the other wanderer, whose life was to enter into the American legend, Corporal Ledyard, of Groton, Connecticut, who set out to walk across Siberia and the American continent, and was to die on his way to look for the sources of the Niger; a corporal of 'lofty sentiment' and literary ambitions. They endured much, these men of diverse origins and qualities, stowed so close through four years in those small ships; they did not pursue honour, but the muster-books are a sort of roll of honour; there are not many names we should wish removed from them.

One name we miss, which we should have been glad to find. It is that of Pickersgill, who had been with Cook on both his previous voyages, and before Cook with Wallis: Pickersgill the romantic and a little the sea-lawyer. Fate and the Admiralty were unkind to Pickersgill: they might have made him third lieutenant in the *Resolution* instead of the deplorable Williamson. He could then have begun another elaborate and ill-fated journal, hearkened once more, as the dusk deepened under benign island trees, to Hymeneal Songs ascending in the mild, the bland and blissful air; he could have been a valuable man. They did make him a lieutenant, and sent him in independent command to Baffin Bay.

There were formal occasions. Some time or other the Speaker of the House of Commons, Sir Fletcher Norton, entertained Cook and the officers to dinner.[1] This was very different from the departure of the *Endeavour*. Early in June the ships were ordered round to Plymouth, but there were still delays. It was while the *Resolution* was lying at Long Reach, on 8 June, that Sandwich, Palliser and some of their fellows of the Admiralty visited the ship to see that all was well. Cook was nobly hospitable—they and 'several other Noblemen and gentlemen' dining with him on Westmoreland ham and pigeon pie and strawberries;[2] and were saluted with 17 guns and three cheers when they came and went. Clerke was in the thick of his battle with the Israelites, and Burney had to take the *Discovery* to Plymouth, to the immense pride of the Burney family. The time grew near for

[1] We know about the occasion through a letter from Molesworth Phillips, 27 April 1832, a few months before he died, to a younger Dr Burney, James's nephew (Mitchell Library, Doc. 1303). After the lapse of between fifty and sixty years Phillips could not remember which inn it was (the letter is annotated, 'The Inn alluded to, was the Gun.'), and was rather vague on the date ('about July 1776'). But from 30 June to the time of their departure the ships were at Plymouth.

[2] It was a very good dinner indeed, as we know in detail from the page in the Day Book of Messrs Birch, Birch and Co, of 15 Cornhill, who supplied it. It included besides the comestibles mentioned in the text a turbout, trout, lobsters, shrimps, chickens, 'raggove mellie', stewed mushrooms, peas, beans, 'Spinage Toasts', cauliflowers, 'Petit patties', venison, a tart, sweetbreads, biscuits, currant jelly, sauces, '24 French Roles'. It cost Cook, or the *Resolution*, £12 2s.

Cook's own farewells to Mile End. The day before the letter which closed his correspondence with Douglas he wrote to his friend Commodore Wilson, at Great Ayton, in terms which reflect both of the great preoccupations of his mind, as well as a smaller matter.

Mile End, June 22nd 1776

I am at last upon the very point of setting out to join the Resolution at the Nore, and proceed on my voyage, the destination of which you have pretty well conjectured. If I am not so fortunate as to make my passage home by the North Pole, I hope at least to determine, whether it is practicable, or not. From what we yet know, the attempt must be hazardous, and must be made with great caution. I am sorry I cannot furnish you with some New Zealand Flax seed, having not one grain of it left. Indeed, I brought hardly one home with me, but left the most of what I had at the Cape, to try to cultivate it there; for of all that was brought home in my former voyage, I have not heard of a single grain vegetating. It is much to be feared, that this fine plant will never be raised in England.

The Journal of my late Voyage, will be published in the course of next winter, and I am to have the sole advantage of the sale. It will want those flourishes which Dr Hawkesworth gave the other, but it will be illustrated and ornamented with about sixty copper plates, which, I am of opinion, will exceed every thing that has been done in a work of this kind; as they are all of them from Drawings made on the spot, by a very able artist. As to the Journal, it must speak for itself. I can only say, that it is my own narrative, and as it was written during the voyage. If you or any of your friends, should want any, care shall be taken that you have of the first impressions. Mrs Cook joins her best respects to you, Mrs Wilson and family. . . .[1]

Early in the morning of 24 June he picked up Omai and left London.

[1] I have not seen the original of this letter, which I take from Young's life of Cook, 304-5.

XX

England to New Zealand Again

HE SAILED from the Nore on 25 June, and down Channel without haste to Plymouth, where he joined the *Discovery* on the 30th. At Plymouth he received his instructions and the crew received their pay—the Admiralty again departing from custom—to enable them to buy 'necessaries' for the voyage. The marines came on board. There were last English letters to write. The one to Banks, of 10 July, adverted to the book, and to a matter that was to be noticed more at length in the book, though not by Cook.

As you was so obliging as to say you would give a description of the New Zealand Spruce tree, or any other plant, the drawing of which might accompany my Journal, I desired Mr Strahan and Mr Stuart, who have the Charge of the Publication, to give you extracts out of the Manuscript of such descriptions as I had given (if any) for you to correct or describe your self, as may be most agreeable. I know not what Plates Mr Forster may have got engraved of Natural History, that will come into my Book, nor do I know of any that will be of use to it, but the Spruce Tree Tea plant and Scurvey Grass and I know not if this last is engraved. The Flax plant is engraved but whether the publishing of this in my Journ[al] will be of any use to seamen, I shall not determine. In short whatever plates of this kind falls to my share, I shall hope for your kind assistance in giving some short account of them. On my arrival here I gave Omai three guineas which sent him on shore in high spirits, indeed he could hardly be otherwise for he is very much carressed here by every person of note, and upon the whole, I think, he rejoices at the prospect of going home.

I now only wait for a Wind to put to sea unless C. Clerke makes good haste down he will have to follow me. Sr Jno Pringle writes me that the Council of the Royal Society have decreed me the Prize Medal of this year. I am obliged to you and my other good friends for this unmerited Honor.

Omai Joins his best respects to you and Dr Soiander. . . .[1]

The 'Prize Medal' was Sir Godfrey Copley's gold medal, awarded to the author of the best paper contributed to the *Transactions* of the

[1] Mitchell Library, Banks Papers; Safe 1/68; printed *Journals* III, 1511.

Royal Society by a Fellow during the year; and this was bestowed on Cook for his report on the methods used by him to preserve the health of his men during his second voyage; read at the Society on 7 March 1776. Sir John Pringle would have his say within a few months.

The others, both of 11 July, had a more domestic theme. That to Sandwich indicates some, at least, heart-searching on Cook's part before he made his great decision. 'My Lord', he writes,

I cannot leave England without taken some method to thank your Lordship for the many favors confered upon me, and in particular for the Very liberal allowance made to Mrs Cook during my absence. This, by enabling my family to live at ease and removing from them every fear of indigency, has set my heart at rest and filled it with gratitude to my Noble benefactor. If a faithfull discharge of that duty which your Lordship has intrusted to my care, be any return, it shall be my first and principal object.

I was to have spoke to your Lordship in behalf of Mrs Mahone, Widow of the late Cook of the Adventure, who is minuted down for a Nurse to Greenwich Hospital, a place she seems very suitable for, if your Lor[d]ship should have an oppertunity to appoint her it will add to the many favors already confered on / My Lord / Your Lordships Most faithfull and Most Obedient Humble Servant / Jam^s Cook[1]

Mrs Mahone, or Mahony, was duly appointed to the Hospital, though certainly not as a tribute to the late dirty and indolent Mortimer Mahony, deceased during the voyage. The third letter was to the Rev. Dr Richard Kaye, F.R.S., another Yorkshireman and chaplain to the King, whom Cook may have encountered both at the Royal Society and as a friend of Banks; and it seems from the sequel that the 'acknowledgement' mentioned in the letter may have been the use of his name on the American coast.

I cannot leave England without answering your very obliging favor of the 12th of last Month, and thanking you for the kind tender of your service to Mrs Cook in my absence. I shall most certainly make an acknowledgment in the way you wish, if it please God to spare me till I reach the place for Discoveries, for I shall be happy in having it known that you are amongst the friends of Dear Sir, Your Most Obe^d Humble Servant Jam^s Cook

P.S. I expect to sail to day July 11th 1776.[2]

It was not, however, until next day in the evening that he sailed, leaving the *Discovery* behind him. The ship was even more tightly

[1] Sandwich Papers; printed ibid., 1512.
[2] Dixson Library MSS, MS 92; printed ibid.

crammed than she had been on her departure just four years earlier. Though there were no natural historians on board, or astronomer, there were others of nature's children: in addition to the usual sheep, goats, pigs, rabbits and poultry there was a bull, with two cows and their calves, presented by the royal bounty for stocking Tahiti and its neighbours; while the Earl of Bessborough, struck with one deficiency in the charms of that island, was sending to it a peacock and his hen. Closer to the point of an exploring expedition, and less demanding on space, was the ample supply of astronomical and nautical instruments which the Board of Longitude provided for Cook and King; among them was the faithful friend, 'Mr Kendall's watch machine' of the second voyage. As the *Resolution* met the Channel waves, the captain, who had read a newspaper report of Spanish reconnoitring north of California, might have been amused had he known of the nervous alarm his departure was causing to the Court of Madrid. If the Spaniards could have read his instructions, they would perhaps not have ordered the viceroy of New Mexico, as they did, to seize and imprison him if possible when he arrived on that coast; for he himself was ordered 'not to touch upon any part of the Spanish dominions on the Western continent of America', unless unavoidably driven there, and then to stay no longer than absolutely necessary, and to be very careful not to give offence. But Spanish susceptibilities about the Pacific remained, as the British government well knew, extremely tender; and Cook had already helped to ruffle them. He might have been still more amused at the persuasion of a French agent in London that the real object of his voyage was to join the Russians of Kamchatka in subjugating Japan.[1]

All ignorant of sinister intention, while the ship began to leak and her company to curse, he made this time for Tenerife and not Madeira as his port of call on the passage to the Cape, thinking he would there get better hay and corn for the stock. That may have been so, and there was no fault to find with the water or the fresh provisions—except the lean oxen; but he was to lament the quality of the Tenerife wine, cheap as it was. Interesting here was his friendly contact with the French captain Borda, of the *Boussole*, and the Spanish Varela, both notable scientific workers as well as naval officers, who, in the process of testing the chronometers of Ferdinand Berthoud (the English were not the only inventors) were also fixing the longitude of Tenerife and making some accurate charts. After a

[1] Charles E. Chapman, *The Founding of Spanish California*, (New York, 1916), 376–80; J. E. Martin-Allanic, *Bougainville navigateur*, II, 1448–51.

stay of three days he left—it was 4 August—being within another week a little eastward of the Cape Verde islands, and on one day within great peril from a reef off Boa Vista. Evidently there was a little piece of careless navigation, on whose part does not appear; but Anderson the surgeon was outraged. One is compelled to suspect either Cook or Bligh the master. He made south till he was about five degrees short of the equator, and then out with the south-east trade wind on a huge curve towards the coast of Brazil, so that he came in to the Cape from the west. It was a common enough course at the time, and gave him an outward passage twelve days shorter than that of his previous voyage: a passage not very eventful, with a good deal of time devoted to keeping the ship dry, and to such observations of current, variation and the like as had become for Cook routine though the subject of ever-renewed thought. We may remark that in crossing the equator he was a traditionalist, when not a few men were beginning to regard old custom as dangerous horseplay 'We had the vile practice of ducking put in execution to afford some fun,' wrote Bligh, 'and to my great surprise most choosed to be ducked rather than pay a bottle of Rum. The ceremony was ended without any accident and made Sail.'[1] Cook did not think the matter worth mentioning. He sighted the Cape on 17 October and next day was anchored in Table Bay.

This was his fourth visit to Cape Town, and he was among friends and admirers, whether they were officials or the merchants who supplied his many needs. He dined in state with the governor. Samwell, who also admired, was delighted: '3 royal Salutes of 21 Guns each were given with the Toasts at Dinner. The Governor & all at the Cape pay Captⁿ Cook extraordinary Respect, he is as famous here & more noted perhaps than in England.'[2] There were people who paid less respect. The bakers were remiss; villains at night put dogs among his sheep, grazing on shore with the cattle, and stole some of the best of them, and he had to buy others. They were not the only animals his sense of duty led him to acquire. Meanwhile his company had due refreshment on shore; Anderson and Nelson the gardener were taken on a tour of the natural

---

[1] Bligh to John Bond, 23 October 1776 (Cape of Good Hope).—Nan Kivell coll., NLA; printed Royal Australian Historical Society *Journal and Proceedings*, 45 (1949), 'Some Correspondence of Captain William Bligh, R.N., with John and Francis Godolphin Bond 1776–1811' ed. George Mackaness. Cf. Anderson, 'the old ridiculous ceremony of ducking those who had not cross'd the Equator before . . . . which every sensible person who has it in his power ought to suppress instead of encouraging.'—*Journals* III, 743. Clerke in the *Discovery* provided a double allowance of grog instead, says Bayly; ibid., 15, n. 1.
[2] *Journals* III, 1515.

curiosities of the country; and one of the crew, seized for coining, was flogged and despatched to England in a homeward bound vessel, in lieu of more condign punishment by the Dutch. A furious storm blew the tents to pieces and endangered the astronomical quadrant, but the ship rode it out successfully. On 10 November Cook at last was gladdened to see the *Discovery*. Clerke had survived his battles with the Israelites and the law, perhaps freed from the Fleet by one of the acts for the enlargement of debtors, had dashed down to Plymouth, paused but a day to make adjustments to his crew consequent on sickness, dashed off letters to the Admiralty and Banks—'Cook sail'd tomorrow it will be 3 Weeks a damn'd long stretch but we must see it out—I shall get hold of him I fear not . . . Huzza my Boys heave away . . . adieu my best friend. . . .'[1]—and on the day of his writing was at sea. Though he had some episodes of bad weather, and when close to port was blown right off the coast for a week, his passage was hardly longer than Cook's; though he lost his corporal of marines overboard his men were as healthy as Cook's—for he had learnt from Cook how to keep a ship's company healthy—and his ship was a good deal drier. He gives us no meditation on compass or current; and that is one difference between the two men.[2]

By the end of November both ships were again ready for sea, caulking done, the last animals on board, the last letters written. We may think Cook extravagant, almost reckless, in his sense of duty to island posterity, when we count up the bulls, heifers, horses, mares, sheep, goats, rabbits and poultry he added to his stock; and they were certainly to give him later troubled thought. His London troubles are, we gather from an earlier letter to Strahan his publisher, melted away: 'I suppose by this time you have got my Voyage in hand, but I am so well satisfied with the hands it is in that I do not give my self a thought about it, I would however give some thing to know what Dr Forster is about.'[3] He writes a friendly note to Hodges the artist, 'for fear you should think I had quite forgot you. . . . I fancy I may now give you joy of a Boy or a Girl. I hope Mrs Hodges is well. . . .'[4] He has written to Sandwich and to Stephens, with more or less familiarity, within a few days of arriving at the Cape, and he now writes again, within a few days of leaving it— among the sheaf of letters to the Navy Board, the Sick and Hurt Board, the Victualling Board which mainly report the expenditure

[1] Clerke to Banks, 1 August 1776; Webster coll., printed ibid., 1513–14.
[2] For Cook on the Atlantic currents see ibid., 20–3.
[3] Cook to Strahan, 5 November 1776; Phillips coll., Salem, Mass., printed ibid., 1516.
[4] Cook to Hodges, 5 November 1776; Princeton University Library, printed ibid., 1517.

of money and bills drawn. To Banks write Clerke, Anderson, Gore, as well as Cook; and Cook, writing in much the same terms as he employs for his last letter to Sandwich, may be here quoted:

Your very obliging favour I received by Captain Clerke who arrived here on the 18th Inst. something more than three weeks after me and nearly the same time as I sailed from Plymouth before him, for I left that place on the 13th of July. We are now ready to proceed on our Voyage, and nothing is wanting but a few females of our own species to make the Resolution a compleate ark for I have added considerably to the Number of Animals I took onboard in England. Omai consented with raptures to give up his Cabbin to make room for four Horses—He continues to enjoy a good state of health and great flow of spirits, and has never once given me the l[e]ast reason to find fault with any part of his conduct. He desires his best respects to you, Dr Solander, Lord Seaford and to a great many more, Ladies as well as Gentlemen, whose names I cannot insert because they would fill up this sheet of paper, I can only say that he does not forget any who have shewed him the least kindness.

I am greatly obliged to you for your readiness to describe the Plants which are to be published in my Journal and I hope Mr Strahan will give you the parts in time. I have no other way of makeing a return for this and many other favours than by using my best endeavours to add to your Collection of Plants & Animals: this you may be assured of, and that the Man you have sent out with Captain Clerke to collect seeds & plants shall have every assistance in my power to give him. . . .[1]

He proceeds to describe the onslaught on his sheep by 'the honest Dutchmen of this place', and sends his best respects to Solander. To Sandwich also he speaks highly of Omai: 'the people here are surprised at his genteel behaviour and deportment'. Omai, it appears, was at his peak. A different note—deeper or merely formal?—follows: 'Permit me to assure your Lordship that my endeavours shall not be wanting to accomplish the great object of the Voyage. . . .'[2] Sandwich was to hear from him no more.

The last of these friendly letters in date is that from Gore to Banks. He too strikes a different note; in part answers the question put by Fanny Burney (the articulate James may have been too articulate), in part states some genial alarm about the ship.

. . . we shall sail hence in a Day or two with Both Ships the manner of our Acquipment you will in all probability Learn from another Quarter, this I have To say we are of Both Ships in Good health and on Board the Resolution have hitherto agreed verry Will and there is a fair Prospect of

[1] Cook to Banks, 26 November 1776; Phillips coll., Salem, Mass., printed ibid., 1521.
[2] Cook to Sandwich, 26 November 1776; Sandwich Papers, printed ibid., 1520.

its Continuing To the End of our Voyage, There has been a Misunder-standing between Charles And Burney,—Sometimes Young Officers Forget there Place, all is well now and is likely To Continue. If I return in the Resolution the next Trip I may Safely Venture in a Ship Built of Ginger Bread.[1]

Cook gave Clerke a copy of his instructions and a rendezvous at Queen Charlotte Sound, and on the last day of November they weighed anchor. In the night it fell calm, and they could not put to sea till early next morning. This was already a month behind the schedule laid down in the instructions. It was still, however, early in the southern summer. Whether they could reach Tahiti in time to leave again, refreshed, by the beginning of February, 'or sooner', if Cook should judge it necessary, may have been a question he had already dropped.

His first objective was a harking back to the conversation he had had at the Cape with the French captain Crozet on his way home in 1775, and to the chart that Crozet had given him. He wanted to verify the islands discovered by Marion du Fresne between the latitudes of 46° and 47°, and so followed a south-east course to pick up the westerlies without delay. It was but two days after finally clearing the land that he lost his mizen topmast in a squall—a loss that gave him no worry, as it was sprung already and he had another to replace it. There was, however, some cause to worry as he got into the roaring forties: the ships pitched and rolled in the cold gale and high following sea, and the miserable shivering sheep and goats began thus early to die. On 12 December he sighted and sailed between the first two of Marion's islands, small, rocky and precipitous, unnamed on his chart, and called them after the young Prince Edward. Having done this, he was prepared to let go Marion's other small group of four, twelve degrees to the east—though he named them after Marion and Crozet[2]—sailing south of them to get into the latitude of Kerguelen's discovery. The weather became colder, and the *Resolution* leaked again, in spite of the Cape caulking. Three weeks through December, when the ships were close to Kerguelen's reported position, fog came down, and they kept in touch only by the sound of their guns. 'This is a most importunate Fog', says Clerke; the confounded foggy atmosphere rendered

[1] Gore to Banks, 27 November 1776; ATL, *Miscellaneous Material relating to Cook's Voyages*, printed ibid., 1522.
[2] The island now called Marion is the more southerly of Cook's Prince Edward islands, lat. 46°53′ S, long. 37°45′ E; its companion, Prince Edward, is twelve miles to the NNE. The other, rather more scattered, group is collectively the Crozet islands, about 46°27′ S, 52° E.

exploring a miserable business.[1] The latitude they wanted was about $48\frac{1}{2}$; and Cook, having reached it, was running east. King, not yet with enough experience of his captain, was worried. If the island was small, they might miss it in the fog altogether; sailing in thick fog also was dangerous, yet to heave to would mean loss of time; 'We who are not acquainted with y^e Plan of ye Voyage, nevertheless indulge Conjectures, & conceive that ye smallest delay would hazard ye Loss of a Season, & even wish the Search for this Land which has already, & may still Longer detain us, had not been a Part of ye Plan.'[2] This passage is interesting. It shows a Cook fairly confident of his whereabouts, whatever the fog, and determined on a particular piece of verification: a Cook also who must have calculated carefully how much time he could afford to lose without losing a season. Cook himself notes the navigation as 'both tedious and dangerous'. We have known already his reputation for keeping his officers in the dark about the programme before them, and one is led to ask how far the habit was constitutional, and how far due to a literal interpretation of 'secret' instructions as secret. Yet intelligent officers, 'unacquainted with the plan of the voyage', made conjectures; and why should King worry about the loss of a season, and wish Kerguelen's land had not come into the programme, if he had no idea what the programme was? He must have had a fair idea of the topics of geographical discussion in England over the previous twelve months. He was at any rate shrewd enough to see, novice as he was, that in the trade of exploring time was not an unlimited commodity. And on the day when he wrote his words, 24 December, the land was seen where and when it was expected to be seen, to the south-south-east.

Kerguelen island, the largest of the scattered spots of land in the Southern Indian Ocean, sprawls untidily over the sea between latitudes (roughly) 48°30′ and 49°45′ S, and longitudes 68°40′ and 70°30′ E: a mass of rocky hills, bog and running water, split on its northern and eastern sides into dozens of sounds and inlets and minor bays, fringed with rocks and giant seaweed swaying deceptively round them, the whole frequently enough lost in fog; with limited vegetation, treeless, its animal life confined to sea-birds, penguins, and seals—few of the last left now, for Cook's observations announced their fate. Kerguelen's own two brief visits, in 1772 and 1773-4, can hardly be classed above sketchy and ignoble recon-

---

[1] '. . . indeed it is impossible to do anything in our way of trade till the Weather in some degree favours us.'—*Journals* III, 26, n. 4.
[2] ibid.

naissance of the western and southern sides, the foundation first of absurd reports and then of embarrassed dejection; the man, indeed, was an adventurer whom on close scrutiny it is not possible to admire. Cook, knowing little about him beyond what he had picked up from Crozet, not knowing even that Kerguelen had made two voyages (there was no published work till 1782), knowing nevertheless that he had to do merely with an island of no very great extent, was willing to take for granted the coasts already charted. He contented himself with a running, and for the time he could spare for it, fairly accurate, survey of the northern and eastern coasts that had not been seen before. One may at this point perhaps generalise a little, and say that when conditions were not too unfavourable, and a discovery seemed important, Cook would insist on getting it all down on paper—as with the New Hebrides; when conditions were most unfavourable, but a key point seemed in question, he would cling grimly to his purpose of settling it until he had succeeded—as over the position of the North Cape of New Zealand; where time was short, or adverse conditions went with unimportance (apart from a sheer geographical interest) in the discovery, he would make the most accurate observations possible, chart what he could, and then be content to leave—as with the South Sandwich islands, and now with Kerguelen.

The land first seen was an islet, Kerguelen's Isle de Croy, off the north-west point of the main island, one of a small group so lying. Cook hauled off round this group, just weathering the high rock he called Bligh's Cap (now Ilot du Rendez-vous). In the afternoon, with a clearer air, the main shore was in view, an extremely indented one; within its northern promontory lay a promising harbour, which Bligh reported on favourably; and next day the ships worked up inside almost to the sandy beach at the head. He called the place Christmas Harbour. It was Kerguelen's Baie de l'Oiseau, and retains this name; but Cook, with the sketchy chart that he had, and altogether ignorant of Kerguelen's second voyage, may be excused for making some wrong identifications, and even for being surprised at finding himself preceded here. There was plenty of water—the whole country was running with it—but not a tree or a shrub or a piece of driftwood; plenty of penguins, innumerable other sea-birds, and seals whose lack of sophistication made it easy to club them for their oil; a little grass for the cattle, few fish; so really the habour's promise was a little illusory, except for shelter. The men, however, were given a day off for a Christmas celebration, and one of them brought back a bottle he had found attached to a rock on the north side. It contained a Latin inscription on parchment recording French visits to the country in 1772 and 1773 (though the French officer who left this record did not land until January 1774). Cook had a new inscription put on the other side—*Naves Resolution & Discovery de Rege Magnæ Britanniæ Decembris 1776*—and returned it to the bottle with a silver twopenny piece, built a pile of stones on a little rise and put the bottle inside; displayed the British flag and gave the place the name he chose. Whether that signified the 'ridiculous' act of taking possession, as the philosophic Anderson feared it did, we are left to guess.

On the afternoon of that day, 28 December, he went on to the high cape that guarded the harbour in the north, to get a view of the coast. Fog hid all, except the higher land within, quite naked and desolate, and some snow-covered hills to the south. Next morning he left the harbour, and fortunately the fog cleared, the sea was still. There followed two days of such intense coastal observation that at the end of his close-packed pages one realises with difficulty that this is the harvest of two days indeed, and not a week. On the whole this observation of a tortuous shore was accurate, and the greater number of the names Cook gave have survived; and glad are we to find not merely those of royalty and naval personages, not merely the inevitable Sandwich, laid upon the ocean from one end to the other, but '*Point Pringle* after my good friend Sr John Pringle Precedent of the Royal Society'. At the end of a day of clearing forelands, islets, rocks, shoals, and even threading the channels between the great beds of kelp, with the lead going all the while, with fog threatening again, the ships put into a small harbour which gave snug enough shelter for the night—Port Palliser. Cook climbed a hill as usual for the view—daylight was long—Gore looked at the land, the masters sounded. Barrenness and desolation again, nothing for cattle, only water, seals, and sea birds for men. So to sea again, and the sight of a lower, more level, less indented piece of country, backed by rocky mountains topped by snow, until Cook had in sight what he was persuaded must be the most southerly point of the land; as night came on a south-west swell added to his conviction that there was no more in that direction, and the wind shifting to the same quarter he stood away from the coast eastwards.

Well: he must summarise his impressions, geographically. The first discoverers, 'with some reason', had imagined the country to be the projection of a southern continent; 'the English' had since proved that no such continent existed. The country, then, was an island; if any further proof of its limited extent were needed that could be found in Furneaux's track in 1773, for he had passed it only about seventeen leagues off Cook's most southerly cape and seen nothing. So in latitude it could not much exceed one degree and a quarter—a remarkably accurate estimate. As to the longitude of its western end he could not say, but it could not stretch as far as 65° E; for he had searched to that point in 1773. And a name? 'Kerguelen's Land', or Kerguelen Island, was not the name he gave: 'from its stirility' he would call it the Island of Desolation. For its natural history he would fall back on Anderson, who had made good use of his four days at Christmas Harbour, and wrote on soil and rocks, the Kerguelen cabbage that he called *Pringlea*—he too celebrating the President—the few other small plants and mosses; three different penguins, clearly described; shags, ducks, albatrosses, gulls; an uninviting fish; the fur seal.[1] What could be eaten was eaten. When the captain looked at his own stock, he could feel even less joy. The young bulls, one of the heifers, the rams, most of the goats, bought at the Cape had died. The islands, it was plain, would not be easily supplied. The animals that were left still ate. Whatever the feelings of animals, there was some relief for men in leaving 'this Cold Blustering Wet Country' (the words of Gore), and 'the Melancholy Croaking of Innumerable Penguins' (the words of Edgar), and steering a course for New Zealand.

The winds were generally favourable, though for a week or more there was thick fog, so that, as Cook said, they ran above three hundred leagues in the dark. Fog brought up the thought of possible separation—it had been not far from the Island of Desolation that he had parted from the *Adventure* in those seas—and that, with the needs of his stock, impelled him on 7 January to give Clerke an intermediate rendezvous, short of New Zealand, at Furneaux's Adventure Bay in Van Diemen's Land. Twelve days later there was a piece of serious trouble. A sudden squall at 4 o'clock in the morning carried away the *Resolution*'s fore topmast and with it the main topgallant mast. The mess of rigging saved them from going overboard, and there was a spare topmast, but the whole day was occupied in clearing the wreck and getting the mast up. The main topgallant mast could not be replaced. Perhaps the necessity of making up time had led to carrying too much sail, meditated King. The Tasmanian coast was sighted on the 24th; as Cook sailed on the westerlies turn to variable light airs and calms, and in two days more to a breeze from the south-east. Cook, examining the land with interest, was not sorry, whatever the pressure of time: it was now in

---

[1] For Cook's description see ibid., 43–7; for Anderson's, 770–5.

his power 'to carry into execution a design I had formed of putting into Adventure Bay to get a little Wood and some grass for our Cattle both of which we were in great want of'. No doubt curiosity had its part also, and the rendezvous he had given Clerke was not merely for the sake of rendezvous. Queen Charlotte Sound was not so far away. He ran with the breeze: on the afternoon of 26 January anchored in the bay and he and Clerke were immediately out in their boats looking for what they wanted. Wood and water were there in plenty; grass was scarce and not good, but necessity gave them no choice.

As smoke was seen up in the woods the shore parties next day were guarded by marines—some of whom stole the available liquor and made themselves dead drunk; there was a good haul of fish in the seine and then everyone was ordered on board to be ready to sail as soon as the wind served. It did not serve on the next day, and the day after that was a calm, so there was more wooding and foraging on shore, the carpenter was sent to cut spars, and Roberts, the master's mate, to survey the bay. In the afternoon of the first of these days the wooders and waterers were visited by a number of the aborigines, amiable uncovetous people, slender, black and naked, with agreeable features, their skin scarred, their hair and beards smeared with red ochre; they were frightened away by a couple of musket shots, not fired at them. Cook left a boar and a sow inside the woods, where he thought they had a fair chance of escaping immediate slaughter, a fate which sheep, goats, or cattle would certainly suffer in the open. When next morning the men were again at work the aborigines returned, in greater numbers, still quite peaceable, and this time brought women and children with them. Primitive they certainly were, showing no interest in fish-hooks or other iron, but not so naïve as to tolerate advances to their women from some of the gentlemen ashore. The women wore a kangaroo skin round the shoulders for carrying their children, otherwise they were as naked as the men—even more naked, for some of them had their heads shaved. These people were obviously shellfish-eaters, though they rejected all other fish; and they seemed to have no canoes or other means of adventuring upon the water. They had a few bark huts, also extremely primitive. Anderson wrote at length about them and the natural history of the country, so far as he could explore it. He did not like the mosquitoes or the ants. Some good grass had been found. Cook went on board, at the end of his three days, with a good opinion of the place. Beyond correcting Furneaux's chart a little, and recording some accurate observations, he added nothing to the

geography of Tasmania; and when he left, far from coasting northward to check Furneaux's verdict, he made a little south of east. Of
the land in general he was content to remark—'I hardly need say it
is the Southern point of New Holland, which if not a Continent is
one of the largest islands in the World.'[1] More time than these three
days might have brought more enlightenment; but Thursday, 30
January, came with a favouring breeze and he put to sea for New
Zealand. It was about this date that his instructions designed he
should be leaving the Society Islands for North America.

The light westerly breeze turned for a day to a violent southerly
storm, then moderated, went to the north-east and finally came
round to the westerly quarter again; the weather was dull, there was
nothing to see but a few petrels and albatrosses. Clerke lost another
man overboard, a marine. On 10 February New Zealand was
sighted at Rocks Point, on the west coast south of Cape Farewell;
rounding the Cape and Stephens' Island, on the morning of the 12th
Cook was in his old anchorage at Ship Cove. He wanted to refresh
his men and his stock, attend to his ships, check his chronometers;
he was also strongly interested in finding out the truth about the
Adventure's slaughtered boat's crew. As for refreshment, it was all
there, the best of water, greens, vegetables planted on the previous
voyage, grass, illimitable fish; and, for the susceptible, refreshment of
the spirit in the melodious wild music that had enraptured Joseph
Banks, and now enraptured Edgar the *Discovery*'s master, 'the Sweet
Harmony' which surpassed anything of the kind he had ever met
with. There were no scurvy cases in the ships, but Cook enforced his
usual regimen, and had hands brewing spruce beer, the substitute
for grog, almost as soon as they were on shore. In all the activity
there was, however, a difference from earlier days. When he arrived
the New Zealanders seemed apprehensive and hesitated to come on
board, even those he knew best and best knew him. On his side,
though he soon convinced them of his friendship, there was not
altogether trust. With his first shore party, clearing the ground for
observatories and tents, he sent an armed guard, and he kept it
there in charge of King until he left. All the workmen had arms
with them. No boat was ever sent any distance unarmed or without
reliable officers. Such precautions he could not believe were strictly
necessary; but after the affair at Grass Cove and the destruction of
Marion and his men at the Bay of Islands in 1772 he was determined
there should be no more massacres. Cook's friendliness soon brought

---

[1] *Journals* III, 56.

the native people in families to the cove: not a spot outside his own encampment where a temporary hut could be raised was unoccupied, and he was struck with the speed and efficiency with which such ground was adapted to domesticity by general co-operation of men and women. He studied the scene one day: 'as to the Children I kept them, as also some of the more aged sufficiently employed in scrambling for beads till I had emptied my pockets and then I left them.'[1] It was a change from cannibalism.

With the characteristics of the people here no one seems to have been as favourably impressed as was Cook—not even Anderson, who had an admirably fair as well as clear mind, and gives us the best single account of Queen Charlotte Sound we have. Cook, possibly, judges together, all the New Zealanders he has seen, and his observations were not confined to the Sound. He does not, on his second and third voyages, set out to give any large deliberate analysis of characteristics. He had done that on his first voyage—perhaps inadequately —and now, apart from one or two almost incidental observations, he is interested in individual incidents and individual persons. It was his habit to deal, so far as was possible, with individual persons, and preferably with persons of influence; so it is he who gives us names and some individual portraiture. We may be able to infer from some incidental phrase how far he agrees with the impressions of greed, suspicion and deceit conveyed by some of his officers, as when he mentions 'a Tribe or Family', whose chief was '*Tomatongeauooranue*, a man about forty five years of age, with a fine cheerful open countenance, two things more or less remarkable throughout the whole tribe.'[2] Fine cheerful open countenances do not seem to have been generally remarkable in the Sound. Gore was scandalised at the common lack of gratitude: 'Give one of them a Hatchet, afterwards Ask the same person for the Claw of a Crawfish he'll not Part with it without being Paid'.[3] It was of course unwise to give away hatchets, which were strictly articles of trade, except on some grand occasion; it was easier to give away mouldy biscuit, or bits of blubber, which were as enthusiastically received, or oil-skimmings; it could be astonishing when they came on board and ate the candles, drained the lamps of oil, even devoured the wicks. Their habitual diet contained little fat. It contained no superfluity of any sort.

Cook carried out no vengeance for the Grass Cove affray; and this was the reason for a sort of contempt which some of his officers thought they detected among the people of the place. Certainly vengeance had been expected by the New Zealanders. Cook, among

[1] ibid., 61.   [2] ibid., 65.   [3] ibid., 66, n. 1.

his own men, noticed the effect of the massacre, which must have been well talked over; and it led to a little meditation, paralleled already in his paragraphs on Van Diemen's Land, on encounters between the sexes on voyages of exploration. He had never been comfortable—no man of humanity could be comfortable—on the subject. On this voyage his discomfort, and that of his officers who had what the age called 'a feeling mind', became increasingly apparent. The matter had more than one aspect. There was first the introduction of disease, about which, it will be recollected, he had said something on his second visit to Queen Charlotte Sound, in May 1773:

I have observed that this Second Visit of ours hath not mended the morals of the Natives of either Sex, the Women of this Country I always looked upon to be more chaste than the generality of Indian Women, whatever favours a few of them might have granted to the crew of the Endeavour it was generally done in a private manner and without the men seeming to intrest themselves in it, but now we find the men are the chief promoters of this Vice, and for a spike nail or any other thing they value will oblige their Wives and Daughters to prostitute themselves whether they will or no and that not with the privicy decency seems to require, such are the concequences of a commerce with Europeans and what is still more to our Shame civilized Christians, we debauch their Morals already too prone to vice and we interduce among them wants and perhaps diseases which they never before knew. . . .[1]

Anderson now in this third voyage remarks on 'very disagreeable commands' laid on the women, in consequence of which the people suffered much 'from a loathsome disease which we have communicated without as yet giving them any real advantage as a recompence.'[2] Meanwhile Cook had modified somewhat his views on the chastity of 'Indian Women', but the general fact of the transmission of disease remained.

There was the other aspect of the matter. Men, husbands, fathers, were not always driven by greed, or women complaisant. There was the little incident of the gentlemen's advances at Adventure Bay.

This conduct to Indian Women is highly blameable, as it creates a jealousy in the men that may be attended with fatal consequences, without answering any one purpose whatever, not even that of the lover obtaining the object of his wishes. I believe it has generally been found amongst uncivilized people that where the Women are easy of access, the Men are the first who offer them to strangers, and where this is not the case they are not easily come at, neither large presents nor privacy will induce them to

[1] *Journals* II, 174–5. [2] *Journals* III, 816.

violate the laws of chastity or custom. This observation I am sure will hold good throughout all parts of the South Sea where I have been why then should men risk their own safety where nothing is to be obtained?[1]

The unusual restraint of the sailors ashore at Ship Cove may indicate that though, unlike their captain, they were not gradually working out a philosophy of the subject—and he had still more to learn—they at least had concluded that amatory adventure should be pursued with caution. Cook renews his argument when telling of visitors for trade.

Their articles of commerce were Curiosities, Fish and Women the two first always came to a good market, which the latter did not: the Seamen had taken a kind of dislike to these people and were either unwilling or affraid to associate with them; it had a good effect as I never knew a man quit his station to go to their habitations. A connection with Women I allow because I cannot prevent it, but never encourage tho many Men are of opinion it is one of the greatest securities amongst Indians, and it may hold good when you intend to settle amongst them; but with travelers and strangers, it is generally otherwise and more men are betrayed than saved by having connection with their women, and how can it be other wise sence all their View are selfish without the least mixture of regard or attachment whatever; at least my observations which have been pretty general, have not pointed out to me one instance to the contrary.[2]

It was no trouble over women, however, that caused the *Adventure* tragedy. This was one of those things, so it appeared in the end, that Cook had always gone to enormous pains to prevent. He did not push his enquiries too soon, but waited until he was out with a large party—five boats, which reflects his caution—cutting grass for hay. They filled the launches, then went over to Grass Cove. Here they found his old friend Pedro of the second voyage, looking rather frightened; from him, when reassured, and two or three others Cook, through Omai, got a fairly coherent story. On the fatal day Rowe and his sailors left the boat with only one man, Furneaux's negro servant, to guard her, and sat down about two hundred yards away to eat their meal. They had only two or three muskets. The account now splits into two, though Cook did not think these were irreconcilable. According to the first, some of the New Zealanders who clustered round the luncheon party snatched at the bread and fish; in the ensuing quarrel two were shot dead, apparently by Rowe, before he and his men were overpowered; and the excited savages immediately knocked all their prisoners on the head. They then despatched the unfortunate negro. According to the second, the

[1] ibid., 55–6.   [2] ibid., 61–2.

quarrel started at the boat, with a native who seized something, was struck a heavy blow by the negro, and called out that he was killed, on which the difference flared up and Rowe fired. It was not a premeditated quarrel. It was undoubtedly Rowe's foolish and hasty behaviour that gave it so grim a turn; and as one of his friends had recorded, he had a contempt for Indians. Once the savage blood was up, general butchery and cannibalism followed easily enough.

The native people were surprised that Cook did not exact *utu*, or payment. He did not behave naturally. It was natural for Gore to kill the man who made off with his cloth at Mercury Bay, on the first voyage: that was *utu*, and not resented. They lived a life of wild passion, warfare, and revenge; had long memories and did not forgive. These people were constantly embroiled with those of Admiralty Bay. Not long before the ships' arrival a chief, one of Cook's old friends in the Sound, had gone there and been slain with about seventy of his followers. There was no large tribe left. One party after another applied to Cook to destroy its enemies; if he had followed the advice of all his pretended friends, he says, he might have extirpated the whole race. One particular man he was urged by many to kill—one who looked a villain, and was by the testimony of all the leader of the murderers at Grass Cove; indeed, he did not deny it, and said outright that he had slaughtered Rowe and most of the others with his own hand. Like his fellows, when he understood there was to be no *utu*, he did not hesitate to come freely on board the ships, even into Cook's cabin. Why did not Cook shoot him? asked Omai, feverish for his death—were not murderers hanged in England? Cook had made his enquiry. He had never killed anybody in cold blood, and he would not start now. He agreed with Clerke that to do so 'cou'd answer no purpose at all'. Kahura at one stage looked as though he expected to be killed; he recovered so much that seeing a portrait of a fellow countryman hanging on the cabin-wall he asked to be drawn too, and sat with great aplomb while Webber made the drawing. Cook summed up the matter: 'I must confess I admired his courage and was not a little pleased at the confidence he put in me. Perhaps in this he placed his whole safety, for I had always declared to those who solicited his death that I had always been a friend to them all and would continue so unless they gave me cause to act otherwise; as to what was past, I should think no more of it as it was some time sence and done when I was not there, but if ever they made a Second attempt of that kind, they might rest assured of feeling the weight of my resentment.'[1]

1 *Journals* III, 69.

A useful sojourn this was at Ship Cove, though of only eleven days, on two of which the ships rode out violent northwest storms. A vast quantity of excellent fish, wild celery and scurvy grass was consumed; the young gentlemen stretched their legs and, so we gather from later reminiscences, indulged in a good deal of high-spirited horseplay;[1] Bayly, or Bayly and King, made over a hundred sets of observations to calculate the longitude again, found that the chronometer was losing only some three seconds a day, checked the astronomical clock, observed the variation of the compass with six needles on board the ship and on shore, observed the dip of the needle; Anderson observed rocks, plants, birds, insects and people; Samwell took down the first native chants ever recorded; Webber drew busily. Omai was here at his best as an interpreter, and managed to push through a plan of his own, which he had conceived before arriving in the country. This was to take home with him from New Zealand a companion, or follower, or servant—it is not quite clear which— and before long his talk had brought out a volunteer, one Tiarooa or Te Weherua, a youth of seventeen or eighteen, who took up his residence on board. Cook, who had disliked Omai's departure from his own island, was disturbed at the proposal, particularly when he found out that the youth was the only son of a chief killed in war and that his mother was a much respected lady. Had Omai promised his return? It was made quite clear that there could be no return. Then this son of a chief had to have a follower or servant: the first candidate was removed by his friends, but another, a boy of ten or twelve years called Coaa, or Loa, was handed over with no sentiment at all. Cook was still troubled. The complete indifference of all the people convinced him that the two adventurers could lose nothing by leaving home, and he let Omai have his way.

While the ships were unmooring and getting under sail two chiefs and a train of others came on board to take leave—or rather, to get what presents they could at the last moment. The chiefs wanted some goats and hogs. Cook had intended to present not only these animals but also sheep and a bull and heifers, had he found a chief powerful enough to protect them or a place safe enough for their natural protection. There was neither, and he determined to leave no stock at all. But the chiefs asked, he made them promise to keep his gifts alive, and as he had animals to spare bestowed on one a

[1] I have given a specimen in the Introduction to *Journals* III, xcviii–xcix, taken from George Home's *Memoirs of an Aristocrat* (London, 1838), which contains some of the reminiscences of the author's father Alexander Home, master's mate in the *Discovery*. 'Ah! those were the glorious days', Alexander is quoted as saying; and quite likely he did say so.

he-goat and she-goat, on the other a boar and sow; and hoped, not very confidently, for the best. Pigs, it seems certain, did survive, from whatever occasion, in the deeps of the New Zealand forest. When at last the captain was ready to go, neither wind nor tide served, and he anchored for the night outside the island Motuara. Next morning he had his last visitors—Kahura, with a whole family, male and female, of over twenty, down to the very children. He got rid of them and, a light breeze springing up, stood out of the Sound only to meet contrary winds in Cook Strait, so that it was two more days before he had Cape Palliser behind him. At 8 a.m. on 27 February, the cape bearing west seven or eight leagues, he steered east-by-north with a fine gale.

XXI

New Zealand to Tonga

COOK WAS to lose his passage. We can see now, our knowledge of the Pacific winds being greater than his, that this was inevitable. The bitter fact had nothing to do with time spent at the Cape or Kerguelen Island or Van Diemen's Land; indeed, he could have spent enough time at the last place to sail all round it, and thus dispose of Furneaux's too hasty verdict, without affecting the large outlines of his voyage. He had lost his passage already when he left England in July 1776. The time-table of his instructions was in fact totally unreal. If he could have sailed (Clerke with him) when he told Walker he expected to be ready to sail, 'about the latter end of April', then we can perhaps—with a flight into the hypothetical— see him leaving the Cape early in September, and Queen Charlotte Sound early in December, and arriving in Tahiti, with some luck— the winds being what they are—in mid-February. He would already be behind his illusory schedule. According to that schedule, he was to be in latitude 65° north on the American coast in the following June. If we now looked ahead on the actual voyage, we shall find him leaving the Society Islands not at the beginning of February, but two months earlier, at the beginning of December; and then he will not reach latitude 65° till early August. Such was the nature of exploration; such were the chances of—we must constantly remind ourselves—the age of sail; such was the fate of plans composed in London. The wisest of all Cook's instructions was that which confided the voyage to his own discretion.

His shortest passage from New Zealand to Tahiti, if it had been possible, would have been one directly north-east. On his previous experience of the winds in the ocean east of New Zealand, in June and July 1773, he had been able to make fifty degrees of easting before he turned north, in latitude 40°, to reach latitude 20°, and then turn west in August over eighteen degrees of longitude to Tahiti, all in ten weeks, though the passage had been tedious and the trade-wind slow in arriving; and sailing on this sort of immense irregular bow, he had had westerlies when he needed them. For seven months of the year, in that part of the Pacific, from the south to latitude 30° S, the westerlies are regular; from 30° to 20° S is a belt of variable winds; at 20° the south-east trade sets in. But from November to March the variables move as far south as New Zealand; they are broken by calms, and at the other extreme now and again by cyclones and hurricanes. These last, at any rate, Cook was to escape. He even had some favourable winds in the first few days: then March became a frustrating month to him, and in 1777 these frustrating conditions, calms, light breezes, faint breezes, from the east, north-east, south-east, extended themselves into April. His journal covers March in a page or two of generalised comment. He was trying to stand to the north-east, he writes for one of the days to which he gives specific mention, the 17th, 'but as the Wind often veered to E and ENE we frequently made no better than a North Course and some times to the Westward of North. But the hopes of the Wind coming more Southerly or meeting with it from the Westward a little without the Tropic, as I had formerly done, incouraged me to Continue this course. Indeed it was necessary I should run all risks as my proceeding to the North this year depended intirely on my making a quick passage to Otaheite or the Society islands.'[1] There was nothing to see except now and again a tropic bird and once a barnacled log. We read of little diversion. On board the *Resolution* the two young New Zealanders for some days gave way to grief and seasickness, which even a red cloak ordered for each by Cook—a princely gift on land—could not assuage, and they sang dolefully and continually a dirge or chant preserved for us by Samwell; after a week or so they recovered and became well-liked, particularly the younger boy, a droll jackanapes. It may have been boredom that led to a small outbreak of theft from certain men of victuals, of which King gives the story: as the crew would not discover the thieves Cook cut the meat allowance of all for a day to two-thirds, which all refused, on the plea that honest men should not be penalised; on which Cook denounced them for 'a very mutinous proceeding' and promised to continue the cut; an episode which we may regard as entirely trivial, but still indicative that Cook himself was not unaffected by the strain on his hopes. He may have felt some additional irritation when he reflected that only a week before, to avoid too great a demand on food for the stock, he had had his own sheep killed, and those belonging to 'the gun-room

1 *Journals* III, 77.

gentlemen', and served to the ship's company. These were matters he did not commit to his journal.[1]

He was, however, making some progress north, and towards the end of March coming up with a group of islands hitherto undiscovered, the group now called after him, the Lower Cooks. The southernmost, Mangaia, was sighted on 29 March, when he was still some five degrees short of the latitude of Tahiti, and ten degrees short in longitude. From the sea it looked well-wooded and attractive, though defended by a formidable reef and a furious surf; and the following day, when the ships bore up for the lee side, it became clear that a large number of inhabitants, much like New Zealanders in appearance, were anxious to defend it too. The Mangaians did not favour visitors. The boats sent to reconnoitre found no place to land; reef, surf, depth of water and sharp coral bottom made it dangerous to anchor. The people, though inhospitable, had enough curiosity to swim off to the boats and prove embarrassing visitors themselves, snatching everything they could lay hands on; but only one had the courage to come on board the ship. Webber drew his portrait, with a knife that was given him stuck through a hole in his ear; other presents, as we know from later enquiries, were long retained by their owners as articles of remarkable value, and Cook was remembered in the island tradition. It was an unprofitable island to him, and he now needed food for his cattle. On the 31st, a little more northerly, another island was sighted, 'Wautieu' or Atiu, where contact with the islanders was on a larger scale. The wind was so slight that the ships could not work up to it till 2 April. Gore was sent off with armed boats to look for anchorage and a landing place; while they were away several canoes came out with small presents for the chiefs, Cook and Clerke—plantains, a pig each, and some coconuts, in return for which they were most anxious for a dog. One of them, who bedded down for the night in Clerke's cabin, proved that he was willing to take anything else—'a most incorrigible. damn'd rogue indeed', summed up the outraged Clerke. Gore returned without success, but with the suggestion that as the natives seemed very friendly they might through Omai be persuaded to bring off to the boats, lying outside the surf, the supplies most wanted. 'Having little or no Wind', thought Cook, 'the delay of a day or two was of no moment', and he determined to try the experiment next morning. It did not reward him much, even after the bestowal of a dog. Gore, Omai, Anderson and Burney all went on the mission, and were landed from canoes on the reef, whence they could walk

[1] We learn about them from King, 15 March, 23 March; ibid., 76, n. 3, 77, n. 1.

ashore; but instead of obtaining what they wanted became themselves both guests and prisoners for the day, almost stifled in an excited and curious crowd who purloined everything loose they had, entertained them with dancing and a mock fight, provided them with no food till towards evening, when they were too exhausted to eat, cross-questioned Omai exhaustively, and got some romance in return. Both men and women were handsome, very like the Tahitians, much-tattooed, proud of a divine origin, yet greatly impressed by the explosion of some loose powder, to illustrate Omai's stories of the might of the ships. Omai himself, as the uncomfortable day advanced, had been nervous over the preparation of an oven, until persuaded that it was to cook a pig and not him. At length the party was returned to the boats, with a few coconuts and plantains, and to a captain whose mind was a good deal eased by their reappearance. One story they brought interested him much: this was of four Tahitians on the island, survivors of a painful drift-voyage from their home, after being driven off course by a strong wind. For years he had asked himself the question, how had the scattered islands of this immense ocean come to be peopled by members so obviously of the same race?—and now it seemed he had the answer, or at least an answer for many of them.

Atiu being unprofitable, the following morning Cook steered for an islet ten miles to the north-west, 'Wennuaete'—Whenua iti or Takutea. It was uninhabited. Despite the great surf even on the lee side he managed to get a quantity of scurvy grass, coconuts, and pandanus branches, soft spongy juicy stuff: 'the Cattle eat it very will when cut up in small pieces, so that it might be said without any impropriety that we fed our Cattle on Billit-wood'.[1] A hatchet and a few nails were left in an empty hut as payment. This was on 4 April. Cook knew that if he kept on the same course he would find within forty or fifty miles his Hervey island, the atoll of his previous voyage, Manuae as we call it, which he thought uninhabited. Although it was so close, he did not reach it till the 6th, when he was surprised to see a number of canoes coming off to the ships. Their occupants would not venture on board, but grasped boldly at everything within reach, even the oars in the *Discovery*'s cutter lying alongside—'great Thieves and horrid Cheats', reports a midshipman; they wore little and were not tattooed, and said they had seen two great ships before, so that the *Resolution* and *Adventure* had not passed by unnoticed in 1773. There was no anchorage. King, who went to look for it, saw signs of hostility among the people. Cook wanted water, as well as

[1] *Journals* III, 88.

grass for his stock. If there was water here, and it could be got at, there would still be the business of transporting it across the reef. There were light airs from the eastward and an easterly swell. The ships' position was now two degrees south and ten degrees west of Tahiti; to reach it had taken Cook six weeks. He made up his mind. The decision he reached must have been forcing itself on him for some time.

Being thus disapointed at all these islands, and the summer in the northern Hemisphere already too far advanced for me to think of doing any thing there this year, It was therefore absolutely necessary to persue such methods as was most likely to preser[v]e the Cattle we had on board in the first place, and save the Ships stores and Provisions in the second the better to enable us to procecute the Discovery's in the high northern latitudes the ensuing summer. I intended to have stood back to the south till I had met with a westerly wind, provided I had got a supply of water and grass at any of these islands; but the consequence of doing this without, would have been the loss of all the Cattle without gaining any one advantage. I therefore determined to bear away for the Friendly Isl^ds where I was sure of being supplied with every thing I wanted; and as it was necessary to run in the night as well as in the day, I ordered Capt. Clerke to keep about a league ahead of the Resolution, as his Ship could better claw of a lee shore than mine.[1]

To help with water he kept his still at work for ten hours a day: it provided a moderate quantity of fresh water at a considerable cost of fuel. Two days later he issued careful, though not harsh, orders for the economical use of the water he had. If he had only known! Within this group he passed by, out of sight, its two largest islands rich and fertile, Rarotonga and Aitutaki, either of which could have given him all the supplies he could possibly need.

When he bore away he had a fine easterly breeze. It fell, and he altered course for Palmerston and Niue, as a sort of insurance, though he must have considered the latter, 'Savage Island', purely a last resort. Where now was the easterly trade wind? On the 10th came thunder squalls from the south, which at least brought heavy rain, channelled into the empty puncheons. And then, as if heaven were simply seeing how malign it could be,

At length about Noon the next day it fixed at NW & WNW and blew a fresh breeze with fair weather, thus we were persecuted with a Wind in our teeth which ever way we directed our course, and the farther Mortification to find here those very winds we had reason to expect 8° or 10°

[1] ibid., 91.

farther South. They came now too late for I durst not trust to their continuance and the event proved that I judged right.[1]

Indeed they turned variable again, but help was at hand. Daybreak on 13 April showed Palmerston. It was more than twenty-four hours before the ships could creep up with it.

Palmerston was a virgin atoll if ever there were such: six sandy islets and a few low cays strung on the reef round its lagoon, with no sign of human touch save a few bits of wreckage driven over the reef on to a beach. The boats were immediately out to look for a landing place, and by early afternoon the starving stock were eating their way through scurvy grass and the green of coconut trees. For the rest of that day and the following three days the foraging parties were hard at work, gathering young coconut trees and an infinity of the nuts, pandanus, 'palm cabbage'; fish was abundant in the lagoon, and Omai excelled himself as a cook; the sea birds stimulated general wonderment. They stood to be stroked and picked off the trees. 'The immense Quantities of these Fowls', writes Clerke, 'which consisted chiefly of Men of War and Tropic Birds, Boobies, Noddies and Egg Birds, are astonishing, the Trees and Bows in many places seem'd absolutely loaded with them; but we were a most unhappy Interruption to their wonted Security, for unfortunately for them we found them very palatable and well-flavour'd.'[2] Anderson was enchanted by the lagoon, its colours, its corals, its fishes 'playing their gambols'; why should Nature conceal a work so elegant so far from the praises of mankind? The only drawback was the half-mile of reef across which the toiling men had to walk, waist-high in water, to get their burdens to the boats. This reef and lagoon, the chained islets and banks of sand, the vegetation, made a strong impression on Cook and his naturalist-surgeon; they both speculated on the formation of coral islands, sensibly enough, within the limits of their observation.

At sunset on the 27th course was set for Nomuka, where Cook proposed first to call. Wind and weather were still quite uncertain, with frequent squalls, thunder, lightning and rain, some high seas and disagreeable heat. While it was impossible to keep the ships dry the rain, on the other hand, provided the ample fresh water of which there was none at Palmerston and which would be only of poor quality in Tonga. Cook laid his still aside. In spite of all the salt food since leaving the Cape there were no sick. After a week of this uncomfortable sailing Savage Island was sighted and passed by, then the sea moderated and fell smooth, tropic birds were again in the sky and

[1] *Journals* III, 92.   [2] ibid., 94, n. 3.

dolphins glowed in the water after dark. On 28 April, in the morning the eastern islets of the great net were visible, Nomuka inside them; Cook was coming into the group a little south of his track of June 1774. He anchored for the night. The old exchanges immediately began, pigs, breadfruit, yams for hatchets and nails.

We are at the beginning of another parenthesis in Cook's exploration. We might almost say that his mature style as an explorer is parenthetical: that is, within the wide discretion conferred upon him by his instructions he finds it possible to investigate, and make a number of statements on, the nature of the world, in a manner subordinate to his main investigation, his main statement; and that without interfering with the general movement of his mind. To the great query of his second voyage he gave the definite answer, There is no southern continent; to the great query of his last voyage he was to give an answer almost as definite, There is no north-west passage; but included in the negatives, what wealth of subordinate clauses tending towards 'the improvement of Geography and Navigation'! True, there is a difference between the two voyages: the masterly parenthesis of the second voyage, that took in the Marquesas, the New Hebrides, New Caledonia, was deliberate, a calculated extension of the voyage in line with its original plan; this one was forced on Cook. As it was forced, he cannot display the same sureness of touch. We have again a difficulty over timing. On his two previous visits to Tonga, in 1773 at 'Eua and Tongatapu, in 1774 at Nomuka, he had spent altogether eleven days enough to convince him that those islands could provide him with all the refreshment he needed. When he made his decision to turn to Tonga he gave Clerke a series of rendezvous, the first at 'Rotterdam' or Nomuka; if there was no meeting within fourteen days then at the other two islands, fourteen days more; failing that at Tahiti and a wait of a month, then to Raiatea until the end of October—when, if Cook had still not appeared, he was to pursue the Admiralty's instructions, 'which you are now at liberty to open'.[1] They would not have told him much that he did not know already. What he would have done with about three months at Raiatea it is difficult to imagine; and sailing thence at the end of October he would presumably gain the American coast in the middle of winter. The questions we ask ourselves are unnecessary except as they illustrate the difficulty Cook was in, at sea in the beginning of April with the wretched winds always contrary. We may note that after a passage of nine weeks and three days from Queen

[1] ibid., 1525–6.

Charlotte Sound to Nomuka he was to spend not eleven days in the group, nor the month he had allowed to Clerke, but eleven weeks. Of this period the lesser part, so far as we can see, was devoted to Geography and Navigation; though Bligh did some excellent charting, and his own observations were as precise as was customary with him. The journals for the reader whose interests are not geographical or navigational in the narrowest sense, have a remarkable importance as accounts of a Polynesian society at a highly mature point, before inner strains and the influence of a foreign world combined to break it in pieces. They also, one or two directly, Cook's own mainly by implication, cast some light on the mind of the captain himself.

Cook provided immediately for trade, with his usual regulations to prevent confusion and quarrelling, and to stop men from acquiring 'curiosities' until the ships were supplied with food, so that in three days he could end all sea diet except grog, and put everybody on fresh pork, fruit and roots. Meanwhile the ships, impeded though they were by canoes, were worked round the shoals and islets to the old anchorage on the northern side of Nomuka. This was 1 May, and here they remained a fortnight, with the people of the island swarming aboard and in general good relations prevailing. The only really untoward incidents, apart from the constant thefts, were the parting of the *Discovery*'s cables on the sharp rocks of the anchorage, which meant some difficult days spent in recovering the anchors. The chiefs, the *eiki*, were well-inclined and helpful, though not disinclined to profit from the thieving which so constantly went on— even, for a start, to take part in it themselves. Cook was determined to put it down. It must have seemed purposeless, apart from a sense of triumph—why, for example, carry off the bolt from the spunyarn winch?—and could be very inconvenient. A minor chief was caught in that particular act, was flogged, carried on shore to the trading place his hands tied firmly behind his back, and released only after some hours when a large hog was brought as ransom. Such punishment was to Anderson extreme: 'after this we were not troubled with thieves of rank', commented Cook, but on their servants or slaves 'a floging made no more impression than it would have done upon the Main-mast'. The chiefs advised him to kill them. He could not quite do that, but we can see a sort of desperation coming upon him. Clerke, in like situation, was rescued by his waggishness. He had the offenders half-shaved, head, face, and beard, before throwing them overboard to become objects of derision; and that was fairly effective.

One of the chiefs who came to visit, from Tongatapu not Nomuka, was obviously a man of great importance, youngish, tall and of a handsomely wild appearance, introduced as 'Feenough', king of all the Friendly Islands. He did not deny the dignity—when he arrived at Nomuka all the natives present bowed their heads to his feet; when he came to dinner with Cook only one other chief was esteemed to be of high enough rank to be present also; he was certainly influential enough to reclaim stolen goods. Cook rather suspected the claim to kingship, but made no doubt of the unusual importance; for Finau Ulukalala Feletoa was indeed a grandee, an arrogant, able and ambitious one, among those isles. It was at his suggestion that Cook, finding at the end of ten days that he had got from Nomuka all that he could get, resolved, instead of going directly to Tongatapu, to visit first an island to the north-east called 'Happi'. It was not a single island, as Cook was to find, but a group, the five largest members of which lie on the water in a twisted green flat line north to south; the central part of the group bordered on the westward or leeward side with innumerable reefs and shoals and islets, on the whole of the windward side, where he did not go, with a barrier reef and the parallel white line of the exploding Pacific. Why Finau should have wished Cook to visit this group, rather than his own island of Vava'u, still farther to the north, is a little hard to understand: perhaps he noticed on Nomuka how far inroads on provisions could go. The ships accordingly weighed anchor and steered a careful way north and north-east, rock-studded reefs on the starboard hand, to the north-west and then west the flat top of volcanic Tofua and the beautiful cone of Kao; then within low islands, skirting further rocks; a night, a second night under sail, 'for although we had land in every direction the sea was unfathomable'; a sudden patch of six fathoms depth then no ground with the lead down eighty fathoms; a third night under sails with land and breakers in every direction, comforted only by a fire lit on shore as a mark by Finau, a partial passenger. At daylight on the 17th anchorage was at last found before what Cook called a creek in the reef—that is, the narrow division between Foa, the second island from the north, and Lifuka, the third and principal island of the five. It was a safe enough anchorage in the trade-wind; in a westerly it would not have been safe. There were sheltering ledges of rock without; down the west coast of Lifuka the maze of underwater reefs. Cook was here for nine days.

Again the ships were immediately surrounded by multitudinous canoes and thronged with the islanders. Finau, closely and constantly attended by Omai, made himself a sort of master of ceremonies. The people were ordered ashore. He took Cook ashore at the northern point of Lifuka, seated him in a house close by the beach, placed himself and other chiefs there with 'the multitude' seated outside in a circle, introduced Cook and proceeded to dictate through a subordinate a harangue on the duties of the populace: Cook was a friend who would remain a few days, they were not to molest or steal from him in any way, they were to bring hogs and fowls and fruit to the ships and would receive defined things in exchange. Cook made presents, there was a second harangue (Omai was the interpreter); Cook was conducted to some tolerably fresh water, presented with a baked hog and yams for dinner, and after dinner with a fine large turtle and more yams. There were plenty of hogs changing hands, with fruit and roots, alongside the ships. This was very satisfactory; but next day there were to be greater ceremonies. Cook was conducted ashore, as before, by Finau. He found a large crowd already assembled. Before long a band of nearly a hundred people came on to the ground from his left bearing various fruits and sugar cane which were piled up in two great heaps; they were followed from his right by another band bringing similar offerings, two smaller heaps; six pigs and two turtles were added on the left, two pigs and six fowls on the right. In front of them, on the left, sat the chief of the island, on the right a lesser chief. The bearers joined the great circle of the crowd, and in came club fighters to exhibit their prowess, their contests broken by wrestling and boxing matches, including some female boxing which distressed the more gallant of the visitors. These diversions came to an end with the morning. The larger quantity of provisions was presented to Cook; it 'far exceeded any present I had ever before received from an Indian Prince'; the smaller, formally, to Omai—who possibly, in his attachment to Finau, had not failed to enlarge on his own importance. The Indian Prince received a very satisfactory return.

Cook's journal has no entry for the following day, 19 May. Anderson's records a pleasant walk all over the island, which is not much over four miles long, and nowhere wider than a mile and a half. He was much impressed by its large plantations, neat fences and spacious roads, though there were few people to see, the populace all thronging about the ships. The party had a guide and protector generously provided by Finau. How Finau spent the day we may perhaps gather from the story told by William Mariner, the very intelligent young man who thirty years later was the prisoner, friend, and close observer of the Tongans, a story which—Mariner's informants being who they were, chiefs who had been concerned, and

Finau's own son—we have no reason to doubt.[1] The chiefs of the island were no doubt carried away by the prospects of the booty and the realisation of the numerical inferiority of their visitors. They conspired together. Finau, the most influential, did not originate the conspiracy, but gave counsel and advice. There should be a great entertainment of night dancing, lit by torches; Cook, his officers, and the marines should be invited, and at a given signal massacred. The ships were then to be taken by assault. Finau objected that taking the ships at night would be difficult, and proposed instead a daylight operation. Entertainment by day was already in train. When Cook and the others present were out of the way, 'the men, who would naturally come in search of him, were to be conducted to the further part of the island under pretence that he was there, and they were then to be destroyed in like manner. Thus the two ships, their crews being so weakened, might be taken (as they supposed) with ease.' We can fancy possible defects in this plan, but it was the one adopted; and we may fancy a connection between it and the first sentence of Cook's journal entry for Tuesday, 20 May: 'Fenough having expressed a desire to see the Marines go through their exercize and being willing to gratify him, I ordered them all ashore from both ships in the Morning of the 20th.' They duly, in an undisciplined way, performed their exercise and fired several volleys. The time came for the Tongan entertainment. The victims were in order. Cook's fate hung by a thread.

It was a sight entirely new, he says—an exciting and most complicated paddle dance, performed most perfectly by a hundred and five men, to the sound of two hollow log drums and a song in which everyone joined, ending with a 'harlequin dance' in front of Cook himself: it 'so far exceeded any thing we had done to amuse them that they seemed to pique themselves in the superiority they had over us.'[2] We can tell from Cook's close account how his attention was rivetted. Could anything be better designed as an aid to dramatic murder? Yet the signal was not given. Finau's vanity and pique had countermanded his treachery. Argument had arisen again: 'a little before the appointed time', (Mariner's tale continues) 'most of the chiefs still expressed their opinion that the night-time would have been better than the day, and Finow, finding that the majority were of this opinion, was much vexed, and immediately forbade it to be done at

---

[1] John Martin, *An Account of the Natives of the Tonga Islands . . . from the extensive communications of Mr William Mariner* (3rd ed., Edinburgh, 1827), II, 71–2. Mariner arrived in Tonga through the cutting-out by the Tongans of his own vessel, the *Port au Prince*, in 1806, while she was lying in Cook's anchorage off Lifuka.

[2] *Journals* III, 109.

all.'[1] Cook went on board to dinner. At night the ground lost by the
marines was regained by fireworks, particularly rockets; but then a
series of dances by torch-light, both by men and by women, carried
away the guests, and also some of their hosts, with admiration:
flower-garlanded heads, soft-voiced song, the regular clapping of
hands and thud of bamboos on the ground, oiled and scented bodies,
naked from the waist up in the Tongan fashion, limbs moving with
the most dexterous unison in the shine of the flaring torches against
the dark trees; some female 'indecency'; admiration even from the
rather prudish Mr Williamson at 'the most beautiful forms that
imagination can conceive in the younger part of the Sex'.[2] Webber's
pencil was furiously busy. Lines and circles changed position,
fingers fluttered; song was varied by savage shouts; at the end of each
dance the pace quickened; the *po me'e*, the night of dancing, was over.
Cook had never before seen such an exhibition; he was never to see
another quite as exhilarating.

   Trade was falling off as supplies dwindled. Only girls remained in
endless plenty, generally at an axe or a shirt the night, payable to the
man who brought the young lady aboard, though the price was known
to go higher. Cook in his turn walked on the island, observed and
admired; had vegetable seeds planted, Indian corn, melons, pump-
kins, to add to its resources; continued the struggle against pilfering.
Careless sentries and sailors were punished as well as the thieves.
Had the commanders been of less humanity than Cook and Clerke,
thought a junior officer, many of these people must have lost their
lives. Chiefs in their canoes came and went. A persuasive liar came
with a story of another ship at anchor in the road at Nomuka, and
Cook's belief was dissipated only by a newly arrived chief, whom he
knew, from that island. To what end such a story?—to get him back
to Nomuka? He had already decided to leave, and was indeed on
the point of unmooring, when Finau announced that he himself was
departing for 'Vaugh Waugh' to get red-feathered caps for the ships'
trade at Tahiti. Two days' sail to the north: Cook proposed to add to
his knowledge by taking the ships there. Finau was discouraging, with
a large lie of his own (perhaps he wished to conserve the resources of
Vava'u). There was neither harbour nor anchorage there, he said.
Cook acquiesced but would stay where he was little longer. He made
his way down the coast to a bay between Lifuka and its next southern
neighbour Uoleva; here he anchored till next day, thinking to attempt
the passage to Nomuka amongst the islands. Thence he would pass
to Tongatapu. The next day brought an unsettled wind and rainy

[1] Martin / Mariner, II, 72.   [2] *Journals* III, 110, n. 3.

squalls, the *Discovery* had already touched on a shoal, and the masters returned from investigating ahead with a too unfavourable report of islets, shoals and breakers. It was clear he would have to reverse his northward course outside the islands.

During this day still another chief arrived, in a large sailing canoe, and was brought on board: the king, the Tu'i Tonga, said the lesser ones, the supreme person in all those isles. It was Cook's policy to pay his court to all these great men, without enquiring too closely into the legality of their titles, but this time it really did appear, from the authority exerted and the reverence paid, that the claim was justified. Finau was abandoned by all who had exalted him before, except Omai: Omai had a vested interest he could not abandon, his identification with Finau had gone to the exchange of names, contradiction was bitter. If Cook had known, Finau was far too slim to be a king; but this person, sedate, sensible, enquiring, was 'the most corporate plump fellow we had met with', outrivalling the fat hogs he had brought with him. Fatafehi Paulaho had all the marks of majesty; after dining with Cook he was carried ashore in a sort of hand barrow: flies were fanned away from him; he would keep no present but a glass bowl; people came on purpose to bow their heads to the sole of his foot; nowhere had the captain seen the like decorum. He presented Cook, before the ship sailed next daybreak, 29 May, with one of the beautiful red feather caps or bonnets, which were never brought in trade; and his reprimand to people who had stayed on board all night without his permission brought tears to their eyes.

This passage to Nomuka turned out to be a difficult and dangerous one of a week. The winds became scant or contrary, or blew fresh and in rain squalls at the worst possible time by night. By the 31st Cook had worked round the more northern islets, tacking at night, then stood for a passage between the islet of Kotu and a reef to the westward, could not make it, was forced to stretch south-west until he feared he would lose the islands, with a cabinfull of islanders on board, tacked back towards the other islet of Fotuhaa, and spent a night between it and Kotu tacking in the squalls under reefed topsails and foresail. There was real danger, and the *Resolution* fired her guns to warn the *Discovery* astern. Cook provides us with another passage that may be taken as illustrative of his philosophy of exploration, a sigh rather than a groan.

I kept the deck till 12 oclock when I left it to the Master, with such direction as I thought would keep the Ships clear of the dangers that lay round us; but after making a trip to the north and standing back again to the south the Ship, by a small shift of the wind fetched farther to windward than was expected; by this means she was very near runing plump upon a low Sandy isle surrounded by breakers. It happened very fortunately that the people had just been turned up to put the Ship about and the most of them at their stations, so that the necessary movements were not only executed with judgement but with alertness and this alone saved the Ship. . . . Such resks as thise are the unavoidable Companions of the Man who goes on Discoveries.[1]

As his frightened passengers were anxious to get ashore, with the first light he landed them on Kotu, and found anchorage himself about two miles off; 'for I was as tired with beating about amongst the islands and shoals as they were and determined to get to an anchor some where or another if possible.' He remained at anchor for three days of strong wind, while Bligh sounded between the islands, Paulaho came off to visit, and he himself walked on Kotu to examine it and the shoals and reefs about it. On 5 June he was again at Nomuka, where the people were digging yams for him; and here arrived Finau from Vava'u, with a tale of canoes lost with the supplies they were bringing, and all their crews perished, during the recent weather—a tale which Cook was disinclined to believe, in view of general native equanimity. Here also Paulaho caught him up, and Finau's inferiority became clear; he made his obeisance, he could not sit at table with the greater one.

This was but a way-station. In four days more the ships were steering for Tongatapu, rapidly outdistanced by a fleet of sailing canoes which set out with them. Finau left pilots in the *Resolution*, knowledgeable men, who followed the course of the canoes; but even then, as on the second day they approached the middle of the island, through what is now called the Lahi passage, with boats sounding ahead, they were 'insensibly' drawn upon a large coral shoal—'a most confounded navigation', to quote Clerke, over 'a continued bed of Coral Rock, very uneven, with here and there a mischievous rascal towering his head above the rest, almost to the water's Edge'.[2] By good luck the water was smooth and clear, the breeze gentle, though both ships touched they both came over without damage, anchored safely for the night, and next afternoon, 10 June, were anchored again, very snugly, in the spot designed for them by their pilots, not far from the shore, sheltered by a congeries of islets—the eastern

---

[1] *Journals* III, 119. The 'low Sandy isle' was Putuputua, about twelve feet high, standing on a reef three miles north-east of Kotu. King: 'the Master whose watch it was (one of the officers being sick) immediately threw all aback & afterwards wore . . . otherwise we might have ended our discoveries here.' Bligh, who undoubtedly acted with excellent decision, has a rather vain comment of his own.—ibid., n. 1.

[2] ibid., 122, n. 2.

reach of Nuku'alofa harbour. Cook landed. On the beach was the king waiting for him. He was to stay for a month.

This seat of royal kings, Tu'i Tonga, lords of Heaven and Earth, was the largest and richest of all the Tongan islands, and Paulaho the king was a truly friendly man. The island is generally speaking a plain on a base of coral, rising to somewhat more than two hundred feet at its south-western quarter, and with a large area occupied by a sort of three-fingered lagoon opening from the sea a little east of Cook's anchorage: a very different spot from Van Diemen's Road outside the narrow western peninsula where he had lain in 1773. Here was a wider prospect—no 'variety of hills and valleys, lawns, rivulets and cascades' for the romantic English soul, no 'grand Landscapes' but the most exuberant fertility, as it was felt by Anderson, great 'Cocoa palms' towering above all. Cook, less expansive on such matters, agreed. Cultivated land or uncultivated showed the same fertility; plantations were large, flowering shrubs were grown about houses for their beauty, fences were neat, roads and lanes well-made. The Tongans, wherever they dwelt, clearly knew well how to tend the land. The larger works of their hands too were impressive: artificial mounds raised as pigeon-snaring areas; *esi* or 'rest-mounds', where men might simply catch the breeze or enjoy a view; the *langi*, royal tombs of stepped masonry the technical expertness of which was so difficult to comprehend. There was little information that could be acquired visually that Cook and Anderson, King and Clerke did not pick up between them. Social relations were a rather different matter. The absolute power of chiefs over commonalty was plain enough; it was plain that there was a hierarchy of chiefs; a king had been found, but what was the standing of a king, sacred, certainly lord of Heaven and Earth, who had sometimes almost surreptitiously to protect himself from the obeisances of his subjects, and yet himself do obeisance to a woman—who, apart from accepting that tribute, seemed to have no political or social or religious function whatever? Not without long study would it be possible to disentangle the family relationships of royalty or near-royalty, to be clear about the functions of sacred king and executive king and the one who came between, or the paternal standing of fathers and uncles and elders, the place of first wives and other wives, the particular position of women in conferring distinction of descent.[1]

[1] The social and political organisation of Tonga was both complex and strictly ordered, and difficult to make clear in a note. But it may be said that there was a sacred 'king', the Tu'i Tonga; at the time of this 1777 visit of Cook's it was Paulaho. Anciently the Tu'i Tonga had been supreme ruler in all secular affairs; in the fifteenth century, for

Cook, who had been so signally misled on his earlier voyage, now had one point of certainty in Paulaho; but with so many other chiefs sharing names and obviously occupying high positions he must have felt not seldom that he wandered in a mist.

Paulaho, somewhat more than the 'indolent, fat, greasy rogue' that Clerke thought him (for Clerke was much taken with that 'active, stirring fellow' Finau) extended his welcome and beneficence. Cook landed close to the point called Holeva, his 'Observatory Point', not far from the northern entrance to the lagoon, was given a small house and had an area virtually made over to him for his convenience; almost immediately was held the first of many kava ceremonies—though Cook, this time put off by the preliminary chewing of the root, passed his cup to Omai. He nevertheless observed the ritual with care. Next morning he got all the cattle ashore under a guard of marines, set up his tents and astronomical instruments, spread out the sails for repair and had a party cutting plank and firewood; the two gunners managed trade; King became resident superintendent; 'our little post was like a fair and the Ships so thronged that we had hardly room to stir on the decks.'[1] Finau was in attendance, and the days settled down. Almost every day brought some present from Paulaho; almost every day brought Paulaho as a guest to dinner, rapidly tolerant of English cooking and very cheerful over his bottle; and this pleased Cook, because it kept the cabin clear of a crowd. There was, however, another great person to meet, the venerable 'Marriwaggy' or Maealiuaki, understood, wrongly, to be Paulaho's father and 'the first man on the island'. If a man had precedence of the king, there lay further confusion; but it was true,

reasons that may be ignored, he made over all these secular affairs to an executive ruler, the Tuʻi Haʻa Takalau. In the following century this ruler similarly passed on executive government to the Tuʻi Kanokupolu, while retaining great prestige and privilege. Among Cook's chiefs Maealiuaki had been the fourteenth and last Tuʻi Haʻa Takalaua (the office then being dropped) and was currently the Tuʻi Kanokupolu, effective principal ruler of the group: hence his vast importance. Cook did not understand the full implications of the word *tamai*, which meant both father and what the anthropologist calls 'classificatory fathers'—i.e. all paternal male affines; hence some confusion in his journals. In the chiefly class nobility descended through the female line, and daughters were superior in rank to sons. This was carried a long way: not only was a sister *fahu*, or superior in rank, to her brother, but so were her children, both male and female, and they were *fahu* to his children. A particular sacredness attached to the eldest daughter of the Tuʻi Tonga by his principal wife, a daughter called the *Tuʻi Tonga fefine* (*fefine*, female); she was so sacred that no Tongan could marry her, a Fijian chief had to be brought in for the purpose, and her first-born daughter was a *tamaha*, or 'sacred child'. There was also one male *tamaha* appointed, the son of Paulaho's aunt, a *Tuʻi Tonga fefine*: this was the chief whom Cook found so stupid, Latunipulu. There were then women to whom Paulaho owed obeisance, as *fahu*; he did not do obeisance to Latunipulu, but could not eat in his presence. The matter may be left at that, but the reader who wishes for more may be referred to the annotation of the Tongan pages in the journal.

[1] *Journals* III, 125.

because the old man was the Tuʻi Kanokupolu, the effective secular ruler of all the islands. When Cook was first taken to see him, up the lagoon at the delightful village of Muʻa, where all the principal men had their houses, he was not there, and Cook suspected Omai of bringing wrong intelligence. The following day, however, very satisfactory visits were exchanged. Maealiuaki was a kindly man and a man of sense: when he came again he gave his chief attention to the cattle and the cross-cut saw.

Two days and evenings were devoted to great entertainments of dancing and presentation of food. The first was Maealiuaki's, when Finau, dressed in English cloth, took a leading part, and the old chief himself did not disdain to beat a drum; the second was Paulaho's, when the yams were piled thirty feet high, crowned with hogs, inside a rectangular framework of posts, and at night the unwieldy king threw himself into the dance. The dances were much the same as those seen at Lifuka, for men, for women, for both sexes, paddle dance, club dances, dances preluded or accompanied by song; and with the dark, pandanus torches flared. The whole population seemed to be making holiday, though it was hard to estimate the size of the crowds who came to watch both dancing and visitors and lay down to sleep on the spot; eight or ten or twelve thousand were various estimates. But such crowds were not a good index to the population of any particular island, thought Cook, because curiosity brought people from afar. If otherwise unoccupied, they entertained themselves with boxing and wrestling, women sometimes as well as men, and boys and girls; and sailors who contemned the Tongan style in these arts of battle as an ignoble variation on British technique were almost invariably worsted—when they won it was by courtesy of their opponents. Cook thought it wise to protect prestige by prohibiting further contests. In return for the dancing the marines were again put through their rather inadequate exercise; and fireworks excited general astonishment and admiration. There was the daily diversion of watching King or Bayly examine the sky. So jealously, so tenderly were the chronometers guarded that it was thought they must be gods.

The presence of such crowds accentuated the old evil of thieving. It was not always trivial. One of the *Discovery*'s anchors was saved only because it got hooked in a chain-plate and could not be disengaged by hand. Trivial thefts—a pewter basin, a sentry's ramrod— were none the less irritating. Anything left lying loose about the ships or a working party was purloined. Cook's effort to protect prestige came too late. Clerke mourned over stolen cats, his rats rioted unmolested. As awe disappeared, workmen and sentries became objects of derision. Cook deprived the men of weapons, lest they should proceed to extremes; the sentries were ordered to fire only with small shot. When the tormentors were driven away by threats, they climbed trees and threw stones and coconuts from the safety of the branches. Paulaho promised protection to any sportsmen or strollers in the country who let him know what they intended; foolish officers ignored this and lost their muskets; Cook, who was rigorous over government property, would take no step to aid the fools, already warned, and was highly displeased when they got Omai to complain to the king. Samwell on an amatory adventure, too lavish in his display of beads, was assaulted, and escaped only by a murderous assault of his own. After the first week, lest the stock should go, Cook thought it best to present to the chiefs the animals he destined for the island—a bull and a cow to Paulaho, a ram and ewes to Maealiuaki, a horse and a mare to Finau. It was done with formality and what explanation of husbandry could be dispensed through Omai. Maealiuaki was not interested; in the end it was Paulaho who was the principal beneficiary, for he got some goats as well. In spite of this, by the next morning two turkey cocks and a kid were gone. Cook determined on strong measures. He seized the canoes lying alongside the ships; he seized the chiefs (though amiably, and drank their kava), and announced that neither canoe nor man would be released until all the stolen property was returned. Fortunately enough was returned to enable him to relent. Yet the thieving went on, and as it did so his exasperation increased. Lashes descended in their dozens; some stone-throwers whom he regarded as hardened offenders were seized; they were not only heavily flogged, but had crosses slashed with a knife on their arms. Cook does not give us these details; the officers who do were shocked. We are troubled to see an unfamiliar Cook rising up, by the side of the scrupulously humane Cook we have known. He was still unwilling to risk a fatal encounter. He remarked, after a sentry had wounded a man with ball, that 'after this they behaved with a little more circumspection and gave us much less trouble. . . . the repeated insolence of the Natives had induced me to load the Sentries Muskets with small shot and authorised them to fire on particular occasions. . . . I could never find out how this Musket came to be charged with ball, there were enough ready to swear that it was only charged with small shot.'[1]

At the end of a fortnight the sails had been repaired, and wooding

[1] *Journals* III, 142.

and watering completed. Little more could be expected from the inhabitants, who, their curiosity sated, were drifting away. The masters returned from an investigation seaward, much against the dangerous channel by which the ships had come in, but pleased with one to the east through the reefs and islets, provided a westerly wind blew. Cook could go. He preferred to wait ten days more, to observe the eclipse of the sun that was due on 5 July. With leisure at his disposal, he walked out over the land and along the lagoon, calling at the king's capital and spending a night with him, strolling with him, inspecting a fishery, houses, plantations, *fa'itoka* or burial mounds, receiving presents, drinking endless kava, participating in a mourning ceremony (the main part of which seemed to be the emptying of a kava bowl holding four or five gallons). He entered up his journal at length; the pages are enchanting for the anthropologist. As the new month began, he got his stock on board, and moved the ship out to a position where he could take early advantage of a wind favourable for departure. The observation of the eclipse was imperfect, spoiled by cloudy weather; no matter, thought Cook—having waited so long for it—the longitude was accurately enough determined by lunar observations. He took aboard everything that remained on shore, including the sheep given to the neglectful Maealiuaki, and was ready to sail. On the morrow neither wind nor tide served. He would have to wait two or three days more. He decided to accept the invitation of Paulaho to a great ceremony that was to take place on the eighth day of the month.

It was held at Mu'a. It was a ceremony called 'inatchee' or *inasi*, and went on to a second day, and Cook's long and close description is quite the best we have. It was complex: what its precise significance was, as a whole or in its separate parts, we do not know. Cook could not find out; his constant enquiries through Omai were met by the answer *tapu*, and Omai had no gift of enquiry himself. It seemed to be both political and religious; there was certainly no doubt—this much information Paulaho was himself free with—that the central figure was the king's son 'the young Prince' with whom Cook was already acquainted; there were elements in it of a celebration of this youth's maturity, of a solemn oath of allegiance taken to him, of his elevation to an equality with his father—marked by their highly symbolical eating of yam together;[1] it was public, in the sense that a large

[1] It seems clear that the name '*inasi*' ('inachi' with Mariner) was not confined to one sort of ceremony, and that the usual great harvest festival or offering of first fruits described by him (Martin / Mariner, II, 168–73) was a quite different thing from this. This one, indeed, may possibly have been unique, which makes Cook's witness all the more important. See *Journals* III, 145, n. 1, 153–4; and for Anderson's account ibid., 913, 916–17.

number of the people were present, and as members of the public
Paulaho had no doubt invited the presence of Cook and his officers;
it was private, in so far as the commonalty was fenced off from sight
of the inner area where the more *tapu* proceedings took place. To
be present at all the visitors had to go bare-headed and let their hair
fall free, and Cook himself was carefully watched lest he should
wander too intimately; but he was able to remedy the fence by
making a hole in it. His boat's crew were not allowed to stir from
their boat. There were processions larger and smaller, of men and
women, chanted sentences and responses, 'Oraisions'—speeches or
set prayers?—the presentation of yams real or 'emblematical', the
emblems being small sticks of wood tied to poles; the investing of the
Prince with cloth. Cook stayed at Mu'a for the night; the king came
to supper with him 'and drank pretty freely of Brandy and Water so
that he went to bed grogish'; and then slept in the house apportioned
to Cook's party. Next morning, after paying a round of visits to the
chiefs, Cook made his own present of English cloth and beads to the
gratified Prince. The ceremony in the afternoon was even more
baffling than that of the previous day. Cook was determined to mark
every detail, and boldly walked on to the forbidden ground. There
was some demur, but finally he was allowed to stay on condition of
stripping to the waist as well as letting his hair flow, and thus he
joined in such of the activity as fell to his group. Did his mind go back
to that other anthropological student, Banks in Tahiti on the first
voyage, stripping and blacking himself to act as a 'chief mourner's'
assistant? His officers, outside the fence and peeping through, were
surprised to see their captain thus in a procession of the chiefs. 'I do
not pretend to dispute the propriety of Captn Cook's conduct, but
I cannot help thinking he rather let himself down', noted the
insufferable Williamson.[1] As for the captain in this ignoble state, 'I
was now partly under the management of a man who seemed very
assiduous to serve me and placed me in such a situation, that if I had
been allowed to make use of my eyes, I might very well have seen
every thing that passed, but it was necessary to sit with down cast
eyes and as demure as Maids.'[2] He made very good use of his eyes,
however; the later student, looking through them, is much in his
debt.

Paulaho pardoned his lack of discipline, and more: he pressed him
to stay still longer, and witness another ceremony, the funeral of
Maealiuaki's wife. Cook was tempted, but the tide was now favourable for taking his ships through the narrows of the Piha passage, the

[1] *Journals* III, 151, n. 1.   [2] ibid., 151.

wind was moderate and settled, and he dared not trust his fortune too long. He had had his gifts of stock brought to Mu'a, and there added an English boar and sow to improve the island breed; Finau had already extracted a pair of rabbits from him. He wanted to call at 'Eua for water, and he was persuaded that he should go. The passage was neither safe nor easy, and it was the morning of the 12th before he was at his anchorage in English Road. He was welcomed by the chief he had met in 1773. The only good water was at a distance from the anchorage; he therefore contented himself with what he had, arranged a trade for yams and the few hogs that were obtainable, and presented to the chief the sheep that had been so unsuccessful at Tongatapu. On his previous brief visit he had seen little of the island, though admiring what he saw; now, on his second afternoon, he made the journey to its topmost point for a general view. Cook had no natural gift for rhapsody, and it is among his officers that we find references to romantick valleys, enchanting walks, and a little Paradise. Nevertheless his mind could not fail to be stirred as he gazed out over the high cliffs to the eastward limitless ocean, then to the green and fertile slopes, and he had his own emotion: 'the SE side from which the hills are not far distant, rises with very great inequalities directly from the Sea, so that the plains and Medows, of which here are some of great extent, lay all on the NW side; and as they are adorned with tufts of trees and here and there plantations, make a very beautiful Landskip from whatever point they are viewed. Whilest I was viewing these delightfull spots, I could not help flatering my self with the idea that some future Navigator may from the very same station behould these Medows stocked with Cattle, the English have planted at these islands.'[1] And, perhaps in the same vein of provident romance, 'The next morning I planted a pine apple and sowed the seeds of Millons &cᵃ in the Cheifs Plantation, and had a dish of Turnips to dinner, being the produce of the seeds I left last Voyage.'[2]

He consented to stay a day or two more to receive the gift of yams and fruit the chief was assembling, and also in the hope that his friends from Tongatapu, who had promised to catch him up, might arrive. There was further entertainment of cudgelling, boxing and wrestling; there was to be night dancing, but Cook would have none of it. His servant William Collett, out on a walk, had been assailed by a mob, his clothes torn from his back, and arrived at the landing place naked except for his shoes. Cook immediately seized two canoes and a hog, demanded instant restitution and the delivery of the

[1] ibid., 157–8.   [2] ibid., 158.

offenders; the people scattered; the chief, much concerned, managed to produce a shirt, a pair of trousers and one young lad, and next morning the rest of the clothes in shreds. What could be done? Cook had already released the canoes. How could he flog one boy? He made the chief a present, paid for the hog, weighed anchor and stood out to sea. A canoe pursued him, with a message just come from the king: Paulaho had ordered him a number of hogs and in two days would be at 'Eua himself. The ships were well supplied; Cook did not feel inclined to return; his course was set for Tahiti.

'Thus'—on 17 July—'we took leave of the *Friendly Islands* and their Inhabitants after a stay of between two and three Months, during which time we lived together in the most cordial friendship, some accidental differences its true now and then happened owing to their great propensity to thieving, but too often incouraged by the negligence of our own people. But these differences were never attended with any fatal consequences, to prevent which all my measures were directed.' In the next three weeks he sat down to make his careful general report, premising the difficulty of being accurate about things that did not come directly under his eyes, or non-material matters, like religion or relationships. Even with translation at hand, informants and Omai alike were casual, the ships put the people on holiday, they had no wish to be examined at length. He had felt the difficulty before. No one was likely to tell him of the plot at Lifuka; it was not till he was at Tongatapu that he realised that Finau was a liar, and that Vava'u had an excellent harbour and everything else he was in need of. Undoubtedly he liked the people, in spite of their great propensity, so constant a trial to him, in spite of their leaning to sheer devilment; one judges that the chiefs, through whom he preferred to deal, with whom the Polynesian custom of exchange of presents was carried on, liked him. Samwell—not a Polynesian chief, it is true—stresses his impartial justice, which 'rendered him highly respected and esteemed by all the Indians.'[1] When D'Entrecasteaux came to Tonga sixteen years later, and the chief Kepa, with whom Cook had had much to do at Nomuka, learnt of his death, he burst into tears, and would have cut himself in the Tongan fashion with a sharks' tooth; but there were others whose memory was a disagreeable one. He may have offended more men

---

[1] '. . . it must be confessed that in all disputes between our People & the Indians, Captn Cook ever acted with the utmost Impartiality, being as ready to hear the Complaint of an Indian and to see justice done to him when injured, as he was to any of his own Men, which equitable way of proceeding rendered him highly respected & esteemed by all the Indians.'—ibid., 1044.

than he knew. Cook could reflect as he flogged, if he so wished, that Tongans were cruel to themselves, as the cheek-scars of mourning showed, or the propitiatory mutilation of fingers; that chiefs could be vilely brutal to commoners; that human sacrifice was not unknown to them—indeed an *inasi* a few months later would include the killing of ten men. Yet he would not himself have thought the reflection a proper one. We may wish that in his struggle he had shown some of the waggish imagination of Clerke. But Cook was not Clerke; nor had Clerke had to bear the strain of the preceding years. Describing this people, their persons, their customs and government, their houses and cookery, their trade, manufactures, their diseases, he forgets his rage. He thinks, as others do, of the wretched, the seemingly inevitable gift he has left behind him, to be an eternal curse, with his cattle, goats, and rabbits—'the Venereal'. Not for the first or the last time has he been deceived by the endemic island yaws.

One matter remains on which we may speculate, in the sphere of Geography and Navigation. The Friendly Islands, he thought, must be a larger group than was comprised by the islands he had himself visited or seen. It must include 'all those that have been discovered nearly under the same Meridian to the north, as well as some others which have never been seen by any European but are under the Dominion of *Tongatabu*, which is the Capital (tho not the largest) and seat of Government.'[1] To the north, 'nearly under the same Meridian', lay the Keppel and Boscawen islands of Wallis (discovered still earlier by Le Maire and Schouten)—Niuatoputapu and Tafahi: he had already, in 1774, concluded that they were part of the group, and his conclusion was reinforced when he was told by Paulaho that a nail he had then seen at Tongatapu came from Niuatoputapu. These two islands are in fact rather too far away to be reckoned as geographically part of Tonga, but there had always been a historical connection, and Paulaho (he said) had been at them himself. They made but two of an archipelago of, in all, one hundred and fifty-three islands, 'if we credet the Inhabitants', who counted them out with bits of leaves and small stones; some no doubt were 'mere spots'— indeed he had seen plenty of those and almost run on to one of them —but there were to the north-west Tasman's Prince Williams islands, which seemed to be identical with a group the Tongans claimed, and put three or four days' sail away (the north-eastern islands of the Fijian group, though Cook's identification was not quite right); there was 'Vaughwaugh'; there was '*Hammoah*' or Samoa, 'also under the dominion of Tongatabu . . . the largest of all

[1] *Journals* III, 161.

the islands'. Well known also was 'Fidgee . . . a high but very fruitfull island', with a cannibal people; but they were not subject to Tonga. Nor, in spite of the Tongan claim, were the Samoans.

Why did Cook make no attempt to visit any of these islands? Can anyone doubt that on his second voyage, if he had heard of the existence of large islands so close to any of his anchorages, he would have been after them, fastened them down securely on his general chart, even at the cost of minor disorganisation of his time-plan? True, for a man whose next objective was Tahiti, they were in the wrong direction; yet he now was not afflicted by a sense of urgency, and the surprise we may feel springs from the absence of mention in his journal of even the rejected possibility of reconnais-sance—except for Vava'u. Paulaho, enlightening him about Vava'u, offered to go there with him. He met Fijians on Tongatapu: their home certainly could not be far away, and the store of red feathers he acquired at Tongatapu came from Fiji. Is it then misguided to speculate on his absence of interest in active exploration? We are anticipated by one of his own men, the young George Gilbert, who also has mentioned Fiji: '. . . it is somewhat surprizing that Capt Cook did not go in search of it accoarding to His usual practice. His reasons for not doing it I can't account for; as we certainly had time while we were lying at Tongataboo.'[1] From other men one would anticipate nothing. Has one simply come to anticipate from Cook the superhuman? Is it possible to think that just as a long but unsuspected strain on his mind was beginning to affect his attitude to the human situation, to make him the victim of his own exasper-ation in dealing with Tongan light-fingeredness, so, in relation to unexpected geographical possibilities, he was beginning to experience a certain inner tiredness?

[1] *Journals* III, 163, n. 3.

XXII

Last Days at Tahiti

IT WAS a four weeks' passage from Tonga to Tahiti, at first with north-easterly, later with more favouring winds: a passage broken by only one untoward incident and one new discovery. The untoward incident was a sudden heavy squall in the evening of 29 July, which blew two of Cook's staysails to pieces and did worse to the *Discovery*, carrying away her maintopmast and causing other damage— fortunately without making for much delay. The discovery, on 9 August, was that of the high island Tubuai, one of the Austral group, in latitude 23°25′ S, a fellow of Rurutu, encountered on the first voyage. The usual canoes approached the ships, without coming alongside. Cook saw no advantage in landing, altered his course to the north, and on the 12th made both the sign-post island Mehetia and Tahiti itself. He was not far from Vaitepiha Bay, but a series of baffling airs and squalls kept him from anchoring there until the next morning. Meanwhile he had his first visitors, learnt that two ships, which must have been Spanish, had called at the island twice since his last departure, and that Spaniards had lived there for almost a year; and had the spectacle before his eyes of Omai, the returning hero. This was much as Cook had foreseen. The hero was ignored until it was found he had red feathers with him. Then he became a dupe. He was not the only one who had red feathers: next morning at daybreak, before the ships had even moved into harbour, they were surrounded by a multitude of canoes and people, and 'not more feathers than might be got from a Tom tit would purchase a hog of 40 or 50 pound weight'.[1] Trade throve. At last anchors went down, Omai's sister came on board, and at last he was welcomed for his own sake. Cook at once began to inspect his provisions and set his caulkers to work; and went on shore.

He gathered the news. Purea was dead, as was the young Vehiatua whom he had known on the last voyage, succeeded by a boy his brother, not yet to be seen. Tu and his friends of the other end of the

[1] *Journals* III, 187.

island were all alive. He was equally interested in the Spaniards, the story of whom took some time to emerge, and did not emerge at all very clearly; but it was clear that they were from Lima, that their commander had died and been buried on shore, that they had returned two of the youths taken away before, had treated the people generously, had left behind them, and afterwards taken away again, three of their number, and had done a good deal of vaunting of their superiority to the British. Cook found a small house they had put up and a little furniture, and a cross, and some animals—goats and dogs and some fine large hogs 'of the Spanish breed'—and was told of cattle. Had all his trouble and anguish in bringing stock from England, then, been needless, irrelevant, as he had been thus preceded? It was a desolating thought. It was in due course relieved; the Spanish cattle turned out to be a solitary bull. The cross had carved upon it the words CHRISTUS VINCIT CAROLUS III IMPERAT 1774. This would not do, the glory of George III was at stake: he had cut on the other side the exclusively secular legend, GEORGIUS TERTIUS REX ANNIS 1767, 69, 73, 74 & 77. We can be clearer about this small piece of Spanish history than Cook could. The visits were at once an ineffectual assertion of sovereignty over Pacific islands and a singularly feeble attempt to convert the islanders; for the two Franciscans who formed the mission were but timorous servants of the Lord and scarcely left their house, while the ship's boy who looked after them, though he enjoyed his stay thoroughly, and wrote an excellent account of his experiences, was neither conqueror or apostle. There was nothing to do with the friars but remove them. A successful mission might possibly have compli-cated the situation for Cook, against whom the Spaniards had warned the people—rather belatedly, to be sure. Without such a thought, and noting the great plenty of coconuts, he went on board after this first expedition and called his crew together. He did what there is no record of his doing before or later, and took them into his confidence. It was another result of the winds and the lost season. He foresaw a shortage of grog in the cold northern climate if the men drank their spirits now. They could on the other hand drink from coconuts now, and save the spirits for future support in the quest for a north-west passage, with a cash reward—perhaps—at the end. They would not be entirely deprived: there would be the usual Saturday night's allowance 'to drink to their feemale friends in England, lest amongst the pretty girls of Otaheite they should be wholy forgotten.'[1] We can almost hear this speech. Clerke made the same proposal in the

1 *Journals* III, 189.

Discovery. The men could decide; and without hesitation they plumped for prudence.

It rained for two days. The people nevertheless flocked to the place with hogs and fruit in the hope of red feathers, Cook made the acquaintance of the young chief and exchanged names and presents with him; when the weather cleared set off some fireworks for the general delectation; and visited what his officers had taken for a Roman Catholic chapel, and turned out to be the decorated house where the embalmed corpse of the last Vehiatua was laid in state, a *fata tupapau,* an extremely *tapu* spot. He met other chiefs, and one or two oddities—a man who was said by Omai to be the god of Borabora, and did bear the god's name, Oro; another man said to be possessed of the spirit of an *atua,* or god, who squeaked, and was probably mad; but nothing occurred that could detain him long from what he considered to be the real centre of Tahitian life at Matavai Bay, and to that bay he steered on 23 August. He was to remain there till the end of September, and he could not complain of the quality of his refreshment.

Tu, whom he continued to regard as the 'king', was at Point Venus next morning, ready to receive presents, with a vast crowd of people. The returning hero knelt at his feet, embraced his legs, and handed over 'a large piece' of red feathers and a length of gold cloth—the sacred colours, red and yellow—and was ignored. Cook's gifts included a linen suit, a gold-laced hat and more red feathers, the principal item being one of the Tongan feather bonnets (for which Tu later made the return of ten large hogs). The whole royal family came on board to dinner, attended by a train of canoes loaded with provisions for the ships; then Cook went on shore to Tu's own district of Pare, to deposit Lord Bessborough's peacock and hen, with turkeys, geese and ducks, and saw the Spanish bull, a fine beast. The following day he relieved this animal's celibacy with three cows, but his own remaining bull, horse, mare and sheep he put ashore at Matavai; and 'now found my self lightened of a very heavy burden, the trouble and vexation that attended the bringing these Animals thus far is hardly to be conceived. But the satisfaction I felt in having been so fortunate as to fulfill His Majestys design in sending such useful Animals to two worthy Nations sufficiently recompenced me for the many anxious hours I had on their account.'[1] One hopes that was true, because he deserved recompense. Meanwhile the observatories and other tents were pitched at Point Venus, under the command of King, and old friends arrived in such numbers that it was difficult

1 ibid., 194.

to know what to do with all the provisions they brought. Meanwhile also there was a change in Omai's fortunes. Tales of his wealth spread quickly, and his friendship was courted by the great; but alas for Omai, he would associate with low fellows, who got from him articles that no chief could extract from anybody else on board; and if it had not been for Cook's intervention, within a few days he would have had little left. Cook still hoped a little: the young man, he seems to have thought, might make a respectable marriage and settle down under Tu's patronage as a sort of farm manager and instructor. This was not Omai's idea of the good life at all. True, at Vaitepiha he had had the sense to rescue a despised grapevine, planted by the Spaniards, from destruction, and had brought away slips; but this was with the ambition of making wine. As the days went by, he continued to fall from grace. It seemed to be a way with protégés: when Hiti-hiti—the charming youth 'Odiddy' of the second voyage, who had adventured in the *Resolution*—came to pay his respects he also was found to have gone rather to seed. Cook gave him some clothes the Admiralty had sent out for him, adding the more useful gift of a chest of tools: Omai took his wife to live with.

There were other things to do than to bestow gifts, tasks that kept seamen from gazing enraptured at too many 'libidinous' dances. The *Discovery*'s main mast, which had suffered in the squall in mid-ocean, was taken ashore and repaired, as were sails and water-casks; Cook had one of his vegetable gardens made and planted, though doubtful whether it would be looked after. Shaddock trees, however, seedlings from Tonga, were to flourish, as Nelson the gardener, who put them in, was to find when he revisited Tahiti with Bligh eleven years later. There was the usual wooding and watering and work about the ships. There was the first of several reports of Spanish ships at Vaitepiha, and this first one was so persuasive that Cook sent a boat to investigate, and at the same time put his own ships in a state of defence, not knowing whether England and Spain were then at peace or war. As all these fictions came from Taiarapu men, he concluded that they aimed at getting him away from Matavai—in which conclusion he was no doubt quite right; for other parts of the island might well think that Matavai, and Tu, were getting far more attention and profit from the visitors than were their due. Tu was not generally liked.

Indeed, it is difficult to find anybody who liked Tu. Cook certainly did not warm to him. Yet his position as an *ari'i rahi*, or high chief, gave him a leading importance, his participation in certain ceremonies was essential; and thus Cook was able to take advantage of his own importance as a familiar of the chief and witness one of the great Tahitian ceremonies, that of a human sacrifice. Cook's sight of the great war fleet drawn up in the bay in 1774 will be recollected, and its occasion, the quarrel between Mahine of Eimeo, or Moorea, and certain chiefs of Tahiti—a quarrel in which Tu was rather a laggard. The fleet had had no glorious victory, and now, three years later, the quarrel continued to smoulder, Tu still a laggard, and the chief whom Cook had then thought to be his admiral, Towha, or To'ofa, still an impatient and fiery leader. Cook had been anchored but a week at Matavai when news was brought of a fresh flare up when 'Otoos friends' on Moorea 'had been obliged to fly to the Mountains'. He was present at a long debate at Tu's house, when it was decided to despatch a strong avenging force—to which, he managed to make plain in his halting Tahitian, he could contribute no aid. Nor could the later eloquence of Tu's father convert him. To'ofa was absent from the meeting, but acting independently to ensure success, killed a man for sacrifice to Oro, the god of war, and sent to demand Tu's presence at that god's *marae* at Utuaimahurau on the southern coast of the island. Tu agreed that Cook should accompany him, and they set out immediately in Cook's pinnace with Anderson, Webber and Omai following in a canoe. On the way they called on To'ofa who was to be absent himself, but gave Tu some feathers and 'a lean half-starved dog' for additional sacrifice. When they arrived at the *marae*, on a small point of land, the seamen were confined to the boat, while Cook, Anderson and Webber had to doff their hats. Before them were many men, some boys, no women; priests, attendants, the great sacrificial drums and those who beat them; the bruised corpse trussed to a pole in a small canoe at the seas edge, some miserable man caught unawares and felled with a stone. The ceremony began at once, a long and complicated affair of prayers and invocations, the production of symbolical articles, the symbolical 'eating' of one of the victim's eyes by Tu, the offering to Oro of red feathers, some of the victim's hairs, the dog's entrails, the sounding of the drums. A kingfisher, the sacred bird, made a noise in the trees: 'It is the *atua*', the god, Tu told Cook. A hole was dug and the dead man buried in it. A boy called out shrilly to the *atua* to eat of the sacrificed dog. The day ended. The next morning there were further ceremonies: renewed offerings of red feathers; the sacrifice of a pig; the careful unwrapping of the 'royal' *maro* of red and yellow feathers fixed to *tapa* cloth and edged with black; the partial unwrapping of what Cook called the 'ark' of the *atua*, a bundle containing something he was not allowed to see, so sacred was it—a simple object of twisted and woven coconut fibre, representing the god—and its re-wrapping with the latest offerings of red feathers added.

To all these proceedings Cook was very attentive. His description of them stands beside that of the *inasi* as an unpretentious classic of anthropological observation.[1] Those sinister sacrificial drums, it might almost be said, throbbed round Europe, which found the paradisal island rather unpleasantly stained with blood. Nor had the eyes or the pencil of Webber been idle: he was to produce a picture that even more, in its way, became a classic, of Pacific illustration. That was for the future, but the first two days of September would remain in their minds. They went back to the ship, with Tu in company. They called again on To‘ofa. He had the morning before tried to enlist Cook as an ally, and been angered by refusal—the refusal of a professed friend to take part in his war! Now he tried again, and was even more angered by the same reply. Well, then: how did Cook like the ceremony he had just seen? Cook, having Omai to help him, did not hesitate to say that he disliked it extremely, and that the *atua* was much more likely to reward it with defeat than victory. This was not an entirely uncalculated answer; for he had noticed that in relation to these hostilities there were three parties, those in favour, those who strongly supported Mahine, and the third perfectly indifferent; and this being so, there was unlikely to be a satisfactory war effort. When Omai, entering into the spirit of the matter, explained that in England a chief guilty of having a man treated so would be hanged To‘ofa was outraged beyond endurance: '*Ma ino, ma ino*'—'Vile, vile'! he bawled (we have Cook's authority for the word), and the company broke up. To‘ofa seems to have been frequently an angry man.

The days passed, without great event involving Cook. There was some pilfering, but not beyond control, and Tu was instrumental in having stolen articles returned. He himself and other chiefs were sometimes victims, and applied to have boxes or chests made for them, with locks, on the model of a few which the Spaniards had left, to keep their valuables safe, and Cook was glad enough to oblige them. Presents of food-stuffs continued, and there were large presents of fine cloth, wrapped ornamentally in the native manner round handsome girls, who were then led on board. Some of the dishes drew forth Cook's admiration: in the course of his life he ate so much that could be recommended as food only because it was

[1] *Journals* III, 199–204; and for Anderson's account, 978–84.

fresh that it is pleasant to find him as gourmet. On the first voyage he had spoken highly of baked Tahitian dog; in these weeks he describes with a sort of affection the whole making of a quite elaborate pudding or *poe*, and adds, 'Some of these puddings are excellent, we can make few in England that equals them, I seldom or never dined without one when I could get it, for they were not always to be got.'[1] Omai entertained royal and naval guests at a dinner-party. Omai dressed up in his suit of armour. Tu's sisters appeared elegantly as actresses in a play. Fireworks caused both delight and alarm. When Cook and Clerke took to riding the horses about the flat ground at Matavai there was general astonishment and pleasure; for though Omai had tried thus to exhibit his skill he had always fallen off. Horses, and this use made of them, says Cook, 'I think . . . gave them a better idea of the greatness of other Nations than all the other things put together that had been carried amongst them.'[2] Cook handed over the remaining stock, a ram and ewes. He inspected another embalmed chiefly corpse. The young New Zealanders enjoyed themselves hugely.

Argument continued about the war. Cook would have attended a second human sacrifice with Tu if he had heard about it in time; the unenthusiastic Tu refused to provide a victim himself for a third. To'ofa, in a burst of impatience, with one or two equally belligerent friends, took a fleet over to Moorea, got into difficulties, and bombarded Tu with demands for assistance—which, though the bay was full of his war canoes, he still withheld. At least he was obliging enough to detach two of these canoes, himself and Cook in one of them, and demonstrate for Cook's information the tactics of a sea-fight. Then, just as Cook found all his work on the ships done, had loaded the observatories and instruments and bent the sails—it was the end of the third week of September—and was fixing a day for departure; at the very moment, indeed, when, that settled, he was stepping into his boat to watch a great review at Pare of Tu's fleet, the news arrived that To'ofa, lacking the help of this fleet, had been forced to make a truce, upon poor terms. The review was cancelled. Controversy and rumour grew excited. It was all Tu's fault. No, argued Tu's father: had not Cook agreed to transport Tu and his whole family to Moorea at the very same time as the fleet went? To'ofa was to blame. To'ofa and Vehiatua, it was said, would join in falling upon Tu in vengeance. Cook thought he, Tu's friend, might go so far as to threaten that in that case he would take vengeance himself on all implicated, when he returned to the island;

[1] *Journals* III, 207.   [2] ibid., 209.

and as a peace-making move this flight of imagination was perhaps justified.

Friendship was evident in another direction. A message came for Tu to be present yet again, next day, at Utuaimahurau, this time for a peace-making ceremony, and Cook was invited. He could not go, he was 'much out of order', but would send King and Omai instead. With him on his return to the ship went Tu's mother and three sisters, and eight other women, who announced their intention of staying all night and curing his disorder, some sort of severe rheumatism on one side. They fell on him simultaneously, as many as could get at him, with the massage called *rumi*, squeezing him 'with both hands from head to foot, but more especially the parts where the pain was, till they made my bones crack and a perfect Mummy of my flesh—in short after being under their hands about a quarter of an hour I was glad to get away from them.'[1] But it gave him relief, and after three more of these assaults he was cured. A day later the party returned from the peace negotiations, or celebrations, the account of which given by King proved that he was an observer not unworthy of Cook.

Although Cook felt he should go, he was still rather reluctant. For the main purpose of his voyage he had time in hand; there were still such quantities of provisions coming forward in this season that he did not need to go to other islands for them, and by now he understood the system of bartering 'presents' so well as to make it a mode of reasonably fair exchange; the trickster's side of Tu, his meanness (he levied toll every morning on the girls coming away from the ships or the tents) did not annul his utility as a chief of power. The complicating factor was Omai. He had to be deposited at some place which would offer him and the two boys the prospect of a tolerable life; he had rejected Tahiti and certainly the people there had had enough of him, unless they could have got hold of his remaining treasures, on which Cook had kept a strict eye. The only profitable exchange he had made himself was with To'ofa, a handful of red feathers for a fine double sailing canoe, round which he hung as many flags and pendants and streamers as he could summon up. Cook also could have taken away a canoe, if there had been any way conveying it, a sixteen-foot well-carved *va'a*—not a war canoe—which Tu wanted to give to the monarch of Britain, as the only thing he could send worth His Majesty's acceptance. It was true that His Majesty had been generous to him; Cook was none the less highly pleased. Tu gave Cook a list of the presents he wished the *ari'i rahi no*

Pretane to send him next time. Cook got from Tu four goats, two for Raiatea, which had none, and two for any other island he might meet with on his passage to the north. Cook had Webber paint his portrait, and gave it to Tu, perhaps as a parting gift. He does not mention this himself, but we know it was done; for it was recognised in later years by visiting seamen, some of whom had sailed on this voyage.[1] We should like to see it too, though Webber's portraits of Cook are not ingratiating. It had its adventures, was for a while snatched away by To'ofa and Mahine, who in the mutabilities of politics had joined forces as enemies of Tu; sank out of sight and no doubt has long since rotted away.

Light westerly breezes and calms detained the ships in the bay a few days longer. At length in the afternoon of 29 September an easterly sprang up, Matavai Bay was saluted with seven guns, Cook obliged Tu with a short run out to sea, and then bore away for Moorea.

One may find it rather odd, as Cook did himself, that he had not before visited this high island, so close to Tahiti and from it visually so striking. He had been told that there were no harbours, which could have been easily enough verified: in fact there were on the north side two excellent harbours, easily accessible through the reef, and others on the eastern coast. One wishes, now that he did pay his visit, that the episode had not happened; for it left him with regrets. It leaves the reader of his journal both regretful and baffled, as at some odd unintelligible phenomenon.

The canoe-borne Omai had preceded him, and marked his way through the reef. He entered Mahine's harbour, the more western of the two, and sailing right up to its head, anchored so close to the shore that he could moor the ships to the hibiscus trees, with the pure water of several rivulets flowing into the bay near by. He looked on this place with a severely practical eye, as 'not inferior to any harbour I have met with in any of the islands' for security 'and the goodness of its bottom'—which hardly conveys an idea of the immensity of the backdrop to the calm sheet of water; for in this dead volcano

---

[1] Bligh saw it in 1788. 'Captn. Cooks Picture which was left by him in 1777 and drawn by Mr Webber was brought to me, With a request to repair it. They said it came from Otoo, that it was Toote Errie no Otaheite. They said Toote told Otoo when he gave it him, that when his son came out he must show it him, and they would always be good Friends. Excepting a little of the background [of] the Picture being eat off, it was not at all defaced. The frame wanted a little repair and as all came within my abilities I assured them it should be done and they left it.'—*Log of the Bounty*, I, 372–3. Cook's midshipman John Watts, when lieutenant in the *Lady Penrhyn*, homeward bound from Botany Bay, also revisited Tahiti in 1788, before Bligh, and had seen the picture.—Phillip, *Voyage to Botany Bay* (1789), 233–4.

strange peaks and buttresses, fire-blasted walls of rock, reach into the sky as if here the world had blown up, and the world's greenness were forever to fall back defeated. But below the heights the green grows thick enough, peaks sink into slopes, the curve of the bay reaches gently to the outer lagoon. It was the bay of Opunohu. Cook called it 'Taloo', getting the name from that of a rock, Tareu, near its mouth; it has acquired the later name of Papetoai; Webber did his best with it in terms of wild romance.[1] The ships were here for ten days. A sort of landing stage was set up, in the hope that some of the *Resolution*'s too many rats would take advantage of it. Hogs, bread-fruit and coconuts were plentiful. The *purau*, or hibiscus, made good firewood, and they loaded up with it. The islanders set no value on it, and no wood had been obtained at Tahiti: 'the geting it at that island is attended with some difficulty, as there is not a tree at Matavai but what is usefull to the Inhabitants.'[2] The humane man speaks.

This was the bay where To'ofa had so recently brought his fleet, and it carried the obvious signs of invasion. There was a suspicion on shore, not unnaturally, that Cook, the friend of Tahitian chiefs, might have come in their support. On the second day only did Mahine, rather hesitantly, visit the captain—a middle-aged chief with what was most unusual in the islands, a bald head, covered by a sort of turban. Was this because the story of shaven heads as a punishment for thieves had spread? Cook noticed that those of his officers who were short of hair had doubtful glances directed at them. In the obligatory, though not extravagant, exchange of presents Mahine got a morning gown, printed all over with large flowers, for which he returned a hog. Amity, Cook thought, was sealed. For a few days all was peace and goodwill, and he put his remaining goats ashore to graze, bringing them off again at night. Mahine asked for two of them. This Cook's plans for the other islands did not allow, but he sent Tu a request, accompanied by still more red feathers, to oblige Mahine with a pair. The fatal 6 October came. A man who shared the charge of the animals took something by force from a native; the native in simple revenge filched a young goat. It had been taken to Mahine, so the story went; Cook chose to fasten the responsibility on him, and next morning sent him a threatening message, demanding both the goat and the criminal. He also put the goats on shore again, and in the evening another was skilfully

---

[1] The neighbouring bay Paopao has no right to the name Cook's Bay which has been given to it.
[2] *Journals* III, 232.

snatched away, as the first was being returned. The thief, coming voluntarily with it, and explaining the circumstances was rather surprised to find himself in irons, though he was later released. Cook, now convinced of Mahine's turpitude, was determined to have this second goat back. He began, acting on information that was dubiously correct, by sending two midshipmen to the other side of the island to claim it. That was Wednesday the 8th. They returned at nightfall without it. Cook was afflicted by a mixture of feelings, of the sort that brings satisfaction to no one. 'I was now very sorry I had proceeded so far, as I could not retreat with any tolerable credet, and without giving incouragement to the people of the other islands we had yet to visit to rob us with impunity.'[1] He applied to Omai (a measure of his desperation) and some elders who had already advised him for suggestions on what to do next; 'they without hesitation, advised me to go with a party of men into the Country, and shoot every Soul I met with.'[2]

'This bloody advice', says Cook, 'I could not follow', but he behaved as if a cold rage had taken possession of him. On Thursday the 9th he marched a strong party right over the island, a hot and wearing journey, burning houses and war-canoes, and being met on the other side by Williamson with three armed boats; on Friday the 10th he warned Mahine by messenger that if the goat were not delivered up he would not leave a canoe on the island, and broke up three or four on the beach at once, taking the timber to build a house for Omai. Then he went to the neighbouring harbour of Paopao and burnt or broke up twice as many, as well as houses. Omai and the sailors took an enthusiastic part in the destruction, and plundered with joy. When he got back to Opunohu in the evening the goat was there. 'Thus the troublesome, and rather unfortunate affair ended, which could not be more regreted on the part of the Natives than it was on mine.'[3] No doubt this was his conclusion; but some of his men, as at Tonga, were troubled. Why had he not taken a chief as a hostage? Why should this people, having suffered from To'ofa, suffer also from them? Canoes were laboriously built. Clerke summed up the case for destruction: 'every social attention . . . the Devil put it in their Heads, to fall in Love with the Goats . . . strange perverseness . . . foolish and unaccountable.'[4] The sorrowful King was candid on the other side.

1 ibid., 229. 2 ibid. 3 ibid., 231–2.
4 More at length—' . . . these good people, whose ridiculous conduct in stealing those Goats, and most absurd obstinacy in keeping them, has brought upon them such damages, inflicted as retaliation and punishment, as they will not recover from these many months to come; but it was wholly their own seeking; we sollicited their friendship at our arrival

Not being able to account for Cap^n Cooks precipitate proceeding in this business, I cannot think it justifiable; less destructive measures might have been adopted & the end gain'd, whether it was simply to get what was of little value or Consequence back again or in future to deter them from thefts; I doubt whether our Ideas of propriety in punishing so many innocent people for the crimes of a few, will be ever reconcileable to any principle one can form of justice.[1]

Next morning friendship seemed to be restored, to judge from the amount of fruit brought early to barter. We may doubt its reality: 'in future they may fear, but never love us', King had added. But there was not time for proof. Cook had been delayed three days beyond his intention. That same morning he put out for Huahine.

It was but a twenty-four hours' passage to Fare harbour. This did not give time enough for Cook's passion to die down entirely. We have King again: 'Just before we got in the harbour, an indian we had brought from Eimaio had been caught with something he had stolen, on which the Captain in a Passion ordered the Barber to shave his head & cut off his ears.'[2] The barber having finished the head was about to start on the ears when an officer standing by (one thinks of King himself) convinced that the rage would have passed, sent him to have his orders confirmed, and the man was made to swim ashore with the loss of only one lobe. But this did not mean a permanent return to gentleness, as will be seen; and the passengers from Moorea—mainly Tahitian women determined to cling to their sailor friends until the last possible moment—creating by their heightened stories of the destruction there a great effect on the people who crowded the ships, may have helped to persuade the captain that he had done well. Apart from his friend the old chief Ori, he was not fond of the anarchic robbers of Huahine; perhaps they would now behave a little better than they had done in the past. It was important that they should do so; for he had determined that if he could make suitable arrangements, he must deposit Omai here. Omai, he thought, had become more prudent since his self-induced misfortunes at Tahiti, but not so prudent that, with his announced ambitions, it would be safe to leave him on his home island of Raiatea.

---

by every social attention, and were upon the best of Terms, till the Devil put it in their Heads, to fall in Love with the Goats: when they had taken these, every gentle method was tryed to recover them, and the consequences of their obstinacy, very clearly and repeatedly explained to them, before any destructive Step was taken; but their strange perverseness in this Business, is I think equally foolish and unaccountable.'—*Journals* III, 232, n. 1.

[1] *Journals* III, 1383.

[2] ibid. Bayly noted (13 October) Cook 'a little indisposed at present'. ibid., 233, n. 4.

28. The Fourth Earl Sandwich, by Thomas Gainsborough

33. Cook in Queen Charlotte Sound, New Zealand
Water-colour drawing by Webber

34. A Tongan Dance
Drawing by Webber

35. 'A Human Sacrifice, in a Morai, in Otaheite'
Drawing by Webber

His father's land was occupied by Borabora people who, Cook thought would be willing to leave amicably. Ignoble, thought Omai: he preferred to arrive as a patriot and a conqueror, and drive all Borabora usurpers off by force of musket, pistol and his suit of armour. There were many, even in Huahine, who looked forward to this entertainment, for the depredations of the Borabora men had not made them loved. Cook would have none of it. Omai's duty, in spite of his armament, was to cultivate the arts of peace; or, if he could cultivate no art, at least to be peaceful.

Although Ori the old chief had been deprived of power and was now at Raiatea the arrival of the ships had brought all the principal people together, and they were more important for Cook's purpose than the new titular *ari'i rahi* of the island, a boy eight or ten years old. After the ceremonies, usual at Huahine, of presentations to the gods as well as the chief, made as impressive by Omai as possible, Cook came at once to the point. He wanted properly conducted relations, he wanted them to make over a piece of land for Omai's settlement, failing which Cook would carry him on to Raiatea, but he would neither aid nor permit any action against the Borabora people. A spokesman rose up and announced with magnificent hyperbole that the whole island and everything in it was Cook's: let him give Omai what he liked. Omai was delighted. Cook preferred something less expansive, and finally a piece of land on the shore of the harbour, something over two hundred yards square, was settled on, at the exchange rate of fifteen axes, with beads and other trifles. In the next few days the ships' carpenters were set to putting up a house, while other hands planted shaddocks, the rescued vines from Tahiti, pine-apples, melons and other desirable vegetables, and nearby Cook established his observatories and trading post. The house was built with as few nails as possible, as a precaution against its being pulled down for their sake; and Cook, thinking of the belongings he had preserved for Omai, and the envy they would bring him, advised him to cultivate some of the most important chiefs by sharing a part of them out as an insurance premium; adding a statement for general consumption that when in due course he came back there would certainly be weighty resentment shown if Omai were worse off. Omai was sensible enough to take his advice; sensible enough also to trade back to the ships a number of the articles for which neither he nor the otherwise rapturously gazing multitude had a use. He kept the barrel organ and the compass and the toys, but as for the wares of British domesticity—he 'now found that a baked hog eat better than a boiled one, that a plantain leafe made as good a dish or plate as pewter and that a Cocoanut shell was as good to drink out of as a black-jack'; and he went for hatchets.

Omai was concerned in another matter, which proved troublesome. More than a week went by before anything appreciable was stolen—a week in which, apart from building and planting, the only notable event was a tremendous but unavailing onslaught on the *Resolution*'s cockroaches—and then on the evening of the 22nd a sextant was taken from Bayly's observatory. A dramatic performance was in progress: Cook put a stop to it and again threatened punishment worse than that at Moorea if both sextant and thief were not delivered up. The criminal, pointed out sitting calmly in the audience denied the crime; Omai flourished a sword and said he would run him through; the chiefs all fled; Cook, a little in doubt, sent the man on board the ship and put him in irons. Omai, by threats and promises wormed a confession out of him, and in the morning the sextant was found unharmed where he had hidden it. He appeared to be 'a hardened Scounderal', says Cook; 'I punished him with greater severity than I had ever done any one before and then dismiss'd him.'[1] That is, this time the man was both shaved and lost his ears. He was not deterred from thoughts of revenge; next night he fell on Omai's garden and destroyed vines and cabbages, following this up with a public promise to kill the owner and burn his house as soon as the ships were gone. Omai may well have been perturbed; for the man was from Borabora and had followers. Cook seized him and put him in irons again, with a view to deporting him from the island, at which the Huahine people were not displeased. Others expected to see him shot. In the early morning of the 30th the sentry standing over him, and the whole watch on the quarterdeck, went to sleep, and he escaped clean away. Cook concluded that he had been able to reach the binnacle drawer, where the key of the irons was kept, and release himself; and Cook was undoubtedly in a fury. Harvey, the mate of the watch, veteran of both the previous voyages, was disrated to midshipman and sent on board the *Discovery* out of his sight; Mackay the midshipman turned before the mast; Morris the marine, the sentry, given a dozen strokes of the lash on three successive days.

By the end of the month Omai was installed in his new house, and again giving dinner parties to the officers, who were quite willing to help him 'drink his wine out.' Besides his New Zealanders he had accumulated retainers at Tahiti and Huahine, so he would not lack for company; and Cook, getting all the ships' belongings on board,

---

[1] *Journals* III, 236.

left with him the horse and mare, a goat and an English boar and sows, as well as some powder and shot for his firearms. This made him happy, though Cook was not happy to see him with firearms at all. A method was devised by which, through sending coloured beads to the ships at Raiatea, he could signify whether his affairs went well or not. One object of the voyage had been accomplished. An inscription was cut on one end of the house recording the ships' visit. On the afternoon of 2 November they sailed with an easterly breeze. Cook conscientiously searched for the best he could say of Omai, as he recorded this last day. 'Whatever faults this Indian had they were more than over ballanced by his great good Nature and docile disposition, during the whole time he was with me I very seldom had reason to find fault with his conduct. His gratifull heart always retained the highest sence of the favours he received in England nor will he ever forget those who honoured him with their protection and friendship during his stay there. He had a tolerable share of understanding. . . . He was not a man of much observation. . . .'[1] He wanted to preserve his glory of being a great traveller; 'he frequently put me in mind that Lord Sandwich told him no more were to come.' Indeed Cook wanted no more visitors from the islands, though if he had been able to see the least chance of a ship going out to New Zealand he would gladly have taken the two boys, who both wished for it. The older, obviously a youth of parts, mild, friendly and dignified, accepted his fate with philosophical grief; the younger, that witty jackanapes and general favourite, had to be parted from the ship by force. As for Omai, he went round both ships bidding farewell—a 'very Afecting Scean', wrote Bayly; for after all he was a friend, manly sorrow did not scorn to weep, it was a weeping age. Omai, though a participant, maintained a measure of sobriety until he came to Cook, when his tears quite overmastered him. The ship was outside the reef before he left her.

Cook wanted to make a last call at Raiatea. He rounded its southern end as usual and was soon off his old harbour at Haamanino, at the northern end of the west coast. The wind blew right out of the entrance, as it always did for him, and it took the whole after-noon of 3 November to warp the ships in. While still anchored off the entrance he was visited by the chief Orio, accompanied by his young son and his son-in-law, husband of the beautiful and well-remembered 'princess', Poetua; and as soon as the ships were inside, there was the usual circle of canoes filled with people, hogs and

1 ibid., 240-1.

fruit, the promise of endless plenty. How long he expected to stay at this island we do not know, but he was to be there a full month and over, a period which could have been extremely pleasant had it not been cluttered up with two periods of desertion; and desertions always gave trouble which could be well done without. He began by repeating the rat operation he had tried at Moorea, mooring the ship head and stern close to the harbour shore on the north side and building a stage, while Clerke did the same opposite. Orio and his family, male and female, were entertained. Not merely did the chief take away presents, but the ladies rejoiced in red feathers, handkerchiefs, gauze, ribbands and beads. The instruments and observatories went on shore and a long series of observations were put in hand by Cook, Bayly and King. Two of Omai's people arrived bearing beads which signified that all was well with him, except that his goat had died in kidding, and he wanted two more, and two more axes. They were sent him. The hardened scoundrel from Huahine, Omai's enemy, turned up casually, announcing that all was now well between them, and pointed out one of the 'young gentlemen' who, he said, had released him from his irons on the night of his escape; the unfortunate sentry may have been too precipitately lashed. We do not know if this arrived at Cook's ears; he preferred to ignore the man. Ori the old friend more than once paid a call, with a train of followers though now 'a private gentleman' only and not a reigning chief. And, we learn from Samwell, 'great Numbers of fine Girls came on board.'

Fine girls on board were not, it seems, enough. Another sentry got into trouble. Just before midnight between the 12th and 13th, the time of his relief, John Harrison, marine, of the *Resolution*, vanished from his post at the observatories and took his arms with him. When morning came Cook got news which way he had gone and sent a party after him, unsuccessfully. The following morning Orio was asked, and promised, to apprehend him; but did not. That day some thefts were committed, and most of the people, including Orio, fled in fear of reprisals. This was the time, thought Cook, to insist on the delivery of the deserter and the following morning himself set off with two armed boats and a native guide for the other side of the island, where he heard that Harrison had taken refuge. He picked up Orio on the way, and leaving the boats, 'marched briskly' up to surprise the stronghold. Needless: the only person surprised was poor Harrison, at his ease in a native house in native dress between two women. It is possible that Cook did not find this little excursion unpleasant; for he uses calm language. The two women rose up to plead for their friend; 'but as it was necessary to descourage such proceedings, I frown'd upon them and bid them begone, at which they burst into tears and walked off.'[1] The peace offering of the local chief was equally abruptly rejected, the captain immediately returned with his prisoner, and 'harmony was again restored.' Harrison, a simple person, explained himself to Cook, and at greater length to others. His particular trouble was, put briefly, 'the engaging females'.[2] It will be recollected that Cook, though he would not tolerate desertion, was not altogether unsympathetic to deserters; and this time, considering that the man had stayed at his post almost until relieved, he inflicted only a moderate punishment.

Not every sailor was moved purely by female blandishments. The idyllic life had other aspects, and there were many invitations quite pressing. There must, after so many weeks in the islands, have been a great deal of talk—of what Alexander Home called 'the spirit of Desertion'. Cook felt it necessary to harangue his crew again. We have more than one witness to this occasion: perhaps the best is the admiring, slightly incoherent Home.

Upon the discovery of this spirit of desertion Captain Cook Turned his men up and Made a Long speech on that head. He Made use both of Entreateys and Threats and with a Deal of Art and Eloquence, for he could speak much to the purpose but this was but one of the Smallest Ackomplishments of that Excellent man. Amoungst Other things he told them they Might run off if they pleased. But they might Depend upon it he would Recover them again: that in Such a Case he had Nothing to do but to seize their Chiefs and although they Might like them very well to stay Amoungst them yet he knew for certain that they liked their Cheifs far better and Indeed with such a degree of partiality that they would Not give A Cheif for A Hundred of us, and they all Must know that his Authority over these Isles was so great that Never Man had a people More under his Command or At his Devotion. They Might fly if they pleased to Omiah King Ottou or to the Most distant Country known to these people. His authority would bring them back and Dead or Alive he'd have them.[3]

These arguments, hard upon the example of John Harrison, seemed unassailable. 'Every man was Convinced and how so ever great Our inclination Might be to taste of these Joys and Bliss that seemed More than Mortal all hopes was now given over.' All hopes in the *Resolution*, perhaps; but not in the *Discovery*, where Clerke had made no tremendous speech. On the night of the 23rd Alexander Mouat,

[1] *Journals* III, 244.
[2] The phrase is that of William Griffin, the *Resolution*'s cooper.—ibid., 247, n. 1, in which note are quoted other tributes.
[3] ibid., cxiii, from the MS in the National Library of Australia, Canberra.

a romantic midshipman aged 16, and Thomas Shaw the gunner's mate went off in a canoe with a Tahitian, taking some provisions and a pistol; their idea seems to have been to get round the north of Raiatea to Huahine, the seat of Mouat's love, or even to Tahiti.

Mouat was the son of Captain Mouat of the navy, who had commanded one of Byron's ships, and to Cook's determination to recover a deserter were added both a wish to stop a young man, however foolish, from blasting his life and a sense of duty to a brother officer. Clerke, although ill, first went fruitlessly with two armed boats and a party of marines to the northern part of the island. Cook then took on the chase, having been told the two had moved to Tahaa, the island a mile or two north of Raiatea, and within the same reef. His expedition also was fruitless; they had fled to Borabora. It was now the 25th. Next morning Orio, his son, daughter and son-in-law came on board the *Resolution*. Cook passed word to Clerke, who was also there, to invite the young people on board his ship and make them hostages, and Orio was invited to secure their release by reclaiming the deserters. He was not, thought Cook, who suspected him of general enticement, being unduly put upon in thus being made responsible; and he did immediately despatch a canoe to Puni, the great chief of Borabora, with the request to seize the men, wherever they were, and send them back. To keep track of everybody else, the ships' companies were mustered morning and evening. Meanwhile a different drama had begun to centre on the *Discovery*. Poetua of the conquering charms, her husband and her brother were all three particular friends of Clerke, and in no fear for their safety settled down comfortably in the great cabin with a sentry at the door; but outside the forces of formal distress were released. It is imperative to use the words of Clerke.

The News of their Confinement of course was blaz'd instantaneously throughout the Isle; old Oreo was half mad, and within an hour afterwards we had a most numerous Congregation of Women under the Stern, cutting their Heads with Sharks Teeth and lamenting the Fate of the Prisoners, in so melancholy a howl, as render'd the Ship whilst it lasted, which was 2 or 3 Hours, a most wretched Habitation; nobody cou'd help in some measure being affected by it; it destroyed the spirits of the Prisoners altogether, who lost all their Chearfullness and joined in this cursed dismal Howl, I made use of every method I cou'd suggest to get them away, but all to no purpose, there they wou'd stand and bleed and cry, till their Strength was exhausted, and they cou'd act the farce no longer. When we got rid of these Tragedians, I soon recover'd my Friends and we set down to Dinner together very chearfully.[1]

[1] *Journals* III, 1318.

Thereafter half a dozen old women came daily with 'a little serenade', but the main action was on shore, and principally on this first day.

If one could plot, thought Orio, another could counter-plot; hostages could be taken on both sides. He knew that Cook went unarmed every evening to bathe in fresh water, and that Clerke was then generally taking a walk. But Cook this day decided not to bathe, although invited to repeatedly by Orio; and Clerke, walking with Gore, was playing visibly, though idly, with a pistol, and even shot at a tree. The ambush retired. Suddenly the people about the harbour and in the canoes began to move off, on the assumption that somebody had been seized and there would be vengeance; while a Huahine girl, the mistress of an officer, 'a Fat Jolly good Natured girl' who had heard of the plot and disliked fighting, had warned the *Discovery*. Those on board called out to Cook on shore: he instantly sent an armed party to rescue Clerke and Gore, and ordered the boats to cut off fleeing canoes from leaving the bay.[1] Within a few minutes the news that the tables had been thus turned was contradicted, the armed party and the boats were recalled, and the surprised and unsuspecting gentlemen returned from their walk. Orio then took seriously the return of the fugitives, and, a little alarmed at the delay, set out for Borabora himself. They had fled even further than that island, to the islet of Tupai, about seven miles north-west of it, where Puni's men had seized them. Orio returned with them on the 30th. Clerke gave Shaw two dozen lashes as soon as he came on board, sent Mouat before the mast, and put them both in irons for the time the ship should remain in harbour. Shaw was released earlier and excused from further punishment on the petition of his shipmates, who promised immaculate behaviour in return. The three hostages were presented to their rejoicing friends. There were threats that the Huahine girl would be killed; her friends therefore removed her from the ship one night and hid her until she could be sent back to her own island. The episode was over, after giving Cook, so he said, more trouble and vexation than the men were

[1] We hear of another prospective desertion from Samwell.—'It is something remarkable that at this time another of the Discovery's People was on the point of deserting and had just embarked in a Canoe for that purpose, when hearing our Boats firing after the Canoes which were paddling out of the Bay & seeing them pull after them immediately concluded they were in pursuit of him, & therefore paddled ashore as fast as he could where joining those people who were going to Captⁿ Clerke's Assistance, he went on board the Ship again withᵗ being in the least suspected of the Design he had just been attempting to put in Execution, & it was not till some time after that he informed his Shipmates of it.' A few days later Samwell himself and a friend, bathing alongside their vessel, took it into their heads to swim ashore, where they informed the people they had deserted, but received scant sympathy and were told to go back again.—ibid., 1077, 1078.

worth. Orio might have been inclined to say the same thing for himself. Clerke and his guests remained on the warmest terms of friendship.

The ships had already been moved from their moorings, and there was nothing but the wind to keep them longer in harbour. Hulls, masts, yards, rigging, sails had all been overhauled. The lamenting women—'our Otaheite sweethearts'[1]—were all sent away, loaded with their lovers' gifts. The last presents had been given—the goats saved from Moorea, an English boar and sow to improve the native breed (before long the native breed all through the islands was improved out of existence). Never had a crew been better fed for weeks on end: until the last day the hogs and plantains came tumbling in—indeed so many hogs were here obtained that quantities had to be salted down. The ships' bread had already been picked over and the rotten part destroyed at Tahiti and Huahine. What could be done to drive away the vermin had been done. No complaints are extant on the deprivation of grog. Both ships' companies were not only well-fed but healthy, except for the wretched gonorrhea they had given and acquired from Tahiti, and a little 'yellow jaundice' which is hard to account for.[2] There were two other exceptions to the clean bill of health, and in neither did the sensual island joys play a part: they were the doomed men Anderson and Clerke. Clerke's uncertainty of health was obvious; Anderson could tell very well what was wrong with him, and Anderson had no illusion about himself. We have a story, which there is no reason to disbelieve, from Burney, who had it from Anderson. At Tahiti, records Burney,

Anderson represented to Captain Clerke their inability to encounter the severities of a frozen climate, and they mutually agreed to ask leave of Captain Cook to resign their situations, that they might remain where they were, and trust themselves to the care of the natives, as the only hope left them of being restored to health. When the time approached for the ships to sail, Captain Clerke's papers and accounts were not in order; and as we were next bound to *Huaheine*, one of the *Society Islands*, it might answer their purpose as well to quit the ship there as at *Otaheite*. At *Huaheine*, the same thing happened, and the execution of their plan was deferred to our going to *Ulietea*, the next island. At *Ulietea*, the ships remained above a month; but that time did not suffice Captain Clerke for the settlement of his accounts. As Captain Cook proposed to stop at *Bolabola*, the last of

---

[1] The phrase is Samwell's.—ibid., 1078.

[2] Nor, probably, did it last long. The information comes from Bayly, 13 October, just after they had arrived at Huahine: 'Omi is very ill at present & Capt Cook is a little indisposed at present . . . We have ½ of our people ill with the fowl disease & 4 or 5 has had the Yellow jaundice.'—ibid., 233, n. 4. Nobody else mentions Omai's illness, and the nature of Cook's indisposition is undefined.

the *Society Islands*, Mr. Anderson consented to the postponement of their intention to our arrival at that place; and there I believe Captain Clerke, if the opportunity had not failed, would have really landed and settled.[1]

This is not a story of mutiny. Anderson, not yet thirty, able and clear-sighted, might well have thought the chance of life and scientific work in the islands worth taking; Clerke might well have been moved by the arguments of so rational a man. Then why, in all those weeks, could Clerke not get his papers and accounts into order? The task could not have been so formidable; Gore, who would have succeeded him, would have had no difficulty in understanding them, and would have made an adequate commander of the *Discovery*. It is improbable, one feels, that Clerke was really willing to leave his ship: probable from what we know of him, that what he failed to master was not his accounts but his sense of duty and his loyalty to his own commander.

It is true that Cook intended to stay a day or two at Borabora, previously unvisited by him. He had heard that the chief Puni had one of the anchors lost by Bougainville at Hitiaa in Tahiti in 1768. This he hoped to acquire, not for use as an anchor, but as old iron which could be converted by the armourer into hatchets and other articles of trade. When, therefore, after a week of waiting, on 7 December a light north-easterly breeze at last sprang up, he set all the boats to towing and, once outside the harbour, steered for Borabora, high-peaked, steep and craggy.

He gave Orio and half-a-dozen other Ruiatcans a passage with him, most of them sorry they were not getting a passage to England. He tacked all night off the south end of Borabora, with its reef and breaking sea; and in the early morning the wind fell scant, so that, short as the passage was in miles, the day had well begun before he was off the harbour of Teavanui, on the western side. It is a good, deep, and sheltered harbour, but tide as well as wind were against him. After some trial, he abandoned the idea of taking the ships in, and rowed in with the boats. Puni that great man was waiting on the beach in the midst of a large crowd. Cook, after paying his respects, came straight to the point; for, as he was not staying, he thought he had not time to lose. Borabora had been outside the lines of trade, and the variety of presents he set out produced a sensation; Puni positively refused to accept them until Cook had seen what he was getting in return. It was certainly only a portion of an anchor; nevertheless it was a lump of iron and he was glad to have it, and

[1] Burney, *Chronological History of North-Eastern Voyages of Discovery* (London, 1819), 233–4.

going for it himself where it lay, he sent Puni the whole intended gift and returned at once on board. Having heard from young Mouat that a Spanish ram had somehow got to the island he put on shore also a ewe from the Cape of Good Hope, hoisted in the boats, and at once made sail to the north. So brief was the visit that we are left with no impression of Puni, the redoubtable conqueror, or his island. Neither Clerke nor Anderson landed; nor is it likely that Clerke, if he had not settled his accounts by the time he sailed from Raiatea, would have done so by the time he reached Borabora. He had his rendezvous on the coast of New Albion.

It may be that Cook was struck with a sudden impatience. He had lost a season, but he was early with the new season, and he would waste none of it. His men were refreshed. There was a great amount of ocean still to be crossed, and beyond it waited the coast of America. It may even be that as he gave the order to steer north, he had the sense of relief. That was not the sense that attended the generality of the ships' companies, if George Gilbert spoke truly for them: 'We left these Islands with the greatest regret, immaginable; as supposing all the pleasures of the voyage to be now at an end: Having nothing to expect in future but excess of cold, Hunger, and every kind of hardship, and distress . . . the Idea of which render'd us quite dejected.'[1] There were pleasures yet stored up; but it was true, there were also miseries.

[1] *Journals* III, 256, n. 1.

XXIII

To New Albion

THE SENSE of relief: perhaps it was also with a sense of release that Cook made north, the islands behind him. He had desperately wanted to reach them, but they had ceased to be an objective; had become, in fact, a sort of entanglement; and now, seventeen months out of Plymouth, with the run to New Albion ahead of him, and nothing as far as he knew in the way, he may at last have felt that the prospect was fair, that he was about to grapple with the real purpose of the voyage. He had enquired of his late hosts if they knew of any islands to the north or north-west: they did not. Nor had the Spanish galleons, passing and repassing the ocean between Acapulco and Manila for two hundred years, ever reported land in the middle of it. A vacant and wintry ocean, then, Cook expected, as he advanced into the northern hemisphere, a passage 'of considerable length both in distance and time', a part of which 'must be performed in the very depth of Winter when gales of Wind and bad Weather must be expected and may possibly occasion a Seperation'; so he wrote in giving Clerke his rendezvous. His own instructions were to be on the American coast, at latitude 65°, a degree and a half short of the Arctic Circle, in June. He had thus six months to get there, from 17° South to 65° North, with the complication that from 45° North, where he was to make his American landfall, the voyage must be a coastwise one; and, in spite of the maps, who knew what the coast would be like?

It would have been useless to try to sail a direct course to that American coast, against the prevailing easterly and north-easterly winds, and Cook's plan is clear enough, to steer north until he should strike the westerlies that drove the galleons home. Even as it was, he was pushed a few degrees to the west. For the first two weeks he did find an empty passage ahead, as he sailed not very far westward of the most southerly of the scattered small Line Islands, with Tongareva, the largest of the Northern Cook group, some 350 miles farther west still, though sea-birds indicated the presence of land;

and he must have been almost within sight of flat sandy Starbuck as he passed it on the east. Clerke describes the plan adopted for getting ahead as quickly as possible, while still exercising a proper caution: 'By Capt Cook's desire, as the Discovery is the fastest Sailing Vessell, I make all sail every morning at daybreak and run as far as I can ahead till Sunset, when I shorten to an easy Sail for the Resolution to come up; by this means we see a good part of the Sea's we cross during the Night.'[1] They crossed the equator in longitude 156°45' West on the night of 22–23 December; and on the 24th, just after daybreak, were in sight of land to the north-east. It was the barren atoll that Cook called Christmas Island, the largest of all atolls in the area of land it provides.[2] There was anchorage on the lee side. All along the shore, so far as could be seen, broke a tremendous surf, though there was good fishing outside it, and it was not until next day that Bligh returned from a boat expedition with news of an opening through the reef—or rather a double opening, divided by a little islet—into the shallow lagoon. Cook therefore decided to land, and changed his anchorage; for he had a mind both to turtling and to observing an eclipse of the sun which was due on the 30th of the month. Christmas was duly celebrated.

The turtling and fishing parties were highly successful, and some of them had good sport, which they remembered long afterwards. The men who had to carry a heavy turtle two or three miles, however, across the sandy land and through coral-bottomed shallows to the boats, might not have thought of sport, and two of them from the *Discovery* had a most unpleasant adventure. They got lost. How they managed to get lost on that flat and almost treeless island, from a good part of which the ships' masts were visible, Cook could not well make out; but lost they were, one for twenty-four hours, the other for two days, blundering about beneath a blistering sun or struck with cold by night, with nothing to drink but turtle's blood, which one of them could not stomach; finally picked up on the beach in the last extremity of distress and fright. For all that terrestrial direction meant to them, they might just as well have dropped from the clouds. Cook meditates again on the nature of his kind: 'Considering what a strange set of beings, the generality of seamen are when on shore, instead of being surprised at these men

[1] 11 December; *Journals* III, 256, n. 2.
[2] The land of Christmas Island is 300,000 acres, though the land is not good for much. On the place of the island and its neighbours in pre-Cook Polynesian history see Peter Buck, *Vikings of the Sunrise*, chapter 11, and Kenneth P. Emory, *Archaeology of the Pacific Equatorial Islands* (Bernice P. Bishop Museum Bulletin 123, Honolulu, 1934)—for Christmas, pp. 17–24.

lossing themselves we ought rather to have been surprised there were no more of them; indeed one of my people lost himself in the same place, but happening to have sagasity enough to know that the ships were to leeward, he got on board almost as soon as it was known he was missing.'[1] While the wanderers were still unreclaimed the eclipse was observed from the small island near the entrance to the lagoon, which King accordingly called Eclipse Island—it is now known as Cook islet. Cook, Bayly and King observed, Clerke being too ill to do so. There was too much cloud for the beginning of the eclipse to be seen, and Cook himself was forced to discontinue observing for a time, under the strain of the awkward angle of his telescope, combined with the fierce heat of the sun reflected by the sand. He is a little apologetic for an added reason: as Bayly and he had the same sort of telescopes his timing for the end of the eclipse should not have differed from Bayly's as much as it did—24″; 'perhaps it was in part, if not wholy owing to a protuberance in the Moon which escaped my notice but was seen by both the other gentlemen'.[2]

Apart from turtles and fish and sea-birds, there was nothing on or about the atoll to support life unless one points to crabs, small lizards, and rats. A few poor coconuts, a few other scrubby trees, one or two shrubs and a like number of creeping plants and grasses, made up its botanical resources. There was no fresh water, though this would not have mattered to islanders. If Cook had made a full exploration of the place he would, none the less, have found signs of earlier habitation, platforms and enclosures of coral stone, memorials of some forgotten Polynesian past. What hurricane or starvation time depopulated it we shall not know. He gave it what he could. Having some coconuts and sprouting yams, he planted them on the observation islet, and sowed melon seeds elsewhere. Also on the islet he left another of those seamen's bottles enclosing its inscription to the honour of *Georgius tertius Rex*. He took from it three hundred excellent green turtle; a spot where they were particularly plentiful was, Samwell tells us, given the name of Alderman's Point. He departed from it at daybreak on 2 January 1778. The same sort of agreeable sea weather continued; in spite of which he had the carpenters caulking the main deck, and on the 6th served out fearnought jackets and trousers, so it is possible he thought that weather must soon come to an end. At the same time Clerke was putting his men on an allowance of water. It seems that neither commander anticipated another tropical or sub-tropical island. The ships made

[1] *Journals* III, 260.   [2] ibid., 259.

northing, the wind dropped, then went round more to the north and freshened. The amenities were observed: a week after leaving Christmas Island, the day being calm, Clerke dined with Cook. This time it was Anderson who was very ill. There were turtle seen now and again in the ocean; there were birds in the oceanic air; these were signs of land. The gentlemen may have consulted together over their dinner, whatever their anticipations. At daybreak on the 18th high land was seen bearing NEBE, and soon after more in the north, quite distinct from the first.

The wind was light, and the ships came up with the land slowly. The following day a fresh breeze blew, right off the first heights seen, and Cook stood for those in the north; a short time later he saw a third piece of land in the north-east, again distinct; certainly here was a set of high islands. He was advancing towards one of his important discoveries, the Hawaiian group, that stretched in a line from north-west to south-east, and these were the three northern islands—the first Oahu, then Kauai, then Niihau. He was off the eastern end of the roughly circular Kauai on the afternoon of the 19th, wondering if this, like the so different Christmas Island, were uninhabited; but before long canoes put off from the shore and were about the ships; to general astonishment the people in them were talking a language clearly close to Tahitian, and intelligible. These too were a branch of that remarkable oceanic race! How, then, was it that at Raiatea there was no knowledge of further islands to the north? Cook did not ask himself that question; but evidently in the centuries there must have been a break of tradition. He had come to the apex of the 'Polynesian triangle'; and here the question he asked himself yet again was, 'How shall we account for this Nation spreading itself so far over this Vast ocean'—from New Zealand to these latest islands, from Easter Island to 'the Hebrides'? He does not recur to the castaways of Atiu, who had seemed to make clear a great deal; and indeed, they had little to contribute to the part of the problem now before him. He did not formulate the problem immediately; his eyes were on the land, as he coasted the south-east shore, with its gradual rise to the great hills and ridges, and on the people who ran from their villages to view the ship, while the canoes alongside traded freely their pigs and potatoes for nails. Another land of plenty this, just as the diet of turtle was coming to an end; the sad gentlemen of the departure from Raiatea did not foresee the day on which they would eat both turtle and fresh pork for their dinner. And within a day or two more their grog would be restored.

People ventured on board, rather nervously, but their surprise at what they saw did not deter them from attempting to take away anything portable. Cook made his usual orders on approaching unsophisticated islanders a little more stringent:[1] no women were to be allowed into the ships, there was to be no connection with them at all, no man with the 'foul disease' was to go out of the ships. Men would not be left on shore at night. He hoped for good effect, though like regulations had broken down at Tonga on his first visit; he knew how reckless were his men; his experience was now enough to make him rather melancholy. He had had conscientious surgeons, but 'It is also a doubt with me, that the most skilfull of the Faculty can tell whether every man who has had the veneral is so far cured as not to communicate it further, I think I could mention some instances to the contrary.' With such thoughts in his mind, but yet with no knowledge of how indignant Hawaiian women might be over a rebuff, he sent off Williamson in command of three armed boats, to look for a landing place, water and anchorage, while the ships stood off and on. It was 20 January. Williamson found what was needed; in doing so, at one spot where the excited people rushed into the sea to grasp at the boats and the oars, he lost his head and shot a man dead. In spite of his self-righteousness he did not tell Cook; and Cook, finding out later, after conducting himself as if nothing untoward had happened, was not pleased. The ships anchored off the village called Waimea, in the bay of that name. Cook immediately went ashore, where several hundred people were assembled on the beach; he was astonished again, the moment he landed, to see them all fall flat on their faces. He could not know that he was being received with the respect and submission paid to very few of the sons of men, to the half-divine Hawaiian 'kings' or *ali'i 'ai moku*. When he got them to rise they brought the ceremonial plantain fronds and pigs and he gave them what he had in return, all was peace, the water proved excellent.

On the morrow, while a brisk trade went forward, and the people helped roll the water-casks, Cook, Anderson (recovered for the time) and Webber took a walk up the river valley, through the taro plantations, to what Cook called a 'Morai'—the more elaborate Hawaiian equivalent of the Tahitian *marae*, that is, called *heiau*. A guide and herald went before them, a train of followers behind; every person they met fell flat as on the day before. The walled enclosure of the *heiau*, with its oracle tower, carved images, sacred

[1] *Journals* III, 265–6. I say 'a little more stringent', going on his description of the measures he took, but he writes, 'It is no more than what I did when I first visited the Friendly Islands yet I afterwards found it did not succeed'; and he adverts to the recklessness there of the gunner of the *Discovery*, in spite of the expostulations of his companions.

buildings, drum house, and chiefly graves, Cook describes with care; Webber made a drawing, and another of the village. At the end of a day of profitable investigation and barter everybody returned to the ships. The people were very honest dealers, 'never once attempting to cheat us'—but why should they, when they wanted nails and makeshift chisels so much?—'Some indeed at first betrayed a thievish disposition', but this did not last. They seemed to have no chiefs (chiefs they had but at that moment these were almost all absent on the other side of the island). Amiability, honesty, plenty provided every inducement to stay; and then the weather went to the bad, with rain, south-east winds which put the ships on a lee shore, breakers astern and a high surf on the beach. After a day and a night of this, with little interval, the wind went round to the north-east, and Cook decided to move the *Resolution* a little further out. The moment his last anchor was up the wind veered to the east, he had some trouble in clearing the shore, was driven to leeward, had a strong current against him as well as the wind when he tried to regain the road, hoped uselessly he might find a better harbour at the west end of the island; and on the morning of the 24th found that in spite of light airs and calms all night the current had carried him right to the west of Kauai, with the other island of Niihau to his own south-west. The morning before, when he found he could not regain the anchorage, he had sent boats ashore for more water and refreshments, and they had come back safely, in spite of the surf. He had also sent a message to Clerke to follow him to sea if it was plain he could not return; for Clerke, anchored outside the *Resolution*, had felt safe enough without moving. Now a northerly breeze sprang up: this, thought Cook, would bring the *Discovery* to sea, and he steered towards Niihau to pick her up, and possibly find a safe anchorage there. She was not in sight, so he determined, rather than risk a separation, to make his way back to Waimea Bay and complete his water there. Next morning, when the bay lay north, he was joined by his consort; and then neither could regain the anchorage. After struggling for four days they found that the currents had again been at work, and they were within three leagues of the south-east point of Niihau. The open bight of Waimea Bay, however attractive to the newcomer, charmed deceptively.

This tedious struggle kept one or two things out of Cook's journal that he would normally have noticed. While the ship tacked off Kauai his quartermaster, Thomas Roberts, died of the dropsy that had plagued him from the first day of the voyage; and Sergeant Gibson of the marines, his captain's great admirer, laying himself down to sleep upon the gangway, 'a little in liquor' (reports King), fell overboard, and was rescued by means of the 'machine' that had been designed for just such a purpose—the ship having not much way on, fortunately for Sergeant Gibson. On the 29th Cook, with his mind on fresh water, resolved to try the west side of Niihau for a landing place. One was found, and the ships anchored on a convenient bank; but Gore, who landed, could find no supply. Nor could he do so next day, though he did get a load of yams and salt—most of which was lost in the surf. The surf was all too high, and increased: Cook was himself following Gore, but, fearful of not getting back again, returned to the ship. Gore had to be left on shore with twenty men for two nights and the day in between, a period of storm and heavy rain: there was no fear for their safety, but what about the safety of the islanders from disease? It was an appalling mischance. Thus, wrote Cook, 'the very thing happened that I had above all others wished to prevent.'[1]

Sheltered water was found inside the south-east point of the island, and a man swam through the surf with a message to Gore to go there. Cook himself went to pick the party up. We have come to the first day of February. He took goats, pigs and seeds that he had intended for Kauai, and bestowed them on a person who seemed to have authority and received him with some ceremony. As he walked inland people ran from all directions, and these too prostrated themselves as he passed. The soil seemed poor, but nurtured the most sweet-smelling plants; the rain had filled a small stream where a few casks were replenished; he returned on board with the intention of landing again next day. Again misfortune descended: soon after sunset, in a heavy swell, his anchor started and the *Resolution* drove from the bank; it took a long time to get in a whole cable, secure the anchor, hoist up the launch alongside and make sail; so that at daybreak next morning the ship was three leagues to leeward of this last anchorage. Cook was not inclined to spend more time in regaining it. He signalled the *Discovery* to join him, and though the surf had gone down and everything was fair for a pleasant trade, there was nothing for Clerke to do but comply. They again stood away northward.

Thus, on 2 February, Cook left the group he called the Sandwich Islands, after a visit that he can hardly have regarded as satisfactory. Out of a fortnight, he had set foot on shore on only three days. He numbered the islands as five—Atoui or Kauai; Enecheeou or Niihau; Orrehoua and Otaoora, or Lehua and Kaula, mere rocky

[1] *Journals* III, 276.

islets, one close off the northern point of Niihau, the second farther off the southern point; and Wouahoo or Oahu, the first seen to the east.[1] To the south-west, not far away, was said to lie another island, small, low and uninhabited, called 'Tammata pappa';[2] but what it was, and precisely where it was, remains quite baffling. At least, when he did set foot on shore, he had found the people friendly, in spite of the murder that had introduced his own men to them; and although he had not been able to complete his water, friendly trade had given him a three weeks' supply of fresh provisions, and Clerke 'roots'—sweet potatoes and yams—enough for two months. He had done his best to reciprocate friendship with his seeds and goats and pigs 'of the English breed'. The observations he and his officers were able to make, in the short time they had, were quite remarkable. The resemblance of the people to the Tahitians was at once obvious: darker in hue they were certainly, from greater exposure to the sun consequent on their very small amount of clothing—the men's maro or loin-cloth, the women's short skirt—but in physique, language and customs the alliance was close. Within the relationship there were differences such as one would expect. These people practised tattooing, but scantly and with poor design compared with the magnificence or the complexity of New Zealand, Tonga, Tahiti, the Marquesas. Their outrigger canoes were highly skilled productions; their double canoes were not the great structures of the Society Islands, there was none of the masterly carving with which the New Zealanders decorated their vessels; but these were speedy and well-handled. The people, too, were gifted swimmers. Their houses, low-walled, high-roofed, large or small, were like so many oblong corn-stacks, wooden framework covered thickly with grass or sedge; they spread finely woven sleeping-mats on the clay floor; they had few domestic utensils beyond gourds and wooden bowls. Weapons also were few: wooden spears and daggers were all that Cook saw. Their working tools were much like those at the other islands. For music they had instruments of percussion, though Cook himself did not see these, and a simple gourd rattle; he did see the stone discs with which they played various games of bowls.

Some of their possessions called forth a good deal of admiration, like the 'neat Tippets made of red and yellow feathers'—no doubt the *lei* worn by distinguished ladies round the head or neck; the brilliant short cloaks, of similar feathers, attached to a finely woven network of vegetable thread—Cook on this visit saw none of the full-

---

[1] On Cook's renderings of these names see p. 653, n. 2 below.
[2] For some remarks on its identification, see *Journals* III, 604, n. 4.

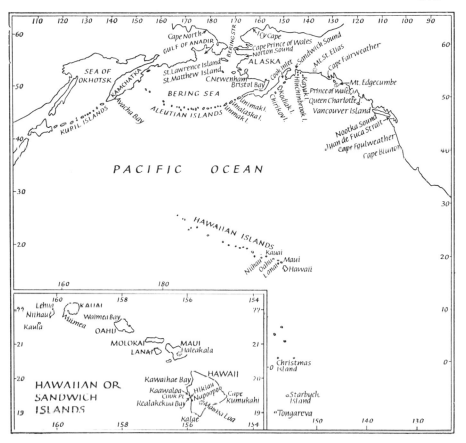

The North Pacific

length garments, which rendered glorious the progress of the greatest chiefs; the ingenious feather-covered 'Caps', as he rather inadequately called them, 'made so as to fit very close to the head with a semicircular protuberance on the crown exactly like the helmets of old. These and also the cloaks they set so high a Value upon that I could not procure one, some were however got.'[1] He does not say how got, in the absence of chiefs. One young Kauai chief, it is true, of the very highest rank, fenced in with divinity and retainers, called on Clerke at the gangway of the *Discovery*; the social Clerke clapped him on the back to make him feel at home—'upon which they gently took away my hand, and beg'd I wou'd not touch him.'[2] The present this personage brought was not a cloak or a helmet, but a fine kava bowl. Less splendid than feather garments, but elegant and pleasing beyond compare, was the bark cloth—not the fabric itself, which could not rival that produced by the women of other islands, but its decorative designs and dyes, the lightness and freedom, variety and colour of which strained the descriptive powers of more men than Cook: 'one might suppose oneself transportd in a Linen drapers shop', declares the susceptible King.

Admiration and ordinary interest were not all to be recorded: there was also matter for a little wonder and conjecture. Not merely were these people anxious to acquire nails, and generous in payment, but they had one or two bits of iron already, used for cutting tools. It followed that eighteenth-century Englishmen were not the first to visit the islands, thought some; were not these helmets a memory of sixteenth-century Spaniards?[3] Others since have been as much convinced, and have adduced a little speculative evidence. It is easily demolished. The pattern of helmets might equally have been derived from Periclean Greeks; Cook was no doubt correct in attributing the iron to its presence in drift-wood. He could not believe that ships had been there before: 'the very great surprise' the people showed at the sight of his, 'and their total ignorance of fire arms seemed to prove the contrary'. Spain, on the other hand, now that the discovery was made, might probably reap some benefit from it, as a way-station for her Pacific galleons. We can agree with Cook that his discovery was the first one. His prophecy was ill-founded. The Spanish showed no interest in Waimea Bay. The era of the galleons was drawing to an end.

Of the passage to the coast of North America, almost five weeks of

---

[1] *Journals* III, 280. [2] ibid., 281, n. 2. His name was Kaneoneo.
[3] ibid., 285–6 for Cook's discussion; and 285, n. 4 for extracts from other journals, and some editorial remarks on the matter.

an empty ocean, with scarcely a sea-bird seen, and no other sign of life, Cook's journal has little to say. It was a not unpleasant passage. A few sentences mention latitude and longitude and prevailing winds—south-easterlies, north-easterlies, south-easterlies again, a calm on the first day of March, when he was as far north as latitude 44°49′ and in longitude 141° West, practically in American waters, when there was a change round to the north. A week earlier than that the weed or kelp that the Spaniards called *porras*, and regarded as a sign that their eastward crossing of the ocean was almost over, was encountered. Other records than the journal supply us with a few details of activity:[1] the carpenters are employed on the *Resolution*'s boats, stove in at Niihau, the sailmakers on the sails; the rats eat a hole in the *Discovery*'s quarter-deck to get at Clerke's yams, and his carpenters are employed on that—'Oh! my poor Cats at Anamooka', he cries; Bayly sees the *Aurora borealis*; in the calm Cook sends his boat to beg a few yams for Sunday dinner for himself and his officers. Quite early, after little more than a week, we get a note from Clerke that reminds us that hedonism is at an end: 'We have been so long Inhabitants of the torrid Zone, that we are all shaking with Cold here with the Thermometer at 60. I depend upon the assistance of a few good N:Westers to give us a hearty rattling and bring us to our natural feelings a little, or the Lord knows how we shall make ourselves acquainted with the frozen secrets of the Artic.' The thermometer continued to go down steadily —in March it was in the forties. With the north wind that succeeded the day's calm Cook turned his course east for the land. He was not far short of the designated 45° latitude. On 6 March life appeared in the sea at last, seals and whales; next morning at daybreak, ten or twelve leagues distant, stretched the land from north-east to south-east, the 'long looked for' coast of New Albion.

The irony that broods over so much of this voyage again appears in the skies. Having lost his passage in the previous year, at least— Cook could have argued—he had made up the loss by being at 45° early in the season this year; and surely, unless luck were badly against him, he could cover twenty degrees of coast line and be in 65° in three months. Luck was badly against him. By a double irony, even if he had been able to move swiftly up that north-west coast, he could not have profited; even if he had been able to reach 65° by the very end of June, which was about the earliest that ice would have allowed him, he could not have pushed much farther till much later. Not having foreknowledge, he could not but be put

[1] Clerke, 11 February, 21 February; Bayly, 1 March; ibid., 288, nn.

out by the three weeks of hard westerly gales, with their rain, hail, sleet and haze, and few fair intervals, which turned the whole American continent, as it were, into a lee shore. On some days, as he tacked off and on, he managed to get a glimpse or two of the land, moderately high, and named some of the capes—including that which formed the northern extreme of the land when he first saw it: 'which I called *Cape Foul Weather* from the very bad weather we soon after met with'.[1] He settled the position of this cape very accurately. Early next morning the weather deteriorated. The worst of it he summarises in his words for the storm which began at midnight of the 11th with a sudden shift of the wind from south-west to west-north-west, soon increasing 'to a very hard gale, with heavy squals attended with Sleet or snow. There was no choice but to stretch to the Southward to get clear of the coast, this was done under courses and two close reefed top sails being rather more sail than the ships could bear but it was necessary to carry it to clear the land.'[2] By the morning of the 13th, when this gale abated, he had been forced back to latitude 42°45'. Clerke records the very heavy westerly swell. 'It is really rather a lamentable business that these NW^ters & this very unsettled Wea^r shou'd so far intrude upon us, that we can neither forward our Matters by tracing the Coast, nor have the Satisfaction of getting into a Harbour to take a look at the Country. . . . we can't look at the shore, but continue to dance about in the Offing here & make the best Weather of it we can.'[3] Then on the 21st there was some fairer weather and the land was seen; then in two days more the gale again; under courses and close-reefed topsails they fought to keep an offing. But they were, slowly, increasing their latitude. The westerlies were not quite continuous. They were varied by storms from the southward, attended by rain and sleet—'it was by the means of these Southerly blasts, that we got [to] the NW attall',[4] writes Cook. It is clear that this unpleasant weather does not put his predecessors out of his mind: he adverts to Martin de Aguilar and, on 22 March, when he wrongly thought he was in latitude 48°, to Juan de Fuca: 'It is in the very latitude we were now in where geographers have placed the pretended *Strait of Juan de Fuca*, but we saw nothing like it, nor is there the least probability that iver any such thing exhisted.' Night swallowed up a large strait before he could see it, providing a sort of subsidiary ironic comment on his own scepticism; for, wherever the real Juan de Fuca went and whatever he saw, here opens the passage that

[1] *Journals* III, 289.   [2] ibid., 292.
[3] ibid., 292, n. 4.   [4] ibid., 294.

now bears his name, not bisecting a continent, certainly, but at least cutting off from that continent a large island which at the end of a week more was to provide Cook with the shelter he so badly needed.

On the morning of the 29th, standing north-east after being well out to sea, he came in with the land again. It was now a land of high snow-crowned forest-covered mountains. On a stretch of the coast that he called Hope Bay—a reflection of his feelings rather than of its real trend—he saw two indentations out of several, and into the more southern of these he determined to go for water. There were inhabitants, whose canoes soon surrounded the ships; their faces were thickly painted, and they were clad in skins; they were eager to trade, and seemed a mild inoffensive people. The inlet, or sound, promised well. Cook decided quickly that it would do for more than merely watering the ships: what appeared to be a snug cove was found for a longer anchorage, and even before they were moored he ordered the sails to be unbent and the *Resolution*'s foremast to be unrigged for repair. On the last day of the month they were moored securely head and stern to the shore, for a stay, as it proved, of four weeks. This anchorage, named then Ship Cove, and since then Resolution Cove, not good, but satisfactory enough for the time, is to be found at the seaward end of an island named (also since then) after Bligh, inside Nootka Sound, on the western side of Vancouver Island. It is not good because, though sheltered from the sea, it is directly exposed to violent south-easterly gales; this was discovered soon enough from the fallen and mutilated trees, as well as from the first gale that blew. There was an infinitely better harbour just inside the south-west point of the sound; but Cook, contemplating a brief stay only, was unwilling to spend more time than he had to in securing the ships. At least there would be no difficulty in wooding and watering.

Vancouver Island is built on vast proportions: no one approaching it from the sea, or even flying down its coast, would take it for an island—the scale of the hills behind hills is too great, the snowy mountains inland recede too far, the line of breakers is too long; the very clouds are almost too immense. The spruce and hemlock and cedar of the forest cover it, to within a few feet of the sea; the flat points reaching a short way into the ocean are covered; the islets off-shore are crowned with trees, like grave barbaric princesses pacing up the coast to some remote festival; trees spring, it seems, from each individual solid rock. The sides of the sound and of the minor inlets that run off it, north, east and south, fall precipitous to the water, with only here and there a naked narrow strip of land marching with it, or a larger ledge. Ship Cove is surprisingly small, its rocky beach perhaps fifty yards long, running back a few yards to where the moss and trees begin—trees of a second growth now, for Cook was not the last to set his axe to the forest, and drifted barkless trunks rub everywhere along the shores of the inlets. But there is the anchorage; there is the rock where the astronomers set up their instruments; there are the steeps that echoed the noise of axe and forge, and the wild cries of Indian companies as they paddled away in the gloom of evening. In this tempestuous and rainy place the explorer's mind might have gone back to the Dusky Sound of the second voyage, far in the south-west corner of the ocean, not altogether unlike though so different in its garment of trees; no doubt in this harbour there were sailors who thought with regret of the warm Polynesian bays, the yellow hibiscus on their sands, their benign and flower-decked girls. Yet the climate here was 'infanately milder' than it was in the same latitude on the east coast of America, in spite of the snow on the heights. Cook found all hands work to do.

Some of the timbers supporting the fore topmast were decayed or sprung. This was remedied within a week, and Cook saw the ships putting to sea again, when it was found that the foremast head itself was damaged, the result of inadequate work in England, and that the mast would have to be taken out and repaired on shore. Meanwhile some of the lower standing rigging being decayed, and there now being time to put it in order, he ordered a new set of main rigging to be fitted and the best of the old to be converted to fore rigging. So far the weather had been fine, but on 8 April a tremendous storm blew across from the opposite side of the sound. In this storm the mizen mast, the only one with its topmast still aloft, gave way at the head; obviously it would have to be taken out too, and as soon as the main rigging was fixed this was done. It was so rotten that the head dropped off in the slings. This meant a whole new mast. A tree was cut and dragged to the shore, and as soon as the carpenters had finished the foremast they set to work on the mizen; they were well advanced when they found that their stick had been sprung in the felling, 'so that their labour was lost and we had a nother tree to get out of the wood which employed all hands half a day.' The new mast was finished and rigged by the 21st, when these hard-labouring men had to produce a new fore topmast.

While all this was going on, with supplementary activity such as caulking, the cutting of firewood and the brewing of spruce beer— which the crew resolved, without effect, not to drink[1]—the people

[1] *Journals* III, 479.

of the sound or the nearby coast were in constant attendance. Cook and Anderson observed them closely, as a quite new people, the wildest and most uncouth of all the Indian tribes of North America; indeed all the journal-keepers poured description and anecdotes into their pages. 'Mild and inoffensive' might be Cook's first impression; before this month was over he had much to add to that. They were a short-statured people, dirty beyond measure from head to foot, smelling strongly of fish, oil and smoke, their broad faces painted thickly with ochre, red, white or black; their legs bowed with long sitting in their canoes. The men dressed generally in nothing more than knee-length cloaks made of the skins of moose or some fur animal; the women rather more completely in a rough fabric woven of bark fibres or goat's hair; copper ornaments hung from their ears or were pinched on to the nose. They had hats of strongly woven straw like inverted flower pots. These women, at any rate, had no attraction for the British seaman, except for some of the more experimentally-minded young gentlemen, who went to work to see what they could do with a tub of warm water and soap, and scrubbed down the startled ladies to a very satisfactory result.[1] The men were constant traders, bringing a variety of furs, weapons and all kinds of other artifacts large or small, bladders of very good oil, even at first human skulls and hands (and did that argue cannibalism?), to exchange for any sort of metal—knives (better than their own, for they had iron knives already), chisels, nails, buttons, unregarded bits of iron or tin, or brass, pewter plates; the ships had hardly a bit of brass left in them by the time they sailed says Cook, 'except what was in the necessary instruments. Whole Suits of cloaths were striped of every button, Bureaus &c^a of their furniture and Copper kettles, Tin canesters, Candle sticks, &c^a all went to wreck; so that these people got a greater middly and variety of things from us than any other people we had visited.'[2] The great attraction for the sailors was the furs, particularly the beautiful pelt of the sea otter. With a very high regard to property on the Indian side—when Cook wanted some common grass for his few remaining stock, he found that every blade was claimed by some separate owner—went a very great disregard for other people's goods, particularly if they were of metal; it was hard to keep the ships and the boats properly guarded, and the captain's own gold watch was abstracted from his cabin, under the noses of the men put there for protection. It was however recovered. This was hardly inoffensive, though one is struck by the fact that Cook had utterly abandoned his

[1] ibid., 1095. Our witness is not Cook but Samwell.   [2] ibid., 302–3.

attempts to deter offenders by punishment. Only once, towards the end, did he in a fit of exasperation fire a load of small shot at a man who refused to give up a misappropriated small piece of iron.[1] Did the memory of Moorea, one wonders, ride hard on his mind, or did he simply feel a futility in counter-measures?

Nor were the Indians mild among themselves, but conducted their many quarrels with a rage of passion that seemed subject only to an odd form of ritual, unless it went on to physical violence; and their sense of property was certainly extended to the two ships, as was evident in the first week in their attitude of defiant hostility towards newcomers whose canoes were brought into the sound by the news of profitable trade. For a time it was Cook and his men who thought they were menaced. Trade with outsiders had to be carried on through those who were there first. But such behaviour did not preclude from all parties a great deal of oratorical display for the benefit of the visitors, in a language that seemed designed to rupture the vocal chords; or a great deal of ceremonial dancing in fantastic costumes surmounted by the animal masks which were here the chief productions of art; or the songs which struck more than one hearer as deeply and excellently harmonious. Nothing could be more different from the sounds of Polynesia; nothing could be more different from the aspect of Polynesian life than the long communal log-framed, heavy-boarded houses in which these people lived on their ledges of land, or their square-sterned, shovel-nosed canoes hollowed out of great cedar trunks, needing no outrigger for stability; or their smoking of fish, or their cooking of food in water heated by stones from the fire; or, among implements, the harpoons with which they pursued the whales off their shore. They always had a supply of fish for the ships, though the seamen could catch none by line, could find no beach from which to cast a net, and were reduced to collecting mussels, which were excellent and in plenty; finding that Cook approved much of a wild garlic, which they did not eat themselves, they kept him supplied also with that. Edible vegetables there were in that place but few: the Indians, like the New Zealanders, ate the rhizomes of bracken fern and, among plants, 'some others unknown

---

[1] Cook passes over the watch incident, which we learn about from others. His small shot, says Bayly, 'wounded three or 4 men in their Backs & backsides—which made the whole party leave us rather apparently in an ill Humour with us.'—ibid., 307, n. 2. He may have consciously fallen back on the policy adopted by Clerke, in the face of 'industrious' and 'audacious' thievery: 'I ever made it a point to reconcile matters as well as I cou'd; determin'd, as our acquaintance was to be of so short a duration, sooner to put up with the loss of some trifles, than bring matters to a serious decision; this plan in short visits answers very good purposes; but had our business detain'd us here any durable term of time, I must have totally changed my scheme of Operations, or these Rogues wou'd have rifled the Ship.'—ibid., 1328–9.

to me which I saw them pull up and eat without so much as shaking of the dirt.' Savage and nasty, then, in some respects their life; but they made the best of their environment. Where they had got their iron Cook could not find out, but attributed it to trade—and indeed it could easily have come northwards up the coast from the Spanish settlements; the copper he rightly understood came from the 'in-Country'. What puzzled him was two small silver tablespoons acquired by Gore from a man who had them hung round his neck as an ornament; it seems that they had been stolen from a Spanish vessel on the coast four years earlier. Of the government and religion of these people, says Cook, persevering with the queries he was directed to satisfy, 'it cannot be supposed that we could learn much'; but he did include in his journal a considerable vocabulary, which we should probably attribute to the laborious Anderson. 'Was I to name them as a Nation', he remarks, 'I would call them *Wak'ashians*, from the word *Wak'ash* which they frequently made use of, but rather more with the Women than the men; it seemed to express applause, approbation and friendship; for when they were satisfied or well pleased with any thing they would with one voice call out Wak'ash wak'ash.'[1]

There are better accounts of the botany of the place than Cook's, it must be confessed; more vivid impressions of birds—the spiring eagles, the beautiful humming birds and their fellows—from King and Clerke and Anderson; but it is Cook who asks the question, why should albatrosses cross the line into the northern hemisphere in the Pacific ocean and not in the Atlantic? Animals, apart from two or three small ones, racoons, squirrels and 'polecats' or ermines, were seen by nobody except in the forms of skins, and from their variety it was apparent that the people were good hunters. Cook's first duty, of course, he esteemed to be geographical, however much else he observed; although not until three weeks had gone by, 'having now got the most of our heavy work out of hand', could he start off early in the morning and have himself rowed all round the sound by his midshipmen. He found better harbours than the one he was in, inlets, islands, huge trees; and the young gentlemen, though tired after thirty miles, did not regret the expedition. A midshipman under Cook must have expected to be hard-worked, as well as taught a great deal, and at times roundly cursed for incompetence. We

---

[1] *Journals* III, 323. The language of the Indians of northern Vancouver island is still known as Wakashan, though there are two very divergent dialects, Nootka on the west coast and Kwakiutl on the east; almost different tongues.

have sometimes a conflict of evidence. When Cook went a second time to choose a tree for a new mizen mast, he says all hands were employed; Samwell on the other hand tells us that 'we soon found another Tree which was cut & hauled to the Beach by the young Gentlemen of the Resolution' under Cook's direction. The young gentlemen very likely cut the tree down; if they exclusively hauled it they must indeed have been exhausted, and perhaps resentful. They do not seem to have been resentful. Trevenen appears to have felt no resentment when he was denounced by the captain for bringing back from a particular rock a set of compass directions that Cook deemed obviously absurd; particularly when it was found on a second trial that for some reason—possibly metal in the rock—the compass and not Trevenen had behaved absurdly, and the captain, the 'despot', had put himself in the wrong. It is Trevenen who gives us some impression of the voyage, and of personality, that we should otherwise lack. He tugged his oar, and bears his witness.

We were fond of such excursions, altho' the labour of them was very great, as, not only this kind of duty, was more agreeable than the humdrum routine on board the ships, but as it gave us an opportunity of viewing the different people & countries, and as another very principal consideration we were sure of having plenty to eat & drink, which was not always the case on board the Ship on our usual allowance. Capt. Cooke also on these occasions, would sometimes relax from his almost constant severity of disposition, & condescend now and then, to converse familiarly with us. But it was only for the time, as soon as we entered the ships, he became again the despot.[1]

The midshipman does not stop at this bald statement: a higher strain, as not infrequently with him, was called for. He treads close behind Thomas Perry, that bard of the second voyage.

> Oh Genius superior, in forming whom Nature
> Had an eye to the moulding of a great navigator;
> And tho' towards thy Mids thou wert not very nice,
> Declaring thoudst have no more cats than catch mice—
> 'Not here do you come to see fashions or folly, but
> To hold on the nippers and row in the jolly-boat'.
> And tho' still thou wouldst send me, when by the wind steering,
> To haul out the weather mizen topsail reef earing,
> Yet not now I'll remember thy wholesome severity,
> Or remember 'twas meant but to give me dexterity:
> No! rather I'll think on that happier season,
> When turned into thy Boat's crew without rhyme or reason,

[1] Another of Trevenen's notes on the printed *Voyage*. It refers to the expedition round the sound, 20 April.

But proud of that office we went a marooning,
And pulling against tide, or before the wind spooning;
Sometimes a shooting, and sometimes surveying,
With pleasure still watching, with pleasure obeying
Through gulf, creek and inlet our jolly boat forcing,
As if the old D– himself had been coursing;
Till pleased with our efforts thy features relax
And thou givst us thy game to take home on our backs.

Or again:

Sometimes more substantial tokens of favour
Than mere empty praises reward our endeavour,
And hunger excites us to use every effort,
While good beef and pudding more solidly pay for't.
Oh Nootka, thy shores can our labour attest
(For 30 long miles in a day are no jest)
When with Sol's earliest beams we launchd forth in thy sound,
Nor till he was setting had we compass'd it round.
Oh Day of hard labour! Oh Day of good living!
When Toote was seized with the humour of giving!
When he cloathd in good nature his looks of authority,
And shook from his eye brows their stern superiority.[1]

'And sure Nootka Sound I shall never forget', affirms the hungry
poet. It is hard to think that any of those ships' companies ever
would.

The day after this expedition the sails were bent, and the observatory tents and instruments got on board. The position of Ship Cove
had been settled with the utmost care, the longitude being the mean
of ninety sets of lunars taken at the observatory, twenty before
arrival and twenty-four after departure, these being reduced by the
chronometer, 134 sets in all; corresponding care, though the process
was not so continuous, was taken with the variation of the compass
and dip of the needle. The tides were closely observed. In two days
more the ships were ready for sea, and at noon on 26 April the
moorings were cast off. As the anchors were weighed, all the nearby
canoes assembled and their occupants sang a parting song, flourishing the more valuable goods they had acquired, while one man,
mounted on a platform, danced to the singing in a succession of
masks. The boats towed the ships out of the cove. There was a final
exchange of presents with a friendly chief, whom a new broad
sword with a brass hilt made 'as happy as a prince. He as also many

[1] The verses occur in the National Maritime Museum MS of Penrose's memoir of
Trevenen, pp. 470–1.

others importuned us much to return to them again', promising a good supply of skins. A northerly breeze sprang up and Cook put to sea.

What name should he confer upon this useful inlet? With no great originality, he hit on King George's Sound. The native Indians, he gathered, called it 'Nookka' or 'Nootka'—which argues some misunderstanding, because that was no Indian word at all. Although he had a leaning for indigenous names, when they could be found out, he neglected this one. Nootka Sound was a decision of the gentlemen in England.

XXIV

The North-west Coast

THICK HAZY weather, a tumbling barometer, all the signs were of a storm from the south; but Cook was anxious to get to sea. Scarcely were the ships outside the sound than the storm fell on them with an instant shift of the wind, squalls, rain and a darkness that made it impossible to see the length of either ship; and to avoid a lee shore again they stretched off to the south-west with all the sail they could bear. Next morning they were clear of the coast, and steered north-west, parallel with what Cook judged to be its trend. As the day wore on the storm increased to a hurricane, and there was nothing to do but lie to. It was just at this time, in the early afternoon—so soon after all the work done in harbour—that the *Resolution* seemed to have sprung a leak, 'which at first alarmed us not a little'; and if Cook was alarmed not a little, what must have been the feelings of others? The fish room, in the after part of the ship, was full of water. There was a leak, but not a serious one; the sound of water rushing in was rather the sound of water washing about, as the coals which lay under the casks of fish kept it from the pumps; bailing and clearing made it possible for one pump to control the danger; apprehension faded. But this unpleasant storm, with some intervals, lasted for most of five days, during which Cook was out of sight of land—out of its sight, that is, for six degrees of latitude; driven right outside—or rather keeping sedulously clear of—the northern part of Vancouver Island, the Queen Charlotte Islands, and Prince of Wales Island. At least he was increasing his latitude, and so far the gale was favourable. In the early morning of 30 April he altered course in order to make the land, 'regreting very much that I could not do it sooner, especially as we were passing the place where Geographers have placed the pretended Strait of Admiral de Fonte.' This fabled admiral's strait, it will be remembered, or river Los Reyes, lay in latitude 53° N. He registered at once his scorn and his reason.

For my own part, I give no credet to such vague and improbable stories, that carry their own confutation along with them nevertheless I was very

591

desirous of keeping the Coast aboard in order to clear up this point beyond dispute; but it would have been highly imprudent in me to have ingaged with the land in such exceeding tempestious weather, or to have lost the advantage of a fair wind by waiting for better weather.[1]

When he sighted land again he was in latitude 55°20′, in the evening of 1 May: a broken coast it was, but he could not distinguish the islands and islets which formed its bays and harbours. Not Spaniards, but Chirikov and Bering were now the predecessors in his mind; he talked of putting into harbour to repair the leak, and oh! thought King and others, that providence would lead them to rescue the miserable men lost by Chirikov hereabouts, surely, thirty-seven years before. Cook was more of a realist: the leak having become inconsequential he would not sacrifice a favourable wind for so romantically improbable a notion.

Once more in sight of that wild tremendous landscape he was determined to keep it in sight, whatever the wind. He would not only remark a general trend of the coast, but fix upon it such an intent gaze that if he could not chart every inch of it, and every inch of the waters lying behind islands and long projections of land, he could at least make fair inferences, and suggestions which his successors would more often verify than deny. To realise how intently he gazed, one must oneself follow slowly and intently the lines of his journal, with their constant record of positions and bearings, with the chart before one's eyes. No swift reading will do. With Mount Edgecumbe and Cape Edgecumbe, in latitude 57°, he resumes his naming of the geographical features, and it is pleasant to record that before long he has a Cape Fairweather to balance the Foulweather of early March. Rising over it was Mount Fairweather, the highest of a ridge parallel to the shore, covered with snow from top to bottom; and then appeared the 18,000 foot peak of what must be Bering's Mount St Elias. These early days of May were days of light airs and calms: 'We are forwarding our business in tracing the Coast, but our breeze enables us to get on but very leisurely', writes Clerke on the 6th; and on the 7th, 'We continue to have most extraordinary fine Weather, with such gentle Breezes that we just crawl along shore'; and Cook could hoist out a boat for the carpenters to work on the leak. He was most anxious to identify Bering's anchorage, but at his distance off shore—some eight leagues—found this difficult. We must turn from his journal to his log and back again, over a period of five days and longer, to see how his mind wavered, set, and then

1 *Journals* III, 335.

went back again;[1] and perhaps the very process of crawling, instead of resolving his doubts, helped to extend them. He had little to go on: only Müller's account of Bering's voyage, and Müller's map. The bay he first decided upon, and charted, and called 'Behring's Bay', was not in fact a bay at all, but (as Vancouver later showed) a deception of low land let into mountains, though he thought he could see low land behind it. Thus on May 6. Four days later, by which time he was beginning to doubt his first identification of Mount St Elias, he found another bay, a real one, only about half a degree farther up the coast, behind a point shooting out towards a small high woody island. This bay, he now supposed, must be the anchorage he sought, and there he might anchor himself to stop the leak which had resisted all efforts at sea. There lay Bering's St Elias Island. The trifling difference of latitude between the reality and the 'Russian Map' could be ignored. He was correct. Why then does he say—again in his log—'On re-considering this matter, I find, this cannot be the place where Bering Anchored, but rather I think it to be the place we passed on the 6th'? He does not explain his reconsiderations, as he has failed to explain reconsiderations once or twice before. Nor has he finished reconsidering. A fortnight later, still trying to determine a point in Bering's track, and confessing near defeat, he casts back. Müller's account is too much abridged, his chart too inaccurate. Bering seems 'to have fell in with the Coast near Mount Fair weather, but I am by no means certain that the Bay to which I have given his Name is the place where he anchored, nor do I know that Mount St Elias is the same as the one to which he gave that name and as to Cape St Elias I can form no judgement where it lies'.[2] The whole process of observation and thought is interesting; it illustrates the attention he paid not only to the coast he could see, but to the only map of that coast he had, and to the history and memory of a man he felt he must respect.

The wind shifting to north on the morning of 11 May, he abandoned the idea of anchoring within the bay and bore up for the west end of the island: later, the wind dropping away, he landed intending to climb its heights and take a view. He found that this also would take too long, and contented himself with leaving a bottle containing the usual inscription and some of the Maundy money presented to him by his friend Dr Kaye.[3] He did not forget his promise to Dr

[1] ibid., 338–41. I have tried to explore the processes of his mind in the notes on the pages.
[2] ibid., 358, entry for 24 May, which is very much a repetition of his log for 9 May, 340, n. 3. Cape St Elias was the outer point of St Elias—i.e. Kayak—island.
[3] ibid., 341.

Kaye, whose name he gave to the island, as a mark of 'esteem and regard', which name, like Bering's of St Elias, has disappeared in favour of the more native one of Kayak Island. But the point and the bay, which might, if it had not been for those unlucky reconsiderations, have justly commemorated Bering, remain Cape Suckling, after the relatively unimportant captain, Maurice Suckling, who succeeded Palliser as Comptroller of the Navy; and Controller (for Cook's Comptrollers) Bay.

After getting out to sea a few leagues, Cook continued to make north-west. He was, in modern terms, sailing into the head of the Gulf of Alaska—the north-east corner, as it were, of the Pacific Ocean; as he went he could see that the coast lay nearly east and west and then trended south-west. At noon on the 12th, when he was in latitude 61°11', he could see also to the WNW the east point of a large inlet. It was at this point that the coast changed direction, and that he was confronted with a complete and critical conflict in his maps. Müller or Stählin? We know very well that to get by sea from 61° N on the coast of America to 65° N Cook would have to turn inside the corner and follow the Alaskan peninsula and the Aleutian islands south-west as Müller's map indicated, however conjectural the shading of his line. We know very well that Cook was instructed not to lose time in exploring rivers or inlets, as he proceeded northward on the American coast until he arrived at the latitude of 65° N. 'Rivers or inlets' implies a suspected passage through the continent. Why then did Cook, who had lost so much time already, now proceed to lose more in precisely this fashion? Simply because the inlets he explored led northward: they indeed might provide the true direction of the American coast, apart from off-lying islands, and take him most directly to latitude 65°. They had nothing to do, in his mind, with a north-west passage. Put in modern terms again, the question was how he could get most quickly from the point he saw 'WNW 3 leagues distant', modern Cape Hinchinbrook, into the Bering Sea? He abandoned Müller and took to Stählin. To use his own words, the southward inclination of the coast was 'a direction so contrary to the Modern Charts, founded upon the late Russian discoveries, that we had reason to expect that by the inlet before us we should find a passage to the North, and that the land to the West and SW was nothing but a group of islands.'[1] We can, if we like, carry this reasoning back to London, before the ships ever left home. Cook has a subsidiary motive. 'Besides the wind was now at SE and we were threatened with both a fog and a storm and I wanted to get

[1] *Journals* III, 343.

into some place to stop the leak before we incountered a nother gale.' So he hauled close round the cape and anchored in a little cove just within. He was not the only *Resolution* man to feel some heightening of curiosity. King, who identifies Stählin with Maty his translator, looked from the ship even with excitement: 'We have Dr Matys map of the N^oern Archipelago constantly in our hands, expecting every opening to the N^oward will afford us an opportunity to seperate the Continent. . . . We are kept in a constant suspense. . . .'[1] And Gore begins a wildly romantic fortnight of his life by conferring on Cook's Cape Hinchingbrook the name Cape Hold with Hope.

When the fog cleared, intermittently, there seemed to be clear sea ahead in one direction at least. Men were set to fish, not very successfully; Gore went over to some small rocky islands to see if he could shoot anything to eat, but he had hardly reached them before two boatloads of Indians appeared and he thought best to return. Indian or Eskimo it is hard to say, because of the mixing of cultures in that place; certainly their canoes, of wooden framework covered with skins, were quite different from those of Nootka Sound, as was the garb they wore, of skins somewhat in the fashion of English waggoners' frocks. They seemed friendly though they would not come close. Next morning, in improving weather, Cook weighed again to look for some place more suitable for repairing the leak than the rather exposed cove he was in, sailing steadily north till late afternoon, when he found a promising harbour on the eastern side of the sound. It was as well; for the weather had gone back, hard squalls with rain turned into violent squalls which nevertheless did not dissipate a thick fog, and by the time darkness had fallen, leading on an 'exceeding stormy' night, he was glad to be anchored securely in that harbour. Bad weather did not deter further Indian visitors in the night, at first three men in kayaks who bore the symbols of friendship, wands with large feathers or birds' wings tied to them, then many more. Some of these ventured on board—once sailors had become hostages by stepping into their boats—and were prepared to trade for a few beads anything they had, even fine seaotter skins. They did not stay long, fortunately, being like other native peoples of a 'thievish' disposition. Indeed, during the course of the following day they attempted, with a sort of naïve effrontery, not merely to take one of the *Resolution*'s boats, but to make general plunder of her consort. A part of them finding the *Discovery*'s deck empty, except for one or two men, while her company were at dinner,

[1] ibid., 342, n. 9.

immediately sent to their fellows at the *Resolution* to reinforce them, drew their knives, invaded the vessel and began to sweep it clean. At the alarm the men from below tumbled up with cutlasses, and the Indians tumbled overboard, rather deliberately, empty-handed but in the best of tempers. At this moment they saw the *Resolution*'s boat out sounding, and all made for her. The officer in charge hastened back to the ship. The boat's crew were hardly on board before the Indians thrust the guard aside, cast her loose and began to tow her away. But the instant they saw a display of arms they desisted, quite unconcerned, and motioned aside the weapons. Cook could hardly feel what he was accustomed to call resentment. Surely these people must be unacquainted with fire-arms: 'for certainly if they had known any thing of their effect they never would have dar'd to take a boat from under a ships guns, in the face of above a hundred men for the most of my people were looking at them at the very time they made the attempt. However after all these tricks, we had the good fortune to leave them as ignorant as we found them, for they neither heard nor saw a musket fired unless at birds.'[1]

This was on 14 May, and the boat was sounding the head of the bay to see if the ship could be laid ashore to stop the leak. The gale came on as hard as before. How long it would last heaven knew. Cook therefore resolved to keel her where she was, and sent out a kedge anchor to moor her to—in which operation a maladroit seaman, tangled in the buoy rope, was nearly drowned. He survived with a badly broken leg. The day had not been without incident. The next morning the ship was given a good heel to port, the leak being in her starboard buttock,[2] and the sheathing ripped off, when the oakum in the seams beneath was found to have so rotted away that two-and-half inch rope had to be stuffed in. It took two days to put the matter right, and while the carpenters were at work all the empty water casks were filled at a stream nearby. The gale had given place to fog and rain. This weather did not keep away the people of the sound, however, who brought their women to inspect the visitors, and this time Cook studied them carefully. Among the books he had on board was the *History of Greenland* by the Moravian missionary David Crantz. These people, small in stature, thick set, good-looking (as Cook thought, or—to quote Clerke—'fine jolly full fac'd Fellows') were much like, though not quite like, those described by Crantz. They wore the same sort of clothing. Their fishing and

---

[1] *Journals* III, 348.
[2] The buttocks of a ship were the timbers on each side of her sternpost, from the bottom of the cabin windows downwards.

hunting instruments were exactly the same. Their boats and canoes, though structurally the same, differed in details such as the prow and the stern. They wore the Greenland clothing, with the addition, on some of the men, of a sort of body armour made of vertical slips of wood fastened together with sinews and tied at the back like European stays. The women tattooed their chins and cheeks, apparently to match the male beards, and this also seemed to be a Greenland custom. But unlike the Greenlanders were they in their passion for bone adornments to the face. Both men and women had the under-part of their lower lips bored, or slit horizontally, so that they could pass through the holes a sort of bone stud, singly or several in a row; attached to these and hanging down over the chin would be short strings of beads or bone. Inside the lip they stuck up like a second set of lower teeth. Their noses were bored for longer bones; their ears were bored all round for small ones or for beads; in addition they painted their faces black and red. With all this they managed to appear very cheerful, as Clerke noted; though by what standard Cook managed to find them good-looking it is hard to imagine. Where their affinities really lay he could not tell. Greenlanders? Esquimaux, said to be of the same nation?[1] He had never seen one or the other; he must defer judgment.

At the end of the second day the weather cleared, and for the first time Cook could examine his surroundings. He called the place of his anchorage Snug Corner Bay, 'and a very snug place it is'. From the purely nautical angle he was probably right, but no one confronted with the crags and icy mountains, snows and few trees and cold sky that Webber and Ellis portray would find it other than forbidding. Certainly their waters are calm. Early next morning Cook made sail to the north-west, thinking that would be the most likely direction for any passage north; by the beginning of the afternoon he was forced to anchor again, having covered only a few leagues and escaped with difficulty the dangers of sunken rocks and a failing wind. He took thought. In the north the land seemed to close. The flood tide came from the south: 'altho this did not make wholly against a passage, it was however nothing in its favour.' He sent

[1] In spite of careful observation of native characteristics, pp. 344–6, 349–50, it was difficult to discriminate. Not very long afterwards Cook writes of the Cook Inlet people 'All the people we have met with in this River are of the same Nation as those who Inhabit *Sandwich Sound*, but differ essentially from those of *Nootka* or *King Georges Sound*, both in their persons and Language.'—371. On which opinion Frederica de Laguna comments (*Archaeology of Cook Inlet, Alaska*, Philadelphia, 1934, 14–15), 'It is by no means certain that this opinion is correct, for we know that the Indians had adopted much of the culture of their Eskimo neighbors'. The people he now met might therefore be either Athapaskan Indians (to which group the Nootka people belonged) or Eskimos.

Gore and Roberts to examine an arm of sea to the north, and Bligh one to the east. Roberts and Bligh came back without hope; Gore differed strongly from Roberts and apparently hoped that he had found the entrance of an actual north-west passage. Cook considered sending him out again. But in the morning—the 17th now—'as the wind . . . came favourable for geting out to sea I resolved to spend no more time in searching for a passage in a place that promised so little success. I, besides, considered, that if the land on the west should prove to be islands agreable to the late Russian descoveries, we could not fail of geting far enough to the north and that in good time, provided it was not spent in searching places where a passage was not only doubtful but improbable.'[1] There were other arms of this sound on its western side, as well as plenty of islands, which he might possibly have searched; but his instinct was as rationally based as Gore's fancy was absurd. He turned back, learning from the native people as he did so that there was a channel to the open sea other than the one he had come in by, to the west of a large and long island lying in the entrance of the sound. Through this channel he made a slow passage, because of the rocks and small islands that studded it, light airs and a period of dead calm. It had become almost tautology to mention whale and seals, declared Clerke, and the innumerable sea fowl that so confoundedly kept their distance. In the evening of 20 May the ships were at sea again. Eight days gone by: and what was there to show for them but a stopped leak and a rough chart? The names on the chart argue a disposition in Cook to celebrate the First Lord in all parts of the globe. The whole sound is Sandwich Sound;[2] the large island in the entrance bears the patronymic Montagu; we have already had the family seat in Cape Hinchingbrook. Gore, for the moment a mournful romantic, confers upon the south-west point of the island a name of his own, Cape Lost Hope.

Cook steered south-west. He was off the south-eastern coast of the Kenai peninsula, turning inside the corner of the Gulf of Alaska, and now, if the land had been continuous, would have sailed down the southern coast of the Alaskan peninsula, projecting like a long finger from the main coast of the continent. But was the land continuous? On the 21st he sighted a high promontory, in latitude 59°10'—Cape Elizabeth, after the princess whose birthday that day was. No land was seen beyond it: perhaps it was the western extremity of the

---

[1] *Journals* III, 353.
[2] After the voyage the gentlemen in London decided that this name should be superseded by that of Prince William Sound, which has remained.

coast? No, there was more land bearing WSW. He was driven off by a heavy north-west gale, came back towards Cape Elizabeth, and on the 23rd saw still more land that seemed to connect the cape with the land farther to the west. Next day he had a closer view of another cape, the north-eastern extremity of an island,[1] beyond which lay the snow-covered mountains of the larger mass. Now there seemed to be not land, but a gap of open water, fifty or sixty miles of it, between the two capes. From the position of the second one, latitude 58°15′, and Müller's account of Bering's voyage, this must be what appeared on Müller's chart as Cape St Hermogenes. Inaccurate as the chart might be, it did leave a space only doubtfully occupied by land north-east of Cape St Hermogenes, where Bering was supposed to have seen none; and here at least there was a tendency towards agreement with Stählin's more sweeping assertion. Stählin made the cape a treeless island, as it looked to be: 'so that every thing inspired us with hopes of finding here a passage Northward without being obliged to proceed any fa[r]ther to the South.'[2] True, they were hopes only, not overstrong. King's study of the books and their maps rather depressed him; nevertheless, 'we do not like to give up all hopes of breaking thro this (as we hope) imaginary continent, although the high Snowy land to the S°ward damps ones expectations. . . .'[3] Clerke enters his journal for 24 May:

We are still in the same predicament as yesterday in respect to our Western Gale. Here's a fine spacious opening, which this wind will not enable us to examine: as the Season now advances so fast, shou'd we leave a passage to the N'ward behind us, it wou'd be a most unfortunate incident; or on the other hand shou'd we get engaged in an extensive Sound, and after searching its various crooks & corners, find ourselves under the necessity of returning, from whence we came, it might have a most unhappy effect upon this Seasons operations.[4]

The heart of one man, however, rose within him. The island of the cape Gore named 'Hopes Return'. He did not make charts, but on the very useful chart that Roberts made of the inlet they were about to enter he had a coruscation of his own names, somewhat different from Cook's, inscribed—'Cape Hope', 'Mount Welcome', 'The Gulf of Good Hope', 'The Land of Good Prospect'. Alas!

The contrary wind sank, a north-east breeze sprang up; in the morning of 25 May Cook steered into the empty space with 'Hopes Return' close aboard. He would not emerge till 6 June, with hopes blasted. He sailed immediately towards what on the 23rd he had

[1] Marmot Island (which Cook called St Hermogenes Isle) and Cape St Hermogenes.
[2] *Journals* III, 358–9.　　　[3] ibid., 358, n. 7.　　　[4] ibid., 359, n. 1.

thought to be intermediary coast between Cape Elizabeth and that to the west: it turned out to be a group of high rocky islands, round which he manoeuvred to the west past a large promontory on his larboard hand, friendship being commemorated again in the name he gave it, Cape Douglas. At daybreak on the 26th, St Augustine's day, while in the north-east the horizon was unbroken, in the north-west there seemed to be a chain of islands: the nearest of these, a cone of vast height, he called Mount St Augustine. Between it and Cape Douglas there seemed to be a passage to the north-west. The haze cleared: Mount St Augustine certainly was an island; its fellows were the summits of a range of mountains, rising from low land everywhere visible. Cook, taking in this sight, at once came to a conclusion on which he might very well have acted and saved ten days' time. He restrained himself. 'This land was every where covered with Snow from the summits of the hills down to the very sea beach, and had every other appearence of being part of a great Continent, so that I was fully persuaided that we should find no passage by this inlet and my persevering in it was more to satisfy other people than to confirm my own opinion.'[1] One suspects some argument from Gore. To depart, after only this short experiment!—and one feels that the captain, though no doubt the midshipman's despot, was not the entire dictator. He stood over to Cape Elizabeth, to examine the shore thereabouts, then west again, in a strong northerly gale, rain and thick weather. Next day, conditions having much improved, he was sailing north, past a deep bay to starboard, and anchored for the night opposite the rounded southern end, Anchor Point, of a tract of low land extending to the NNE—'in the Middle of the inlet . . . but as this was supposed to be an island it did not discourage us.' An island on the evidence of the deep bay of which it formed the northern shore, perhaps; but it proved in fact to be the eastern side of almost the whole inlet, backed by a range of high mountains.

In the next few days there was slow advance only, partly because of contrary gales and squalls, occasional mist and drizzle, partly because of dangerous shoal patches—more because of the strength of the tide, which rose and fell twenty feet and in places ran like a race; the farther up the inlet the ships pushed the stronger it was, and in the end the boats could make no headway against it at all. Cook was reduced to sailing with the flood and anchoring with the ebb. He first remarked this difficulty off Anchor Point, after his stationary night there, when the *Resolution* began to drive. He dropped a kedge anchor to stop her, the hawser parted, and he lost hawser and

[1] *Journals* III, 361.

anchor; no effort of a day's 'creeping and sweaping' by Bligh could recover them. His log betrays a touch of irritation; for 'they hooked the Hawser the first trial, but lost or spit it before it was got up to the boat and no one in the boats thought of letting go a grapling to mark the place, so that it never could be hooked again.'[1] This day too he first noticed the driftwood coming down with the ebb, while the water changed colour, becoming 'thick like that in Rivers', though still as salt as the ocean. The following day, a fairly clear one, there was still no land to be seen north-north-east; the continuous ridges of cloud-covered mountains on either side showed no sign of closing in on each other. On the 30th, the ships being anchored under a bluff point on the eastern shore, facing another opposite, they had their first visit from the people of this inlet, two men in kayaks, who obviously wanted someone to land. Instead of this Cook stood with the flood over to the other side, past the opposite point, and followed that shore as it turned to the east. Between the two headlands, which here narrowed the channel, ran a 'prodigious' tide. Whether the agitation of the water was due to the strength of the stream or to rocks or shoals above them was hard to say, but Cook decided on the former. It was these two points, virtually attracted as it were, that stimulated Gore's last romantic outburst: that on the eastern shore became 'Nancy's Foreland', after his 'Favourite Female Acquaintance'; the other 'Gore's Head'. A later, less tender, cartography affirmed them to be simply East Foreland and West Foreland. Cook, also, was less tenderly employed; he was weighing the water. At low water it was perfectly fresh to the taste, and its light weight seemed conclusive, 'in so much that I was convinced that we were in a large River and Not a Strait that would communicate with the Northern Seas. But as we had proceeded so far I was desireous of having stronger proofs and therefore weighed with the next flood and plyed higher up or rather drove up with the tide for we had but little wind.'[2]

The last day of May and the first day of June determined the matter for Cook. Most of his men were of the same opinion as he was, but Gore still stood out. The inlet had definitely turned east. At clear intervals in misty drizzling weather there were indications that beyond an area of shoals it divided into two arms, one running directly east, the other north-east. Bligh was sent to examine the north-east arm, and returned to report a deep and navigable river for the ten or twelve miles he had been up it, between continued ridges of mountains. Cook tried to get the ships into the eastern arm, but was stopped by a breeze directly against him and by the ebb

[1] ibid., 362, n. 1. [2] ibid., 364.

tide; King with two boats also could make no headway against the tide. All that was found out was that the fancied large island on the eastern side of the inlet must be part of the main. The arm was called the Turnagain river. As for the inlet itself, what was its real nature? The fresh water on its surface persuaded Cook it must be a river. 'Besides this we had many other & but too evident proofs of being in a great River; such as low shores, very thick and Muddy water, large trees and all manner of dirt and rubbish floating up and down with the tide.'[1] River it was not, we know, though there were plenty of rivers to carry this sort of rubbish into it; it was 'thick' and discoloured because of the glacial silt it carried, and glacial silt was a concept unknown to Cook; some of the rubbish was probably also glacial. They had traced it, ice-free, seventy leagues or more from its entrance, to latitude 61°30', without seeing the least appearance of its source. He went on to something more general.

If the discovery of this River should prove of use, either to the present or future ages, the time spent in exploring it ought to be the less regreted, but to us who had a much greater object in View it was an essential loss; the season was advancing apace, we knew not how far we might have to proceed to the South and we were now convinced that the Continent extended farther to the west than from the Modern Charts we had reason to expect and made a passage into Baffin or Hudson bays far less probable, or at least made it of greater extent. But if I had not examined this place it would have been concluded, nay asserted that it communicated with the Sea to the North, or with one of these bays to the east.[2]

Even this moderate man, clearly, was not exempt from the vanity of human thought. Neither he nor King had seen with eyes, had laid down on paper the end of that eastern arm he had called the 'river' Turnagain. Sixteen years later his midshipman Vancouver came again and did both. Had the 'great and first discoverer of it', wrote Vancouver, 'dedicated one day more to its further examination, he would have spared the theoretical navigators, who have followed him in their closets, the task of ingeniously ascribing to this arm of the ocean a channel, through which a north-west passage existing according to their doctrines, might ultimately be discovered.'[3]

He sent King away again to land and take possession of the country and the 'river'. King's party was met by a friendly band of natives, who were happy to observe a turf turned and the flag flown, share the bottled porter in which King George's health was drunk, and accept the empty bottles. The other bottle, containing the relevant

---

[1] *Journals* III, 365.   [2] ibid., 368.
[3] Vancouver, *Voyage of Discovery* (London, 1798), III, 125.

paper and further Maundy money, the zealous officer buried under some rocks by the side of a stunted tree, 'where if it escapes the Indians, in many ages hence it may Puzle Antiquarians'.[1] Anderson might therefore have moralised a little more on the pointless nature of acts of possession, but poor Anderson, two days after this first afternoon of June, was forced to stop his writing. The 'Indians' had been equally friendly whenever they had come to the ships, which was almost every day since their first appearance, flying one of their leather frocks on a pole as a sign of peace, or standing with arms spread wide. They continued to come as the ships slowly returned down the inlet. They seemed in every way like the people of Sandwich Sound, except that they had more iron, in the form of spears and long knives, and made no attempt to depart with anything that they had not acquired by honest trade. This iron must have come from people directly in touch with Russian traders, thought Cook, which these people could not be; for if Russians had been here, sea otter skins could not have been a common article of clothing. He was right. He was right, too, in thinking that though there were prospects of a very profitable fur trade on this coast, it was not one in which the British could play a great part, 'unless a northern passage is found'. Meanwhile the speculators among his men got what they could in exchange for old clothes and beads. Cook was possibly more interested in the 'large quantity of very fine Salmon', and a supply of cranberries. The country itself, what was seen of it, provided no great promise: a few trees, spruce, birch, willow, grew in a poor light soil, a few shrubs and currant bushes, a few berries, a little grass.

Cook turned his back; and as he did so the wind, which had been in his teeth for the last nine days, went round to the south. Fortunately it blew no gales, and now anchoring with the flood and tiding with the ebb, he plyed his way back. He had one lucky escape from disaster. His judgment over the agitated water between the two headlands, that it was due simply to the strength of the stream, will be remembered. He was wrong. It was on the first day of this return passage, as he sailed down the middle of the inlet, that, 'by the inattention and neglect of the Man at the lead', the *Resolution* struck the eastern side of a great bank or ridge of hard sand and rock above the headlands and stuck fast.[2] She at once signalled the

[1] *Journals* III, 1421.
[2] Vancouver was to write later, in his own *Voyage* (p. 120), that 'it must be considered as a most fortunate circumstance, that neither Captain Cook nor ourselves had attempted to pass on the south side of that shoal'. On Chart LI the thing is called 'The Snare'. Its name is now Middle Ground Shoal.

Discovery to anchor, which prevented her narrowly from running on the other side. No damage was done, the ship floated off with the flood, and Cook worked round the northern end of the bank into deep water and anchored. If he had had time to investigate, he might have been glad that his luck had kept him away from the bank's southern end, a cruel jungle of perpendicular rocks rising from quite deep water. Perhaps the leadsman was not highly to blame. Next day, the 3rd, while they were anchored two miles below the western headland, the mountains cleared for the first time since they came into the inlet, among them a volcano 'emitting a white smoke but no fire'.[1] Cook did not know it, but he was on the edge of a restless part of the earth's surface. With the wind still southerly as he crossed over to the eastern side of the inlet and anchored, weighed, and anchored again, on the 5th he found himself at the spot where he had lost his kedge anchor. He made a last vain effort to reclaim it; weighed with the ebb; anchored for the last time inside the inlet, a little north of Cape Hinchinbrook; and in the earliest morning of 6 June, a fresh breeze springing up from the west, got under sail, passed outside the rocky islands, and stretched away for Cape St Hermogenes. That episode was over.

Cook found no name for this gash in the land. King referred to it merely as the Great River. Bayly, sharing the no doubt general feeling that they had been 'had', hit on 'Seduction River'. Gore fell silent. Later on, in London, Lord Sandwich ordered that it should be called Cook's River. Vancouver, who in the end knew more than them all, in 1792 altered the word River to Inlet. Cook summed up his feelings in his log for 6 June, in a passage that refers to both the inlets he had just explored. It is an interesting passage for more than one reason. It registers the state of his own mind—a sort of disgust at being swindled and at being a party to the process himself—while at the same time he had to admit that he had learnt something. It illustrates the fashion in which he composed his journal; for some of these phrases form the substance, expanded, distributed, of passages in the journal which hinge on different and earlier dates. Certainly in the journal he took some care to speak with less acerbity of his officers.

It is now sixteen days since we came in sight of the land before us, which time has been spent to very little purpose, and is the more to be regretted as the wind has been favourable the most of the time for ranging the Coast to the South or sw and would probably have carried us to its extremity in

---

[1] *Journals* III, 370. Redoubt Volcano, 10,198 feet high. There was another, Iliamua, almost as high, not far to the south—at the time, it must be supposed, concealed by cloud.

that direction. I was induced, very much against my own opinion and judgment, to pursue the Course I did, as it was the opinion of some of the Officers that we should certainly find a passage to the North, and the late pretended Discoveries of the Russians tended to confirm it. Had we succeeded, a good deal of time would certainly have been saved but as we did not, nothing but a triffling point in Geography has been determined, and a River discovered that probably opens a very extensive communication with the Inland parts, and the climate seemed to be as favorable for a settlement as any part of the world under the same degree of latitude.[1]

'Late pretended Discoveries': the Russians are now classed with de Fonte and de Fuca. And it is unusual to find Cook referring to any point in geography as trifling. We have Clerke giving his own succinct summary: 'a fine spacious river . . . but a cursed unfortunate one to us'.

A cursed unfortunate one. Latitude 65° N in June? On the first day of June they were in latitude 61°30', and turning from Stählin's map to Müller's, were confronted by the prospect of sailing WSW down a conjecturally hatched in, but none the less continental coast, to latitude 53° before they could turn north again. True, Müller showed a number of islands, but they were nothing like Stählin's; and Cook, in his three weeks of coasting, was to find a quite large number of islands—some which were without doubt islands, some which were perhaps rather a highly indented mainland coast, perhaps only islands which (to use his own phrase) locked in one behind another. In any case, in all those three weeks he saw no way through. He found a way through, finally, at a point that in no way resembled anything on Müller's map, except vaguely in latitude; and on the last day of June, as he lay in harbour on the northern side of the great projection, he was in latitude 53°55'. On the map, towards the western end of the projection, was indicated a Mt St Johns, overlooking a cluster of offshore islands, which proved of no use at all as a point of reference; the only other names to which he could refer, apart from Cape St Hermogenes (and he was not sure that he had correctly identified that) were Bering's two, Tumannoi or Foggy Island and Schumagin Island. Foggy Island, where there were so many foggy islands, nagged at him day after day, and he never did see it. Schumagin, or Shumagin, or the group of which it was one, called after a sailor whom Bering buried there, gave him surprisingly little trouble. He conferred comparatively few names of his own, and of those fewer still have survived. Overhead flew

[1] *Journals* III, 368, n. 2.

seabirds of all kinds, sometimes in large flocks; sometimes ducks and geese and swans; seals and whales were constant companions in those waters.

Cook, with only one gale, had much better fortune with the weather than Bering had had; but it was a tedious and sometimes anxious navigation, off shores barren and rugged, brown with the dead herbage of the previous summer, fringed with steep cliffs and formidable rocks. Inland were snowy mountains; in places snow covered the lower hills and deep valleys, and came down beaches almost to the edge of the sea. Land could not always be seen; nor did the two ships always pick up the same points of land. There was only one gale: the difficulties came rather from frequent contrary, though not strong, winds, and a combination of misty, drizzling and rainy weather that gave way to fog, and fog that turned to rain and drizzle again. The first three days were clear enough, then came three on which there was hardly a sight of the coast, and when it was seen it could be all too close. The absence of a sight of the sun was embarrassing to accurate navigation and Cook is more sparing with daily positions than usual; but he never lost a chance of a sight, and when he fixes a position for some natural feature, a cape or an island, he is rarely more than a minute or two out. His journal preserves the level unimpassioned tone of a man whose only interest is observation. Not quite so Clerke: 'the confounded fog. . . . A thick fog and a foul Wind are rather disagreeable intruders, to people engaged in surveying and tracing a Coast'; or again, 'These have been 24 Hours more of wretched Weather for our Work, however we are getting forward as fast as we can, and hope & trust that soon, our darkness will be enlighten'd.'[1] Not for almost a week more would the physical darkness be much lightened, and on one matter enlightenment never came; they were at this time not coasting the mainland at all, but a complex of islands the largest of which is Kodiak—which, though it certainly in its bulk had the look of mainland, was cut off from it by the considerable Shelikof Strait; and the existence of this was something Cook had suspected as he sailed into the 'Great River'.

On 14 June, close in with the land, he saw and named Trinity Island, a sort of small appendix to the massive Kodiak and its neighbours. From this point onwards, if the weather had been clear, he would have had most of the Alaskan peninsula in sight, behind its fringe of islands and islets. Could Trinity Island be Bering's Foggy Island? No, because Bering's island was supposed to be thirty leagues from the coast. On this day he saw his first Eskimos, two men

---

[1] *Journals* III, 375, n. 2. Clerke writes thus for 10 June, 11 June.

paddling a kayak, but they would not come near the ships. Then the wind went to the south, and he stretched out to sea for safety. He saw another island, quite clearly, and so did the *Discovery*'s people. Foggy Island?—he thought not. Vancouver saw it again, in the same position, in 1794; and now it has vanished. The gale came, and the journal, still in its level tone, illustrates the anxieties of that navigation. It was the 15th.

At 8, being flatered with the hopes of the weather clearing up, ster'd WNW and at 10 NW. But at Noon seeing no land and the gale increasing with a thick fog and rain, I steer'd WNW under such sail as we could haul the wind with; for I was very well apprised of the danger runing before a strong gale in a thick fog, exposed us to. It was however necessary to run some risk when the wind favoured us, for clear weather was generally accompaned with a Westerly wind. Between two and three PM land was seen through the fog bearing NW not more than 3 or 4 Miles distant, upon which we immediately hauled up South close to the Wind. Soon after the two Courses we had bent were split so that we had others to bring to the yards, and several others of our sails recieved considerable damage. At 9 the gale abated the weather cleared up and we got sight of the coast extending from WBS to NNW about 4 or 5 leagues distant.[1]

'This was no agreeable discovery', says the log; the fog soon returned, there was little wind all night, and 'a prodigious swell' rolled them by morning half the distance towards the land. The north-eastern point of 'the Main' that could be seen Cook called Foggy Cape, in latitude 56°31' (its modern determination is latitude 56°32', and it is the eastern extremity of an island, Sutwik, which here masks a bay in the mainland). Lying off it eight or nine leagues (in reality about twenty miles) was an indubitable island—surely, at last, '*Foggy Island*, a name given it by Behring'. He was wrong: this was one of the group called the Semidi islands; it was precisely the fog that concealed from him Bering's island, a little farther east. But the name, placed on the chart, remained; and when Vancouver in 1794 made the correct identification he called it, with a due sense of history, Chirikov island. Let Clerke be again our summary: 'I hope and trust Providence will favour us with a little clear Weather: never had a set of fellows more need of it, here's such a Labyrinth of rocks and Isles, that without a tolerable distinct vision, they will puzzle our accounts, confoundedly.'[2]

Providence was indeed for a few days kind, though accompanying its gift with a first day's calm. Cook lost no time in making observations for longitude and variation. Then, with a fair wind, he steered

---

[1] ibid., 379.   [2] ibid., 380, n. 2.

his way into a channel between groups of islands lying parallel off the land, fearing that if he kept the main coast aboard he might mistake some point for an island, become embayed, and lose his fair wind. The group to which belonged the island of Schumagin's burial was unmistakable; from there the eye was filled with islands, 'most of them of a good height', (it seemed as the ships ran past them) 'very barren and rugged, ending in pointed rocks steep clifts and other romantic appearences'; well-watered but quite without trees or bushes and some still laden with snow, like those parts of the continent that could be seen—and this day was 19 June, mid-summer. It was on the same day that alarm was caused by guns from the *Discovery*, two miles astern. But she had no sudden accident to report, merely a visit from pursuing kayaks, which had delivered, to Clerke a sort of small box containing a message written in Russian, 'as was supposed'; and it was at first supposed to come from shipwrecked sailors in distress. Cook would have none of this idea: much more likely it was some note connected with Russian trade, and in spite of an upset crew he refused to delay. He was to prove right. Russian influence was confirmed two days later. While the crew were fishing, very profitably, for halibut during a calm, three or four miles from the shore, a single man came off in his canoe, took off his cap and bowed very politely, as the *Discovery*'s visitors had done; he wore breeches and jacket of cloth instead of fur beneath his waterproof frock of whale-gut, and had little to barter. His physical likeness to the Sandwich Sound people was marked, but his face was unpainted and he wore no ornament in the perforation of his lip. The wind failed more than once during this period. Fortunately it did not fail so soon as to let the ships drift in the early morning of the 20th, and the weather was then clear; for of the two fearful dangers they survived on the Alaskan–Aleutian coast this provided the first. They were running westward with a gentle north-east breeze: at 2 a.m.

some breakers were seen within us at 2 Miles distance; two hours after others were seen ahead and on our larboard bow and between us and the land they were innumerable, and we did but just clear them with a south course. These breakers were occasioned by rocks some of which are above and others under water; they extend 7 leagues from the land and are very dangerous especially in thick weather, which this coast seems subject to.[1]

Cook never made an understatement more laconic. His seamanship must have been as masterly as it ever was, because what he had 'just cleared'—indeed he must have been within them—was the Sandman

[1] *Journals* III, 384.

reefs, a region still, two hundred years later, inadequately surveyed, which vessels are forthrightly warned not to enter.

As the men fished in the calm the ships lay off the Sanak islands. Over them could be seen high mainland covered with snow, some summits in particular towering above the clouds 'to a most stupendious height', the most south-westerly a pure cone, a volcano from whose top rose a column of smoke vast enough to stain the sky. But Cook was not now looking at the mainland; the great peninsula had come to an end; the volcano was Shishaldin, the highest summit, over 9000 feet, of the island of Unimak, separated from the continent by the narrowest of straits. He had arrived at the north-eastern end of the thousand mile-long thread of the Aleutian islands. Müller's hatched coast was still continuous; but the wearied student of Müller, if he cared to sail all down it, would find ample opportunities of sailing through it into an open sea. Curiously enough, Cook, who had desired and sought that open sea so long and so pertinaciously, missed his first chance to do so; and looking back, without a considerable effort to understand his mind, one may find his alternation of caution and boldness curious too. For three days the weather was dark and gloomy, with few gleams of sunshine, even when the fog did not settle down. He kept off the land, making very slowly west. On the 24th he saw land to the north-west—still, he was convinced, a continuation of the continent, though it was in fact Unimak; and to the south-west more land, obviously islands. Next day there was the unusual combination of an easterly breeze and clear weather, and the whole coast was plain. He thought he could see the mainland terminate at a point to his north-west (the end of Unimak), and a large opening between this and the neighbouring islands, and he steered for it. Then he raised land beyond the opening, which might not be part of the continent—but on the other hand might. He had second thoughts about the land to the south-west, and a recurrence of his reluctance to run any risk of embaying: if all were continent, 'the opening would be a deep bay or inlet into which, if we entered with an Easterly wind we could not so easily get out'. He turned about; and thus he turned his back on the Unimak pass, ten miles wide at its narrowest part, and quite the best passage through the Fox group of the Aleutian islands.

After getting away from the land he steered west. They were islands after all south-west of the opening he had abandoned. He passed three of them and had more to the west, but the most south-westerly part of them bore WNW. The weather in the afternoon took on its normal composition, gloom and mist turning steadily thicker, with a fresh easterly breeze. He hauled to the south again for the night, out of danger, and at daybreak of the 26th resumed his westerly course. This time there was no visible sign of peril; indeed beyond the ship there was nothing visible at all. To quote the journal, 'Day light availed us little as the Weather was so thick that we could not see a hundred yards before us, but as the wind was now very moderate I ventured to run. At half past 4 we were alarmed at hearing the Sound of breakers on our larboard bow; on heaving the lead found 28 fathom water and the next cast 25; I immideately brought the ship to with her head to the Northward and anchored in this last depth over a bottom of Coarse Sand, and called to the Discovery who was close by us to anchor also. A few hours after, the fog cleared away a little, and it was perceived we had scaped very emminant danger . . .'.[1] The sound of breakers had been the sound of salvation; the ships had been running straight for the shore, which was only three quarters of a mile off, the head of a bay guarded at each side by a high rock, with lesser ones attendant—so that it was disputed whether they had passed between, or somehow outside them. Cook was clear: 'Providence had conducted us through between these rocks where I should not have ventured in a clear day and to such an anchoring place that I could not have chosen a better.'[2] There were other journal-keepers more inclined to indulge in sentiments of horror, terror and astonishment, but Clerke's ironical note may suffice: 'very nice pilotage, considering our perfect Ignorance of our situation'.[3] Cook improved the situation by sending a boat on shore to see what it produced, and was highly pleased by the salad that was brought back.

He stayed where he was for twenty-four hours, at the end of which the fog had dispersed enough for him to weigh again, and work through one channel between islands to another leading north. But for a further day he was uncertain about the prospect. It was possible that the land might trend away to the northward; on the other hand, he might find a passage to the west or the south-west. Surely he could not be merely in another inlet! Anchor in a failing wind; weigh with a light north-east breeze and the flood tide; anchor with the ebb for the night—a trifling tide here, but half a mile north-east 'a race that looked frightfull.' Weigh at daybreak next morning, the 28th, with a light southerly, then variable light airs from every direction. The *Resolution* nevertheless got through the channel with the last of the flood tide from the south; the *Discovery* astern got caught in the ebb, was twirled round and round with the sea breaking

---

[1] *Journals* III, 388–9.   [2] ibid., 389.   [3] ibid., 389, n. 1.

on the decks, 'confoundedly tumbled about for an hour or two', until she drove clear of the race, and then she too was through. On one side the coast trended, as before, west and south-west; on the other, north. Nine weeks from Nootka Sound, and the continent had at last taken a favourable turn. There was not wind enough to govern the ships, and they were in danger of being carried back through the channel; Cook was forced to anchor again until low water, when they were towed by their boats into a bay not far distant that promised good shelter. We can identify the places of these hazards. The spot where they were nearly ashore is a small bight just south of the north-east extremity of an island called Sedanka or Biorka, which itself lies off the north-eastern coast of the large island of Unalaska. Cook did not perceive their separation, and until he learnt the indigenous name proposed to give Unalaska the grateful one of Providence Island. He worked his way into the Unalga pass, between Unalaska and the small Unalga island to the north-east, where the tide can run at the rate of eight or nine knots; and the secure harbour into which the ships were towed, 'Samgo-onoodha' or Samgunuda, is now known as English Bay.

Cook's purpose in putting in here was to get water. He had all he wanted by the evening of the following day, 29 June, but the thickest of fogs and a northerly wind kept him in harbour until 2 July. The second day of July, and latitude 53°55'; how long to 65°? Fog was not continuously so thick that men could not walk on shore, and a surprising amount of information, for three days, was collected about the place and the people that were encountered—Eskimos of the Aleut branch, obviously affected by their Russian contacts. Cook received from them another note like the one that had caused so great a sensation ten days before; he returned it with one of his own, in English and Latin, giving the names of the ships and their commanders. King, ascending the highest hill nearby in spite of snow and ice, as if he were Cook himself, to take a view, lost the view in the fog, and fell down a crevasse. He was lucky enough to be able to walk out of it. A large amount of wild pease, angelica, celery and sorrel was gathered. The air was clear enough at one moment, while the watering was going on, to make observations that settled the position of the place very accurately.[1]

The fog thinned, the wind went round to the south; they put to

---

[1] On what precise spot the observations were made we do not know. They gave the result lat. 53°55' N, long. 193°30' E (= 166°30' W); which is remarkably close to the position now given for the eastern entrance point, lat. 53°57' N, long. 166°14' W.

sea and steered north, where now it seemed all open. Cook had, however, to trace the coast, and the coast turned north-east: that is, he had to run up the northern side of the Alaskan peninsula as a preliminary to anything else, and it was slow work. After a first short gale there were weeks of light and often contrary winds that died away into calms; and after the first week, as the peninsula began to change direction and merged into the continent, notice was given, in a lessening of the depth of the sea, that one of the perils of that coast was its shoals. It was not a notice, however general, that could then be understood. There were some early fine days, more fog, much 'cloudy gloomy weather', rain, mist. At least the calms off the peninsula provided such fishing weather, and the ships were stationary over such teeming cod banks that the men grew bored with hauling in. Cook cut the allowance of salt meat. The land levelled out in front of the great mountain spine of the peninsula, and on 10 July, at the head of a bay at its northern angle, surrounded by a large plain, he was in some danger from the sand bottom the rivers had built up. Anchoring during the unfavourable flood tide, plying to windward on the ebb, he managed to get out of this danger to the south-west, and then make a little distance to the north-west; it was light airs, calms, and cod-fishing, with unavailing attempts to harpoon the walrus that now began to appear, sometimes in fog so thick that again one end of the ship could not be seen from the other. Thus the days went by till the 16th, when the weather cleared. The ships were off a barren promontory in latitude 58°42′, where the coast changed direction north. Williamson, sent to examine it and take the requisite view from it, was allowed the privilege of naming it, and called it Cape Newenham, after an Irish friend. He also took possession of the country, for what that was worth. The cape seemed to Cook to be the northern limit of a great bay or gulf which extended south-west to Unimak island, and this he himself called Bristol Bay, his old friend Augustus Hervey having succeeded to that earldom. The name has become much more confined.

He got easily enough round Cape Newenham before the wind failed again, and then he found himself over the fearful shoals of Kuskokwim Bay, parallel hard banks of sand and stones and mud flats, some of which dry at low water, stretching far out of sight of land. He was well within sight of land, and anchored. At the first attempt the *Resolution*'s cable parted from her anchor. While the masters were away sounding for a channel he managed to recover it. He was determined about this, because he had lost one anchor already; he had a 'very excellent swimmer' on board, who was sent down when something was caught in the sweep and reported a rock, although it turned out to be the anchor; and a little sign of irritation shows in the log entry, that there was reason to think the man perhaps, instead of being mistaken, 'had wilfully deceived us'. A possible channel to the north was narrow, intricate, too risky; to the south-west was no channel at all. It remained to go back the way they had come. Clerke had taken his own look around: a country appearing just as destitute as a country could be, the surrounding seas scarcely navigable for their numberless shoals—'a damn'd unhappy part of the World'.[1] They turned back with three boats ahead to direct them, and before long had to anchor again to avoid a shoal with only five feet of water on it. When they could clear it they edged in for the land, where the water was deepest, and by the evening of the 22nd were safe. Five days had gone on that episode.[2] While the ships had been at anchor a fleet of kayaks had paddled out to see them, appearing to express peaceable intentions, each man in his own canoe—like the Unalaska people, but far less sophisticated, dirtier, less well clothed. Pieces of iron they had somehow got hold of, however, and had made into primitive knives. They were anxious for more and were willing to give in exchange anything they had about them—skin dresses, bows and arrows, darts. They were Eskimos, of different stock from the Aleuts, and Cook judged that they had had no Russian contact, nor seen European ships before his.

Instead of following the coast north, he was now forced into a sort of large semi-circular cast out into the Bering Sea. To be sure of clearing the shoals he steered south and south-west, the *Discovery*, drawing less water, in the lead; then west, then west-north-west in a northerly wind, anchoring for the worst of the fog, then for a few hours one day even north till the wind went round again. The 28th gave a space of clear sunshine: lunars were taken, the position worked out—latitude 59°55', longitude 190°06' East. They were gradually working north—were, approximately, in the middle of the Bering Sea, and according to Müller's map, were in the middle of the land; according to Stählin's, in the middle of an ungainly mass of islands. Next day an island was indeed seen through the mist, with an 'incredable' number of the picturesque birds called Tufted Puffins about it, whence the name (not given by Cook) Bird Island; it was in fact St Matthew Island, earlier discovered by Sindt. One of Stählin's many islands, supposed Cook; 'we expected every moment

---

[1] Clerke for 18 July: *Journals* III, 401, n. 2.

[2] 'Whoever will reflect on what we have already encounter'd for these last 5 days will Allow that we have been in no small danger, which might have proved very serious, had not the Wea^r all that time been remarkably Moderate & fine.'—King, ibid., 1429.

to meet with more of them.' Then the fog came down again, and the ships were in a noise of guns, drums and bells in their efforts to keep together. They stood alternately north-west and north-east. Saturday, 1 August, came: latitude 60°58', longitude 191° East, the wind north-east, cloudy gloomy weather. The next day brought variable light winds with showers of rain, and a 'nasty jumbling' disconcerting sea, which made the *Discovery* unmanageable. Monday the 3rd, two degrees further north, a degree and a half further east, a south-east breeze and a course to the northward: but this day brought an expected grief. Anderson died. Cook, no great hand at obituary phrases, does his awkward best; we feel that there was an unspoken affection within him.

He was a Sensible Young Man, an agreeable companion, well skilld in his profession, and had acquired much knowlidge in other Sciences, that had it pleased God to have spar'd his life might have been usefull in the Course of the Voyage. Soon after land was Seen to the Westward, 12 leagues distant, it was supposed to be an Island and to perpetuate the Memory of the deceased for whom I had a very great regard, I named [it] *Andersons Island*.[1]

He would—a further touch of sentiment—have preferred to bury his friend ashore; but when the time came, next morning, there was no land to be seen. Not many deaths at sea can have been more felt than that of this attractive modest man.[2] Seniority brought Law to the *Resolution* to take his place; his friend Samwell, to whom he had left his books, went as surgeon to the *Discovery*.

Anderson's Island was not quite a new discovery: it was St Lawrence Island, sighted and named by Bering almost exactly fifty years before. Cook maintained his northward course, with a favouring wind though in thick weather. On the afternoon of the 4th he saw land again, extending north-east to north-west, low next the sea, swelling inland to high hills; bare, so far as he could see, of either wood or snow. He judged it was the American continent again, though he had not laid eyes on that since he put the shoals of Kuskokwim Bay behind him. There was a small high island close by. He anchored seven or eight miles off the main and next morning ran down between it and the island and anchored again. He was anxious,

---

[1] *Journals* III, 406.

[2] Clerke: 'The Death of this Gentleman, is a most unfortunate Stroke to our Expedition alltogether; his distinguished Abilities as a Surgeon, & unbounded humanity, render'd him a most respectable and much esteemed Member of our little Society; and the loss of his superior Knowledge of, and wonted attention to the Science of Natural History, will leave a Void in the Voyage much to be regretted.' King writes at length with the greatest admiration, concluding, 'If we except our Commander, he is the greatest publick loss the Voyage could have sustaind.'—ibid., 406, n. 1, 1429-30.

as ever, to climb a hill. To the west the fog was so thick that he might
as well have stayed in the ship as set foot on the island, but to the
north, after a westerly swing, high land could be seen a great way off.
There was more to be seen on the island—some grass, wild vegetables, a fox, a few birds, decayed human habitations, a beaten path,
and an extremely well-made sledge, about ten feet long but narrow,
such as Cook had seen described as Kamchatkan. He was enough
struck to call the small spot of land Sledge Island, and he noted its
latitude, 64°30'. The next morning he began to follow the main
north-west, slowly and cautiously, because the winds were light, the
air thick and drizzling; anchoring when the wind fell to a calm or
near-calm and the current carried him towards the shoal-bordered
shore. He hoped for a few hours that a short cut to the north-east
might serve him; it did not exist, nor, he found immediately after,
was it needed. When morning came upon him at anchor on 9 August
the air had cleared and he could see about him. To the west lay a
high steep rock he had perceived through the mist the evening
before, and an island north of it; to the east the main rising to a
peaked hill over a flat point. Beyond this point the coast turned
north-east, and a strong current set in the same direction. He had no
doubt of where he was in one particular at least; 'This Point of land
which I named *Cape Prince of Wales*, is the more remarkable by being
the Western extremity of all America hitherto known'; and when the
pale sun shone for a few minutes at noon he was able to settle its
position fairly well—latitude 65°46' North, longitude 191° plus an
indeterminate distance East, the observations being 'liable to some
small error on account of the haziness of the weather.'[1] So: now, if he
adhered to his instructions, would begin the detailed exploration of
the American coast.

One can say more circumstantially where he was. He was
anchored in Bering Strait, about three miles off Cape Prince of
Wales; his high steep rock was Fairway Rock, his island was Little
Diomede, with its larger companion rising close behind it, in the
middle of the strait. The strait is fifty-five miles across at its narrowest, and he could not see the other side. It is hard not to assume that
he knew that if he sailed across he would arrive at Asia, like a
sixteenth-century cartographer skirting the Strait of Anian; and
indeed Müller's map told him he would. But Stählin's map told him
he would arrive, anyhow as an intermediate stage, at a large island
called Alaschka; and though neither map, in certain respects, was

[1] ibid., 409. The position of the cape now accepted is lat. 65°37' N, long. 168°06' W
(191°54' E), so that, taking the haze into account, Cook's error was again indeed small.

in touch with reality, at least both showed an American continent sloping away north-east from its western cape, and so far could claim to be authentic. Cook was at once plunged into investigation of the matter. He did not intend to be, because when he weighed anchor with the first faint northerly breeze on this morning of 9 August it was the coast of America he wanted to follow, and he plied to windward. The faint breeze immediately turned to a hard gale, with the usual thick rainy weather, and a sea so high, from the conflicting directions of wind and current, that it kept on breaking into the ships. Early in the afternoon he bore up westward for the island he had seen, thinking he would anchor under it; there were two islands, neither large enough to provide shelter from the violent wind that howled over and between them, and he continued to stretch to the west. The weather clearing somewhat, in the evening he saw land twenty or thirty miles off, and after tacking to the east for the night, next morning came in again and anchored on the north side of a bay he called after St Lawrence, whose day it was: for once a 'fine cheerly day'—to revert to Clerke—which 'gives even this wretched, barren Country a most pleasing appearance; we all feel this morning as though we were risen in a new World.'[1]

A new world virtually it was; and inhabited. As the ships were standing in Cook saw a village, from which people were departing hurriedly inland with burdens on their backs; and when he went with the boats to land near the place he found a band of forty or fifty men drawn up to receive him, all armed with spears and bows and arrows. They had sent their women and children away. He did not know what we know, that these people, Chukchi, a Mongoloid group tenacious of their freedom, took the ships for Russian, and they had no love for the Russians. They could see very well that the boats were armed. Cook's behaviour illustrates clearly his attitude and policy on first meeting a strange and potentially hostile people; and the man who had made such contacts at Dusky Sound and on the beaches of the New Hebrides would perhaps have admitted that the behaviour of the people themselves was also a model. The account he gives us is equally illuminating as an unconscious portrait of himself.

As we drew near three of them came down towards the shore and were so polite as to take of their Caps and make us a low bow: we returned the Compliment but this did not inspire them with sufficient confidence to

---

[1] He continued, 'we had almost forgot the cheerful & pleasing Sensations, instilled by a clear Atmosphere & enlivening rays of the Sun.—Got every thing from between Decks & clean'd Ship.'—ibid., 410, n. 1.

wait our landing, for the Moment we put the boats a shore they retired. I followed them alone without any thing in my hand, and by signs and actions got them to stop and receive some trifles I presented them with and in return they gave me two fox skins and a couple of Sea horse teeth. I cannot say whether they or I made the first present, for these things they brought down with them for this very purpose and would have given me them without my making any return. They seemed very fearfull and causious, making signs for no more of our people to come up, and on my laying my hand on one mans Shoulder he started back several paces. In proportion as I advanced they retreated backwards always in the attitude of being ready to make use of their Spears, while those on the hill behind them stood ready to support them with thier arrows. Insensibly my self and two or three more got in amongst them, a few beads distributed to those about us brought on a kind of confidence so that two or three more of our people joining us did not Alarm them, and by degrees a sort of traffick between us commenced.[1]

Their weapons, however, they would not part with: even when they danced they kept them within reach. But cautious as they were, they let Cook examine everything he wished—their persons, their extremely well made clothing of skins or leather, their winter houses partly sunk in the ground, their tent-like summer huts, the high stages built of bones on which they dried their skins and fish. They were a taller, longer-faced people than the northern Americans, they did not wear the Eskimo frock, though certainly their boats and canoes were of the same pattern and, like them, they depended on the sea for their living. Cook's observations, for the two or three hours that he stayed, were remarkably wide. Soon after he returned to the ship the wind veered to the south, and he at once stood out of the bay and steered north-east between the coast he was on and the two islands, through the strait.

He was uncertain where he had been. In his log he refers tentatively to the Island of Alaschka 'or the Westland'; in his journal he more directly registers his doubt.

This land we supposed to be a part of the island of *Alaschka* laid down in Mr Staehlins Map before q[u]oted though from the figure of the Coast, the situation of the opposite coast of America, and the longitude it appeared rather more probable to be the Country of the Tchuktschians explored by Behring in 1728. But to have admitted this at first sight I must have concluded Mr Staehlins Map and account to be either exceeding erronious even in latitude or else a mere fiction, a Sentance I had no right to pass upon it without farther proof.[2]

[1] *Journals* III, 410–11. [2] ibid., 414.

Nor was this immediately important. The important thing was the
passage north, and all eyes were on the lie of the land. As they left
the two capes, east and west, of the strait behind them, Alaschka or
Asia did not seem to matter. How close the captain came to the
feelings of King we do not know, but that lieutenant looked cheerfully at the prospect. 'Which conjecture is right we cannot determine,
but we are in high spirits in seeing the land to the N⁰ward of these
Extremitys trend away so far to the NE, and the other NW, which
bespeaks an open sea to the N⁰ward free of land, and we hope of Ice,
as we have hitherto seen no signs of any.'[1] The northern ice-free sea!
That was after two days, and though shoal water and gales followed
hard, and thick weather and rain swallowed up the eastern shore,
which here changed direction north-west for a short distance to the
north of Kotzebue Sound, in three days more the sun shone out—
latitude 68°18′—'All our Sanguine hopes begin to revive, & we
already begin to compute the distance of our Situation from known
parts of Baffins bay.'[2] The air was sharp. Next day, 17 August, both
sun and moon were seen, and some 'flying observations' gave the
position as latitude 70°33′, longitude 197°41′ E. As the morning
advanced towards noon there was a brightness in the northern sky, of
a sort that Cook had known in high southern latitudes. It was ice-
blink. He had not expected to meet with ice quite so soon; but after
all, he was four degrees beyond the arctic circle, and in the afternoon
was forced to tack off an immense field of it, quite impenetrable, that
filled the whole northern view. He was in latitude 70°41′. There
were, however, living things—sea horses or walruses in the water,
more with their great carcasses flopped upon the ice. He considered
killing some for meat, until the freshening wind persuaded him to
ply to the westward—or rather to try to do so, because next day he
was about twenty miles farther east and three farther north. This
point was his, and the expedition's, northern extreme. He was still
close to the edge of the ice, which rose like a solid wall ten or twelve
feet above the water, and seemed to rise much higher in the distance;
and for the next eleven days his concern was with the ice-field, a
moving mass, whether with an abrupt and definite edge as here, or
breaking away into a fringe of dangerously rotting pieces, cakes and
lumps, iron-hard reefs drifting underwater. One danger he was
spared: this sea had no fringing glaciers, and no vast bergs continually thrust into its currents. But the drift of the ice was dangerous
enough, as he found.

In that highest latitude of 70°44′ Cook was out of sight of land,

[1] 13 August, ibid., 414, n. 2.   [2] 16 August, ibid.

more through haze than distance. He stood south for six leagues, when through a clearing haze he could see the shore three or four miles distant, its most prominent point, 'much incumbered with ice', being given the name of Icy Cape. The wind was from the west. The water shoaled. They were on a lee shore, the *Discovery* a mile astern, with the main body of ice driving down on them, and it would certainly drive them right on shore unless it took the ground before they did—or unless they could get away to the south-west, where was the only opening. 'Our situation was now more and more critical': both ships tacked together; 'the Wind proved rather favourable', the water deepened; for a third time in a few weeks disaster was skimmed by.[1]

This might have seemed not merely baffling but decisive, to a man who wished to follow a coast that ran north-east, and it must have been shattering to King's computation of the distance to Baffin Bay. Cook, on the other hand, clearly did not intend to abandon the ice yet, and even (it also seems fairly clear) for a short time considered the chances of forcing his way into it and so working north. By the time the wind went round to the west again, next morning, he was well away from the land, and tacked to the north through drift ice to the edge of the main field again. It was not quite continuous; there were in it a number of clear places like pools (thus his log), 'so that had there been a necessity the ships might probably have been forced into it, had they been strengthened and armed against Ice like Greenland ships; but even if they had, it would not have been prudent to have done it at this advanced season of the year.'[2] In the mean time there was something else that could be done. On the ice lay a 'prodigious' number of walruses, that potential fresh food; boats were sent from both ships, and between them slew a dozen of the animals. They were huge; they provided a great deal of meat; Cook was delighted and stopped all normal rations except bread; Clerke found it good eating; the men, at first rapaciously hungry for something other than the contents of the harness cask, in general agreed till the novelty wore off; some swore it was not intended to be eaten by Christians, and there were some whose stomachs positively rejected it. Very well, said Cook: it might be coarse, black, and strong in taste, the fat might melt down into train-oil, but it was wholesome, and the alternative to wholesome food would be ship's bread alone. With the utmost difficulty was he persuaded to restore salt meat to those who would other wise have

1 ibid., 418.
2 Log: ibid., 418, n. 4.

starved.[1] He found the habits of the animal interesting, and gives an interesting description; he went to pains to have the dimensions of one, 'none of the largest', measured in most possible ways. And then the oil was excellent for lamps, the thick hides very useful about the rigging. These, though the largest living things to be seen—for whales had disappeared—were not the only ones. Day after day flights of ducks and other birds went by, on their way to the south: did not this argue land, a home of migratory species in the north?

The larder was replenished, but when it was done, on this 19 August, the drifting ice was all around them, and it was necessary to beat a retreat to the south. Cook would not yet abandon the ice in this part of the sea, and for three days he tacked back and forth about latitude 69°30', while the light breezes went round from north to east to west to south, in gloom and fog. The sun might not go beneath the horizon, but did little to illuminate the waste, and the direction of the main ice edge, as it slowly moved southward, was announced by the roaring of walruses or the noise of the sea surging upon it. On the 21st the fog cleared, and to the south the American shore appeared again, a low-lying coast marked only at its furthest limit by the bare precipitous hill of Cape Lisburne—a name not conferred by Cook himself, who was this month not fertile with names, nor had much use for them. He went in to the land to get a nearer view 'and to look for a harbour'—but what would he have done with a harbour just then? He would surely not have immobilised himself before the advancing mass? There was none. He returned to the north till he heard the midnight surge and grinding of the ice. A calm was succeeded by a north-east wind, the fog cleared for a while, and he came to a decision: 'finding I could not get to the North near the Coast for the ice, I resolved to try what could be done at a distance from it', and he steered west. The northerly brought a raw, sharp, cold air, and the weather now was varied by showers of snow or sleet. By the 26th he was once more close to the ice, about ten degrees of longitude west of where he had

[1] See the conflicting opinions quoted in the long note 3 of p. 419 of *Journals* III. Cf. also King, ibid., 1453–4, on the determination of Cook to conquer 'Prejudice and caprice' in the cause of fresh food: 'when we first fell in with the Sea horses which we calld by the name of Sea Cows, we were full of the Idea of the excellent repast they would afford, accordingly eat of them with good appetites. The Captn finding this, was more precipitate than his usual good sense & penetration warrant'd, for he stopt the allowance of Salt provisions altogether. At the same time some of the Sailors on board, who had been to Greenland, spread the report that these were only Sea horses, & that they were consider'd to be such bad food, that no one in these voyages ever thought of eating any parts but the heart.' If Cook had held back only half the allowance of salt meat, thought King, and left the sea horse to free choice, he was convinced that as Cook at his table, and the officers at theirs had nothing else, 'the whole would have been very happy at eating what was far preferable to any salt meat.'

left it, and in much the same latitude. That is, he had sailed three-quarters of the distance across this southern part of the arctic ocean, to meet exactly the same phenomenon—a solid compact main ice-field, with a fringe, at first scattered and then jostling, in strange broken shapes, large and small, of what Cook called heavy loose ice. For a while he was embayed until he could escape to the east, where only there was a clear sea. Obviously there was no better prospect of getting to the north here than there was close to the American shore.

But the ice-edge seems to have had a fascination for him. Next day he tacked back again, and the wind falling, went in the boats to examine it at close quarters. The separate broken pieces were so tight-packed that it was difficult to get a boat between them, and it would have been quite impossible for the ships. He observed the surface. He sounded the underwater ledges. He killed a few out of the almost incredible number of walruses that drifted upon it; and then, a blinding fog coming down, had to return to the ships rather prematurely—so he thought—finding them not without difficulty, and with only one walrus for each. The fog lifting a little the following morning, he sent the boats out again for this 'marine beef'; for he was persuaded, against some at least of the evidence, that by this time his men began to relish it. His latitude was still above 69°, but the ice had advanced twenty miles in the previous forty-eight hours, a wind from the south made it a lee shore again, and not until midnight, with a shift of the wind to north-west, could he feel agreeably situated. He stretched to the south-west close-hauled. The morning of 29 August came. In the north the main ice-field was still visible. In the south-west and west was land. As he approached it the water shoaled rapidly, repeating the pattern of the American shore; and the coast was very like that of America, low next the sea, except for a cape or two, rising steadily inland, without wood or snow, brown with dried herbage. One point stood out steep and rocky. King called it Cape North; it was the present Cape Mys Shmidta. Beyond it the coast trended west. There Cook must go. But he could not weather the cape, the wind freshened, the air once more turned to thick fog, with snow added, 'and being fearfull of the ice coming down upon us, I gave up the design I had formed of plying to the Westward and stood off shore again after standing into 10 fathoms water.' The decision had to be taken.

The season was now so very far advanced and the time when the frost is expected to set in so near at hand, that I did not think it consistant with prudence to make any farther attempts to find a passage this year in any direction so little was the prospect of succeeding. My attention was now directed towards finding out some place where we could Wood and Water, and in the considering how I should spend the Winter, so as to make some improvement to Geography and Navigation and at the same time be in a condition to return to the North in further search of a Passage the ensuing summer.[1]

The ice had beaten him. He meditated on the nature of the enemy, though not at such length as he had done in the southern hemisphere, where also he had been defeated. There were some certainties. Quite certainly the great mass stretched from shore to shore, east to west, was as impenetrable as the shore, was a 'moveable Mass', advanced and retreated with the seasons. Quite certainly it was not river ice; for how could so vast an extent, of such height and depth, float from rivers 'in which there is hardly water for a boat'? He must have been generalising, in this estimate of arctic streams, from Samuel Hearne's account of the Coppermine river as it debouched through shallows into a shallow sea. Nor did this ice carry with it anything that originated in the land. It must have been all formed at sea. There may be a tribute to the force of European dogma in that even now, with all his experience, he would not assert, or guess, that the sea froze. 'It appeared to be intirely composed of frozen Snow.' It could not be produced by one winter only, one summer could not destroy a tenth part of it. None the less it waned as well as waxed—then how? He thought the sun, whose rays he had so infrequently seen, must be an ineffectual agent; and where he saw from the masthead a rugged surface and pools of water could hardly assume that this was the typical appearance of old ice where summer melting had taken place. It was the surge of the sea that undermined, that broke, that ground the great pieces together, that washed away, that left for a while submerged platforms over which a ship might sail, on which upper lumps and fragments stood like rocks on a reef. 'Thus it may happen that more ice is distroyed in one Stormy Season, than is formed in several Winter[s] and an endless accumulation prevented, but that there is always a remaining store, none who had been upon the spot will deny and none but Closet studdying Philosiphers will dispute.'[2] Poor Barrington; poor Samuel Engel!

Beaten: he might himself have preferred to say baffled, and baffled to fight better; for he would try again in the ensuing summer and then undoubtedly he would be earlier on the scene of struggle. Nothing need stop him from being at latitude 65° in June. He simply

[1] *Journals* III, 427. [2] ibid., 425.

did not know enough—how could he, or anyone, know enough?—about the arctic and sub-arctic ice in this part of the hemisphere. Hudson, in 1607, west of Spitsbergen, had reached a latitude of 80°23' N. Phipps, on the Spitsbergen coast in 1773, had not been stopped till 80°37'; many Greenland whalers had been up to 80°. Cook might therefore well be surprised at meeting impenetrable ice in latitude 70°41'. It was in mid-August as against Phipps's mid-July, but should a month, even at the end of summer, make all that difference? There was a good deal of enquiry necessary about the distribution of ice. One may believe that Cook, quite unwittingly, was on the whole fortunate to arrive in the north when he did, and have the season he had, whatever the fog and the winds. In June he would have found ice in Bering Strait, and most probably in the Bering Sea; if he had not reached the strait till the very end of June, he would have found the sea beyond it, probably, just beginning to clear. The latitude of 70°41' was about the average latitude for the summer retreat of the pack. In a bad year he might have met it further south, in an exceptionally good year much further north; and if 1778 had been such a good year he might have been lured round the American coast, past Point Barrow into the Beaufort Sea, towards where Samuel Hearne had stood and looked on the grey and narrow margin of water, in the direction of the veritable Passage, and have been lost for ever. Or in an August even a little better than this one of 1778 he might have been tempted up a lane of clear sea next the coast beyond Icy Cape while the easterly wind blew back the ice, and with a change of wind it would have closed on him over the shoals with irretrievable disaster, as he had felt it might only the day after he first sighted that compact moving wall. That was a lesson he may have learned at once. There was little enough time for study before the book was closed.

With useful experience in his mind, nevertheless, he bore away eastward and later south-eastward to trace this new coast, through four days of heavy snow with but few intervals, and a freezing air. This did not impede the general cheerfulness that the ice had been left behind, or the prospect of warm joys to come. At times the lead was the only guide. Fortunately the clear intervals, though not many, gave a far enough view for Cook to see that the coast, now barren white instead of brown, was continuous, and to settle its main features. By the first day of September he was 'well assured' that this was 'the coast of Tchuktschi, or the NE coast of Asia'—in modern terms, the Chukotskiy peninsula, truly the north-eastern extremity of Siberia—and that he could connect it with the sightings of Bering's first voyage in 1728. On the 2nd the snow at last ceased, the sun broke out to provide a precise latitude, 66°37'30'' N, and the view of a few people and their hillock-like habitations on shore, even there; and in the evening he passed once more the 'Eastern Cape'. He both described it and fixed its position with great accuracy.[1] Next forenoon, in pleasant weather, he was looking into St Lawrence Bay, somewhat surprised that none of the people whom he could see would come off to the ship; even some out to sea towing a dead whale seemed to hide themselves behind it. He wanted to find a harbour which he could use in the spring; but he wanted one with a supply of wood and he had seen none here. Further to the south the bays he passed were guarded by shoal water; then the coast changed direction west towards the Gulf of Anadyr, into which he did not want to go. He did want to get a sight of the St Lawrence island of Bering, so he continued his southerly course till he picked up its western end in the distance—the evening of 4 September—and then steered over for the American shore. He had made a careful check of Bering on this side of the northern sea—that is, of the accounts of Bering's first voyage, so much clearer than anything that could be learnt of the second—and concluded that his predecessor had done well.[2]

Why, then, having merely ascertained the existence of an island in the reported position of St Lawrence island did Cook without further investigation steer for the American shore? True, his store of firewood was diminishing. But also the purely geographical problem of Stählin's Alaschka continued to gnaw at him. If he had just left the Asian coast now, at the beginning of September, it was crystal clear that he had been on the coast of Asia, and not of an island, at the beginning of August. What then had happened to Alaschka? The comparative width of the large strait between America and Alaschka and the narrow strait between Alaschka and Asia, on Stählin's map, could be ignored: the map contained other things just as extraordinary as that. Although in escaping from the shoals north of Cape Newenham he had had to sacrifice his view of the land, he had concluded that the land formed one continuous coast from Cape Newenham north to Cape Prince of Wales. Was that conclusion wrong? Was part of that coast insular, and had he

---

[1] 'It is a Peninsula of considerable height, joined to the continent by a very low and to appearence narrow neck of land; it shew[s] a steep rocky clift next the Sea and off the very point are some rocks like Spires. It is Situated in the latitude of 66°06' N, longitude 190°22' East . . .'.—ibid., 431. The now accepted position is lat. 66°5' N, long. 169°40' W (190°20' E).

[2] ibid., 433.

somehow missed in the distance or the fog a strait that could be equated, by whatever violence, with Stählin's? Had he, that is, sailed in his ignorance past the west coast, and not the east coast, of Alaschka? Some of his men thought he probably had. We may note that King writes in his journal, of the view of the main from Sledge Island, 'The Map of Dr Matty's places the large Island of Alashka in this latitude & therefore many suppose this to be it.' Well: what then? If the Stählin strait indeed existed, where might it lead? —to an ice-free sea?—to a passage into Baffin Bay? To resolve the dubiety was important; not to waste time the following summer in fruitless quests was important. 'It was with me a matter of some Consequence to clear up this point this Season, that I might have but one object in View the next. . . .'

A matter of less consequence was let go, therefore, when next day, the 5th, land was seen bearing south-east, 'which we tooke to be Andersons island or some other land near it, therefore did not wait to examine it.'[1] The next day again the American coast was in sight, near Sledge Island. Cook had no doubt that if there were an Alaschka, it must be here; for here he had felt, it seems, when at anchor at the beginning of August, that the direction of the tides east and west indicated that he had the option of sailing either way; and he had chosen west. Coming slowly in with the land, this time in fine and pleasant weather though with light contrary breezes, he found it trend to the east, and on the 8th followed it in that direction, his progress even more retarded by the shoaling of the water. Off a large projection, later called Cape Darby, he anchored for the night; beyond this projection the coast turned northerly, and at daybreak on the 9th he continued to follow it. South-east there was an island, east another as he thought; in the morning haze hills seemed so many islands in that direction, and there was quite high land far beyond. For a moment it seemed that the problem was solved: the high land was the continent, the land to the north and west was Alaschka, the ships were in the entrance to a strait. If strait then useless; for the water shoaled more and more, and the shoals were not merely a passage to deeper water. At one point the *Resolution*'s keel brought up the mud from the bottom. Return was imperative, and in the face of the wind. The admired captain had done what perhaps no other man in the world would have done, thought the later Trevenen; and perhaps he had been imprudent. His luck held; after plying all night he was in safety, and could land to inspect the country. There was plenty of excellent drift wood, as well as small

[1] ibid., 434.

spruce, birch and willows, and an ample supply of berries of various sorts. A change of wind sent him over to anchor for the succeeding night in the shelter of what he had taken for an island, which proved next day to be the peninsula he called Cape Denbigh—how the land joined up!—with a quite large bay beyond, a sort of flattened semi-circle lined with shoals; everywhere shoals, and a bottom of mud. It was difficult to load the boats with wood from the peninsula, because they grounded so far from the shore. He stood over to the other shore again, inside Cape Darby. Here it was easy to get drift wood from the beach, more difficult to load with water.

There is a curious air, not exactly of leisure, but of relief from pressure, about the days spent in this not very ingratiating gap in the land—Norton Sound, as Cook called it in honour of the Speaker who had provided that valedictory dinner. The weather was through-out fine and favourable. Certainly every time he weighed anchor and moved to a fresh position his sailors had to bow their backs; and when he sent King away with the cutters to complete the exploration of the inlet from which the ships had been rebuffed, so emulous of good was that young officer that he made his crew row till they collapsed asleep at the oars. He had been given a week's provisions and a rendezvous at 'Samganoodha', in case he should find a channel or the ships should have to leave before his return; he was back in two days with a report of nothing but sandbanks and mud and marsh, a small river, hills and distant mountains; and when he arrived on board at Cape Denbigh (where Cook had moved the ships again, and climbed another hill) he found the captain already 'pretty certain of the Event'. The men had been given leisure to wander on shore and pick berries; shooting parties of officers had tried their luck, with no brilliant success, among the geese and bustards, snipe and grouse; spruce had been cut for beer; there had been many friendly encounters with the people of the place, a people very like all other Americans encountered north of Nootka Sound, and as generous—much more generous indeed trading their skins and fish than the sailor whom Clerke overheard 'damning his Eyes very heartily because they gave him only 2 Salmon for a small yellow Bead.'[1] Perhaps the astronomers worked as hard as anybody, with their seventy-seven sets of lunar observations to determine the longitude, 197°13' East. The latitude was still as far north as 64°31'.

Meanwhile, Cook had been giving some thought to his next move-ments, and the paragraph in which he summarises his cogitations

---

[1] *Journals* III, 439, n. 3.

is so characteristic as to be not merely a statement of intention but again a comment on himself.

Haveing now fully satisfied myself that Mr Stæhlin's Map must be erroneous and not mine it was high time to think of leaving these Northern parts, and to retire to some place to spend the Winter where I could procure refreshments for the people and a small supply of provisions. *Petropaulowska* in *Kamtschatka*, did not appear to me a place where I could procure either the one or the other for so large a number of men, and besides I had other reasons for not going there at this time, the first and on which all the others depended was the great dislike I had to lay inactive for Six or Seven Months, which must have been the case had I wintered in any of these Northern parts. No place was so conveniently within our reach where we could expect to meet with these necessary articles, as *Sandwich Islands*, to these islands, therefore, I intended to proceed, but before this could be carried into execution it was necessary to have a supply of Water. With this View I resolved to search the America coast for a harbour, by proceeding along it to the Southward and endeavour to connect the Survey of this coast with that to the North of Cape Newenham. If I failed of finding a harb. then to proceed to *Samgoonoodha* which was fixed upon for a Rendezvous in case of Separ[a]tion.[1]

He weighed anchor again on 17 September and slowly, with a light wind and the boats ahead, skirted the shore of the sound outside its islands. Anchoring for the night, he was not outside until the end of the following day, when he steered for the southernmost point of the continent he could see. In vain: he ran into shoals again; forty or fifty miles, as he judged, off the coast he had only four fathoms beneath him, and had to steer directly away from it. That southernmost point he called Point Shallow Water, and suspected the disemboguing of a considerable river. He was right, except that his 'point' was rather a bulge, the northern part of the delta of the river Yukon, and of land so flat, only a foot or two high, and so with an invisible shore, that he largely overestimated his distance from it. When he steered west he was retreating from the Yukon flats. Cape Newenham he would not see again; the coast for three degrees of latitude, 63° to 60°, from Point Shallow Water to the equally dangerous shore of Kuskokwim Bay, must remain 'intirely unexploared'. That being so, there was no harbour and for water he must go to Samgunuda.

So at least he had determined; but other possibilities began to come forward. After getting away from the shoals he set a more southerly course, for the land he had sighted on the 5th, a fortnight before, 'Andersons island or some other land near it.' He came up

[1] ibid., 441–2.

with it on the 20th, and presents us with a pretty problem. The problem is not the identity of this piece of land, but why Cook failed to identify it. It was an odd lapse of perception. He now says, 'As I found this land laid two [*sic*] far to the West to be Andersons island I named it'—and he leaves a blank, filled in by a later hand as Clerke's Island. But he had given no position for the Anderson's Island of 3 August, his first sighting, only a bearing, 'to the Westward, 12 leagues distant'. He had sighted the island of St Lawrence on 4 September, and on the following day 'Andersons island or some other land near it'—and if other, why not St Lawrence? Why should Cook assume that his position for 'Clerke's Island' was correct, when he got sight of it in a fresh northerly gale with showers of hail and snow and a high sea? Was he misled by Stählin's shamble of islands to think that four separate sightings must be sightings of four or, at the least, three separate islands? They were, we know, all sightings of St Lawrence, which is the largest island in the Bering Sea. We can hardly upbraid Cook for not knowing that. But he could see a reason in his own experience why Russians should multiply islands, and was plain enough about it in his log, precisely on the subject of Clerke's Island.

From what we have seen of this Island it cannot be less than 35 or 40 leagues in circuit, and is composed of Mountains and plains, so that [at] a distance it looks like several islands, each hill or mountain appearing as one, and this may be the reason why we find a group of Islands, nearly in this situation, in the map of the New Northern Archipelago discovered by the Russians; for unless these Navigators have taken every hill for an Island, many of their Islands must either have no existence, or a very different situation to that which they have in the above mentioned Map.[1]

Then why did he suspect no flaw in his own conception? Assuredly the Cook of the second voyage would have disentangled the truth.

He hung about the northern side of this island, fruitlessly looking for a harbour, until noon the following day, when he stood south-

---

[1] *Journals* III, 445, n. 1. Summarising, we may say that Cook made four imperfect sightings of the same island: his St Lawrence is Cape Chibukak, the north-west extreme, and a small part of the land adjoining; his Clerke's is large parts of both eastern and western halves though unconnected on the charts then made; his Anderson's is the high land of the eastern end between East Cape and North-east Cape, some eleven miles. A 'gross mistake', says Bligh, quoted in the note here cited; and also, 'This unaccountable error arose only from sheer ignorance not knowing how to investigate the fact, & it is a disgrace to us as Navigators to lay down what does not exist. I know it does not from a perfect knowledge of the lands. . . .'—Bligh to Burney, 26 July 1791, Dixson Library MSS, printed *Journals* III, 1565. But even this positive expression did not make Bligh's knowledge quite perfect: he merely reduced the number of islands to two—(1) St Lawrence (2) Clerke's—'for Anderson's I^d and the East end of Clerke's I^d is one and the same land'.

south-west for a further island he regarded as discovered by himself, on 29 July, the one King called Bird island—the St Matthew of Sindt. He was up with it, and its attendant islets, on 23 September: still another of those islands that looked from a distance like a group, among which he had hopes of finding shelter. There were now few birds, and shelter there was none about what Clerke called 'this rascally Place'; Samgunuda after all must be the aim, and for Samgunuda the ships steered with a pleasant breeze behind them, the captain 'being resolved to spend no more time in searching for a harbour amongst islands which I now began to susspect had no existance, at least not in the latitude and longitude the Modern Mapmakers have placed them.'[1] He was unaware of the little irony this remark cast on his own division of St Lawrence Island into three. The passage was not to be all pleasant: in a day or two the wind went round to the south and blew an increasing and violent gale. A clear sea and a good depth of water counterbalanced that discomfort, even though the *Resolution* sprung a starboard leak which gave trouble as long as she was heeled over on a western tack. Cook was fearful of heading eastward prematurely lest he should fall on the Kuskokwim shoals, but that danger and the gale came to an end together. The wind remained contrary; it was not until 2 October that he raised the coast of Unalaska, and the day after that, having tried one unsatisfactory anchorage, he was returned to his previous harbour, and the spendthrift sailors were handing over their precious tobacco for dried fish.

Cook had come to a pause. He remained in this harbour for three weeks. There was much work to do on his ship and the *Discovery's* carpenters were put to it as well as his own. The leak was in the starboard buttock again, fortunately above the water-line, but under the sheathing many of the seams were found quite open. To get the water freely to the pumps, in case of further leaks, he re-stowed his spirit room—which had filled during the last leak—fish room and after hold; and in addition cleared his fore hold right out and took in new ballast. There was no lack of fresh water, and both ships completed their supply. Fish was equally abundant: every morning a boat went out and returned with enough halibut and salmon to feed all hands. If fishing might be regarded as part of the ships' labours, there was compensation in leave to wander ashore berrying, and in the softer side of Unalaskan custom; and whatever penalties might be consequent on the latter, half a dozen different sorts of berry in

[1] *Journals* III, 446.

unlimited quantities, together with the spruce beer that supplanted grog every other day, effectually banished any possible taint of scurvy. This the captain observed with pleasure.

There was ample to observe in the place besides its dietary advantages. The Aleut people were of a sort Cook had not encountered before. The 'Indians' of his previous Pacific experience whom he had been able to study at leisure—Tongans, Tahitians, New Zealanders —had been in their original state, their societies unaffected, even in Tahiti, by the touch of an outside influence, except in so far as he brought it himself. At Samgunuda there was a difference. It was not simply that these were 'the most peaceable inoffensive people I ever met with'—though they had not ever, it seems, been a markedly warlike people. They were under a Russian yoke: from Cook's paragraphs, added to by his officers, we get an account of a primitive society under the first impact of commercial exploitation that is rare in the records of exploration. It was a society which had ceased to be quite savage without becoming civilised; it had, for instance, been deprived of its weapons without being given new and deadlier ones. The Russians, after losing a few of their own men to the defenders of freedom, were nothing if not precautionary. So Cook was received with politeness by Aleuts and with geniality by Russians, and had no difficulty in examining what he wanted to, whether public matters or private—if private matters could be said to exist in that very open society. They were an Eskimo people, short of stature, round-faced and 'plump', wearing the frock and trousers standard on that northern part of the coast, the women's of seal skin, the men's of tough bird skins, all made by the women, who were skilful sempstresses with their bone needles; all of both sexes had their underlips pierced for ornaments, but the men wore none. The article of clothing that most interested Cook was the 'snouted' painted wooden cap or eye-shade, stuck over with bristles of seal or walrus, worn by all the men: but why, if an eye-shade, he wondered, in that sunless clime? Interesting were the capacious communal houses, dug into the ground, but high enough above it, with their frames of driftwood and covering of grass and earth, to look like so many small hillocks; fish-houses and tanneries as well as living quarters and the centres of a surprisingly amoral (at least in the European sense) hospitality. Domestic furnishings and implements were few. It was an economy based on the sea, in a treeless country, where few plants grew besides grass and berry-bushes, and birds and land animals were not many. But the sea still offered abundance, fishing and hunting gear was well made, and though large boats there were none, except in Russian possession, the small canoes or kayaks and their double-bladed paddles were perfect of their kind, waterproof and swift. Such things Cook described with a workman-like and admirable brevity, yet with a gift for being inclusive, that make his remarks models for the student of material culture. Other men—Clerke, King, Edgar, Samwell—may give us more, and in-valuable, material on certain topics or events. The captain, con-sidering birds or stones or 'a kind of Scurvy grass', or words or dialects, may have sighed for Anderson. Yet, when one has read the others, one realises again how much lies compacted in his pages, and how safely: even Bligh, in whom the spirit of contradiction ran so perversely, found nothing to contradict here.

The Russians, it was clear from all accounts, when they first came here for furs on Bering's report, did not have it all their own way; but now, in the islands that they knew, they did, and were gradually pushing up towards the peninsula. They were the masters, adopted a lofty tone, they took the sea otter skins, they bestowed payment of chewing tobacco and snuff; and chewing tobacco had become a necessity of life for their subjects, an indispensable currency for Cook's sailors. But where were the Russians? Only on the fifth day was contact made, when an Aleut brought Cook and Clerke each a present of a sort of pie or loaf of rye flour with a salmon baked inside it, and an incomprehensible note. Cook reciprocated with a few bottles of rum, wine and porter, and sent with them as ambassador Corporal Ledyard of the marines, nothing loth to make a name for himself, and perfectly willing to travel stowed away inside a kayak. He was taken to the bay where Cook had failed to find good anchor-age on his arrival, and a settlement called 'Egoochshac'—apparently the modern Unalaska or Iliukliuk harbour, where a small band of Russians, with their Kamchatkan followers and Unalaskan servants, maintained storehouses and a joint dwelling, and the rum, wine and porter was drunk out with an intense Russian devotion. There was no tendency to deny that the newcomers were English, Friends, and Allies; and not, as a cautious peep over the hill had led on the suspicion, Chinese, Japanese, Spanish or French; and if French, enemies. Ledyard returned with three Russian seamen or furriers, intelligent persons, and Cook's geographical enquiries immediately began. Language was the difficulty, interpreter there was none, yet somehow through the production of maps, and signs and nods, information filtered through. One of these men, Cook understood, claimed to have been with Bering, but Cook's chart of the American coast meant nothing to him. Nor, to any of them, did Stählin's map;

indeed, till Cook told them, they had no idea of what part of the world it referred to; and then it appeared that another of the three had sailed over Stählin's islands. They promised to bring a chart of the islands between Unalaska and Kamchatka. Although they failed to do so, that disappointment was swallowed up in the discussions with still another Russian, the chief man on the island, the factor Gerassim Gregoriev Ismailov.

This man, who appeared first on the 14th, adopted some state, though susceptible to the power of Cook's liquor; he was clever and shrewd, and knew a good deal, though not as much as he pretended to—or he may have had reasons of his own for denying certain things that Cook knew to be so; he had travelled to Canton and France, though he spoke no language but his own; he had been with Sindt; he was well acquainted, naturally enough, with the extent of the fur trade and of Russian discoveries; and during mutual hospitalities Cook both picked up a good deal and reciprocated, in spite of the gap of tongues. 'I felt no small Mortification in not being able to converse with him any other way then by signs assisted by figures and other Characters which however was a very great help.'[1] Ismailov, through his own experience, had made some adjustments to the chart of the Kamchatkan coast, and could assure Cook that it afforded only two harbours; but that chart, which included also the Sea of Okhotsk and its Asian coast and the Kurile islands, was of less interest to Cook than his other manuscript. This 'comprehended all the discoveries made by the Russians to the Eastward of Kamtschatka towards America, which if we exclude the Voyage of *Bering* and *Tcherikoff*, will amount to little or nothing.'[2] But latitudes and longitudes differed much from Müller's. As for Müller's islands between Kamchatka and America—what we should call the Aleutian islands—Ismailov was full of scorn. He struck out a third of them as non-existent, and altered the situation of others. To some of this condemnation Cook was quite prepared to accede. Yet, he thought, Muller must have had some authority for some of his islands—and the authority indeed was that of Bering, and good. Provisionally, if not finally, Ismailov's word could be taken, and islands sorted out by the names and situations he gave, but Cook, in doing so, would by no means guarantee his own chart, so built up, until he came to the Unalaska group, where the position of Samgunuda was fixed by himself, by the usual multiplicity of observations. Indeed Ismailov, who so uncompromisingly destroyed islands, had not been everywhere as overseer of the fur trade; he was not at

[1] *Journals* III, 450.   [2] ibid., 453.

all good at putting them in. It can be allowed that fur traders were not scientific navigators; and Cook, who pointed out that because of their different reckonings they might easily think they had made a new discovery when they had not, had done the same thing more than once, as we have seen, and for the same reason. Müller, at any rate, who had remained tentative, however unhappy some of his conjectures, did not incur a hanging condemnation. But what was to be said of Stählin and his accurate new map? No one had seen the continent to the north; no one had ever heard of Stachtan Nitada; Alaska, far from being an island, was the continent, and the name was the proper Indian name for it, 'and probably means no more than that part adjoining to *Ooneemak*, however the Indians as well as the Russians call the whole by that name and know very well that it is a great land.'[1] Cook's indignant judgment of Stählin, which in spite of all temptation and all provocation, he had been heretofore so scrupulous to withhold, at last boils over. And Stählin had been so foolish in self-satisfaction as to refer to 'the illiterate accounts of our sea-faring men'.

If M*r Stæhlin* was not greatly imposed upon what could induce him to publish so erroneous a Map? in which many of these islands are jumbled in in regular confusion, without the least regard to truth and yet he is pleased to call it a very accurate little Map? A Map that the most illiterate of his illiterate Sea-faring men would have been ashamed to put his name to.[2]

Cook, quite clearly, felt that he had been imposed upon. He had paid attention to a worthless document, and had spent weeks of time in trying to verify it. Yet he had been imposed upon to the world's advantage; for his incidental discoveries had not been unimportant. Nor—as we can see though Cook could not—did the maps available to him have any relevance to his arctic adventure; if Stählin had in fact been extremely accurate, it would not have advanced one inch the discovery of the North-west Passage. He was just as much imposed upon by Daines Barrington's theory of the formation of arctic ice. His real enemy, whose victory was foreordained, was ice; gales, shoals, fog, blind alleys, were but supplementary forces or obstacles, which patience, seamanship, luck could triumph over; but the ice outlasted patience, out-manoeuvred

---

[1] ibid., 456.
[2] ibid. And King, p. 1448, 'We felt ourselves not a little vext & Chagrind at the Publication of such a Map, under the title of an Accurate one, & the attention we had paid to it.' Stählin's unlucky phrase had come on p. 16 of his little book.

seamanship, was insusceptible to luck. All these hypotheses of closet-studying philosophers, months of preparation, grapplings with adverse circumstance, to end with three weeks beyond latitude 65°, eight days glimpsing the American shore! So it is useful at this point in time, when Cook had been scrutinising the maps of the northern archipelago, to scrutinise his own northern map and, leaving his observations of mankind on one side, measure his positive geographical achievement. It is interesting to note, first of all, what stood out to the eye of an observer close to him, who made a lengthy and closely reasoned analysis of the whole result. This is the admiring but not fulsome King.

Amongst the many grand discoveries of C. Cook, this event of ascertaining the true distance between the Continent of Asia & America will surely not be deemd the least splendid. Philosophers will no longer find any difficulty in accounting for the Population of America. The Grand bounds of the four Quarters of the Globe are known, & one part of Geography is Perfect, at least as far as it can be of use.[1]

One may summarise a little more soberly, in modern terms, from the first sighting of the American coast. Its general line was settled from Cape Blanco north to Nootka Sound, and from a few degrees beyond Nootka to the 'Great River' or Cook Inlet. Storm had driven the ships away from island groups, and fog had made it impossible to separate islands from mainland. Nevertheless the general line of the Alaskan peninsula, south and north, was firmly placed, and the true nature and direction of the Aleutian chain realised. The American side of the Bering Sea from Bristol Bay to about latitude 60°, and from about 63° (where we may say Norton Sound begins to open) to Cape Prince of Wales, was clear; and the arctic coast up to about the entrance of Kotzebue Sound. From there to a little beyond Icy Cape the line is partly firm, partly conjectural: its direction may be called correct. On the Asian side we have a remarkable degree of correctness from Mys Shmidta through Bering Strait down to about the north-east limit of the Gulf of Anadyr. With all this, it was not merely a general trend that was indicated; it was a line firmly based on coordinates of latitude and longitude, ascertained, in spite of all difficulties, with quite remarkable scientific exactitude. It was the product, still, of a running survey, not of what Cook called a survey 'in its literal sence';[2] and that, instead of being matter of apology, makes it all the more remarkable. The one piece of confusion is that

[1] *Journals* III, 1436.
[2] We are taken back to the New Hebrides: *Journals* II, 509, n. 4.

over St Lawrence island; which, because of its confusion, may seem remarkable also.

Not the coast of America only, but the whole voyage, was in Cook's mind as he composed a letter to the Admiralty, the first such communication since he had left the Cape almost two years before. Ismailov would send it to Petropavlovsk in the spring, it would reach St Petersburg the following winter, and London perhaps, if there were no delay, at the end of 1779. It was dated very precisely, 'Resolution at the Island of Unalaschka on the Coast of America, in the Latitude of 53°55′ North—Longitude 192 30 East from Greenwich the 20th of October 1778.' It sketched his proceedings and his intentions. He would go to the Sandwich Islands and after refreshing return to the north by way of Kamchatka; from there he would use the summer to make another and final attempt to find the Passage.

But I must confess I have little hopes of succeeding; Ice though an obstacle not easily surmounted, is perhaps not the only one in the way. The Coast of the two Continents is flat for some distance off; and even in the middle between the two the depth of water is inconsiderable: this, and some other circumstances, all tending to prove that there is more land in the frozen sea than as yet we know of, where the ice has its source, and that the Polar part is far from being an open Sea.[1]

Here was new reasoning. What were the 'other circumstances', apart from the flight of birds? And why, having already disposed of the theory of land-formed ice, should he now recur to it? Did he want to let the philosophers down lightly, or would he not permit himself to believe he had disproved that particular hypothesis unless he had scoured the whole arctic extent? He may, possibly, merely have been going through a phase of worried thought, as he considered the chart he had just had 'hastily copied' for his masters, running off into polar ignorance; for he disliked extremely leaving an unsolved problem behind him. But an end to effort must come, even if apologetically.

Stores and Provisions we have sufficient for twelve Months, and longer without a supply of both it will hardly be possible for us to remain in these seas, but whatever time we do remain, shall be spent in the improvement of Geography and Navigation. . . .[2]

We may, as we gaze also over the shoulder of King, filling his journal pages with experience reflected upon, catch again his pride in being the lieutenant of such a commander, and see that he had long since

[1] *Journals* III, 1532. The original letter and a copy are in PRO, Adm 1/1612.
[2] ibid.

ceased to calculate the distance to Baffin Bay: 'It would greatly add to a self complacency one cannot help indulging, in being an humble assistant in these events, could one look forward to any prospect of success in our grand object the next Season: but I hardly know in what light to consider matters, to give Rational ground of hopes.'[1]

The day after the letter was written, Ismailov departed with it and a Hadley's octant Cook gave him; for the man seemed able and educated enough to use such an instrument with profit. He in his turn gave Cook letters to the governor of Kamchatka and the commandant at Petropavlovsk. The brief international interval had pleased everybody. Though rough, the fur traders—people who were not Indians—appeared in that savage ambience like an unexpected group of old friends and neighbours. Officers went over to Egoochshac, and were received with merriment and hard drinking. Still another Russian came to visit, a man so European as to have been born in Moscow, and the total reverse of his fellows in his modesty and soberness. He was Jacob Ivanovich, the master of the sloop who was to have charge of Cook's letter, and as he was anxious to take some token to the governor, who would forward the letter, Cook sent a small spy-glass. Ivanovich, arriving late, met Cook only because a first attempt to get to sea had miscarried; for while the *Resolution*, having unmoored on the 22nd, was warping to windward in a south-east breeze, to get under sail, the wind suddenly fell, and some puffs blowing into the harbour with the ebbing tide set her stern fast aground. It was a minor misadventure, although it meant a few days' delay: on the morning of 26 October the ships put to sea, once more with a southerly wind, and Cook stood west.

[1] *Journals* III, 1454.

XXV

Kealakekua Bay

HE STOOD west, one can hardly do otherwise than think, in the hope of clearing the confusion that lay upon the further islands, whether their existence were affirmed or denied. If he could do that he would put out of the way one more problem that might tempt him from his single purpose when he came north again; and he had his time-plan laid down in the instructions he gave to Clerke—rendezvous at the Sandwich Islands till March, Petropavlovsk till the end of May, then the further search for (it is interesting) 'a NE or NW Passage'. But any hope he had of verifying or supplementing Ismailov was blown to pieces by four days of gales all round the compass, hard and vicious, sometimes with rain, hail or snow, sometimes with all three together. In the early morning of the 28th, in a fearful gust of wind, the *Discovery*'s main tack gave way, killed a seaman and badly injured others; there had hardly been four days' worse weather in the voyage than in this little cruise, thought King, and Cook gave it up on the 29th, deciding to reverse his course through the uninviting but known strait eastward of Unalaska. Westward he had certainly picked up some land through the gloom—probably Umnak, but impossible for him to identify. In a continuing north-westerly gale and a snowstorm on the 30th he bore away for the strait, passed safely through and steered south, the weather clearing though the gale still blew. Within three days it veered round to a violent southerly storm, which played havoc with the *Discovery*'s headsails and brought her to a dead stop: both ships had to lie to, parted for the night, and it was fortunate that from this peak of bad weather the storm fell away by morning—the morning of 3 November—and the wind became favourable again. It went almost entirely for a while on the 7th, while a weary lost shag flew heavily round the ships, Clerke visited the *Resolution* to compare notes, and Cook first learnt of the fatality his consort had suffered so soon after leaving Samgunuda.

By this time they were, reckoning in latitude, half-way to their destination; but it took twice as long to cover the second half of the distance. There was one more severe northerly gale, tearing the *Resolution*'s main topsail, just repaired, to pieces; on the whole, how-ever, the weather was fair, the temperature—which had begun to rise from the end of October—went up steadily to pass 80°, the men sat on deck sewing old sails, putting old rigging into order, and working up junk; the stores were aired, the carpenters repaired the boats; all no doubt thought of joys to come. After a short diversion easterly, Cook steered steadily south. On the morning of 25 Novem-ber his latitude, 20°55′, put him a degree south of his reckoning for his Kauai anchorage at Waimea Bay, while his longitude was about four degrees to the east. He therefore, full of expectation, spread the ships and steered west till nightfall, and at midnight brought to. Next morning there lay the land, the island of Maui, with its 'ele-vated saddle hill'—the extinct 10,000 foot volcano Haleakala—raising its summit above the clouds, and descending gently towards the deep ravines and falling waters of that steep rocky coast, where the trade wind hurled other waters into perpetual surf. The coast he approached ran a little north of west, and he thought best to follow it. Before long people, houses and plantations could be seen; at noon he was only three or four miles from the shore, and the canoes began to come off. The regulations, few and basic, which he pub-lished this day to govern the conduct of his men nevertheless prove that he was determined on a strict discipline, both in their own inter-ests and in those of the islanders. A steady supply of provisions being of the highest importance, and the ships' articles of trade now being few (and no wonder) private trade was strictly forbidden. This was an old rule. A new one shows, perhaps, that the captain had been reflecting on his Tongan experience (we can think of the 'Officers and others' implicated):

And whereas it has frequently happened that by Officers and others travelling in the Country with Fire-Arms and other Weapons, in order to obtain which, the Natives have committed thefts and outrages, they other-wise would not have attempted; it is therefore Ordered that no Officer or other person (not sent on duty) shall carry with him out of the Ships, or into the Country, any fire Arms whatever, and great care is to be taken to keep the Natives ignorant of the method of charging such as we may be under a necessity to make use of.[1]

The third treated of disease. It was well enough known that Unalaska had been a great encouragement to 'the Venereal'; some days before all the men had been examined by the surgeons; the complaints

[1] 26 November 1778; *Journals* III, 1534, printed from a copy sent to Clerke, in Dixson Library MSS.

remained. Cook was specific: 'in order to prevent as much as possible
the communicating this fatal disease to a set of innocent people',
no woman was to be admitted on any pretence into either ship without the captain's permission; any man party to such an entry would
be punished; any man having the disease, or under suspicion of
having it, who lay with a woman would be severely punished; no
suspected person would be allowed on shore on any pretence whatever.[1] After reading out these articles to his assembled crew, Cook
made what King calls 'a sensible speech' to reinforce them. He had
done as much before, in January of this same year, in the leeward
islands; and now, among the first people who came on board, who
knew of that earlier visit, he found too much, and too melancholy,
evidence that his efforts had been unsuccessful. Or could it be that,
after all, in the islands of the Pacific Ocean, there were original roots
of the malady? Some men tried to make themselves believe so. Cook
did not. The island women certainly seemed to carry no fear in their
handsome bosoms: repulsed from the ships, they were highly indignant, and the words they shouted were unambiguously words of
abuse.

Nails, bits of iron, even iron tools, the only things that could be
used for trade, were exchanged on this and the succeeding days for
roots and small pigs. Cook made no attempt to land, but going close
inshore by day, stood off again as trade slackened and brought to
for the night. Lying to on his second night, he noticed that a current
carried him to windward, in spite of the strength of the wind, and
he changed his mind about the course he would pursue: he decided
to take advantage of the current and ply to windward with it, and so
getting round the east end of the island have its whole lee side before
him—one presumes at this time with the hope of finding a harbour
there. The islanders continued to come off to the ships, sometimes
with obvious chiefs among them, making no attempt to cheat or
thieve, even rescuing and returning to the *Discovery* a small cat that
had fallen overboard and gone astern. This was admirable, and as
the decks became thronged native amiability was expressed in dance
and singing, though the women were still turned away. Among those
on board on the last afternoon of the month was a chief who was
important indeed, handed up the side with great care by his followers, partly because of his rank, partly because of the feebleness
to which he had been reduced by excessive drinking of kava, mani-
fested in his scab-encrusted skin and his red inflamed eyes. But he
was observant and good-natured, visited the captain's cabin, and

[1] ibid., 1534-5.

presented Cook with the very beautiful cap of yellow and black feathers that he wore, and his feather cloak—princely gifts; Cook heard his name as Terryaboo. When he departed he allowed a few of his noble followers to remain on board all night, and they suggested a possible anchorage near the east end of the island. But Cook had seen another island to windward, which the natives called 'O'why'he'. He was close up with its northern side as the first day of December ended. The next morning revealed high mountains with snowy summits, pieces of white cloth flying on shore, canoes coming out flying white streamers; Cook flew his ensign in reply. The paddlers of the canoes, at first rather shy, soon understood the possibilities of trade; and by evening Cook had determined to ply further to windward round this island.

Possibly he was relying on the favourable current. If so, his reliance was misplaced, as he found within a few days, and working to the east became a singularly tedious exercise. He himself, aided by King, had the short-lived diversion of observing an eclipse of the moon;[1] King and a few others had the intellectual exercise of entering up their journals; but that did not take long when there was nothing to record but the weather and the ship's position. As for the crews, what was there for them to do but haul on the ropes and look at the shore? Had they known, as they passed from the Maui to the Hawaii shore, how long they were to do this they might have shown more restiveness than they did. Their idea of refreshment, as they turned back from the ice, had not been this sort of hovering on the edge of Paradise. It begins to look as if Cook, for whatever reason, had lost touch with his men. His own sheer weariness may have been the cause. He had never been very communicative about his intentions, though once or twice, as at Vaitepiha Bay the previous year, when it was a question of conserving grog, he had taken the people into his confidence. Now, in December 1778, he seems to have had a policy. Precisely when he arrived at it we do not know; and he explained it to neither officers nor men. King, writing at some length when they were safely in harbour, five weeks after this, thought he could see it; but he could do no more than 'presume' his captain's

---

[1] He goes to some pains to elaborate on the imperfections of his method: 'Indeed these observations were made only as an experiment without aiming at much niciety.' This done, they immediately proceeded to observe 'the distance of each limb of the Moon from Pollux and Arietis, the one being to the east and the other to the west. An oppertunity to observe under all these circumstances seldom happens, but when it does it ought not to be omited, as in this case the local errors these observations are liable to, destroy one the other, which in all other cases would require the observations of a whole Moon.'— *Journals* III, 477. They were settling the longitude, and we have indicated not merely Cook's passion for exactitude but the refinement of technique which he had attained. His results and King's differed by a little over one minute.

motives. The policy was to keep the sea as long as possible; and we do not know, either, whether to begin with the captain was clear about all his motives himself. To ply to windward so stubbornly was a good enough way of ensuring that he would have to keep the sea; for it took nineteen days for the ships to arrive at the eastern point of Hawaii; blown off it, the *Resolution* was six days in regaining it, and was parted from the *Discovery* for a fortnight. Both ships' companies were by then heartily sick of the process. There had been signs of strain in the *Resolution* before.

In his first trade with the Hawaii people Cook had acquired a quantity of sugar cane. Always experimental, he found that a 'strong decoction' of this made what he considered 'a very palatable and wholesome beer which was esteemed by every man on board'; and we have King's testimony that both the captain and the officers liked it. Cook therefore ordered more to be brewed, with the same view that he had had at Tahiti, to save his spirits for the future push into the arctic cold. He came close in with the shore again on 6 December, by which time the favourable current had ceased. 'Here', he writes, 'we had some traffick with the Natives, but as it proved but trifling I stood in again the next Morning, when a good many visited us and we lay trading with them till 2 PM then made sail and stood off; having procured Pork, fruit and roots sufficient for four or five days.'[1] For a crew excluded from inner councils it was exasperating; and we have further to note that their rations were still on short allowance, well after they might have expected plenty. Cook seems simply to have forgotten. As was not unnatural, exasperation broke out indirectly. The men baulked at the sugar cane beer, alleging that it was injurious to their health: 'my mutinous turbulent crew refused even so much as to taste it and demanded their grog. . . . I took no step either to oblige, or perswaid them to drink it; for as we had plenty of other vegetable there was no danger of the Scurvey.'[2] He had stopped their grog; which might or might not be taken as a measure of persuasion. His account of this incident is inadequate. There was a letter we should much like to inspect—'a very mutinous letter', in King's opinion—and we are fortunate to have a longer story from John Watts, midshipman, a young person of intelligence. The people disliking the Decoction, says Watts,

remonstrated with ye Captn by Letter, at same time mentioning the scanty Allowance of Provisions serv'd them, which they thought might be

[1] ibid., 478.
[2] Cook felt so strongly over this matter that he deleted two or three sentences about it in his journal and substituted for them a whole circumstantial indignant paragraph.— *Journals* III, 479–80.

increas'd where there was such Plenty & that bought for mere trifles. This Morning therefore ye Captⁿ order'd the Hands aft, & told them, that it was the first time He had heard any thing relative to ye shortness of ye Allowance, that he thought they had had the same Quantity usually serv'd them at the other Islands, that if they had not enough, they should have more & that had He known it sooner, it should have been rectified. He likewise understood He said they would not drink the Decoction of Sugar Cane imagining it prejudicial to their Healths, he told them it was something extraordinary they should suppose the Decoction unwholesome when they could steal ye Sugar Cane & eat it raw without Scruple he continued to tell them that if they did not chuse to drink the Decoction he could not help it, they would be the Sufferers as they should have Grog every other day provided they drank ye Sugar Cane, but if not the Brandy Cask should be struck down into ye Hold & they might content themselves with Water, intimating to them that He did not chuse to keep turning & working among these Isles without having some Profit. He gave them 24 Hours to consider of it.[1]

Twenty-four hours did not alter their resolve, and the brandy cask went down into the hold. The following entry is equally indicative of a captain and crew at loggerheads:

Standing off & on. Punish'd Willᵐ Griffiths, (Cooper) with 12 Lashes for starting ye Cask of Decoction which was sour. At the same time ye Captⁿ address'd ye Ships Company, telling them He look'd upon their Letter as a very mutinous Proceeding & that in future they might not expect the least indulgence from him.'[2]

When else did Cook write of his crew as mutinous and turbulent over such a matter?—or, in spite of giving himself no trouble to oblige or persuade, address them like an outraged schoolmaster? If there ever was such an incident, we have no record of it. We certainly have records enough of distaste for food or drink; and now for the first time, it appears, the captain heard of the men's abortive decision over spruce beer at Nootka Sound. For the first time, also, he seems to feel it necessary to go on the defensive, as if he had never written the famous paper for the Royal Society. He even harks back to the first voyage. Injurious to their healths!

Every innovation whatever tho ever so much to their advantage is sure to meet with the highest disapprobation from Seamen, Portable Soup and Sour Krout were at first both condemned by them as stuff not fit for human beings to eat. Few men have introduced into their Ship's more novelties in the way of victuals and drink than I have done; indeed few men have had the same oppertunity or been driven to the same necessity.

[1] 10 December; ibid., 479, n. 4.   [2] 12 December; ibid.

It has however in a great measure been owing to such little innovations that I have always kept my people generally speaking free from that dreadful distemper the Scurvy.[1]

The matter blew over. How much sugar cane beer was in the end drunk we do not know. As for indulgence, Cook had already, on his second approach to Hawaii, relaxed his rule on women; for it was too apparent that nothing he could do now would avail to keep the islanders unharmed. True, that was of little use to seamen as long as the ships were so far out of the reach of canoes.

In six days they were six leagues further to windward. Cook stood in for a little more trade; then, with a wind slightly less unfavourable, he thought he might stretch eastward to round, or at least get a sight of, that end of the island. Then conditions deteriorated; squalls were varied by calms with thunder, lightning and rain. On the evening of 18 December he was north-east of the point he had to weather, Cape Kumukahi, and had no doubt he would clear it; but at one o'clock in the morning the wind fell and he was at the mercy of a north-easterly swell heaving him fast towards the land, in a rainy darkness which thunder and lightning did little to improve. At daylight the surf on the shore was not more than a mile and a half away. Fortunately the cape has no offshore dangers, and a breeze that had sprung up just enabled him to clear the land with all possible sail set —additionally fortunate, in that just at the peak of anxiety ropes gave way, and the main topsail and both topgallant sails were rent in two. A narrow escape, thought King; indeed, it was as narrow an escape as Cook ever had from losing his ship. Once in safety, he made another attempt, the same day, to weather the cape. It was fruitless, and he ran down to join the *Discovery*, so far astern that she had not been in danger. Clerke had inconveniences enough; having dressed his ship in her old clothes, as it were, for the agreeable informality of weeks of refreshment in balmy weather, he found some worn decayed garment constantly giving way, and his men were as constantly knotting and splicing the ropes, unbending and sewing and bending his sails. The *Resolution* was in no better state, as they heaved and pitched in the highest sea Cook had ever known in the tropics, irrespective of the winds: it might shift its direction three or four points, but never seemed to go down. Hence, general experience culminating in the crisis of escape, a second explosion so soon—a few days—after the first, which rocks the pages of the captain's journal; and now administration rather than trifling mutiny receives the

[1] ibid. ,479–80.

blast. The passage is worth giving as a whole; for it shows that Cook was willing to pit himself against the Navy Board.

On this occasion I cannot hilp observing, that I have always found that the bolt-ropes to our sails have not been of sufficient strength, or substance to even half wear out the Canvas: this at different times has been the occasion of much expence of canvas and infinate trouble and vexation. Nor are the cordage and canvas or indeed hardly any other stores made use of in the Navy, of equal goodness with those in general used in the Merchant service, of this I had incontestable proof last voyage. When the Resolution was purchased for the King her standing rigging, some runing rigging, blocks and sails were also purchased along with her, and altho the most of these things had been in wear fourteen Months yet they wore longer than any of those of the same kind put on board new out of the Kings stores. The fore rigging are yet over the mast head, the brace blocks and some others in equal use still in their places and as good as ever. And yet on my return home last voyage these very blocks were condemned by the yard officers and thrown amongst other decayed blocks from which they permited my Boatswain to select them when the ship was again fited out. These evils are likely never to be redressed, for besides the difficulty of procuring stores for the Crown of equal goodness with [those] purchased by private people for their own use, it is a general received opinion amongst Naval officers of all ranks that no stores are equal in goodness to those of the Crown and that no ships are found like those of the Navy. In the latter they are right but it is in the quantity and not in the quallity of the stores, this last is seldom tried, for things are generally Condemned or converted to some other use by such time as they are half wore out. It is only on such Voyages as these we have an oppertunity to make the trial where every thing is obliged to be worn to the very utmost.[1]

This onslaught may well have startled Palliser, as Comptroller of the Navy, when he later came to read it; for he, of all men, was responsible for the dockyards and what came out of them; and he, certainly, was one of those who held the article of faith that stores from the royal yards were best. Sometimes the navy, he was willing to admit, particularly in wartime, was driven to use cordage made by contract. Cook might be 'in part' right, if he spoke of such cordage; but it was improper of him—said the Comptroller, deleting from publication all of the passage that defined Cook's personal experience—to make charges that implied abuse or mismanagement, the economical regulations of the yards were out of his line. Undoubtedly all the stores taken on a ship of discovery should be of the best that were made.[2] If Palliser had been wholly ingenuous, he might have let

[1] *Journals* III, 481–2.
[2] Dr Douglas when editing the journal took Palliser into consultation, and Palliser's letter is extant, B.M., Egerton MS 2180, f. 171. Douglas printed the gist of this as a

Cook's detailed complaints stand, even the word 'evils', and have commented on them more at large, as he was perfectly entitled to do, in the published history of the voyage. Certainly Cook's canvas and cordage underwent unusual strains, beyond those normally provided for by the regulations of the royal dockyards; but it is unlikely that he did not know what he was talking about, in a very thorough way. Possibly, if he had had leisure to revise, he would have removed all trace of vehemence from his words. They may not seem particularly vehement to us, as we look back in calmness over all his career and the naval history of his time. But they are vehement, almost with the tone he has reserved hitherto for bad charts and dishonest chart-publishers. Possibly also, coming where it does, this vehemence is another sign of the strain within himself.

'Be that as it may'—he has long given up this once favourite phrase —he continued to ply, convinced that the least shift of wind in his favour must carry him round the point; trading when he was close enough to the land, with varying luck, and full of admiration for the straightforwardness of the native people in their exchanges. Sometimes he had small boats out himself as intermediaries, but that did not stop eager ones, men and women, from swimming to the ships with their breadfruit or plantains or personal charms and piling up noise and confusion. In the early morning of the 23rd, between two of these commercial occasions, he was on a south-east tack, when again the wind died away and left him at the mercy of the landward-moving swell. It was not so hair-raising an experience as that a few days earlier; for he was six or seven miles from the shore and the wind returned in puffs enough to make the ship manoeuvrable. He wanted no further lesson on this unreliable wind, the sight of furiously breaking surf was no pretty one, he would keep well away from it; and the spirits of his men continued to sink. Nevertheless, it seems to have become a point of honour to double the cape. In the middle of the night between the 23rd and 24th, while the ships were stretching to the north, Cook decided to tack to the south-east once more, and thinking the *Discovery* could see him, omitted the usual signal. She could not, and in the morning they were apart. This day Cook succeeded in getting to windward of Kumukahi, where he cruised, well off the land, in the expectation that Clerke would join him, trading when he could, until the first day of the new year. Through that period wind and weather were unsettled, and there was the discomfort of a great deal of rain, but by the time he

footnote in *Voyage*, II, 538. He omitted from Cook's words the passage 'of this I had incontestable proof . . . . purchased by private people for their own use'.

came to his next resolve the wind had gone to the south. He had
concluded that Clerke must have abandoned Kumakahi, and gone
to leeward to round the island in the other direction; and so he
himself would round the southern point and meet him as he sailed
down the opposing coast. It was not till the morning of 5 January
that the *Resolution* doubled the point, Ka Lae, short as the distance
was; for the nights were spent tacking and part of each day lying to
and trading, up to twenty miles out at sea; nor, indeed, was it an
inviting shore that she passed by, with the bare slopes of its lava
flows, its masses of volcanic rock, and a whole desert at the foot of
the great mountains. Ka Lae itself was flat and grassy, with a considerable village standing on it, whence men and women thronged
to the ship. Cook was fairly well provisioned, but he needed water;
and now, sheltered at last by the land from the almost remorseless
easterly wind and the vast swell, thinking at last of anchorage, he
found none. Bligh sounded in vain a quarter of a mile from the
shore with a line of 160 fathoms; where he landed he found only rain
water, brackish with spray, lying in holes in the rocks. At that
moment the *Discovery* appeared, after a separation of thirteen days.
This at least was satisfactory. Cook's guess had been wrong. She had
not gone to leeward. Clerke, with as much persistence as his own,
had cruised five days about their place of separation, then had got
far to the eastward before coming in with the land again south of
Kumukahi, and in two days more had caught up.

It was 6 January 1779, but eleven days still were to pass before
the anchors went down. Cook realised that he could not stay at sea
indefinitely, and had the master out sounding more than once. The
Resolution was leaking again, the *Discovery* so leaky in her upper works
that they could not wash down the decks; both ships were 'in a most
tattered condition', so much so that Clerke had bought a quantity of
small cordage from the islanders for repairs.[1] The supply of fruit and
roots was now irregular, and not large; a great amount of salt had
been obtained, for salting down hogs, but there were not enough
hogs; at one stage Cook was driven back, disappointingly, on his
'sea provisions'. The ships gradually worked along the coast, northwards as it trended here, off and on, driven back twice by current or
wind to its south-west point, and visited by fewer canoes. The country
seemed poorer. But on the 15th there was a change: a fine pleasant
morning, plenty of company, abundant supplies of all sorts. With the
following daybreak appeared the shape of a bay. Bligh was sent the
distance of three leagues to examine it, with a boat from each ship.

[1] Burney, *Journals* III, 490, n. 5; and Edgar, 489, n. 2.

While he was away and the ships slowly plied to the north more canoes came off than ever before: not less than a thousand were counted surrounding the ships, with perhaps ten thousand people in them or in the water or crowding on board, universally curious, bearing such quantities of provisions that half had to be refused, even though the process of killing and salting hogs was at once begun. Not a man brought a weapon of any sort. Among so many there were bound to be light fingers, and Cook had two or three muskets and four pounders fired over one offending canoe. The effect, he noticed, was surprise rather than fright. The evening brought back Bligh, reporting good anchorage, fresh water, peaceable and friendly people. Cook could defer no longer. Next morning, 17 January, he stood into Kealakekua Bay and anchored, a quarter of a mile from the shore, in 13 fathoms of water.

Excitement on the Hawaiian side was balanced by relief on the seamen's: 'we were jaded & very heartily tir'd', wrote King, 'with Cruising off these Islands for near two months. . . . The Disappointment in not trying for a place of Anchorage had a bad effect on the Spirits of our Ships Company'—and he harks back to the rather absurd but so indicative sugar cane beer quarrel and the short rations. He tries to account for his captain's course of action, and it is hard to believe that Cook, though he did not explain himself at length, had not dropped some hints.

Captain Cook has observ'd that in a harbour, from the impossibility of bringing the Natives to a proper understanding of the advantage of a regular supply, it was always either a glut or a Scarcity, particularly in respect to Vegetables, more would be brought to the Ship in one day than would serve a Month; if it was purchas'd the greatest part would spoil, & if the people were sent away, they would not return again, both parties were therefore injured; by cruising off he had it in his power to proportion the quantity, & keeping up the Value of his Iron, which began to be a scarce article, & of course getting a more plentiful supply for the length of time we might stay, & of hogs for Salting; as by this means every part of the Island had opportunities to dispose of its produce. Besides these reasons, there was another, founded on the Safety of the Ships; for from what we had observ'd of the Islands to leeward last year, & of Mowee & Owhyhe now, there appeard little chance of finding any harbour, & nothing better than an open bay like that at Atoui, which would be very insecure: Cruising about was therefore the safest way. These were I presume the motives that made us keep the Sea to the great mortification of almost all in both Ships.[1]

[1] *Journals* III, 503-4.

From what we know of Cook, we may guess at other motives. The longer the policy of trading at sea continued, the fewer the opportunities of theft presented to the islanders, and the fewer the difficulties arising thereby. The more passing the contacts of his men with the people, the fewer the quarrels, the fewer the opportunities for irresponsible officers wandering with fire-arms to get into trouble. The longer from the land—he may have thought at first—and the longer the separation of his men from the island women, the greater the chance of controlling the 'foul disease'. We may possibly add, once he had decided on a plan, his own obstinacy in continuing it. The faithful, jaded, and knowledge-hungry King could think of an objection that his captain may have thought of also, but was prepared to ignore.

If it be an object, & if there be one amongst us, whose abilities & leisure would have enabled him to have made enquiries into the Customs of the Natives, & of the produce of the Islands, it certainly by this mode of proceeding was greatly frustrated, our connexions were with the lowest & most ignorant of the people, who were too much occupied in selling their goods & getting on shore again, to attend to ones enquiries: & of the land we could speak but very superficially.

Nevertheless he was to learn a good deal.[1]

Kealakekua Bay—'Karakakooa'—though not a harbour, is the best anchorage on the west side of Hawaii, safe at all times except in south-westerly storms, which are not frequent. It is not large: from Cook Point in the north to Palemano Point south-south-east the direct distance is no more than a mile and a quarter; from Kaawaloa in the north-western corner of the bay, the seat of old Hawaiian royalty, across the water, to the great *heiau* or religious structure then called Hikiau, at the modern village of Napoopoo. once Waipunaula, is perhaps seven eighths of a mile. The *Resolution* was anchored closer to Kaawaloa, the *Discovery* a little farther within the bay towards the *heiau* and a beach which gave easy landing. They were both opposite the precipitous rugged long cliff, the *pali*, which cuts apart Kaawaloa and the southern half of the bay, and was passable only at low water; covered on its heights, like so much of the lower land, with the *pili* grass that was the staple of Hawaiian housing, roof and walls. It is a volcanic place: almost everywhere a rough lava lip meets the water, where the great mountain Mauna Loa anciently poured out its liquid fires. But the ground within was fertile enough,

[1] *Journals* III, 504,

the mountain flanks supported a vast forest, whence came canoe hulls and the images of the gods; the bay and the country about supported the largest population of any part of the island. The weather was fine as the ships unbent their sails and struck their yards and topmasts: and Cook observes 'The Ships very much Crouded with Indians and surrounded by a multitude of Canoes. I have no where in this Sea seen such a number of people assembled at one place, besides those in the Canoes all the Shore of the bay was covered with people and hundreds were swimming about the Ships like shoals of fish.'[1] The *Discovery* heeled over with the number clinging to her side. It would have been impossible to do anything had not two handsome chiefs, Parea or Palea, and Kanina, come to the rescue and driven the mob, temporarily, overboard. There was one other visitor, at least, who did not get this summary treatment—'a man named *Tou-ah-ah*, who we soon found belonged to the Church'; Koaa or Koa, a little, old, kava-affected, highly important priest. This man introduced himself with much ceremony, presenting Cook with a small pig and two coconuts, and wrapping a piece of red cloth around him, gifts supplemented with a long sort of prayer, a large hog and a quantity of fruit and roots. Ceremony did not end thus; indeed it became surprising and baffling. 'In the after noon', records Cook, 'I went a shore to view the place, accompaned by Touahah, Parea, Mr King and others; as soon as we landed Touahah took me by the hand and conducted me to a large Morai, the other gentlemen with Parea and four or five more of the Natives followed.'[2] These, because of the fortunes of documents, are the last words we have from his hand. There is no lack of information otherwise.

It became immediately clear that he was not for the time being a free agent. The party landed on the beach below a stone wall that fronted a grove of coconut trees. At the north end of the beach was a village, at the other end the *heiau*, built up with stones from the sloping beach sixteen or eighteen feet to its flat surface. Close about the huts of the village their occupants had cast themselves down prostrate, like the people of Kauai when Cook landed there; otherwise the place was empty, except for three or four men who held wands tipped with dog's hair—and silent, except for some sentence they kept repeating, always including the word 'Erono'. Cook and his supporters were conducted by these officers to the *heiau*, a paved

---

[1] ibid., 490–1. There is here a little difference in observation from King, who says, 'There were not many regarding us from the Shore'—although he estimates the number of canoes at not less than 1500, and thinks 'we should not exagerate, in saying we saw at this time 10 000 of the Inhabitants.'—ibid., 503.

[2] ibid., 491.

quadrangle about twenty yards by forty, with a stout railing all
round it, adorned with a score of human skulls. At its seaward end
were two huts; at the end opposite stood an insecure scaffolding of
high poles and loose sticks, a ramshackle 'oracle tower'. Near the huts
were two crude wooden images, balefully grinning; in front of the
scaffolding a semicircle of twelve more, with an elevated 'altar', or
stand for offerings, facing its middle, a decayed hog on top and a
variety of fruits at the foot. Dividing this part of the area from the
rest were a short wall and the framework of a hut; and in the centre
of all was a sunken square of ten or twelve feet, with still two images
more on one side of it. This was a much more elaborate structure
than the Tahitian *marae*, and every part had some significance in
Hawaiian ritual; but it was natural that the visitors should be left in
some wonderment.

Cook, attended by King and Bayly, and led on to the *heiau* near
the seaward end, was halted at the two images there, for an exchange
of words between Koa and a tall grave young man called
'Kaireekeea'—Keli'ikea; they then proceeded to the scaffold end.
Koa placed Cook under the 'altar', took the rotting hog and uttered
what seemed to be a prayer, let it drop, and holding Cook's hand,
climbed the risky scaffolding with him. A procession of ten men
came round the railing to the short wall bearing a hog and a large
piece of red cloth (the sacred colour red); Keli'ikea took the cloth to
Koa, who wrapped it round Cook; the hog was handed up to Koa;
he worked through a sort of litany with Keli'ikea and dropped it
again, and he and Cook came down to the ground. He now conducted
Cook round the semicircle of images, addressing each, 'in a very
ludicrous and slighting tone', except one in the middle, which was
only three feet high—half the height of the others—and covered
with cloth; 'to this he prostrated himself, & afterwards kiss'd, &
desird the Captn to do the same, who was quite passive, & sufferd
Koah to do with him as he chose.'[1] King, Bayly and Palea had been
left at the seaward end of the *heiua*: they were now brought forward,
Cook was seated between the images by the sunken square, one arm
supported by King, the other by Koa; and here they remained while
another procession led by Keli'ikea brought an offering of a baked
hog and other provisions. Keli'ikea, holding the pig and facing
Cook, made a series of rapid speeches, which became shorter and
shorter—perhaps incantations or invocations—with responses from
the others, who in the end chanted only the single word or name
'Erono!' The company then sat down to prepare the food for eating,

[1] *Journals* III, 505-6.

while Keli'ikea chewed up coconut kernel, with which, wrapped in cloth, he anointed very thoroughly Cook, King and Bayly, and very slightly Palea and Koa. The end of the long and rather tiresome ceremony is described for us by King: Palea and Koa 'now insist'd upon Cramming us with hog, but not till after taseting the Kava; I had no objection to have the hog handled by Pareea, but the Captn recollecting what offices Koah had officiated when he handled the Putrid hog could not get a Morsel down, not even when the old fellow very Politely chew'd it for him We rose as soon as we could with decency, & the Captn gave some pieces of Iron, & other trifles which he said was for the Eatooa at which they were well pleas'd, but took care to divide the Spoil between them.'[1]

This was not the end of the ceremony, however. When the party walked by the houses along the shore to the south they were preceded by wand-bearers repeating the magic word Erono, at which all the people fell on their faces. It seemed too abject; it probably signified co-operation and assistance; but how much preferable, just then, seemed the cheerful shouts, the enthusiastic hindrances, of the Friendly Islanders! There was something in the air far beyond the relatively simple veneration of Kauai in the preceding January.

Nevertheless quiet co-operation and assistance had value. Close to the *heiau* and the beach was a walled-off sweet potato or *uala* field. No difficulty was experienced, on the promise of compensation, in securing this for the observatories and tents, and having it *tapu*-ed by the priests; added protection was given, though hardly needful, by a few marines in their regimentals, with Lieutenant Phillips himself in command to enforce Cook's regulations on keeping fire-arms from the people. Men would sit on the boundary wall, but not venture inside unless with permission; nothing would induce any woman ever to brave the *tapu*, even for a red-garbed marine. The only people habitually near by were the priests and their dependants who lived in a few huts about a rather dirty pond behind the coconut grove, and with these from the start there was an entire understanding and trust. No canoe would land opposite the observatories, though that might have been from a religious respect for the *heiau*; and all trade was carried on at the ships. Fresh water enough came from a spring at the northern end of the beach—not enough to replenish the ships fully, but that could be done at Kauai; so little disturbance occurred there. In charge of this post was King: very tranquil, he thought, getting on with his observations. The ships

[1] ibid., 506.

were less tranquil, and a general clearance was made several times a day by Palea, who began the morning by driving off the super-abundant overnight women. Women alone would have stopped all the caulking that was necessary. When after ten days that was done the *Resolution*'s rudder was sent ashore for repair; then plank had to be cut for some of her rail work. Certainly the carpenters were busy. Certainly also thieves began to be busy, in a very honest sort of way—like those who swam off with small flint-pointed chisels to prise the nails out of the ships' sheathing and were surprised to be the object of small shot: to quote Law the surgeon, 'they seemed when they were desired to Go Away not to have any Idea they were doing wrong.'[1] It was a commentary on all Cook's troubles.

To Cook continued to be paid the most remarkable observances, a quite extraordinary homage. When he first went to visit some houses, priests were at hand; he was placed at the foot of a clearly important image, King again supporting him, and once again dressed in red cloth; there was the most ceremonious presentation and sacrifice of a pig, much ritual recitation, the making and drinking of kava, the feeding of pork. Whenever he went on shore to the astronomers' marquee, the priest Keli'ikea—'the Taboo-man', as the English called him—bearing a long wand stood at the bow of his pinnace announcing the approach of Erono, people in canoes immediately squatted down, on the beach they prostrated them-selves, none but priests or chiefs would approach him. He was always received by a priest, once he was in the marquee Keli'ikea and his train came with the ceremonial food—always as a duty, thought King, and with no expectation of a return; inferior chiefs might bring some pig-offering, but while they held it, not without trembling and marks of dread, the priests 'pronounced the necessary Orizon'. Curiously enough, there is no mention of such abasement among the people who thronged the ships, as if—there is a little paradox—people could be more at ease in Erono's natural sphere, and even abstract what suited them. Cook, although embarrassed in his movements, seems to have accepted it all, so bafflingly beyond anything in his experience of other islands, philosophically. As a matter of policy, he deemed it duty on his side to co-operate for a week or two in island custom. He could hardly have been overjoyed. Clerke, when he went on shore, was less tolerant of form. There was no attempt to confer on him what could hardly be other than a religious aura; but he was obviously a great chief, and was accorded the *kapu moe*, the sacred prostration. He would have none of it, he

[1] *Journals* III, 491, n. 1.

'disliked exceedingly putting so many people to such a confounded inconvenience', and he had the honour withdrawn.'[1]

The priesthood was generous: trade was quite unnecessary for the astronomical party, whatever the consumption of the ships. The abundance came in the name of an absent elder called Kao, who seemed to be the principal priest, Keli'ikea's grandfather. But where was the secular power? Its encouragement might be very useful. Chiefs of secondary importance there were: Palea and Kanina, for example, exerted considerable authority. The really great man, the 'king' of the whole island, whose dependants they were, whose dependant it seemed also the priest Koa was (he seemed to have a rather different interest from the establishment at the *heiau*), was also absent. He was at Maui pursuing, as we know, matters of conquest, not very successfully. His return in a few days to Hawaii was expected and Palea and Koa left to escort him. His approach was announced on the 24th, when a solemn *tapu* was pronounced over the whole bay, which kept people in their houses, canoes on shore, and the ships short of vegetables. Neither on that day nor through most of the next did he come, so that a few unorthodox and daring spirits were prevailed on to bring a small supply of provisions; at last, as evening fell, a long line of large sailing and paddling canoes came round the north point, and some visited the *Resolution*. King Terreeoboo, or Kerrioboo—or Kalei'opu'u the *ali'i 'ai aupuni*[2]—went on board. To Cook's surprise, he was the same Terryaboo who had visited him off the coast of Maui eight weeks before, tall, emaciated, red-eyed,

---

[1] ibid., 596—'by application to the Arees I got this troublesome ceremony taken off.' Again, 597: 'At my first landing they got me to their Morai and with a vast deal of ceremony, singing and fuss, sacrificed a small Pig to me with as much respect as though I had been a being of a superior Nature; this they very frequently did to Captain Cook and afterwards would often have done to me but I always avoided it as a very disagreeable kind of amusement. . . .'

[2] In the present pages this chief's—or 'king's'—name is given as Kalei'opu'u, a shortened and correctly alternative rendering of Kalani'opu'u, simply as the accepted modern version. The pronunciation was certainly heard by Cook and others as Terreeoboo, though not by all others; for Samwell's version is Kariopoo, and some write Kerrioboo. The difficulty is that the Hawaiian language as spoken was at that time undergoing a consonantal change, working up from south-east to north-west, but still rather dubious when the early nineteenth-century missionaries reduced it to written form. The Polynesian *t* and *k*, *l* and *r*, *v* and *w*, *b* and *p* were all affected, and spellings in the journals vary accordingly, according to the progress of change as well as to the acuteness of the listening ear. King notes a geographical difference. Samwell registers one change, but not others (still delayed) in the name of the village 'Kavaroa'—i.e. modern Kaawaloa—in the island of Hawaii; but to the north-west he has, like everybody else, a *t*, not a *k*—Atowai, not Kauai—and writes, no doubt with accuracy, 'Bootaberry' for the place name Pu'ukapeli. The matter of glottal stops and the rendering of vowels are also interesting, though they need not be touched on here. We may say compendiously that the versions of Polynesian names we get in Cook and his officers are not the work of ignorant and careless seamen, but an invaluable index to linguistic change in the Pacific. Cook himself seems to have had a good ear.

scabby, shaking—with all the signs of long-continued excessive consumption of kava, in fact—but amiable. He was perhaps sixty years of age. His queen, Kaneikapolei, was with him, and his two young sons, as well as attendant chiefs. After exchanging names with Cook and receiving presents he retired highly satisfied to his town of Kaawaloa to sleep. The *tapu* was off the bay, and ladies—'our old Sweethearts', in Samwell's phrase—were restored to their lovers.

Next day there was a water-procession from Kaawaloa that captured all eyes. Though only three canoes took part, they were large double ones. In the first stood Kalei'opu'u and a crowd of his chiefly retainers, glorious in feather cloaks and helmets of yellow and red, the royal and sacred colours, most brilliant raiment of the whole ocean; in the second were chanting priests, led by the old Kao, who had returned with the king, escorting four images of gods, feather-covered basket work with distorted furious features, dog's teeth, eyes of pearl-oyster shell; in the third was a vast load of hogs, coconuts and vegetables. They passed by but did not stop at the ships, making for the tents, where King turned out the guard, and Cook followed them. On their meeting Kalei'opu'u threw round Cook's shoulders his own cloak, placed on his head a helmet and in his hand a feathered *kahili* or fly-flap, part of the royal insignia; and at his feet laid half a dozen more cloaks—a truly regal gift. Then came venerable Kao at the head of the priests; he wrapped round Cook the ritual cloth and made oblation of the ritual pig, while Keli'ikea and his fellows recited the customary chants. Once again, while all this went on, visible commoners were prostrate, and not a canoe stirred on the waters of the bay. The king went back to the ship with Cook for dinner, and himself received presents valuable in his eyes, iron hatchets and such things. Presents came constantly from the chiefs to Cook and Clerke in the remaining days; somehow the captains summoned up enough to give in return, with the armourer hard at work at old iron at his forge. Cook managed a tool-chest complete for Kalei'opu'u. Kao, familiarly known at the ships as 'the bishop', retired to the settlement of priests, whence he exercised his benevolence; Keli'ikea—'the curate'— was frequently his agent.

An unarmed party that attempted to climb the 'snowy mountain', Mauna Loa, and was away for five days in the forest without succeeding, was guided and watched over by men whom Kao sent with them; the carpenters on their timber-cutting expedition were similarly aided by natives who bore their heavy loads; gentlemen on their rambles were fed and entertained, welcome to inspect anything from surf-riding or mourning over the dead to a game of draughts;

all apprehension was banished. There were exhibitions of boxing and wrestling, in which the visitors, no doubt with memories of Tongan experience, declined to participate though invited; Cook replied with his few remaining fireworks. The 'enquiries into the Customs of the Natives, & of the produce of the Islands', earlier desiderated by King, were given full scope. We are told a great deal about this island. Nor was benevolence confined to priests or chiefs, or even to one race, in spite of the brutality which common sailors tended to show to those they considered their inferiors. 'A constant exchange of good offices, & mutual little acts of friendship obtained among us', wrote Trevenen, thinking of an occasion when he and fellow-midshipmen were swamped off their beach in a canoe, and children took part in their rescue. Only one Hawaiian seems to have suffered flogging for theft, in the *Discovery*; sailors suffered more for their usual mindless offences. In the last few days, as it was evident the ships would not go short of provisions, Cook threw trade open to everyone.

January passed, and February began with two incidents which are not only part of the voyage, but cast some light on Hawaiian religion. The first concerns one of Cook's necessities, firewood. Why he did not follow his usual practice, and seek permission to fell trees near by, we do not know: there may have been none suitable near by, or his men may have been otherwise too busily employed. He could anyhow see, surrounding the space of the *heiau*, a fence which, though stout enough, looked as if it were being let go to decay; from which, indeed, from time to time people appropriated palings to use for purposes of their own. There could hardly be any impropriety or impiety in offering to buy the whole thing for the needed firewood, and King was sent to treat with Kao. The old man was most accommodating, and did not trouble to put a price on it at all, though a handsome price was paid; and on the morning of 1 February the ships' launches took it off. The men were also taking, they said at native bidding and with native help, the carved images, and had actually got the whole principal semicircle out of the ground and down to the boats before the alarmed King could take notice and run to Kao. He was still unruffled, asking only that the small central clothed image should be returned, and the two others by the sunken square left standing. Hence the first burning, at European hands, of Hawaiian 'gods'; but it is clear that those were mistaken who later declared Cook guilty of some vast blasphemy in Hawaiian eyes. Neither the enclosing fence nor this particular class of images (however much Cook or King would have respected them) had any sanctity; a Hawaiian in need would have burnt them without incurring the awful penalties implicit in *tapu*.

The second incident was the death on this day of William Watman, the old seaman who had followed Cook from Greenwich Hospital. He had been ailing for some time but was convalescent when he fell paralysed under a stroke. The chiefs, acquainted with his death, asked that he should be buried on shore, and he accordingly was, in the *heiau*, at the foot of one of the images that had been left, to which a board was affixed with wooden pegs (to circumvent nail-stealers) —'HIC JACET GULIELMUS WATMAN'.[1] When Cook had read the service, and the grave was being filled, Kao and his brethren, silent spectators in their turn of an alien ceremony, threw in a dead pig, coconuts and plantains, their sacrifice to mortality and sorrow, and embarked on ceremonies and invocations of their own. For three nights, says King, 'and in one it lasted the best part of it', they 'surrounded the grave, killd hogs, sung a great deal, in which Acts of Piety & good will they were left undisturb'd'; and one trusts that William Watman, old and beloved of his shipmates, was left undisturbed too, under the paving of Hikiau. Certainly the episode exhibits good will.

Cook now waited only for the carpenters' return to take his departure. The fortnight had been crowded and profitable, to the ships, to the astronomers, to the amateur anthropologists, to Nelson the botanically-minded gardener, to the bird-collectors; the ordinary carnal man had no cause to complain. Nowhere else in the ocean had they been supplied so generously. It was time to look at the leeward side of Maui and investigate the other islands of the group, to water the ships at Kauai if no other source of supply was found, before striking north to Kamchatka and the cold. The chiefs, Kalei'opu'u no less than the rest, were beginning to enquire when they proposed to leave, and unlike Tongans and Tahitians, seemed pleased that it was to be soon. From this general wish they excepted King, whose politeness and consideration had obviously ingratiated him in no small degree; it was proposed to him that he should 'elope', and be hidden in the hills, and made a great man. Kalei'opu'u and Kao, finding him unreceptive, and persuaded that he was Cook's son, approached Cook himself with the more honest proposal that he should be left behind; and Cook felt himself forced to temporise that

[1] This at least is Samwell's version. King says 'at the head of the grave a post was Erect'd & a Square piece of board naild on it, with the name of the desceased, his age, & the date, this they promised shou'd always remain, & we have no doubt but it will as long as the post lasts & be a monument of our being the first Discoverers of this Group of Islands.'—*Journals* III, 517. This was optimistic.

perhaps the next year it could be arranged. The modest King reflected that in every island there was a wish to retain some individual person, 'often from no better motive than what Actuates Children, to be possess'd of a Curious play thing'; and this was true enough, however it undervalued his own merit. There was a final collection from the common people, by order of Kalei'opu'u and Kao, of a vast quantity of sugar cane and vegetables, as well as hogs, heaped up with bundles of tapa cloth and red and yellow feathers, and another bundle of ironware from the ships; but the ceremony on this last day was rather complicated, because Kao presented the iron and the feathers to Kalei'opu'u, who presented part of the feathers and the cloth to Cook, the provisions to Cook and King; while Cook, having picked out the large hogs and as much of the other food as he had room for, presented the remainder to the commoners from whom it had come in the first place. By the end of the day everything belonging to the ships was on board, and all their company—even King, the last to leave, had escaped from his lamenting friends. The huts on the *heiau* where the sailmakers had worked went up in flames, when men with torches ransacked it for possible booty; the field below, *tapu* removed, had already been rushed and explored. Early next morning, 4 February, the ships unmoored and sailed out of the bay, with an escort of canoes.

We may not unnaturally ask, as they steer north, why Cook should have received such extraordinary notice at this particular island. He had been presented with pigs before, and with large quantities of produce, but he knew that this was part of the Polynesian life-pattern, it was a gift-pattern that was also a trade-pattern. It was far transcended by what was now happening at Kealakekua Bay. He had seen *moe*, the abasement with which commoners approached the feet of Paulaho, the royal person of Tonga, and Paulaho approached the feet of one other person, a woman. He had experienced the *kapu*, or *tapu*, *moe*, at Kauai, and he saw it again at the feet of Kalei'opu'u as that chief went on his way, as well as at his own; and Clerke, who was also a great chief, had had expressly to forbid it. It made chief-ship a rather absurdly and inconveniently puffed up thing, he could see, it conferred a measure of sanctity; but even this was nothing compared to the ceremony, the ritual, the chanting, the anointing, the exalting in a savage (or if the word is too unjust, an 'Indian') place of worship that had here befallen him. It was as if he had been given divine honours. Those were precisely the honours, one is driven to conclude (though there has been argument about it) that were given him. The *kapu moe*, the sacred obeisance, was itself a semi-divine thing; for the highest chiefs of Hawaii, to whom it was accorded, the *ali'i kapu*, had a tinge of the god in their blood, as much as the Tu'i Tonga—a virtue beyond that of ordinary men or ordinary chiefs. To such a virtue, to such beings, veneration, obviously, was due. How large is the step from veneration to adoration?

Gods could appear on earth, if they were the right sort of gods. Such an event might be unlikely, but it could not be ruled out. Again, as when Cook was in the New Hebrides, we must not forget the thinness of the line between the seen and the unseen, the ease with which, for these islanders, the trembling veil could be split. The ghosts, the enemies, the ancestor-spirits, the white-faced ones, at Eromanga, were all around, in the forest, on an off-shore islet, they came in from the sea. We must consider, too, the nature of the gods. They also, in a more or less remote degree, were ancestral. The primal god begat other gods, and they still others, and they in turn begat human beings. In a more literal sense than that of Christian thought, the Polynesians were all children of God—or at least of a god: not immediately, perhaps, of a primal god, but of some divine ancestor-spirit. But the ancestor-spirit might reflect the nature of the primal god: so was it on the island of Hawaii. There the greatest of gods was Ku, in whose honour would be built the *luakini*, the royal *heiau*. No one, however, could have a warm feeling for Ku, creative as he was; for he was also terrible, the god of war and of human sacrifice. Of a different nature was Lono or Rono, also great, known elsewhere in Polynesia as Rongo, Ro'o, 'Ono: the god of light and peace, of the tilling of the earth, of abundance and the games of peace. There were very many lesser gods—lesser in status but none the less *atua* or *akua*. Thus Lono was also, in the legends of Hawaiian antiquity, a divine chief who participated in the name as well as the benevolence of the primal god, an ancestor who had worked good for his people, of whom it had been prophesied—as of other gods—that he would come again, bearing gifts. Now with the Hawaiian there was a season called *makahiki*, four months beginning in October or November, when warfare was forbidden and hard work was in abeyance, a season of games and sports beyond the ordinary, a season of abundance which was also that of the gathering of taxes. The god of this season was Lono, *Lono makua*, 'Father Lono'; and the gathering of taxes, the produce of the earth, was done on a slow clockwise progress round the island, the presence of the god being symbolised by a long staff bearing a banner of *tapa*, attached to a cross-piece somewhat like the yard of a ship's mast, and in form much like a ship's square sail. And now, proceeding slowly round the island in the festival direction, bearing the banners of Lono, bearing articles which were as good as gifts, though dispensed in trade, came vessels from afar captained by a chief of goodwill. Possibly the white cloth flying on the shore and on the canoes were emblems of Lono, and Cook's ensign seemed a divine acknowledgement of them. We seem to be right in saying, without too much discrimination between aspects of the divine, that Lono had returned incarnate in Cook. The constant repetition of the name among the humble people, as he was led through them by the wand-bearing priest, indicates it. The long ceremony on the *heiau* with which his visit was inaugurated went in its totality far beyond the greeting of the greatest chief, though what exactly was contained in all the formulae and incantations used we cannot know. The apparently despiteful words used by Koa to the images of inferior divinities, those who merely waited on, as it were, the central figure; the central, though smaller, figure of Ku, sacredly wrapped, *Ku-nui-akea*, 'Great Widespread Ku', the lord of the *heiau* and of all, which Koa, having prostrated himself, kissed, and caused Cook to kiss—all this was bringing together of god and god. The ceremonies continued day after day, the red cloth, the prayers that accompanied the proffered pigs, the nervousness of inferior chiefs making their oblations, the mediation of Keli'ikea and his train of priests—all this was appropriate to a god, not to a sea-captain. In Clerke's plain words, in a report that eschewed all mention of Lono, the respect the islanders upon all occasions paid Cook more resembled that due to a Deity than a human being.[1] The continual good offices of old Kao, who may be called the high priest, need hardly be treated as an argument, because they could simply have been the kindness of his own heart; and simple good nature may—though this seems less likely—have been the explanation for the daily supply by the priests of all the wants of King's party. It does not appear that the common people of the ships were regarded as being in any way heavenly beings. A god could have earthly retainers. Yet King—who was, it is true, in a favoured position—could write, 'As they certainly regarded us as a Superior race of people to themselves, they would often say, that the great Eatooa liv'd with us.'[2] Now the Eatooa was the *atua* or *akua*, the god. There could be only one person to whom this could refer.

---

[1] In his report to the Admiralty from Petropavlovsk, 8 June 1779, Adm 1/1612: printed in *Journals* III, 1535 ff.

[2] ibid., 621. The tradition that Cook was taken for a god, here supported, has not met with universal acceptance. The opposing case was put by Sir Peter Buck, 'Cook's Discovery of the Hawaiian Islands', in his *Report of the Director for 1944*, B. P. Bishop

We have in King's pages another passage on this theme, which does not, however, bear on the god; which meditates earlier on Hawaiian well-doing, and the subjection of the people to their chiefs. 'What praise soever we may bestow on our Otaheite friends & still more on those at the friendly Islands, we must nevertheless own, that we durst never trust them with such entire confidence as we have done these people. . . . It is very clear . . . that they regard us as a Set of beings infinitely their superiors; should this respect wear away from familiarity, or by length of intercourse, their behaviour may change. . . .'[1] But this was written as he put the bay behind him, with its priests, its people and their chiefs. There was no more to do here, for god or for men.

They were back in a week. In winds at first light and variable they made their way slowly north, a few miles off the shore. They had a number of Hawaiians on board, men and women, bound for Maui, including Koa, who announced that his name was now 'Brittanee'; canoes came off in crowds, and if anyone thought food might be running short on the island, the supply these carried would have been an ample contradiction. On 6 February they were off a large bay, Kawaihae, which runs in between the western and the northern points of the island. Here, according to Koa, would be found shelter and water, and Bligh put off with him in the pinnace to look. There was no shelter, and no water near the shore, and Koa preferred not to return. At noon the weather became squally, canoes coming out put back; the squalls off the land became so heavy that the ships had to bring to, and Bligh himself returned with three natives he had rescued when their canoe was thrown over. Another canoe was hoisted on board, and its company added to the seasick unhappy women already there. The weather moderated and grew more boisterous in turn. Still another canoe was rescued, with exhausted occupants. The night of the 7th brought a succession of strong gales, the canvas was double-reefed, the topgallant yards got down. In the morning the head of the *Resolution*'s foremast was found to be badly sprung—that mast that had given so much trouble to the carpenters at Nootka Sound ten months before. The two fishes then bolted on had been made from what seemed well seasoned drift wood, but King now thought he remembered some suspicion attaching to it.

Museum Bulletin 186 (Honolulu, 1945), 26–7, beginning, 'Another popular fallacy associated with Captain Cook is the theory of his alleged deification by the people of the island of Hawaii.' I have discussed this opposing case, up to a point, in my note on p. cxliv of *Journals* III.

[1] *Journals* III., 524–5.

Whether or no, they had both split, and both must be replaced without delay. The misadventure was hastened by slack topmast rigging, noticed as soon as the ship had left the bay; but that was no comfort. How to proceed? The mast would have to be taken out before it could be repaired, and for this a sheltered harbour was necessary. There was Kealakekua Bay. Cook was not eager to return: he was not enamoured of the place as a harbour, he felt he had worn out his welcome there, and probably gone through the provisions available close about, it was not good for water. If he went back he might have to abandon all prospect of seeing the other islands. He might find something better to leeward, but he could not depend upon it; Waimea Bay, which he knew, was too exposed. He decided to go back. 'At 10 we bore away for Karakakooa,' says King, a person not habitually given to strong language, 'all hands much chagrin'd & damning the Foremast.'[1]

There were continued gales and squalls, one of which carried the *Resolution* too close to the breakers; without further misadventure, however, by the morning of the 11th both ships were anchored within the north point of the bay, and the necessary labour started immediately. The preceding afternoon Koa had turned up again, with his customary pigs and coconuts for the captains; and another visitor to the *Discovery* had been an unprepossessing but highly important chief, already familiar, called Kamehameha. He was related to Kalei'opu'u; he was to be the first ruler of a consolidated Hawaiian kingdom. There was no glimpse of the future as Clerke bargained with him for his elegant feather cloak; but there was perhaps something a little symbolic in the price that had to be paid—not adzes, but nine long iron daggers, which product of the armourer the people had latterly preferred, and certainly preferred to their own wooden ones. That afternoon of 10 February Samwell had cast his memory back from priests and chiefs and savage sweethearts: 'It is three Years to day since the two Ships were put in Commission.' Three years, and the voyage might be about half over; but losses had been few, health and spirits were good, and into his mind, that welcomed so much miscellaneous poetry, came almost inevitably a Virgilian tag: 'tho' we have still a long prospect before us and an arduous Undertaking in hand yet when we consider the Man who is to lead us through it we all agree that

"Nil desperandum
Teucro Duce et Auspice Teucro".'[2]

---

[1] ibid., 527.   [2] ibid., 1191.

Indeed it would have been hard for anyone to imagine worse storms, narrower escapes, more forbidding cold and darkness than they had already triumphantly encountered, behind that indestructible leader.

No time was lost. The main topmast of the *Discovery* was requisitioned, with that of the *Resolution*, to use as sheers, and on the morning of the 13th the wounded foremast got out and sent on shore. The work was unimpeded because there had been no rush of natives to the ships, and the bay was strangely empty of canoes. This, however advantageous, was rather hurtful to British vanity, which had expected a crowd and general rejoicing; it was sufficiently explained by the information that Kalei'opu'u, then absent, had laid a *tapu* on the bay until he should pay the first visit himself. He arrived this same morning, inquisitive about the reason for the ships' return, and not (at least so Burney thought) very satisfied to see it.[1] This was natural, if he had been glad to see them go. In the meantime the priests had been as obliging as before, and we know that he was angry that they should have been so. Close to the *heiau* was a house that they lent for the carpenters and sailmakers to live in; in front of this they allowed a marquee and a tent to be raised for the guard of marines and the astronomers and *tapu*-ed the mast to keep away meddlers; the observatories were placed for King and Bayly on the *heiau* itself, where the two huts had been burnt down the night before the ships sailed. The heel of the foremast also was found to have rotted with a hole in it 'large enough to hold a coconut', so there was further repair to be done. Timber cut at Moorea for anchor sticks was to be used as fishes. With these arrangements on shore, and the ships surrounded with canoes, 'full of Hogs & roots of all kinds, such was the Situation of affairs on the 13th at Noon', says King, who commanded this shore detachment. He was not quite all-inclusive; for a number of large canoes had arrived at Kaawaloa, where their occupants added to the population, putting up temporary huts for the period of the ships' stay; and a distressing affair had already happened on board the *Discovery*. A man who had stolen the armourer's tongs was somehow identified, seized up to the main shrouds, given the severe punishment of forty lashes, and kept there till the tongs were returned, which they fortunately were in half an hour. The 'propensity to theft', thought Clerke, was stronger than on the first visit; he finished by turning all the people out of his ship except chiefs, and indeed it was in the afternoon of this day that he had a visit

---

[1] Kerrioboo 'appeared much dissatisfied at it', indeed; these are the words in the Mitchell Library MS of Burney's journal: ibid., 528, n. 3.

from Kalei'opu'u, who presented a cloak and a hog to him. There might be reason for irritation, but not for alarm.

Not for alarm; for the irritation had been undergone often enough before, and surmounted. Yet why should the wretched propensity be stronger now, and why should it be exercised so much more effectively on the *Discovery* than on her consort? Did some aura of the god lie upon the *Resolution,* even in her maimed state, a sort of discouragement to itching fingers, or was it that the *Discovery* lay nearer the beach, or was it pure chance? Did the reappearance of the ships, with that obvious damage to one of them, lower the esteem in which they had been held? Should the ship of a god have suffered damage at all? Had the prestige of Lono been damaged too? Had the people never really believed in Cook—Lono—or, after initial belief, had a week's reflection convinced them or influential chiefs to the contrary? We may remember King's words on the superiority the Hawaiians attributed to their visitors—'a Set of beings infinitely their superiors'—and the possibility of their respectful behaviour changing with greater familiarity. He had added a further reflection: 'the common people which are generally the most troublesome, are I am afraid here kept in so slavish a subordination to their Chiefs, that I doubt whether they would venture to give us offence without great encouragement in so doing from their Masters, whose passions & desires are as great as any of their brethren to possess such Novelties as we have.'[1] Had the time of familiarity, or fancied familiarity, now come, had the chiefs loosened their hold? The questions are really impossible to answer; but we seem to be confronted by a sudden shift in Hawaiian feeling. The propensity to theft was matched by a propensity to mischief, as if the return had released some instinct in the people that had hitherto been pent up, something like the devilry that had made the Tongans, after a while, their awe departed, throw stones at working-parties and laugh among the bushes. Then Cook had insisted on the letter of his orders: sentries must not fire with ball.

We get a partial answer to one of our questions from an incident of the afternoon of this 13 February. While the carpenters were busy over the mast beneath the *heiau,* at the other end of the short beach a party of sailors and Hawaiians, who had been paid for their help, were filling water for the *Discovery,* with her quartermaster, William Hollamby, in charge. A chief hindered the Hawaiians, and together with a mob of others caused a good deal of trouble; Hollamby therefore came to King and asked for a marine to act as a

[1] *Journals* III, 525.

guard. King gave him one, with only side-arms, who was quite ineffectual, and Hollamby returned to say that the Indians had now taken up stones and were still more 'insolent'. King went himself with another marine, armed with a musket, at which the stones were thrown away, at King's request the chiefs present drove off the mob, and the watering party, including its Hawaiians, was left in peace. King met Cook, who was coming on shore to inspect the carpentry, and reported what had happened. Cook's answer warns us that there may have been in him too a sudden shift of feeling: 'he gave orders to me', says King, 'that on the first appearance of throwing stones or behaving insolently, to fire ball at the offenders: this made me give orders to the Corporal, to have the Centries pieces loaded with Ball instead of Shot.'[1] The air, we are almost conscious, has taken on a slight tremor.

Much worse occurred in the later part of the afternoon. Kalei'opu'u had left the *Discovery*, and Clerke was entertaining in his cabin Palea, the chief whose spontaneous good offices had been so useful earlier. While he was doing so a 'rascal' (the word is Clerke's) somehow got up the ship's side, dashed across the deck, seized the armourer's tongs—the fatal attraction of that piece of equipment!—and a chisel, and was overboard again almost before anyone saw what he was about. A canoe—Palea's canoe—immediately picked him up and made for the shore. Clerke, hearing the alarm, ran up on deck and ordered muskets fired at her, but as she was rapidly getting out of range despatched his master, Edgar, after her in his small cutter with Vancouver the midshipman and two men, in such a hurry that they took no arms. The canoe won the race to the beach, and the thief vanished; but as Edgar was following her in he was met by another canoe, bringing back both the tongs and the chisel, and a third article which had not been missed, the lid of the water-cask. Meanwhile several other things happened. Palea told Clerke he would see that the stolen property was returned, and went on shore to do so, though not in his own canoe. The *Resolution*'s pinnace, with a few men in her, rowing off the beach waiting for Cook, saw the chase, and pulled to the cutter's assistance. Cook and King, both busy, the one with the carpenters, the other in his observatory, heard the firing and saw the beginning of the chase. They could see that something valuable had been stolen. Cook called to King, and together with the corporal of marines and a private carrying his musket, they set off as fast as they could to intercept the thief as he reached the shore. King, outrunning the others, was too late even

1 *Journals* III, 529.

then; he could but call out to Vancouver and get a gesticulation towards the shore in reply, because no words were audible against the noise of the great crowd that had collected. So, still ignorant over what exactly had happened, he devoted himself to rejoining Cook, which was difficult; for Cook, ignoring the *Discovery*'s boat, had gone on at a great rate to catch the thief—quite misled by his informants for miles as to direction, and threatening that the marine would fire if they did not produce the man. There was a mob close about, and other bodies gathering as the dark came on; at first when the marine made as if to present his piece, the mob would fall back; then they began to laugh. Where now was the respect, where now were the prostrations before Lono, the murmurs of awe? Cook, the victim of a wild-goose chase, in an impossible and ridiculous position, simply had to accept the fact, and walk back to his boat; 'but I believe', records King, 'it was not from the smallest Idea of any danger.' The Hawaiians led him back by a different way.

Reaching the tents he heard another tale of woe from his coxswain, which must have been very like that recorded by Edgar. When Edgar was joined by the pinnace he assumed that she was armed—which she was not—and in addition seeing Cook and King running along the shore he assumed that he now had the advantage, and by seizing the thief's canoe could impose some punishment on evil-doing. The canoe, however, was Palea's, and he quite naturally objected. When Edgar persisted Palea took hold of him, on which one of the pinnace's men struck Palea on the head with an oar; and this provoked a shower of stones from part of the crowd on shore and a rush on the pinnace. She was aground; her crew leapt out and swam to some rocks not far off, where the cutter took them in. Edgar's story becomes a little confused, but it is clear that he and Vancouver were being stoned and beaten, while the pinnace was being gutted of her oars and moveables, and that Palea was their saviour; the chief stopped the mob, returned the pinnace with a whole oar and a broken one, and sent them off. They were joined by the cutter, which, wisely though ingloriously, had been lying out of stone's throw, and set off to report to Cook. As they went they were pursued by Palea in a canoe, bringing Vancouver's cap, snatched from him when he was knocked down in a separate mêlée; and with the question whether it would be safe for him to come on board next morning. He seems to have been an admirable man. He went on to Kaawaloa, where no doubt he gave his own version of the story, in which the emphasis would have been rather different from that of

Edgar's. Cook was furious with his coxswain, both for acting without orders, and for his folly in acting as he did, unarmed. But Cook, we reflect, had been armed only with the musket of one marine, and had had no sense of folly. We can see that familiarity had its dangers for both sides. King transmits another remark that has the significance of heightened tension: 'In going on board, the Captⁿ expressd his sorrow, that the behaviour of the Indians would at last oblige him to use force; for that they must not he said imagine they have gaind an advantage over us.'[1] He relieved his mind immediately by turning all the visiting women and others out of the ship.

Before King returned on shore he enquired for orders. Cook told him to call at the *Discovery* and hear all Edgar's details, and report on them in the morning when he came to take the chronometer on shore. King, with his mind a little perturbed, thought it wise to give the sentry particular instructions: if potential marauders were descried lurking at any distance, he was to be called; if any came so close that their intentions must undoubtedly be bad, the sentry was to fire at once. Half a dozen did come creeping warily at the bottom of the *heiau* during the night; shoot if one came on top, said King; and about midnight one appeared close to the observatory. We must suppose a nervous sentry; he seems to have dropped his piece, and when he at last let fly the intruder was gone. The rest of the night was peaceful; but in the dark hours something else happened. The *Discovery*'s larger cutter was taken away. She was lying moored to one of the anchor buoys, sunk to the level of the water to prevent her plank from splitting in the hot sun, and she had gone without a sound, her moorings plainly cut through. This was a most serious loss, if it should prove a loss; for, though the Hawaiians might enjoy pulling a boat to pieces for the sake of the ironwork in her, she was the only large boat the ship had, and she could not cheerfully be let go. The people of the bay later put the blame on Palea. After the attempted impounding of his canoe and the blow on the head the evening before, he might quite well have wanted to solace some sense of injury, and presumably iron was as valuable to him as it was to his fellows. But he was anxious over his standing with Cook, and this would have been no way to improve it; in the light of his behaviour before and later such a plot seems unlikely; while it is not impossible that the Hawaiians, for reasons of their own, should have named him as someone known to the ships—or even named him at random.

Clerke hastened to the *Resolution* to inform Cook of the matter, and after some consultation Cook proposed sending the boats to the

[1] *Journals* III, 530.

two points of the bay to prevent any canoes from leaving. Such a blockade, and the holding of canoes as security for the cutter would, he thought, soon result in her return. Clerke agreed, rowed back to his own ship to give the necessary orders, sent off his launch and small cutter, this time well armed and with marines in them, under the command of Rickman, towards the southern point, and returned to inform Cook. A large double sailing canoe was already making out of the bay, and the *Resolution*'s great cutter was sent after her. The cutter could not get up with her, but forced her ashore within the point. While Clerke was away, Cook came to another, apparently sudden, decision. King arrived on board, and 'found them all arming themselves & the Captⁿ loading his double Barreld piece; on my going to acquaint him with the last nights adventure, he interruptd me & said we are not arming for the last nights affairs, they have stolen the Discoverys Cutter, & it is for that we are making ˙preparations.'[1] Some of the ship's guns were fired at large canoes in movement to send them back to shore. King was himself sent back to shore with the chronometer and orders to be on his guard and keep his people together. He thought it wise to go to Kao and the priests, explain the situation to them, and plead for general peace and quiet in their part of the bay; and certainly they did not wish for trouble. In the meantime, Clerke had returned in his small jolly-boat, all he had left, to the *Resolution*, to confirm that he had done as agreed. He found not Cook but Gore. Cook had gone on shore at Kaawaloa, his own musket loaded, one barrel with small shot, the other with ball, with an armed escort of Lieutenant Molesworth Phillips and nine marines, also ready with ball. He had resolved to make Kalei'opu'u his hostage for the return of the cutter. As he went, he saw the canoe that his cutter had forced ashore, and remarked that she could not possibly escape, though the cutter was held off by the rocks. How if her people resisted? asked somebody; 'he answered there could be no great difficulty, for he was very positive the Indians would not stand the Fire of a single Musket.'[2]

But what did he—or anyone else, for that matter—know about the reaction of Hawaiians to musket fire? He had had no experience of it at all. Everybody thought the same, says Burney, who tells this story, founding the opinion on 'so many instances' of Indian

[1] ibid., 549.

[2] Burney, Mitchell MS, Safe 1/79; ibid., 529, n. 1. Burney can hardly have heard the words himself, unless he were just then accidentally on board the *Resolution*, and he was certainly not at the scene of action, but he seems to have collected his information carefully. He adds to the words quoted, 'indeed, so many instances have occurred which have all helped to confirm this Opinion, that it is not to be wondered at, if every body thought the same.' Of course, the instances did not need to be Hawaiian ones.

behaviour 'which have all helped to confirm' it. The generalisation was too wide. There were instances to the contrary, which nobody troubled to think of, even among Indians who were not Hawaiians. It is worth while, therefore, at this stage to examine the Cook who steps into his pinnace to go ashore at Kaawaloa, between six and seven o'clock on this morning of 14 February, however tentative may be the statement that one makes. We have a Cook who—it has been said before—disliked bloodshed, and had spent a great deal of his energies on keeping his ignorant, irresponsible, often stupid men out of the sorts of trouble that entailed bloodshed. They had no great plans in view, were not gifted with foresight, got into a scuffle with remarkable facility. Why should Cook now lose his sense of proportion—as one is compelled to think he did: why should he act with less than real foresight? There can hardly be doubt that, if Cook wanted to make Kalei'opu'u a hostage, he could at a more normal hour, in a more normal manner, easily get him to come to the ship. He had decided on the abnormal—that is, on an immediate descent on the village, with the marines at his back, and marines armed as if for battle. Did anybody think there was a battle in prospect? Hawaiians were used to marines, standing about as sentries, amiably hobnobbing or pursuing their women; but this was a set piece of menace, 'things carried on in a quite different manner from formerly' (the words are King's). He might have tact in mind, but if so, he was supporting it with a threat; and threats do not always work, as he had already proved at Moorea, when he wished he had not started the miserable business. They sometimes work in quite the wrong way. Besides, how were the people to know what the threat was? Did Cook himself know what it was? It was certainly not a carefully calculated one. Unless the Hawaiians were already convinced of the deadly nature of fire with ball, and were convinced that the muskets were loaded with ball, what use would Phillips's nine ill-trained men be? It is possible that Cook merely thought in terms of more than the one man he had had with him the previous afternoon. Or it may be an indication that not force but a slight show of force was all he had in mind. But that does not tally with loading ball. If he was serious about the ball then he had parted with his general theory that it was better to frighten than to slaughter the unsophisticated. There were persons serving under him who did not agree: who thought it better to kill a man or two on the first sign of disagreement and save trouble in the future—and, giving their argument a humanitarian twist, in saving trouble save also future slaughter. Nothing could be more repugnant to Cook's soul;

but he did, as we have seen, share with these murderous logicians an overestimate of the effect of muskets fired to kill.

Looking back on this wearing, this worrying voyage we have remarked times of irritation, points at which the cautious, deliberate man was less than cautious and deliberate, and we have seen reasons for this. We have seen the problem of theft on all the voyages, so much a problem because to the islanders it carried no taint of crime —what should they know of crime?—but was, apart from being the means of acquiring articles useful or useless, both an amusement and a battle of wits. Multifarious as were the things that had been taken or attempted, a boat had never been stolen before—and one of the ships' best and most useful boats. It was too much. When King came on board the *Resolution*, then, this morning, after Clerke had left her with a clear understanding of what was to be done, he found a Cook—we must conclude—whose patience had been tried beyond its limit; who felt in some rather obscure way that the time had come when, once and for all, he would put an end to the burden these Polynesians not Hawaiians only—put upon him. His hasty preparations themselves cast a light on the exasperation of his mind. We may, of course, throw away all this hypothesis and think only of calm action in a calm atmosphere. But then the action becomes almost casual: it is hard to see the connection with events. The hypothesis does not presuppose that Cook should not maintain the appearance, and a considerable measure, of calm.

Cook went away from the ship with three boats, himself in the pinnace, accompanied by the small cutter and the launch. The cutter, under Lanyon, the master's mate, was sent to lie off the north-west point of the bay to prevent canoes from leaving, according to the arrangement with Clerke. Cook, Molesworth Phillips, and the nine marines landed in a little cove of the rocks close to the village; the launch under Williamson and the pinnace under Roberts withdrew separately a few yards to keep off the bottom, hereabouts almost a labyrinth of lava. Of what was to happen from this moment we have a number of accounts, and a great deal of circumstantial evidence, all interesting, and mostly unreliable. Only Phillips was with Cook. He does not seem to have been an imaginative man, and is probably to be relied on. He reported to Clerke, who probed him before writing his own journal, and was careful in statement. What was seen from the pinnace, fairly close to the shore, is obviously important, though it is equally obvious that this was one of those affairs, the dramatic, emotional, swift-moving moments in history, of which every witness gives a different story, and every story is confused by subsequent hearsay. Hawaiian evidence of any value is exiguous, but one or two scraps, almost accidentally transmitted, may be believed.[1]

Cook and the marines marched into the village, where Cook enquired for Kalei'opu'u and his two lively young sons, who spent much of their time on board the *Resolution*. The boys soon came and took him and Phillips to their father's hut. After waiting some time Cook began to doubt whether he was there and sent in Phillips to see. He was just awake, but came out to see Cook at once. A few words made it obvious that he knew nothing of the stolen cutter, and he very readily accepted the invitation to the ship. He started off for the beach with Cook and Phillips; one of the boys ran ahead and jumped happily into the pinnace. So far all was well; but near the waterside Kalei'opu'u's wife and two lesser chiefs came up, began to argue with him, and made him sit down. There was a change in the chief: he 'appear'd dejected and frighten'd', says Phillips; apparently he was being told he would be killed. A great crowd had now gathered, quite clearly not well-disposed. So many muskets, and the obvious lack of friendliness, had caused alarm. Cook pressed the chief; his friends insisted he should not go; the noise increased. The few marines were huddled in the midst of the Hawaiians; Phillips proposed to Cook that they should form a line along the rocks by the water, facing the crowd; Cook agreed, and the people quite willingly made way for them. Nevertheless the Hawaiians were arming themselves with spears and stones—to repel any force that might be exerted on Kalei'opu'u, so Phillips thought: many had daggers, some of them the iron ones obtained from the English. Then, remarks Phillips, 'an Artful Rascal of a Priest was singing & making a ceremonious offering of a coco Nut to the Capt and Terre'oboo to divert their attention from the Manœuvres of

---

[1] In analysing what actually happened, once Cook was on shore, I have leant heavily on Phillips. There is a large amount of contributory evidence, apart from the accounts given by Clerke and King, *Journals* III, 533 ff. Not much of it is really revealing, and little of it comes from people who knew anything directly. I have collected most of it in the long footnote on pp. 536–8, and in other smaller pieces of annotation, pp. cxlix–clvii. Samwell obviously made a considerable effort to sift out a clear, circumstantial and honest account, ibid., 1194–1202, and did not feel that King as printed had the whole truth; but he himself did not wholly satisfy Trevenen. Trevenen, says Penrose (*Memoirs*, Turnbull MS, 14) 'was highly pleased with the general spirit with which his friend Samwell's account of that transaction was written; yet he expressed himself not so thoroughly satisfied as he expected to have been from the very high opinion he entertained of that gentleman's abilities.' He thought Samwell's pamphlet (*Narrative of the Death of Captain James Cook*, London, 1786) was highly useful; yet 'it is not what I expected from him— some things are represented different from my conception, and in situations which should seem to render minute detail impossible.' This is a criticism which could be made of most of the accounts. Trevenen himself was in the small cutter with Lanyon and three other midshipmen.

the surrounding multitude.' It is not clear what these manœuvres were, or why Kaleiʻopuʻu's attention should be diverted. The look of things was such that Cook decided to abandon his plan, and said to Phillips, 'We can never think of compelling him to go on board without killing a number of these People.' Cook undoubtedly still believed he had the initiative. Clerke considering the matter later, agreed with this: there was nothing at this time to stop Cook, in spite of the clamour, from walking peaceably down to the boat and embarking; nothing to stop him from taking off the marines. He did begin to walk slowly down.

Two things now happened difficult to put in order, nor is their precise order particularly important. One, in relation to Cook, was a mere chance. At the other end of the bay, to keep a canoe from escaping, muskets had been fired—by Rickman among others—and a man killed. The man was Kalimu, a chief of high rank. Another chief hastening to the ships in indignation to pour out the story to Cook was disregarded, and forthwith made for the beach. It was Cook he wanted, not the crowd. It was the crowd that got the news, spreading like wildfire, not Cook; and the news was enough, with the other thing, to carry them over the borderline of excitement into attack. The other thing was Cook's own act. As he made his way to the boat he was threatened by one of the mob with a dagger and a stone—seriously or in mere bravado we cannot tell. Cook fired one barrel of his musket, loaded with small shot, at this person, and at that moment, when, we must think, the strained cord of his temper snapped, he lost the initiative. The man being protected by his heavy war mat, the shot did no damage—except that it further enraged the Hawaiians. Kaleiʻopuʻu's young son in the pinnace was frightened and was put ashore; but even then the men in the boats saw no particular reason for alarm. In the next second the wave broke. A chief attempted to stab Phillips, stones were hurled, a marine was knocked down, Cook fired his other barrel, loaded with ball, and killed a man; Phillips fired, there was a general attack, Cook ordered the marines to fire, and the boats joined in unordered. Phillips had time to reload his musket. The overwhelmed marines did not. Cook shouted 'Take to the boats!', an order hardly necessary, as the unfortunate and ill-trained men were already scrambling into the water and towards the pinnace, 'totally vanquish'd', as Phillips said. Phillips himself was knocked down by a stone and stabbed in the shoulder, shot his assailant dead and managed to get to the pinnace; and then out of it again to save the life of a drowning man. In all this tumult he lost sight of Cook. The men in the pinnace saw Cook's last moments. He was close to the lava edge waving to the boats to come in[1] when he was hit from behind with a club; while he staggered he was stabbed in the neck, or the shoulder, with one of the iron daggers—a blow which, not in itself fatal, was enough to fell him, strong as he was, face down in the water. There was a great shout, and a rush to hold him under and finish him off with daggers and clubs. The pinnace had gone in as close to the shore as possible to rescue the floundering marines; the launch had not—Williamson, that strange man incomprehensibly mistaking the meaning of Cook's wave, had even moved further out. The overloaded pinnace pulled off, the cutter came round and fired till she was recalled: the *Resolution*, hearing the uproar and the firing, and seeing, whatever might be the meaning of it all, that there was trouble on shore, fired those of her own four-pounders that could be brought to bear. It seems that the crowd had retired somewhat, and there was a space of time enough to reclaim bodies. The men in the boats may have been shocked out of all awareness of this. Leaving the dead, Cook and four marines, where they lay, the boats rowed back in silence to the ships; and the ships fell silent.

[1] There is no justification for the statement commonly made that he was waving to the boats to stop firing.

36. Poetua, by John Webber

37. The *Resolution* at anchor in Nootka Sound
Drawing by Webber

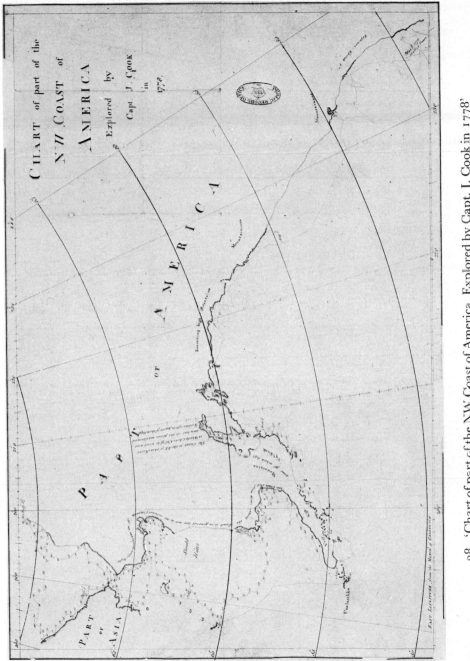

38. 'Chart of part of the NW Coast of America Explored by Capt. J. Cook in 1778'
By Cook. Showing the track and discoveries of the *Resolution* and *Discovery*,
7 March–3 October 1778

39. The ships in the ice off Icy Cape, 18 August 1778
Drawing by Webber

2c. Meeting with the Chukchi at St Lawrence Bay
Drawing by Webber

41. 'An Offering before Capt. Cook in the Sandwich Islands'
Engraving by S. Middiman and J. Hall after Webber

42. Keaiakekua Bay with the ships at anchor
Unsigned drawing, possibly by William Ellis

43. Mrs Elizabeth Cook
Oil painting by unknown artist

XXVI

End of a Voyage

ON NO one did the inconceivable fall more heavily than on the sick man Clerke. If he had been crushed, or if he had been swept into an excess of excitement, in either case it could have been understood; but the wasting away of his body did not disturb the quality of his mind. He briefly entertained, and discarded, the idea of summary vengeance. His level-headedness made even King, unbalanced for a day or two and ready for extreme measures, think that he was unable to reach any decision at all: in reality his perceptiveness was matched by his tact and his firmness, and made him the master of a situation which could quite easily have gone from disaster to disaster. His men would have turned the bay into a shambles; the Hawaiians might have put the ships into such a state of siege as to cancel the rest of the voyage. Vengeance on a grand scale would certainly have been both difficult and inept. It was not possible to maintain a complete control. In some sporadic skirmishing round the *heiau* and the spring the men of a watering party showed how savage sailors could be were guilty, in the words of a King who had regained his balance, of 'many reprehensible things'; the people, at once appalled and exultant at what they had done, did not omit to provide temptation. A few guns were fired; there was no assault on canoes. On both sides, as the days passed, the temperature was lowered. It may have helped, in the ships, that the immediate rage for revenge was mingled with a rage against Williamson over his conduct at the crisis. He faced a storm of accusation, as the person who could have saved Cook's life and did not. Clerke felt compelled to make some sort of specific enquiry. He could not be convinced of any real degree of turpitude, whatever he thought of the man's power of judgment, and the matter dropped. Phillips, who hated Williamson as much as anyone did, was clear that nothing he could have done would have had that sort of utility. The first conclusion Clerke came to we may regard as a determining thought in all his policy of these last days at Kealakekua Bay: 'Upon the whole I firmly believe

673

matters would not have been carried to the extremities they were had not Capt Cook attempted to chastise a man in the midst of this multitude'—relying, in the last resort, on the fire of the marines to disperse it.[1] How, then, could he give a free hand to retaliatory violence? But if Cook had been to blame, the whole transaction had not been simple, he was to reflect as in due course he departed from the islands and summed up his impressions: he 'must leave it to superior Judgments to settle the secret springs and original causes of action, with once more observing that the unhappy catastrophe which befell us I do think appears by no means the effect of pre-meditated intention, but of an unfortunate string of circumstances tending to the same unlucky point, one action irritating another till they terminated in the fatal manner as has been represented.'[2]

Whatever might be thought on that matter, there could be no divergence on two immediately necessary things. The first was to get back the abandoned bodies—or anyhow Cook's. The second was to secure the mast and put the *Resolution* into order—for 'we were now really in a tatter'd condition'. There was less difficulty about the second than the first. A strong armed party brought off everything on shore at the *heiau*, and the mast was placed fore and aft on the forecastle and quarterdeck for the carpenters to work on it. In the evening the boats were sent with King and Burney to demand the bodies. The people seemed pleased to see a flag of truce and discarded their weapons; the priest Koa swam out to King and said that Cook's body, carried far into the country, could not be delivered till the morrow; other people told Burney that it had already been cut up. Of the marines there was little mention. When the unsuccessful party returned Clerke got the impression that next day, in some state or other, the remains would be returned. No one knew the Hawaiian habit with the bodies of great men, especially great men—perhaps gods—killed in war, and those in the ships could but speculate during the night on the meaning of the lights flickering high up on the hill above the *pali* and the obvious fires that burnt there. The new day brought nothing but old Koa and a companion in a canoe with a white flag, some little pigs, and fair promises; and Koa became both tedious and suspect. There was no reason, indeed, why the Hawaiians should have readily fallen in with British sentiment, which they in their turn would have found quite incomprehensible; and after all, they were the victors, even if they had lost more men in the wretched affray than the defeated—four chiefs, in fact (including two who had been very good friends to the ships),

[1] *Journals* III, 538–9. [2] *Journals* III, 593–4.

and thirteen others. It was not till after dark on this second day, the
15th, therefore, that anything significant happened: when the
younger priest, Keliʻikea, appeared with a piece of flesh from Cook's
thigh which he had brought at the risk of his life as a mark of
particular friendship. All the rest, Clerke understood, had been
burnt; only the bones remained, and Kaleiʻopuʻu had them.
Keliʻikea may have been surprised at the horror and rage that
swept through the ship when his parcel was unwrapped. It was
gathered from him that there was by no means unity of feeling
between the priests of the *heiau* and the chiefs of the other end of the
bay: the priesthood remained as benevolent and generous as always.
The exception was Koa, against whom he gave warning. Kaleiʻopuʻu
all through these days seems to have played an entirely passive part,
though for the ultimate decision to return the bones his consent, at
least, must certainly have been necessary.

Clerke made it clear that he wanted these last remains. There
was still delay. Meanwhile, as Cook's successor in leadership, he
re-arranged the command on orthodox lines. Gore went to the
Discovery as her captain; King became first lieutenant, and Williamson (by virtue of seniority) second lieutenant of the *Resolution*; while
Harvey, the banished midshipman of Huahine fame, was brought
back to her as third. He had outlived Cook's resentment, and Clerke
could reflect that the promotion was something already designed.
Then there was the episode of the watering party, its stoning by
natives still belligerent, the brutal retaliation, the firing of a village
and the belongings of priests who had been promised immunity.
Outrageous as this was, it brought submission, the green boughs and
white flags of peace, a revived trade in provisions; perhaps helped
on the resolve to surrender sacred trophies. On the 19th, the day
that work on the mast was finished, Kaleiʻopuʻu sent a present as
earnest of his desire for peace. First, said Clerke, the remains of
Captain Cook. Next morning the mast was stepped, not without
difficulty; and at noon a procession came down the hill opposite the
ship, with hogs, fruit and roots, bearing flags, beating drums,
uttering loud cries; the chief in the lead handed over a bundle 'very
decently wrap'd up', and covered with a cloak of black and white
feathers. Good, said Clerke, who was prepared to be hospitable; but
what about the marines? They, alas, it was explained, had been
distributed among various chiefs in different parts of the island, to
collect them would be impossible; it was different with Cook, the
property of the king. Clerke thought best to drop the subject. The
bundle was opened in the cabin of the *Resolution*. It contained,

according to Hawaiian custom, the scalp, all the long bones, thighs, legs, arms, and the skull; the jawbone of the latter was missing, as were the feet, and the hands were separate. All had been scraped clean except the hands, which had been preserved with salt stuffed into a number of gashes. There was a means of identification: the right hand bore the well known great scar between the thumb and forefinger, the legacy of the exploding powder-horn on the New-foundland coast. The backbone and ribs had been consumed with the flesh in the fire.[1] The following morning the chief came again, bringing the jawbone and the feet, together with Cook's shoes and the bent and battered barrels of his musket. The remains were put into a coffin, and late in the afternoon of this day, 21 February, amid all the marks of naval grief, flags at half mast, crossed yards, and half-minute guns, they were sunk in the waters of the bay.

There was one more day. The fatal mast was now in place and rigged; trade was plentiful and theft unknown. Kalei'opu'u remained invisible, though he had sent to claim a red baize cloak edged with green that had been promised to him before the disastrous event, and let one of his sons, a charming and accomplished beggar, come on board the *Resolution*. Women had never entirely deserted the ships; they had even stood on deck and admired the flames of the burning village. Some, as they saw the preparations for departure, took passage for another island—they did not seem to care which. It was a pattern repeated. How really friendly the people were in general, and how they regarded the deeds of the lapsed week, it is impossible to say. Some wept over the death of Cook, and asked when Erono would return—a curious question, thought King. Some enquired what he would do to them when he returned; some said he would return in two months, and begged their English friends to mediate with him.[2] Clerke could not worry about this. In the evening of the 22nd there was a light breeze off the land, and for the second time

---

[1] Such trophies were normally distributed among great chiefs, and accordingly with Cook's remains there was a little problem in collecting them again. King learnt that the head or skull had gone to 'kahoo-opeou' (? Kekuhaupio, a warrior of immense distinction); the hair to 'Maia-maia' (Kamehameha, the future king); 'and the legs, thighs and arms to Terreeoboo.'—*Voyage to the Pacific*, III, 78. The missionary William Ellis, later collecting what information he could, was told that some bones were still retained, considered sacred, kept in a *heiau* dedicated to Lono on the other side of the island, and carried in annual religious procession—until, with the 'abolition of idolatry' in 1819, they disappeared, probably hidden in some secret cave. Almost everything else that could be called a relic of Cook's visit was venerated, he adds.—*Narrative of a Tour through Hawaii* (London, 1827), 117–18.

[2] King, *Journals* III, 561; Trevenen, ibid., n.; Samwell, ibid., 1217. On the general question of Cook's godhead, and the sceptical case put by Sir Peter Buck, cf. the note on p. cxliv of that volume—which includes also relevant remarks by Ellis (*Narrative*) and Colnett.

the ships put Kealakekua Bay behind them, amid a good deal of gloom. Clerke would follow Cook's plan: see if he could get better water and more sea stores at the other islands, and settle the positions of those which lay between Hawaii and Kauai; and then steer north to Avacha Bay, in Kamchatka, which would be the base for a further attempt on the Arctic.

The winds were not good, and progress was rather slow and painful, as close in as possible to the westward coasts of Kahoolawe, Maui with its great extinct crater, Lanai, the mountain mass of Molokai, and between that island and Oahu, tracing another eastern shore, well populated, green, fertile, most beautiful. Rounding its northeastern point, Clerke anchored for a few hours in a promising bay; landing, he was received with prostration and pigs, but found only a brackish supply of water. Obviously he must make for Kauai, where he hoped also for yams, good keepers at sea; and having got rid of all his women on Oahu, lest they should talk too much of Hawaiian misfortune, he was at the old anchorage in Waimea Bay on 1 March, prepared for a stay of some days. He at once sent a watering party on shore. Whether or not the news of Cook's death had arrived, and lowered the prestige of the visitors, the people were at first truculent, and on that day in defence a man was shot dead. It could not be called a cruel or gratuitous act, like that of Williamson the year before—the careful King was in command, there was little further conflict, and watering was completed without trouble. Trade went on apace; Kauai, thought Clerke, was 'the most extraordinary Hog Island we ever met with', and there was fruit; but the season, as luck would have it, was bad for yams. As there was plenty of salt, a large amount of pork was cured for future needs. The everlasting problem of the *Resolution*'s leaky sides was again evident, and all the carpenters were employed on them. Chiefs, even a 'queen' came on board the ships; a great deal was learnt about the tangled politics of the island, which possessed some extraordinary personalities and a lively civil war—in which Cook's goats had perished; great inducements were held out to likely persons to stay and lend their aid in the struggle; but the idea of desertion, which had seemed so fair at Tahiti or Raiatea, had become not at all attractive, and there was no trouble on that score. After a week the ships crossed to Niihau, to try again for yams. Here also the supply was disappointing, and another week was productive of little beyond boisterous weather. On 15 March they departed south-west on a brief unavailing search for the elusive turtle island 'Modoopapappa', which remained an object of curiosity from the earlier visit, and then steered west. They were without joy. It was a mission of conscience rather than hope. The gloom of Kealakekua Bay sailed with them. There was further gloom for Clerke—and it was shared by most of his officers—in the reflection that he was leaving behind in the Sandwich Islands not merely his friend but, visibly and horribly alive, a disease compared to the ravages of which musket-balls were gifts of love. Samwell might try to convince himself, and the world, that it was there before Cook discovered the group. Clerke, like Cook, was without illusions, and did not encourage them in others; and the Hawaiians were not such fools that they could not put cause and effect together. Clerke had at one stage been too sanguine. 'Captain Cook did take such preventive methods as I hop'd and flatter'd myself would prove effectual,' he writes, 'but our Seamen are in these matters so infernal and dissolute a Crew that for the gratification of the present passion that affects them they would entail universal destruction upon the whole of the Human Species.'[1]

At Niihau Clerke's longitude was about 200° E, his latitude a little short of 22° N. His plan—which may have been Cook's, or perhaps was a modification of it—was to stand to the west in latitude 20°–21° as far as longitude 170° E before turning north, so as to cover as much of the unknown part of the ocean as possible, though he could hardly avoid crossing the Manila galleons' course at some stage; but with the varying weather and baffling breezes that he had he was no farther on this course than longitude 180° by the end of March. He therefore decided at that time to haul to the northward for Kamchatka, confident that he would still be on a course not previously sailed, and be as likely to pick up new discoveries as on the one he had set out to follow. There were no new discoveries. There were old trials. In April gales old rigging gave way, old sails split; both ships leaked, especially the *Resolution*, though in new places. As the ships got farther north the men, who had traded most of their clothes for female favours in the islands, felt the cold; fortunately the warm jackets that had been issued for the Arctic had all been collected on the passage south from Unalaska and were in store, and these, together with a few slops that still remained, saved them from too bitter a frost-biting. They were abundantly fed. On 19 April the temperature was 29½ degrees, a fall of 53 degrees since

---

[1] *Journals* III, 576. Clerke attributes the severity of the visitation in Hawaii, in contrast to the Friendly and Society islands, to the quantity of salt the Hawaiians made use of in their customary diet.—'It certainly is a most unfortunate and ever to be lamented incident, here's a most miserable curse entail'd upon these poor Creatures which never can end but with the general dissolution of Nature.'

the first day of the month, and the ships were covered with snow; in four days more they looked like sheets of ice. It's the sudden change that pinches, confided Clerke to his journal, considering the state of his men. He confided nothing of his own malady, either throughout these weeks or much later; and by now it had gone so far that he was unable to leave his cabin. Land, rising in snow-covered hills, was sighted through the fog on 23 April; on the 25th the ships, not surprisingly under the conditions, parted company. So close to port that was of no great moment; it was of greater moment to discover next morning that the *Resolution*'s chronometer, 'the Time Keeper', the 'trusty guide', had broken down. As the month ended the ice which blocked Avacha Bay was clearing; on the 29th the *Resolution* got inside, and within a mile of the village of Petropavlovsk before she was stopped; on 1 May she was joined by the *Discovery*, and everybody could shudder at the idea of a winter spent at that place.

Avacha Bay was the only harbour on the east coast of Kamchatka. Petropavlovsk, like a few other villages in the southern part of the country, was supposed to be a fortified post; but when King and Webber, despatched as linguists, reached it by stumbling painfully over the ice, they found that its armament and its scurvy-ridden exiguous military force, as the Kamchatkan winter drew to a close, could stimulate nothing but sad laughter. The sergeant in charge was most obliging, and concealed the alarm he felt at the appearance of two armed ships, large by his standards, before the few log houses and native huts of his command in that dreary snow-covered wilderness. The country had, indeed, been largely depopulated by smallpox, and what supplies were to be obtained must obviously be sent for and bestowed by higher authority. The only place of account was Bolsheretsk on the other side of the peninsula, the seat of government and of trade, and the sergeant was willing enough to pass on to the governor, Major Behm, the letters which Ismailov had given Cook at Unalaska. When two persons came in reply to this to inspect the situation it was clear that Ismailov had badly misrepresented the ships, and Clerke decided to send King, Webber and Gore (the last eager to go for the novelty, though useless on an embassy as he spoke nothing but English) on the river and sledge journey overland to interview Behm. They were absent a fortnight, while the ice cleared and the early herbage appeared above ground, and the carpenters set once more to work on the rotting heart-breaking *Resolution*. Cook's regimen in diet was in full force, nettle-tops and wild onions were collected, fish was obtained in vast quantities, under the surgeons' directions even the Russian garrison was restored to health. Among the mutual good offices ranked high those of the priest of Paratunka, a village some miles away, who supplied Clerke with the comforts of bread, milk and fresh butter. King's journey was interesting; Major Behm, at the end of it, once he understood its cause, was sympathetic and generous, refusing to consider payment in any form for the cattle and flour and tobacco Clerke wanted, and sure—alas for his future!—that his Government would nourish the same generous sentiments. He was a highly intelligent man, interested in discovery. It was perhaps a stroke of luck that King's arrival coincided with the news from a northern outpost of the favourable effect on Russian-Chukchi relations of Cook's visit to the Bay of St Lawrence; for he had been taken for a Russian, of an amiability earlier unknown, and the Chukchi were now themselves inclined to be friendly, even to pay tribute. Behm's qualities cancelled out the less engaging ones of his subordinate, shortly to be his successor, a Captain Shmalev, who could see no scientific purpose in the voyage; and when King came back Behm insisted on accompanying him, both to wait upon Clerke and to ensure that the orders he had himself given were carried out. So much a friend did he prove that, as he was about to return to St Petersburg on relinquishing his command, Clerke decided to entrust to him Cook's journal, a long letter and the journal in which he continued Cook's, some important charts, and reports from King and Bayly, lest the ships should even now encounter disaster—and considering their state, that possibility could not be ignored. Behm was glad to undertake the trust; and in this way, seven months later, after a trans-Asian journey, was the crushing news to fall upon the Admiralty.

The governor was amazed at the healthy appearance of the seamen, three years out from home, in so much better order than their ships were. Yet one more man had died, Alexander McIntosh, a respected carpenter's mate of the *Resolution*, of a long-lasting 'flux'— the only man to perish of sickness, it was thought, who was not doomed from the start of the voyage. As June began the vessels had been made seaworthy once more, though ropes and cables would stand little strain. Ropes could be spliced, or some substitute found: the Time Keeper presented a more difficult problem. It had been religiously guarded and wound by Cook and King, and no one could imagine why it should have stopped. Among the *Resolution*'s people was Benjamin Lyon, a seaman who had served his apprenticeship to a watchmaker, and had kept his hand in by odd work on the voyage. Clerke called him into consultation: he found a little dirt in one of the wheels and got the thing going, not quite accurately. After three weeks it stopped again, was cleaned a little more, re-started and satisfactorily regulated, 'when at last we flattered ourselves with having once more a valuable machine in our possession'—only to stop a third time with a broken pendulum spring; and although Lyon made a new spring its utility on that voyage in the finding of longitude was over. It had still honourable work before it.[1]

By the middle of June, after final exercises of friendship, the ships were engaged in the tedious process of getting away from Petro-pavlovsk and out of the bay, weighing, anchoring, weighing, towing, the dismal gloom of fog intensified by the ash and cinders thrown over them by a tremendous eruption of Avachinskaya, the most active of the volcanoes that stud the land for some distance north. On the 18th they were safely at sea, and for the next two and a half weeks followed the Kamchatkan coast amid much foggy weather, in which still the true nature of St Lawrence island could not be made out. They were through the strait by 6 July, and at once among heavy drift ice. The following period of three weeks was one of utter frustration. Cook could have done no more, on this attempt to do what Cook had failed to do. Clerke first made over to the American shore, to investigate the piece of coast from Kotzebue Sound northwards that had been missed the previous season. He was blocked by ice, still firm. He bore away to the west, in latitude 68° 12′ —the penalty of being so early in the season was that the main ice field was farther south than Cook had found it—running through the drift ice and trying to force a passage northward, the ships brought to a dead stop with battered bows when they hit some formidable lump, finding the ice bent round south-westward towards the Asian shore; finding that to keep in touch with its main line they must be always among the drift. Obstinate and unconquerable the barrier remained. Clerke persisted in his effort until the early morning of 19 July, when, at the end of a deep bay formed by solid ice, he was in latitude 70°33′, a few miles short of Cook's farthest north, and about one degree of longitude to the west of it. Then there was nothing he could do but follow the line of ice south-

---

[1] King gave a full account of the difficulties in a letter to the secretary of the Board of Longitude from Petropavlovsk, 10 June 1779, a copy of which is in the Banks Papers in the Mitchell Library MS A 78.1, printed in *Journals* III, 1541–2. He hoped for the best, but Bayly (*Astronomical Observations*, 69) says it was rendered 'in a manner useless during the remaining part of the voyage'. After repair by Kendall it went with Captain Phillip in the First Fleet to Australia, returned to England in the *Supply* in 1792, and seems to have served with Jarvis/St Vincent till 1802. See Derek Howse, 'Captain Cook's Marine Timekeepers', in *Antiquarian Horology*, 1969, 190–9.

ward. This was the triumphant day when two white bears were killed. They provided 'palatable and wholesome fresh meat in the idea of every body'; more palatable, it seems, than walrus. It could not restore Clerke to health. His strength was running out. On 21 July he registered his despair of the American side of the ocean—'It is now clearly impossible to proceed in the least farther to the N°ward': but he would not quite give up. 'I therefore think it the best step I can take for the good of the service to trace the Ice over to the Asiatic Coast, try if I can find a Hole that will admit me any farther North, if not see whats to be done upon that Coast where I hope but cannot much flatter myself with meeting better success, for this Sea is now so Choak'd with Ice that a passage I fear is totally out of the question.'[1] With these words this devoted man put down his pen.

There was no hole leading to the north; there was no passage to the west; the Asian coast was thickly bordered with ice; the *Discovery*, having survived some frightening danger from entanglement in the ice, emerged with much of her sheathing gone and a bad leak; the attempt was on the 27th abandoned, and on 30 July the ships re-passed Bering Strait. They made their passage south farther out to sea than on the way north, to the east of the Komandorski islands, Bering and Medni, before turning into the coast. On 10 August Clerke dictated to King, his 'very dear and particular friend', his last letter to another friend, 'ever honoured', Banks—the document that carries most pathos in all the records of these voyages.[2] There was nothing for him to be jovial about now; he had a sense that he had faithfully done his duty, he hoped his friends would 'have no occasion to blush in owning themselves such'; he recommended to them persons in the ship of less importance. He managed to write a firm signature. Though he was too weak for greater physical effort, he continued to command the ship until 15 August, when he relinquished it to King, and on the 22nd, the day after the Kamchatkan coast was sighted, he died. He was thirty-eight.

Two days more and they were in harbour, gazing with a lift of the heart at the transformed country, the Kamchatka of summer. Gore, now commander of the expedition, returned to the *Resolution*, bringing with him Burney and Rickman as the senior lieutenants; King took command of the *Discovery*, to which went also Williamson and William Lanyon, a master's mate in the *Resolution* and a veteran

---

[1] *Journals* III, 696–7. The position for this day was later added to his entry—latitude 69°37′ N, longitude 193°7′ E.
[2] Mitchell Library, Brabourne Papers, MS A 78⁻¹; *Journals* III, 1542–4.

of the second voyage, and four midshipmen who had been very useful to King in astronomical calculations; to keep observations going in both ships, Bayly exchanged into the *Resolution*. It was a stay of seven weeks, and some men found it tedious. Tents were at once set up for wooders, waterers, sailmakers and coopers; the forge was taken ashore; there were hands gathering greens and hauling the seine. There was much to be done to both ships: planks were stove, ironwork twisted, rudders damaged, sails in rags, rigging unkempt. On the 29th Clerke was given burial ashore, with salutes and all the dignity that could be provided; his shipmates planted willows round his grave, and Gore himself composed inscriptions for it and for the 'escutcheon' which the good pastor agreed should be hung in the church at Paratunka. Bullocks were driven to Petropavolvsk from the interior; other stores were brought from Okhotsk. An interpreter, who understood French and German, and played the fiddle, was provided by the Russians; he was the exile Ivashkin, strange figure of an alien romance, thus given fame;[1] for he would have sunk obscure like other exiles had it not been for the published account of the voyage. Governor Shmalev—less suspicious, it appears, than he had been—came from Bolsheretsk to see that all was well. The priest lost no opportunity for benevolence. The officers went to Paratunka to visit him and to shoot wild ducks, and even tried their hands, unsuccessfully, at a bear-hunt. Country-dancing, Russian, Kamchatkan and English, took place on board the *Resolution* and at the tents for the local ladies. The ships' freemasons held lodge meetings. Anniversaries were appropriately celebrated: the British monarch's coronation, the name day of the Russian empress. The talk of furs from America brought merchants across the country from Bolsheretsk, who paid well for them; as there was neither gin nor tobacco to spend money on, observes King, the sailors were before long kicking their roubles about the deck. Other, more responsible, sailors now had time to consider the prospects of a regular fur-trade with the American coast. Spruce beer was again brewed, and before long it had to be drunk, if men were to drink anything besides water: on 5 October the last of the grog ran out. The short summer came to an end, and the winter began to set in; the leaves fell, the country became desolate and barren, the inland mountains were covered with snow; it was high time to be gone. One man wanted to stay, the *Discovery*'s drummer, not from love of island ease but of a Kamchadale woman. He was torn from her arms. Gore felt it incumbent on himself to address the British Ambassador at the

---

[1] *Journals* III, clxvi, 1276.

Court of Russia in praise of his hosts: 'Behm leads, Ismyloff [Shmalev] follows, and so on down to the poor, useful, inoffensive Kamtschadale . . . I do assure your Excellency, that I have been most agreeably disappointed in meeting with so much polite civilization in a Country so remote as Kamtschatka really is.'[1]

The instructions for the voyage left it to Cook, if he were debarred from returning home by a north-west or north-east passage, to adopt what route he thought fit. Gore, inheriting them, had no dictatorial instinct, and took his officers into consultation. They agreed that the best plan would be to trace the eastern sides of the very inadequately known Kurile islands and Japan and settle some latitudes and longitudes, then call at Canton for supplies, and make directly for the Cape, altogether avoiding Batavia. This, it was hoped, would add something to Geography and Navigation. It added very little. They sailed from Avancha Bay on 10 October, were deprived by contrary winds of any sight of the Kuriles and by fierce gales of anything beyond fleeting glimpses of the Japanese islands, so that the next land to be sighted clearly, and rather unexpectedly, was the Volcano or Kazan islands, far to the east of Formosa; they missed the Bashi, or Batan, islands, where Gore thought he might call for refreshment, south of Formosa, and passing through the Bashi channel into the China Sea narrowly missed running on the deadly Pratas shoal. Reading between King's lines, one feels some unstated reserve about Gore's quality as a scientific navigator, however just his reputation as a practical seaman. By then it was almost the end of November, and the north-east monsoon season; but a fortunate shift in the wind let them make the coast of China, and on 4 December they were moored on 'the Typa', a sort of shallow harbour between the islands which lie off the Portuguese settlement of Macao, at the mouth of the Canton river. A few days before this all journals, charts, and other papers relevant to the voyage had been surrendered. As the Portuguese had nothing they could dispose of, and the Chinese were difficult, it was necessary to get in touch with the merchants of the English factory at Canton to arrange for supplies, and King was sent up the river to expedite them. The merchants were full of courtesies. There was news at Macao that France, as well as the American colonies, was waging war against England. Surely the Americans had given up long ago! Burney set busily about preparing for the worst by making that minutely-written copy of his journal on China paper which is one of the curiosities of the voyage:

[1] The greater part of the letter was a formal explanation of the reason for putting into Petropavlovsk: 5 October 1779.—*Journals* III, 1546.

which the Lords of the Admiralty, fortunately for themselves, never had to read. This unsettling information was balanced by later news at Canton, where they had both the public news and private letters, that the French, in their regard for science and admiration for Cook, had exempted his ships from molestation, and that their example had been followed by the American congress.[1] While King was away, furs were sold to Chinese merchants at high prices; and when two men deserted at Macao, taking a ship's boat with them, it was opined that they intended to make their fortunes in the fur trade. The period of waiting came to an end; the ships got their supplies; the English merchants got their bills on the Admiralty; on 13 January 1780 the ships sailed.

In the China Sea they called for a week at Pulo Condore, a small high island where they were able to buy a number of buffaloes for fresh meat, to cut wood, and fish; then coasted Sumatra, passed the Strait of Sunda, watering at Prince's Island, and steered for the Cape—or rather, Gore not wishing to call there, for St Helena. The Indian Ocean provided pleasant sailing weather, except in the second week, when a violent storm tore to pieces every sail set, and— probably—started the strain on the *Resolution*'s rudder which made it necessary for her to seek an earlier port. She could not even turn up round the Cape into Table Bay, and was forced to put in to False Bay—to Simonstown, as we should say—for repair. This was on 12 April. At the Cape the tidings of Cook's death brought dismay. Phillips and Williamson are said to have fought a duel, somewhat to the discredit of the latter. Gore was met by a communication from the Admiralty, addressed to Cook, apprising him of the French care for the safety of the ships, and learnt from the governor that the Spanish, who had come into the war, had ordered the same immunity. He therefore decided he had better not sail in company with any other British vessel; for if she were attacked how could he refrain from battle?—and that could cancel out the benefit conferred on neutral science. In case of any accident that might happen to the *Resolution* ('She being very Weak in her Hull'), he informed Their Lordships in the letter that contained this thought, he was sending by His Majesty's Ship *Sybil* journals, observations and drawings, together with 'a Gentleman (One of our Masters Mates) who goes

[1] On this, see Martin-Allanic, *Bougainville*, II, 1455, 1459; the text of Benjamin Franklin's recommendation to American privateers, 10 March 1779, printed in *Journals* III, 1535; and the letter of J. H. de Magellan to Banks, 23 June 1779, ibid., 1542. The American Congress was slow to follow the example of Franklin. After the war the Admiralty showed its appreciation of his gesture by presenting him with a copy of the printed *Voyage*, and the Royal Society sent him one of its gold Cook memorial medals.

with Capt Pasely as an Assistant In making the Lunar Observations . . . the above Gentleman Mr Portlock will be able to point out to their Lordships somewhat more of our Passage From Kamtschatka Than can be understood by the Map.'[1] By the time of this letter the ships were almost ready to sail themselves. They did so on 9 May. Any contrary wind or calm was now infuriating to impatient men, and they had both these in the Atlantic, where on 13 July, the *Resolution*'s 'birthday' was celebrated—the fourth anniversary of her leaving England; opening the Channel on 9 August they were shut out of it by an easterly, tried in vain for a port on the west of Ireland, and anchored for the first time since the Cape in the Orkney islands, at Stromness, on 22 August. Here Gore waited a month for a favourable wind, to the disgust, the indignation, of midshipmen who wanted to see first their mothers, and then prize-money—was there not a war still going on? Was this immobility in tune with 'the sublime & soaring genius of a Cook?' King was sent overland to London for the benefit of the Admiralty. Sergeant Gibson of the marines, now one of the seniors of circumnavigation, improved the time by getting married. Gore at length thought fit to sail, round the Orkneys and down the east coast that Cook had known so well. Sergeant Gibson, and another man, died. On 4 October the ships were in the Thames; without Cook; without Anderson; without Clerke.

There could be pleasure over their arrival, there could be no vast official excitement. The Admiralty had had the essential information early in the year. England, Europe knew that Cook was dead. The poetasters were at work on their afflicting verse. There was nothing to tell about the great central purpose of the voyage. The ships were paid off. There was no twenty thousand pounds to distribute. There were promotions and appointments. Gore and King became post-captains, and Gore went to Cook's vacant berth at Greenwich Hospital; there was a crop of lieutenants; Molesworth Phillips became a captain. There was scrambling among collectors for the bird-skins and other 'curiosities' brought home: Sir Ashton Lever competed with Banks, Mrs Anna Blackburne of Fairfield nourished a hope. Banks got his dried plants. The booksellers began to scout for anything that could be called an account or a journal. Those returned adventurers who knew on what grand lines their adventure had been planned, and were inquisitive, could enquire into that other expedition, the instructions for which had been made known to

[1] Gore to Admiralty Secretary, 1 May 1780; P.R.O. Adm 1/1839, *Journals* III, 1556–7.

Cook—the one that was to try the Passage from Baffin Bay, and perhaps to lead him from half-way back to the Atlantic, the expedition to command which Pickersgill had been appointed.

Unfortunate Pickersgill! Everything was against him, the task he was given to do, the circumstances of his appointment, his own temperament. The task was impossible. His ship was the armed brig *Lyon*, which had spent several seasons surveying on the Newfoundland coast under Michael Lane, who had been Cook's mate in the *Grenville* on that duty, and had succeeded him in it, with distinction. Lane was now superseded by Pickersgill, and appointed to serve under him which could not have been pleasant for either of them. The Admiralty, or the Navy Board, in preparing the ship for service, was quite irresponsible: it saw no reason to strengthen her for a sea in which the stoutest whalers alone normally ventured, or even to overhaul her properly: half the crew were landsmen, none had proper clothing, the charts which could be supplied were of no service whatever. Pickersgill left Deptford in the middle of May 1776, two months before Cook, two months too late for useful work. He had a preliminary task, to protect the English whaling fleet from the Americans. After a slow passage he reached Greenland in early July, was at once amongst ice, in latitude 60°, and learnt from a stray vessel that the whalers had finished their season and left their base at Disco Island for home. It was still possible to get on to the eastern coast of Davis Strait and find a small harbour which supplied wood and water immediately, and could be of use in the following season. The highest latitude reached was 68°26′ N; whalers regularly went further; Baffin had been to 78°. Pickersgill was beaten by ice and icebergs, managed to make his way painfully to Labrador for a month's stay, to recruit his men, repair his ship, and drink hard; and reached Deptford at the end of October, five and a half months after he had left it. He retained his command until January 1777, when it was decided on Lane's allegations of his constant drunkenness to court-martial him, and he was dismissed from the navy. One sighs for Pickersgill, the romantic, the man of good intentions and less than iron will, who could take a lunar and draw a chart, had been round the world three times, had a sense of justice, and, like so many of his naval contemporaries, drowned his disappointments in the bottle.[1]

He was followed in the *Lyon* not by Lane, who at least might have

[1] J. R. Forster had something to say in his praise, and Forster is the authority for all we know of his end: after his dismissal from the navy he got command of a privateer, fell into the Thames one night while going off to her drunk, and was drowned.—*History of the Voyages and Discoveries made in the North* (London, 1786), 407–8.

brought back some accurate observation, but by Lieutenant Walter Young, a good fighting officer, but one of the most inefficient explorers that ever existed. Young was instructed to winter in the north if that was necessary to his mission. No improvement was made to the ship, though the men were this time given warm clothing. He sailed from England in mid-March 1777, on 8 June reached latitude 72°45', was stopped by ice; coasted it to the northern end of Disco, where he found it 'fixed to the land and impenetrable'; was persuaded of the impossibility of penetrating further northward because of fog, was convinced that his ship was in imminent danger, and on 22 June sailed straight back home. Young may have been correct in his judgment of the situation; but it was not thus that Baffin, in whose bay he was, had made discoveries. The Admiralty must wait for Cook, and Cook was then no farther on his voyage than Tongatapu.

XXVII

Epilogue

'DEAR SIR', wrote Sandwich to Banks, on 10 January 1780, 'what is uppermost in our mind allways must come out first, poor captain Cooke is no more . . .'.[1] It was the day the letters from Unalaska and Petropavlovsk were opened. The *London Gazette* made the news public next day. Letter-writers less closely implicated were quick to spread it. The Rev. William Cox, his account of the Russian discoveries between Asia and America then in the press, told his young friend George Herbert, travelling in Italy: 'I am sure you will be much concerned at the loss of so good and able a man'; and Herbert returned, 'Poor Cooke is truly a great loss to the Universe.'[2] The press took note of the deep feelings of the Empress of Russia, and was not behindhand with evidence of British feeling. The king is said to have shed tears, which is not improbable, and at once to have ordered Mrs Cook a pension of £200. Poor Elizabeth: she was but 38, and the cup of her sorrows was by no means filled. She had given birth to six children. The two eldest, James and Nathaniel, were those whose names had begun to 'earn time' for them, at the ages of six and five respectively, as members of their father's crew in the *Endeavour*; and now, at ages more mature, they were pursuing their careers in the navy more actively. James had entered the naval Royal Academy at Portsmouth when eleven, Nathaniel was shortly to follow him, and in 1780 they were up and coming young midshipmen. The youngest son was Hugh, the child of 1776, Palliser's godson. Three children had died prematurely (as the custom was, one might say): Elizabeth, the only daughter, at the age of four, in 1771, three months before the *Endeavour's* return; Joseph, at the age of a month, in September 1768; George, at the age of four months, in October 1772. These losses the wife bore with her husband absent.[3] Before the year 1780 was out the next blow

---

[1] Dixson Library, MS Q 158; *Journals* III, 1552–3.

[2] Coxe to Herbert, 16 January 1780, in Lord Herbert (ed.), *Henry, Elizabeth and George* (London, 1939), 393; Herbert to Coxe, 16 February 1780, ibid., 413.

[3] The precise dates, as recorded on the family memorial in the church of St Andrew the Great at Cambridge, were Elizabeth 9 April 1771; Joseph 13 September 1768; George 1 October 1772.

fell. Young Nathaniel was serving in the *Thunderer*, 74, Captain Boyle Walsingham, on the West Indian station. In a famous and fearful hurricane that sank thirteen vessels of the royal navy his ship went down, off the coast of Jamaica, on 3 October, with all her company; and it may well be thought that Elizabeth Cook had sustained enough.

At least she would not be materially cast on the world. The indications are that she was not an extravagant woman. During the last voyage, as Cook's wife, she had been allowed by the Admiralty the yearly sum of £300, which had been paid up to August 1779, though her pension would begin with the date of Cook's death. The Navy Board, though willing to be generous, had to have specific direction on the matter from their Lordships; Sandwich went to the king immediately, and the over-payment was approved.[1] There was the pension. There were the provisions of Cook's will. It is a simple yet interesting will, the expression of an habitually prudent mind, the will of any careful respectable citizen of Mile End Old Town, well enough off to own the leasehold of his house, with a proper amount of family feeling and regard to the conventions.[2] It is dated 14 June 1776. Time had made it in one small respect out of date; for it began by bequeathing to the testator's father, 'Mr James Cook of Redcar in the County of York'—where he lived with his daughter Margaret, the wife of the fisherman James Fleck—an annuity of ten guineas; and James Cook the elder, though he outlived his son, had died on 1 April 1779 at the age of 84. There were four other minor legacies—to each of Cook's sisters, Christiana Cocker and Margaret Fleck, £10; and £10 to each of his 'good friends Thomas Dyall of Mile end old Town Gentleman and Richard Wise of Rumford Essex, Gentleman . . . as a Mark of the great Regard I have for them.' This is the only time these good friends come into the record. They, with Mrs Cook, were to execute the will. To Mrs Cook went the house and its furniture for her life, with reversion to the children in equal shares. There was the residue of the estate. One cannot tell what it was, but it would include accumulated pay and the property in the published second voyage and its plates. A third went to Mrs Cook, the other two thirds were to be put into appropriate securities for the children in equal shares; their shares of the principal were to be paid over to the sons when they came of age, to a daughter or daughters—for the baby who was Hugh might appear as a girl or

---

[1] Navy Board to Admiralty Secretary, 30 May 1780, ADM/BP/1, loose paper; Admiralty to Navy Board, 1 June 1780, ADM/A/2752, loose paper; *Journals* III, 1557–8.
[2] P.R.O. Probate 11/1060 (10).

even more than one girl—at the age of 21 or at marriage, whichever should be the earlier, 'Provided Nevertheless such Marriage be had with the Consent of my said Wife but not otherwise'. There was further prudential provision. Such part of the individual children's portions as the trustees might think fit might be spent in placing them out as apprentices 'or otherwise in their Advancement in the world', the interest in the mean time going towards maintenance and education. The portion of any who might die before it became payable was to go to the survivors. There were no delays of the law: probate was granted to Mrs Cook and Dyall on 24 January, the out-of-town Wise not coming on to the scene till March. One begins to get the impression that Mrs Cook was a good woman of business, or had good advisers.

She was not affected financially by Nathaniel's death, in the week that the returning ships anchored in the Thames, the beneficiaries thereby being James and Hugh. But the ships' return brought King and Bayly before the Board of Longitude to report on their activities; and as the presence of Cook and King jointly in the *Resolution* had saved the Board the salary of an astronomer, it was resolved to pay Mrs Cook, as well as King, a gratuity of £500—for 'the use of herself and children in such way as she shall judge most proper.' This was settled between November 1780 and April 1781.[1] In the following June Elizabeth was addressing Lord Sandwich most respectfully, 'upon the presumption that the History of the Voyage in which my dear Husband lost his Life will soon be laide before the Public', through which his Lordship might be able to confer some benefit upon herself and her family. Sandwich was not loath to ensure this. The matter was not so advanced, however. It was not till June of 1784, two years after the fall of Sandwich from office, that the *Voyage to the Pacific Ocean . . . for Making Discoveries in the Northern Hemisphere* appeared, in three volumes quarto. The first two of these were edited by Douglas from Cook's journal, with considerable interpolations from Anderson's; the third was written by King. The delay in publication, so much deplored by an avid public, was occasioned much by the complications of the unusually large number of engraved pictures and charts. There was no need, one may think, for the tremendous irony of bringing in for a while as adviser on the latter, and attempted meddler in them, of Alexander Dalrymple.[2] It was not

[1] Board of Longitude Minutes, VI, 4 November 1780, 3 March 1781, Royal Observatory, Herstmonceux; *Journals* III, 1561–2, 1563.
[2] According to Banks, a committee sat on the drawings and the charts, and selected those for reproduction, Banks and Webber were to supervise the engraving of the drawings, Dalrymple ('at Lord Sandwich's desire') that of the charts and the coastal views—except

till July 1785, when Howe had succeeded Keppel after Sandwich as First Lord, that the division of profits was determined. Half was to go to Cook's family, the interest on it to Mrs Cook for her life, the principal thereafter in equal sums to the surviving children. A quarter was for the heirs of King, who had died in the preceding October. One eighth was to go to Clerke's legal representatives. The remaining eighth, after the deduction of one hundred guineas for Anderson's executors to dispose of, was for a disgruntled Bligh, in recognition of his work as surveyor and cartographer.[1] The first edition of the book was sold out in three days, at four and a half guineas, and eager purchasers offered ten guineas for a copy. Second and third editions appeared in 1785. The Cook share certainly amounted to over £2000. But oh! lamented Nicol the publisher at a later date, that the generosity of the Admiralty and the liberal notions of Sir Joseph Banks had not fixed the price at 'little more than prime cost': a fair price would have brought in £12,000.[2]

Elizabeth Cook continued to live in her house in Assembly Row for some years more, with her sons James, when he was at home, and Hugh. It is possible that as the widow of a post-captain and author and famous man, contemplating—possibly—his posthumously granted coat of arms, she maintained a personal state that was a little too much for some of her neighbours to bear; for in July 1788 a correspondent in America was being informed, 'Mrs Cook has left Mile End, gon to Live in Surry but where Cannot Tell nor neither Do Mutch Care.'[3] She had taken a house in High Street, Clapham, which remained hers through forty-seven years. It is possible also that there is a little trace of envy as well as of moral disapprobation in another letter to the same correspondent, from a different writer in 1792; 'can say but little for Mrs Cook who I think might have found time to have sent you a few lines tho she lives in high Life at Clapham & keeps a Footman—her eldest son is a Lietenant has a Horse and lives in stile; the youngest is design'd for a Clergyman, he is a fine tall

---

the general chart by Henry Roberts, 'which was not then constructed'. He adds, 'the Charts & views which were under Mr Dalrymples direction were elegantly engraved at Reasonable prices, but the general chart which was under the sole direction of the admiralty cost a large Sum of money.'—Undated memorandum, Banks Papers, Sutro Library, San Francisco.

[1] ibid., and Memorandum by Banks confined to the division of the profits, dated Thursday, 28 July 1785. Grey MSS 59 Auckland Public Library.

[2] George Nicol to Banks, 14 January 1801. Grey MSS 71, Auckland Public Library.

[3] Sade and Mary Blade, Mile End, to Mrs Frances McAllister, Philadelphia, 6 July 1788; National Library of Australia, Canberra, NK 9528. Mrs McAllister, born Frances Wardale, was the cousin of Cook's who had lived with Mrs Cook at the time of the first voyage.

youth—'.[1] If the poor lady did in fact nourish any delusion of grandeur it was before long unhappily dispelled. In 1784 she had received from the Royal Society a gold exemplar of the medal it had struck in Cook's honour, at the hands of Banks, now its president; and, in assuring him of her gratitude, had written, 'My greatest pleasure now remaining is in my sons, who, I hope, will ever strive to copy after so good an example, and, animated by the honours bestowed on their Father's memory, be ambitious of attaining by their own merits your notice and approbation.'[2] Fate preferred its own twist. The fine tall youth designed for a clergyman (it was usually clergymen's sons who became post-captains, not the reverse) was in 1793 entered at Christ's College, Cambridge, and there, having caught some violent fever, he died on 21 December of that year, aged seventeen. In that year, too, the thirty-year-old James was promoted commander. While his mother was still struggling under the death of her youngest son, this, her eldest, perished. He was at Poole, on 25 January 1794, when he received orders to join his vessel, the *Spitfire* sloop of war, at Portsmouth, without delay, and in spite of weather working up to a hard blow, embarked in an open boat. His body was found on the shore of the Isle of Wight, with a head wound how inflicted it was impossible to say, with pockets empty of money or valuables, and the damaged boat not far away. Of the boat's crew no trace was ever found. At that the mother collapsed utterly.[3] She did not recover for many months.

Yet she must have had enormous physical strength; she had forty-one years more to live. She lived many of them with her cousin Isaac Smith, who on his promotion to superannuated rear-admiral retired to Clapham. Between him and his brother Charles of Merton Abbey close by, and herself, there was great mutual affection; and when Charles died in 1827 and left his Merton Abbey property to Isaac, she went there with him till his death in 1831. Then she returned to her house at Clapham. In her old age handsome, with good bones and a great deal of dignity, rather than warmly beautiful, her white hair rolled back in an eighteenth century fashion, her face a rather squarish oval, nose aquiline, mouth good but rather too

[1] Elizabeth Honeychurch, Mile End, to Mrs McAllister, 29 March 1792, National Library of Australia, Canberra, NK 9528.
[2] Mrs Cook to Banks, 16 August 1784; *Notes and Queries*, 8th series, iv (1893), 165.
[3] E. Honeychurch wrote to Mrs McAllister, 12 September 1794, about her, that the news of the drowning 'quite overcame her, and she has not been able to come down stairs, or eat a bit of bread since, within these few weeks she has eat a small bit of Veal, or Lamb, or a little Fish, since which she has thought herself rather better tho' she has two fits every day Night and Morning and they hold her an hour, and I am afraid they will never leave her, it is a long time to be in such a state. . . .'—National Library of Australia, Canberra, NK 9528.

thin, strong jaw—erect, dressed in black satin, her head surmounted by a large cap with goffered edge, tied over a sort of ruff, she must have conferred distinction upon the street. If one is inclined to see in her somewhat of the intimidating, one may remember the ring she wore with her husband's hair in it, the four private days of mourning and fasting that she kept, the anniversaries of those on which she was bereaved of her husband and three sons; the nights of wind through which she lay awake like any fisherman's wife, thinking of men at sea.[1] She was not inhospitable. Young relatives and friends would visit the old people to hear stories of the great voyages—to hear above all, it seems, how when landing at Botany Bay the captain had said, 'Isaac, you shall go first'—or to inspect the relics and curiosities and maps with which the High Street house was crammed; or listen with a correct attention to the reproof which she addressed to them or an ill-behaved world, 'Mr Cook would never have done so.' To more mature persons who sought for information she was quite incommunicative. For her, obviously, private life was private. She did not in 1830 have in her possession, she bade Admiral Smith say, any letter or even a paper of any sort of her husband's writing.[2] This may not have been absolutely true; for as late as 1852 her executor, and residuary legatee, John Leach Bennett, the husband of one of the Admiral's nieces and a man of whom she was extremely fond, could find a portion of a journal to send to a distant connection; but, he wrote, 'very few memorials of Capt Cook came into my hands as executor of his widow. In fact for a few years before her death Mrs Cook had employed herself in destroying letters and papers and in giving away, or settling to whom they should be given after her death, articles of more value.'[3] We may regret, though respect, her destructive passion. Certainly, when her time came, she had property enough to give away, though no descendants to give it to: money and stocks, furniture and household goods, from which Flecks and Smiths, friends and neighbours, servants, charities, and the British Museum all profited.[4] Her time came when she had survived

---

[1] The preceding paragraph is a good deal founded on the childhood reminiscences of Canon Frederick Bennett, son of John Leach Bennett, Mrs Cook's executor, supplied to Sir Walter Besant for his *Captain Cook* (1890), 190; and of Miss Eliza Elliotson, of Clapham, as recorded by Louisa Jane Mackrell, great-niece of Isaac Smith.

[2] Smith to E. H. Locker, 8 October 1830; Mitchell Library (Safe 1/83).

[3] J. L. Bennett to John McAllister Jr., 7 April 1852; National Library of Australia, Canberra, NK 9528.

[4] Her will is preserved in P.R.O., Probate 11/1847 (346). Cook's Copley medal and Mrs Cook's Royal Society gold medal went to the British Museum. There was evidently some discontent. William Slaughter of South Shields, a Fleck connection, writes to McAllister, 30 November 1854, 'Mrs Cook died worth between £50,000 and £60,000 of which, not more than £3,000 came to all the Family of Marg^t Fleck, the only surviving

her husband for fifty-sx years, on 13 May 1835, seventy-two years since she walked across the fields with him to Barking church; she was ninety-three. She was buried in the grave where her son James had joined her son Hugh beneath the middle aisle of the church of St Andrew the Great at Cambridge: on the north wall of the sanctuary of that church is a stone that commemorates at length James Cook the navigator, Elizabeth his wife, and all their children.

There is one remark by Mrs Cook recorded which has a domestic interest. Among her possessions was a painting by Webber of Cook which she disliked because it made him look severe, and she was 'hurt' by the idea that he was severe.[1] If this portrait was the one that now hangs in the National Art Gallery of New Zealand, as it appears to have been, she was right in finding it uningratiating. Her judgment of her husband, of course, was not altogether correct, but then she had never been to sea with him. It does imply that when at home he was an agreeable person, and there is no evidence to imply anything else. If 'the despot', as he was on shipboard, we may guess that he was a benevolent despot. Clearly he took thought for his sons' future. How far he had real talents for domesticity we do not know, in spite of more than one conventional tribute; what precisely one of his panegyrists meant by 'the benevolent and amiable affections of the heart' we do not know. We are too much thrown back upon the panegyrists, and it is too easy to be one.

The Royal Society's medal, following hard on the *Voyage*, the armorial bearings of a year later, were themselves panegyrics. The medal, proposed by Banks, the work of Lewis Pingo, the engraver to the Royal Mint, was struck at the mint in gold, silver and bronze for subscribers, and for presentation gratis to a few favoured persons. It is not a remarkably distinguished medal, Pingo being no great artist though technically proficient, but its inscriptions are not infelicitous: *Jac. Cook Oceani Investigator Acerrimus*, Horace's tag

---

relative of the Capt; how it is I know not; but I am inclined to think there has been a Screw loose somewhere.'—NLA, Canberra, NK 9528. Certainly the will was sworn for probate at under £60,000. On the other hand, Mrs Fleck had not done badly out of Mrs Cook in earlier years.

[1] Smith to E. H. Locker, 8 October 1830; Mitchell Library (Safe 1/83). Locker himself writes, on the Dance portrait, 'His widow, who preserves all her faculties on the verge of ninety, has more than once expressed to the author of this memoir, her regret that a portrait in all other respects so perfect, should convey this erroneous expression to the eye of a stranger. For she, with the tenderness peculiar to her sex, regards him still with the lively recollection of a husband uniformly kind and affectionate, and of a father dearly loving his children.'—*Gallery of Greenwich Hospital*, part I (1831), 16. There must, it seems have been some confusion between the two pictures. It is hard to see severity in Dance, not hard in Webber.

Nil Intentatum Nostri Liquere. Cook had indeed been a most zealous explorer of the ocean; there was little hyperbole in the declaration that he and his men—'our' men, for were they not Britons?—had left nothing unattempted; there was some pride that he was of the fellowship, *socio suo*. The obverse was adapted to decorate the title-page of the second edition of the *Voyage*. The coat of arms was granted to the family in September 1785. It is a curious exercise, not so much in mediaevalism as in a sort of late eighteenth century romantic realism. The shield azure bears between its two golden 'polar stars' no heraldic symbol but a map of the Pacific hemisphere, with every tenth degree of latitude marked and every fifteenth of longitude; superimposed are Cook's tracks in red, ending precisely at Hawaii. 'And for a crest, on a wreath of the colours, is an arm imbowed, vested in the uniform of a captain of the Royal Navy. In the hand is the Union Jack on a staff proper. The arm is encircled by a wreath of palm and laurel.' Two mottos, an unusual distinction, accompany these bearings: above the crest the words *Circa orbem*, below the shield another adaptation from the Royal Society, the biographical statement *Nil intentatum reliquit*. Mrs Cook did not keep a carriage, and what she did with this fantasy is not recorded. It is curious that no addition to the naval monuments in St Paul's Cathedral seems to have been contemplated. The sculptors were ready.

It is easier to write, and one may note that the greatest panegyrists have been sailors or those who sailed with him—King, Samwell, Trevenen—or his contempories in that full age of sail, or later biographers who have known like conditions; or men who gave his work a specialised attention, like Sir John Pringle. We may not wish to accept as final truth every word of the testimony borne by Admiral John Forbes, 'one . . . not more distinguished by the elevation of rank, than by the dignity of private virtues', which Douglas appended to his introduction to the voyage as a 'monumental inscription'; and, long as it was as an inscription, Palliser had it carved on the four-sided monument he erected in the grounds of his estate at Chalfont in Buckinghamshire, a long way from the sea; but, for all its stately progression, it indicates the feelings entertained by seamen and men of humanity. 'To the memory of Captain James Cook, The ablest and most renowned Navigator this or any country hath produced', going on to a long list of the virtues the admiral was so well qualified to recognise. 'Traveller! contemplate, admire, revere and emulate this great master in his profession; whose skill and labours have enlarged natural philosophy; have extended nautical science; and have disclosed the long concealed and admirable

44. Captain Cook, by John Webber, 1776

arrangements of the Almighty in the formation of this globe, and, at the same time, the arrogance of mortals, in presuming to account, by their speculations, for the laws by which he was pleased to create it.' We may ignore this blow at the geographers; and if we cannot emulate, contemplate—or at least examine, as best we can, the qualities of 'this extraordinary man'.[1]

Physically, as he grew older, nothing occurred to mar the impression he would have made in his thirties, that of a tall, large-boned, powerful man, with strongly marked features. It was a Yorkshire type. No doubt the mature lines were deeper, the nose and mouth still stronger, for they would not have been softened by easy living. There was the scar on the hand. He was good-looking, obviously, in a plain sort of way. We have one contradiction in description: Samwell says his head was small, with small eyes, but Dance's portrait, declared by Samwell himself to be 'a most excellent likeness', gives us a head to match the body, and large eyes that match the large nose and large forehead, the prominent eyebrows. Webber also gives us a large head, and a heavy, dull one. The engraving from Hodges prefixed to the 1777 volumes provide an impression of a smaller head, and certainly a lively countenance—and large eyes; but neither Webber nor Hodges was a very competent painter of portraits. The eyes were brown, 'quick and piercing', which we may well believe; hair brown, tied behind, though Hodges has a crop of springy curls, Dance and Webber what appears to be a dark grey wig. It was an expressive face, and in the 'most excellent likeness' expresses a disposition friendly and humane. What his voice, that sometimes valuable index to character, was like, no one tells us. Presumably it could be loud, to compete with storms and human misdemeanours. One would infer a provincial accent, from one whose access to the polite world was limited and showed no sign of wishing to enlarge it, some provincial turns of speech, some provincial pronunciations which would stand behind the spellings in his journals. Strong and perspicacious understanding says King; in whatever related to the services on which he was employed, of quick and sure judgment. Of an agreeable lively conversation, says Samwell, sensible and intelligent, rather bashful—by which we are to understand the earlier implication of that otherwise surprising word, that of a sensitive modesty. A sensitive modesty does not conflict with the confidence of assimilated experience, or with some deep convictions on professional matters; nor is it incompatible with losing one's temper.

[1] *Voyage to the Pacific Ocean*, I, lxxxv, lxxxvii–lxxxix.

We still lack the quantity of intimate description we should like, the analysis of character that with all men, great or little, we feel would somehow make all things plain. It is possible not to regret this: he was a man of action, and the tendency is to regard a man of action as adequately described by his acts, his biography a succession of things done. It is not quite so, any more than it would be a sufficient paradox to say that the acts of a man of action are the least important thing about him. But acts are public things, and we want to enter the mind. We hanker after someone who might be supposed to have hold of a thread. What would we not give for a conversation with Clerke, that companionable man, the knowledgeable, the amused, the unabashed? We are not, however, devoid of all the aid we need: by assiduous reading between the lines of all those journals, we may even interrogate Cook himself, and get some honest answers. Indeed we have already done so.

He was not (to proceed in negatives) romantic, dramatic—though his death was one of the great dramatic points in Pacific history—imaginative in any cloudy way; he was not semi-mystical, striving as some rarefied explorers have done after the meaning of existence or some absolute human affirmation; he was not searching for or fleeing from himself. He had, so far as one can see, no religion. His was not the poetic mind, or the profoundly scientific mind. He was the genius of the matter of fact. He was profoundly competent in his calling as seaman. He was completely professional in his trade as explorer. He had, in large part, the sceptical mind: he did not like taking on trust. He was therefore the great dispeller of illusion. He did have imagination, but it was a controlled imagination that could think out a great voyage in terms of what was possible for his own competence. He could think, he could plan, he could reason; he liked to be able to plan clearly for a specific object. But he liked to be elastic: there was always in his mind, as he planned, the possibility of something more, the parenthesis or addendum; there was also the sense of proportion that made him, more than once, refuse to waste time looking for what he was not sure to find. He had New Holland up his sleeve; he would not gratify Dalrymple by producing an island that would fit something on the map devised, for all he knew, by Dalrymple. So he would carry out his mass of instructions with a devoted literalness—perhaps because, as has been suggested before, that sort of honest obedience had been bred into him or came natural to him, perhaps because of an equally natural passion for completeness. That called at times for a great deal of patience, a great deal of persistence, some falling back on nervous reserves. Having done it, he could draw breath—less metaphorically, find an anchorage, fresh water and scurvy grass, for the recruitment of his men—and consider the work of supererogation. As he said to young Latouche–Tréville, a man who merely stuck to his orders would never make a great figure in discovery. The question strikes us, did he want to make a great figure? Its answer is almost inevitably No. Obviously he had ambitions: in the southern hemisphere he wanted not merely to reach a higher latitude than any man before him, but to go as far as a man could go: but that is a different thing from making a great figure. He was willing to presume, as his first voyage was drawing to a close, that it was as complete as any before made to the South Seas on the same account. After his second voyage, he could well have recurred to the phrase he had then rejected, 'as compleat if not more so'. It did not occur to him. It did not seem to occur to him that he was a great figure. He was more concerned in pointing out that if his latest discovery, Sandwich Land, was indeed part of the southern continent, the southern continent would not be of much use to anybody. At this point one may remind oneself that it was the controlled imagination, superimposed on the powerful matter-of-factness, that put in the place of dispelled illusion so many positive discoveries, and laid the foundations of Pacific geography as a science, of Pacific anthropology, of antarctic hydrography. If one does not make even greater claims, and bring in the sciences of natural history, it is because one is speaking of Cook, and not of his voyages. As a commander of ships he very efficiently brought the scientists to their material, when that chimed with his own larger purposes; he had an observant eye, he could ask relevant questions, he could learn; but without Banks and Solander, Anderson, the Forsters, the artists, the voyages would not, in natural science, have been great.

They were all great, all sailors who have studied them are agreed, as exhibitions of seamanship, in an age when good seamen were common. It is practical seamanship, rather than scientific navigation, that one is here concerned with. Among men with Pacific service Wallis, Carteret, Furneaux, Clerke, Bligh were good seamen; any master in the navy had to be a good seaman; it was part of Cook's job to train young officers into good seamen, and when John Elliott went for his lieutenant's examination it was enough for his examiners to know that he had been with Cook. But there were good seamen who would not feel happy under certain conditions: the captain of an East Indiaman, the master of a line-of-battle ship who would face an Atlantic storm with equanimity, might be little at ease in the midst of the Tuamotu archipelago. It was not merely Cook's familiarity

that New Zealand had been wrongly placed on the chart by a few minutes? 'The situation of few parts of the world are better determined than these islands are. . . .' Well: it remained true. It was the navigator and stubborn seaman, as well as the surveyor, who had made that possible. Was it the navigator, or the seaman, or the original root of stubbornness in the man, that made him fight for so long the contrary winds eastward of New Zealand on the third voyage, the winds that made him lose his passage?

Navigation, we learn, may be a matter not quite easy to define. King, having sketched the contributions of his hero to geography, proceeds: 'As a navigator, his services were not perhaps less splendid; certainly not less important and meritorious. The method which he discovered, and so successfully pursued, of preserving the health of seamen, forms a new era in navigation, and will transmit his name to future ages, amongst the friends and benefactors of mankind.'[1] With that judgment the Royal Society was fully in accord. This respectable Body, said Sir John Pringle in his presidential discourse of 1776, delivering the Copley medal, 'never more cordially nor more meritoriously bestowed that faithful symbol of their esteem and affection. For if Rome decreed the *Civic Crown* to him who saved the life of a single citizen, what wreaths are due to that Man, who, having himself saved many, perpetuates in your Transactions the means by which Britain may now, on the most distant voyages, preserve numbers of her intrepid sons, her *Mariners*; who, braving every danger, have so liberally contributed to the fame, to the opulence, and to the maritime empire, of their Country!' It may be doubtful if Cook was interested, as a professional man, in any of those things. The preservation of the health of seamen was for him an aspect at once of humanity and efficiency—and hence of navigation; for, with all the instruments in the world, it is difficult for a commander to navigate if he is surrounded with men dying of scurvy. Of course any good sea-captain was a humanitarian. The interesting thing about Cook is that without being a scientist any more than he was a sentimentalist, without being original, he was able to get the remarkable results he did get; or perhaps he was original in this, that having proved a point pragmatically, he made it part of a system, which he maintained as persistently as he maintained his astronomical observations. He found his men a little more intractable than the planets and the stars, but they had to accept the system. How much he had studied the problem of health at sea in the current books it is impossible to say. If he had read Lind's *Treatise of the Scurvy*, of which

[1] *Voyage to the Pacific Ocean*, III, 51.

the second edition published in 1762 would have been close enough to his hand, he would have embraced every opportunity to accumulate lemons. He never mentions lemons, or Lind; and among the antiscorbutic substances experimentally placed in his ships by the Admiralty, it is no wonder he thought meanly of the rob of lemons and oranges, from which the unsuspected vitamins had been assiduously boiled out; he preferred even the wort, 'the inspissated juice of malt', which certainly was no cure. 'Sour Krout' had a value. Changes could be tried in the proportions of raisins and sugar fed to the men. Portable soup could be used to make some mess attractive. There was little that could be done about salt beef and salt pork. There were navy surgeons and captains who saw clearly enough the defects of the conventional diet, the virtue of fresh food. There were Admiralty instructions enough on cleanliness and ventilation of ships, if they had been taken seriously. What Cook did was to take such instructions seriously, and add orders of his own. What other captain inspected his men's hands, and fined in grog the owners of dirty ones? His crew, so far as he could ensure it, was to be clean and dry, in a clean ship, and they were not to eat and sleep in a noisome den. But the sovereign thing was the unremitting insistence on fresh food at every conceivable opportunity, fish, flesh and fowl—walrus, penguins—'scurvy grass' and every other variety of wild vegetables, the fruits and roots of the islands, the berries of Tierra del Fuego and the Arctic, a new batch of spruce beer—anything, as long as it was fresh.[1] Cook could carry out no chemical analysis, but his experience was enough. Where he had no experience, he was willing enough to experiment on himself, and to use himself as an example, with the result that we know a good deal about his tastes and tolerances in eating. 'His stomach bore, without difficulty, the coarsest and most ungrateful food. Indeed, temperance for him was scarcely a virtue; so great was the indifference with which he submitted to every kind

---

[1] Cook summarised his practice clearly enough in his letter to the Admiralty secretary at the end of July 1775, printed in *Journals* II, 954–5, of which his Royal Society paper was not much more than a reduplication. After giving his opinion of a number of articles of diet, both normal and experimental, he proceeds: 'But ye Introduction of ye most Salutary Provisions or Medecines will sometimes lose their Effects unless supported by some well regulated rules. I hope it will not be taken amiss my Mentioning these which I caused to be observed during ye Whole Voyage, as they are founded on many Years experience & some information I had from Sr Hugh Pallisser, Capt: Campbell, Captain Wallis & other experienced Officers & which certainly contributed not a little to that good State of health we, I may say, constantly enjoyed.' He details his principles of enforced cleanliness, dryness of clothes and bedding, and so on, and then reverts to diet: 'We came to few places w[h]ere either ye art of Man or Nature had not provided some sort of refreshments or other, either in ye Animal or Vegitable way, & it was first care to procure them by every Means in my power & Oblig'd ye people to make use of them, both by example & authority.'—And he points the contrast with the effects of ignorance in the *Adventure* on the passage from New Zealand to Tahiti, June–August 1773.

of self-denial.'[1] Thus King; and Samwell protested. 'He had no repugnance to good living; he always kept a good table, though he could bear the reverse without murmuring.'[2] Surely, thought Trevenen, discussing walrus as a food, the taste of his captain was 'the coarsest that ever mortal was endued with.'[3] Having remarked on a number of Cook's judgments of food, and his reasons for giving them, we must think that Samwell was probably right. The captain could not say that penguins were good eating: 'I have indeed made several good meals of them but it was for want of better victuals.'[4] A fresh penguin was at any rate better than salt beef or salt pork after three years in the harness-cask; and certainly more wholesome. A sea-lion cub was very palatable, though not a sea-lion; so was a young shag, or the haunch of a Tahitian dog baked in the island way.

As a disciplinarian and a psychologist, he was generally successful in getting the unorthodox stuff into his men. From what he says himself, and from independent testimony, we can see that in the end he even got these hard-bitten and restive conservatives on his side. Thomas Perry the poet will be remembered.

> Thanks be to the Captain he has proved so good
> Amongst all the Islands to give us fresh food.

A more valuable, because more circumstantial witness is Alexander Home, the admirer of his captain's eloquence; more valuable, too, as from the lower deck, than his superior officers. He describes the habit that had grown up among the men, when on shore, of eating 'almost Every Herb plant Root and kinds of Fruit they Could Possibly Light upon', without enquiry or hesitation:

it is highly probable this disposition has been the principle Means of preserving Our Healths for such a Number of Years Almost Constantly on the water. Captain Cook raised this spirit Amoungst us by his Example for scarc[e]ly any thing Came wrong to him that was Green and he was as Carefull in providing Vegitables for the Messess of the Crews as for his own Table and I do Belive that in this Means Consisted his graund Art of preserving his people in Health During so Many of the Longest and Hardest voyages that was Ever Made.

Green stuff boiled in quantity with pease soup or wheat sometimes offended the taste of seamen.

---

[1] *Voyage to the Pacific Ocean*, III, 48.
[2] *A Narrative . . . To which are added some Particulars concerning his Life and Character. . . .*
[3] *Journals* III, 419, n. 3.
[4] *Journals* II, 613.

But as there was Nothing Else to be got they were Obledged to Eat them and it was No Uncommon thing when Swallowing Over these Mess[es] to Curse him heartyly and wish for gods Sake that he Might be Obledged to Eat such Damned Stuff Mixed with his Broth as Long as he lived. Yet for all that there were None so Ignorant as Not to know how Right a thing it was.

We have, too, the half-days in port for recreation: 'He would Frequently Order them on shore in partys to walk about the Country and smell the Fresh Earth and Herbage'—a reminiscence, as it were, of eighteenth century minor poetry, or some benevolent schoolmaster; and as he himself was constantly seen gathering wild stuff, 'in time the Men adopted the same Humour and Disposition as by Infectsin and perhaps in Many it Might be with a Veiw of making their Court to him, for they knew it was A great Recommendation to be seen Coming on board from A pleasure Jaunt with A Handkerchif full of greens.'[1]

Beside this a great deal of the discussion on the prevention and cure of scurvy—and most other ills of the sea—becomes irrelevant. It also explains why Cook, in spite of the wreaths that Sir John Pringle would have conferred upon him, had less to contribute to the future than one might have thought. Is there a paradox? Given a voyage under somewhat like conditions, and a commander somewhat like him a similar result might be expected. For ordinary voyages and ordinary persons there was needed something easier in the application. The method adopted by Cook reveals a great deal of Cook, the humanitarian persistent and thoroughly efficient; the same Cook that exhorts sea-officers not to be alarmed at the idea of making mathematical calculations from astronomical observations, who is surprised at the notion of an officer's not demanding the best possible sextant whatever the price; who blistered the hands of his young gentlemen pulling a boat round Nootka Sound in teaching them to be sailors, and their minds for sundry derogations from perfection on their part.

Another aspect of the humane captain is a fundamental sympathy for his men, rather wider than the few specific affections or likings that we can trace, not entirely based on the determination to extract the maximum of efficiency. After all, he had been an apprentice of the benevolent John Walker. Desertion was not a thing he could tolerate, but he could very well understand, even sympathise with, the deserter. He saw no sense in working men to exhaustion. He

1 *Journals* III, 1456.

believed in the system of putting a ship's company into three watches instead of two. He had his men under control not only for the ordinary reasons, but because his strict rules of hygiene required it. Captains who visited Cook, not knowing his habits, might be quite astonished to find an air of religious observance, a clean and tidy ship, a clean crew: on board Cook's ships, they said, it was always Sunday. Officers who came under his command from other vessels, on the other hand, were inclined to find his discipline too loose. They learnt better soon enough. There was no need for a man who put first things first to set up as a martinet. Woe indeed for the person who sinned on first things. Yet it was Cook who gave up the great cabin to the sail-maker for his work when the conditions on deck were so desperately discouraging; it was he who insisted, when there was any shortage of food, on a strictly even distribution, from captain to ship's boy. He could unbend to the midshipmen on a hard day's rowing, and throw them as a bonus the ducks that had been shot. If they called him a despot, they also called him Toote. He allowed some customs to be kept up, one presumes as things traditionally held valuable by seamen, on which there was in his day another school of thought. The equator-crossing ceremony was by no means a gentle one, and Furneaux would have none of it. The drunken fighting of Christmas Day was permissible only after the ship's safety had been provided for. We must see it as an emotional outburst that was part of the pattern of a brutal century. Considering it thus, we may be able to tolerate more easily the floggings that Cook inflicted, which did not, it appears, trouble either the conscience of his officers of the feelings of his men. He could not be said to have flogged his way round the world, but he was a naval officer, he needed some means of punishment, and he used the standard navy means. He certainly did not flog for the pleasure it gave him. It was thought by George Forster, a landsman and a sensitive youth, that he punished rarely and unwillingly.[1] If, reading in the logs and journals of half-a-dozen lashes, a dozen lashes, once or twice two dozen lashes, our sensations are not agreeable, we may study the records of the fleet on the American station in which Cook served, and decide that his floggings do not modify his essential humanity.

In his relations with the 'Indians' of the Pacific was another aspect of his humanity, as well as examples of its breakdown. He took seriously Lord Morton's 'Hints', as we have seen. He was aware that most humane, and inexperienced, men would censure his conduct in

---

[1] George Forster gives his impressions in an essay entitled 'Cook der Entdecker' ('Cook the Discoverer') of 1787, printed in Vol. I of his *Kleine Schriften* (Leipzig, 1789 . . .).

Poverty Bay, and he would not attempt to justify it. He was much concerned about his first approach to islanders, or other people he did not know, and, as we have seen, developed a technique that put his life much more than theirs at immediate risk. Obviously the main difficulty on either side was the difficulty of communication. It is easy enough for us to see that, if misunderstandings were not to occur, then what had to be communicated, back and forth, was an instant knowledge of two different ways of life—cultures, as the anthropologist would say, in his effort to subsume thoughts on property and the gods and the observances of polite society. Discoverers tended to be as naïve as the people they discovered. Good intentions were inadequate if they could not be understood. The enlargement of Geography and Navigation was all very well, but Polynesians and Melanesians were not interested in that; they were not anxious to be discovered; intruders they naturally regarded as enemies. Savage Island was not more savage than other islands: the Niueans merely acted with greater decision than their fellows. Cook was not prepared to force his presence when it was obviously not desired. A larger population with fewer fears and wider contacts—as Tonga had contacts with Fiji—might be prepared to wait longer; there might be some treaty-making ceremony Cook went through, without in the least understanding the conditions of peace to which he was agreeing; there was certainly a whole code of behaviour between hosts and guests that he was assumed to accept. He records in his journal from time to time his baffled sense of this sort of thing. Easy as it was for him to make errors, to disregard propriety—and easier for his men, who did not try to avoid them—it was as easy for the islanders, though theirs tended to concentrate in the cardinal one of 'theft'. Cook could see as clearly as we can that they did not regard visitors' property in the European or British or naval way; but what was he to do? He merely wanted to indulge in honest trade for provisions, fresh water and firewood, and observe for a time the life of the land. It is possible that some of the chiefs and priests tried as hard as he did to bring a sympathetic imagination to bear on the problems—that they too were tolerant and humane. He could see himself as they, quite simply, saw him. We go back to the second voyage. One cannot blame the Tanese for hostile behaviour, he says, when one considers their position:

its impossible for them to know our real design, we enter their Ports without their daring to make opposition, we attempt to land in a peaceable manner, if this succeeds its well, if not we land nevertheless and mentain the footing we thus got by the Superiority of our fire arms, in what other light can they than at first look upon us but as invaders of their Country. . . .[1]

He thought the best way to deal with certain situations was to make hostages of chiefs. He did not consider that this might be an outrageous insult, even an act of impiety—was it not better than a punitive expedition and the shedding of blood?—but he could understand the island attitude, the tears and outcry, when his friend Ori, the 'Brave old Chief' of Huahine, made himself a voluntary hostage.

It may be asked what he had to fear, to which I must answer nothing, for it never was my intention to hurt a hair of his head or to detain him one single moment longer than he desired, but how was he or the people to know this, they were not ignorant that if he was once in my power, the whole force of the isle could not take him from me, and that let my demands for his ransom been [sic] ever so high they must have comply'd with it; thus far their fears both for his and their own safety were justly founded.[2]

Here speaks the humanely imaginative man. That particular episode was happy because of the man that Ori was. There were other chiefs made prisoner under easy conditions who were less gratified. We may wish that Cook had not adopted a different procedure at Moorea, on the third voyage. We may wish that, before he did adopt that procedure at Kealakekua Bay, he had allowed his imagination to play at length all round the circumstances.

We have seen him punish islanders severely for their cardinal offence, until his own men were shocked. We know that he was anxious that the islanders should see justice done on his own men who had committed offences against them. He does not talk, as some people do, of native 'insolence', and the weight of his 'resentment'. He can feel rage at the truculent stupidity of seamen and marines. He can feel regret. For nothing does he feel more regret—do he and his responsible officers feel more a sense of guilt as the emissaries of western civilisation—than over the spread of the venereal disease that the ships inevitably brought to the Polynesians, the 'incurable disorder which will for ever embitter their quiet & happy lives, & make them curse the hour they ever saw us.'[3] But the eloquence

[1] Cook's 'than' = 'then'; *Journals* II, 493. For the context see p. 407 above.
[2] *Journals* II, 220, n. 1.
[3] These are the words of King, *Journals* III, 174, n. 3. He begins his sentence by saying, 'We see many things worthy of imitation, few of blame; wou'd to God they cou'd say the same of us, but we have left them an incurable disorder', etc.

and indignation of those conscience-driven men were misplaced. The nature of men and women, accident as well as intention, outflanked all the stringent orders that Cook attempted to impose. He was beaten from the moment he dropped anchor. He had an ally over most of the Pacific, however, in the endemic island disease yaws, so often taken for syphilis, with which syphilis could not co-exist. The variety of the disease first transmitted to the islands was gonorrhea, and if the precautions taken by the surgeons are to be trusted, it must have been transmitted by carriers, of whose role surgeons were ignorant. Cook had experience enough to distrust 'the faculty'. The micro-organisms spread, sailors in their turn were infected or re-infected, and passed the disease on. Cook was depressed. As fortune would have it, however, far from embittering quiet and happy lives for ever, from one generation to another, gonorrhea in the islands had a relatively short life: Cook's successors in Tonga found hardly a trace of it. Quite otherwise was it with syphilis in Hawaii, untouched by yaws; there was nothing to hold it back, or its partner; the spirochaetes and gonococci swarmed ashore in the ships' boats. There could be no possible doubt what ships the boats belonged to. There was a point, then, where the humanity of the most humane of men must prove of no avail.

We are confronted by the fact that Cook, with all his humanity, coolness, patience, temperance of expression in the written word, was a passionate man. He could be hot, as we have seen, about sloppy work, false pretences, plain stupidity; he could be impatient when he was prevented from pushing on his work; he could be most intemperate, obviously, in his spoken words. Our witnesses here are of one accord: in temper subject to hastiness and passion, says King; somewhat hasty, says Samwell; cross-grained, 'sometimes . . . carried away by a hasty temper', says John Reinhold Forster, who cannot in the end but 'acknowledge him to have been one of the greatest men of his age';[1] Trevenen gives us a quite illuminating footnote to his account of the Nootka Sound incident when Cook thought he had been careless over observations, 'Of course

[1] 'If we consider his extreme abilities, both natural and acquired, the firmness and constancy of his mind, his truly paternal care for the crew entrusted to him, the amiable manner with which he knew how to gain the friendship of all the savage and uncultivated nations, and even his conduct towards his friends and acquaintance, we must acknowledge him to have been one of the greatest men of his age, and that Reason justifies the tear which Friendship pays to his memory. He was not free from faults, but these were more than counterbalanced by his superior qualities; and it is very unfortunate that on this last voyage he should have had no friend with him, who by his wisdom and prudence might have with-held and prevented him from giving vent to his passions, which in fact became so detrimental to himself, as to occasion his destruction.'—J. R. Forster, *History of the Voyages and Discoveries made in the North*, 404.

I had a *heiva* of the old boy' (and the phrase 'the old boy', is also illuminating).

Heiva the name of the dances of the Southern Islanders, which bore so great a resemblance to the violent motions and stampings on the Deck of Capt Cooke in the paroxysms of passion, into which he often threw himself upon the slightest occasion that they were universally known by the same name, & it was a common saying amongst both officers & people: 'The old boy has been tipping a *heiva* to such or such a one'.[1]

This was a sort of catharsis, no doubt; was not the effect of self-importance or vanity, was not vindictive; caused some amusement, did no one harm. The swearing that upset Sparrman as the ship came down on the reef off Tahiti was quite disinterested. Most of the evidence we have on the matter, it may be pointed out, comes from the third voyage—though that may merely be because more persons wrote about the third voyage. Isaac Smith, on the first and second voyages, never thought him severe: he was both 'loved' and 'properly feared' by the crew,[2] and the general concern over his illness was obviously not concern over the welfare of a tyrant improperly feared. We may discern a little in Cook's own pages, in some deleted passage of personal criticism; and that is also evidence that Cook knew his own failing, and preferred that others should not suffer from it. The third voyage evidence is of course linked with that of his harsh, his quite inhumane, treatment of native pilferers—outbursts of rage as uncontrollable, evidently, as the 'heivas' which his men got to know and to tolerate so well. It shows a character almost on two planes, and a hypothesis of some physical cause is hard to resist. The strains of the voyage were wearing and worrying, a continuation of the strains of two other voyages. A tired man, fundamentally, the commander must have been. Continued responsibility for his own men, continued wrestling with geographical, nautical and human emergencies might, had his physical and mental constitution been less powerful, have made him go limp. He did not do so, but the inner tensions of an able mind were set up, and exacerbated. To that sort of tiredness add the effect of the violent illness from which he had suffered on the second voyage, the 'indispositions' to which he was subject on this third voyage. We have a man tired, not physically in any observable way, but with that almost imperceptible blunting of the brain that makes him, under a light searching

---

[1] Note by Trevenen on the difficulties encountered in taking bearings for 'our Sketch of the Sound', *Journals* III, cliii, 306, n.
[2] Smith to E. H. Locker, 8 October 1830; Mitchell Library (Safe 1/83).

enough, a perceptibly different man. His apprehensions as a discoverer were not so constantly fine as they had been; his understanding of other minds was not so ready or sympathetic. He 'flared
up' like a man with a stomach ulcer. That is not to say that an ulcer
is necessarily the answer to our problem.

How is one to complete a portrait? He was not a solitary man,
but he must have had a good many solitary thoughts, like many
another commander who has had to wrestle with particular angels.
Some people—notably Forster—were struck by the small degree to
which he took his officers—or his scientific passengers—into his
confidence. He certainly did not conduct his voyages by consensus.
There was discussion enough where discussion could be of any use.
It is quite probable that, having arrived at a solution to a problem—
as, for example, by what route to return to England after having
circumnavigated New Zealand—he consulted his officers, as he
said he did, but he made known what he would call his own 'strong
inclination', at which few would have inclination to demur. After all,
it was he who had been given the instructions, and authority, and
discretion. He was quite willing to test the incidental fancies of other
men. In matters where he had no claim to exert authority, he seems
to have been a tolerant, sober, civilised man of the world. His
general knowledge was extensive and various, we are told by Samwell,
with no indication of what fields it embraced, or how he acquired it.
A great deal must have rubbed off on him from Banks and Anderson
and Wales, from acquaintances in the coffee houses, and at dinner
with the Royal Society gentlemen, where he listened as well as
talked. It does not seem to have been literary. He seems to have had
no politics. The names he gives to prominent geographical features,
names of admirals, noble lords, Lords of the Admiralty, do not
necessarily imply personal acquaintance or admiration. His conversation was agreeable and lively, but also the conversation, we are
to gather, of a modest, or 'bashful' man. We have Boswell's account
of it, its judgment and veracity. We presume that it must largely
have been concerned with facts. We can tell that in the literature of
discovery he read deeply, a professional thing. We know that he
read Hakluyt for amusement, and he must have discussed explorers of all times. Sparrman remembered 'as well, as if it had passed
yesterday, when the old Cooke blamed Magellan for his unnecessary
braving the indians, who killed him, and now this is his own case'.[1]
We know some of the technical books he read, Maskelyne's *British*

---

[1] Sparrman to George Forster, 5 September 1780; *Johann Georg Forster's Briefwechse*
(Leipzig, 1829), II, 748.

Mariner's Guide, Samuel Dunn's *Navigator's Guide to the Oriental or Indian Seas.* He gives no hint that he ever ventured on works of the imagination—glanced for example at Wales's copy of *The Seasons* in Dusky Sound—or of morals. Geography provided him with the imaginative, Navigation with morals. He was happy with the literal side of Hodges and of Webber, their judiciously chosen views, their masterly execution; they provided facts, and that was what they were employed for. Any other side he did not notice. He was happy with any music he heard Tahitian nose-flute, Tongan drums, Scottish bagpipes. He did not devote imagination, or emotion, or time to the other sex, apart from his Elizabeth, and from proposing, it is said, on Saturday nights at sea, the toast of all beautiful women. Any reputation he earned in the matter in the Pacific was, however, not so much for an habitual iron disdain as for obvious age and impotence. The passionately professional man was an idea rather beyond Polynesian conception. In other human relationships his feelings were warm: he remembered old friends—Holland, Walker, Richard Ellerton his commander in the *Friendship,* Ori of Huahine. One may be inclined to say, after gazing hard and long, and considering this way of understanding and that way, that he had a plain heroic magnitude of mind. It is a judgment. It does not make him a simple man.

There are statues and inscriptions; but Geography and Navigation are his memorials. We may find others for ourselves, if we would indulge in sentiment. There are the words of John Elliott, who sailed in the *Resolution* in 1772 at the age of fourteen. He was rather proud of the chart he made showing the ship's track, which, like all other records, was impounded at the end of the voyage. But Cook asked Elliott, now a mature youth of seventeen, to breakfast, and promised he should have the precious document back. So Elliott, writing memoirs for his descendants, can say, 'I attended to his invitation, and did recieve my Chart &c with my Name *Elliotts Chart and Ships Track,* written on it, in his own hand, and which writing I venerate to this day, and never look at Without feeling the deepest regret at the melancholy loss of so great a Man.'[1] There are the words of the New Zealand chief Te Horeta, the ancient hook-nosed warrior with much blood on his hands, who had been an excited small boy at Mercury Bay when the *Endeavour* called there in 1769. There was one supreme man in that ship, who did not talk much, but looked well into everything, and was good to small boys; and Te Horeta would repeat the Maori saying, *e kore te tino tangata e*

[1] British Museum. Add. MS 42,714, f. 48–48v.

ngaro i roto i te tokomaha, a veritable man is not hid among many.[1] Such things; Geography and Navigation; if we wish for more, an ocean is enough, where the waves fall on innumerable reefs, and a great wind blows from the south-east with the revolving world.

[1] Cf. p. 206 above.

Bibliography

A list of manuscripts, charts and miscellaneous publications, to which reference is made in the text. For fuller information on manuscripts relating to the Pacific voyages see *The Journals of Captain James Cook on his Voyages of Discovery* [with] *(Addenda and Corrigenda to Volume I* and *Volume II)*, ed. J. C. Beaglehole, *(Charts & Views* [with] *Corrigenda)*, ed. R. A. Skelton, 3 vols in 4 and portfolio, *Hakluyt Society*, Cambridge, 1955–69. Some manuscripts relevant to the voyages are printed or described in *The Endeavour Journal of Joseph Banks 1768–1771*, ed. J. C. Beaglehole, 2 vols, Sydney, 1962.

MANUSCRIPTS

ADAMS, WILLIAM. Log, H.M.S. *Northumberland*, P.R.O., Adm 51/3925.

ADMIRALTY. Correspondence, see names of correspondents; journals and logs, see names of ships, captains and masters; musters, see names of ships.

ADMIRALTY. Minutes, 5, 12 April 1768, P.R.O., Adm 3/76.

ADMIRALTY. Orders and Instructions, 19 April 1763 to Cook/Test, P.R.O., Adm 2/90; 19 April, 2, 3, 27 May 1763 to Graves, P.R.O., Adm 2/90; 2 May 1763 to Graves, National Maritime Museum, GRV/106, Section 9; 24 April 1764 to Captains of H.M. Ships *Spy, Pearl,* and *Tweed,* P.R.O., Adm 2/90; 24 April 1764 to Captain of H.M.S. *Lark,* P.R.O., Adm 2/91.

ANTELOPE, H.M.S. Muster, May 1763, P.R.O., Adm 36/4887.

BANKS, Sir JOSEPH. Reminiscences of Banks supplied to Dawson Turner, Kenneth A. Webster Collection.

BATEMAN, NATHANIEL. Log, H.M.S. *Northumberland,* P.R.O., Adm 51/3925.

BISSET, THOMAS. Log, H.M.S. *Eagle,* P.R.O., Adm 52/578.

BLIGH, WILLIAM. ALS 23 Oct. 1776 to John Bond, National Library of Australia, MS 4038 (NanKivell Collection 34). Printed in Royal Australian Historical Society, *Journal of Proceedings,* vol. 45, 1949.

CLEADER, JOHN. Log, H.M.S. *Pembroke,* P.R.O., Adm 52/978.

COLVILLE, ALEXANDER, LORD COLVILLE OF CULROSS. Letters to

715

Admiralty, 10 April 1761, 25 Oct., 30 Dec. 1762, P.R.O., Adm 1/482.

—— Journal, H.M.S. *Northumberland*, P.R.O., Adm 50/22.

COOK, CLIFFORD. Letter from Mr C. Cook of Ashby de la Zouch, Leicestershire, to Dr J. C. Beaglehole giving information on the family of Captain James Cook.

COOK, ELIZABETH. Will, P.R.O., Prerogative Court of Canterbury, Probate 11/1847(346).

COOK, JAMES. Journals and Logs, P.R.O., Adm 52 and Alexander Turnbull Library: *Eagle*, 27 June 1755–31 Dec. 1756, Alexander Turnbull Library; *Solebays*, 30 July–7 Sept. 1757, Adm 52/1033; *Pembroke*, 27 Oct. 1757–30 Sept. 1759, Adm 52/978; *Northumberland*, 30 Sept. 1759–11 Nov. 1762, Adm 52/959; *Grenville*, 14 June 1764–15 Nov. 1767, Adm 52/1263.

—— *Grenville* Letter-Book. Stray leaves survive bearing correspondence between Cook and Admiralty, Navy Board and Victualling Board, also Palliser's Instructions to Cook [1764]. There are three leaves possibly torn from the letter-book in the Dixson Library, MS Q140 (Palliser's Instructions form the first item); one leaf is inserted at the beginning of Zachary Hicks's *Endeavour* log, Alexander Turnbull Library; one leaf is in Alexander Turnbull Library, Holograph Letters and Documents of and relative to Captain James Cook.

—— Letters from: 7 March 1764 to Palliser, P.R.O., Adm 1/2300; 15 March 1764 to Graves, National Maritime Museum, GRV/106; 21 April 1764 to Admiralty, Alexander Turnbull Library, Holograph Letters and Documents of and relative to Captain James Cook; 10 Dec. 1771 to Joseph Cockfield, Mitchell Library, Papers in the Autograph of Captain James Cook, Safe 1/80, 11; 24 Feb. 1776 to John Harrison, attorney at law, National Library of Australia, MS 7.

—— Letters from Admiralty, chiefly P.R.O., Adm 2: 13, 18 April 1763, Adm 2/722; 23 April 1764, Adm 2/724 and Alexander Turnbull Library, Holograph Letters and Documents of and relative to Captain James Cook; 18 Dec. 1764, Adm 2/725 and Dixson Library, MS Q140; 5 April 1765, Adm 2/725; 15, 17 March, 27 Nov. 1766, Adm 2/726; 24 March, 12, 13 Nov. 1767, 11 April 1768, Adm 2/727.

—— Order from Admiralty, 19 April 1763, P.R.O., Adm 2/90.

—— Warrant from Navy Board to take charge of the *Grenville* 18 April 1764, Alexander Turnbull Library, Holograph Letters and Documents of and relative to Captain James Cook.

—— *Biography*:

Baptism. Copy of extract 3 Nov. 1728 from the Parish Register of the Church of St Cuthbert, Marton, Yorkshire, National Library of Australia, MS 7, Mitchell Library, Document 1409.

Marriage certificate, 21 Dec. 1762, of James Cook and Elizabeth Batts, St Margaret's Church, Barking, Essex, National Library of Australia, MS 7.

Master's certificate, Royal Navy, Trinity House, Deptford, Books, 29 June 1757.

Will, P.R.O., Prerogative Court of Canterbury, Probate 11/1

CRAIG, ROBERT. Log, H.M.S. *Solebays*, P.R.O., Adm 51/908.

DALRYMPLE, ALEXANDER. Letters: 24 Nov. 1766 to Sir Petty, 2nd Earl of Shelburne, P.R.O., Chatham Papers, 30/8, vol. 31, f.11; 7 Dec. 1767 to Dr Charles Morton, Secr the Royal Society, Miscellaneous MSS III, f.14.

DOUGLAS, CHARLES. Letters to Admiralty: [1763], 3 Ma₁ P.R.O., Adm 1/1704.

— — Log, H.M.S. *Tweed*, P.R.O., Adm 51/1016.

DOUGLAS, JAMES, 14th EARL OF MORTON. Letter 15 Augu from Admiralty, P.R.O., Adm 2/540.

DOUGLAS, JOHN. Correspondence 1776–1784, British Museum, F MS 2180.

EAGLE, H.M.S., Captain's log, Hamar, Palliser, P.R.O., Adm 5 Master's log, Bisset, P.R.O., Adm 52/578, Cook, Alexander Tι Library.

— — Muster, July 1755, P.R.O., Adm 36/5533.

GRAVES, THOMAS. Letters to Admiralty, 2 Jan., 5, 12, 15, 1 29 April, 8 May 1763, P.R.O., Adm 1/1836; draft of letter 2c letter 30 Oct. 1768, National Maritime Museum, GRV/106.

— — Orders and Instructions from Admiralty, 19 April, 2, 3, 27, 1763, P.R.O., Adm 2/90; 2 May 1763, National Maritime Mu GRV/106, Section 9.

GRENVILLE, H.M.S., Log and Journal, Cook, P.R.O., Adm 52/1

HAMAR, JOSEPH. Log/Journal, H.M.S. *Eagle*, P.R.O., Adm 51/2

HAWKESWORTH, JOHN. Letter n.d. to David Garrick, British Mu: Add. MS 28104, ff. 45–6; copy of letter n.d. (August 1773) tc dear Madam', Yale University Library, Osborn Collection.

LIND, JAMES. Letter 30 Jan. 1775 to Maskelyne, copy, British Mu (Natural History), Botany Library, Banks Correspondence, Da Turner Transcripts I, 82–3.

McALLISTER FAMILY, Philadelphia. Correspondence concerning family connections of Captain James Cook, including letters Sade and Mary Blade, Mile End, 6 July 1788; Elizabeth Ho church, Mile End, 29 March 1792 and 12 Sept. 1794; J McAllister Jr. 17 Oct. 1851 to John Leach Bennett; John Lι Bennett 7 April 1852 to John McAllister Jr.; William Slaug 30 Nov. 1854 to John McAllister Jr., National Library of Austrι MS 4263 (NanKivell Collection 9528).

MONTAGU, JOHN, 4th EARL OF SANDWICH. Correspondence 177 with Daines Barrington, Johann Reinhold Forster, and Jaι Stuart concerning the official account of Cook's second voyage the Pacific, Sandwich Papers, Mapperton, Dorset.

— — Letter 25 Dec. 1771 to Lord Rochdale, P.R.O., State Papι Domestic, *Naval*, 42/48, no. 51.

SMITH, ADAM. Part of typescript copy of letter 12 Feb. 1767 to Sir William Petty, 2nd Earl of Shelburne, concerning Dalrymple, Alexander Turnbull Library, Carrington Papers, MS Papers 79, Folder 7.

SMITH, ISAAC. ALS 8 Oct. 1830 to Edward Hawke Locker, Mitchell Library, Cook Documents from the Australian Museum, Safe 1/83.

SOLANDER, DANIEL CARL. Letter 5 Sept. 1775 to Banks, British Museum (Natural History), Botany Library, Banks Correspondence, Dawson Turner Transcripts I, 98–9.

SOLEBAYS, H.M.S., Captain's log, Craig, P.R.O., Adm 51/908; Master's log, Cook, P.R.O., Adm 52/1033.

TEST, WILLIAM. Order from Admiralty 19 April 1763, P.R.O., Adm 2/90.

TWEED, H.M.S., Captain's log, Douglas, P.R.O., Adm 51/1016.

—— Musters, June, July, August 1763, P.R.O., Adm 36/6901.

WALKER, JOHN. Draft of reply 2 April 1776 written on Cook's letter 14 Feb. 1776, Dixson Library, MS Q140.

WALLIS, SAMUEL. Copy of Journal 1766–8, *Dolphin*, Alexander Turnbull Library. A note by Wallis in this copy records that the longitude of Tahiti was ascertained by John Harrison according to Dr Maskelyne's method.

WHEELOCK, JOHN. Log, H.M.S. *Pembroke*, P.R.O., Adm 51/686.

SUMMARY LIST OF MANUSCRIPTS PRINTED OR DESCRIBED IN PUBLISHED JOURNALS OF COOK'S AND BANKS'S PACIFIC VOYAGES
ED. J. C. BEAGLEHOLE

Journals and Logs, First Voyage

COOK, JAMES. Journal on H.M.S. *Endeavour*, National Library of Australia, MS 1.

—— Journal on H.M.S. *Endeavour*, Corner copy, Mitchell Library, Safe 1/71.

—— Journal on H.M.S. *Endeavour*, National Maritime Museum. Transcript formerly in the Royal Library, Windsor.

—— Log. British Museum, Add. MS 27955.

BANKS, Sir JOSEPH. Journal on H.M.S. *Endeavour*, Mitchell Library, Safe 1/12–13.

HICKS, ZACHARY. Log, Alexander Turnbull Library. No owner's name but clearly by Hicks.

MOLYNEUX, ROBERT. Journal, P.R.O., Adm 51/4546/152.

—— Log, P.R.O., Adm 55/39.

PICKERSGILL, RICHARD. Journal, P.R.O., Adm 51/4547/140–1, Log, Adm 51/4547/142.

Journals and Logs, Second Voyage

COOK, JAMES. Log Book and Journal, British Museum, Add. MS 27886, Journal, Add. MS 27888.

—— Journal, P.R.O., Adm 55/108.

BAYLY, WILLIAM. Journal, Alexander Turnbull Library.

BURNEY, JAMES. Log and Journal, P.R.O., Adm 51/4523/1–4.

——Journal, National Library of Australia, MS 3244 (Ferguson MS).

CLERKE, CHARLES. Log, British Museum, Add. MS 8951–3. Clerke's original MS, a fair copy is in P.R.O., Adm 55/103.

ELLIOTT, JOHN. Memoirs, British Museum, Add. MS 42714, ff. 72–452 give an account of the second voyage.

FURNEAUX, TOBIAS. Journal and Log, P.R.O., Adm 55/1.

—— Narrative 13 July 1772–3 March 1774, transcript, British Museum, Add. MS 27890.

MITCHEL, BOWLES. Log, P.R.O., Adm 51/4555/194–5.

Journals and Logs, Third Voyage

COOK, JAMES. Journal, British Museum, Egerton MS 2177A, Fragment of Log 7–17 Jan. 1779, British Museum, Egerton MS 2177B.

ANDERSON, WILLIAM. Journal, P.R.O., Adm 51/4560/203–4. Vol. 3 is missing.

BAYLY, WILLIAM. Log and Journal, P.R.O., Adm 55/20.

—— Log, Alexander Turnbull Library, Journal, Alexander Turnbull Library.

BURNEY, JAMES. Journal, 4 vols in 2, Mitchell Library, Safe 1/64, 79.

EDGAR, THOMAS. Journal, British Museum, Add. MS 37528.

—— Log, P.R.O., Adm 55/21, 24.

GORE, JOHN. Log, P.R.O., Adm 55/120.

KING, JAMES. Log and proceedings, P.R.O., Adm 55/116, 122. King's 'Running Journal' Kamchatka to the Cape 1779–80 has been discovered recently (1973) in the Hydrographic Department, Ministry of Defence.

Letters and Papers

ADMIRALTY

Official correspondence and documents are preserved in Admiralty records in the Public Record Office and the National Maritime Museum. Additional copies as well as letters missing from official files are found in libraries and private collections. References occur to the following volumes of official files:

First Voyage

P.R.O., Adm 1/1609	Captains' letters.
,, ,, 2/94	Out-letters, Orders and Instructions.
,, ,, 2/237–8	Admiralty letters to Navy Board.
,, ,, 2/541	Out-letters including letters to Royal Society.

     ,,   ,,   2/731   Out-letters.
     ,,   ,,   3/76, 78 Minutes of the Board of Admiralty.
     ,,   ,,   106/1163 Navy Board, miscellaneous In-letters.
     ,,   ,,   106/3315 Deptford Yard Letter Books, Series I.
National Maritime Museum
  ADM/A/2606, 2609, 2647 Admiralty to Navy Board.

Second Voyage
P.R.O., Adm 1/1609, 1610 Captains' letters.
     ,,   ,,   2/1992   Secret Orders and Instructions.
     ,,   ,,   3/78–9   Minutes of the Board of Admiralty.
     ,,   ,,   12/4806   Digests and Indexes, Series III.
     ,,   ,,   106/1208   Navy Board, In-letters.
National Maritime Museum
  ADM/A/2647, 2655 Admiralty to Navy Board.
  ADM/B/185 Navy Board to Admiralty.

Third Voyage
P.R.O., Adm 1/1611, 1612 Captains' letters.
     ,,   ,,   2/1334   Secret Orders and Instructions.
     ,,   ,,   106/2204   Navy Board to Admiralty.
     ,,   ,,   106/3318   Deptford Yard Letter Books, Series I.

National Maritime Museum
  ADM/A/2694, 2695, 2698, 2700, 2752 Admiralty Orders to Navy Board.
  ADM/B/191 Navy Board to Admiralty.

BANKS, Sir JOSEPH. Memo. n.d. concerning the committee on drawings and charts for reproduction in the published account of the third voyage, Sutro Library, San Francisco, Banks Papers.

— — Memo. 28 July 1785 on profits from the published account of the third voyage, Auckland Public Library, Grey Collection. MS 59.

CLERKE, CHARLES. Letters to Banks 1772, Mitchell Library, Banks Papers, vol. 2.

— — Letter 1 August 1776 to Banks, Kenneth Webster Collection.

COOK, JAMES. Letter Books 1768–78, 2 vols, National Library of Australia, MSS 2, 6. Dr J. C. Beaglehole refers to these vols as 'CLB' (Canberra Letter Books). MS 2, 1768–71, Cook's correspondence with the Admiralty, Navy Board, Sick and Hurt Board, Victualling Board and Royal Society; copy of Cook's letter 11 Oct. 1770 to the Governor-General, Batavia; letters 6 and 16 Nov. 1770 William Perry to Cook; secret instructions 30 July 1768. MS 6, 1771–8, correspondence similar to that in MS 2 with departments of the Admiralty; Cook's orders to his officers; letters 25 May 1774 from the Board of Longitude to Cook and Bayly; secret instructions 25 June 1772.

— — Letter to Banks 11 August 1771, British Museum (Natural History), Botany Department Library, Dawson Turner Transcripts, I, 32.

— — Letters to Banks 1772, 1776, 4 letters, Mitchell Library, Safe 1/68. Printed in *Historical Records of New South Wales*, vol. I, pt I, 1893.

— — Letter to Banks 26 Nov. 1776, Phillips Collection, Salem, Mass.

— — Letter to William Hammond 3 Jan. 1772, Whitby Museum.

— — Letter to William Hodges 5 Nov. 1776, Princeton University Library.

— — Letter to Rev. Dr Richard Kaye 11 July 1776, Dixson Library, MS 92.

— — Letters to Latouche-Tréville 6 Sept. 1775, 10 Feb. 1776, Bibliothèque Nationale, Nouv. Acq. Fr. 9439. Printed by J. Forsyth, *Mariner's Mirror*, xlv, 1959, letter 6 Sept. 1775 also printed by E. T. Hamy, *Bulletin de Géographie Historique et Descriptive*, 1904, 207.

— — Letter to William Strahan 5 Nov. 1776, Phillips Collection, Salem, Mass.

— — Letters to John Walker, 17 August 1771, Gloucestershire Records Office, copy in Mitchell Library MS A1713-2; 20 Nov. 1772, General Assembly Library, Wellington; 19 August 1775, Phillips Collection, Salem, Mass.; 14 Sept. 1775, Dixson Library, MS Q141.

KING, JAMES. Letter 4 Nov. 1776 to Edmund Burke, Sheffield City Library, Wentworth Woodhouse Papers.

SAMWELL, DAVID. Letters 22 Oct. 1776, 20 Nov. 1781 to Matthew Gregson, Liverpool Public Library, Gregson Correspondence XVII.

SANDWICH PAPERS. Correspondence and papers of John Montagu, 4th Earl of Sandwich, cited by J. C. Beaglehole as Sandwich Papers, Hinchingbrooke, these papers are now at Mapperton, Dorset in the possession of V. Montagu, Esq. Letters quoted: 20 Dec. 1771 from Lord Rochford, correspondence 1772 concerning Banks's withdrawal from the second voyage, letters 11 July, 26 Nov. 1776 Cook to Sandwich, June 1781 Mrs Cook to Sandwich.

SOLANDER, DANIEL CARL. Letters 1 August, 14 August 1775 to Banks, Mitchell Library As 24.

TREVENEN, JAMES. Annotations in vols II and III of a copy of *A Voyage to the Pacific Ocean*, London, 1784, copies in manuscript copies of 'Memoirs of James Trevenen' by Rev. John Penrose in the National Maritime Museum and the Alexander Turnbull Library. There is a full transcription of the annotations in the Archives of British Columbia, Victoria, B.C.

Collections of Documents

Collections includes fragments of journals and many letters.

AUCKLAND PUBLIC LIBRARY. Grey MSS 47–75 relate to Cook. They include Sir Joseph Banks's memo. 28 July 1785 concerning the profits from the publication of the journal of Cook's third voyage, MS 59; letter from Jean Hyacinthe de Magellan 23 June 1779 to Banks quoting a letter he has received from the duc de Croy; letter from George Nicol 14 Jan. 1801 to Banks, MS 71.

BRITISH MUSEUM. 'Cook's Second Voyage. Fragments', Add. MS 27889. The volume includes (ff. 83–96) William Brougham Monkhouse's Journal 6–21 Oct. 1769.

— — Add. MS 37425. The volume includes (f. 134) a letter from Cook 4 July 1772 to Navy Board.

DIXSON LIBRARY, LIBRARY OF N.S.W. Captain James Cook Relics and Manuscripts, MS F1.

An album containing some of Cook's letters to the Victualling Board; a fair copy in Cook's hand of entries in his journal 18–27 Dec. 1774; draft of the General Introduction for the published account of the second voyage with deletions and alterations by Cook and Douglas; manuscript copy, contemporary, of verses by Thomas Perry beginning 'It is now my brave boys we are clear of the Ice . . .' A broadsheet of the verses is in the Mitchell Library, Cook Documents from the Australian Museum, Safe 1/83.

— — James Cook. Correspondence 1764–79, MS Q140. Includes autograph letters 13 Sept. 1771 and 14 Feb. 1776 Cook to John Walker, the latter with draft reply 2 April 1776; autograph letter 28 May 1772 Cook to William Hammond; order 26 Nov. 1778 signed James Cook, prohibiting unauthorised dealings by officers and crew with the natives of the Hawaiian Islands; copy of Pass by Benjamin Franklin 10 March 1779 requesting captains and commanders of American armed ships not to molest Cook's ships.

— — Sir Joseph Banks and Associates. Papers, MS Q158. Includes autograph letter 10 Jan. 1780 John Montagu, 4th Earl of Sandwich to Banks. Another volume of papers of Sir Joseph Banks and Associates, MS Q161 includes an autograph letter [Dec. 1771] Solander to Dr James Lind (incomplete).

MITCHELL LIBRARY, LIBRARY OF N.S.W. Banks Papers, vol. 2 (Brabourne Papers), MS A78-1. Includes autograph letters Clerke to Banks 1772–9; copy of letter 10 June 1779 King to Secretary, Board of Longitude; autograph letters Oct.–Nov. 1779 Sir James Harris to Lord Weymouth.

— — Banks Papers, Voluntiers, Instructions, Provision for Second Voyage, Safe 1/11.

— — Original Manuscripts in the Handwriting of Captain Cook relating to his Second Voyage, Safe 1/82. Includes autograph letter 6 Feb. 1772 Cook to the Earl of Sandwich.

— — Cook Documents from the Australian Museum, Safe 1/83. Includes Cook's draft journal and notes 9 Oct.–27 Nov. 1769; description of Tonga Oct. 1773; drafts of letters 23 Oct. 1770 Cook to Admiralty and Royal Society.

NATIONAL LIBRARY OF AUSTRALIA. Letters and Papers of Associates of Captain James Cook, MS 9. Include Banks's autograph extracts 5 June 1766–9 June 1768 from the 'Transactions of the Royal Society relative to the sending out people to Observe the transit of Venus in 1769'; 'Hints offered to the consideration of Captain Cooke, Mr Bankes, Doctor Solander, and the other Gentlemen who go upon the Expedition on Board the Endeavour', by James Douglas, 14th Earl of Morton 10 August 1768; autograph letters 1777–90 from the Forsters.

ROYAL GREENWICH OBSERVATORY, HERSTMONCEUX CASTLE, SUSSEX. Board of Longitude, Minutes 10 Dec. 1771, 25 Jan., 7 March, 14 May 1772; 4 Nov. 1780, 3 March 1781.

ROYAL SOCIETY. Certificates 1767–1778 include the record of Cook's election 29 Feb. 1776.

—— Council Minutes 19 Nov. 18 Dec. 1767, see also Banks's abstract of Minutes 1766–8 in National Library of Australia, MS 9, Minutes 11 July 1771 include a letter 9 May 1771 Cook to Maskelyne.

—— Letters and Papers V, no. 116 is a letter 28 Nov. 1768 Green to the Royal Society.

—— Miscellaneous Manuscripts III, f. 14, letter 7 Dec. 1767 Dalrymple to Morton.

ALEXANDER TURNBULL LIBRARY, WELLINGTON. Holograph Letters and Documents of and relative to Captain James Cook, 1764–77. Include a copy of James Burney's report to Furneaux on his expedition in search of the massacred boat's crew with a chart; a fair copy of part of Furneaux's journal 8 Feb.–19 May 1773; autograph letter 19 August Solander to a Scottish correspondent, Lind or Burney, concerning Omai.

—— Miscellaneous Material relating to Cook's Voyages. Includes a fragment of a journal May–August 1768 perhaps by Jonathan Monkhouse; autograph letters 12 July, 27 Nov. 1776 Gore to Banks and 26 Feb. 1781 Samwell to Miss Anna Seward.

CHARTS AND SAILING DIRECTIONS
FOR THE EAST COAST OF NORTH AMERICA
(MS and printed)

James Cook

[1758] Directions for sailing in and out of the Harbour of Louisbourg in Cape Breton, MS in the Houghton Library, Harvard.

[1758–62] A Sketch of Harbour Grace and Carbonere in Newfoundland. [with other documents including] Description of the Sea Coast of Nova Scotia, *etc.* and Descriptions for Sailing in and out of Ports [Gulf of St Lawrence], National Library of Australia, MS 5. The Description of the Sea Coast of Nova Scotia, *etc.* is printed in *Report of the Board of Trustees of the Public Archives of Nova Scotia For the Year 1958*, Halifax, N.S., 1959. Copies of the sailing directions are in the Public Archives of Canada and in the Naval Library, Ministry of Defence, Naval Historical Branch, the copy in the latter accompanied by charts and views.

[1759?] *To the Right Hon.ble the Master and Wardens of the Trinity House of Deptford Strond This Draught of the Bay and Harbour of Gaspee in the Gulf of S.ᵗ Laurence taken in 1758 is humbly presented by* . . . *James Cook*, London.

[1759? Halifax Harbour, three manuscript charts], Public Archives of Canada, T. 50/4, British Museum, Add. MS 31360.9, Naval Library, Ministry of Defence, Naval Historical Branch, MS 20.

[1759?] A Plan of the Traverse or Passage from Cape Torment into the South-Channel of Orleams by Jamˢ Cook, British Museum, Add. MS 31360, f. 14.

[1760] *A New Chart of the River Sᵗ. Laurence . . . Also Particular Directions for Navigating the River with Safety. Taken by Order of Charles Saunders, Esq.ʳ . . . Engraved by Thomas Jefferys*, 12 sheets, London.

1760 *Directions for Navigating the Gulf and River of St. Laurence*, London, 1760.

[1762?] To the Right Honᵇˡᵉ the *Lord Colvill . . . This Chart of the River St. Laurence . . . is most Humbly Dedicated by* . . . Jamˢ Cook, MS chart from the Hydrographic Office in the National Maritime Museum.

[1763] A Plan of the Islands of St Peter's, Langly, and Miquelong, British Museum, Add. MS 17963, fair copy for the King, British Museum, Dept. of Maps, K. Top, cxix, III.

[1763 A plan of York or Chateaux Harbour with sailing directions and views], Ministry of Defence, Hydrographic Department, B. 188.

1763 A Sketch of the Island of Newfoundland, Naval Library, Ministry of Defence, Naval Historical Branch, America, Vol. I, No. 21.

1764 A Chart of the Sea Coast, Bays, and Harbours, in Newfoundland between Green Island and Point Ferrolle, Ministry of Defence, Hydrographic Department, 342.

1766 *A Chart of the Straights of Bellisle with part of the coast of Newfoundland and Labradore*, London, 1766.

1766 *Directions for Navigating on Part of the North East Side of Newfoundland and in the Streights of Bell-Isle*, London, 1766.

1766 *A Chart, of Part of the South Coast, of Newfoundland, including the Islands of Sᵗ Peters and Miquelon*, London, 1766.

1766 *Directions for Navigating on Part of the South Coast of Newfoundland*, London, 1766.

1767 *A Chart of Part of the South Coast of Newfoundland including the Islands of Sᵗ. Peters and Miquelon with the Southern Entrance to the Gulph of Sᵗ. Laurence*, London, 1767.

1768 *A Chart of the West Coast of Newfoundland*, London, 1768.

1768 *Directions for Navigating the West-Coast of Newfoundland*, London, 1768.

[1769–70] *A Collection of Charts Of the Coasts of Newfoundland and Labradore, &c. . . . Drawn from Original Surveys taken by James Cook and Michael Lane, Surveyors, Joseph Gilbert, and other Officers in the King's Service . . . Chiefly engraved by Thomas Jeffreys* [i.e. Jefferys], London.
[Facsimile, entitled] *James Cook Surveyor of Newfoundland Being a Collection of Charts of the Coasts of Newfoundland and Labradore . . . with an Introductory Essay by R. A. Skelton*, Grabhorn Press, San Francisco, 1965.

1769 *The Newfoundland Pilot: Containing A Collection of Directions for sailing round the whole Island, Including the Streights of Bell-Isle, And Part of the Coast of Labradore . . . Printed for Thomas Jeffreys* [i.e. Jefferys], London, 1769. [Five tracts, three by James Cook].

1775 *The North-American Pilot for Newfoundland, Labradore, the Gulf and River St. Laurence: Being a Collection of Sixty Accurate Charts and Plans, Drawn from Original Surveys: Taken by James Cook and Michael Lane, Surveyors, and Joseph Gilbert, and other Officers in the King's Service . . . Chiefly Engraved by the Late Mr. Thomas Jefferys*, London, 1775.

1775 *Sailing Directions for the North-American Pilot*, London, 1775.

Other Surveyors

The English Pilot, The Fourth Book, London, 1794. This publication remained uninfluenced by Cook. A delineation of Newfoundland 1677 was first published in *The English Pilot, The Fourth Book* in 1689.

HOLLAND, SAMUEL. [Coastal plans by his deputies], Ministry of Defence, Hydrographic Department, 9/73, A7353/77.

Bibliographical References

SKELTON, RALEIGH ASHLIN. 'Captain James Cook as a Hydrographer' *Mariner's Mirror*, Vol. 40, 1954, 92–119.

— — 'James Cook Surveyor of Newfoundland', introductory essay in the Grabhorn Press facsimile edition 1965 of *A Collection of Charts of the Coasts of Newfoundland and Labradore*, first published [1769–70].

— — Cook's *Northumberland* MSS, typescript notes lent to J. C. Beaglehole.

SKELTON, RALEIGH ASHLIN, and TOOLEY, RONALD VERE. *The Marine Surveys of James Cook in North America 1758–1768, particularly the Survey of Newfoundland, A bibliography*, London, 1967.

PUBLICATIONS

ADMIRALTY. [Cook's instructions for the voyage of H.M.S. *Endeavour*, printed from P.R.O., Adm 2/1332]. Navy Records Society, *Naval Miscellany*, III, 1928, 343–50.

ANDERSEN, JOHANNES CARL. *Maori Place-Names*, Wellington, 1942.

ANSON, GEORGE, BARON ANSON, see WALTER, RICHARD.

BAFFIN, WILLIAM. *The Voyages of W. Baffin, 1612–1622*, ed. C. R. Markham, *Hakluyt Society*, London, 1881.

BANKS, Sir JOSEPH. *The Endeavour Journal of Joseph Banks 1768–1771*, ed. J. C. Beaglehole, 2 vols, Sydney, 1962.

BARRINGTON, DAINES. *Summary Observations and Facts . . . to show the Practicability and good Prospect of Success in Enterprises to discover a Northern Passage*, London, 1776.

BAYLY, WILLIAM. *The Original Astronomic Observations made in the course of a voyage to the Northern Pacific Ocean*, ed. W. Bayly, London, 1782.

BEAGLEHOLE, JOHN CAWTE. *The Discovery of New Zealand*, 2nd ed., London, 1961.

BEALE, EDGAR. 'Cook's First Landing Attempt in New South Wales', Royal Australian Historical Society, *Journal and Proceedings*, 50, 1964, 191–204.

BEGG, ALEXANDER CHARLES, and BEGG, NEIL COLQUHOUN. *Dusky Bay*, Christchurch. 1966.

— — *James Cook and New Zealand*, Wellington, 1969.

BESANT, Sir WALTER. *Captain Cook*, London, 1890.

BLIGH, WILLIAM. *The Log of the Bounty*, 2 vols, London, [1936].

— — 'Some correspondence of Captain William Bligh, R.N. with John and Francis Godolphin Bond 1776–1811', ed. George Mackaness, Royal Australian Historical Society, *Journal and Proceedings*, 45, 1949. Original letters in National Library of Australia, MS 4038 (NanKivell Collection 34).

BOSWELL, JAMES. *Private Papers of James Boswell*, ed. G. Scott and F. A. Pottle, 18 vols, New York, [1928]–1934.

BOUGAINVILLE, LOUIS ANTOINE DE, COUNT. *A Voyage round the World . . . Translated from the French by John Reinold Forster*, London, 1772.

BROSSES, CHARLES DE. *Histoire des Navigations aux Terres Australes*, 2 vols, Paris, 1756.

BUCK, Sir PETER HENRY. 'Cook's Discovery of the Hawaiian Islands', in *Report of the Director for 1944*, B. P. Bishop Museum Bulletin 186, Honolulu, 1945, 26–44.

— — *Vikings of the Sunrise*, New Zealand edition, Christchurch, 1954.

BURNEY, FRANCES. *The Early Diary of Frances Burney*, 2 vols, London, 1913.

— — *Memoirs of Doctor Burney*, 3 vols, London, 1832.

BURNEY, JAMES. *Chronological History of North-Eastern Voyages of Discovery*, London, 1819.

BURRIEL, ANDRÉS MARCOS, see VENEGAS, MIGUEL.

BYRON, JOHN. *Byron's Journal of his Circumnavigation 1764–1766*, ed. R. E. Gallagher, *Hakluyt Society*, Cambridge, 1964.

CALLANDER, JOHN. *Terra Australis Cognita: or, Voyages to the Terra Australis, or Southern Hemisphere*, 3 vols, Edinburgh, 1766–8.

CARRINGTON, ARTHUR HUGH. *Life of Captain Cook*, London, 1939.

CARTERET, PHILIP. *Carteret's Voyage Round the World*, ed. Helen Wallis, 2 vols, *Hakluyt Society*, London, 1965.

CHAPMAN, CHARLES EDWARD. *The Founding of Spanish California*, New York, 1916.

CHARNOCK, JOHN. *Biographia Navalis*, 6 vols, London, 1794–8.

CODRINGTON, ROBERT HENRY. *The Melanesians*, Oxford, 1891.

COOK, ELIZABETH. Letter 16 August 1784 to Sir Joseph Banks, *Notes and Queries*, 8th series, iv, 1893, 165.

COOK, JAMES. 'An Account of the Flowing of the Tides in the South Sea . . . in a Letter to Nevil Maskelyne, Astronomer Royal, and F.R.S.', Royal Society, *Phil. Trans.* LXII, 1772, 357–8.

—— *Captain Cook's Journal during his First Voyage round the World*, ed. W. J. L. Wharton, London, 1893.

—— *The Journals of Captain James Cook on his Voyages of Discovery* [with] (*Addenda and Corrigenda to Volume I* and *Volume II*), ed. J. C. Beaglehole, (*Charts & Views* [with] *Corrigenda*), ed. R. A. Skelton, 3 vols in 4 and portfolio, *Hakluyt Society*, Cambridge, 1955–69.

—— Letter 26 Feb. 1776 to Robert Sayer, printed in copies of *The North-American Pilot* issued after Sayer received the letter.

—— Letter 22 June 1776 to Commodore Wilson, in Young, George, *The Life and Voyages of Captain James Cook*, London, 1836, 304–5.

—— 'The Method taken for preserving the Health of the Crew of His Majesty's Ship the Resolution . . . By Captain James Cook F.R.S. Addressed to Sir John Pringle March 5, 1776', [with] ('Extract of a Letter from Captain Cook to Sir John Pringle . . . July 7, 1776'), Royal Society, *Phil. Trans.* LXVI, 1776, 402–6.

—— 'An Observation of an Eclipse of the Sun at the Island of New-found-land, August 5, 1766, by Mr. James Cook . . . Communicated by J. Bevis', Royal Society, *Phil. Trans.* LVIII, 1767, 215–16.

—— 'Observations made, by appointment of the Royal Society, at King George's Island in the South Sea, by Mr. Charles Green . . . and Lieut. James Cook', Royal Society, *Phil. Trans.* LXI, 1771, 397–421.

—— 'Variation of the Compass, as observed on board the Endeavour Bark . . . Communicated by Lieut. James Cook', Royal Society, *Phil. Trans.* LXI, 1771, 422–32.

—— *A Voyage to the Pacific Ocean in the years 1776, 1777, 1778, 1779, and 1780 . . . Vol. I and II written by Captain J. Cook, vol. III by Captain J. King*, ed. John Douglas, 3 vols, London, 1784.

—— *A Voyage towards the South Pole and round the World . . . In the Years 1772, 1773, 1774, and 1775*, 2 vols, London, 1777.

COXE, WILLIAM. *An Account of the Russian Discoveries between Asia and America*, London, 1780.

CROZET, JULIEN MARIE. *Crozet's Voyage to Tasmania . . . Translated by H. L. Roth*, London, 1891.

DALRYMPLE, ALEXANDER. *An Account of the Discoveries made in the South Pacifick Ocean previous to 1764*, London, 1769.

—— *A Collection of Voyages, chiefly in the Southern Atlantick Ocean*, 5 pts, London, 1775.

—— *An Historical Collection of the Several Voyages and Discoveries in the South Pacific Ocean*, 2 vols, London, 1770–1.

—— 'Memoirs of Alexander Dalrymple, Esq.', *European Magazine*, XLII, 1802, 323*–328*, 421–4.

—— 'Biographical Memoir of Alexander Dalrymple, Esq.', *The Naval Chronicle*, XXXV, 1816, 177–204. A new edition of the Memoirs of 1802, continued to Dalrymple's death in 1808.

DAMPIER, WILLIAM. *Dampier's Voyages*, ed. John Masefield, 2 vols, London, 1906.

DAVIES, JOHN. *The History of the Tahitian Mission 1799–1830*, ed. C. W. Newbury, *Hakluyt Society*, Cambridge, 1961.

DAVIS, GEORGE. Letter 14 March 1764 to Cook, *Historical Records of New South Wales*, I, pt I, 1893, 300–1.

DAWSON, WARREN ROYAL. *The Banks Letters. A Calendar of the manuscript correspondence of Sir Joseph Banks*, ed. W. R. Dawson, London, 1958.

DOBBS, ARTHUR. *An Account of the Countries adjoining to Hudson's Bay*, London, 1744.

DUNMORE, JOHN. *French Explorers in the Pacific*, 2 vols, Oxford, 1965–9.

DUNN, SAMUEL. *The Navigator's Guide to the Oriental or Indian Seas*, London, [1775].

EDGEWORTH, RICHARD LOVELL. *Memoirs of Richard Lovell Edgeworth . . . Begun by Himself and Concluded by his Daughter, Maria Edgeworth*, 2 vols, London, 1820.

ELLIS, JOHN. Letter 19 August 1768 to Linnaeus, in Smith, Sir James Edward, *A Selection of the Correspondence of Linnaeus, and other Naturalists*, London, 1821, I, 230–2.

ELLIS, WILLIAM. *Narrative of a Tour through Hawaii*, London, 1827.

EMORY, KENNETH PIKE. *Archaeology of the Pacific Equatorial Islands*, B.P. Bishop Museum Bulletin 123, Honolulu, 1934.

FALCONER, WILLIAM. *An Universal Dictionary of the Marine*, London, 1789.

FLINDERS, MATTHEW. *A Voyage to Terra Australis*, 2 vols with an atlas, London, 1814.

FONTE, BARTHOLOMEW DE. 'Letter from Admiral Bartholomew d Fonte, then Admiral of New Spain and Peru, and now Prince Chili', *Monthly Miscellany or Memoirs for the Curious*, 1708. Fictiti account of a journey across North America by water by a ficti 'Admiral'.

FORSTER, JOHANN GEORG ADAM. 'Cook der Entdecker', in *Schriften*, I, 1–232, Leipzig, 1789.

—— *Letter to the Rt. Hon. the Earl of Sandwich*, London, 1778.

—— *Reply to Mᵣ Wales's Remarks*, London, 1778.

—— *A Voyage round the World in his Britannic Majesty's Sloop, R during the Years 1772, 3, 4, and 5*, 2 vols, London, 1777.

FORSTER, JOHANN REINHOLD. *History of the Voyages made in the North*, London, 1786.

—— *Observations made during a Voyage Round the World*, Lc

FRY, HOWARD TYRRELL. *Alexander Dalrymple (17. Expansion of British Trade*, London, 1970.

FURNEAUX, RUPERT. *Tobias Furneaux, Circumnaviga*

GONZALEZ, FELIPE. *The Voyage of Captain Don F Easter Island in 1770–1*, ed. B. G. Corney, *Hakl* 1908.

GOULD, RUPERT THOMAS. *Captain Cook*, Lond

GRAVES, JOHN. *The History of Cleveland*, Carlisle, 1808.

HALLEY, EDMUND. 'Methodus singularis quâ Solis Parallaxis sive distantia à Terra, ope Veneris intra Solem conspiciendae, tuto determinari poterit', Royal Society, *Phil. Trans.* XXIX, 1716, 460.

HARRIS, JOHN. *Navigantium atque Itinerantium Bibliotheca . . . Carefully revised* [by John Campbell], 2 vols, London, 1744–8.

HAWKESWORTH, JOHN. *An Account of the Voyages undertaken . . . for making Discoveries in the Southern Hemisphere*, 3 vols, London, 1773.

HEARNE, SAMUEL. *A Journey . . . to the Northern Ocean*, London, 1795.

HENRY, TEUIRA. *Ancient Tahiti*, Honolulu, 1928.

HERBERT, SIDNEY CHARLES, 16th EARL OF PEMBROKE. *Henry, Elizabeth and George, 1734–80*, ed. Lord Herbert, 2 vols, London, 1939, 1950.

HINTON, COLIN JACK-. *In Search of the Islands of Solomon 1567–1838*, Oxford, 1969.

Historical Records of New South Wales, vol. I, pt I, Sydney, 1893.

HOLLAND, SAMUEL. Letter 11 Jan. 1792 to Lieutenant-Governor John Graves Simcoe, Ontario Historical Society, *Papers and Records*, XXI, 1924, 18–19.

HOME, GEORGE. *Memoirs of an Aristocrat*, London, 1838.

HORNSBY, THOMAS. 'On the Transit of Venus in 1769', Royal Society, *Phil. Trans.* Abridged by Charles Hutton, George Shaw, and Richard Pearson, XII, 1763–9, London, 1809, 265–74.

HOWSE, DEREK. 'Captain Cook's Marine Timekeepers', *Antiquarian Horology*, 1969, 190–9.

HOWSE, DEREK, and HUTCHINSON, BERESFORD. *The Clocks and Watches of Captain James Cook 1769–1969*, London, 1969. Reprinted from *Antiquarian Horology*, 1969.

HUMPHREYS, C. B. *The Southern New Hebrides*, Cambridge, 1926.

HUTCHINSON, WILLIAM. *The Second Edition, considerably enlarged, of a Treatise on Practical Seamanship*, Liverpool, 1787.

A Journal of a Voyage round the World in His Majesty's Ship Endeavour, London, 1771. Perhaps by J. M. Magra.

KELLY, CELSUS. *La Austrialia del Espiritu Santo*, ed. Celsus Kelly, 2 vols, Haklyut Society, Cambridge, 1966.

KENDALL, HUGH P. *Captain James Cook*, Whitby Literary and Philosophical Society, Whitby, 1951.

KING, JAMES. *A Voyage to the Pacific Ocean . . . In the Years 1776, 1777, 1778, 1779, and 1780 . . . Vol. I and II written by Captain J. Cook, vol. III by Captain J King*, ed. John Douglas, 3 vols, London, 1784.

KIPPIS, ANDREW. *The Life of Captain James Cook*, London, 1788.

KITSON, ARTHUR. *Captain James Cook*, London, 1907.

KNOX, JOHN. *An Historical Journal of the Campaigns in North America for the years 1757, 1758, 1759, and 1760*, 2 vols, London, 1769.

LAGUNA, FREDERICA DE. *Archaeology of Cook Inlet, Alaska*, Philadelphia, 1934.

LASCELLES, EDWARD CHARLES PONSONBY. *Granville Sharp and the Freedom of the Slaves in England*, London, 1928.

LEADBETTER, CHARLES. *A Compleat System of Astronomy*, 2 vols, London, 1728.

—— *The Young Mathematician's Companion*, London, 1739, 2nd ed. 1748.

LEWIS, MICHAEL ARTHUR. *England's Sea-Officers*, London, 1948.

LIND, JAMES. *A Treatise of the Scurvy*, Edinburgh, 1753.

LIPSON, EPHRAIM. *The Economic History of England*, 5th ed., vol. II, London, 1948.

LOCKER, EDWARD HAWKE. *Naval Gallery of Greenwich Hospital*, London, 1831, [1832].

MACBRIDE, DAVID. *Experimental Essays*, 2nd ed., London, 1767.

McNAB, ROBERT. *Historical Records of New Zealand*, 2 vols, Wellington, 1908, 1914.

—— *Muruhiku: a history of the South Island of New Zealand and the islands adjacent*, Wellington, 1909.

MAGRA, (afterwards MATRA), JAMES MARIA. *A Journal of a Voyage round the World in His Majesty's Ship Endeavour*, London, 1771. Perhaps by J. M. Magra.

MARRA, JOHN. *Journal of the Resolution's Voyage in 1772, 1773, 1774, and 1775*, London, 1775.

MARTIN, JOHN. *An Account of the Natives of the Tonga Islands . . . from the extensive communications of Mr William Mariner*, 3rd ed., 2 vols, Edinburgh, 1826–7.

MARTIN-ALLANIC, JEAN ETIENNE. *Bougainville navigateur et les découvertes de son temps*, 2 vols, Paris, 1964.

MASKELYNE, NEVIL. *The British Mariner's Guide*, London, 1763.

MAUDE, HENRY EVANS. *Of Islands and Men*, Melbourne, 1968.

MAXIMILIANUS, *Transylvanus. Maximiliani Transylvani . . . Epistola de . . . novissima Hispanorum in Orientem navigatione*, Romae, 1523.

MAYER, TOBIAS. *Tabulae lunares ad Meridianum Parisinum quas putavit T. Mayer*, Vindobanae, 1763.

MUELLER, GERHARD FRIEDRICH. *Voyages from Asia to America*, London, 1761.

NATIONAL MARITIME MUSEUM. [Catalogue] *Captain Cook Special Exhibition held . . . 1956–7*. [A collection of printed labels . . . with prefatory matter, reproduced from typewriting].

NEWSPAPER EXTRACTS
1768 *Gazetteer*, 13, 20 June, 18 August; *Public Advertiser*, 20 June. Reports of a projected voyage of the Royal Navy to observe the Transit of Venus from 'King George's Island' discovered by Wallis, and to make discoveries in the South Seas.

1770 *Bingley's Journal*, 28 Sept. Report that H.M.S. *Endeavour* had been sunk by enemy action.

1771 *General Evening Post*, 8 Jan.; *London Evening Post*, 9, 16 May. Reports of the safe arrival of H.M.S. *Endeavour* at Batavia. Further newspaper extracts for the year 1771 are listed in *The Journals of Captain James Cook on his Voyages of Discovery*, èd. J. C. Beaglehole, I, 643–55.

1772 *General Evening Post*, 3 April. Report of death of the goat which sailed with Wallis in the *Dolphin* and Cook in the *Endeavour*.

1773 *General Evening Post*, 2, 21 August; *London Evening Post*, 18 August, Publishers' advertisements for accounts of voyages.

1774 *The Daily Advertiser*, 19 July. Letter from Dr Solander to a Scottish correspondent concerning Omai.

1780 *London Gazette*, 11 Jan. News of Cook's death.

ORD, JOHN WALKER. *History and Antiquities of Cleveland*, London, 1846.

PALLISER, Sir HUGH. Letter from Admiralty 2 May 1764, in Carrington, A. H., *Life of Captain Cook*, London, 1939, 38.

PARKINSON, SYDNEY. *A Journal of a Voyage to the South Seas in His Majesty's ship, the Endeavour*, London, 1773.

PEMBROKE, 16th EARL OF, see HERBERT, SIDNEY CHARLES.

PHILIP, ARTHUR. *Voyage to Botany Bay*, London, 1789.

POLO, MARCO. *The Book of Ser Marco Polo*, ed. H. Yule, 3rd ed., 2 vols, London, 1903.

PURCHAS, SAMUEL. *Hakluytus Posthumus; or, Purchas His Pilgrimes*, 20 vols, Glasgow, 1905–7.

RAINAUD, ARMAND. *Le Continent Australe*, Paris, 1893.

RICKMAN, JOHN. *The Journal of Captain Cook's last Voyage to the Pacific Ocean*, London, 1781. Published anon.

— — *Tagebuch einer Entdeckungs Reise nach der Südsee in den Jahren 1776 bis 1780*, [translated with preface by J. R. Forster], Berlin, 1781.

ROBERTSON, GEORGE. *The Discovery of Tahiti*, ed. A. H. Carrington, Hakluyt Society, London, 1948.

ROBERTSON, JOHN. *The Elements of Navigation*, [containing] (A Dissertation on the Rise and Progress of the Modern Art of Navigation) [by James Wilson], 3rd ed. 2 vols, London, 1772.

ROGGEVEEN, JACOB. *The Journal of Jacob Roggeveen*, ed. Andrew Sharp, Oxford, 1970.

SAMWELL, DAVID. *A Narrative of the Death of Captain James Cook*, London, 1786.

SCOTT, DUNCAN CAMPBELL. *John Graves Simcoe*, Toronto, 1905.

A Second Voyage round the World . . . Drawn up from Authentic Papers, London, 1776. A fake although it claimed to be by Captain Cook.

SEWARD, ANNA. *Elegy on Cook*, London, 1780.

SHARP, ANDREW. *The Discovery of Australia*, Oxford, 1963.

SHORTLAND, EDWARD. *The Southern Districts of New Zealand*, London, 1851.

SMITH, ALAN WILLIAM. 'Captain James Cook, Londoner', *East London Papers*, 11, no. 2, 1968, 94–7.

SOLANDER, DANIEL CARL. Letter 1 Dec. 1768 to Linnaeus, in Uggla,

A.H.J., 'Daniel Solander och Linné', *Svenska Linné-Sallskapets Arrskrift*, xxxvii–xxxviii, 1954–5, 64.

—— Letter July 1774 to a Scottish correspondent concerning Omai, *The Daily Advertiser*, 19 July 1774.

SPARRMAN, ANDERS. Letter 5 Sept. 1780, in *Johann Georg Forsters Briefwechsel*, Leipzig, 1829, II, 748.

—— *A Voyage round the World*, London, 1953.

STACEY, CHARLES PERRY. *Quebec, 1759*, Toronto, 1959.

STAEHLIN STORCKSBURG, JACOB VON. *An Account of the New Northern Archipelago, Lately Discovered by the Russians in the Seas of Kamtschatka and Anadir*, London, 1774.

TAYLOR, EVA GERMAINE RIMINGTON. *The Mathematical Practitioners of Hanoverian England 1714–1840*, Cambridge, 1966.

TAYLOR, HENRY. *Memoirs of the Principal Events in the Life of Henry Taylor*, North Shields, 1811.

TUKE, JOHN. *A General View of the Agriculture of the North Riding of Yorkshire*, London, 1794.

VANCOUVER, GEORGE. [Claim to have been farthest south with Cook], *Naval Chronicle*, I, 1799, 125.

—— *A Voyage of Discovery*, 3 vols, London, 1798.

VENEGAS, MIGUEL. *A Natural and Civil History of California*, 2 vols, London, 1759.

—— *Noticia de la California, y de su conquista temporal y espiritual*, [compiled from the manuscript of Venegas by A. M. Burriel], 3 vols, Madrid, 1757.

VILLIERS, ALAN JOHN. *Captain Cook*, London, 1967.

WALES, WILLIAM. *Astronomical Observations made in the Voyages . . . for making Discoveries in the Southern Hemisphere*. London, 1788.

—— Memoir of Charles Green, in Kippis, A., *Life of Captain James Cook*, London, 1788, 176–8.

—— *Remarks on Mr Forster's Account of Captain Cook's last Voyage round the World in the Years 1772, 1773, 1774, and 1775*, London, 1778.

WALTER, RICHARD. *A Voyage round the World in the years MDCCXL, I, II, III, IV, by George Anson*, compiled by Richard Walter, London, 1748.

WEATHERILL, RICHARD. *The Ancient Port of Whitby and its Shipping*, Whitby, 1908.

WHITE, JOHN. *Ancient History of the Maori*, vol. V, Wellington, 1889.

WILLIAMS, GLYNDWR. *The British Search of the Northwest Passage in the Eighteenth Century*, London, 1962.

WOLFE, JAMES. Letter 30 August 1759 to Charles Saunders, in Willson, Beckles, *Life and Letters of James Wolfe*, London, 1909, 461.

WOOLF, HARRY. *The Transits of Venus*, Princeton, 1959.

WRAY, DANIEL. Letter 10 August 1775 to the Earl of Hardwicke, in Nichols, John, *Illustrations of the Literary History of the Eighteenth Century*, vol. I, London, 1817, 150.

WROTH, LAWRENCE COUNSELMAN. *The Early Cartography of the Pacific*, New York, 1944.

YOUNG, GEORGE. *The Life and Voyages of Captain James Cook*, London, 1836.

ZIMMERMAN, HEINRICH. *Reise um die Welt mit Capitain Cook*, Mannheim, 1781.

Index

For the voyages of discovery the activities of Cook, ships' officers, masters and professional supernumeraries are not indexed in detail. They are covered by the movements and visits of the ships in which they served, under the following abbreviations:

(1768–71) *Endeavour End.*
(1772–5) *Resolution* and *Adventure Res.*(1) *Adv. Res. : Adv.*
(1776–80) *Resolution* and *Discovery Res.*(2) *Dis. Res. : Dis.*

Adv., End., Dis., Res.(1) and *Res.*(2) are used with names of persons to denote voyage and ship; with place names they indicate where the ship is sailing alone. *Res. : Adv.* and *Res. : Dis.* are used when the ships are sailing in company.

Names of ships are under the heading Ships; the heading Ships (Cook's) lists the ships in which Cook served and includes the *Adventure* and *Discovery*.

Maxwell, James, A.B. *Res.*(1), 299
Mayer, Tobias, astronomer, 116
Mediterranean Sea, 7, 32, 54
Medni I., Komandorskiye Is., 682
Medway R., Newfoundland, 97
Mehetia I. (Osnaburg), Society Is., 169, 340, 549
Melanesia, 401, 708-9; *see* New Caledonia; New Hebrides
Melanesians, 397-8, 400-1, 405-6, 414-15, 658
Mendaña, Alvaro de, navigator, 110, 111, 375
Mera Lava I. (Pic de l'Etoile), New Hebrides, 394
Mercator, Gerard, cartographer, 108, 475
Merchant service (ships), 8-9, 14, 15, 644
Mercury, transit of, 205, 221
Mercury Bay, N.Z., 205-7, 213, 230, 522
Merrin, Mt, Tana I., 402
Merton Abbey, Surrey, 693
Mewburn, –, of Marton, 3
Mexico, 112, 479
Middelburg I. *see* 'Eua I.
Middle Arm, B. of Islands, Newfoundland, 93
Middleburg, Flanders, 11
Middle Ground Shoal, Cook Inlet, 603-4
Middlesbrough, Yorks, 1, 5
Middleton, Capt. Christopher, 477
Mile End, London, 75, 97, 131, 275, 291, 444, 505
Milner, Thomas, owner *Earl of Pembroke*, 129
Miquelon I. *see* St Pierre et Miquelon
Mississippi, R., 58
Mitchel, Bowles, midshipman *Res.*(1), 320
Mitchell, John, map (1755), 77
Mitre Tavern, London, 450, 452
Modoopapappa or Tammata pappa, Hawaiian Is., 578, 677
Mohawk, R., New York, 53
Molokai I., Hawaiian Is., 677
Moluccas Is., 110
Molyneux, Robert, master *End.*, 139, 179-182, 191, 234, 241-4; death, 268
Monboddo, Lord, 451
Monckton, Brig. Robert, 47
Monk, Simon, butcher *Res.*(1), 412-13
Monkhouse, George, of Cumberland, 274
Monkhouse, Jonathan, midshipman *End.*, 140, 191, 238; death, 265
Monkhouse, William Brougham, surgeon *End.*, 139, 162, 170, 178, 179, 183; death, 262
Monson, Lady Anne, 145
Montagu, John, earl of Sandwich, first lord Admiralty, 143, 275-6, 281-2, 285, 304, 442, 444, 448, 482; publication of Cooks journal, 289, 290, 457-8; correspondence with Cook, 285, 286-7, 507, 511; dealings with Banks, 291, 293, 294-6; with J. R. Forster, 461-2, 468-70

Montagu I. *see* Emau I.
Montagu I., Prince Wm Sound, 598
Montcalm, Louis, marquis de, 42, 43, 45, 46, 48, 49, 123
Monthly Miscellany, 479
Montmorency, R., Quebec, 42, 46, 48
Montreal, 40, 53
Monument rock, New Hebrides, 398-9
Moorea I., Society Is., 557-8; politics, 381, 383, 553, 555; *End.* party, 183-4; *Res.*: *Dis.*, 557-60; punishment for theft, 558-60
Mopihaa I., Pacific, 389
Moreton (Morton) Bay, Aus., 232
Morlaix, Brittany, 21
Morris, Thomas, marine *Res.*(2), 562
Morton, Charles, secretary Royal Society, 103, 450
Morton, earl of *see* Douglas, James
Morton, Yorks, 2
Motane I., Marquesas Is., 375
Motuara I., Q. Charlotte Sd, N.Z., 214-215, 333, 335, 421, 525
Motu Arohia I., N.Z., 208
Motu Iti atoll, Society Is., 194, 567
Motu Tu'a atoll, Tuamotu Is., 339n
Mouat, Alexander, midshipman *Dis.*, 565-7, 570
Mount and Page, publishers, 34, 85, 86
Mount Edgecumbe, Alaska, 592
Mu'a, Tongatapu, 541, 543, 544, 545
Mulgrave, Lord *see* Phipps
Mulgrave, Yorks, 448
Müller, Gerhard Friedrich, map, 486-7, 593, 594, 599, 605, 609, 613, 615, 632, 633; *Voyages from Asia to America* (1761), 486
Murderers Bay *see* Tasman Bay
Murray, Brig. James, 50, 53
Musgrave, Christopher, vicar St Margaret's, 61n
Mylne, Robert, architect, 450

Napoopoo, Kealakekua Bay, 648
Narborough, Sir John, 479
Narom, of Eromanga I., 400, 401
Natal, S. Africa, 266
National Maritime Museum, Greenwich, 11n, 52n, 387n
natural history equipment, 146, 296
Nautical Almanac, 116, 301
navigation, 12-14, 109-10, 117; instruments, 13, 114-15, 136-7, 288; *see also* chronometers; latitude; longitude
Navy Board, 26; payments, 73n, 78, 79n, 86n; purchase of ships, 128-30, 279-280, 493; supplies, 67, 90, 135, 136, 282, 474
    correspondence with Cook, 82, 140-1, 304n, 510, 644
    comptroller *see* Palliser, Hugh
Nelson, David, gardener *Dis.*, 501, 509, 510, 552, 656